AF412603

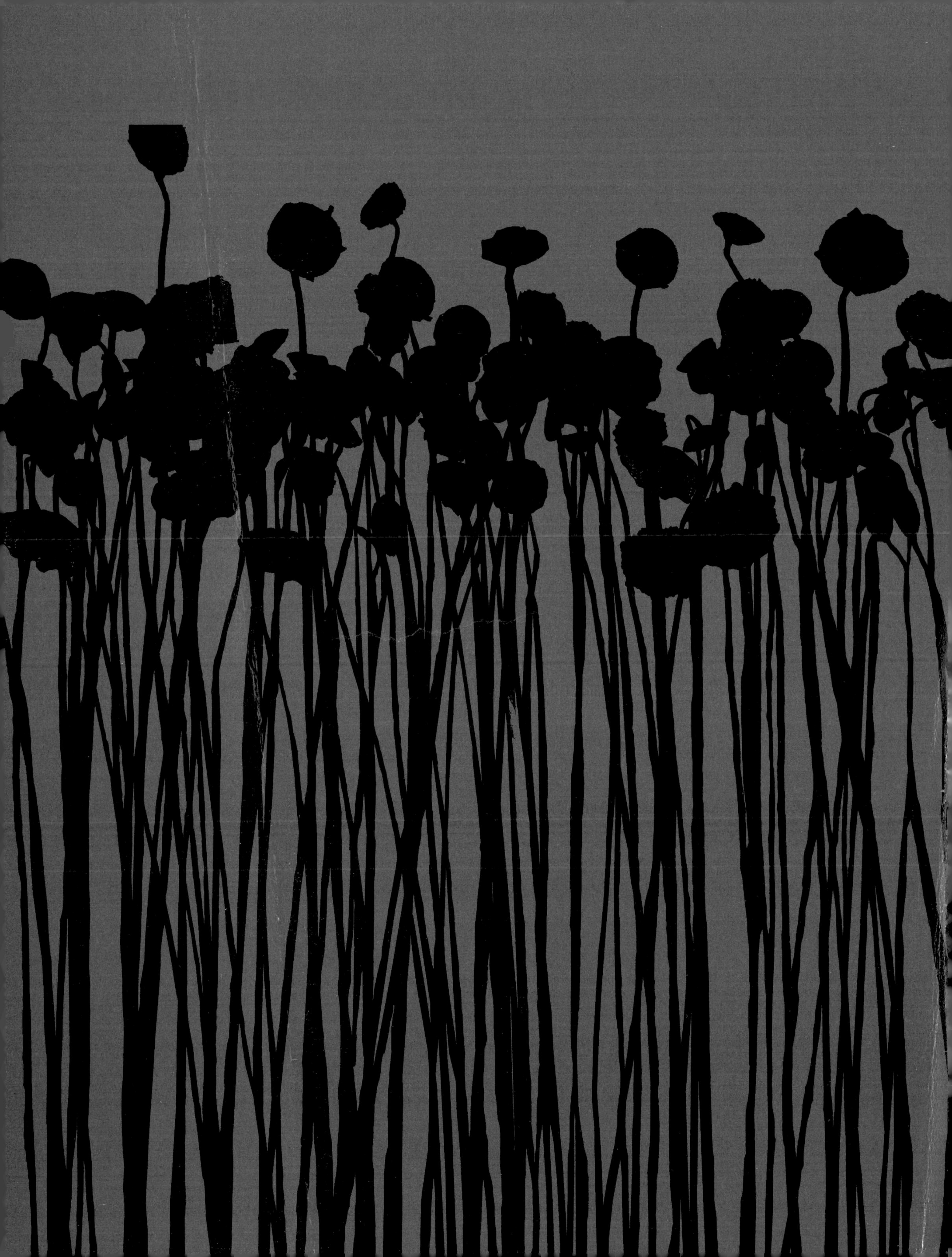

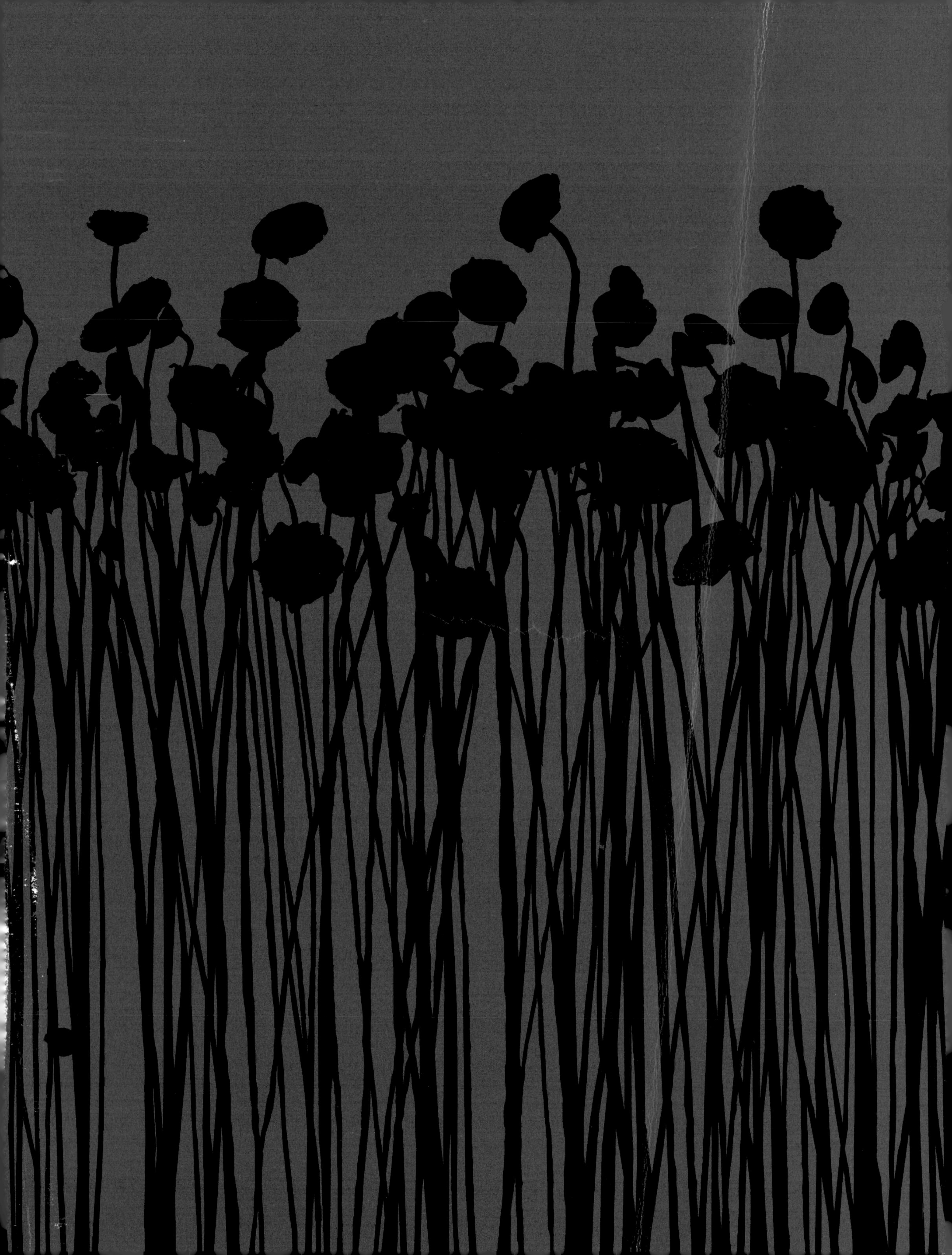

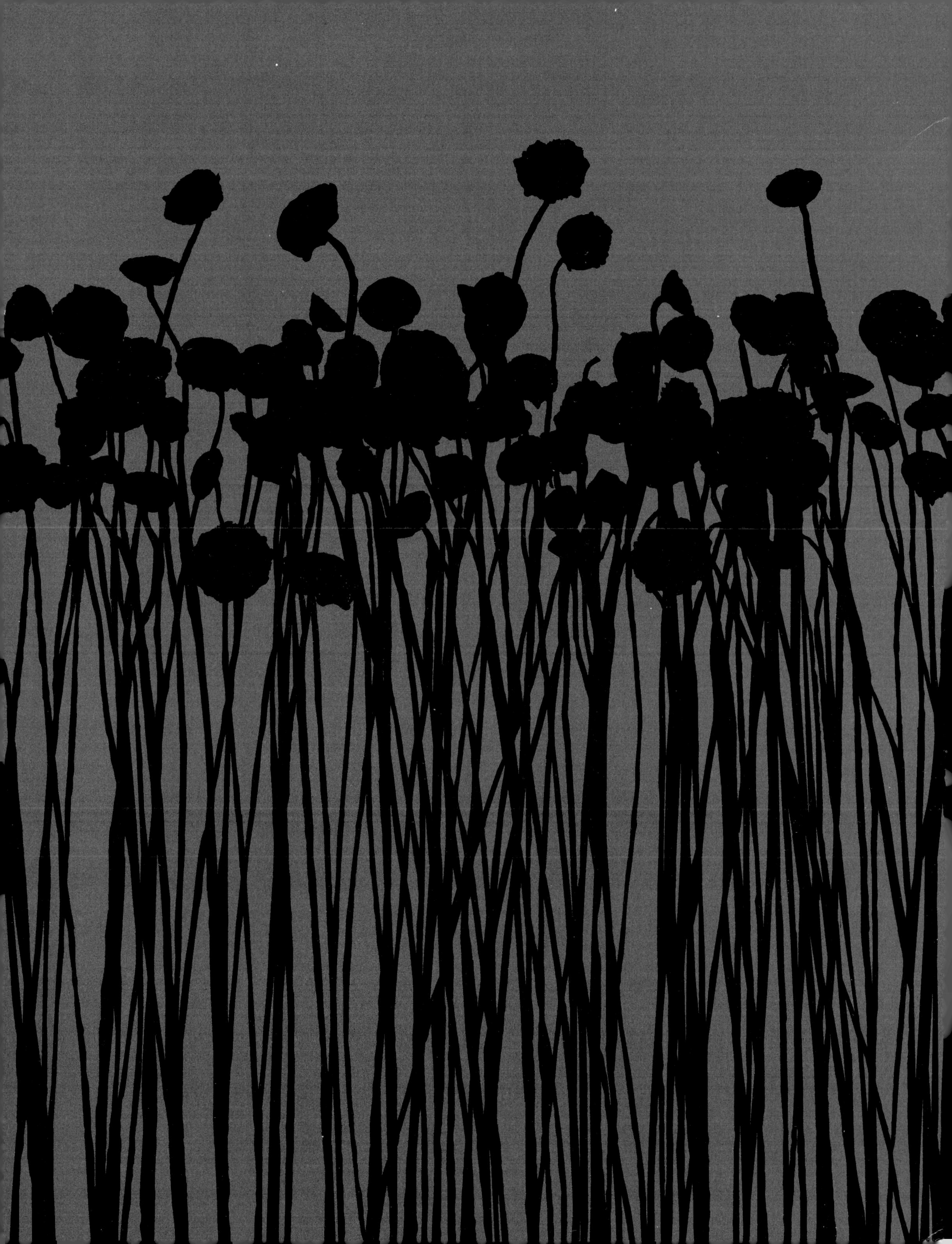

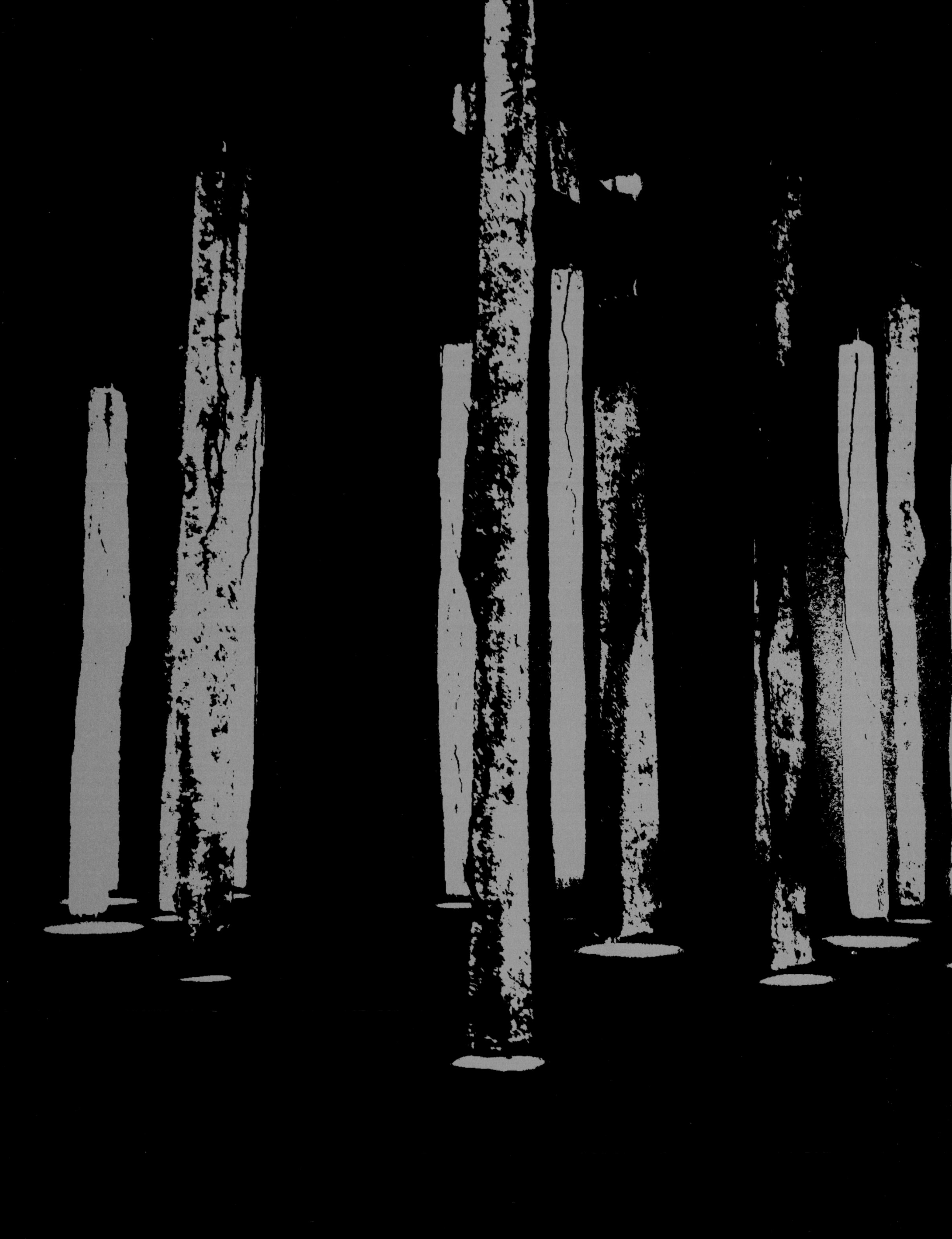

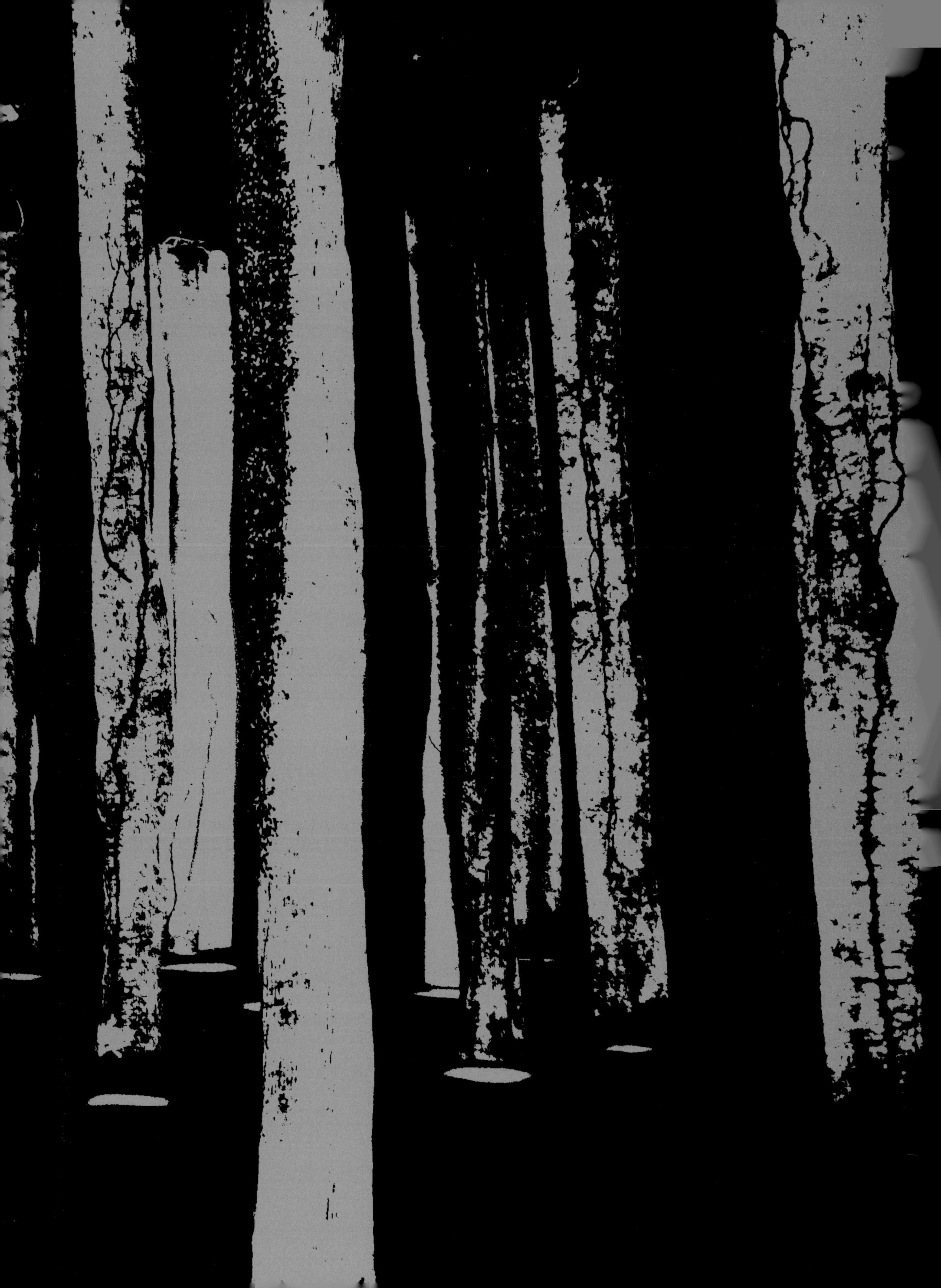

Flourishing Spirits   Blüte des Geistes

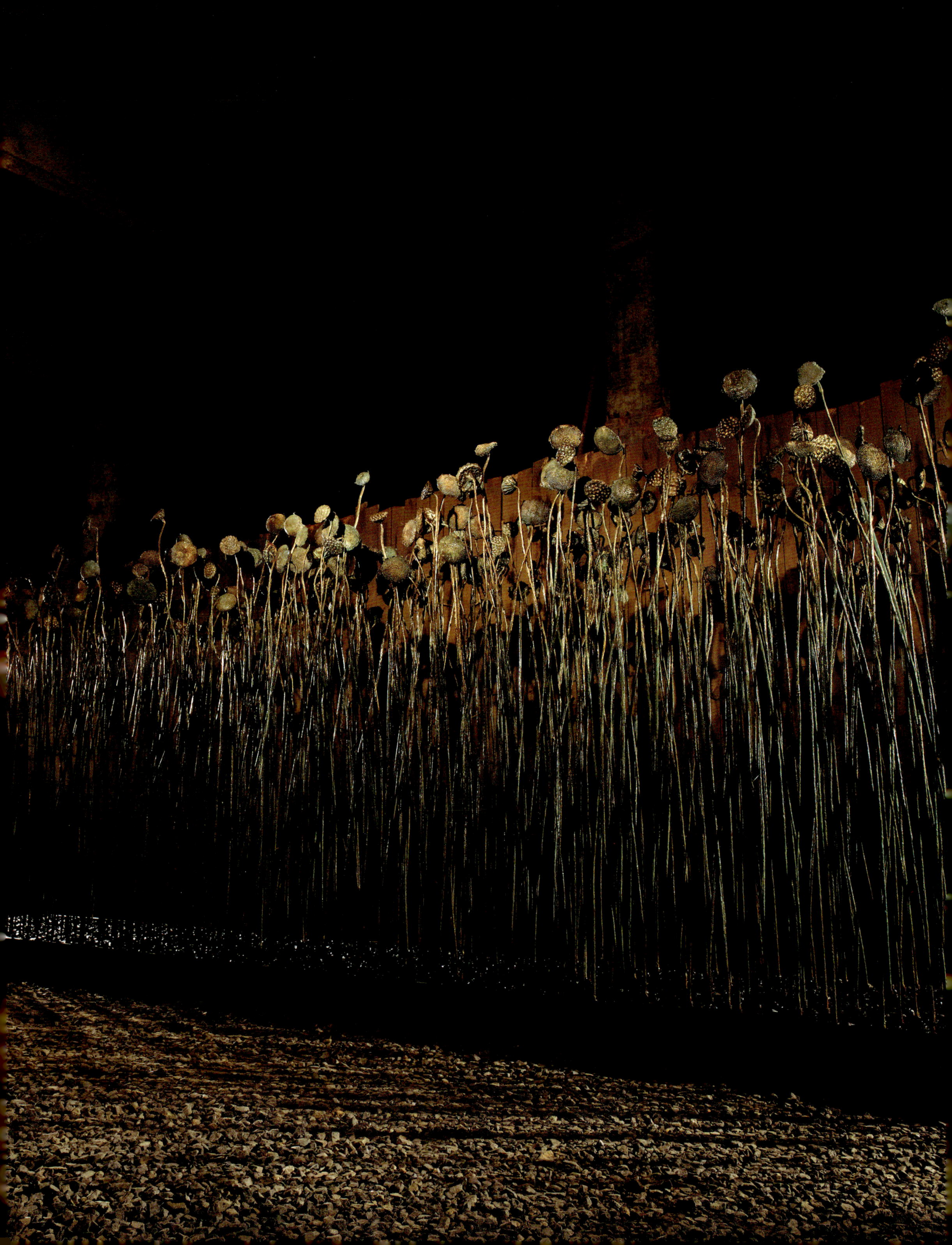

Symbolic Nature
Beate Reifenscheid

Symbolische Natur
Beate Reifenscheid

Xu Jiang
Landscape as Testimony

There are many different ways to depict landscape and nature in images. These possibilities have rarely been exploited as extensively as in Xu Jiang's 'Sunflower paintings' – for the purpose of reductively converting them, in the form of a single motif, into the mirror of an entire epoch and spiritual state. For over a decade, Xu Jiang has dedicated himself to this subject matter and has been able to convert his botanical raw material into a fabric of historical retrospection symbolizing recent Chinese history.

Xu Jiang was born in the province of Fujian in 1955, shortly before the unleashing of the Cultural Revolution, which was introduced by Mao Zedong, then President of the Chinese state. Xu Jiang grew up during a period of great turmoil, which involved enormous societal and cultural changes, and – above all – at a time characterized by permanent unrest and instability: a decade when intellectuals, in particular, were no longer to have anything to say and when traditional, fundamental cultural values were largely negated, if not destroyed. Upon the initiative of Mao, the Cultural Revolution began to be introduced in 1966; it was originally meant to last only a few months, but it would come to dominate China

Xu Jiang
Landschaft als Zeugnis

Es gibt vielerlei Möglichkeiten, Landschaft und Natur im Bild wiederzugeben. Selten wurden ihre Möglichkeiten derart genutzt, um sie so reduziert auf ein einziges Motiv zum Spiegel einer ganzen Epoche und geistigen Verfassung werden zu lassen, wie in Xu Jiangs „Sonnenblumenbildern". Seit einer Dekade widmet sich Xu Jiang diesem Sujet und vermag es, diesen pflanzlichen Rohstoff zu einem Gewebe eines geschichtlichen Rückblicks werden zu lassen, das die jüngere Geschichte Chinas symbolisiert.

Kurz vor Ausbruch der durch den Vorsitzenden Mao eingeleiteten Kulturrevolution wird Xu Jiang 1955 in der Provinz Fujian geboren. Er wächst dort in einer Zeit des großen Umbruchs auf, mit enormen gesellschaftlichen und kulturellen Veränderungen und vor allem in Zeiten, die von permanenter Unruhe und Instabilität gekennzeichnet sind. In einem Jahrzehnt, in dem insbesondere die Intellektuellen nichts mehr zu sagen haben und in dem die alten kulturellen Grundwerte weitgehend negiert, wenn nicht sogar vernichtet wurden. Auf Maos Betreiben hin wird ab 1966 die Kultur-revolution eingeleitet, die ursprünglich nur wenige Monate dauern, dann aber zehn lange Jahre China beherrschen

1 China's Xinhua News Agency, 23 August 1966. The English here is translated from the German version in: VR China im Wandel, ed. by Ostkolleg der Bundeszentrale für politische Bildung (Bonn, 1988), p. 235.

for ten long years. In the end, it would briefly outlive Mao, who died in September 1976. It was only through Mao's successor – Deng Xiaoping, who was able to return to power in July 1977, despite numerous adversities and intrigues within the Communist Party – that the Cultural Revolution could finally be brought to an end. This Cultural Revolution had turned inside out the whole of China's development up to that time, and it radically interrupted dynamic processes within Chinese society; what is more, it attempted to use force to restore the population back to a state of unity and simplicity that – in the end, even as early as the 1960s – was already inappropriate. Today it must thus be understood not in terms of a cultural revolution in the positive sense, but as a gigantic campaign serving the cult of personality surrounding Mao and directed against all those forces that he considered to be opposed to his will and his political goals. Many of the measures taken were aimed purely at political 're-education' and effectively took the form of punishment for those affected, who had no way of knowing when they would end. Thus, in the 'Programme of the Red Guard in Peking of 23 August 1966', Mao decreed that '14. The intellectuals should work in the villages' and the following under points 21–23: '21. The old painting, whose subjects are not political themes, must disappear. 22. It cannot be tolerated that images be distributed, which do not correspond to the thought of Mao Zedong. 23. Books that do not record the thought of Mao Zedong must be burned.'[1] This was a radical declaration of war on traditional China: Mao combatted its feudal structures, but he went so far that he essentially sought to destroy the entire cultural heritage of this giant empire – all of those great achievements that elevate China to a status high above that of other cultures – and also its living legacy, which, of course, can only be passed on and maintain its vibrancy by means of tradition.

Accordingly, the CC (Central Committee) of the Chinese

1 Chinas Xinhua Nachrichtenagentur vom 23.8.1966. Deutsche Übersetzung in: Ostkolleg der Bundeszentrale für politische Bildung (Hrsg.), VR China im Wandel, Bonn 1988: 235.

sollte. Am Ende sollte sie Mao noch kurz überleben, der im September 1976 stirbt. Erst durch seinen Nachfolger Deng Xiaoping, der sich im Oktober 1977 vielen Widrigkeiten und Intrigen innerhalb der Partei zum Trotz an die Spitze des Staates katapultieren konnte, kann sie endgültig beendet werden. Diese Kulturrevolution hat alles umgekrempelt, was sich bis dahin in China entwickelt hatte und sie unterbrach radikal dynamische Prozesse innerhalb der Gesellschaft, mehr noch, sie versuchte mit Gewalt das Volk zu einer Einheit und Einfachheit zurückzuführen, die letztlich bereits in den 1960er Jahren unangemessen waren. Sie muss heute deshalb weniger als Kulturrevolution im positiven Sinne verstanden werden, als vielmehr als eine großangelegte Kampagne im Sinne des Personenkults um Mao Zedong und gegen alle Kräfte, die sich seiner Auffassung nach gegen seinen Willen und seine politischen Ziele stellten. Viele Maßnahmen waren reine Umerziehungsmaßnahmen, die sich als Abstrafungen für die Betroffenen auswirkten, ohne dass diese selbst wussten, wann diese ihr Ende nehmen würden. So verfügte Mao Zedong z.B. im „Programm der Roten Garden" in Peking am 23. August 1966, unter Punkt 14 „Die Intellektuellen sollen auf den Dörfern arbeiten" und unter Punkt 21-23 folgendes: „21. Die alte Malerei, die nicht politische Themen zum Gegenstand hat, muss verschwinden. 22. Es kann nicht geduldet werden, dass Bilder verbreitet werden, die nicht dem Denken Mao Zedongs entsprechen. 23. Bücher, die nicht das Denken Mao Zedongs wiedergeben, müssen verbrannt werden."[1] Es war eine radikale Kampfansage an das alte China, dessen feudalistische Strukturen Mao bekämpfte, dabei aber so weit ging, dass er im Grunde den gesamten kulturellen Schatz dieses Riesenreiches, alle großartigen Errungenschaften, die China weit über die anderen Kulturen erhaben machte und das lebendige Erbe, das sich eben nur durch Tradition weiter reichen und vital erhalten läßt, zunichte machen wollte.

2 This resolution presents the programme of the Cultural Revolution; it is also known as the '16 Points', on account of the structuring of its text. The selection from the source is based on the summary outline found in: Oskar Weggel, Geschichte Chinas im 20. Jahrhundert, pp. 252 f. The English version here is based on the official English translation of the source, available online at: http://www.rrojasdatabank.info/16points.htm [accessed 15 January 2013].

Communist Party's (CCP) resolution of 8 August 1966 regarding the GPCR (Great Proletarian Cultural Revolution) expresses this unambiguously: '1. The GPCR constitutes a new stage of the socialist revolution, whose primary goal is "struggle-criticism-transformation", specifically to "struggle" against those persons in authority who are taking the capitalist road, the "criticism" of "reactionary bourgeois academic authorities" who preach the four relics (old ideas, culture, customs, and habits), and to "transform" education, literature, and art and all other parts of the superstructure not in correspondence with the socialist economic base.'[2]

But a land that robs itself of its own culture is on the brink of the abyss. During the Second World War, the National Socialists carried out the Holocaust upon the Jewish people with precise and lethal efficiency. In doing so, they wiped out Germany's cultural life and, in particular, a substantial part of its intellectual strength. What had been a flourishing land, which surely earned its title as home of the poets and thinkers, was replaced by an intellectual and spiritual void, a cultural vacuum. To date, Germany has still not recovered from these events – and not just in regard to the moral guilt with which the country has burdened itself. While it is true that Mao did not introduce a genocidal apparatus directed against ethnic minorities, he vehemently insisted upon the elimination of those forces that failed to prove submissive. It is easier to understand why he directed his efforts primarily against the intellectual forces of his land – against the artists, intelligentsia, and the theatre – when it becomes clear how much power he attributed to the arts. Precisely because of the fact that they provided the source of intellectual impulses and formulated the ideas behind every significant development, they also presented a major threat to purely political reforms. Art and culture are always appropriated and

2 Dieser Beschluß stellt das Programm der Kulturrevolution dar, der wegen seiner Gliederung auch unter der Bezeichnung „16 Punkte" bekannt geworden ist. Er wird hier stichwortartig zusammengefasst. Dazu siehe Oskar Weggel: Geschichte Chinas im 20. Jahrhundert, 252f.

Im Beschluß des ZK der KPCh über die GPKR (Große Proletarische Kulturrevolution) vom 8. August 1966 heißt es deshalb schon unzweideutig: „(1) Die GPKR ist ihrem Charakter nach eine neue Etappe in der Sozialistischen Revolution, deren Hauptziel 'Kampf-Kritik-Umgestaltung' lautet, nämlich 'Kampf' gegen die Machthaber, die den kapitalistischen Weg gingen, 'Kritik' an den 'bürgerlichen, reaktionären, akademischen Autoritäten', die die Vier Relikte (altes Denken, alte Gewohnheiten, alte Kultur und alte Gebräuche) predigten, und 'Umgestaltung' des Erziehungswesens, der Literatur und Kunst sowie all jener Teile des Überbaus, die keine detailgetreue Widerspiegelung der ökonomischen Basis seien."[2]

Ein Land aber, das sich seiner eigenen Kultur beraubt, steht am Abgrund. Als im Zweiten Weltkrieg durch die Nazi der Holokaust gegen die Juden mit präziser, tödlicher Effizienz ausgeführt wurde und das kulturelle Leben und vor allem wesentliche Teile der intellektuellen Kräfte in Deutschland damit ausgerottet wurden, trat eine geistige Leere, ein kulturelles Vakuum an die Stelle eines ehemals blühenden Landes, das sicherlich zu Recht als das der Dichter und Denker bezeichnet worden war. Deutschland hat sich bis heute davon nicht erholt, auch jenseits der moralischen Schuld nicht, die das Land auf sich genommen hat. Mao Zedong hat zwar keine Tötungsmaschinerie gegen ethnische Gruppen in Gang gesetzt, aber er hat doch sehr dezidiert auf die Beseitigung von Kräften gepocht, die sich als nicht gefügig erwiesen. Dass er dies vor allem auch gegen die geistigen Kräfte im Lande richtete, gegen die Künstler und Literaten sowie gegen das Theater, mag nur dann verständlich sein, wenn man begreift, welche Macht er diesen Künsten zugemessen haben mag. Gerade weil von ihnen die geistigen Impulse ausgehen und die Ideen für alle wesentlichen

instrumentalized whenever they can be utilized for maintaining or establishing power. Art then becomes devoid of will; it becomes an instrument within the grand machinery of propaganda. All dictators take advantage of precisely this condition – initially with great success. In the first years after the Cultural Revolution, China was still struggling with these shadows. In the course of the gradual opening of China since 1985, it has become all too clear that the new art, vehemently oriented towards that of the West, makes use of precisely this idiom by concealing it beneath that other culture of the everyday – Pop Art. Works by Wang Guangyi, for example, have become symbols of a Chinese art that has achieved liberation after Mao and his Great Proletarian Cultural Revolution. However, the wounds that the Cultural Revolution inflicted upon the young, developing generation and the spiritual injury that it has caused, in particular, to the emerging artists of that time are immense. Initial indications of a gradual success seem to be appearing in the developing reflection upon and, above all, in the developing of a distinctive idiom capable of dealing with these memories, these scars burned into the cultural memory. Xu Jiang has found his own form within the language of art, one that permits him to bundle into a single image something that, in its full dimensions, can be grasped only partially – and also allows him to cause this form to resonate and to articulate itself by means of variations.

In May 2012, during a podium discussion accompanying his exhibition at Dresden's Kunsthalle im Lipsiusbau, Xu Jiang vividly described how he, like others during the Cultural Revolution, was forced to undergo the painful experience of being sent to the country as a young student – in order to take part in the 're-education' measures ordered by Mao. Worse than the physical labour there was the fact that he was able to paint only in secret, which he then did to the limits of his endurance. The pressure caused sores on the palms of his hands, which were

Weiterentwicklungen formuliert werden, stellen sie zugleich eine große Bedrohung dar, wenn es um rein politische Reformen geht. Die Kunst und Kultur wird immer dann vereinnahmt und instrumentalisiert, wenn sie zum Erhalt bzw. zur Fundamentierung des Machtaufbaus eingesetzt werden kann. Kunst wird dann willenlos, wird zum Werkzeug der großen Propagandamaschinerie. Genau dieser haben sich alle Diktatoren zunächst höchst erfolgreich bedient. In den ersten Jahren nach der Kulturrevolution hat China mit diesen Schatten noch zu kämpfen und bei der allmählichen Öffnung Chinas nach 1985 wird nur allzu deutlich, dass die neue Kunst, die sich vehement nach Westen hin orientiert, sich genau dieser Sprache bedient, indem sie sie mit der zweiten Alltagskultur überblendet, die der Pop-Art. Werke z.B. von Wang Guangyi werden zu neuen Symbolen einer befreiten chinesischen Kunst nach Mao und seiner Großen Proletarischen Kulturrevolution. - Die Wunden, die diese jedoch in der jungen herangewachsenen Generation geschlagen hat und die seelischen Verletzungen, die sie vor allem bei den damals angehenden Künstlern hinterlassen hat, waren immens und erst allmählich scheint es zu gelingen, hierüber ein Nachdenken und vor allem eine eigene Sprache zu entwickeln, die mit diesen Erinnerungen, mit diesen Brandmalen des kulturellen Gedächtnisses umzugehen lernt. Xu Jiang hat eine eigene Form der künstlerischen Sprache gefunden, die es ihm ermöglicht, das zum Teil in seinen ganzen Ausmaßen nicht Faßbare in eine einzige Form zu bringen und diese in Variationen zum Klingen und zum Sprechen zu bringen.

In einem Diskussionsforum zu seiner Ausstellung im Lipsiusbau in Dresden im Mai des Jahres 2012 beschrieb Xu Jiang eindrücklich, wie schmerzhaft auch er erfahren musste, im Rahmen der Großen Kulturrevolution als junger

3 Torsten Klaus, 'Ganz ohne Gelb: Xu Jiang's Sonnenblumen erinnern an Chinas Kulturrevolution', interview of 31 May 2012, 22:13.

3 Ganz ohne Gelb. Xu Jiang's Sonnenblumen erinnern an Chinas Kulturrevolution, von Torsten Klaus, vom 31. Mai 2012, 22:13.

like the flagellant's marks of the second existence that he was living out in secret. Despite the fact that, after the Cultural Revolution, he was ultimately able to persevere in making his living as an artist, the scars on his soul remain. As someone who has undergone such an elementary experience, he is sensitive to nuances, little signs and symbols that have grown into an individual iconography. The fact that, for a decade now, he has been painting sunflowers in a directly excessive form – which he has since expanded to include monumental installations – is fundamentally connected to this experience of the countryside in extreme psychological isolation. Despite the fact that the motif caught his attention only much later, during a stay in Turkey in 2003, the motifs of the sun and the sunflower are closely linked to China. Among other things, he once emphasized in an interview that, in his native China, they are 'two of the most typical images of the Cultural Revolution'. The badges of young pioneers, for example, had a sun on them. The people of his generation share a common store of memories from that time: 'one that brings tears to their eyes', he says. 'The flowers are the image of an epoch, of his epoch …' 3

Sunflowers are wondrous creations. As flowers, they are astonishingly beautiful; their form and their pattern of growth are simultaneously soaring and solid, while the exterior of their stalk is somewhat unwieldy and coarse. Everything is robust, suited to a vertical growth that sends it soaring above its surroundings, but it is also endowed with so much flexibility that the flowers can always turn to face the current position of the sun. They are sun worshippers in the truest sense of the word. Only the sun is capable of assisting them in fulfilling their actual purpose: bearing fruit and, in their seeds, providing that which is meant to serve both nature and humanity. Their seeds and the oil pressed from them are both a valuable sources of nourishment. The ripening of the fruit is completed

Student aufs Land verschickt zu werden, um an den von Mao befohlenen Umerziehungsmaßnahmen teilzunehmen. Schlimmer noch als die körperliche Arbeit dort war es für ihn, nur heimlich malen zu dürfen und dieses dann bis zur Schmerzgrenze zu exerzieren. Die Handinnenflächen wurden wund von dem Druck und waren ihm wie Geißelungsmale seiner in Heimlichkeit gelebten zweiten Existenz. Auch wenn er seine künstlerische Existenz schließlich nach der Kulturrevolution doch durchsetzten konnte, die Wundmale der Seele sind geblieben. Jemand, der solch grundlegende Erfahrungen gemacht hat, ist empfänglich für Nuancen, für kleine Zeichen und Symbole, die sich bei ihm zu einer eigenen Ikonographie ausgewachsen haben. Dass er nun seit einer Dekade geradezu exzessiv Sonnenblumen malt und sie mittlerweile zu großen Installationen ausweitet, hat elementar mit dieser Erfahrung auf dem Lande – in großer psychischer Isolation – zu tun. Auch wenn ihm das Motiv erst sehr viel später, bei einem Aufenthalt in der Türkei 2003 augenfällig wurde, so sind die Sujets Sonne und Sonnenblume eng mit China verknüpft. Unter anderem betonte er in einem Interview, dass sie „zwei der typischsten Bilder der Kulturrevolution" in seiner Heimat (seien. (Anm. B.R.).). Das Abzeichen junger Pioniere habe beispielsweise eine Sonne gezeigt. Die Menschen seiner Generation hätten einen gemeinsamen Erinnerungsschatz aus jener Zeit:„einen, bei dem die Tränen kommen", sagt er. Die Blumen sind das Abbild einer, seiner Epoche ..."3

Sonnenblumen sind wundersame Geschöpfe: sie sind als Blüte erstaunlich schön, die Gestalt und Ihr Wuchs hingegen sind hoch aufragend, solide, der äußere Schaft des Stengels eher etwas sperrig und ruppig. Alles ist robust, ausgerichtet auf das Wachstum in die Höhe, das alles andere überragt und zugleich so flexibel ausgestattet ist, dass die Blüten sich immer nach dem Stand der Sonne richten können. Sie sind

only upon the death of the flowers – actually, of the entire plant. In death the sunflower reveals the full extent of its power. This is – to put it in emphatic terms – one of the most striking symbols of life and death: something that has long been interpreted in philosophical and political, as well as religious, terms. The life of the sunflower is a parable of life and the purpose of life (providing sustenance – in a figurative sense), and it thus also offers a guarantee that this principle of life will be passed on to subsequent generations.

In the work of Xu Jiang, sunflowers are often invested with this connotation of strictly regulated growth, of the ambition to mature and grow higher and to renounce all individuality for the sake of a common goal that is in accord with nature. Xu Jiang's sunflowers appear in masses; their stems suggest the arching lash of a whip that had once striven up into the sky but has since expended all of its force. In their amalgamation they reflect the expansiveness of the giant sunflower fields after the period of blossoming: they are never shown as symbols of the sun and beauty, but always only in the state of their maturity, their dying. It is thus possible to associate the connotation of his generation's sense of life with the sunflower fields. An association with that of his father's generation would surely also be appropriate, with those who – regardless of whether voluntarily or because forced to do so – submitted to so many sacrifices and now, as though after a long battle, pass on their fruit to those to come. A feeling of helplessness casts its shadow across the stalks of these dying plants. However, Xu Jiang's sunflowers also express a solidarity that this generation may have experienced as equally binding. Their destiny binds them together, and this may be an indication of why he always seeks to apply colour to his works in a largely homogeneous form. A single tone of colour defines each image: a strong grey, an almost acidic green, or an ochre yellow like that so vividly exemplified in the 2005 series 'Twelve

Sonnenanbeterinnen im wahrsten Sinne des Wortes. Nur die Sonne vermag es, ihnen zu ihrer eigentlichen Bestimmung zu verhelfen: Frucht zu tragen und in den Samen das bereitzuhalten, was der Natur und dem Menschen dienen soll. Ihre Kerne und das aus ihnen gepresste Öl, sind beides Nahrungsmittel von hohem Wert. Die Reife der Frucht ist erst dann abgeschlossen, wenn die Blüte, ja die ganze Pflanze, abstirbt. Im Tod offenbart sie ihre ganze Kraft. Das ist – pathetisch gesprochen - eines der sinnfälligsten Symbole von Leben und Tod, etwas, das seit langem schon sowohl philosophisch, politisch als auch religiös gedeutet wurde. Das Leben der Sonnenblume ist eine Parabel des Lebens, des Lebensziels (Nahrung zu liefern – im übertragenen Sinne) und damit Sicherung der Weitergabe dieses Lebensprinzips an nachfolgende Generationen.

Bei Xu Jiang erhalten sie vielfach diese Konnotation von streng geregeltem Wachstum, dem Eifern nach Höhe und Reife, nach Aufgabe von allem Individuellen zugunsten des gemeinsamen – naturgewollten – Zieles. Seine Sonnenblumen treten in Massen auf, ihre Pflanzenstengel muten wie Peitschenhiebe an, die einst in den Himmel strebten, nun aber ihre Kraft eingebüßt haben. In ihrer Vermassung spiegeln sie zum einen die Weite riesiger Sonnenblumenfelder nach der Blüte, denn nie werden sie als Symbol für die Sonne und die Schönheit gezeigt, sondern immer im Zustand ihrer Reife, ihres Absterbens. Deshalb kann man seine Sonnenblumenfelder auch mit dem Lebensgefühl seiner Generation konnotieren, oder wohl auch mit der seiner Vätergeneration, jener also, die nun abtritt, die sich aber vielfach aufgeopfert haben – ob willentlich oder gezwungener Maßen sei dahin gestellt – und die nun, wie nach einer langen Schlacht ihre Früchte weiterreichen an die, die nachkommen werden. Es liegt ein Gefühl der Ohnmacht über diesen dahin-

views of a sunflower field V'. Here, the sharply defined horizon is also remarkable: it leaves little space free for the sky and – except for a single version – the individual plants are never allowed to penetrate across it. Xu Jiang also makes use of the atmospheric play of light and shadow, and he endows the entire picture plane with a vibrating tension evoked by means of his agitated and, so to speak, shimmering brushstroke. This deliberately agitated use of the brush can already be seen in his early works, where it causes the actual image to remain unidentifiable. The glimmering introduces an unsettled aspect into the visual experience of the work; in turn, viewers are unable to regain their composure or, in the end, to arrive at a definitive point of view. Instead, they are themselves cast into this state of uncertainty. In its ambiguity, the composition once again becomes entirely unambiguous. Ultimately, those works created around 2000 and 2001 – featuring views of Berlin, Beijing, and Shanghai – already testify to this energetic force that manifests both destruction and resistance in equal parts. Many of his views of Berlin recall old photographs from the Second World War, when the city had been reduced to ashes and rubble and scarcely anyone could have imagined that it would be able to rise up out of the ashes like a phoenix. The dramatic energy instilled in Xu Jiang's paintings, particularly the sum effect of their use of colour, causes them to resemble memorial images – like images that conjure up the portents of destruction. However, in light of a city that – since the fall of the Berlin wall in 1989 – has found itself in the midst of a gigantic project of reconstruction and whose integrative process could be observed on a daily basis, the works seem to simultaneously incorporate the dimension of the future and not just that of the past. Destruction on the one hand and fragmentation on the other need not necessarily be opposites; instead, they can also simply represent the two sides of a single coin. It becomes clear that the history of this place

sterbenden Pflanzenstengeln. Xu Jiangs Sonnenblumenfelder drücken aber auch einen Zusammenhalt aus, der gleichermaßen für diese Generation verbindlich gewesen sein mag. Ihr Schicksal eint sie und dies mag ein Zeichen dafür sein, weshalb er in seinen Bildwerken immer eine große farbliche Homogenität sucht. Es ist nur ein Farbklang, der das jeweilige Bild bestimmt: ein kräftiges Grau, ein fast giftiges Grün oder ein ockerfarbiges Gelb wie dies in der Serie „Twelve Views of a Sunflower Field V", von 2005 sehr anschaulich verdeutlicht. Auffällig sind hier zudem der scharf gezogene Horizont, der nur wenig Raum für den Himmel freilässt und in den die einzelne Pflanze – bis auf eine Bildfassung – niemals hineinragen darf. Zudem spielt Xu Jiang mit dem atmosphärischen Spiel von Licht und Schatten und bringt die gesamte Bildfläche in eine vibrierende Anspannung, die er durch seinen unruhigen, gleichsam flirrenden Pinselduktus evoziert. Diese bewußt in Unruhe versetzte Handschrift konnte man bereits an früheren Bildern Xu Jiangs beobachten, durch die das eigentliche Abbild unfassbar blieb. Da durch das Flirren ein unstetes Moment in die Betrachtung eindringt, kommt auch der Betrachtende seinerseits nicht zur Ruhe, kann letztlich keinen definitiven Standpunkt ausmachen, sondern muss selbst in diesen Schwebezustand geraten. In der Uneindeutigkeit wird dann die Komposition wieder vollkommen eindeutig. Letztlich zeugen bereits die um 2000 und 2001 entstandenen Werke mit Ansichten von Berlin, Beijing und Shanghai von dieser energetischen Kraft, die gleichermaßen Zerstörung wie auch Widerstand manifestiert. Viele seiner Ansichten von Berlin erinnern an alte Fotografien aus dem Zweiten Weltkrieg, als die Stadt in Schutt und Asche lag und sich wohl kaum einer vorzustellen vermochte, dass diese Stadt wie ein Phönix aus der Asche auferstehen könnte. Die Bilder Xu Jiangs erscheinen durch ihrer dramatische Aufladung, insbesondere durch die farbliche Gesamtwirkung, wie Erin-

4 Yang Xiaoyan, 'Xu Jaing's fragmentation: Cross-cultural art practices and
   their implications on the post-revolution era', in exh. cat., Re-Generation
   (Dresden, 2012), p. 27.

and its people are linked to destruction and downfall and, at the
same time, that the future can only be envisioned in terms of the
continuing course of an unstable and uncertain development.
Interestingly, Xu Jiang also instils his views of Beijing and
Shanghai with this dynamic unrest, the insecurity that nothing will
remain as it seems. The pattern that he designs in this process is
typically subjected to a view from above – as though seen from
a bomber – and is abstracted to the greatest degree possible,
causing its subject matter to be more intuited than recognized.
Subsequently, the impression arises that Xu Jiang, with his
pictorial structures, essentially provides a view of his own and
foreign cultures subsumed under the same ambivalent pattern
of destruction, resistance, and construction. Particularly works
such as "Great Beijing: Drum and bell tower I", of 2001, can
be interpreted as an image of potential, as a visionary view of
history. A hand reaches out from the clouds of the sky, as though
it wished to intervene in the course of history. Or is it, instead of
a divine power, only a symbol for the players in the great game
of history, those who direct the destinies of human beings as
though playing chess – often simply wasting them? "Chess
Match of the Century: Walled City II" (1998) or "Landscapes of
history: Wall and power" (200) enable us to recognize that Xu
Jiang's interest is always in the grand, the historical dimension of
cities and landscapes.

Yang Xiaoyan is correct in using the term 'fragmentation' to
refer to Xu Jiang's painterly style. He goes on to elaborate: 'In
a sense, Xu Jiang's art practices are embedded in fragmentation, and this has become their overarching symbolism.'[4] Here,
fragmentation refers much less to an outward structure than
to that fracturing into the different levels of experience which
governed life and work during and after the Cultural Revolution.
In a certain sense, Xu Jiang achieves both, specifically: (1) he
actual fragments the subject matter into thousands of individual

nerungsbilder – wie Bilder, die das Menetel der Zerstörung
beschwören. Angesichts einer Stadt, die sich nach dem Fall
der Mauer 1989 jedoch in einem gigantischen Wiederaufbau
befand und deren Zusammenwachsen man täglich verfolgen
konnte, scheinen sie deshalb zugleich die Dimension der
Zukunft – und eben nicht nur die der Vergangenheit – in
sich aufzunehmen. Zerstörung auf der einen und Fragmentierung auf der anderen Seite müssen nicht zwangsläufig
Gegensätze sein, sondern können nur die jeweils andere
Seite derselben Medaille sein. Es macht vielmehr deutlich,
dass die Geschichte des Ortes und seiner Menschen mit
Zerstörung und Untergang in Beziehung gesetzt werden und
zugleich auch die Zukunft nur als eine visioniert werden kann,
in der sich der Prozess des Unsteten, des nicht Gewissen,
weiterhin fortsetzt. Interessanterweise überzieht Xu Jiang
auch seine Ansichten von Beijing und Shanghai mit dieser
dynamisierten Unruhe, der Unsicherheit, das nichts bleibt
wie es scheint. Das Muster, das er dabei entwirft, unterliegt
dabei zumeist dem Blick von oben, wie von einem Flieger-
bomber aus gesehen und mit der größtmöglichen Abstraktion,
die mehr ahnen als erkennen läßt. In der Folge entsteht so
der Eindruck, dass Xu Jiang mit der bildnerischen Textur
ganz wesentlich eine Sicht auf die eigene und die femde
Kultur wirft, die er unter das gleiche ambivalente Muster
von Zerstörtheit, Widerstand und Konstruktion stellt. Gerade ein
Werk wie „Great Beijing: Drum and Bell Tower I" von 2001 mag
als ein Möglichkeitsbild, eine visionäre Sicht auf die Geschichte,
verstanden werden. Eine Hand reicht aus den Wolken vom Himmel
herab, so als wolle sie eingreifen in den Lauf der Geschichte. Oder
ist – statt eine göttliche Macht – diese nur ein Symbol für die Spieler
auf dem großen Feld der Geschichte, die wie im Schachspiel die
Geschicke der Menschheit lenken und nicht selten auch einfach
nur verspielen? „Chess Match of the Century: Walled City II" (1998)
oder „Landscapes of History: Wall and Power" (2000) lassen erkennbar

4 Yang Xiaoyan, Xu Jaing's fragmentation: Cross-cultural art practices and their implications on th epost-revolution era, in Ausst.-Kat.: Re-Generation, Dresden 2012, S. 27.

elements, which, however, he then situates within a unified space-time continuum by means of the rhythm of the forceful blows of his brush and his reductive tonalities, and (2) he is simultaneously able to invest this individual iconography with a historical presence by means of his obsessive interpretation of the sunflower. Experience and the present are sublimated within a single symbol. Neither his individual store of experiences, nor his own pain, nor anything that could possibly be related to his own biography is expressed directly; instead, these works reflect the historical dimension and, with it, the existential horizon of a whole generation. They thus achieve something that only a very few artists have been able to give life to through their art. In this sense, the works can best be compared with those of Gerhard Richter, who appropriated documentary photos from the Second World War for his detached, deliberately blurred paintings (blurred precisely in light of the – sought-after – forgetting of historical facts). Xu Jiang's paintings develop a greater emotionality; they do not make use of Richter's detachment. Nonetheless, Xu Jiang's views of Berlin do sometimes pursue a similar historical perspective. A great number of Anselm Kiefer's works are, however, comparable to those of Xu Jiang in terms of subject matter. It is the same melancholy and historical memory that resides in Kiefer's monumental views of Bohemian landscapes and in Xu Jiang's sunflower fields, with their bent stalks. The thickly applied paint, the emphatically dynamic brushstroke, the taste for materiality, and finally, the expansion of the image into an installation – all of these clearly illustrate the two artists' thematic proximity.

However, the absolutely essential nature of signs, the articulation of an iconography of signs become symbols, is also demonstrated, for example, by Ai Weiwei's work "Sunflower Seeds", which was realized for the Tate Modern in 2010. The

werden, dass es ihm immer um die große, um die geschichtliche Dimension von Städten und Landschaften geht.

Mit Recht wird in einem Beitrag von Yang Xiaoyan der malerische Stil Xu Jiangs mit „Fragmentierung" bezeichnet. Er führt dazu aus: „In a sense, Xu Jiang's art practices are embedded in fragmentation, and this has become their overarching symbolism." 4 Fragmentation ist dabei weniger als äußere Struktur gemeint, sondern vielmehr ein Aufspalten in die unterschiedlichen Ebenen von Erfahrung, die während und nach der Kulturrevolution das Leben und Wirken bestimmt haben. Xu Jiang leistet in gewissem Sinne beides: nämlich tatsächlich die Aufsplitterung des Sujets in tausende von Einzelelementen, die er dann jedoch durch den Rhythmus seiner heftigen Pinselschläge und durch die reduzierte Farbigkeit in ein einheitliches Raum-Zeitkontinuum gießt und zugleich vermag er es, durch die obsessive Ausdeutung der Sonnenblumen diesen eine eigene Ikonographie der ge-schichtlichen Präsenz zu verleihen. Erfahrung und Gegenwart werden in einem einzigen Symbol sublimiert. Nicht der individuelle Erfahrungsschatz, nicht der eigene Schmerz, nichts, was mit der eigenen Biographie zu tun haben könnte, werden direkt ausgedrückt, sondern die geschichtliche Dimension und mit ihr der Erfahrungshorizont einer ganzen Generation spiegeln sich in diesen Werken. Sie leisten damit etwas, was nur wenige Künstler mit ihrer Kunst zu verlebendigen schaffen. In diesem Sinne sind sie noch am ehesten in Beziehung zu setzen mit Werken von Gerhard Richter, der Dokumentarphotos aus dem Zweiten Weltkrieg in seine sachliche, bewußt unscharfe Malerei übernommen hat (Unschärfe gerade in Anbetracht des Vergessen von geschichtlichen Fakten). Xu Jiangs Bilder entwickeln mehr Pathos, bedienen sich nicht der Sachlichkeit eines Gerhard Richters, aber seine Berlin-Ansichten intendieren zuweilen eine ähnliche historische

5 N-tv, 11 October 2010.

6 See Xu Jiang's series of watercolours 'Depth of winter' (2009), in Re-Generation, pp. 74–75.

artist had 150 tonnes of porcelain sunflower seeds manu-factured and then painted by hand. He stated that, in this way, he wished to draw attention to the culture of porcelain in his native country. 'With the Sunflower seeds, Ai Weiwei also wished to call attention to the theme of poverty in his native China. Sunflower seeds are one of the most important sources of sustenance for many people in China.' [5] The ambiguity between culture and food, but certainly also the connotations of the historical dimension, become only too clear in the work of Ai Weiwei. If Xu Jiang has erected a large field with eight-metre aluminium sunflowers for recent exhibitions, then this installation holds an entirely new perspective and interpretation in store. The formerly broken stalks, the hordes of exhausted sunflowers that suggested warriors returning home after a long battle, or the fields that seemed to be fenced off with barbed wire [6] have now become plants that soar high into the air. The old pain seems to have been overcome and the seed to have finally sprouted. Viewers now find self-confident figures standing before them and – if the statement were not so susceptible to political misunder-standing – it could also be said that, here, the self-sacrificing sunflowers have awoken into beautiful queens.

5 N-tv, 11. Oktober 2010.

6 Siehe hierzu Xu Jiang's Aquarellserie „Depth of Winter, 2009, Ausst.-Kat.
   Dresden, S. 74-75.

Sichtweise. Aber auch zahlreiche Werke von Anselm Kiefer sind inhaltlich mit Xu Jiangs Werken vergleichbar. Kiefers große Landschaftsprospekte von Böhmen tragen die gleiche Melancholie und geschicht-liches Gedächtnis in sich wie die Sonneblumenfelder mit ihren geknickten Stengeln bei Xu Jiang. Die Pastosität der Farbe, die heftige Dynamik im Pin-selduktus, die Vorliebe zur Material-haftigkeit, schließlich auch die Ausweitung des Bildes zur Installation – all dies lässt die inhaltliche Nähe des Künstlers deutlich werden.

Wie wesentlich jedoch die Zeichen sind, das Ausformulieren einer Ikonographie der Zeichen, die zu Symbolen werden, zeigt u.a. auch die Arbeit von Ai Weiwei „Sunflower Seeds", die dieser für die Tate Modern 2010 realisierte. Er ließ 150 Tonnen Porzellansamenkörper fertigen und von Hand bemalen. Er wolle damit auf die Porzellankultur in seinem Heimatland aufmerksam machen. „Mit den 'Sunflower Seeds' will Ai Weiwei auch an die Not in seinem Heimatland China erinnern. Sonnenblumenkerne sind für viele Chinesen eines der wichtigsten Nahrungsmittel." [5] Die Doppeldeutigkeit zwischen Kultur und Nahrungsmittel, zugleich sicherlich aber auch die Konnotation der geschichtlichen Dimension, wird bei Ai Weiwei nur allzu deutlich. Wenn Xu Jiang für seine neueren Ausstellungen ein großen Feld mit acht Meter hohen Alu-miniumsonnenblumen errichtet, dann trägt diese Installation eine ganz neue Sicht- und Deutungsweise in sich. Von den ehemals gebrochenen Stengeln, den Heerscharen von müden Sonnenblumen, die wie Krieger aus einer langen Schlacht heimzukehren scheinen, oder deren Felder, die wie von Stacheldraht umzäunt wirken,[6] sind nun hoch aufragende Pflanzen geworden. Es scheint, der alte Schmerz ist überwunden und die Saat ist endlich aufgegangen. Vor dem Betrachter stehen nun selbstbewußte Größen und wäre es politisch nicht völlig missverständlich könnte man auch behaupten, dass hier aus den sich aufopfernden Sonnen-blumen schöne Königinnen erwacht sind.

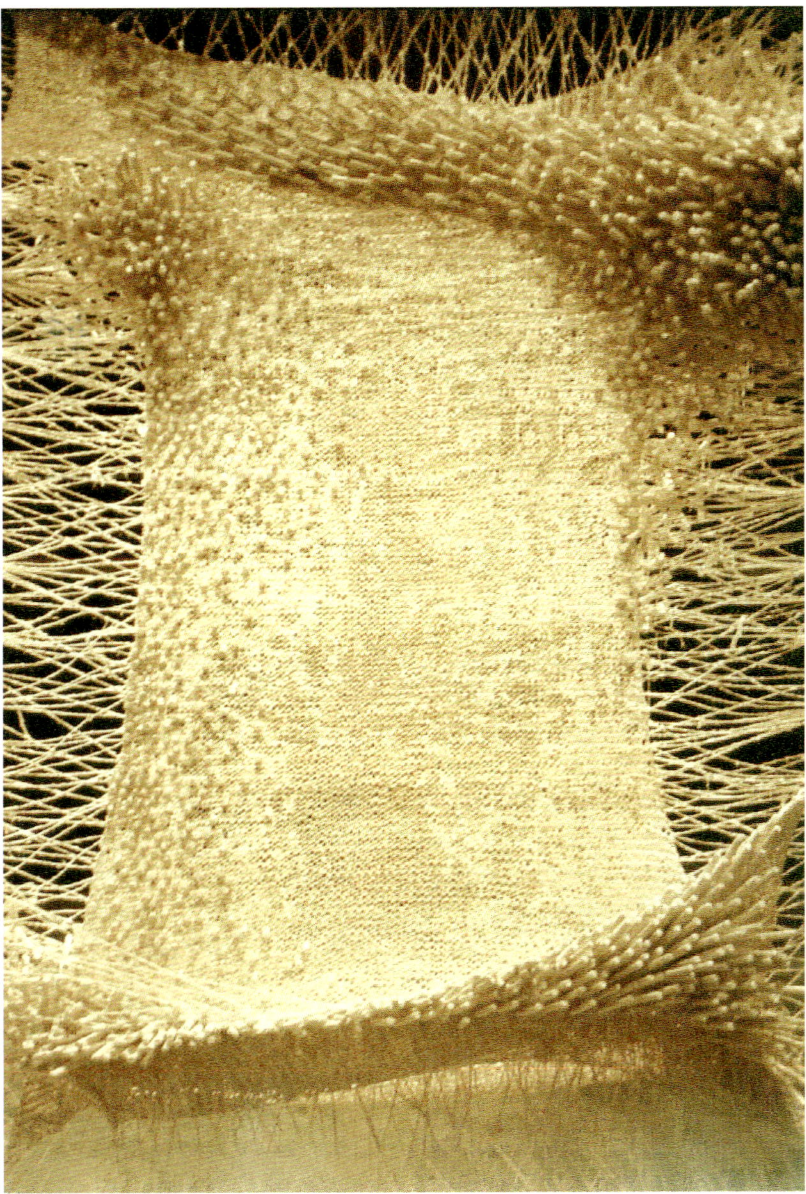

1998   Struture·III · Installation · 188cm×130cm×20cm
Knoten·III · Installation · 188cm×130cm×20cm

Shi Hui
The Fabric of Nature

At least since the Surrealists, the use of natural materials has been a part of the art of the twentieth century. Artists such as André Masson and André Bréton used sand or found objects, for example, in order to develop different surface textures or to establish associative contexts. However, it was among the protagonists of Art Informel, particularly among German artists, that a genuinely new artistic impulse first developed – at the moment they began to incorporate natural materials into their abstract images. This is particularly true in the case of Emil Schumacher, who fixed rocks or also tar to his large cotton duck canvasses, or Gerhard Hoehme, who was led to incorporate volcanic rock from Mount Etna into the paintings of his series, the "Ätna-Zyklus" [Etna cycle] (1980–84). These developments were directly related to the historical and social aftermath of the Second World War: after the propagandistic painting of the National Socialists, the artists of America and particularly those of Europe had no choice but to create abstract works. They were convinced that non-objective art offered greater spiritual and intellectual freedom and also a more productive path for gaining access to philosophical or purely spiritual concepts. This was demonstrated, above all, by the American artists, with the powerful and gestural works of the New York School, followed by the Art Informel of Europe. It is interesting that Pop artists took up the mass-produced surfeit of the industrial age to develop an opposing position – a position adopted in Europe by the Nouveaux Réalistes, who, for their part, cast themselves primarily upon everyday objects that had already been manufactured (Arman, for example, with his 'accumulations'). In contrast, positions related to what is referred to as 'Land Art', as developed in the 1960s by Robert Smithson or Peter Hutchinson and provided with an expanded dimension in Europe – for example, through the walks of Richard Long and Hamish Fulton – seemed to reside entirely beyond the previously familiar horizons of art. In Italy, as well, Arte Povera developed entirely new possibilities and radical changes in thinking. All of

Shi Hui
Der Stoff der Natur

Die Nutzung von Naturmaterialien ist in der Kunst des 20. Jahrhunderts spätestens seit den Surrealisten gegenwärtig. Künstler wie André Masson und André Bréton nutzten beispielsweise Sand oder gefundene Objekte, um andere Oberflächenstrukturen zu entwickeln oder assoziative Kontexte herzustellen. Aber einen wirklich neuen Impuls für die Kunst entwickelten erst die Künstler des Informel, insbesondere die deutschen Künstler, als sie anfingen, Naturstoffe in ihre abstrakten Bildwerke mit einzubeziehen. Dies trifft insbesondere bei Emil Schumacher zu, der Gesteinsbrocken oder auch Teer auf seine großen Nesselstoffe brachte oder führte Gerhard Hoehme dazu, in seinem "Ätna-Zyklus" (1980-84) eigens Lavasteine vom Ätna in seine opulente Bilderserie einzufügen. Die Entwicklungen standen in unmittelbarem Zusammenhang mit den geschichtlichen und gesellschaftlichen Auswirkungen des Zweiten Weltkriegs, als nach der propagandistischen Malerei des Nationalsozialismus die Künstler in Amerika und vor allem in Europa nicht anders als abstrakt malen konnten. In der gegenstandslosen Kunst, so ihre Überzeugung, lägen eine größere Freiheit des Geistes und zugleich eine tiefere Einmündung in philosophische oder rein geistige Konzepte. Dies zeigten allen voran die amerikanischen Künstler mit ihren kraftvollen gestischen Arbeiten der New York School, denen das Informel in Europa folgte. Als Gegenposition nahmen Künstler der Pop-Art sich interessanterweise der Materialflut des Industriezeitalters an, dem sich in Europa die Künstler der Nouveaux Réalistes annahmen und die sich ihrerseits vornehmlich auf bereits fertig produzierte Alltagsgegenstände stürzten (z. B. Arman mit seinen "accumulations"). Dagegen wirkten dann Positionen wie sie in der sogenannten Land-Art durch Robert Smithson oder Peter Hutchinson in den 1960er Jahren entwickelt wurden und beispielsweise in den Wanderungen von Robert Long oder Hamish Fulton in Europa eine erweiterte Dimension

1 Theodor Adorno, Aesthetic Theory, trans. by Robert Hullot-Kentor (London, 1997), p. 148.

these artists had long since bid farewell to the pure studio and to the traditional space of the museum; in a sense, they reinvented their material itself and reflected upon nature in a new way – and thus also upon the materials that it constantly brings forth in its process of becoming and passing away. Artists such as Mario Merz, Jannis Kounellis, or Giuseppe Penone worked primarily in wood, stone, glass, and many other materials. They did this not only for the sake of the material, but also in order to shed light on a contested aspect of society by means of their artistic statements, a subject matter articulated by means of natural materials. Arte Povera also began as a counter-movement to and a reflex against the consumerism of the reinvigorated industrialized countries and existed in a state of critical opposition to a world ever more dominated by technology. The desire to extend the limits of art and life also led to process-based approaches. Temporary installations and actions conceived for the moment defined the image of Arte Povera at the end of the sixties.

In his *Aesthetic Theory*, which was written at approximately the same time as these stylistic developments although it was first published posthumously, Theodor Adorno granted material – and thus, in a more narrow sense, natural material as well – the title of "emancipated" and understood it as being equal in value to previous artistic materials, such as canvas, paint, chalk, etc. However, what is most interesting is his remark that he does not value the material as timeless – as might seem likely in the case of the products of nature, such as twigs, wood, stone, etc. He goes on to elaborate: 'Thus material is not natural material even if it appears so to artists; rather, it is thoroughly historical.' [1]

Looking at the works of the artist Shi Hui, who – for over twenty years – has been dealing exclusively with natural

erhielten, vollkommen außerhalb der bis dato geläufigen künstlerischen Horizonte. Auch die in Italien initiierte Arte Povera erschloss völlig neue Möglichkeiten und radikales Umdenken. Sie alle hatten sich längst vom reinen Studio oder auch vom klassischen musealen Raum verabschiedet und erfanden sich gleichsam durch das Material selbst neu und reflektierten auf eine neue Art die Natur und damit auch ihre Materialien, die diese im Prozess des Werdens und Vergehens immer wieder selbst hervorbrachte. Künstler wie Mario Merz, Jannis Kounellis, Giuseppe Penone u.a. haben vornehmlich mit Holz, Stein, Glas und vielem mehr gearbeitet. Dies geschah nicht nur um des Materials willens, sondern auch, um mit ihrer künstlerischen Aussage ein gesellschaftliches Spannungsfeld aufzuzeigen, das über das Naturmaterial formuliert wurde. Auch die arte povera wurde als Gegenbewegung und Reflex auf die Konsumhaltung der wieder erstarkten Industrienationen initiiert und stand im kritischen Gegensatz zur immer technologischer werdenden Umwelt. Der Wunsch, die Grenzen von Kunst und Leben zu erweitern, hatte zudem zu einer prozessualen Vorgehensweise geführt. Vergängliche Installationen und für den Augenblick gedachte Aktionen bestimmten Ende der sechziger Jahre das Bild der Arte Povera.

Theodor Adorno hat in seiner etwa zeitgleich zu diesen Stilrichtungen entstandenen – aber erst posthum erschienenen – Schrift "Ästhetische Theorie" das Material, und damit im engeren Sinne auch das Naturmaterial, als "emanzipiert" tituliert und es gleichwertig zu vorher gegangenen künstlerischen Materialien wie Leinwand, Farbe, Stift etc. begriffen. Interessant ist aber vor allem seine Ausführung, dass er dieses nicht als zeitlos gewertet hat, was möglicherweise bei einem Naturprodukt wie Zweigen, Holz, Steine etc. naheliegen könnte. Er geht noch weiter, wenn er ausführt. "Material ist auch dann kein Naturmaterial, wenn es den Künstler als

1 Theodor Adorno, Ästhetische Theorie, Surkamp 1973, S. 223.

materials, the scope of her statements becomes more vivid when placed before this historical background. Seen superficially, it might seem to viewers that the paper, the plants, and the fans folded out of paper and bearing traces of ink are the expression of a very feminine style. While this cannot be entirely denied, Shi Hui is focussed on something else. In my opinion, several different readings are possible: on the one hand, paper is a traditional support for images – particularly in China. The entirety of Chinese ink painting, which, even to present, has always retained its status as the highest artistic discipline, is founded upon paper – alongside the early use of silk as support up. Despite the fact that paper derives from a manufacturing process, its raw material is nonetheless purely a product of nature. In this sense, Shi Hui's objects achieve a reflective interaction with nature and her own culture. However, she does not use this material for a traditional ink painting but, from the very beginning, creates and manufactures it herself – precisely as she would like to have it perceived in terms of its texture, permeability, and also surface. In this way, she has consciously distanced herself from a form of its use that has become almost normative; instead, she reinterprets the material. This step must have seemed far more revolutionary in the China of the early nineties than it would have seemed in Europe or America. By incorporating fibreglass, cotton, canvasses, rice, and other materials, Shi Hui has been able to stake out an extended radius of action over the course of two decades and, at the same time, interrogate the concepts of sculpture and space as well as form and anti-form. Within the historical context of the gigantic paradigm shift realized in contemporary Chinese art since 1985, this was a courageous step and, at the same time, the sign of an individual's opening herself up to influence by developments in Western art. It is thus no less interesting than enlightening to accept the forms of Shi Hui and to find an interpretation that goes beyond pure surface.

solchen präsentiert, sondern geschichtlich durch und durch." 1

Betrachtet man die Arbeiten der Künstlerin Shi Hui, die sich bereits seit über zwanzig Jahren ausschließlich mit Naturmaterialien befasst, wird die Dimension ihrer Aussagen vor diesem geschichtlichen Hintergrund noch eindrücklicher. Oberflächlich betrachtet könnte man meinen, dass sich im Papier, in den Pflanzen, in den aus Papier gefalteten Fächern, auf denen Spuren von Tusche zu finden sind, sich eine sehr weibliche Handschrift ausdrückt. Wenngleich dies nicht völlig zu negieren ist, so liegt der Fokus bei ihr jedoch auf etwas Anderem. Es bieten sich m.E. mehrerlei Lesarten an: zum einen ist Papier eines der klassischen Trägermaterialien für Bilder, insbesondere aber in China. Die gesamte chinesische Tuschmalerei, die bis heute ungebrochen die Königsdisziplin der Kunst ist, begründet sich – neben anfänglicher Nutzung von Seide als Malgrund – auf Papier. Wenngleich dem Papier bereits ein Herstellungsprozess vorangeht, so ist der Ausgangsstoff dennoch ein reines Naturprodukt. Insofern leistet Shi Hui mit ihren Objekten einen reflektierten Umgang mit Natur und mit der eigenen Kultur. Indem sie jedoch dieses Material nicht für die traditionelle Tuschmalerei nutzt, sondern von Anfang an das Material selbst schöpft und herstellt, so wie sie es in der Textur, der Durchlässigkeit und zugleich in der Oberfläche wahrgenommen haben möchte, distanziert sie sich bewusst von der geradezu normativ gewordenen Nutzung und interpretiert stattdessen das Material neu. Anfang der 1990er Jahre in China muss dieser Schritt weit revolutionärer gewirkt haben als dies in Europa oder Amerika wahrgenommen werden konnte. Durch Einbeziehung von Fiberglas, Baumwolle, Leinwänden, Reis und andere Materialien konnte Shi Hui in den beiden Dezennien neue Radien abstecken und zugleich die Begriffe von Skulptur und Raum sowie von Form und Antiform hinterfragen. Im

Therefore, it may not be insignificant that the artist was first trained in weaving – another ancient tradition in human history – nor that it was not until 1990 that she gave up working in two dimensions for the sake of a multidimensional applicability within space and even installations occupying space. The gesture of weaving nonetheless remains – she has repeatedly spun threads that anchor, connect, and give support – but it has taken on a completely different aspect. This can already be seen in one of her first works, structure 1, of 1995, in which she has stretched white and occasionally black threads across open frames in various ways. Like a large folding screen, the individual elements of the frames are attached together to form a wall whose weavings produce an expansive overall pattern. There are structures that recall spiders' webs, however, they are not random: they are also repeated in later works by the artist. The nearness to nature, her mentor, is always maintained (see also: structure V; the nest of 1992; or the pillars of 2002). The operation of light and shadow has already attained a significant intensity here, and the two already forge their remarkable path through the taut threads. Here a structure, whose form provides substance, and a material, which – for its part – permits light to pass through it, already play a complementary role and are conceived in terms of their mutual relationship. In Shi Hui's work, what seems to be a wall is always also articulated in terms of a permeable, transparent situation.

The themes of screens and walls repeatedly appear in Shi Hui's work, and it almost seems as though she were seeking to draw attention to complementary interpretations in this way. When she created "Old Wall" in 2003, it appeared to be built of large, rough stones. Stone upon stone, solid and – above all – massive, it defines space. However, upon closer view, the surface proves to resemble a woven texture that

historischen Kontext eines sicherlich gewaltigen Paradigmenwechsels, den die zeitgenössische chinesischen Kunst seit 1985 vollzogen hat, war dies ein mutiger Schritt und zugleich ein Signal einer individuellen Öffnung gegenüber westlichen Kunstströmungen. Es ist deshalb ebenso interessant wie aufschlussreich, sich den Formen von Shi Hui anzunehmen und eine Lesart hinter der reinen Oberfläche zu finden.

Es mag deshalb nicht unerheblich sein, dass die Künstlerin ursprünglich das Weben gelernt hat – ebenfalls eine alte Tradition innerhalb der Menschheitsgeschichte und sie erst um 1990 die Zweidimensionalität zugunsten einer mehrdimensionalen Einsetzbarkeit im Raum bis hin zu raumfüllenden Installationen aufgegeben hat. Das Weben als Gestus jedoch ist geblieben – immer wieder spinnt sie Fäden, die verankern, verbinden und Halt ermöglichen – allerdings auf eine ganz andere Weise. Das zeigt bereits eine ihrer ersten Arbeiten, "Structure I" von 1995, in der sie offene Rahmen unterschiedlich mit weißen und vereinzelt auch schwarzen Fäden bespannt. Wie ein großer Paravent sind die einzelnen Rahmenelemente zu einer Wand gefügt, deren Verwebungen ein großzügiges Gesamtmuster ergeben. Strukturen, die an Spinnweben erinnern, sind dabei nicht zufällig, sondern wiederholen sich auch in späteren Arbeiten bei ihr. Die Nähe zur Lehrmeisterin Natur bleibt durchgängig erhalten (siehe auch: Structure V, Nest von 1992 oder Säule von 2002). Bedeutsam ist bereits hier, wie intensiv Licht und Schatten wirksam werden, wie sehr sie sich ihre Bahn durch die Fadenverstrebungen brechen. Struktur als substanzgebende Form und Material, das seinerseits Durchlässigkeit ermöglicht, spielen bereits hier eine wechselseitige Rolle und sind abhängig aufeinander hin konzipiert. Die scheinbare Wand wird bei Shi Hui immer auch als eine durchlässige, transparente Gegebenheit artikuliert. Wand und Mauer tauchen als Sujet immer wieder im Werk von

through the white which covers it completely is also imbued with a lightness which entirely contradicts its visual weight and the association of masonry work. Modified and piled up into a soaring block that reaches from the floor to the ceiling, the motif of the wall appears once more in "Old Wall 2", of 2008. In 2006, however, Shi Hui had already articulated this subject matter in an entirely different manner one that allowed her to further increase the work's transparency and its extreme permeation with light, two aspects that had already been apparent in earlier works. In the installation entitled "Fluid Shadow and Flutter Wall", she discovers an equivalent of nature that both in its materiality and also in the light shining through it mirrors nature while simultaneously allowing her to disregard it. It is neither the material source that is decisive nor, ultimately, the realized form, but much rather the overcoming of both for the sake of a freedom newly won by means of the renunciation of traditional perspectives. In "Frozen Wind" and "Float" (both 2007), Shi Hui takes up these elementary forces of wind and light as her explicit subject matter and rids them, so to speak, of their gravity. As in other works, here she once again remains true to her woven structures, through which the one element arises, as it were, from the other in such a way that they remain linked together in every detail. Even the large openings or also the twigs which are woven into the cell-like structure and appear as though they were wrapped in a cocoon push both the materiality and the permeability of the structure to its limits.

In the "Compendium of Materia Medica", the "Book of Healing Herbs", which Shi Hui realized in 2009, the artist not only links together natural materials, such as paper and dried plants, but is primarily concerned with opening our eyes to traditional knowledge by seemingly tracing it back to its origins. In doing so, she takes up that which traditional Chinese medicine (TCM) still continues to teach today, whereby it makes use of many

Shi Hui auf und fast hat es den Anschein, als wolle sie damit auch auf die wechselseitigen Lesarten hinweisen. Als sie 2003 die „Old Wall" realisiert, erscheint diese wie eine mit großen, groben Steinen gemauert. Stein auf Stein, solide und vor allem massiv, bestimmt sie den Raum. Die Oberfläche jedoch erweist sich bei näherer Betrachtung wie als gewebte Struktur, die durch das Weiß, in das sie gänzlich getaucht ist, zugleich eine Leichtigkeit erhält, die der optischen Schwere und Assoziation von Mauerwerk gänzlich zuwiderläuft. Modifiziert und in einen hoch aufragenden Block aufgetürmt, der vom Boden bis zur Decke reicht, erscheint das Mauerthema in „Old Wall 2" noch einmal 2008. Bereits 2006 jedoch formuliert Shi Hui dieses Sujet auf eine gänzlich andere Art, durch die sie die Transparenz und enorme Lichtdurchlässigkeit, die schon in den früheren Arbeiten zu beobachten waren, nochmals steigert. In der „Fluid Shadow and Flutter Wall" betitelten Installation findet sie ein Äquivalent zur Natur, das sowohl in der Materialität als auch in der Durchlichtung desselben gespiegelt wird und mit dem sie sich zugleich über diese hinwegsetzt. Nicht das Ursprungsmaterial bleibt entscheidend, auch die Formgebung letztlich nicht, sondern eher die Überwindung beider zugunsten einer neu gewonnenen Freiheit durch die Aufhebung herkömmlicher Sichtweisen. In „Frozen Wind" und „Float" (beide 2007 entstanden) greift Shi Hui diese elementare Kraft von Wind und Licht thematisch explizit auf und enthebt sie gewissermaßen der Schwerkraft. Wie schon in anderen Werken bleibt sie auch hier der gewebten Struktur treu, durch die sich gleichsam ein Element aus dem Andere ergibt und damit in allen Details miteinander verknüpft bleibt. Selbst die großzügigen Öffnungen oder die in der zellulosen Struktur eingewebten Zweige, die wie in einem Kokon eingehüllt erscheinen, treiben sowohl die Materialität als auch die Durchlässigkeit derselben an ihre jeweiligen Grenzen.

Im „Compendium Materia Medica", dem „Buch der heilenden Kräuter", das sie 2009 realisiert, verbindet sie nicht nur naturhafte Materialien wie Papier und getrocknete Pflanzen

centuries of cultural tradition, and she – purely theoretically – pairs it together with comparable insights that, within the European cultural sphere, were utilized during the Middle ages by the still-famous nun Hildegard von Bingen (1098–1178). Here, in an inconspicuous but nevertheless enduring manner, Eastern and Western culture are linked together: both formally and in terms of content.

Regardless of the fact that Shi Hui's works always derive from the material itself and seem to originate within nature itself, in the impression that they evoke and in their interpretation they go significantly beyond these elements. In turning to nature, Shi Hui manifests a return to the roots of humanity, which – within the germinal situation that existed in China following its opening in 1985 – may have gone against general trends. There was nothing comparable at that time in China and, for this reason, numerous impulses from the European art scene were encompassed within the horizon of her journeys abroad. Everything develops towards a spiritual or intellectual opening, an inner dialogue with her own culture, which she sees within a network of other tendencies and cultural influences. The motif of the wall, which she has worked with multiple times, clearly exhibits an overcoming of borders and buffers and a development towards an openness that continues to offer protection but – with its transparency and permeability – leaves an independent field of influence and action to the elements and other forces. Her works invite a reading in the sense of nature, but they also point beyond this and – in Adorno's words – are, in their own way, not only 'emancipated', but 'thoroughly historical'.

miteinander, sondern eröffnet vornehmlich einen Blick auf überliefertes Wissen, indem sie dieses zu seinen Ursprüngen zurückzuführen scheint. Sie greift dabei auf das zurück, was die traditionelle chinesische Medizin (TCM) bis heute lehrt, wobei diese aus einer Jahrhunderte alten Kultur schöpft, und rein theoretisch ein solch profundes Wissen paart mit vergleichbaren Erkenntnissen, die im europäischen Kulturkreis von der bis heute berühmten Klosterfrau Ⅰ Iildegard von Bingen (1098-1178) im Mittelalter Anwendung fand. Auf unmerkliche, aber dennoch nachhaltige Weise verbinden sich hier östliche und westliche Kultur und zwar sowohl formal als auch inhaltlich.

Wenngleich sich Shi Huis Werke immer aus dem Material selbst verdanken und aus der Natur selbst zu entstammen scheinen, so gehen sie in ihrer Anmutung und Deutung deutlich darüber hinaus. Mit der Hinwendung zur Natur manifestiert sie eine (Rück-)Besinnung auf die Wurzeln der Menschheit, die in der Aufbruchsituation, in der sich China seit seiner Öffnung 1985 befand, den allgemeinen Tendenzen zuwidergelaufen sein mag. Es gab nichts Vergleichbares in der Zeit in China und zahlreiche Impulse aus der europäischen Kunstszene liegen deshalb im Horizont ihrer Auslandsreisen. Alles entwickelt sich hin zu einer geistigen Öffnung, zu einem inneren Dialog mit der eigenen Kultur, die sie in einem Netzwerk mit anderen Strömungen und kulturellen Einflüssen begreift. Das Sujet der Mauer, dessen sie sich mehrfach angenommen hat, erweist deutlich die Überwindung von Grenze und Abschirmung hin zu einer Offenheit, die zwar Schutz noch bietet, aber mit seiner Transparenz und Offenheit den Elementen und anderen Kräften ihr eigenes Spiel- und Wirkfeld überlässt. Ihre Werke eröffnen eine Lesart im Sinne der Natur, weisen darüber hinaus und sind auf ihre Art mit Adornos Terminus nicht nur „emanzipiert", sondern auch „geschichtlich, durch und durch."

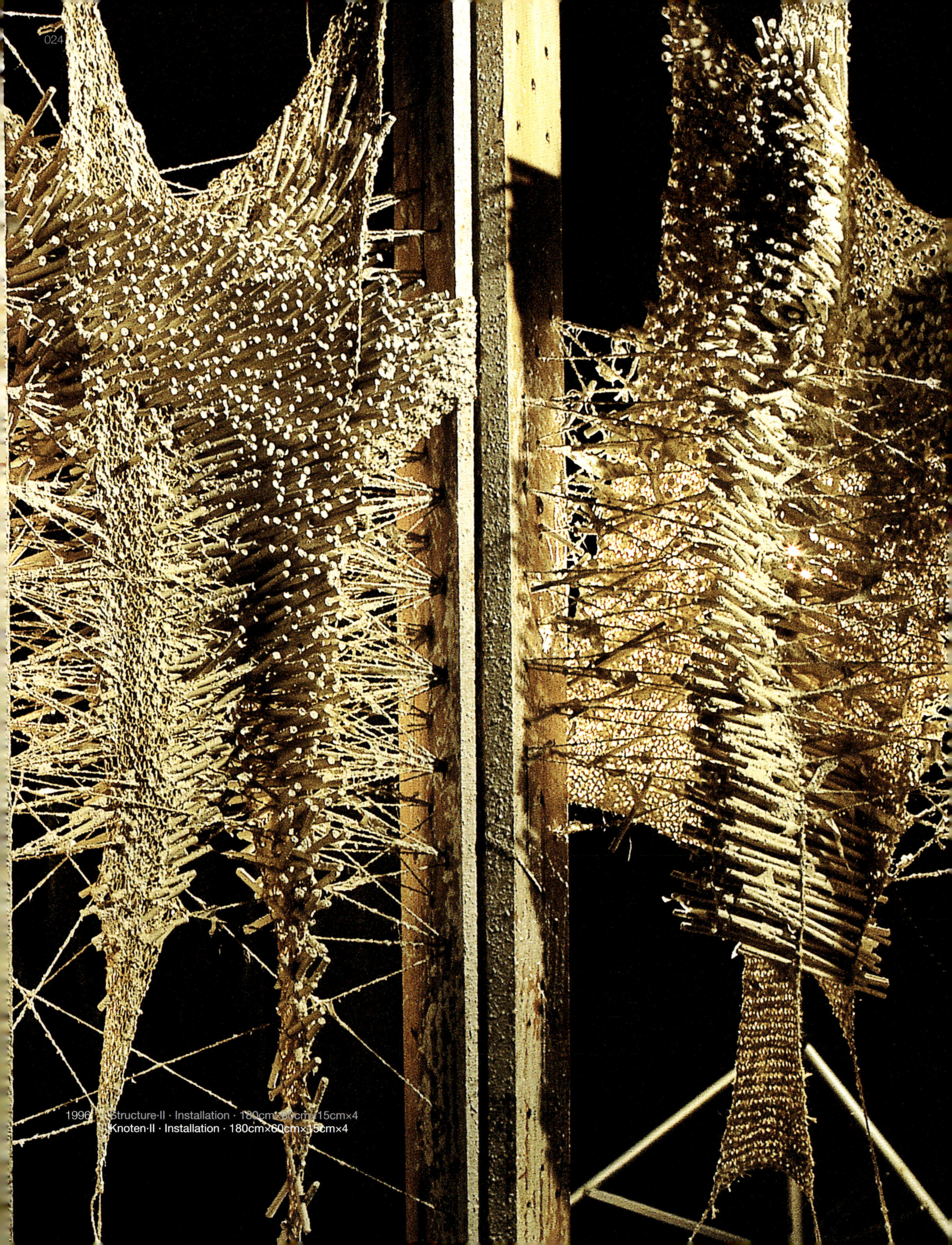

024
1996 · Structure·II · Installation · 180cm×60cm×15cm×4
Knoten·II · Installation · 180cm×60cm×15cm×4

Blossoming Spirits
Gao Shiming

Blühender Geist
Gao Shiming

From acquaintance to intimate knowledge to lifelong companionship, Xu Jiang and Shi Hui have always maintained a reciprocity and tension between their respective artistic careers. Their creative output differs in both form and medium, but what unites their approaches is a kind of expectation and commitment that 'dwells in art itself' during this limited lifetime.

I.

For the European audience, this exhibition, titled 'Blossoming Spirits', may invoke a sense of anachronism. On the one hand, the term 'spirit' has come under increasing scrutiny and questioning in the philosophical and political discourses of the last half century. On the other hand, since the heyday of conceptual art, international exhibitions have been littered with a heady brew of social participation, institutional critique, relational aesthetics, and the European art community has not often been exposed to the kind of sincerity of the visual language and natural objects as exemplified in this exhibition. Yet we would be ill-advised to consider this exhibition as a return to the European modernist tradition, nor should we claim that the two Chinese artists work within a 'cultural

Vom ersten Kennenlernen bis zur engen Vertrautheit und lebenslangen Freundschaft haben Xu Jiang und Shi Hui immer eine gewisse Spannung zwischen ihren individuellen künst-lerischen Karrieren gewahrt. Ihre künstlerische Produktion unterscheidet sich zwar hinsichtlich Form und Medium, aber beide teilen das gleiche Bestreben, die gleiche innere Verpflichtung, in ihrem künstlerischen Dasein tatsächlich in der Kunst „beheimatet" zu sein.

I.

Für das europäische Publikum mag der Titel der Ausstellung „Blühender Geist" alte Erinnerungen wachrufen. Einerseits wurde der Begriff „Geist" im philosophischen und politischen Diskurs des letzten halben Jahrhunderts immer wieder in Frage gestellt. Andererseits konnte man seit dem Aufkommen der Konzeptkunst bei großen internationalen Ausstellungen immer wieder die verschiedensten, aber im Grunde doch immer gleichen diskursiven Praktiken von sozialer Teilnahme, Institutionskritik und relationaler Ästhetik antreffen, und die europäische Kunst-Community war kaum mehr mit einer solchen Aufrichtigkeit der visuellen Sprache und der Natur-objekte konfrontiert wie in dieser Ausstellung. Aber wir dürfen diese Ausstellung keinesfalls als Rückkehr zur europäischen modernen Tradition betrachten, und noch weniger dürfen wir von der Annahme ausgehen, dass diese beiden chinesischen Künstler „kulturelle Nachzügler" innerhalb der Kunstgeschichte

time-warp' of art history. Linear models in history and their grand narratives have long bankrupted themselves, and Chinese artists have their own practical context and specific creative situations.

The artistic couple first got to know each other towards the end of the Cultural Revolution, one of the most exciting acts in the drama of contemporary Chinese art history. Chinese art education was resuscitated from its ashes. In the three decades that followed, their artistic careers have borne witness to the special significance of academia in the ecology of contemporary Chinese art. Quite contrary to the situation in the West, Chinese contemporary artists come mostly from an academic background. In the 1980s, academia was the main origin of the Avant-Garde art movement of China. Most of the main figures of the '85 Avant-Garde started their rebellious acts from within academia, which also happened to supply them with critical weapons and resources for rebellion. Up till now, the most outstanding of them are still teaching within academia. The 1980s also saw Xu Jiang and Shi Hui immersed in the avant-garde art movement: Shi Hui studied with the Bulgarian artist Maryn Varbanov, who was teaching in Hangzhou and took up the intermedia creative work of contemporary fibre art. Xu Jiang went to study at the University of Fine Arts of Hamburg, which marked the beginning of his explorations between East and West, local and global, ideological and formal experimentation.

By the 1990s, the Chinese art scene started to fall into two distinct schools of artists. One was composed of Wang Guangyi, Fang Lijun, Zhang Xiaogang, Zhang Peili, Huang Yongping and Cai Guoqiang, a list of names with which the western audience has been familiar. They have been featured in many international exhibitions and created a basic picture of 'Contemporary Chinese Art'. In the international context after 1989, this is an

sind. Lineare historische Modelle und ihre großen Narrative sind schon längst bankrott gegangen, und chinesische Künstler arbeiten innerhalb ihres eigenen praktischen Kontexts und unter spezifischen kreativen Bedingungen.

Das Künstlerpaar Xu Jiang und Shi Hui hat sich gegen Ende der Kulturrevolution kennen gelernt, also während eines der aufregendsten Kapitel in der zeitgenössischen Kunst-geschichte Chinas, als die Kunstausbildung gerade aus ihren Trümmern wiedererstand. In ihren sich über drei Jahrzehnte spannenden künstlerischen Karrieren kann man die spezielle Bedeutung ablesen, die das akademische Umfeld für die Ökologie der zeitgenössischen chinesischen Kunst hat. Im Gegensatz zu westlichen Künstlern haben die meisten zeitgenössischen chinesischen Künstler einen akademischen Hintergrund. In den 1980er Jahren bildeten die Kunstakademien den Ausgangspunkt für die Bewegung der chinesischen Avantgarde. Die Teilnehmer der bahnbrechenden „Bewegung '85" begannen ihre Rebellion innerhalb der Kunstakademien, wo sie auch ihre Waffen der Kritik und die Ressourcen für ihren Widerstand fanden. Bis heute unterrichten die herausragendsten Vertreter dieser Bewegung an den Kunstakademien. In den 1980er Jahren wurden Xu Jiang und Shi Hui in die Bewegung der Avantgarde-Kunst initiiert: Shi Hui studierte bei dem bulgarischen Künstler Marin Varvanov, der in Hangzhou unterrichtete, und begann sich mit der zeitgenössischen medienüberschreitenden Textilkunst auseinanderzusetzen. Xu Jiang ging zum Studium an die Kunstakademie Hamburg und pendelte zwischen Ost und West, zwischen lokal und global, zwischen ideologischen und formellen Experimenten.

In den 1990er Jahren kristallisierten sich in der chinesischen Kunstszene zwei Kunstströmungen heraus. Zu der einen zählen dem westlichen Publikum wohl bekannte Künstler wie Wang Guangyi, Fang Lijun, Zhang Xiaogang, Zhang Peili, Huang Yongping und Cai Guoqiang, die immer wieder bei internationalen Ausstellungen präsent waren und das Image der „chinesischen zeitgenössischen Kunst" prägten. Im internationalen

easily recognizable picture and echoes the post-Cold War discourse of identity politics and post-revolutionary narrative. The second school includes the artists that have not been featured in the family portrait known as 'Contemporary Chinese Art'. Despite their exclusion from the international version of the 'Contemporary Chinese Art' scene, they are profoundly internal to the construction of subject of contemporary Chinese art. In the cultural milieu since the 1990s, academia has provided a shelter for their artistic creativity. Within academia, they either inherit tradition and revitalize it through transformation, or face up to contemporary challenges and experimentation, or root themselves in the local in a resistant position. Their practice outlines a picture of diversity on the contemporary Chinese art scene, where we often see the active roles played by Xu Jiang and Shi Hui. As representatives of this group, they have been committed to experimentation and built up extensive experience.

At the turn of the 21st century, while Neoliberalism is promoting its spectacle governance on a global scale, 'contemporary Chinese art' as the West knows it has become a topic celebrated by fashion media in China as well as preys that yield the highest profit on the art market. Academia, however, has turned into a laboratory in this consumerist-centred, market-oriented art world. Xu Jiang has now become President of the most important art college in China and displays a great passion and vigour in terms of both creativity and thinking. Shi Hui has also grown to be one of the most important female artists in the country and the main driving force behind China's fibre art. A 'contemporary' outlook has gradually taken shape in their individual creativity and educational practice. This new 'contemporaneity' is entirely different from the kind of 'contemporary Chinese' quality shaped and whetted by the Western exhibition-market system

Kontext nach 1989 hatte dieses Image großen Wiedererkennungswert und bildete eine Reaktion auf den Diskurs der Identitätspolitik nach dem Kalten Krieg sowie auf das postrevolutionäre Narrativ. Zur zweiten Strömung zählen jene Künstler, die nicht ins Gruppenbild, das unter dem Titel „zeitgenössische chinesische Kunst" firmiert, aufgenommen wurden. Obwohl sie aus der internationalen Version der „zeitgenössischen chinesischen Kunst" ausgeschlossen waren, gehörten sie zum inneren Kreis jener, die das Subjekt der zeitgenössischen chinesischen Kunst konstruierten. Im kulturellen Milieu der 1990er Jahre boten ihnen die Kunstakademien eine Zufluchtsstätte für ihr künstlerisches Schaffen. In den Kunstakademien setzten sie entweder die Tradition fort und wiederbelebten sie, indem sie sie transformierten, oder sie stellten sich in ihren Experimenten der zeitgenössischen Herausforderung. Oder aber sie verwurzelten sich im Lokalen in einer Position des Widerstands. Ihre Praktiken schufen das diversifizierte Bild der chinesischen zeitgenössischen Kunst, wobei Xu Jiang und Shi Hui dabei eine sehr aktive Rolle spielten. Als Vertreter dieser Gruppe haben sie sich dem Weg des mühsamen Experiments verschrieben und dabei einen reichhaltigen Erfahrungsschatz angesammelt.

Am Beginn des 21. Jahrhunderts, wo der Neoliberalismus sein Spektakel-Regime in globalem Maßstab betreibt, stellt die „zeitgenössische chinesische Kunst", wie sie der Westen kennt, in China bereits das Lieblingsthema der trendigen Medien und eine begehrte Beute auf dem internationalen Kunstmarkt, verspricht sie doch den höchsten Profit. Die Kunstakademien hingegen hatten sich in ein Labor inmitten dieser konsum- und marktorientierten Welt der Kunst verwandelt. Xu Jiang ist inzwischen Rektor der wichtigsten Kunstakademie Chinas geworden und entfaltet eine enorme Leidenschaft und Lebendigkeit, wenn es um Kreativität und kritisches Denken geht. Shi Hui ist eine der bedeutendsten Künstlerinnen Chinas und die treibende Kraft hinter der chinesischen Textilkunst. Aus ihrer individuellen Kreativität und Unterrichtspraxis hat sich nach und nach eine neue Sicht des „Zeitgenössischen" entwickelt. Dieses neue „Zeitgenössische" unterscheidet sich

and discursive mechanism. It grows out of its interaction with China's own historical context and social reality. Rooted in local culture and oriented towards contemporary reality, with a decided emphasis on subjective consciousness, it is inextricably linked to Chinese society in transition and maintains an introspective and constructivist attitude. Such self-constituted Chinese contemporaneity has offered a possibility of self-explanation that goes beyond the discursive system of twentieth century Western art history, and opened up a new space for local historical imagination for contemporary Chinese art.

II.

All the narrative above is intended to furnish a context necessary for the European audience to understand the Chinese artist couple. Let us temporarily put aside the linear narrative of western art history and jettison the ideological imagination vis-à-vis contemporary Chinese art in order to delve into the works in exhibition themselves. This way we may reap some enduring reflections.

This exhibition juxtaposes two worlds at the opposite ends of a spectrum. Xu Jiang's works are themed 'Bathing in Life-giving Fire', and feature stalks of age-old sunflowers, burning like fire under the rays of sunlight as if caught in a cycle of samsara. In a recent solo exhibition at the Staatliche Kunstsammlungen Dresden, Kunsthalle im Lipsiusbau, Xu Jiang told the story of 'Re-generation' of his generation with his sunflowers. This was a tale characterized by life renewed in ruptures and redeemed from history. The generation of 'regeneration' is not unlike old sunflowers standing on the wasteland, who have just survived revolutionary fervour and post-revolutionary disillusionment, before being plunged into the most rapid social change and intellectual shifts in Chinese history. They have gone through all vicissitudes and shouldered the burden of hope and responsibility.

grundlegend von jenem „zeitgenössischen Chinesischen", das vom westlichen System des Ausstellungsmarkts und seiner diskursiven Mechanismen geformt und inspiriert wird. Dieses neue Zeitgenössische ist innerhalb des historischen Kontextes, auf dem Boden der gesellschaftlichen Realität Chinas gewachsen und geschärft worden. Es wurzelt in der lokalen Kultur und richtet sich an die aktuelle Wirklichkeit. Es betont das subjektive Bewusstsein, es ist untrennbar mit der sich in ständiger Transformation befindlichen Wirklichkeit Chinas verbunden und nimmt eine introspektive, konstruktivistische Haltung ein. Dieses sich selbst konstituierende chinesische Zeitgenössische verweist auf eine Möglichkeit der Selbsterklärung, die über das diskursive System der westlichen Kunstgeschichte des 20. Jahrhunderts hinausreicht und der zeitgenössischen chinesischen Kunst einen neuen Raum für eine im Lokalen verankerte historische Imagination eröffnet.

II.

Das bis jetzt Gesagte will lediglich einen Kontext herstellen, den das europäische Publikum braucht, um dieses chinesische Künstlerpaar zu verstehen. Lassen wir einmal das lineare Narrativ der westlichen Kunstgeschichte beiseite und werfen wir die ideologisch behafteten Vorstellungen von chinesischer zeitgenössischer Kunst über Bord. Wenn wir uns voll und ganz auf die in dieser Ausstellung versammelten Arbeiten einlassen, werden wir einige nachhaltige Eindrücke mitnehmen können.

Die Ausstellung umfasst Werke aus zwei einander entgegengesetzten Welten. Xu Jiangs Arbeiten stehen unter dem Motto „Wiedergeburt aus dem Feuer" und zeigen verwelkte Sonnenblumen, die wie Feuer brennen unter der sengenden Sonne, als wären sie im Zyklus der Wiedergeburten gefangen. In einer kürzlich gezeigten Ausstellung in der Kunsthalle im Lipsiusbau der Staatlichen Kunstsammlung Dresden erzählte Xu Jiang anhand dieser Sonnenblumen die Geschichte der „Re-Generation" seiner Generation. Dies ist die Geschichte der Wiedergeburt aus Brüchen und Sprüngen, die Geschichte der Erlösung aus der Geschichte. Die Generation dieser „Re-Generation"

Now these sunflowers are gathered in groves and bundles, echoing one another and offering mutual support. The sunflower is integrated into the earth, from where it stands upright and lonesome, through life and death. The sunflower grows toward the skies, towards the sun, which lends the sunflower its glory and commitment. Heavy with harvest, the sunflower droops its head and converts to the faith of the earth, where its origin and destiny lie. In this antagonism between heaven and earth, between life and earth, the sunflower spawns a kind of intrepid will and blinding spirituality. Therefore the sunflower is reincarnated in the flames on the wasteland which spread towards the horizons filled with the warmth of life and hope for redemption.

In the cycle of seasons of the sunflower, Xu Jiang tries to grasp the Being-towards-Death that is immanent in all life. In the fields riven by reminiscing and desire, the sunflower, a natural gift, fortune bestowed by heaven and earth, is returning to the depth of the earth. This is a story between life and death, an elegy of rebirth by fire.

In stark contrast to the torrential weightiness of Xu Jiang, Shi Hui's work displays a kind of lightness of touch and tranquillity. Against the 'rebirth by fire', she adopts water as her theme. 'Quiet water runs deep' aptly captures the latent, ubiquitous existence of her peaceful, unassuming world. Her technique is weaving, of both fibre and thought. Her work constitutes an epic for life and for women in everyday life.

Shi Hui's artistic creativity takes weaving as its point of departure. Weaving is related as much to a special material or craftsmanship as to creative approaches or form. Moreover, weaving is for her a way of making sense of the world. It is both instrumental and significant epistemologically and onto-

ähnelt in vielem diesen alten Sonnenblumen in der Ödnis, die den revolutionären Eifer und die post-revolutionäre Desillusionierung überlebt haben, nur um dann die rasanteste intellektuelle und gesellschaftliche Transformation zu durchlaufen, die China je erlebt hat. Sie haben alle Wechselfälle des Lebens durchgemacht und trugen die Last von Hoffnung und Verantwortung.

Nun sind diese sich der Sonne zuwendenden Blumen in Bündeln und Büscheln zusammengebunden und sind einander Stütze und Widerhall. Die Sonnenblume reicht tief in den Boden, nur um aus ihm hoch und einsam herauszuragen, in einem Kreislauf von Entstehen und Vergehen. Die Sonnenblume drängt zum Himmel, zur Sonne. Es ist die Sonne, die der Sonnenblume Halt und Glanz verleiht. Unter der Last der Frucht lässt sie ihren Kopf hängen und nimmt Zuflucht zum Boden, der ihr Ursprung und Schicksal zugleich ist. In dieser Durchdringung von Himmel und Erde, von Leben und Tod verströmt die Sonnenblume einen fast tapferen Willen, eine blendende Geistigkeit. Daher reinkarniert sich die Sonnenblume in den Flammen der Ödnis, die sich, durchdrungen von einer Leidenschaft fürs Leben und einer Hoffnung auf Erlösung, bis ans Ende der Welt erstreckt.

Im Zyklus der Jahreszeiten der Sonnenblume versucht Xu Jiang das „Sein-zum-Tode" zu erfassen, das jedem Leben innewohnt. Im weiten Feld, wo Erinnerung und Begehren untrennbar verbunden sind, kehrt die Sonnenblume, jenes Geschenk der Natur, von Himmel und Erde, in die Tiefen der Erde zurück. Es ist eine Geschichte zwischen Leben und Tod, eine Elegie der Wiedergeburt aus dem Feuer.

In krassem Gegensatz zum aufwühlenden und wuchtigen Werk von Xu Jiang verströmen die Arbeiten von Shi Hui eine gewisse Leichtigkeit und Ruhe. Als Kontrapunkt zur „Wiedergeburt aus dem Feuer" macht sie das Wasser zu ihrem Thema. „Stille Wasser sind tief" beschreibt wohl am besten das Latente, alles Durchdringende ihrer ruhigen, schlichten Welt. Ihre Technik ist das Weben, das Weben von Fäden und Gedanken. Ihre Arbeit

logically. Excavating the constitutive nature of the microscopic world from the natural composition of fibre furnishes Shi Hui with a crucial framework of reference. It is an ancient art of mimesis, a kind of construction that resonates with nature in a methodological sense. In fibre and weaving, the artist has extrapolated a unique understanding of things – all kinds of material, all objects, exquisitely constituted either naturally or artificially.

In Shi Hui's world, whiteness and modesty constitute the basic representation of colour for everything in the world. Be it 'Nest', or 'Knots', or 'Drifting', or 'Column', whether it takes the form of literati rockery or ragged walls, everything returns to the modest, neutral hue of white. This is a distilled, rarefied world. And what Shi Hui has presented is a process of 'making everything even' through purification. In such a process, all the sensational colour representations are reduced and siphoned off. What is left is form only. This is a world view from the microscopic field, where everything is a formal construction weaved, entwined, stocked and connected through specific means.

Christopher Landini, the famous humanist, writes about the origin of poetic creativity in his *On Dante* (1481), 'the word "poet" in Greek comes from the verb "piin"(sic), whose meaning falls somewhere between "create" and "make". The former is the power of God to create *ex nihilo*, and the latter is the creative activity of ordinary people that involves form and material in any art.' For Landini, the poet's work is no longer 'making' but 'creating'. The poet creates like God, therefore 'God is the highest poet, and the world is His poetry'. However, in Shi Hui's world, the 'creative activity that involves form and material in any art' has been transformed into creativity in another sense, since the objectivity of 'things' is no longer ascribed to its material form but to its constitution. This is the Chain of Creation in the fundamental sense of the word. Therefore the modest agency

ist eine Ode ans Leben und an die Frau im Alltagsleben.

Shi Huis künstlerisches Schaffen beginnt beim Weben. Das Weben bezieht sich aber nicht nur auf ein spezielles Material oder eine besondere Technik oder auf kreative Ansätze und Formen. In einem weiteren Sinn ist es für sie eine Methode, die Welt zu verstehen. Es ist sowohl Instrument als auch von erkenntnistheoretischer und ontologischer Bedeutung durchdrungen. Aus der natürlichen Struktur der Faser die konstitutive Natur einer mikroskopischen Welt abzuleiten, bildet einen wichtigen Referenzrahmen für Shi Huis Schaffen. Das ist die alte Kunst der Mimesis, eine Konstruktion, die in einem methodologischen Sinn mit der Natur in Resonanz steht. Aus der Faser und dem Weben extrapoliert die Künstlerin ein besonderes Verständnis über die Dinge – allen Arten von Materialien, alle Objekte, egal ob natürlich oder künstlich, ist eine subtile Struktur eigen.

In Shi Huis Welt bilden das Weiße und das Schlichte die grundlegendste Farbe für alles in der Welt. Egal ob „Nest", „Knoten", „Dahintreiben" oder „Säule", egal ob es als schroffer „falscher Berg" oder als fleckige alte Mauer erscheint – alle Gegenstände kehren ins Schlichte und Neutrale der Farbe Weiß zurück. Es ist eine destillierte, gereinigte Welt, und was Shi Hui uns hier demonstriert, ist ein Prozess des „Ausgleichens der Dinge" durch Reinigung. In einem derartigen Prozess wird die sinnlich erfassbare Farbe des Materials reduziert und abgeschabt, sodass nur mehr die Form zurückbleibt. Das ist eine Weltsicht, die sich aus dem Mikroskopischen herleitet, wo alles eine formale Konstruktion bildet, die durch spezielle Methoden gewebt, gewickelt, geschichtet und verknüpft wird.

Der berühmte Humanist Cristoforo Landino schreibt über den Ursprung der dichterischen Kreativität in seinem Kommentar zu Dante (1481), dass das griechische Wort „Poet" sich vom Verb „piin" (sic) ableitet, dessen Bedeutung irgendwo zwischen „Erschaffen" und „Machen" angesiedelt ist. Ersteres bezieht sich auf die Macht Gottes, etwas ex nihilo zu erschaffen,

and constitutive action of manual labour has become the only myth, in which *creatio ex nihilo* stands no longer at the origin of creativity. Instead the everyday power of weaving-labour is the key driving force. Here, a creative attitude deeply rooted in the feminine experience has emerged: creation does not have to imply genesis from nothing to eternity, but rather reproduction, expansion, proliferation and gestation.

III.

One is concentrated, the other expansive; one is tranquil as water, the other burning as fire. This fire and water contrast has yielded many interpretations of the ancient world views of the East. On Xu Jiang's canvas, fire rises along with ashes; in Shi Hui's works, under the tranquil surface run deep currents.

On a certain day of May 2011, on the train to Koblenz, Shi Hui described the imagery of 'rope' that persisted in her creative mind. The rope she referred to was woven with different techniques and stood in space without apparent use, just like the giant tree in Zhuang Zi's 'Enjoyment in Untroubled Ease'. As I see it, the rope which is yet to be, is not unlike the 'one stroke' in Shi Tao's Words on Painting, something most fundamental and constitutive about fibre art, the 'fleeing One' in Shi Hui's artistic career.

Similarly, from the ruins of the 1990s through the turn-of-century historical landscape to the sunflower gardens of the recent years, Xu Jiang's creative work has gradually crystallised in one leitmotiv, the sunflower. The revolutionary sunflower, once identified by the generation of the Cultural Revolution, has now been transformed into seasoned soldiers that stand upright on Xu's canvas. Of course there has always been a tangential relation between the sunflower as object and Xu Jiang's selfhood. In his creative work, the sunflower

während letzteres die schöpferische Handlung gewöhnlicher Menschen beschreibt, woran wie bei jeder Art von Kunst Form und Material beteiligt sind. Für Landino ist die Arbeit des Dichters nicht ein „Machen", sondern ein „Erschaffen". Der Dichter erschafft wie Gott, daher ist Gott der höchste Dichter, und die Welt ist das Gedicht Gottes. Aber in Shi Huis Welt hat sich die kreative Aktivität, wo Form und Material wie in jeder Art von Kunst involviert sind, in ein kreatives Tun in einem anderen Sinn verwandelt, denn die Dinghaftigkeit von „Dingen" wird nicht länger ihrem Material, sondern ihrer Struktur zugeschrieben. Das ist die Kette des Schöpferischen im grundlegendsten Sinn des Wortes. Daher ist Handarbeit, diese schlichte, aber wirksame konstitutive Handlung, zum einzigen Mythos geworden, in dem eine creatio ex nihilo nicht länger den Ursprung von Kreativität bildet. Stattdessen bildet die alltägliche Kraft der Web-Arbeit die zentrale treibende Kraft. Hier zeigt sich eine schöpferische Haltung, die tief verwurzelt ist in der Erfahrung einer Frau: Schöpferisches Handeln bedeutet nicht zwingend Genese aus dem Nichts hin in die Ewigkeit, sondern vielmehr Fortpflanzung, Ausdehnung, Vermehrung und Reifung.

III.

Das eine ist konzentriert, das andere ist expansiv; das eine ist ruhig wie Wasser, das andere brennt wie Feuer. Dieser Kontrast zwischen Feuer und Wasser hat die Weltsicht des Ostens hervorgebracht. Auf Xu Jiangs Leinwand steigen Flammen gemeinsam mit Aschen auf; in Shi Huis Arbeiten ziehen tiefe Strömungen unter der stillen Wasseroberfläche.

An einem gewissen Tag im Mai 2011 beschrieb Shi Hui im Zug nach Koblenz das Bild eines „Seils", das in ihrer schöpferischen Vorstellung ständig präsent ist. Dieses Seil wurde mittels verschiedener Techniken gewebt und steht mitten im Raum, ohne einen speziellen Zweck zu erfüllen, wie der riesige Baum in Zhuangzis „Sorgloses Wandern". Meiner Meinung nach ähnelt dieses noch im Werden begriffene Seil dem „einen Strich" in Shitaos „Worte über das Malen" und ist das grundlegendste

has transcended self-confession and all symbolism and transfigured into a medium of lived experience, from which Xu's art departs and touches on a kind of fundamental Geschehen (happening) played out between self and the world. This Geschehen is a kind of 'production' in terms of creativity. And the Greek word for production shares with technology the same root 'tec'. For the ancient Greeks, the meaning of this root lies in a kind of 'showing'. Birth by fire, linguistic ruptures, the repeated fragmentation and reconstruction of phenomena, the repeated erasures and new starts on the canvas, the convergence and divergence of shape and colour, of ink and water…everything that takes place on the canvas is geared up to the intertwined Geschehen, production and showing. And in the quintessential Geschehen, production and showing, we see spirits blossom. Here what blossoms is not something of the spirit of an individual subject, but the flames passed by the sun into the sunflowers, which, although growing into a forest on the wasteland, remain solitary. Waldeinsamkeit, or the solitude in the forest. This would be the abyss of existence. Here Xu Jiang has discovered his unique 'Oneness'. Be it oil painting or water colour, sculpture or painting, Xu Jiang's sunflowers are always a group repatriated by history. And the collective group or mass points in the end to thousands of 'individual stalks'. This dialectic, between individual stalks, demonstrates the at once collective and absolutely solitary lived experience of the generation that grew up following the sun. The stalks and masses have congealed into a facial expression, an image, a state of mind. The prisoner of sun, who has just been revived by fire, stands old, dilapidated, firm, intractable, alone yet not decadent, melancholic yet not morose.

Spirits blossom in the Ludwig Museum, Koblenz. It is not what Hegel termed Weltgeist or Zeitgeist that is blossoming here. Rather they are the 'changing shapes of cloud and life-force of flora and fauna' that spring out of life. This spirit is carefully kept

gestaltende Ding in der Textilkunst, das „Fliehende Eine" in Shi Huis künstlerischer Karriere.

In ähnlicher Weise hat sich in Xu Jiangs schöpferischem Werk aus den Ruinen der 1990er Jahre und den historischen Landschaften um die Jahrtausendwende nach und nach ein Leitmotiv herauskristallisiert: die Sonnenblume. Diese revolutionäre Sonnenblume, von der Generation der Kulturrevolution zum Symbol erkoren, hat sich heute transformiert in bewährte Soldaten, die aufrecht auf Xus Leinwand stehen. Natürlich hat es immer schon eine gewisse Distanz wahrende Beziehung zwischen der Sonnenblume als Objekt und Xu Jiangs Ich gegeben. In seinem kreativen Schaffen hat die Sonnenblume schon früh Selbstausdruck und alle Symbolismen transzendiert und sich in ein Medium gelebter Erfahrung gewandelt, aus dem heraus Xu Jiangs Malerei ein fundamentales Geschehen berührt, das gemeinsam von Selbst und Welt in Szene gesetzt wird. Dieses Geschehen ist aus dem Blickwinkel des kreativen Schaffens als eine Art von „Produktion" zu werten, wobei das griechische Wort für „Produktion" dieselbe Wortwurzel „tec" besitzt wie „Technologie". Für die alten Griechen hatte diese Wortwurzel die Bedeutung von „Erscheinen". Geburt aus dem Feuer, linguistische Brüche, wiederholte Fragmentierung und Rekonstruktion von Phänomenen, wiederholtes Löschen und Neubeginnen, Zusammen- und Auseinanderfließen von Form und Farbe, Tinte und Wasser … alles, was auf der Leinwand stattfindet, wird zu diesem Geschehen hin hochgeschaukelt, Produktion und Erscheinen. In diesem essenziellen Geschehen – Produktion – Erscheinen sehen wir das Aufblühen des Geistes. Was hier aufblüht, ist nicht der Geist eines individuellen Subjekts, sondern die Flammen, die die Sonnenblumen von der Sonne empfangen haben und die zwar einen Wald in der Ödnis bilden, aber nur schwer ihre Einsamkeit verbergen können. *Waldeinsamkeit* ist der Abgrund der Existenz. Darin hat Xu Jiang sein einzigartiges „Eins-Sein" gefunden. Egal ob Ölgemälde oder Aquarell, Skulptur oder Zeichnung, Xu Jiangs Sonnenblumen sind immer eine Gruppe, die von der Geschichte abgeschoben wird. Und diese kollektive Masse

within and displayed without. The more one wants to turn inward for it, the more inexhaustible one feels it to be. Hence expectations arise out of the interplay between heart and this spirit, just as Sikong Tu aptly put it, 'nature as it stands, whose immortal hand has created it?' here 'nature' refers to what *Physis* in the world of the ancient Greeks used to mean – emergence, growth and blossoming.

Spirits blossom at the Deutsches Eck. Xu Jiang and Shi Hui, the artist couple from China, are playing out the churning fire and tranquil water in their own works. Fire emerges above water, and according to the *Book of Changes* (which Ecke Bonk terms 'a topology that systematically creates contingencies'), happens to coincide with the last of the 64 hexagrams, namely 'the incompletion of fire and water'. According to Zhu Xi (1130 – 1200), here 'incompletion' does not imply failure to reach a state of completion. Rather, it suggests an unending cycle, and the 'incompletion' here points to the way of nature, just as the geomancy of 49 in the *Book of Changes*, the so called recourse to 'spirituality', is exactly the 'Oneness' that hides itself from view.

oder Gruppe besteht letzten Endes immer aus Tausenden „individueller-Stängel". Diese Dialektik von Gruppe und Einem steht für eine sowohl im Kollektiv als auch in absoluter Einsamkeit durchlebte Erfahrung einer Generation, die der Sonne gefolgt ist. Die Stängel und Massen sind zu einem Gesichtsausdruck geronnen, einem Bild, einem Geisteszustand. Diese Gefangenen der Sonne, die durch das Feuer neu belebt werden, sind gebrechlich, marode, entschlossen, verbissen, allein, aber nicht mutlos, sie sind melancholisch, aber nicht traurig.

Der Geist blüht im Ludwig Museum in Koblenz. Was hier blüht, ist aber nicht das, was Hegel „Weltgeist" oder „Zeitgeist" genannt hat, es sind eher die „sich wandelnden Muster der Wolken, die Lebenskraft von Flora und Fauna", die aus dem Leben der Natur entspringen. Dieser Geist, sorgfältig im Inneren gehütet, erscheint im Äußeren. Je mehr man sich auf der Suche danach nach innen wendet, desto unerschöpflicher scheint er zu sein. Aus diesem Zusammenspiel zwischen Herz und Geist erwachsen Erwartungen, wie es Sikong Tu formuliert hat: „Die Natur, wie sie ist, wessen unsterbliche Hände haben sie geschaffen?" Hier bezieht sich „Natur" auf das, was die alten Griechen mit „Physis" meinten – Emergenz, Wachsen und Blühen.

Im Deutschen Eck blüht der Geist. Xu Jiang und Shi Hui, das Künstlerpaar aus China, spielen in ihren Arbeiten mit dem lodernden Feuer und dem stillen Wasser. Feuer lodert über dem Wasser, und gemäß dem Buch der Wandlungen (das der deutsche Künstler Ecke Bonk als „Typologie, die systematisch Zufälle erzeugt" bezeichnet) bildet es das letzte der 64 Hexagramme: „Feuer und Wasser vor der Vollendung". Nach dem Philosophen Zhu Xi (1130 – 1200) bedeutet „vor der Vollendung" hier nicht, dass der Zustand der Vollendung nicht erreicht werden kann, sondern verweist auf einen endlosen Kreislauf, und „Nicht-Vollendung" bezieht sich hier auf den Weg der Natur, so wie im Orakel zum Hexagramm 49 des Buchs der Wandlungen mit „Spiritualität" das Eins-Sein gemeint ist, das sich dem Blick entzieht.

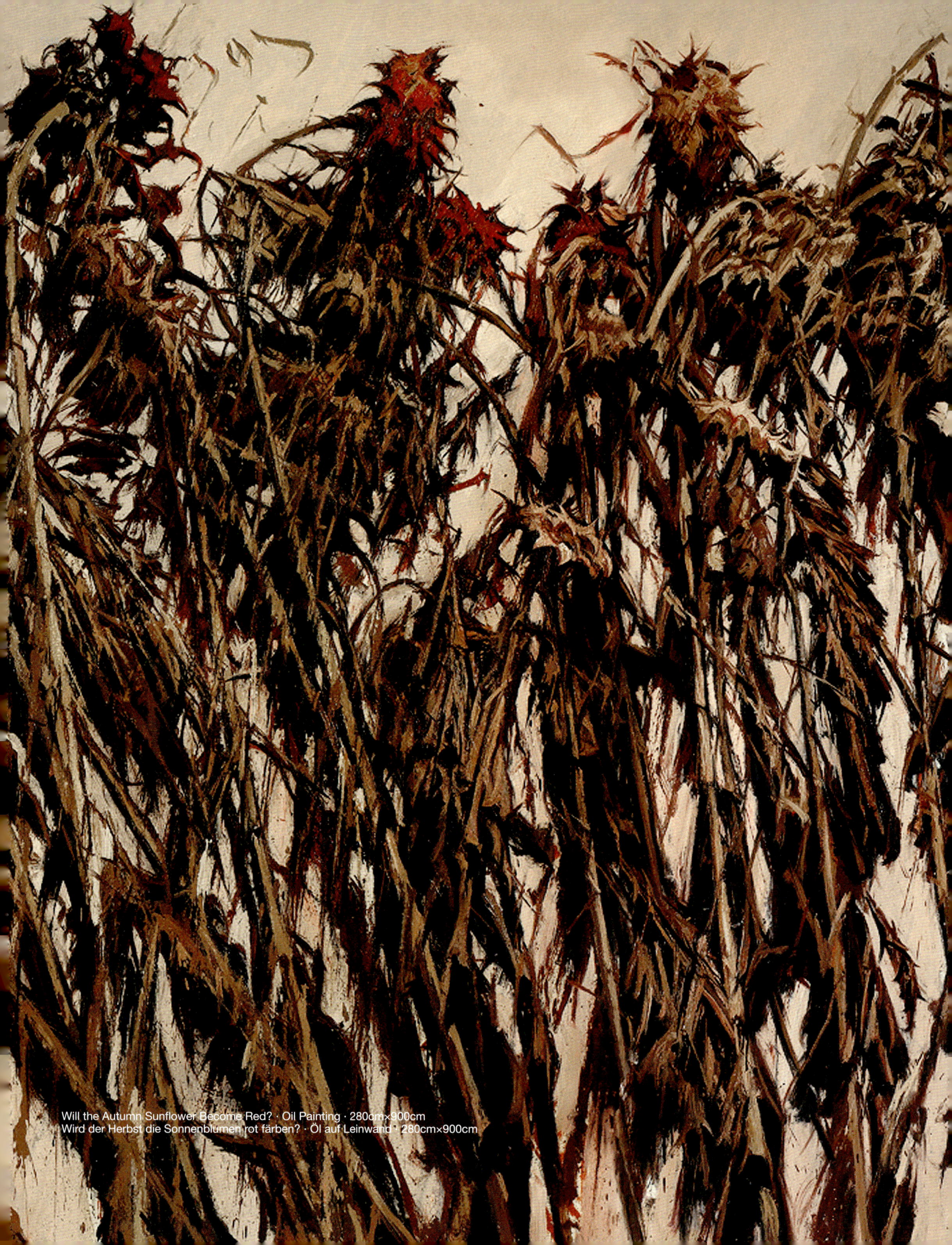

Will the Autumn Sunflower Become Red? · Oil Painting · 280cm×900cm
Wird der Herbst die Sonnenblumen rot färben? · Öl auf Leinwand · 280cm×900cm

The Thread and the Sunflower
Material and Symbolism in the Artwork of Shi Hui and Xu Jiang
Claus Mewes

Der Faden und die Sonnenblume
Material und Symbol in der Kunst von Shi Hui und Xu Jiang
Claus Mewes

At first glance the artwork of Shi Hui and Xu Jiang hardly resembles each other:While the artist Shi Hui concentrates on fibre structures based on natural or synthetic fibres, threads, ductile and soft materials, such as paper maché and bamboo wattle, Xu Jiang creates lively pictures in his drawings, paintings and sculptures that can be read symbolically. Yet, this brief comparison leaves some doubts about the analogy. Both of them belong to a generation of artists that not only appear to have great influence on the aesthetic discourse in China at present but also co-determine the latter with their art, their work and public role. Shi Hui and Xu Jiang are active as longterm professors and advisors at the renowned China Academy of Art, Hangzhou. Among the long list of their cultural responsibilities, Shi Hui currently acts in the role of director of the "Varbanov Tapestry Research Center" in Hangzhou, where she also lectures. There she initiated and implemented the first "Triennale of Fibre Art" in 2013. Xu Jiang, president of the China Academy of Art, Hangzhou since 2001, has stimulated the Biennial of Contemporary Art in Shanghai since 1996. In 2004 he functioned as chief-curator of the latter ("Techniques of the Visible"). Both artists take credit in an impressive series of substantial exhibitions in

Auf den ersten Blick ähneln sich die künstlerischen Arbeiten von Shi Hui und Xu Jiang kaum: Während sich die Künstlerin Shi Hui mit textilen Strukturen auf der Basis unterschiedlicher pflanzlicher, aus der Natur gewonnener oder synthetisch hergestellter Fasern, Fäden, formbarer weicher Stoffe wie Pappmaché und Bambusflechtwerk auseinandersetzt, schafft der Künstler Xu Jiang in Zeichnungen, Gemälden und Plastiken Bilder, die sich symbolisch lesen lassen. Doch täuscht diese schnelle Unterscheidung über das Gemeinsame hinweg; beide gehören einer Generation von Künstlerinnen und Künstlern an, die zur Zeit in China großen Einfluss ausüben und den ästhetischen Diskurs mitbestimmen durch ihre Werke, Tätigkeiten und Funktionen. Shi Hui und Xu Jiang sind langjährig als Vermittler mit Professuren an der angesehenen Akademie für bildende Künste China in Hangzhou aktiv. Aus der Vielzahl der kulturellen Verantwortlichkeiten beider sei nur erwähnt, dass Shi Hui, Dozentin und heutige Direktorin des „Varbanov Tapestry Research Center" („Varbanov-Tapisserie-Zentrum") in Hangzhou, die erste „Triennal of Fiber Art" („Triennale textiler Kunst") 2013 initiiert hat und vorbereitet, - dass Xu Jiang, seit 2001 Präsident der Akademie in Hangzhou, die Biennale für zeitgenössische

China and abroad.

Both born in 1955, Shi Hui, originally from Shanghai and Xu Jiang, originally from Fujian, met in Hangzhou during their studies. The artist couple to-be graduates in 1982. Since their childhood they were affected by China's ample social changes. During their youth they witness the three phases of the Cultural Revolution, 1966-1976. As students they faced the beginning of the political and economic reform movement and its revisions. Caught up in the spirit of cultural and economic liberalization the artistically trained teachers took part in the so-called '85-Avant Garde' movement. While Shi Hui engages in post-graduate studies with the fibre artist Maryn Varbanov (1932 Bulgaria - 1989 China) at the academy in Hanghzou, Xu Jiang grasped the opportunity to study one term, 1988/89, at the University of Fine Arts of Hamburg. There he studied with KP Brehmer (1938 Berlin -1997 Hamburg) who has previously been a visiting professor in Hangzhou. The exposure to the distinct cultures of East and West during the past decades has left traces in the artists' work. It has also provoked an expansion of their aesthetic repertoire, as well as their orientation in context of cultural policy.

Motivated by a natural spectacle in Turkey in 2003, the motif of the sunflower, constitutes a central theme in Xu Jiang's work. Hence, the artist grouped a field of oversized sunflowers made of bronze and aluminum in front of the Fridericianum in Kassel, in 2011 ("Re-Generation"). Stems, six meters of height, and closely arranged side by side convey an association of a well-fortified regiment with erect lances. The solid metal stems embody an unyielding power, while the blossoms on top signal movement among one another and seem to turn in all geographic directions. In contrast to the

bildende Kunst in Shanghai seit Gründung 1996 stimuliert und 2004 als Chefkurator gestaltet hat („Techniques of the Visible"). Beide können auf eine beeindruckende Reihe umfangreicher Ausstellungen in China und im internationalen Kunstbetrieb verweisen.

Im gleichen Jahr 1955 geboren, traf sich - sie aus Shanghai und er aus Fujian kommend - das spätere Künstlerehepaar zum Studium in Hangzhou und absolvierte 1982 zeitgleich das Diplom. Jeweils sind sie seit ihrer Kindheit geprägt durch die großen gesellschaftlichen Umbrüche in China. Als Jugendliche erlebten sie die drei Phasen der Kulturrevolution von 1966 bis 1976, als junge Studenten den Beginn der politischen wie wirtschaftlichen Reformbewegungen und deren Revisionen, als künstlerisch Ausgebildete und bereits lehrend sind sie Teil der sogenannten '85er-Generation im Rahmen des kulturellen Aufbruchs und der Liberalisierung des chinesischen Wirtschaftssystems. Während sich Shi Hui an der Akademie in Hangzhou durch ein Aufbaustudium bei dem Textilkünstler Marin Varbanov (Bulgarien 1932 - 1989 China) spezialisierte, nahm Xu Jiang 1988/89 ein Auslandssemester an der Hochschule für bildende Künste in Hamburg bei KP Brehmer (Berlin 1938 - 1997 Hamburg) wahr, der zuvor mehrfach in Hangzhou als Gastprofessor aus dem Westen gewirkt hatte. Die Berührungen mit den verschiedenen ost- und westeuropäischen Kulturen der letzten Jahrzehnte haben im Werk beider Spuren hinterlassen und zu einer Erweiterung sowohl des ästhetischen Repertoires als auch der kultur- politischen Orientierung geführt.

Angeregt durch ein Naturschauspiel in der Türkei 2003 bildet das Motiv der Sonnenblume einen Schwerpunkt im Werk von Xu Jiang. So platzierte der Künstler 2012 einen feldgroßen Block überdimensionierter Sonnenblumen aus Bronze und Aluminium vor den Schlossbau des Fridericianums in Kassel („Re-Generation"). Sechs Meter hoch und Stiel an

bright and clearly contoured face of the neo-classical piece of representative architecture, the field of flowers does not increase the courtly grandeur and order but offers with its dark auburn color an antagonism of effulgence and morbidity, rigidness and mobility. In opposition to their natural feature of uniformly orienting themselves towards the sun, Xu Jiang's plants of varied heights turn their creased heads into random directions. The memory of the bright yellow sunflower field seems blurred by the image of the drooping blossoms. The perspective of the dispersal of its seeds anew, compensates for the loss of the bright blossom.

The confrontation of power structure and the unhierarchical field of plants is tied to metaphors in the West, as well as in the East alike. These metaphors do not only allude to social order but are commonly understood beyond cultural borders: On one side there is the Sun King to whom his subjects bow. On the other side there are the collective masses that unveil their idea of taking action under the millionfold duplicated emblem of the sunflower, as during the period of the Cultural Revolution in China. By the beginning of the 20th century when Vincent van Gogh's paintings of cut sunflowers, banned in vases, circled in large quantities, the vanity-thought has come to the fore in popular consciousness: The drooping sunflower as a symbol for vanity of life and power. Yet, even as the signet of the international anti-nuclear movement, the complex symbolism of evolution and decline has become omnipresent. The auburn and black sunflowers in his numerous drawings, gigantic paintings and sculptures, Xu Jiang explicitly alludes to his generation. As an expression of a historical period in China, Xu Jiang's sunflowers can be read in the dialectics of group identity and individual demeanor. This may be compared to Auguste Rodin's monument for the inhabitants of the city of Calais, marking the end of the

Stiel gedrängt, stellt sich die Assoziation eines wehrhaften Regiments mit aufgerichteten Lanzen ein, deren Schäfte metallisch massiv eine unbeugsame Macht verkörpern, während nach oben hin die geneigten Blütenköpfe Bewegung untereinander und Wendung in alle Himmelsrichtungen signalisieren. Im Gegensatz zur hellen und mit Profilen sauber abgesetzten Fassade des klassizistischen Repräsentationsbaus steigert das Blumenrevier nicht die höfische Würdeform und Ordnung, sondern bietet im Kontrast dunkel rotbrauner Verfärbung einen Widerspruch zwischen Glanz und Morbidität, Starrheit und Mobilität. Entgegen der natürlichen Eigenschaft, sich einheitlich am Licht der Sonne auszurichten, wenden sich bei Xu Jiang die unterschiedlich großen Pflanzen mit ihren zerknitterten Köpfen beliebig in die Gegend. Die Erinnerung an strahlend gelbe Sonnenblumenfelder wird getrübt durch das Bild der welkenden Blüte, deren Verlust des hellen Scheins abgelöst wird durch die Perspektive neuerlicher Verbreitung der freiwerdenden Samenkerne.

In der Konfrontation von Herrschaftsarchitektur und unhierarchischem Pflanzenfeld verknüpfen sich im Westen als auch im Osten gleichermaßen Metaphern, die auf gesellschaftliche Organisation anspielen und über die Kulturen hinweg für jeden verständlich sind: Hier der Sonnenkönig, dem sich die Untertanen zuneigen - dort die kollektiven Massen, die unter dem millionenfach vervielfältigten Emblem einer Sonnenblume die Idee ihres Handelns sichtbar machen, wie zur Zeit der Kulturrevolution in China. Spätestens seit Anfang des 20. Jahrhunderts Vincent van Goghs Bilder von abgeschnittenen und in Vasen verbannten Sonnenblumen massenhafte Verbreitung fanden, ist damit im populären Bewusstsein der Vanitas-Gedanke in den Vordergrund gerückt: die welkende Sonnenblume als Zeichen der Vergänglichkeit von Leben und Macht. Bis hinein in das Signet der weltweit wirkenden Anti-Atomkraft-Bewegung reicht die komplexe Symbolik der Sonnenblume zwischen Entfaltung

empire and the begin of a civil constitution. Six sculptures of reputable inhabitants of the city, which Auguste Rodin created on the occasion of the anniversary of the French Revolution, 1889, should recall the bravery of the small group in the face of the imminent repression of the city of Calais during the Hundred Years' War between England and France. The monument serves as a model for a new social identity. Therewith, Xu Jiang's work reflects his conviction of building bridges between history and presence, between Asia and Europe.

By displaying the image of the sunflower, Xu Jiang revitalizes numerous old Eastern, as well as Western cultural traditions, whose imagery memory derived from natural scenes. Shi Hui's focus on texture and material demonstrates a different reflection of the relationship towards nature and cultural identity.

As one of the few female artists among the '85-Avant Garde' movement, Shi Hui has programmatically tied in with the rich tradition of specific manual techniques of fabric manufacture, such as spinning, dyeing, ladle, weaving, Knotting and knitting. Moreover, Shi Hui uses ductile material, such as paper maché for her sculptures. The dimensions of her works, like for example "Suspending Foundation Stones" (2012) are space filling. The different pieces of her art work appear in varying conditions, some standing, some hanging, some rigging, in polydirectional alignment in indoor and outdoor settings. At the same time, the different structure of the materials interacts with incidence of natural or artificial light. Fragile webs of light and dark percolate and amplify different sections of the room in changing directions. The empty exhibition space hence becomes an unusual area, in which the beholder has to coordinate perception and movement afresh ("Structure 4", 1998) The "soft sculptures", which outweigh the empirical values of mass and weight, rigidity and firmness, as well as flexible softness, seem just as much

und Untergang. Ausdrücklich bezieht Xu Jiang seine vielen als Zeichnungen, monumentale Gemälde und Plastiken in Rotbraun und Schwarz gehaltenen Sonnenblumenarbeiten auf seine Generation. Als Ausdruck einer historischen Phase Chinas lässt sich das Monument der Sonnenblumen von Xu Jiang in der Dialektik von Gruppenidentität und individueller Haltung lesen im Vergleich etwa zu dem Denkmal für die Bürger der Stadt Calais von Auguste Rodin nach dem Ende des Kaisertums und zu Beginn einer bürgerlichen Staatsverfassung in Frankreich. Mit sechs portraithaften Darstellungen angesehener Stadtbewohner verschiedenen Alters, die Auguste Rodin aus Anlass zur Jubiläumsfeier der Französischen Revolution 1889 modellierte, sollte an den individuellen Mut der kleinen Gruppe angesichts drohender Unterwerfung der ganzen Stadt Calais im hundertjährigen Krieg zwischen England und Frankreich erinnert werden - als Vorbild einer neuen sozialen Identität. Damit entsprechen die Werke dem Konzept Xu Jiangs, mit Kunst Brücken zu schlagen zwischen Geschichte und Gegenwart, zwischen Asien und Europa.

Mit Darstellungen der Sonnenblume aktualisiert Xu Jiang zahlreiche alte, östliche und westliche Kulturtraditionen, die ihr Bildgedächtnis an Naturvorgängen herausgebildet haben. Shi Hui's Konzentration auf Stofflichkeit und Material hat einen anderen Fokus auf die Reflexion des Verhältnisses zur Natur und zur kulturellen Identität.

Zu den wenigen Künstlerinnen der '85er Generation gehörend, hat Shi Hui programmatisch angeknüpft an den traditionellen Reichtum spezifischer Handwerkstechniken der Stoffherstellung wie -gestaltung vom Spinnen, Färben und Schöpfen bis zum Weben, Knüpfen und Sticken. Darüber hinaus nutzt die Künstlerin plastisch formbares Material wie Papiermaché zur Herstellung von Objekten, deren Dimensionen raumgreifend sind, wie die Installation „Suspending Foundation Stones" aus dem Jahr 2012. Shi Huis Werke variieren Zustände

surprising. Seemingly heavy chunks hang from the ceiling. Yet, they are made from paper maché. Firmly contoured, oval-shaped panels on the wall seem to fray and trickle ("Fan", 2002). Dense surfaces are translucent. Altogether, Shi Hui questions with her work habits of conduct and assessment. The material oriented aesthetic can also be linked to Western art history, as for example to the "Bauhaus" school, which was founded in Weimar in 1919. Bauhaus combines crafts and fine arts with the aim to provide modern models to the industrial production, as well as ideas of a concept art that utilizes everyday life items and -materials.

The conclusion to this brief abstract on Shi Hui's and Xu Jiang's art work discloses a mutual mindset that not only implements aesthetically what is reflected in the present discourse in China but also guides their approach towards cultural policy in this context. Their common aim is to create designs that deal with global trends in the arts, without compromising their Chinese cultural identity between the agrarian tradition, social failure and industrial dynamics.

des Stehens, Hängens, der Verspannung und allseitigen Ausrichtung im architektonischen Innen- und öffentlichen Außenraum. Dabei reagieren die unterschiedlichen Material-strukturen auf den natürlichen oder künstlichen Lichtein-fall. Feine Helldunkel-Gespinste filtern und vervielfältigen Raumzonen in wechselnden Richtungen und machen den vormals leeren Ausstellungsort zu einem ungewohnten Arreal, in dem der Betrachter Wahrnehmung und Bewegung neu koordinieren muss („Structure 4", 1998); ebenso überraschend sind für ihn die „Soft Sculptures", die jegliche Erfahrungswerte von Masse und Gewicht, von Härte, Festigkeit und flexibler Weichheit aufheben. Scheinbar schwere Brocken hängen an der Decke, sind jedoch nur aus Papiermaché. Festumrissene, ovale Scheibenobjekte an der Wand scheinen auszufransen und zu tropfen („Fan", 2002), dichte Oberflächen sind licht-durchlässig. Insgesamt fordert Shi Hui mit ihren Arbeiten heraus, Gewohnheiten des Verhaltens und der Beurteilung zu hinterfragen. Die materialorientierte Ästhetik der Künstlerin lässt sich auch mit westlicher Kunstgeschichte verbinden - nur erwähnt seien sowohl das Programm des 1919 in Weimar gegründeten „Bauhaus", die freien und angewandten Künste zu vereinen, um der industriell geprägten Produktion moderne Modelle zu liefern, als auch die Ideen einer auf Alltagsgegen-stände und -materialien zugreifenden Concept Art.

Das Fazit zum kurzen Abriss der Arbeiten von Shi Hui und Xu Jiang offenbart eine gemeinsame Position, die ästhetisch und kulturpolitisch umsetzt, was im aktuellen Diskurs in China reflektiert wird: Formen zu entwickeln, die sich mit globalen Tendenzen in der Kunst auseinandersetzen, ohne dabei eigene chinesische kulturelle Identität zwischen agrarischer Tradition, gesellschaftlichen Brüchen und industrieller Dynamik aufzugeben.

Bathing in Life-Giving Fire

Wiedergeburt aus dem Feuer

Longing For Life
Foreword to the 'Re-Generation' Exhibition
Xu Jiang

Sehnsucht nach Leben
Vorwort zur Ausstellung 'Re-Generation'
Xu Jiang

The Sunflower Whisperer

I have been in the company of sunflowers for a while. Each day I try to paint one sunflower and over the years they populate the fields. Seen from afar, sunflowers that grow in droves remind one of the all-pervasive passing of time. A closer look would, however, yield a distinct sensitivity that runs through them, which endures the alternating seasons. Take the sunflower stalks left in wall corners for over ten years. They are a ripe yellow from dehydration, and may command no special attention day after day, yet an occasional glimpse would perhaps persuade one to notice the survivor's sensitivity and joie de vivre.

Sunflowers grow in sandy soil. The humidity of the soil in South China means that large stretches of sunflower fields are rarely seen. Usually a few stalks will grow at the corner of a field. When I was little, I was a boarder at a high school in a faraway suburb of a city. The high school is located on top of a hill called *Fucang* (the floating storage) whose shape is like an upside down bushel. The entire hill is covered by dense forestation, like a large botanic garden. Each summer,

Der Sonnenblumenmensch

Die Sonnenblumen sind meine steten Begleiter schon seit vielen Jahren. Jeden Tag eine Sonnenblume – so entstand im Laufe der Zeit ein ganzer Sonnenblumengarten. Aus der Ferne betrachtet erscheinen sie konturlos, wie die verschwommene Erinnerung an eine ferne Vergangenheit, doch nähert man sich ihnen, so verströmen sie eine besondere Aura, trotz oder gerade wegen ihrer unscheinbaren und unansehnlichen Gestalt: Für einen Augenblick können wir in ihren verwitterten Gestalten nachempfinden, was es heißt, vom Leben gezeichnet zu sein, seine Höhen und Tiefen erfahren zu haben.

Sonnenblumen wachsen auf trocken-sandigem Untergrund. Im Süden Chinas herrscht jedoch feuchtes Klima, große Sonnenblumenfelder sind daher selten. Lediglich einzelne Exemplare wachsen bisweilen an Feldrändern. Als ich klein war, wohnte ich am Rande einer größeren Stadt in einer Mittelschule. Diese wiederum lag auf einem trichterförmigen Berg, der mit seiner dichten Vegetation an einen botanischen Garten erinnerte. Auch einige Sonnenblumen wagten sich

on the narrow slopes halfway up the hill, a few sunflowers would be spotted growing. They sank their roots into the soft and spongy loess, stretching their limbs with difficulty. The sunlight of South China lent them a special brilliance. A few times I climbed up the steep slope and groped into the yet tender blooms and touched the florets to feel the mystery of the plant's texture, imagining a mysterious exchange of natural energy. I was naturally given many dressing downs for such pranks. The sunflowers, however, would not endure, as they often disappeared altogether from the slope a few days after the summer typhoons. It was during the Cultural Revolution, and the sunflowers were often likened to the people. On the blackboard bulletins in my school, stylised sunflower ornaments were an all-time favourite. When I was drawing the sunflower head with crayon in the popular style, I could not help wondering the sunflowers whose lives were cut short by the typhoons. The group symbolism of that time coincided with the social transformations of the time, brewing in my memories for decades until they assumed a metallic shape. So far I have cast a few thousand bronze sunflowers, yet each time I look at one of them I feel like it's a first encounter.

Comparisons to sunflowers are often made because of their heliotropism, as is often seen both at home and abroad. Heliotropism isn't a rarity in plants, yet that of the sunflower is quite unusual in its combination of flower and fruit, and its daily motion towards the sun for as long as the entire season. The enduring brilliance always triggers cosmic inspirations and a belief in supernatural forces of transformation. Its flower head is the size of the human face, its height also comparable to that of an adult human. People compare themselves to this plant, grafting their own selves into the sunflower and indulging in such flight of fancy. Cao Shu (?-308AD) of the West Jin Dynasty (265-317AD) wrote, 'As the sun moves

jeden Sommer auf seine langen schmalen Hänge hinauf. Sie kämpften sich dort durch die lockere gelbe Erde, der südlichen Sonne entgegen, die sie in ihrer ganzen Pracht erstrahlen ließ. Was ich gerne tat, auch wenn es mir manchen Ärger einbrachte, war zu den Sonnenblumen hinaufzusteigen, meine Hand in die Knospen zu schieben und dabei die Tiefe des Blütenkelches bis hinunter zum Blütenteller zu ertasten. Ich bildete mir ein, dabei die geheimnisvolle Kraft natürlichen Wachsens zu fühlen. Die Sonnenblumen selber jedoch überdauerten nicht lange, nach einigen Taifunen zu Beginn des Sommers mussten sie sich den Naturgewalten beugen und waren jedes Mal bald wieder verschwunden. Damals war die Zeit der sogenannten „Kulturrevolution" und die Sonnenblume galt als etwas, womit die Menschen sich selber gerne verglichen. Sonnenblumenmotive waren auch die beliebteste Dekoration auf den sogenannten „Wandzeitungen", den obligatorischen schwarzen Brettern in den Klassenzimmern. Jedes Mal wenn ich eine bunte Kreide in die Hand nahm, um im Stil der Zeit einen Blütenteller zu skizzieren, dachte ich insgeheim an ihre Vorbilder auf den Hängen, die viel zu früh dem Taifun zum Opfer gefallen waren. Wir alle waren Opfer des Kollektivismus und sind stark durch unsere Erfahrungen geprägt worden. All diese Erinnerungen haben sich in meinem Gedächtnis überlagert und konnten nach Jahrzehnten der Latenz schließlich in Kupfer modelliert und Eisen gegossen werden. Die Zahl dieser Kupfer-Eisenblumen geht mittlerweile in die Tausende, doch jedes Mal, wenn ich sie betrachte ist der Eindruck so frisch wie beim ersten Mal.

Warum verglich man sich selber so gerne mit der Sonnenblume? Der Grund hat offensichtlich mit der allgemein bekannten Heliotaxis zu tun: Zwar richten sich alle Blumen nach der Sonne aus, das erstaunliche Phänomen, das Pflanzen ihrem Tageslauf jedoch über Monate hinweg in synchroner Abstimmung folgen, findet man jedoch nicht so häufig und es hat zu allerhand wilden Spekulationen über verborgen wirkende Kräfte Anlass gegeben. Außerdem

into another house, the sunflowers and pulse leaves turn their heads, filled with longing.' The sun moves solemnly from one zodiac house to another, and the sunflowers on the earth longingly follow its course. What a devoted and all-encompassing passion between heaven and earth! 'The heart of an inch-long grass welcomes the eternal sun; I compare my own to that of the sunflower.' (Zhan Wujiu of the Song Dynasty [960-1279 AD]) 'The yellow flower stands there cold and unattended, the sun it alone turns to with longing.' (Liu Ban of the Song Dynasty) Chinese poets have bestowed on the yellow flower a human heart, and a loyalty kept alive by a longing. Chinese style transference, characterised by comparing the self to almost every object in the cosmos, always tends to describe the sunflower as withering and pertinacious. Since the flower has a colour yet carries no scent, and since it seems to be flower yet in fact it is the fruit. Unlike ordinary flower appreciation, it is more likely to see a kind of commiseration as described in Sikong Tu (837-908AD)'s line 'The grand way is diminishing day by day, what can the hero possibly do?' Therefore, each time I encounter the last stanza of the chapter 'Commiseration' in Sikong Tu's *Twenty Four Poetic Categories*, 'Fallen leaves rustle, while the dripping rain spills onto the moss.' Such desolation belongs to the sunflower fields on the cold and sterile earth.

Sofia Loren starred in *Sunflower*, a film set in World War II. The film tells the story of a couple's forced parting of ways during the war and the post-war loss of contact. The wife, played by Loren, travels to Eastern Europe in search of her husband. As she makes her way through a sunflower field, the guide tells her that this was once a battleground with piles of bodies. War dead from both sides are buried under this sunflower field, which remains silent and sways gently to the wind. The dead souls shuck off their armours, and now become

entspricht die Größe eines Blütentellers ungefähr dem eines menschlichen Gesichtes, die Höhe der ausgewachsenen Pflanze ungefähr der Körperhöhe des Menschen; der Vergleich zum Menschen liegt daher nahe und es ist geradezu verlockend, sich selbst in die Blume hineinzuprojizieren. Bei vielen Dichtern aus alter Zeit tritt uns die Sonnenblume entgegen als beseeltes Wesen, treu und standhaft bis in den eigenen tragischen Untergang. An die kalte Trostlosigkeit eines solchen Sonnenblumenfeldes muss ich jedes Mal denken, wenn ich die letzte Zeile von Si Kongtus Gedicht „Schwermut" aus der Tang-Zeit lese: Trauer, Hilflosigkeit und Einsamkeit, all dies bündelt sich im Bild des feucht raschelnden Herbstlaubes, im regenglänzenden Moos.

Sonnenblumen spielen auch eine Rolle in einem nach ihnen benannten Film. Dieser Film erzählt, wie ein Ehepaar während des zweiten Weltkrieges getrennt wird und sich aus den Augen verliert. Nach Ende des Krieges macht sich Giovanna, gespielt von Sophia Loren, dann auf die Suche nach ihrem verschollenen Mann. Während Giovanna eines Tages zusammen mit ihrem Führer ein Sonnenblumenfeld durchquert, weist dieser Giovanna darauf hin, dass an dieser Stelle früher schwere Kämpfe tobten und Leichen sich auf dem Boden stapelten. Doch ganz gleich auf welcher Seite sie einst kämpften, jetzt ruhen die Gefallenen gemeinsam unter diesem Garten aus Sonnenblumen. Und die Sonnenblumen schweigen und wiegen sich im Wind; die Soldaten dort im Sand haben ihre Uniformen ausgezogen, ihre Seelen kennen weder Freund noch Feind. Am Ende findet Giovanna ihren Mann wieder, der in der Fremde eine neue Familie gegründet hat. Beide haben den Krieg zwar überlebt, aber die Jahre der Trennung lassen sich nicht wieder ungeschehen machen.

Ein Buch des bekannten Gelehrten Simon Wiesenthal trägt ebenfalls die Sonnenblume im Titel. Es ist kein Roman, keine Autobiographie und auch kein historisches oder politisches Buch. Es beschreibt, wie eine Sonnenblume auf dem Grab

inseparable from one another! In the end the wife finds her husband, who has already built a new family in a faraway place. The war did not cost them their lives, but their previous life together.

Simon Wiesenthal wrote a book, *The Sunflower: On the Possibilities and Limits of Forgiveness*. It is neither fiction nor biography, neither history nor political doctrine. Yet this book questions the collective destiny of humanity. The book tells of the story of how sunflowers growing on the tombs of dead German soldiers became a major concern of a dying Jew. In fact, man's conscience is the sunflower standing between the historical earth and the ubiquitous heavenly way. It makes generations after generations of men carry an awe in their heart, and listen to the calls of the heavenly way when faced with the entwined choices in destiny. It reveals the strength in the depth of human spirit, and offers consolations for the sadness in life. It redeems humanity from the current pains and sense of loss. And with the light of the heavenly way, it looks down on all generations and tells an eternal narrative.

The real sunflower field can be found both on earth and in man's heart. It exists in the images of historical memories, as well as in the everyday world we face on a daily basis.

Learning About Death Prior to Learning About Life

In winter 2008, the writer Yu Hua came to my studio and could not help exclaiming at the room full of sunflowers. The next day he wrote in his article, 'the sunflower is a common memory shared by all of us, an image capable of bringing tears to the eyes for this generation of Chinese.'…'After many years, finally we have someone here to revive our sunflowers.'…'Sunflowers gather at the canvases of Xu Jiang,

eines deutschen Soldaten zum Gegenstand der Sorge der jüdischen Gefangenen wird. Das Gewissen der Menschen gleicht in der Tat einer goldenen Sonnenblume, die den Gesetzen des Himmels folgend versucht, sich einen Weg durch die irdischen Verstrickungen zu bahnen.

Sonnenblumengärten sind daher genauso in den Herzen der Menschen beheimatet wie in der Natur, wir begegnen ihnen in Zeugnissen der Vergangenheit genauso wie in unserer heutigen Alltagswelt.

Den Tod kennenlernen um das Leben zu verstehen

Im Winter des Jahres 2008 besuchte mich der Schriftsteller Xu Hua in meinem Atelier. Als er die Unmengen von Sonnenblumen sah, konnte er ein Seufzen nicht unterdrücken. Am nächsten Tag schrieb er in einem Artikel: „Die Sonnenblumen haben sich in unser gemeinsames Gedächtnis eingebrannt, bei ihrem Anblick treten uns heiße Tränen in die Augen… Nach so vielen Jahren hat endlich jemand unsere Sonnenblumen ins Leben zurückgerufen… In Xu Jiangs Bildern bündeln sich unsere widerspruchsvollen Gefühle und mannigfaltigen Erinnerungen an die Sonnenblumen. "Viele der Besucher meiner Ausstellungen im Shanghai Art Museum (2009) und im Zhejiang Art Museum (2010) fühlten sich von den Sonnenblumen stark berührt, denn sie hatten die „Kulturrevolution" am eigenen Leib erfahren, sind während dieses finsteren Abschnitts der Geschichte aufgewachsen und erzogen worden. Die Sonnenblumen waren Teil unserer gemeinsamen Lebenswirklichkeit, sie symbolisieren den Kollektivismus der damaligen Zeit. Die Kulturrevolution kannte auch eine beliebte Symbolfarbe: Rot. Rot war die Sonne, rot war das Volk, das sich so gerne mit den Sonnenblumen verglich. Diese Symbolik hatte sich über die Jahre hinweg in die Seele einer ganzen Generation eingebrannt und ist zu deren Erkennungszeichen geworden. Die „widerspruchsvollen Gefühle und mannigfaltigen Erinnerungen", von denen Xu Hua spricht,

full of emotions…' At my solo exhibitions in 2009 and 2010 respectively at the Shanghai Art Museum and Zhejiang Art Museum, many eye-witnesses of the Cultural Revolution, especially those growing up in that sterile era, were all sighing with emotion. The sunflower was once the common life or our generation, encompassing the collective spiritual imagery of that era. The billions of red badges circulating in the Cultural Revolution, bore images of the people likening themselves to sunflowers, apart from those of the Red Sun himself. The symbolic value of such imagery, the expression of the *Zeitgeist* of that era, crystallise into the sentimental symptoms of an entire generation of youths. 'Full of emotions', as Yu aptly puts it, was exactly the generation's perception of their own drifting destinies. At that time, folly and madness spread like winds whirling past the plateau, and finally died out in an endless stretch of desert. Youthful passions underwent debate, armed fighting, defence, until finally the millions of 'educated youths' were sent to their fate's cutting edge. Generations of youths died young after a glorious blossoming, just like the sunflower. Prior to the termination of the Cultural Revolution in 1976, they seemed to have all experienced death for at least once. As society reawakened, they started to meet with opportunities for life. They seized each of them, trying once again to make their youth blossom. They knew full well the hardships and transformations over time, so they held dear the meanings of life just as they held dear the sunflower heads. They had learned about death before they learned about life.

This generation of youths experienced unprecedented ruptures in their value system. Such ruptures were not confined to the revolutionary *Sturm & Drang* of the 1960s and the waves of reform since the late 1970s. More importantly it entailed breaking through the constrictions of the

betreffen die im Bild der Sonnenblume verdichtete Erfahrung der Ohnmacht und Selbstentfremdung. Zu dieser Zeit war eine Raserei ausgebrochen, die in Windeseile das ganze Land erfasste, bevor sie später irgendwann in der Wildnis versandete. Euphorisch hatte sich die rotgardistische Jugend in den Kampf um die richtige Theorie gestürzt, zunächst in Debatten, dann in Handgemengen bis schließlich alles in einer Schlacht auf Leben und Tod mit einem Schlag sein Ende fand. Wie Sonnenblumen, deren Leben nach kurzer Blüte jäh erlischt, so war diese Jugend bei Ende der Kulturrevolution 1976 in gewisser Weise um ihr Leben betrogen worden. Umso kostbarer waren ihnen daher die Gelegenheiten, die sich Ihnen während des Wiederaufbaus der Gesellschaft boten und sie nutzten jede Möglichkeit um ihren Entwicklungsrückstand aufzuholen. Sie mussten erst den Tod kennenlernen bevor sie das Leben verstehen konnten.

Diese Generation erlebte in ihrer Jugend einen Wertewandel, der historisch einmalig ist. Er beschränkt sich nicht auf die revolutionären Stürme der 60er Jahre und die in den späten 70er Jahren einsetzenden Reformen, viel wichtiger ist die Frage, wie es den Menschen gelungen ist, den Bann solcher propagandistischer Zauberwörter wie „Revolution", „Selbstlosigkeit", „Neuanfang" zu brechen, und den blinden Irrsinn der sogenannten Kulturrevolution hinter sich zu lassen, um sich wieder ein Stück menschliche Normalität zurückzuerobern. Die Schwierigkeit bei der Rückkehr zur Normalität lag darin, dass man in der Gedankenwelt der Kulturrevolution sozialisiert und zu einem roboterhaften Denken erzogen worden war: „frühere Epochen" = „Feudalismus", „der Westen" = „Kapitalismus", „Ich" = „Revisionismus" – ein radikales Schwarz-Weiß-Denken, dem das Kritisieren zur Droge geworden war, an der es sich selbst berauschte. Dieselben Denkschablonen behielt man jedoch bei, nachdem die Zeiten sich geändert hatten und nunmehr im Zuge der Internationalisierung eine westlichere Weltsicht gefordert war: Mit missionarischem Eifer wurde jetzt das Auslandsstudium propagiert, um mit dem

discourse marked by such words as 'revolution', 'altruism', and 'rupture', and penetrating the passion and loss of the Cultural Revolution in order to observe the true reparation and restoration of humanity of an entire era. Such reparation and restoration are difficult because of a certain absolute, mechanic mental pattern that is deeply embedded in the ruptures of the Cultural Revolution thinking: the black-and-white, one-dimensional critical passion and radical mental pattern that once ascribed history to feudalism, the West to capitalism, the self to revisionism. Such a pattern, in the historical corrections afterwards, such as the establishment of a globalised, i.e. fundamentally Westernised outlook, and the surge in the number of students going abroad to keep abreast with the world, has morphed into a one-dimensional collective conscious and self-inflicted stricture capable of diminishing the originally progressive historical motivations in waves of social reform.

This generation of youths have suffered the most severe case of identity loss. Identity was used in an obstructionist way to divide people into hierarchies. The underlying reason for such divisions was marked by ideology, the theory of pedigree characteristic of feudalism. The social identities of one's ancestor, private ownership, as well as the intellectual, all carried an inexplicable sense of historical guilt. The definition of a good man was completely overthrown. Historical subjects were reduced to slogans of the radical rebels. Individual subjectivity was completely lost in the traps set by presupposed identity divisions. So profound was this loss, that the recovery of humanity took a rather long path, and engendered many eschatological readers in history and quests. Up till now, such readers are still used to describing and explaining the extent of openness of contemporaneity and have survived in the depth of the memories of a generation. Perhaps there

globalisierten Zeitgeist Schritt halten zu können – die gleiche monotone Konformität, die gleiche Art von selbstauferlegtem Sprüchezauber, für die der positive Impuls zu einer gesellschaftlichen Neuordnung verschwendet wurde.

Diese Jugend hatte den größten Selbstverlust der Geschichte zu verkraften. Die eigene Identität, das sind im Normalfall die Leitplanken, die einem helfen, Menschen zu klassifizieren, doch der Anlass zu solcher Klassifizierung liegt immer in einer bestimmten Bewusstseinshaltung, nicht zuletzt zeigt hier der Feudalismus seine verhasste Fratze. Familienzugehörigkeit, Vermögensverhältnisse, Bildungsgrad - alles identitätsstiftende Merkmale, die dem einzelnen historisches Schuldbewusstsein aufluden. Die Definition dessen, was einen guten Menschen ausmacht, wurde völlig neu geschrieben, als Geschichtssubjekt ließ man lediglich die radikalen Revolutionäre gelten. Der Mensch als autonomes Subjekt seiner Handlungen ging inmitten der vorgefertigten Klassenklischees völlig unter. Dieser Selbst-verlust war so gravierend, dass er noch auf dem langen Weg zur Normalität für allerlei Kalamitäten sorgte. Die damaligen Denkkategorien hatten sich so tief ins Gedächtnis eingebrannt, dass sie selbst den Beschreibungen und Kommentaren zur späteren Öffnungspolitik übergestülpt wurden. Es gab wohl kaum einen Zeitabschnitt, in dem Millionen von Schulabgänger auf entlegene Dörfer oder ins Gebirge geschickt wurden, um die Mühsal des bäuerlichen Lebens am eigenen Leib zu erfahren. Nach Ende der Kulturrevolution wiederum sandte man zahlreiche Mittelschulabsolventen zum Studium nach Europa oder in die USA. Die ersteren waren Ziel einer einfachen Umerziehung während die letzteren sich auf einer Art Mission befanden, auf der es galt, sich zu bewähren und abzuhärten. Innerhalb von gut zehn Jahren hatte das Schicksal der Jugend einen komplett neuen Lauf genommen: Aus Schülern, die ausgesandt waren, um das chinesische Bauernleben zu studieren (*tu chadui*), wurden „studentische Gesandte" im Ausland (*yang chadui*), ein Wandel, der tiefere seelische Spuren hinterließ als manche Kriegserfahrung.

was hardly a time like this, when millions of 'educated youths' were sent to faraway villages and mountainous areas to eke out a living with manual labour. Later, after the Cultural Revolution was over, quite many of them went to Europe and America, through means both private an official, to study. The former group is called *tu chadui,* 'the local production brigade' and the latter *yang chadui,* 'the foreign production brigade'. The former went on an exile in the disguise of re-education, while the latter had to complete trying exercises, as they had a certain historical task at hand. In just over a decade, the production brigade went from local to foreign. The fate of this generation of youths underwent more drastic transformation of worlds than an ordinary war.

This generation also went through a twofold ideological suffering which is quite rare in human history. Openness and closure, traditional and contemporary, global and local, modernisation and westernisation, the past that cannot die and the future that is yet to be born. They have to survive in the fissures between a twofold trap, feel the painful entanglement on the inevitably conflicting paths, demonstrating a hesitant and overlapping *Zeitgeist*. On the one hand they were courageous enough to break free from the closed-minded nationalism in their reflections on and critique of its ignorance, backwardness and vanity. On the other hand they are consciously resisting the tendency of sycophant westernisation as they are often alerted by the oppression and hegemony of the dominant culture and quick to denounce it. On the one hand they borrow freely from international cultural achievements in an attempt to keep abreast with the theoretical cutting edge of Internationalisation and to broaden their horizon. On the other hand, they have replaced the obscure aristocratic language with a vernacular, thereby substituting the outdated, alien language with that of a living,

Die Schizophrenien, mit denen diese Jugend konfrontiert waren, sind historisch gesehen wohl einzigartig: Abschottung und Öffnung, Tradition und Moderne, Globalisierung und Nationalisierung, Modernisierung und Verwestlichung, eine Vergangenheit, die nicht vergehen will und eine Zukunft, die nicht kommen will. Die Jugend fand sich umringt von Widersprüchen, denen sie sich stellen musste, ohne sie jedoch lösen zu können. Die hieraus entstandenen seelischen Narben sind Kennzeichen dieser Generation. Einerseits kämpfen sie mutig für die Überwindung nationaler Beschränktheit, stehen sich selbstkritisch gegenüber und verurteilen jede Form von Ignoranz, Rückständigkeit und Hohlheit. Auf der anderen Seite widerstrebt ihnen die Verherrlichung westlicher Werte, sie prangern kulturelle Unterdrückung und imperialistische Tendenzen an. Einerseits sind sie in den Genuss einer hervorragenden internationalen Ausbildung gekommen und hoffen, sich im Zuge der Globali-sierung als Theoretiker profilieren zu können. Auf der anderen Seite vermeiden sie die Verwendung schwer verständlicher, als „aristokratisch" empfundener Ausdrücke zugunsten einer einfachen volkstümlichen Sprache, die Benutzung antiquierter Wendungen und fremdländischer Ausdrücke zugunsten der lebendigen Sprache des Volkes, denn Kultur entsteht für sie aus dem Hier und Jetzt. Noch bezeichnender aber ist, dass sie erst lernen müssen, wie man die „Dichotomiefalle" vermeidet, das Schwarz-Weiß-Denken überwindet und sich durch Versuch und Irrtum einen dritten Weg ebnet, einen Weg zur seelischen Wiedergeburt.

Ein Besucher der Ausstellung *A Tribute to the Garden* (Zhejiang Art Museum, Hangzhou, 2010) schrieb nach der Besichtigung ins Gästebuch: „Eine oder zwei verdorrte Sonnenblumen sind nichts weiter als verdorrte Sonnenblumen; ein Feld verdorrter Sonnenblumen – das ist eine Jahreszeit, das ist eine Generation".

Der Marsch der Re-Generation

1989 bin ich vom Studium in Deutschland in meine Heimat

contemporary national reality. They build on the firm base of their own circumstances, and look at their own cultural production from within the matrix in a local perspective. More importantly, they have to learn to avoid the dual traps of dichotomy and transcend the black-and-white, one-dimensional judgment, and construct a 'Third Way' that is repeatedly engaged in dissection and reconstruction in search of a contemporary regeneration, out of the interaction between many conflicting yet mutually dependent factors.

After seeing the *To the Sunflower Fields*, my solo exhibition held in September 2010 at Zhejiang Art Museum,a member of the audience left a note on the guestbook, 'The desolation of one or two stalks of sunflowers is desolation pure and simple. The desolation of a whole field of sunflowers is the destiny of a season,an entire generation.'

The March Towards Re-Generation.

It has been twenty-three years since I returned from my studies in Germany in 1989. It is an age marked by great transformations in China, and my generation are at their prime. As our homeland, the Chinese art community has undergone continuous opening up and expansion, mod-ernisation and internationalisation. Many artists are going with the flow and become the 'comrades of the time'. I have experienced an alternative formation thanks to my studies in Germany.

Six years ago, my solo exhibition *Looking Afar* was held at the National Art Museum of China, Beijing. Some art critics summarised my case as a return from conceptual art to the easel, from composite material to painting and from the heaven to the earth, and dubbed it 'a retrospective history

zurückgekehrt, die 23 Jahre, die seitdem vergangen sind, waren die Zeit der größten Umwälzungen, die China je erlebt hatte und auch die Zeit, in der unsere Generation im Zenit Ihrer Schaffenskraft stand. Die chinesische Kunstszene hat in dieser Zeit einen stetigen Prozess der Öffnung, Modern-isierung und Internationalisierung erlebt. Viele Künstler haben sich dem Zeitgeist angepasst und reiten mit auf dieser Welle. Bei mir verlief die Entwicklung jedoch aufgrund meiner Studi-enerfahrung in Deutschland etwas anders.

Vor sechs Jahren fand in der National Chinese Art Gallery in Peking die Ausstellung „Yuan Wang" (Fernsicht) statt. Ein Kritiker resümierte meinen Entwicklungsweg als „Rückwendung vom Konzept zur Staffelei, von integrierten Materialien zur Farbe und als Rückkehr vom Himmel zur Erde" und nannte ihn eine „Reise durch die Kunstgeschichte". Der Grund für diesen Eindruck liegt darin, dass sich China zur Zeit der Reform und Öffnung vor mehr als dreißig Jahren auf einen Schlag mit einer jahrhundertealten westlichen Kunsttradition konfrontiert sah, die mit modernen und zeitgenössischen Ansätzen zu den unterschiedlichsten Strömungen verschmolz. All dieses strömte plötzlich ins Land und traf auf ein altes Kulturvolk, dessen menschliche Empfindungskraft durch die Kulturrevolution verkümmert war und erweckte diese zu neuem Leben. Eine ganze Generation junger Menschen ergriff teilweise unter großen Schwierigkeiten ihre Chance auf ein Auslandsstudium, um sich über die aktuellen Entwicklungen auf dem Laufenden zu halten. Mit einem verklärten Blick auf die sogenannte Globalisierung, die in Wirklichkeit eine Verwestlichung ist, eiferten sie den aktuellen Trends der internationalen Kunstszene nach in der Hoffnung, dort Anerkennung zu finden. Als wir damals aus dem Ausland zurückkehrten, erging es uns ganz ähnlich wie Odysseus: Wir mussten uns zu Hause ganz neu einrichten und uns einen eigenen Weg zurück in die Heimat bahnen.
Die experimentellen Arbeiten, die während meines kurzen

of art'. This individual case of retrospection in an open age is derived from the century of Western art history faced by the Chinese artist during the three-decade long opening up and reforms era. The diachronic waves entwined with the modern and contemporary history of the West have synchronically entered China, an ancient culture that has just survived the destruction of human sensitivity wrecked by the Cultural Revolution and waits to be reactivated. A generation of overseas Chinese students have seized all sorts of opportunities and overcome mounting difficulties in order to have an up-close and personal look at the West. They used to uphold the doctrine that internationalisation was in essence a Westernised, utopic outlook, and tried to catch up with the avant garde of contemporary international art in the hope of getting internationalised recognition. So upon returning to our homeland, we were faced with an Odyssean dilemma, namely the reconstruction of our homeland and selfhood from the foundation up.

In the short period I spent studying in Germany, my main experimental works were interpretations of the conflicting yet mutually generative relationship between Chinese and Western cultures with an approach characteristic of Chinese chess. Within it, the characteristic symbol system of Chinese chess can produce many changes in conceptual images, and the differentiated game model between Chinese chess and Western chess keep people perpetually wondering about the intrinsic modes of different cultures. This is a game with an imagined enemy, and the chess board is often likened to a battleground. I once used real people as chess pieces, and once I used the pictures of many colleagues in a 'game' with that of Voltaire, a representative of the European Enlightenment, the plaster cast version of whose head most Chinese art students were familiar with at the very beginning at their

Deutschlandaufenthaltes entstanden, waren konzeptionell an das chinesische Schachspiel angelehnt. In ihm versuchte ich allegorisch, die Beziehung zwischen China und dem Westen widerzuspiegeln: Ein Wechselspiel von Abwehr und Herausforderung auf beiden Seiten. Der ausgeprägte symbolische Gehalt der chinesischen Figuren und die vom westlichen Schachspiel abweichenden Spielregeln lassen unwillkürlich an verborgene unterschiedliche kulturelle Muster denken, deren eingebildete Feindschaft sich auf dem symbolischen Schlachtfeld des Spielbrettes manifestiert. In einer solchen Schachpartie ließ ich einmal über mehrere Tage hinweg zwei Seiten gegeneinander antreten: Auf der einen Seite standen als Figuren Porträts meiner Kollegen, auf der anderen Seite Nachbildungen der den Liebhabern westlicher Malerei allzu bekannte Gipsbüste des großen Aufklärers Voltaire. Bei einem anderen Projekt im Künstlerhaus Bethanien nahe der Berliner Mauer präsentierte ich im Rahmen einer Ausstellung die Berliner Mauer selbst als Figur in einem Schachspiel, bei einer weiteren Ausstellung erschien dieses Schachspiel in Form der Gegenüberstellung chinesischer Stoffschuhe und westlicher Lederschuhe. Als Künstler, der weit gereist ist, aber dennoch stets seine Heimat vor Augen hat, erlebte ich eine Art Wiedergeburt, als ich mich experimenteller Kunst zuzuwenden begann, die sich von Denkverboten befreit und von Bindungen an traditionelle Formen gelöst hatte. Wie dies bei avantgardistischen Formen häufig der Fall ist, so schlugen auch mir hier seitens der Kritiker viele Zweifel und Vorbehalte entgegen.

Aus Anlass der 50-Jahr-Feiern zum Ende des 2. Weltkriegs und des bevorstehenden Jahrtausendwechsels griff ich Ende der 90er Jahre des vorigen Jahrhunderts wieder zum Pinsel, um mich Ruinen als Zeugen der Geschichte zu widmen, besonders den Ruinen des 2. Weltkriegs. In meiner Serie „Wechselhände" (*fanshou yu fushou*), bei der ich sehr viele

studies. I once exhibited a work of chess with the Berlin Wall as the trench at Kunstquartier Bethanien near the Berlin Wall itself. I also created a series of works about the game between Chinese cloth shoes and Western leather shoes with composite materials. As an artist who travelled across the world yet constantly kept watch on my homeland, I experienced a being-towards-death kind of trailblazing experiment that marched towards uninhibited conceptual contemplations and completely given up my previous approaches to art. Meanwhile I also encountered questioning of understanding and interpretation that always confronted any avant-garde form.

In late 1990s, in the run-up to the 50th anniversary of World War II and the advent of the new century, I returned to the easel looking down at the ruins of history, especially those of World War II. I first adopted a holistic approach to the site of historical ruins in order to reveal the historical forces lying behind them. The manipulative hand of history seemed to be planting clouds and evoking rain in thick smog. This series was exhibited at the 48th Sao Paolo Biennale in 1998. In the meantime, I engaged with the historical firmament of old Beijing and Shanghai, looking down at the disappeared and disappearing landscape in the history of great metropolises. As the painting process eased up and my physical perception deepened, the holistic approach was gradually phased out, and examination of the historical firmament has given way to that of urban presence. In the winter of 2000/2001, I spent three months working at Kunstquartier Bethanien in Berlin. Each night I walked along the alleyways and riverside in Berlin's Old Town, imagining the skies casting glances down on the earth. The old architecture prior to World War II seemed so clear in my mind's eye; the smoke rising out of the ruins shrouded everything as if in a landscape. Back

unterschiedliche Materialien einsetzte , versuchte ich, mich den Trümmern zu nähern und diese zu ergründen, durch welche ungeheure historische Kraft diese Ruinen hervorgebracht worden waren. Einige der so entstanden Werke wurden auf der Biennale in Sao Paolo ausgestellt. Zur gleichen Zeit tauchte ich tief in die Vergangenheit Pekings und Shanghais ein, um mich mit dem Thema der Vergänglichkeit von Großstadtlandschaften auseinanderzusetzten. Im Laufe des Malprozesses und der Vertiefung der Anschauung wandte ich mich nach und nach wieder von der in den „Wechselhände"- Arbeiten angewandten Technik ab und begann, den historischen Blickwinkel gegen eine Gegenwarts-perspektive einzutauschen. Während des Winters 2000-2001 verbrachte ich drei Monate im Berliner Künstlerhaus Bethanien und pflegte abends durch die Straßen zu schlendern. Während dieser Spaziergänge stellte ich mir Berlin immer wieder aus der Vogelperspektive vor, das Stadtbild der Vorkriegszeit erschien mir lebendig vor Augen und fast war es, als wehte mir der Rauch aus den Kriegsruinen um die Nase. Wenn ich dann auf dem Rückweg wieder an der Bethanienkirche mit ihrer wechsel-vollen Geschichte vorbeikam, wurde mir wieder schmerzlich bewusst, wie kurz das Leben doch war und welche Bitternis in ihm schlummerte, schwermütig dachte ich dann oft an mein Heimatland. In solche Betrachtungen versunken fühlte ich mich, als ginge ich den langen Korridor der Geschichte entlang, das leise Lied des ewigen Wandels auf den Lippen während meine Augen an den Wänden des Flurs den Linien entlangglitten, die wir Kultur nennen - indem die Hand des Malers der Geschichte ein Antlitz gibt, rührt er an versunkene Erinnerungen und verborgene Wunden. Im Februar 2001 fand im Künstlerhaus Bethanien die Ausstellung „Landscapes of History" statt. Der künstlerische Leiter meinte jedoch, so etwas wie Landschaften der Geschichte gebe es gar nicht. Ich dagegen bin nach wie vor der Meinung, die historische Perspektive ist eine seelische und besitzt

to the vault of the old church in Bethanien that had been rebuilt several times, I felt entangled in the reflections on the transience of life and homeland. The retrospective look on the historical firmament, however, is like a downward glance at cultural geography, with certain traces of cultural topology, as if a minstrel was reciting an epic in the long corridor of history, at once with a heavy heart and a lightness of touch. The historical landscape unravels under my hand, and the past is resurrected 'in' my pen, as I stroke my heart with all its throbbing pains. In early Feb. 2001, I held a solo exhibition titled 'Historical Landscape at the Exhibition Hall of Kunstquartier Bethanien, Christoph Tannert the art director proposed the name 'A Geographic Outlook'. He believed there is no landscape in history, while I thought looking down from the historical firmament was a spiritual gaze without anything to do with geography. The two propositions tell of the differences of two distinct cultural poetics. This happened ten years ago, and I could still not banish that moment from my mind.

Summer 2003 saw me travelling as a member of the 'Karmic Affinity of the Earth' delegation on a tour around Asia to study the contemporary culture of these nations. At the Asian plains near the Sea of Marmara in the Euro-Asian state of Turkey, I encountered old sunflowers in the wilderness. They struck me as cast in bronze. On the other hand I encountered the relics of the ancient city of Troy. The melancholic beauty by the ancient highway in a wilderness was as striking as the flaps of the shepherd's whip from afar. Keeping watch for a season or a year was equally epic and touching as everlasting steadfastness. It also made me realise that one season of life matters as much as eternity. This thickness of the here and now made us reflect on the richness and history of the earth. Only in this moment did history happen once more. The history of the sunflower, the sun-adoring flower, overwhelmed

keine geographischen Konnotationen. Derartige Differenzen entstammen meiner Meinung nach aus unterschiedlichen poetischen Traditionen. Auch wenn das Ganze schon zehn Jahre her ist und ich die Sache für längst abgeschlossen halte, regt sie mich doch manches Mal zum Nachdenken an.

Im Sommer des Jahres 2008 nahm ich als Mitglied der Delegation *Edges of Earth* an einer Erkundungsreise zur Gegenwartskunst in verschiedenen asiatischen Ländern teil. Am westlichsten Zipfel Asiens, auf einer Ebene in der Nähe des Marmara-Meeres stieß ich unvermittelt auf ein weites Feld aus Sonnenblumen, die leuchteten wie kupferüberzogene Eisenskulpturen - welch unvergesslicher Anblick! Hier eine Wiederbegegnung mit den Ruinen des alten Troja und dort, jenseits der Ödnis am Rande antiker Wege, karge Schönheit, die mich ins Mark trifft, wie der ferne Peitschenknall eines Hirtenjungen. Den Zeiten trotzen - eine Saison, ein Jahr oder Äonen - das ist der Kern jedes Heldenepos. Dies mit eigenen Augen sehen zu dürfen rührt das Herz und erweckt den Geist: Es ist die Dichte des Moments und nicht dessen Dauer, die uns des Reichtums und der Vergangenheit eines Ortes teilhaftig werden lässt. Geschichte wird nur im Moment geschrieben, und zwar in jedem einzelnen aufs Neue. Der Dichter Kuang Zhouyi war Ende des 19., Anfang des 20. Jahrhunderts ein großer Theoretiker des „Ci", einer freien Gedichtform. Einer seiner zentralen Begriffe lautete „Cixin", womit er den Gefühlskern einer Anschauungsform bezeichnete, der einerseits der Kontrolle des Künstlers entzogen ist, anderer-seits diesem aber als Quelle der Inspiration dient. Auf dieser Basis entstand zwischen 2004 und 2006 die Serie „12 Ansichten eines Sonnenblumengartens". Die Schmerzhaftigkeit des „Zeit"-Empfindens dient dabei als Wegweiser zu Rekonstruktion einer durch Ödnis gekennzeichneten Jugend und zum distanzierten Blick auf ein geistloses Leben. Jenseits solcher Gefühlsverwirrung zeichnet sich jedoch eine Vision am Horizont ab, klar

me. 'I observe the storms and I traverse the country. Often I feel there is something ineluctable beyond this whole scene. And the ineluctable is at the heart of a lyric.' (Kuang Zhouyi [1859-1926]) It was precisely this ineluctable element that prompted me to work on *Twelve Scenes in the Sunflower Fields* from 2004 to 2006 *Twelve Scenes in the Sunflower Fields* was an attempt to trace the youth that was once caught up in the wilderness through the sentimentality of 'time'. Casting a look on the wild atmosphere of life, although one was full of emotions, one could still make out the solemn atmosphere of the twilight of the gods with a blurred horizon. Nostalgia was used to amplify the lamentation of life at the moment. Especially Chinese-style landscape was adopted to express an ego-trip of an entire generation, which was quite novel in Chinese art back then. As I wrote in an article later, *Twelve Scenes in the Sunflower Fields* was not intended to express a specific *Zeitgeist* or scenery and to lend it a touch of brilliance, as the twelve scenes by West Lake was, but it came with an outlook that was characteristic of Chinese landscape painting, namely the delineation of a vista within one's heart in order to capture the blossoming of the image of a poet-like life. *"Twelve Scenes"* was not like the kind of spectacle afforded by installing stones in a garden, or filled with Chinese symbols, rather it was an attempt to dissolve the nostalgic sense of history into contemporary life, or to work out the nostalgia for youth and remembrance of the past and life's cycles through the mind's writing, so as to get closer to the wordlessness of the world of Chinese landscape painting. *"Twelve Scenes"* was not a pointless adaptation of the old scenes, or a grafted bonsai, rather it was the life of experience of grafting of the self into the body of the sunflower, and the heart into that of the sunflower, the reincarnation of the kind of profound Chinese concerns with landscape.

After *Twelve Scenes*, the outlook for the sunflower no longer sufficed. I started to put myself in large-scale 'sunflower

und majestätisch: Durch Rückbesinnung auf den klassischen Geist die Gegenwart zu beleben, wobei die chinesische Landschaftsmalerei der Darstellung des Lebensweges unserer Generation hierzu eine geeignete Formensprache bietet. Doch stecken diese Ansätze noch in den Kinderschuhen. Wie ich bereits in einem früheren Artikel schrieb, orientieren sich „12 Ansichten eines Sonnenblumengartens" weniger an der stark stilisierten Malweise beispielsweise der populären 12 Ansichten des Westsees, wo die einzelnen Bilder lediglich durch hinzugefügte typische Wahrzeichen variieren, sondern stärker an der klassischen chinesischen Landschaftsmalerei, in deren Bildern eine tiefe Sehnsucht nach Weite angelegt ist. In fast poetischer Weise wird dort eine Aura der Lebendigkeit erzeugt. Keineswegs beabsichtigt ist jedoch, durch Einarbeitung spezieller chinesischer Symbolelemente einen oberflächlichen ästhetischen Effekt zu erzielen, etwa in der Art, wie ihn die in vielen chinesischen Parks platzierten Ornamentfelsen hervorrufen. Stattdessen erfolgt in meinen „12 Ansichten" eine Annäherung an die für die chinesische Landschaftsmalerei so charakteristischen Stille, indem die Gegenwart historisch aufgeladen wird, Erinnerungen an Jugend und Wiedergeburt greifbar gemacht werden. Es geht nicht darum, Altbekanntes in neuem Gewande zu präsentieren oder transplantierbare Miniaturlandschaften zu schaffen, sondern um die elementare Erfahrung, der Sonnenblume den eigenen Körper, ja, das eigene Herz einzupflanzen – solches leisten zu wollen, das ist die Seele der chinesischen Landschaftsmalerei.

Nach der Fertigstellung der „12 Ansichten" fühlte ich, dass es noch an Weite und Distanz mangelte und so begann ich, die Dimensionen der Sonnenblumengärten auszuweiten. Im Bild „Wird der Herbst die Sonnenblumen rot färben?" ist ein Sonnenblumenfeld in verschiedenen Rotschattierungen dargestellt. Die roten Sonnenblumen stehen sowohl für eine reale Absurdität als auch für authentische Erinnerungen, sie

fields'. *Would the Autumn Sunflower Turn Red* creates a stretch of red sunflower fields. The red sunflower was both a realistic absurdity, but also a real memory, entwined in a kind of sobriety and vivacity. *The Green Sunflower* depicts a field full of black sunflowers standing against the light like calligraphic works. *The Suspended Sunflower* is like the suspended Yellow River, its topsy-turvy existence resembling an upside-down cosmic order, filled with the desolation Sikong Tu described as 'a storm carrying water that destroys entire expanses of forestation'. The sunflower groves in *Flower Without Soil* stand like wild growths, firm and recalcitrant, as if slayed. Yet what really stands there is our selfhood. *For Whom the Nocturnal Wind Chases* expresses with a heavy stroke an atmosphere of sunflower fields standing against the twilight of the gods. These large-scale works on sunflower fields are as much about the ineluctable course of the cosmos as the strength in being-towards-death. They are concerned with the multiplying absurdities of culture, as well as with a sobriety full of emotions. Yet behind this entangled, ineluctable scheme of things there stands a jaded, earnest, sublime feeling like the stalk of the sunflower. I have increasingly poured my flesh into the sunflower head, where I could experience the hardships and consolations of regeneration over and over again, and the heroic sense of spiritual burden and self-redemption, day after day.

For several years running, I have been taking my sunflower fields on the road, from Beijing to Guangzhou, from Shanghai to Taipei, from West Lake to Suzhou's gardens. What I found particularly impressive is the invitation extended to the sunflower fields by the historical landscape of cities, and by the old-new cultural sites. This is basically the kind of invitation extended by a certain history towards its new phase, by a certain organism towards regeneration. Now I have taken up the invitation to Dresden, to the site of prosperity and ruin by the Elbe. A great river runs in front of the façade of the entrance hall, and my sunflowers long for a new season of life.

verbinden Ernst mit Vitalität. Mit ihrem vertikalen Linienverlauf und den kräftigen, im Gegenlicht grün-schwarz wirkenden Silhouetten erinnern die „Grünen Sonnenblumen" dagegen an ein Stück Kalligraphie. Die „Hängenden Sonnenblumen" wiederum scheinen wie ein Wasserfall vom Himmel herabzufließen, ihre nach unten hängenden Köpfe erwecken unwillkürlich Assoziationen an Verwüstungen nach einem Sturm. Die kahlen dichtstehenden Stängel in „Blumen ohne Erde", das sind wir selber, unbeugsam und aufrecht. Der kräftige Farbauftrag bei „Für wen weht der Abendwind?" bewirkt eine beinahe apokalyptische Stimmung. All diesen großformatigen Bildern gemeinsam ist die von Ödnis und Vergänglichkeit gekennzeichnete Atmosphäre. Doch die Unbeugsamkeit der Sonnenblumen verspricht neues Leben im nahen Tod. Inmitten von düsteren Erinnerungen, ohnmächtig angesichts bitterer Erfahrungen und unauflösbarer Verstrickungen und hilflos gegen die Absurditäten dessen, was wir Kultur nennen, suche ich so Trost im unbeugsamen Willen zur Selbsterlösung.

Seit Jahren präsentiere ich meine Sonnenblumengärten im ganzen Land, von Peking bis nach Guangzhou, von Shanghai bis nach Taibei, und was mir auffällt, ist die positive Aufnahme, die sie in den historischen Vierteln der Großstädte oder anderen Reservaten traditioneller Kultur finden. Mir scheint, als habe die Geschichte selbst hier eine Einladung ausgesprochen, eine Einladung zur Wiederauferstehung. So sind wir dieser gefolgt, hier nach Dresden. Gegenüber dem Elbufer, umgeben von pulsierender Gegenwart und beredten Zeugnissen der Vergangeheit hofft mein Sonnenblumengarten auf ein neues Leben.

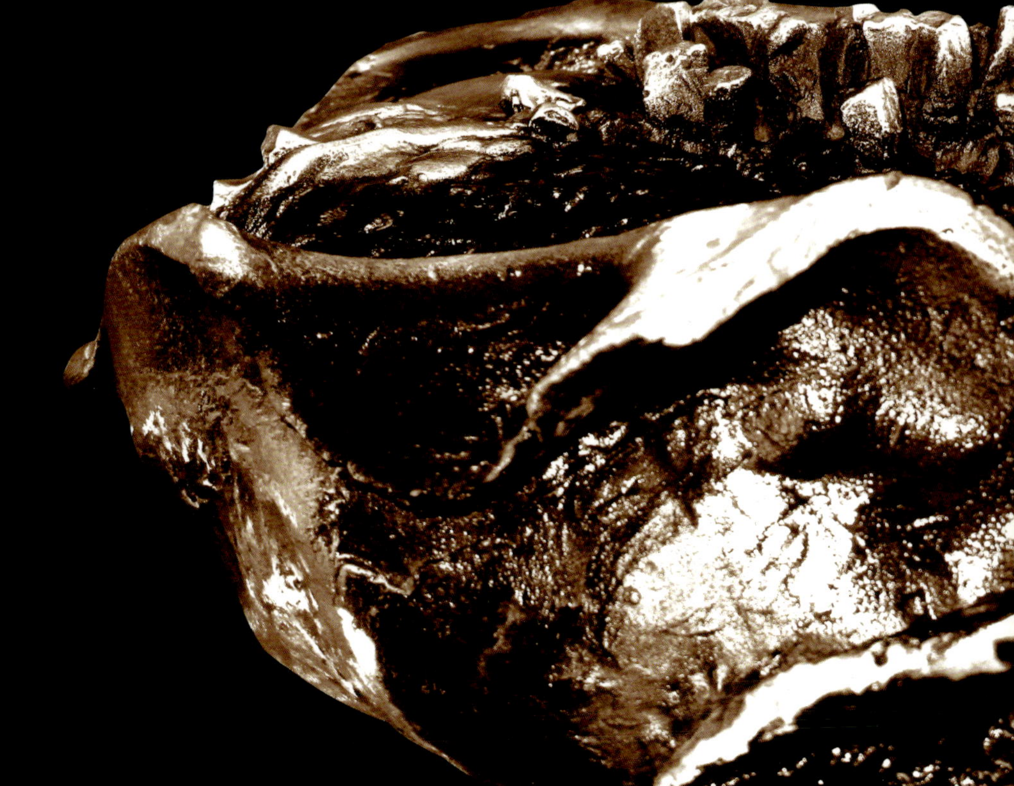

2012   Re-Generation · Installation
Re-Generation · Installation

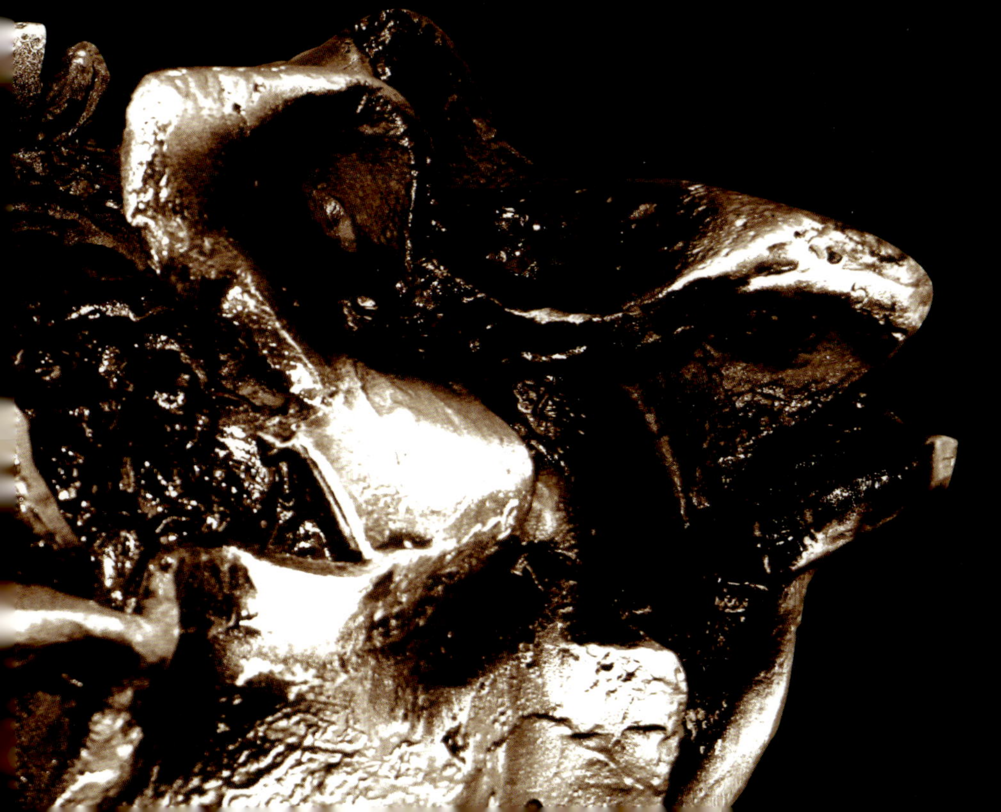

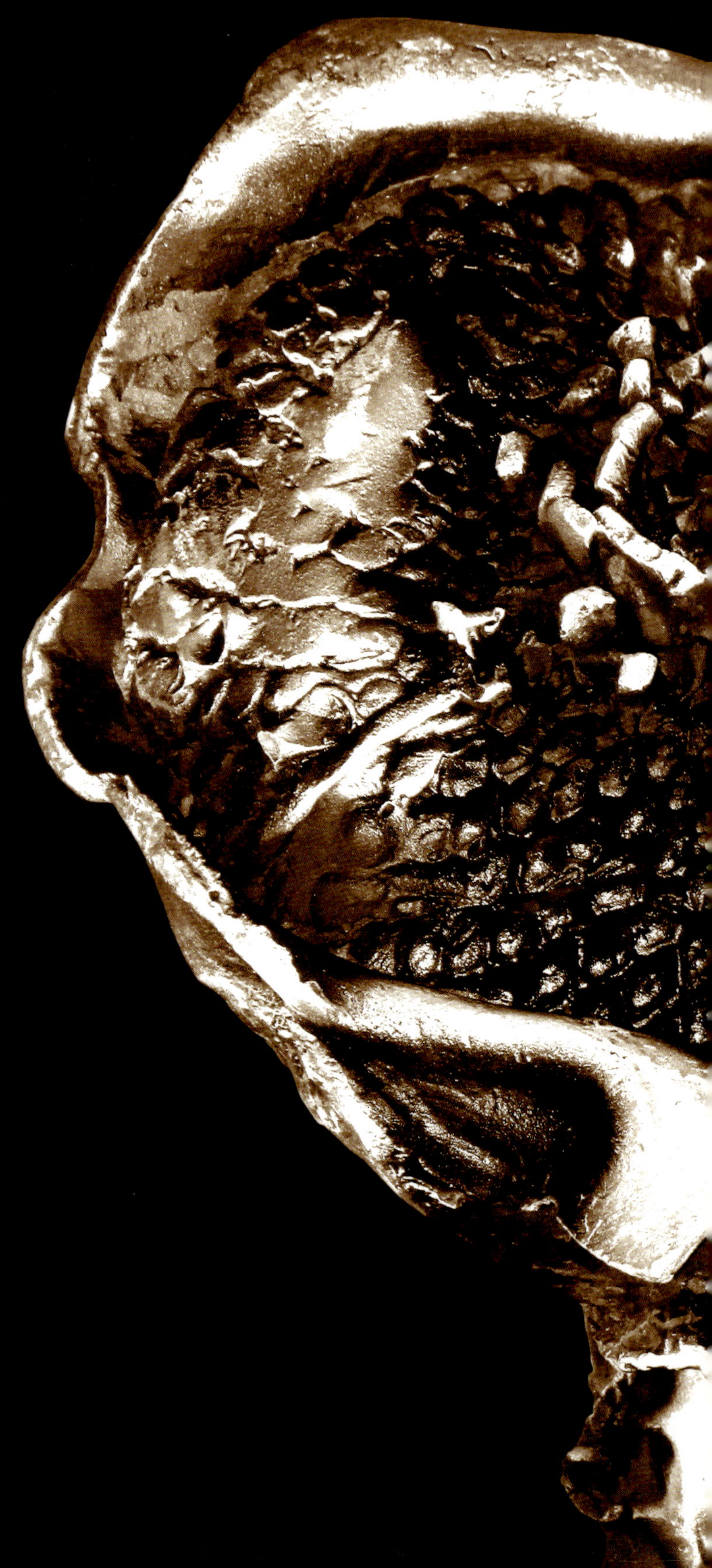

2012 Re-Generation · Installation
Re-Generation · Installation

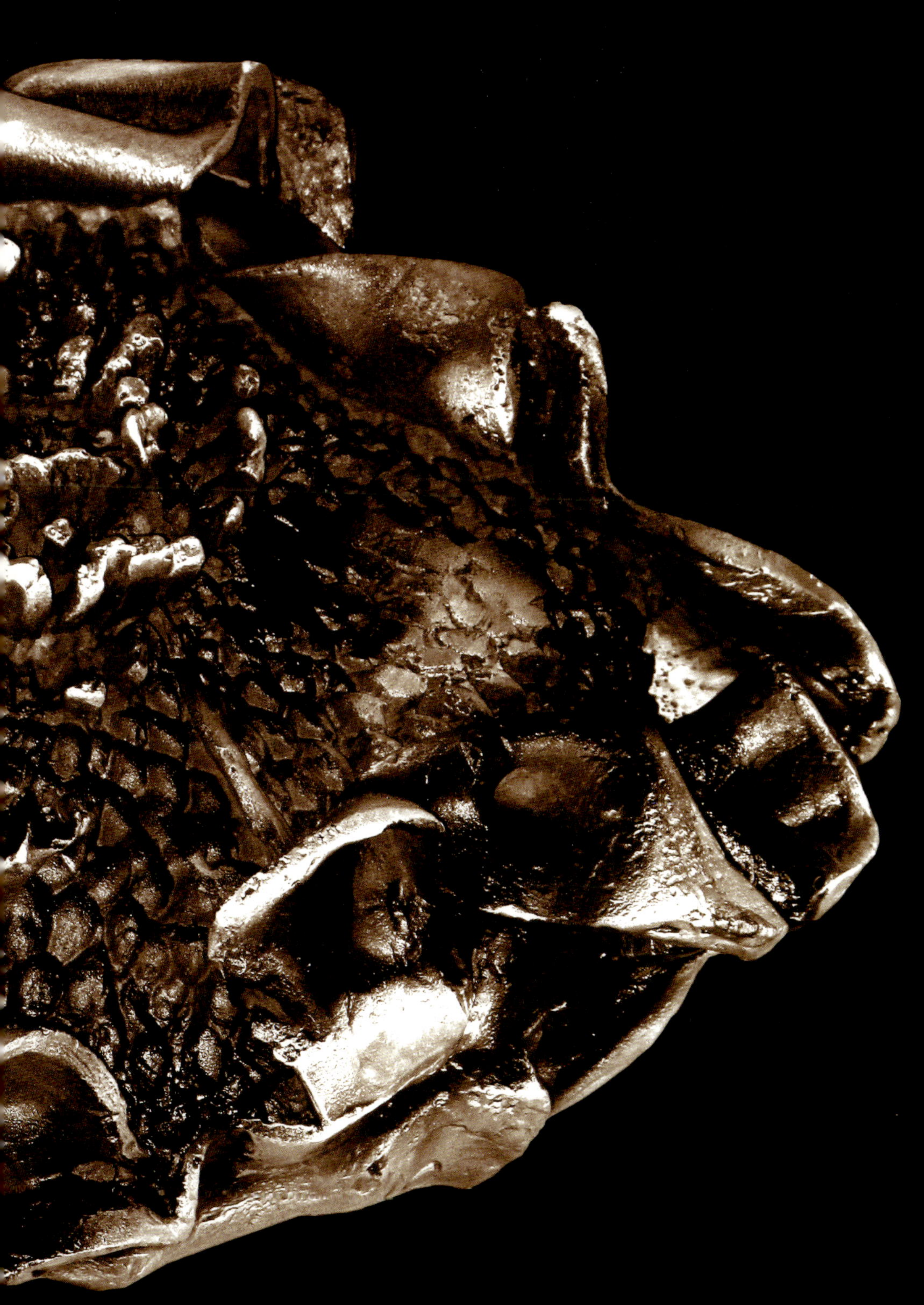

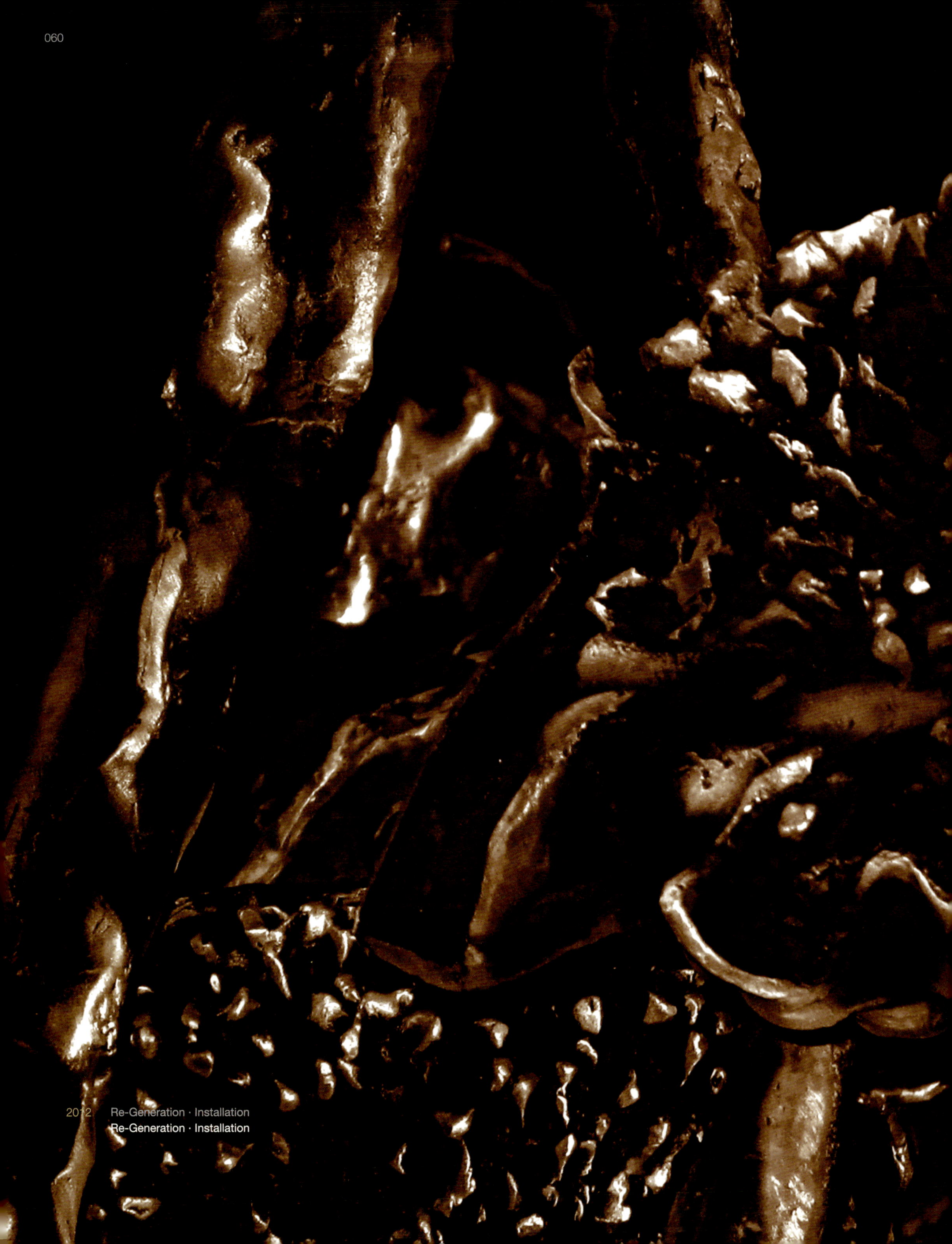

Re-Generation · Installation

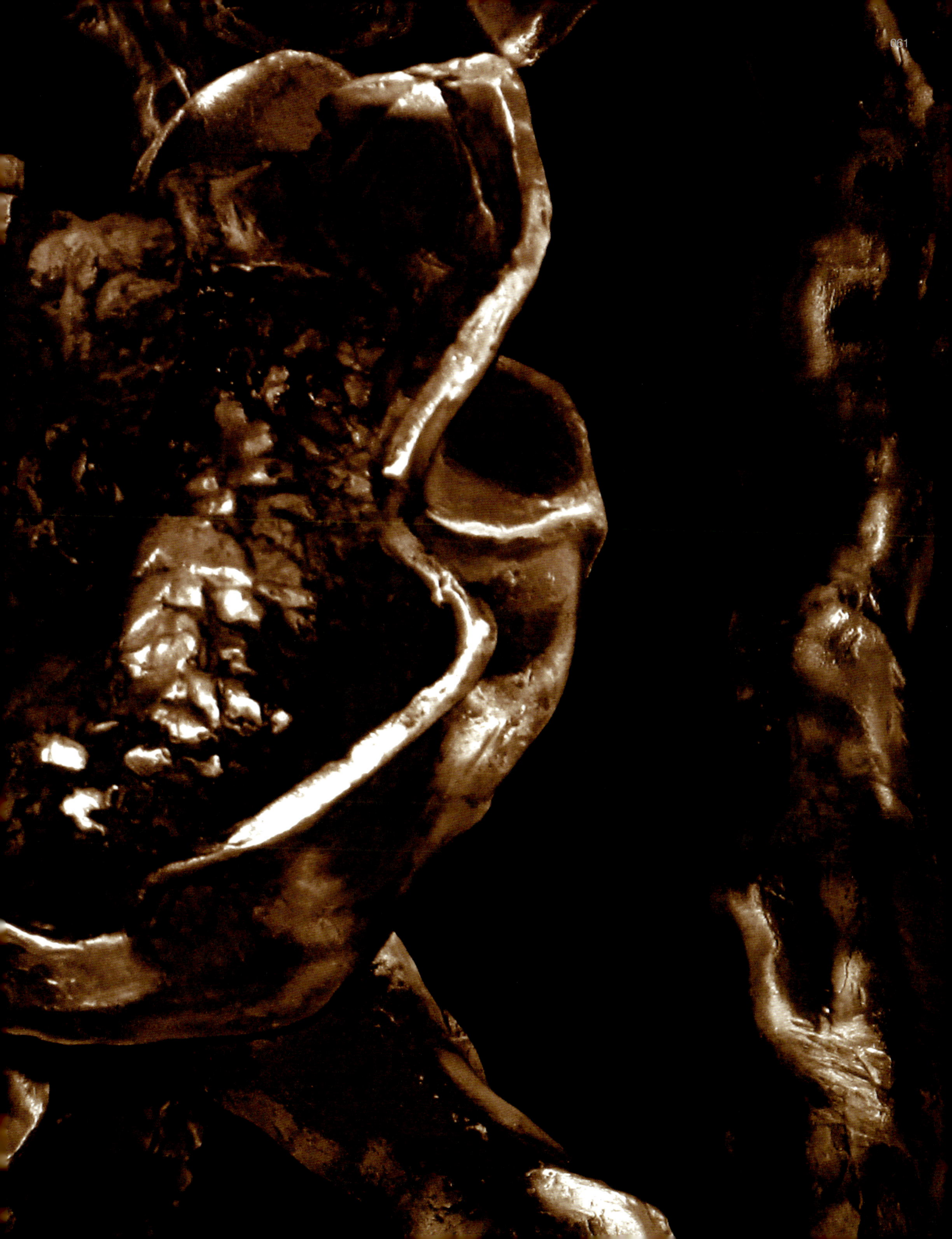

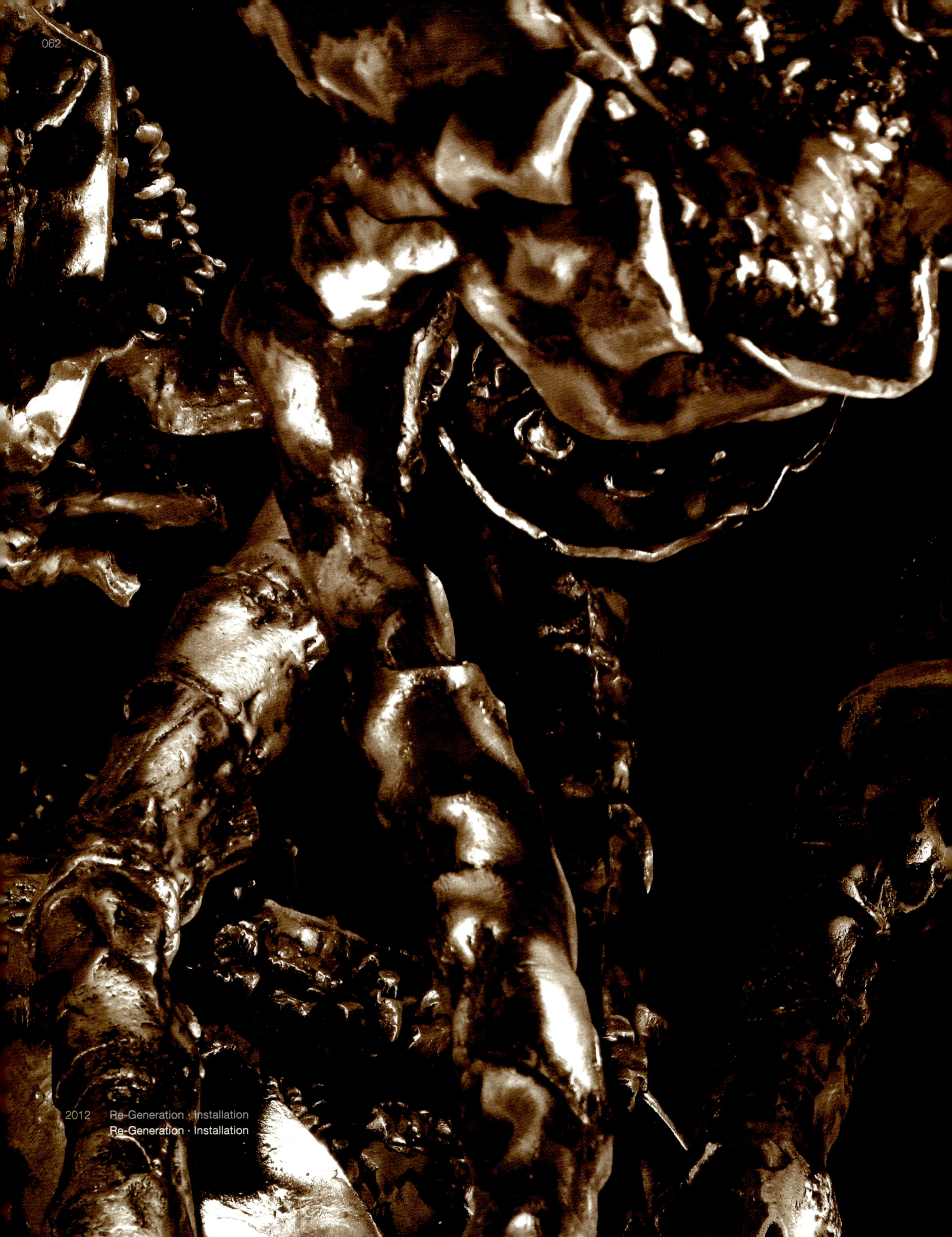

2012   Re-Generation · Installation
Re-Generation · Installation

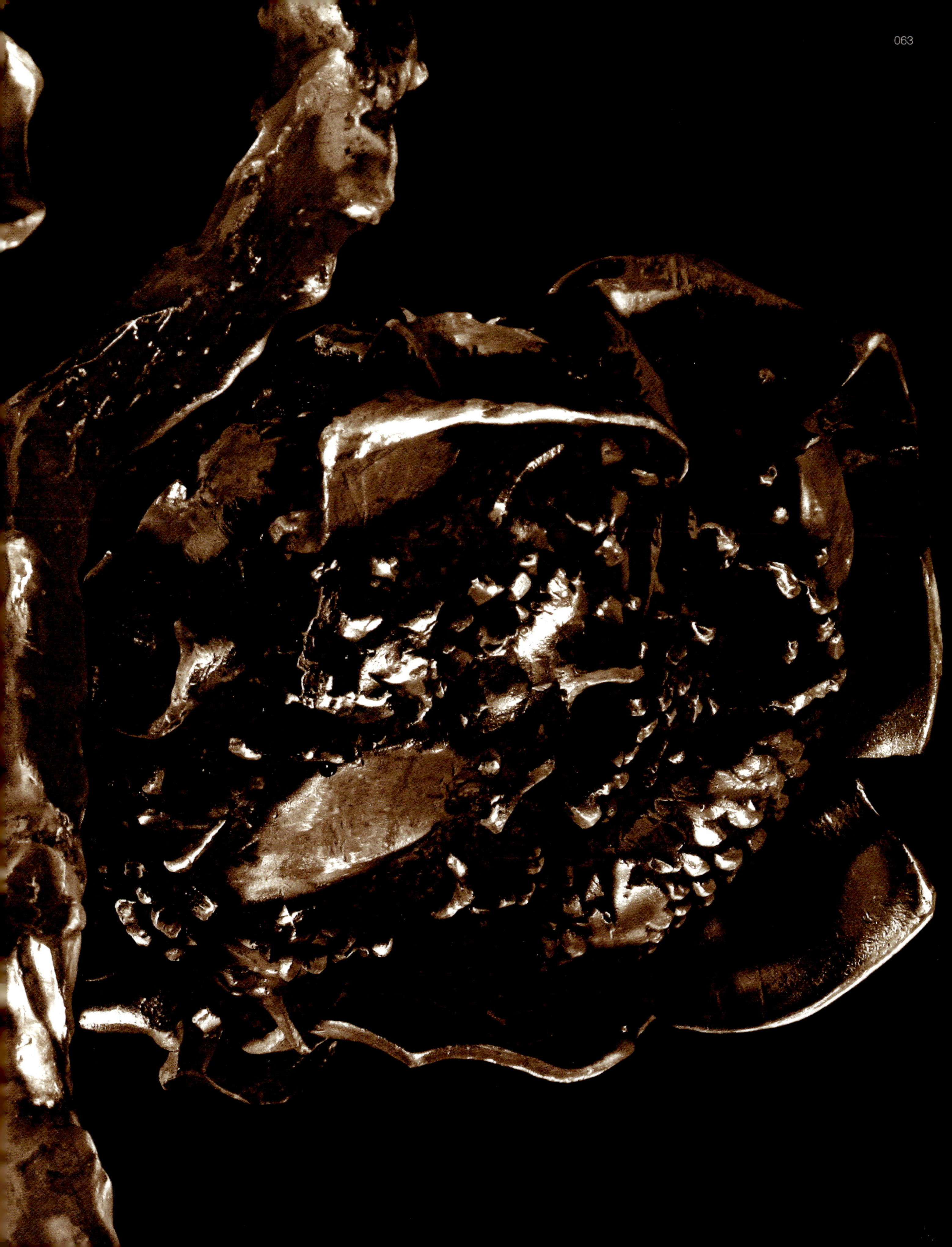

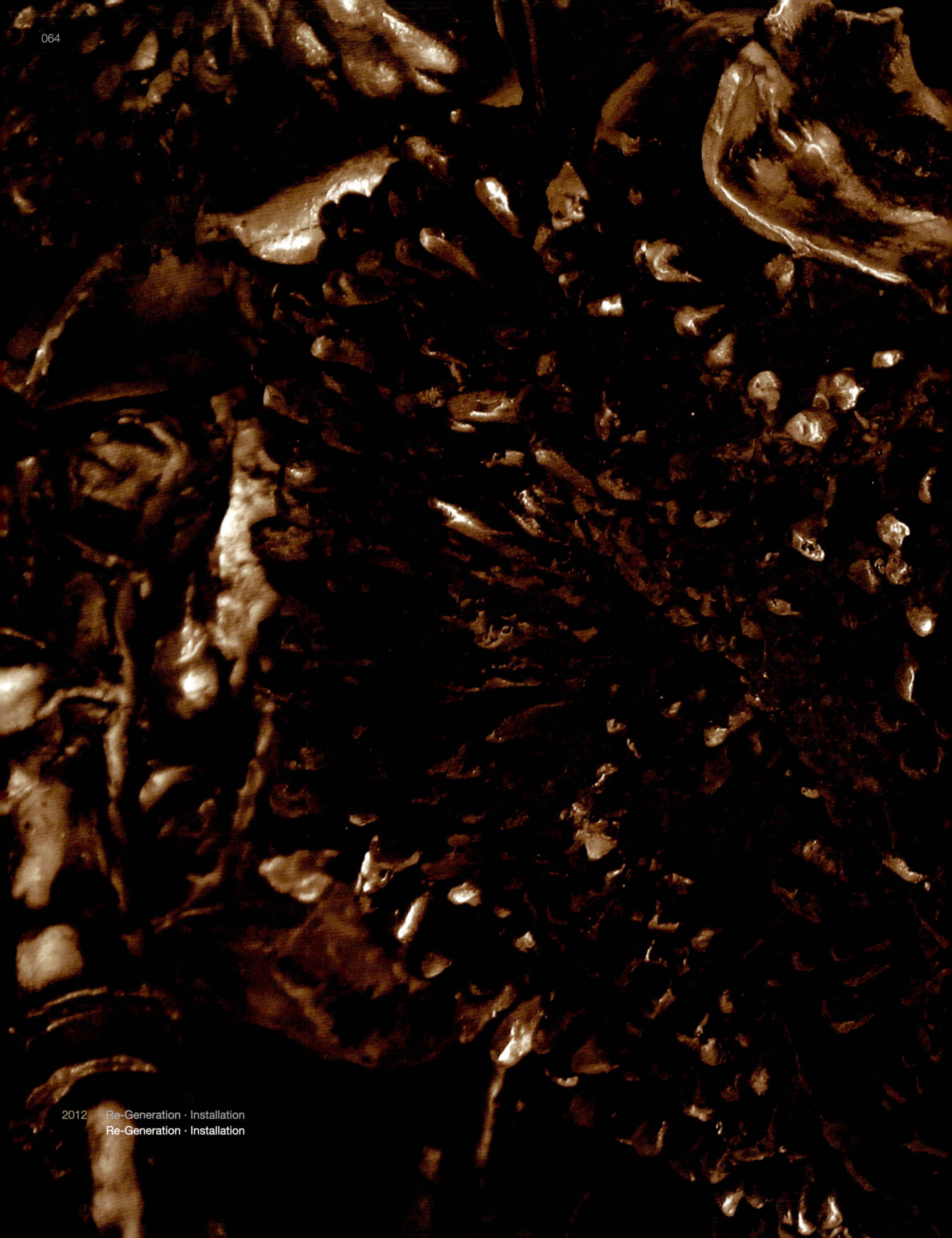

2012   Re-Generation · Installation
Re-Generation · Installation

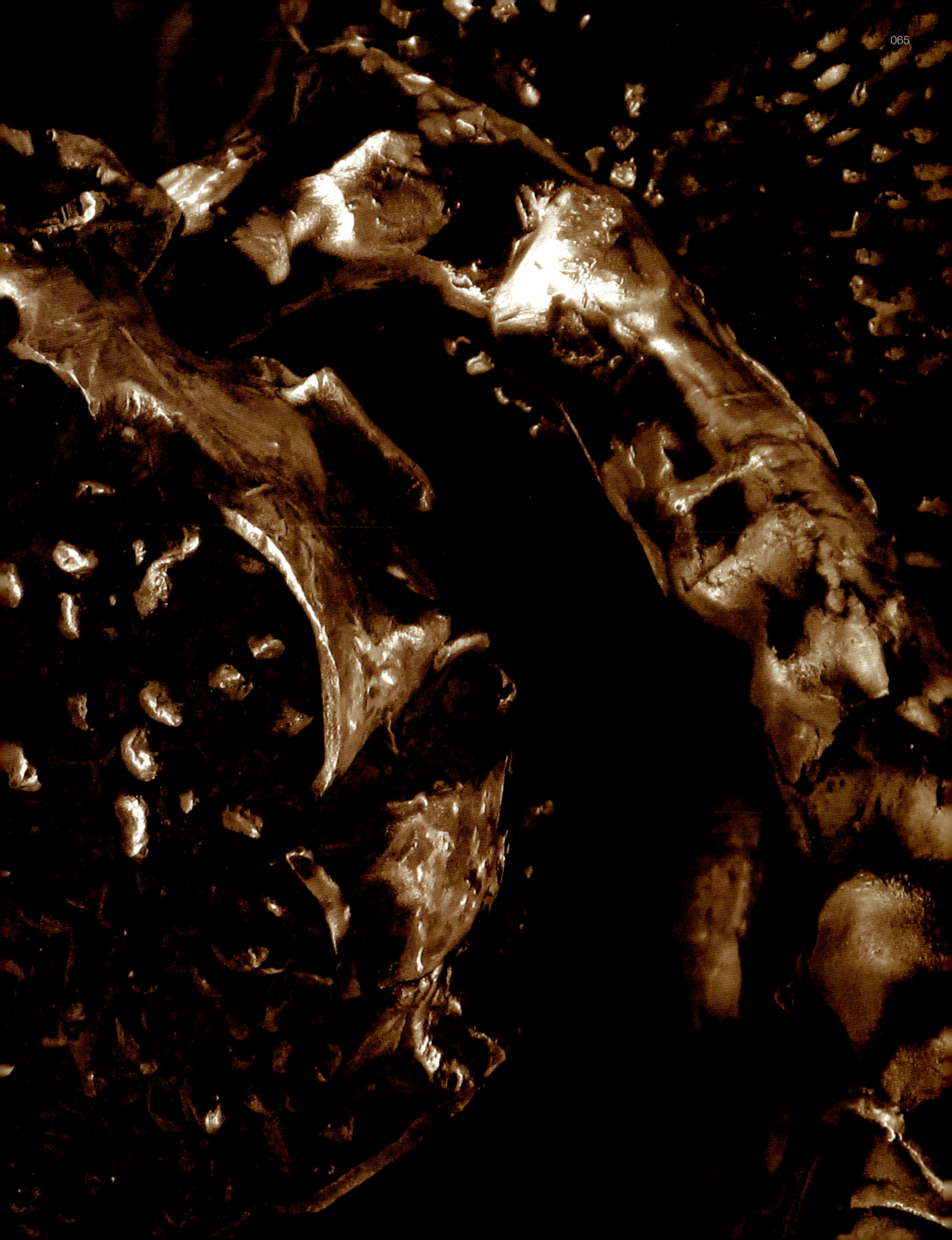

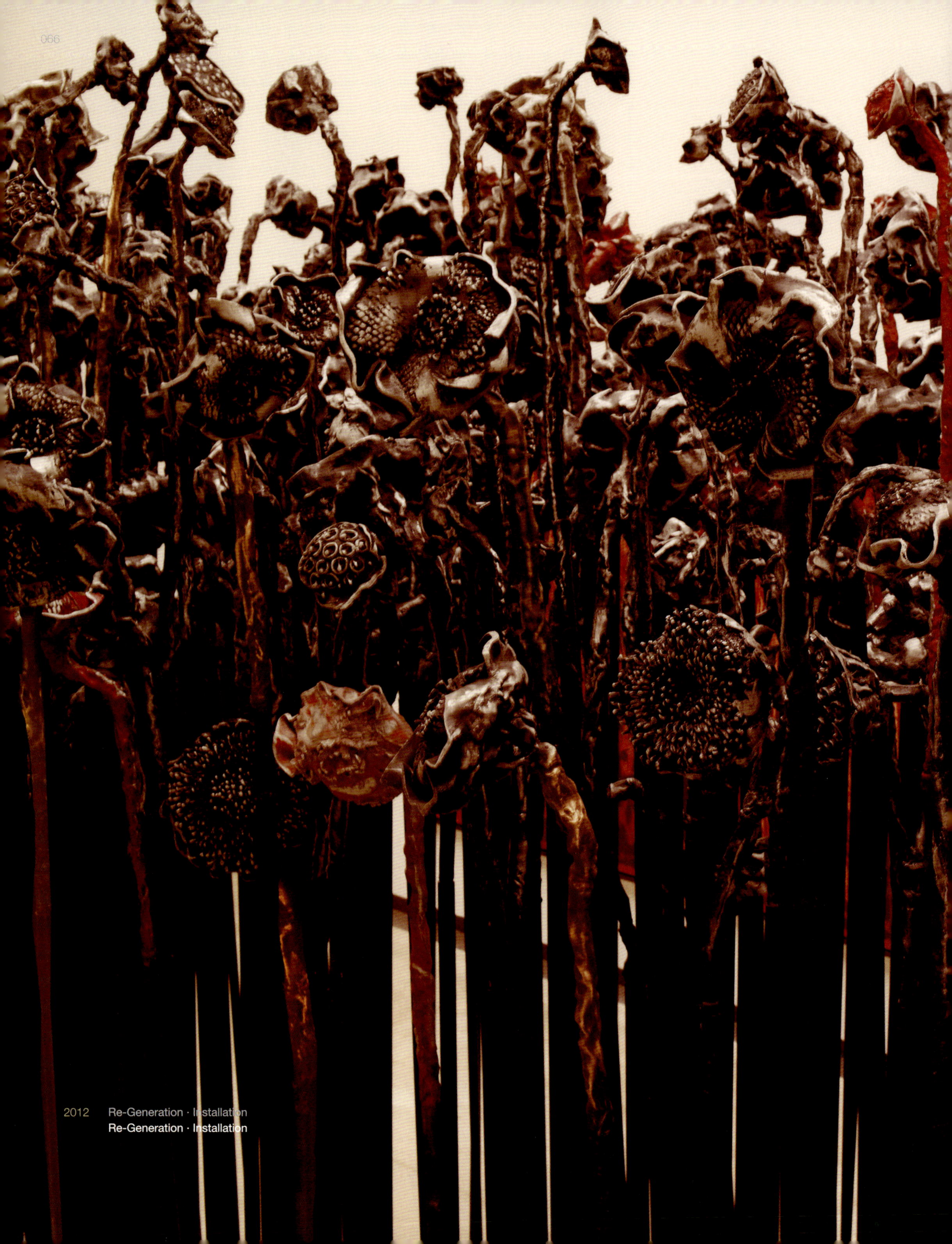

Re-Generation · Installation

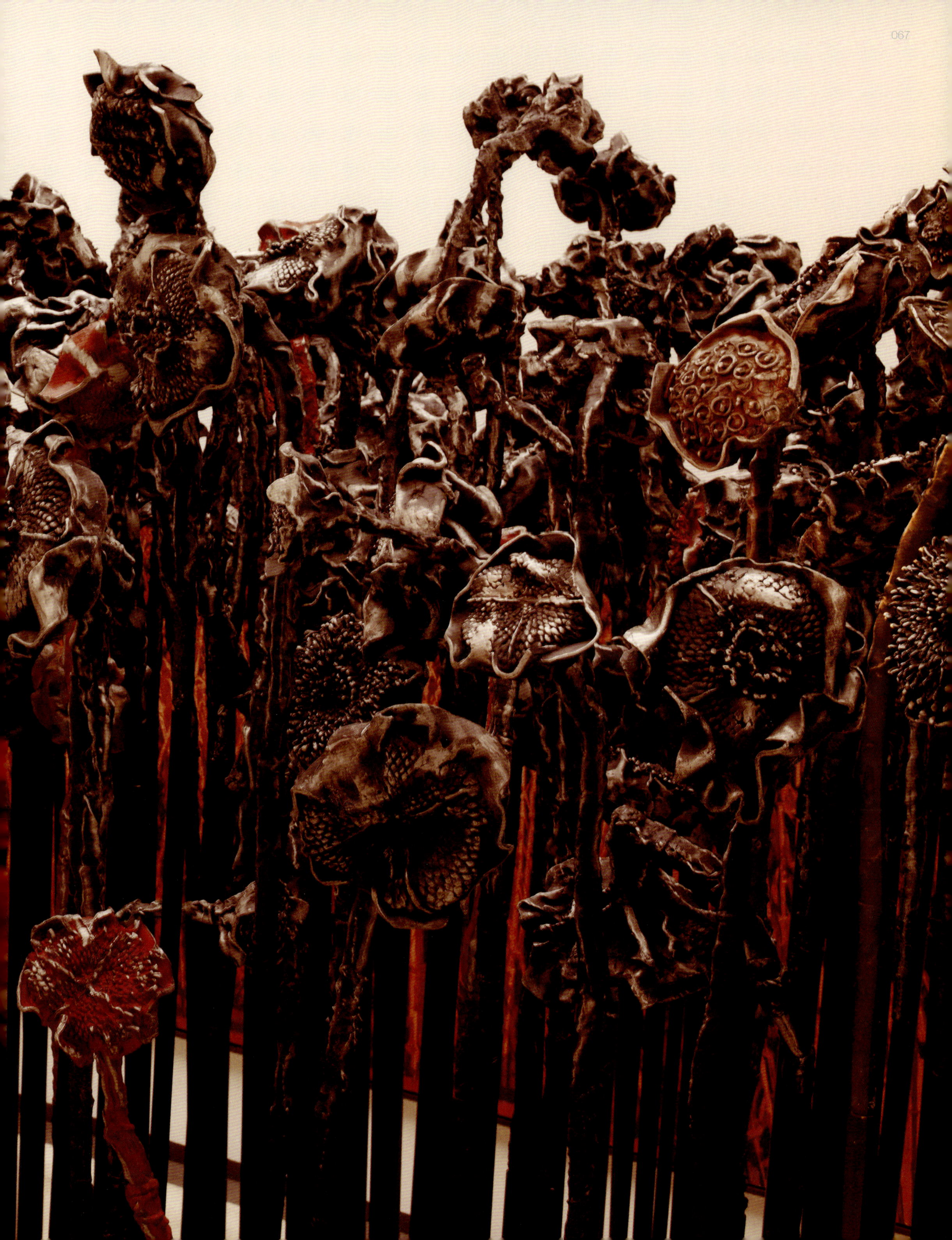

2012 Re-Generation · Installation
Re-Generation · Installation

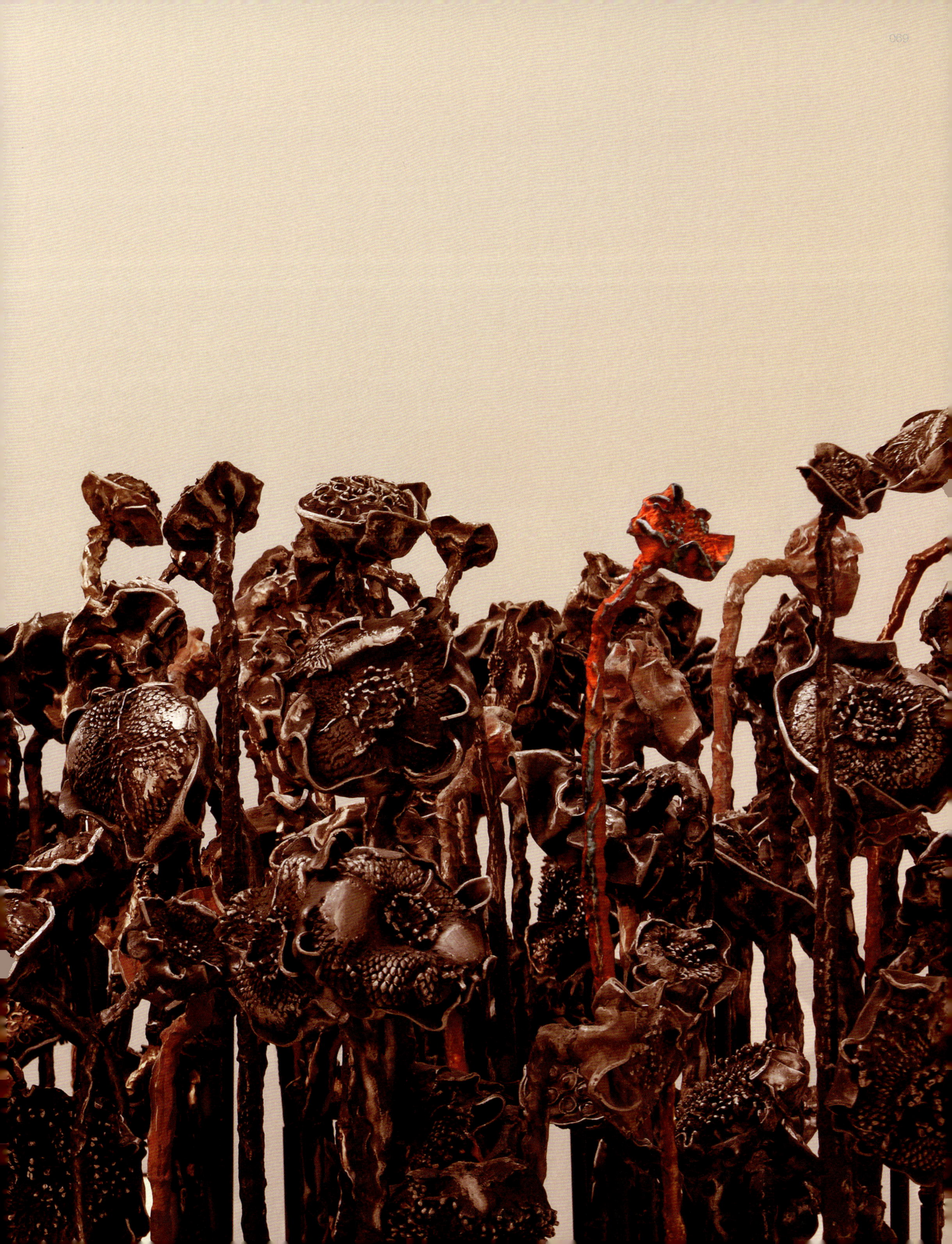

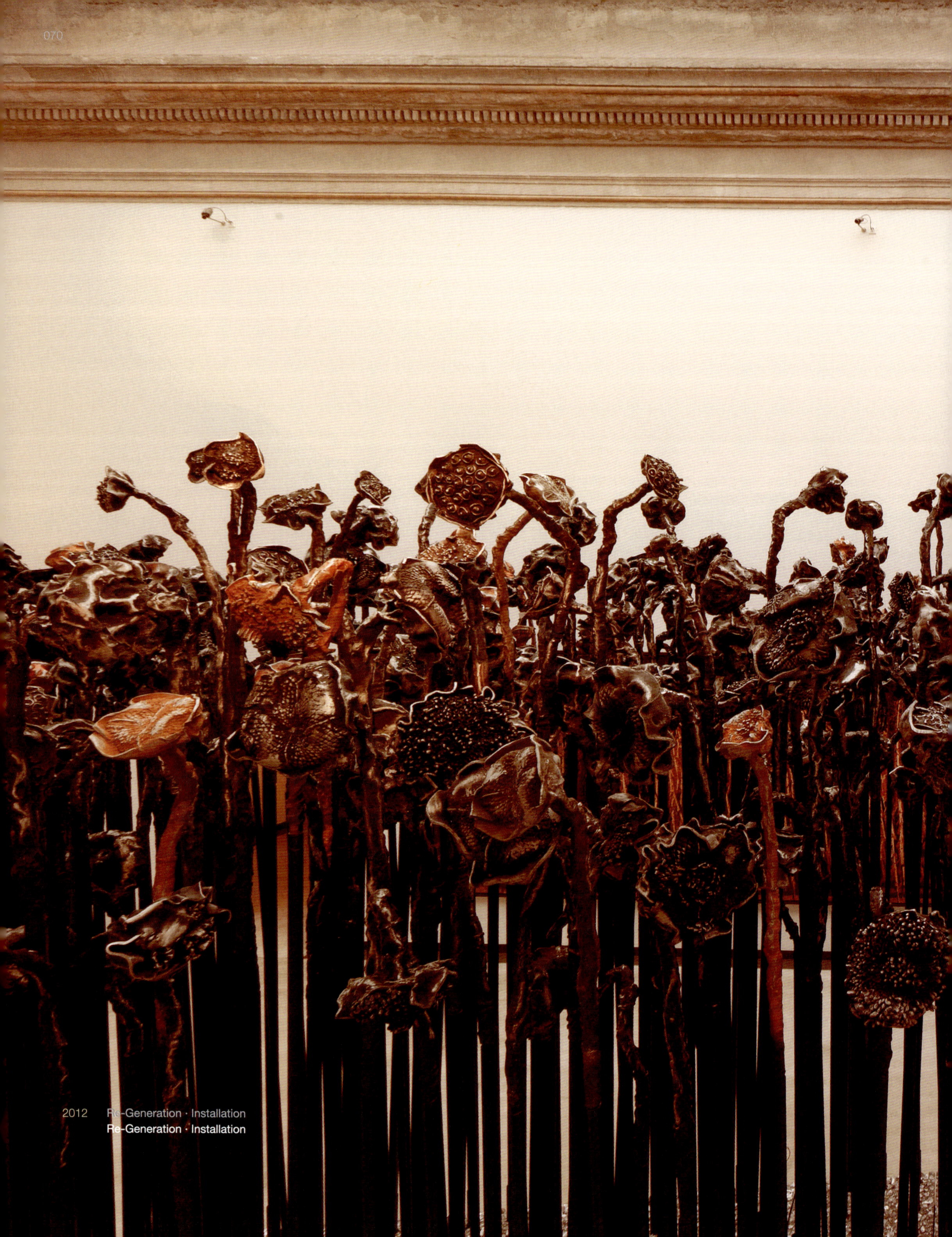

2012　Re-Generation · Installation
Re-Generation · Installation

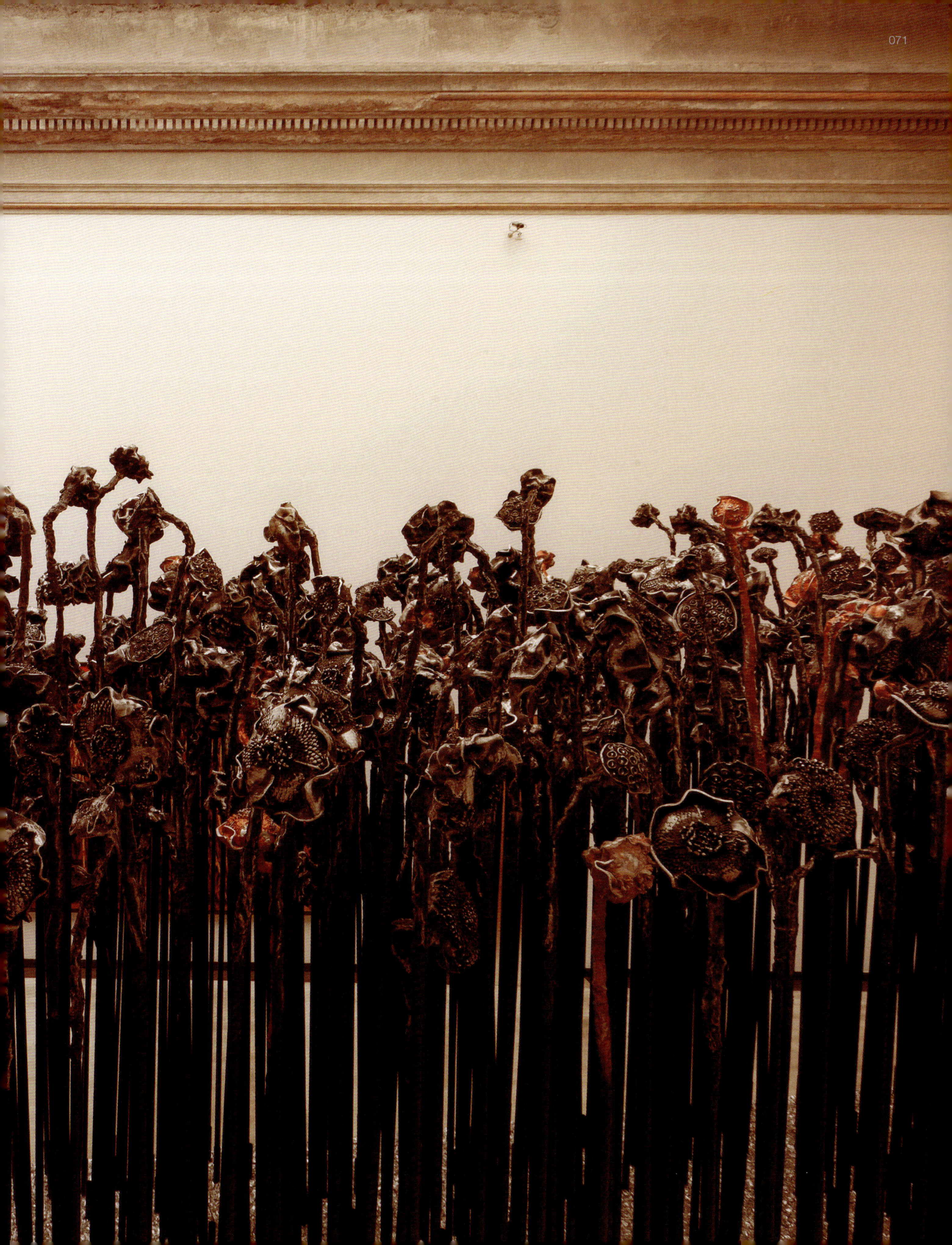

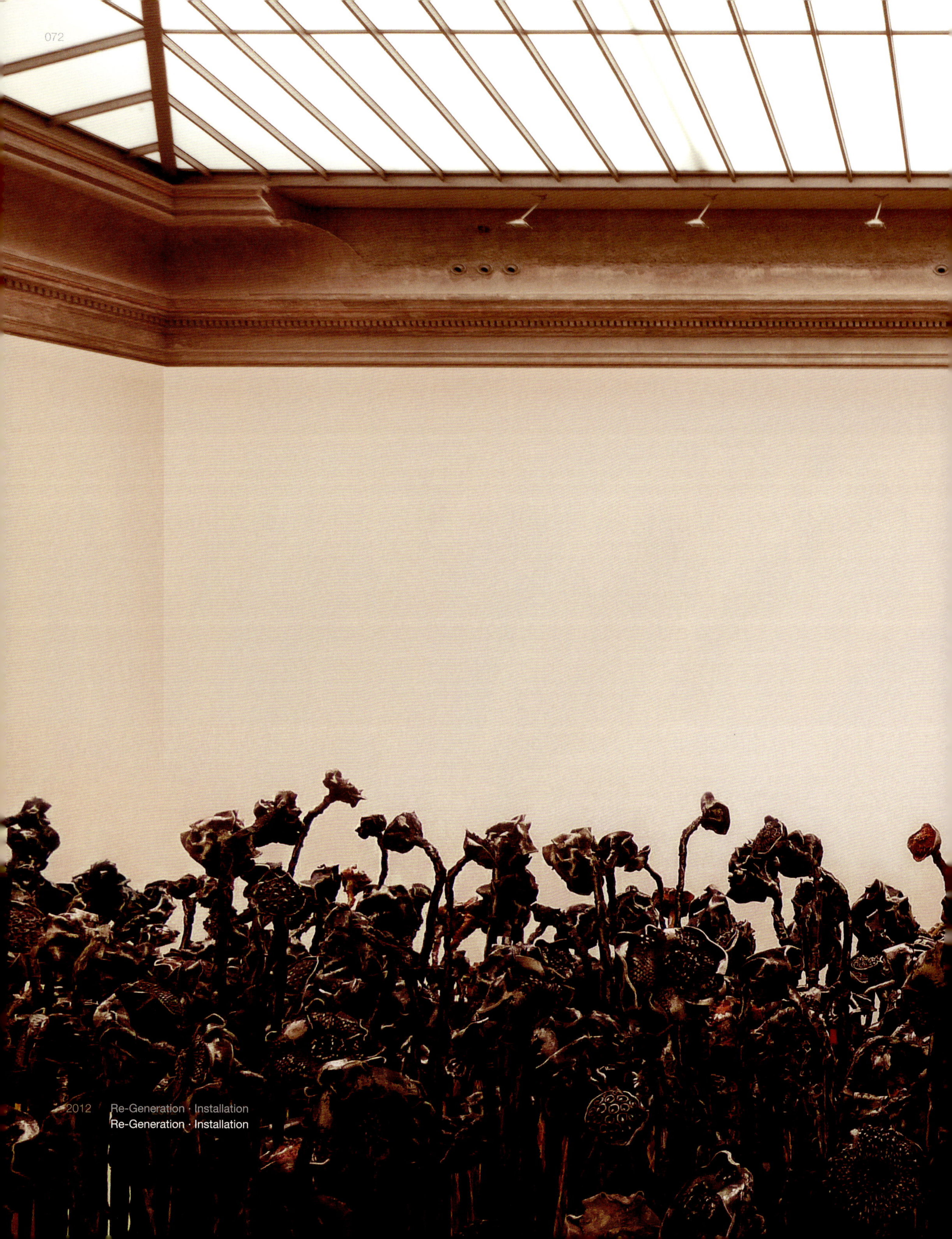
2012　Re-Generation · Installation
Re-Generation · Installation

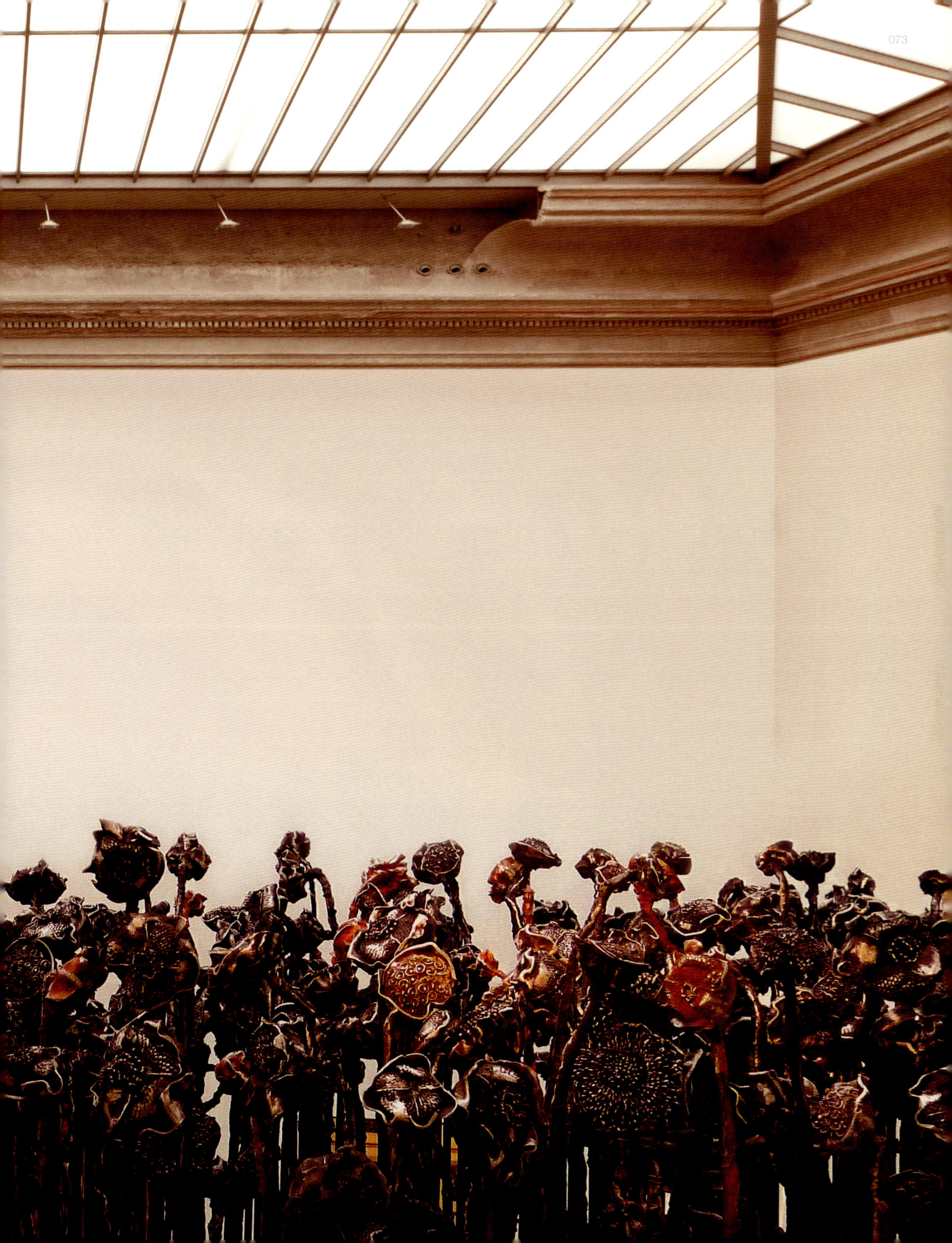

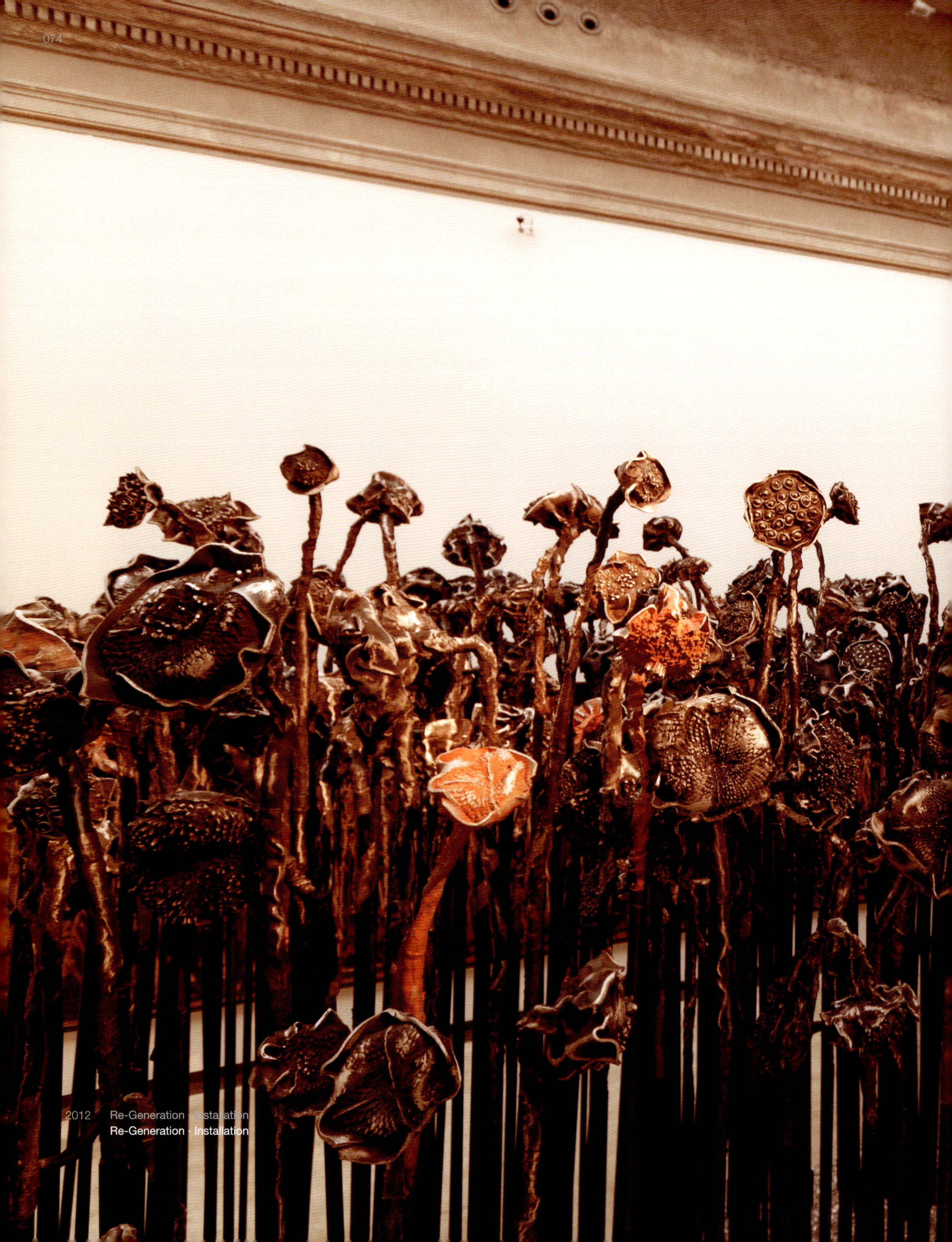

2012　Re-Generation · Installation
Re-Generation · Installation

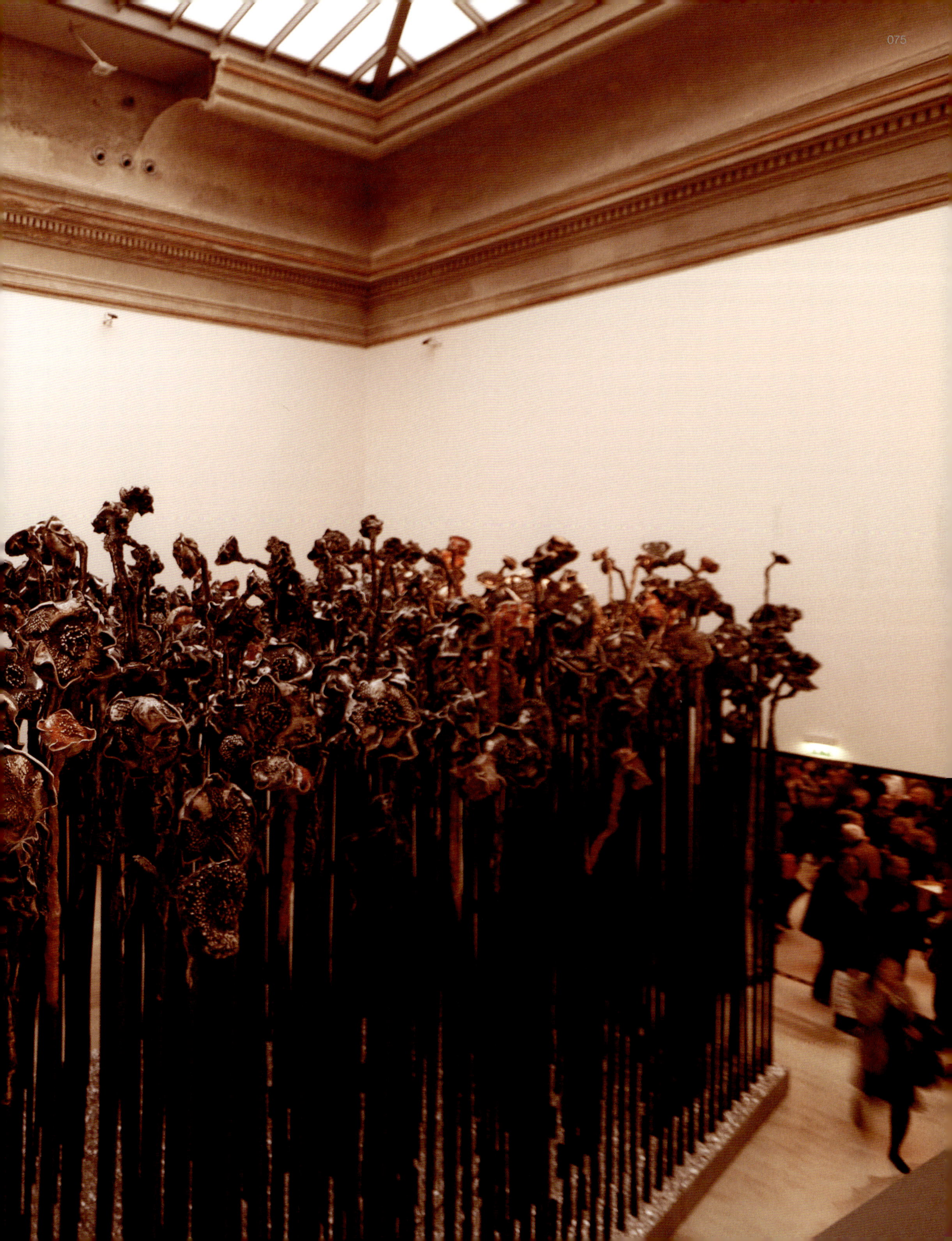

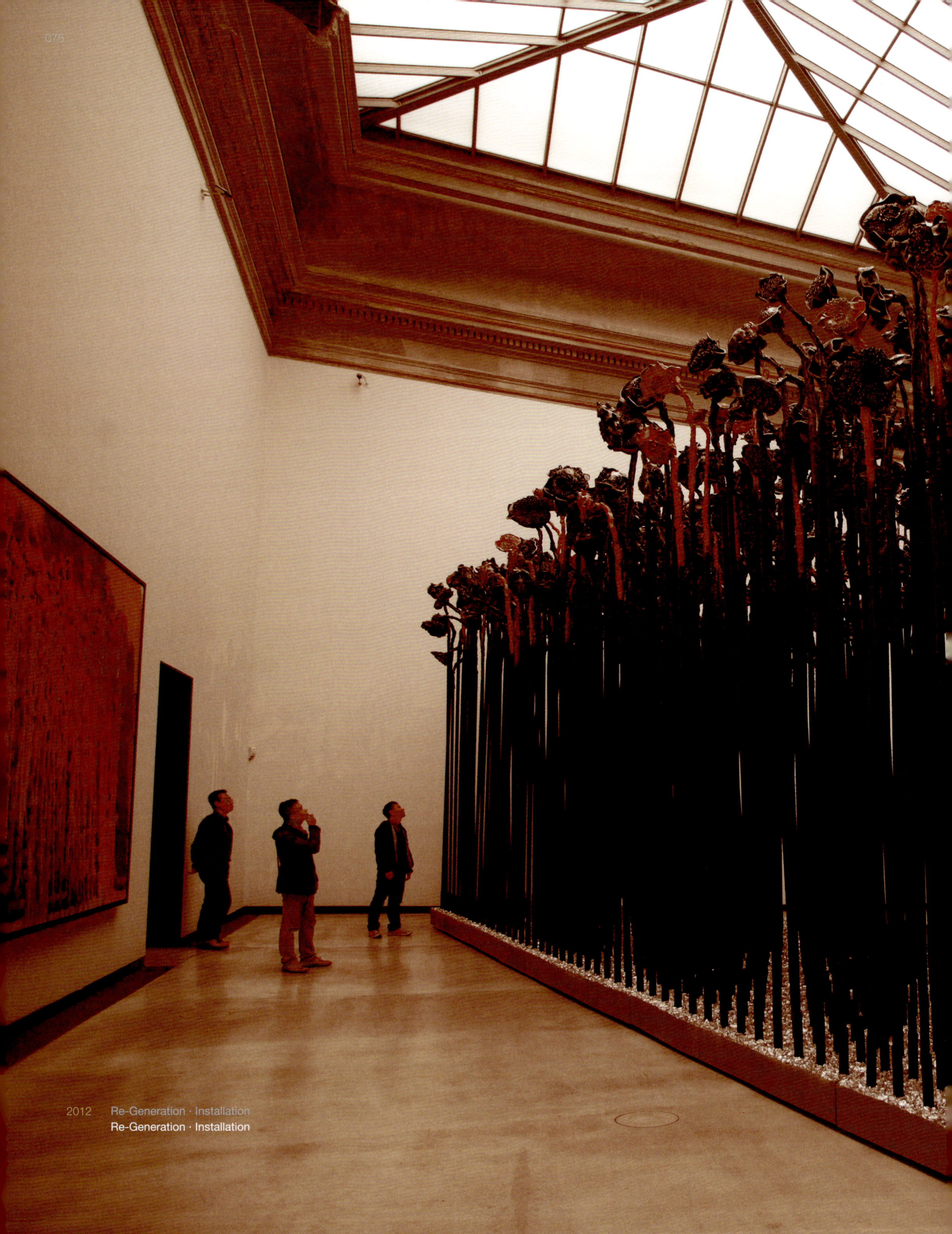

2012   Re-Generation · Installation
Re-Generation · Installation

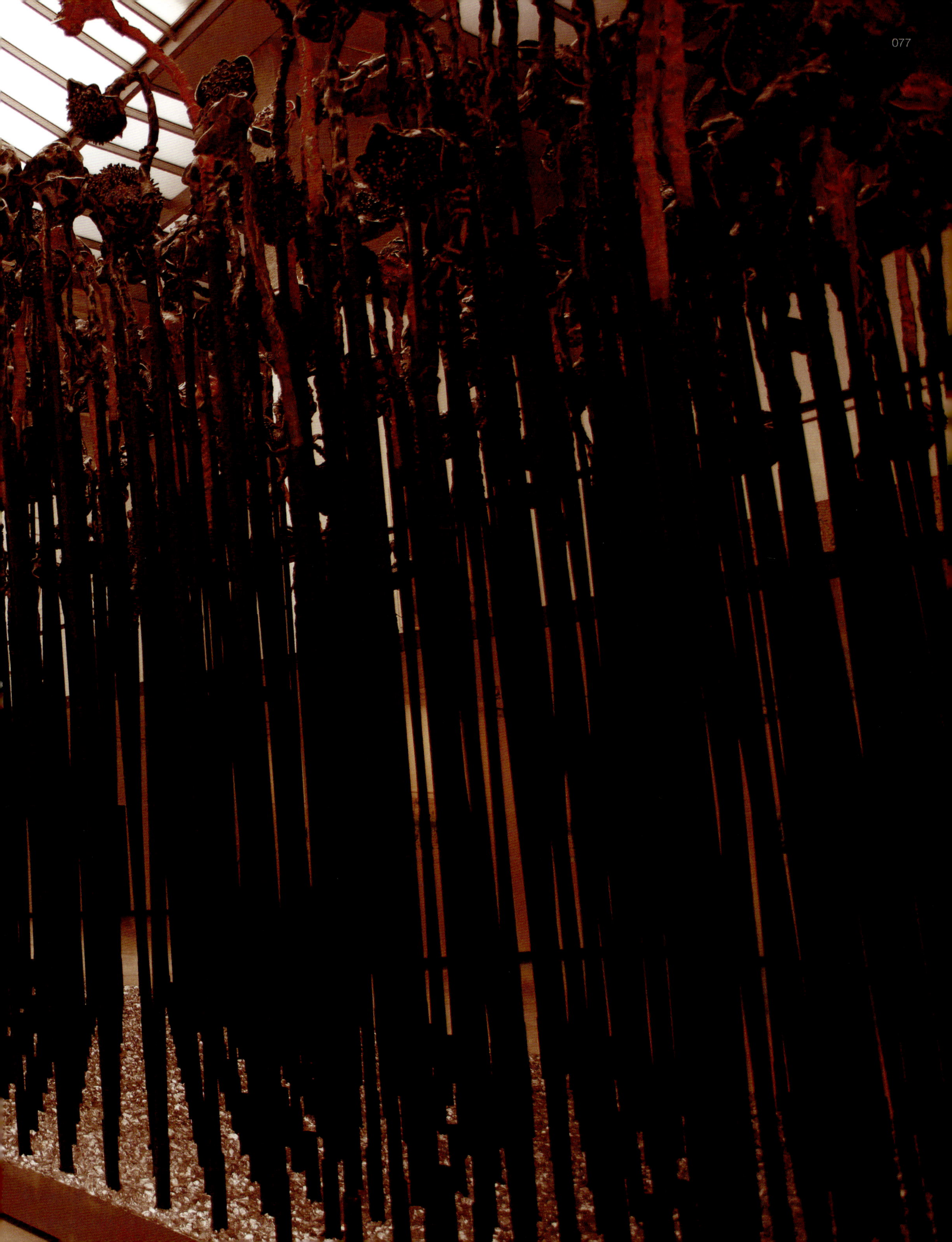

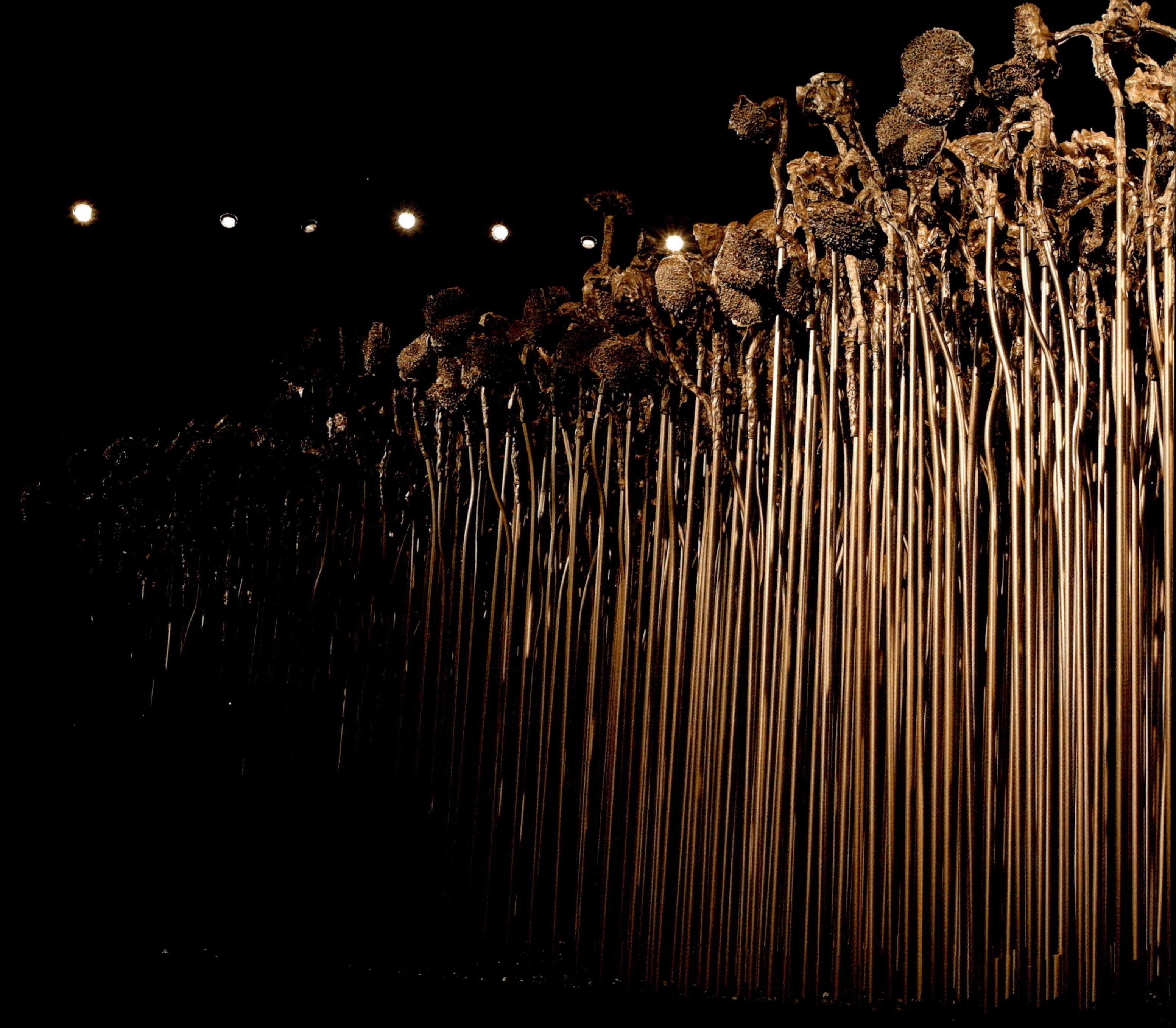

2010   Is It Possible for Them to Live Together? · Installation
Gibt es die Möglichkeit zur Symbiose? · Installation

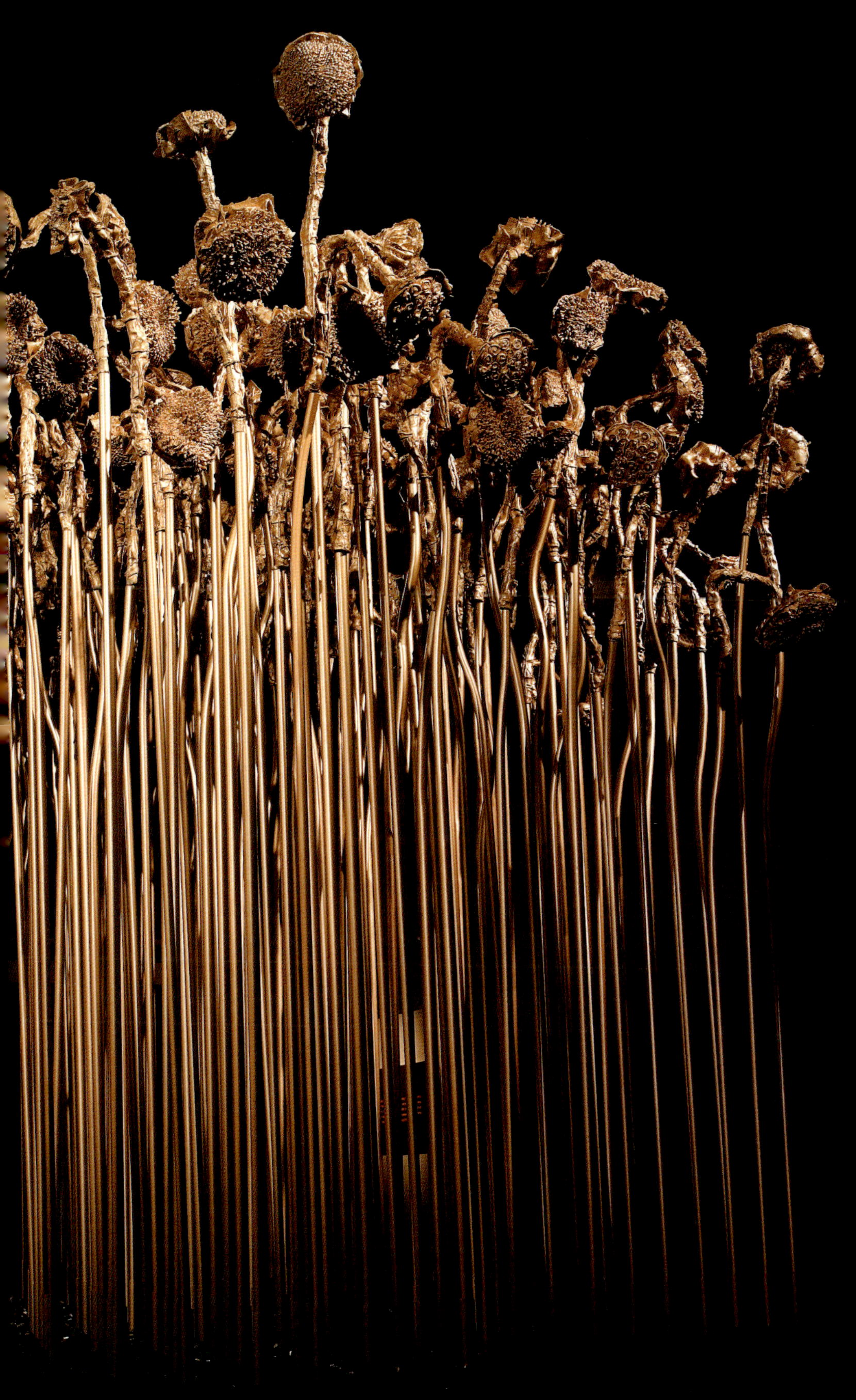

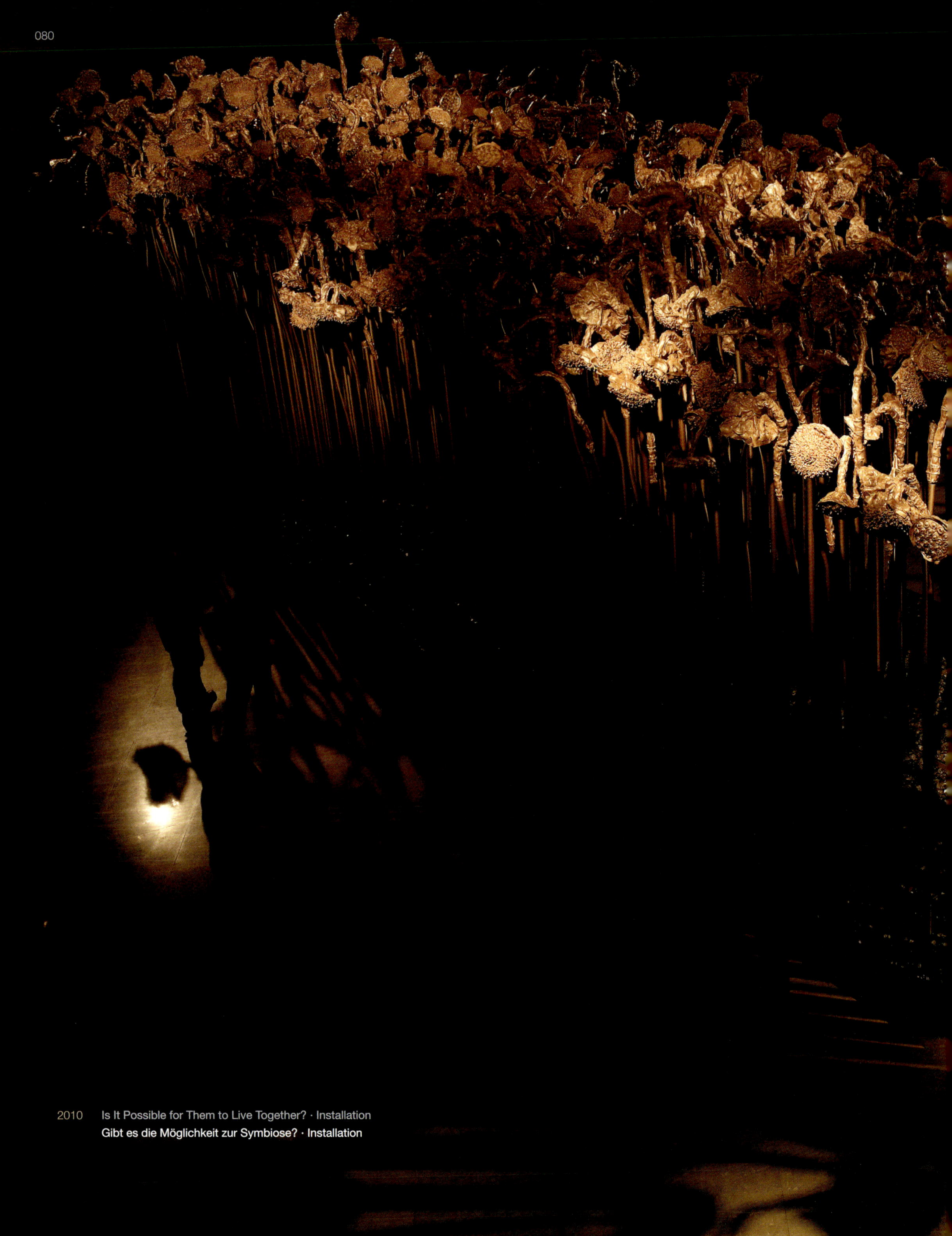

2010 Is It Possible for Them to Live Together? · Installation
Gibt es die Möglichkeit zur Symbiose? · Installation

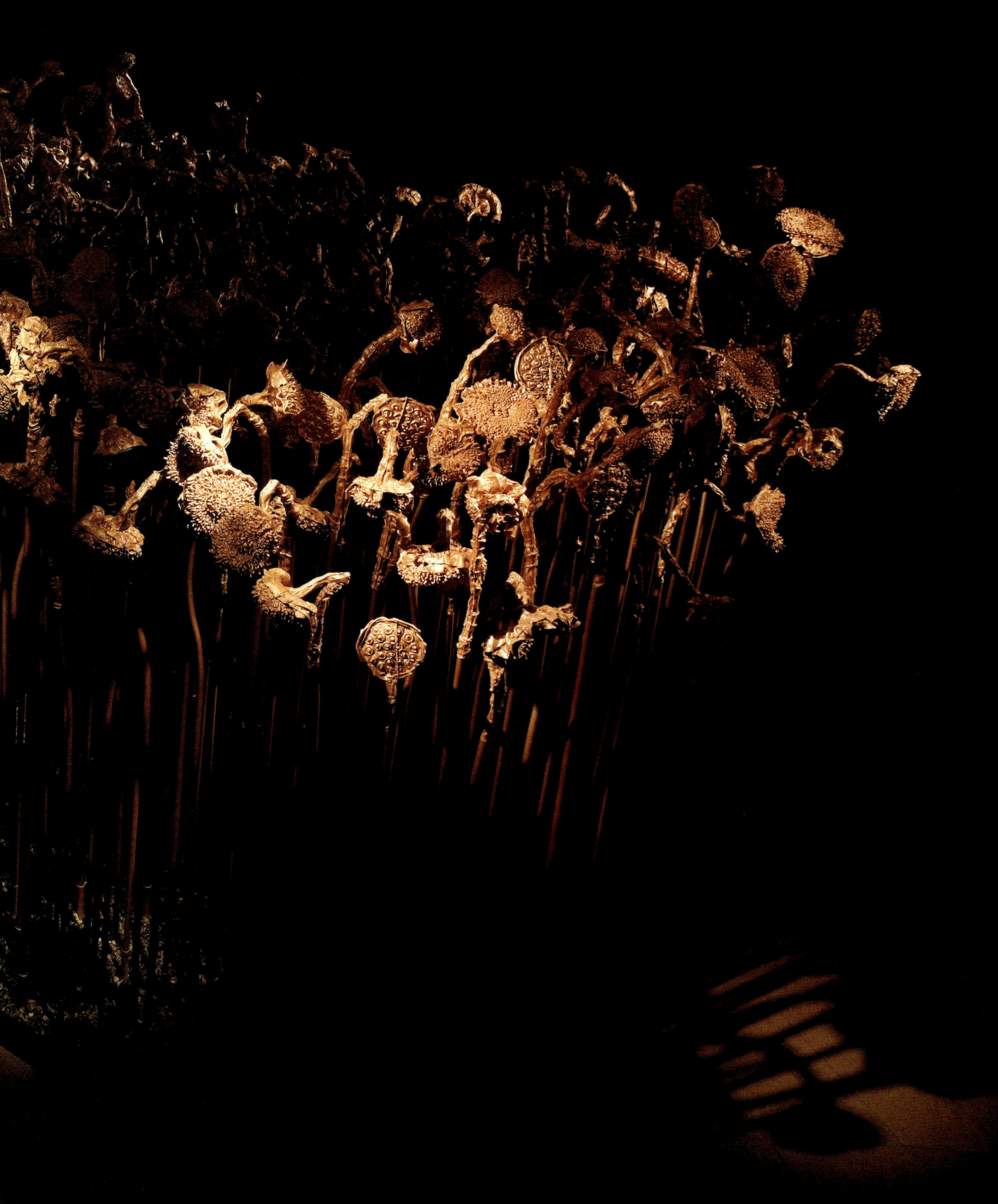

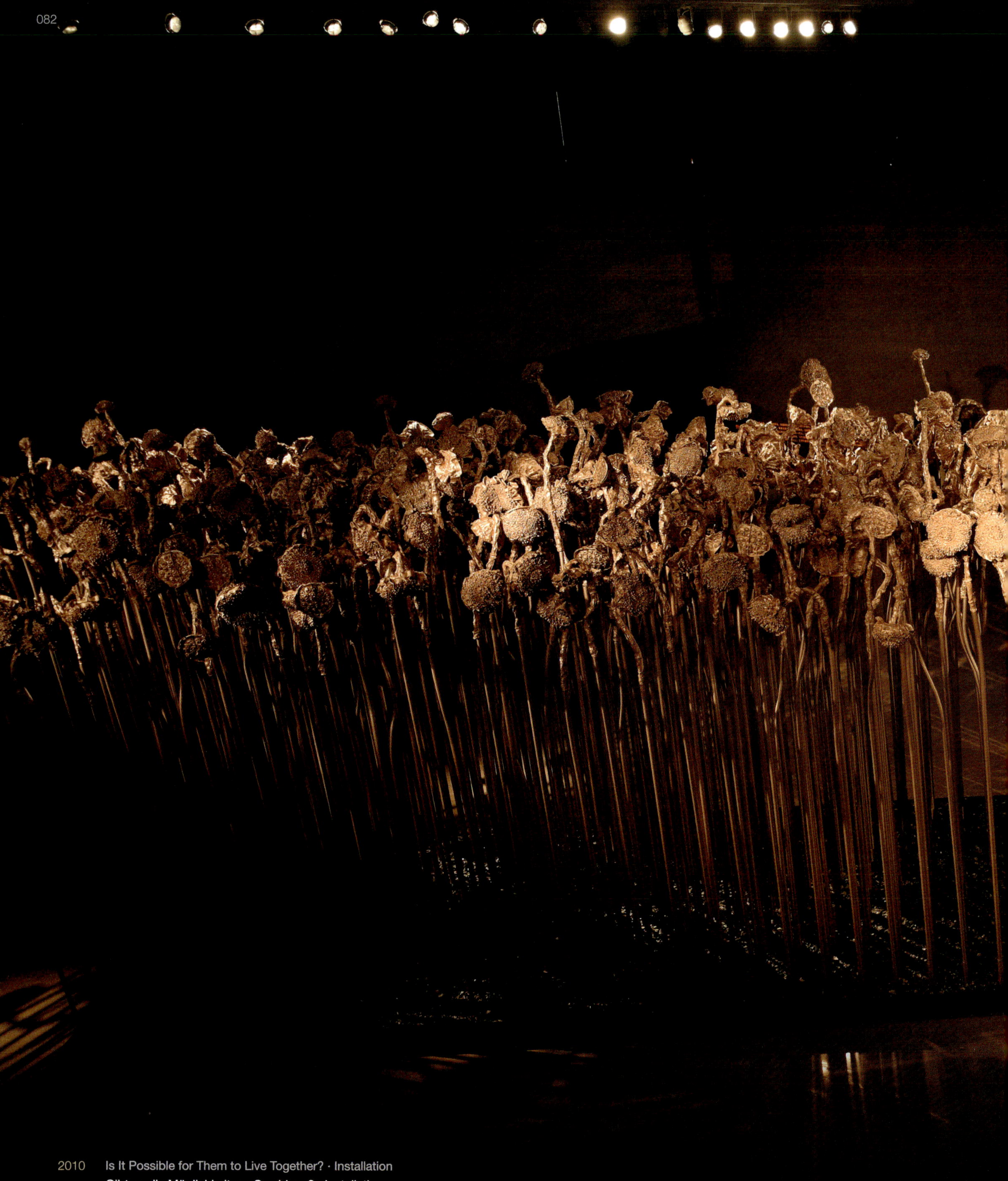

2010   Is It Possible for Them to Live Together? · Installation
Gibt es die Möglichkeit zur Symbiose? · Installation

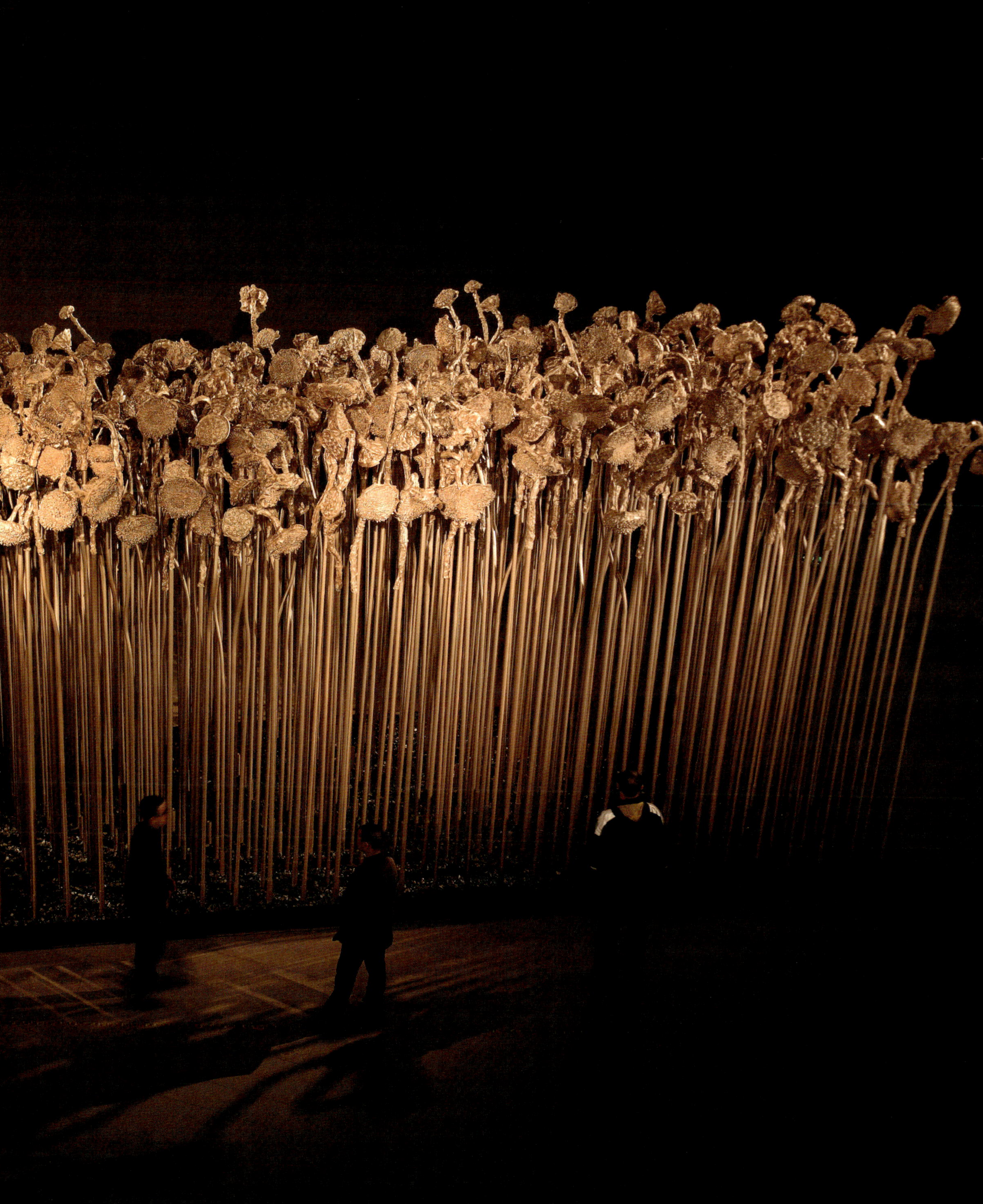

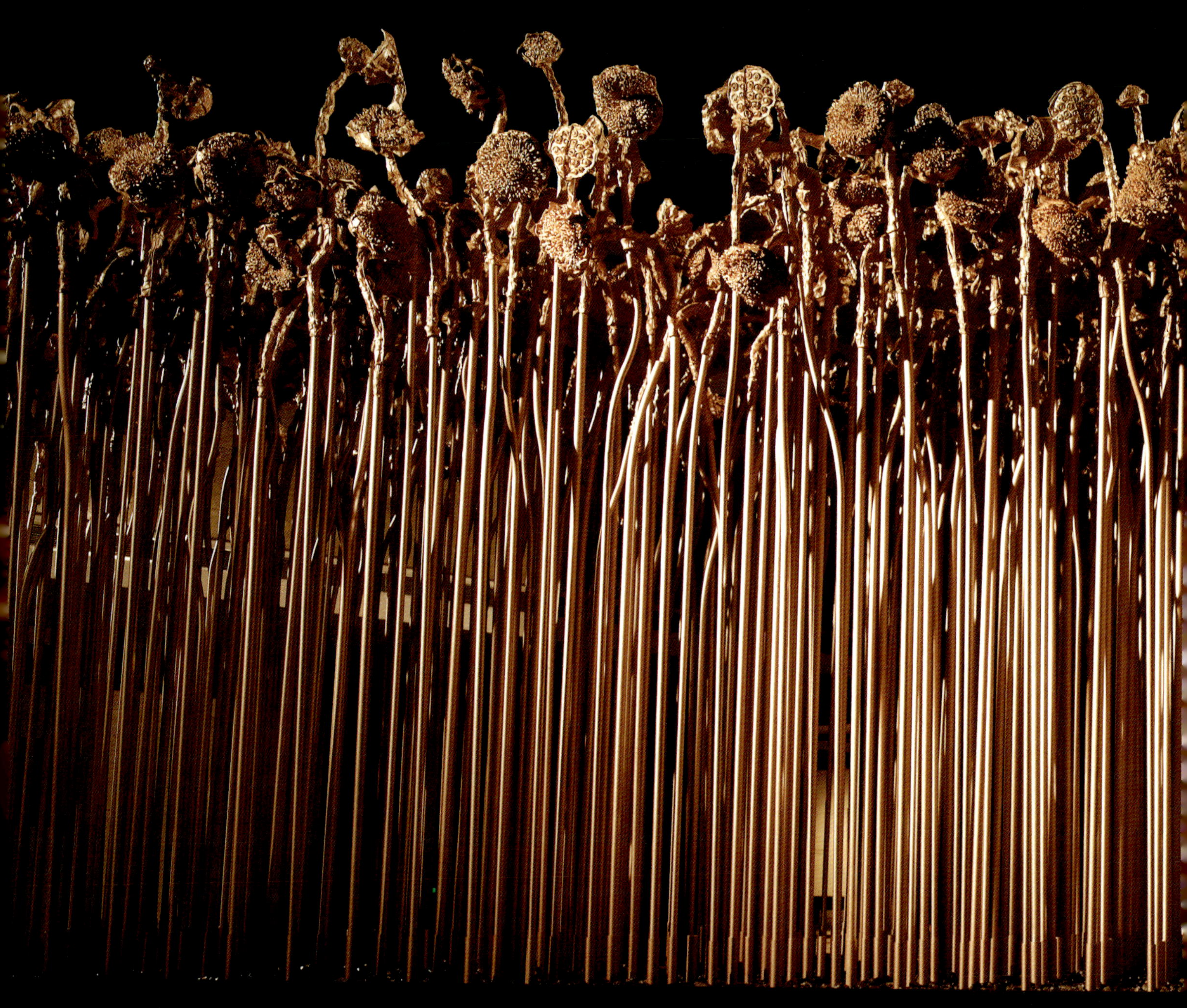

2010   Is It Possible for Them to Live Together? · Installation
Gibt es die Möglichkeit zur Symbiose? · Installation

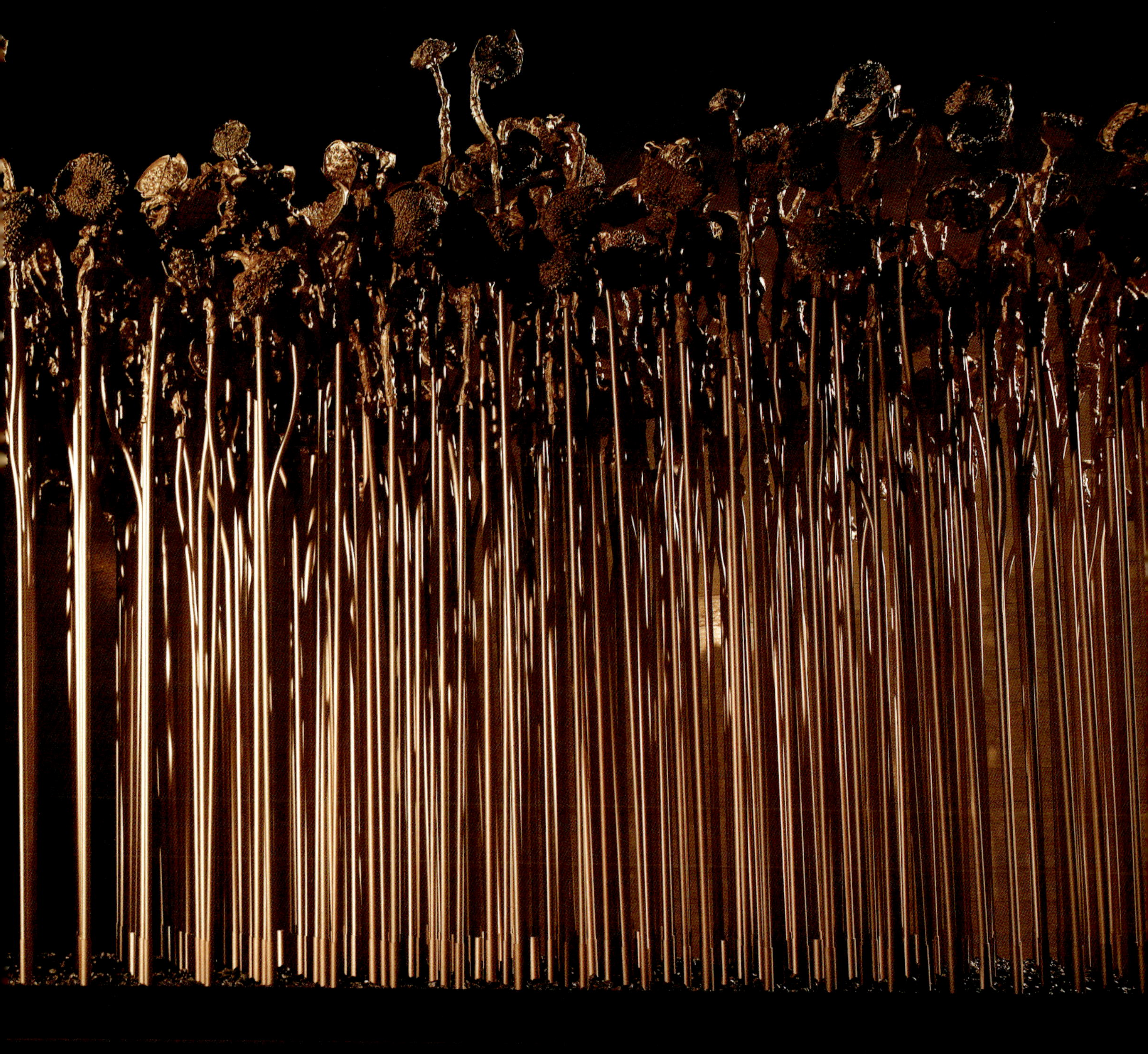

Complexity and Poetics of the Painting
Xu Jiang

Komplexität und Poesie des Gemäldes
Xu Jiang

A few months ago, I was a bit overwhelmed as I came across a newspaper report about the bankruptcy filing of Kodak. In March 1912, the English explorer Robert Falcon Scott and his teammates met their death on the way back from the South Pole. A few rolls of Kodak film were also buried in the snow alongside their bodies, until they were discovered eight months later. The film survived the icy coldness and bore witness to what they last saw. A century later, Kodak filed for bankruptcy. Credited with recording the life of generations of middle classes both within the States and worldwide, Kodak has not only nurtured the art and industry of photography, but also replaced text with image culture as a truthful representation of its time. Today, Kodak's bankruptcy has been ascribed to the company's rather conservative approaches in the 1970s and 1980s.

I agree with Bernardo Bertolucci's claim that the individual is taken hostage by history. Not only is the individual held for ransom by his own time, the invention of a specific technology also bears the imprint of its own time, with which it is inextricably associated. Kodak was destined to flourish during an industrial boom, and similarly to fall at a time of industrial

Als ich vor einigen Monaten in der Zeitung vom Konkurs des Traditionsunternehmens Kodak las, konnte ich einen Seufzer des Bedauerns nicht unterdrücken… Im März 1912 kam der englische Entdecker Robert Scott mit seinem Kameraden am Südpol ums Leben. Unter Schnee und Eis fand man viel später zusammen mit den Leichen einige Kodak-Filme, die der Kälte widerstanden hatten. Klar und deutlich war darauf für die Nachwelt alles dokumentiert, was die Expedition zuletzt gesehen hatte. Hundert Jahre später ist Kodak insolvent, ein Unternehmen, mit dessen Produkten die Mittelschicht nicht nur in den USA sich selbst dokumentiert hatte, ein Unternehmen, das die Fotografie zu einer Kunst und das Fotografieren zu einem Geschäft entwickelte, und maßgeblich daran mitwirkte, dass in unserem Zeitalter die Bildkultur die Schriftkultur abzulösen begann. Paradoxerweise wird Kodaks Niedergang heutzutage meist auf die konservative Unternehmenspolitik in den 80er Jahren des vorigen Jahrhunderts zurückgeführt.

Ich schließe mich Bertolucci an, wenn er sagt „Der Mensch ist die Geisel der Geschichte." Doch nicht nur der Einzelne ist seinem Zeitalter gewissermaßen hilflos ausgeliefert, auch bestimmte Techniken und Erfindungen tragen den

transformation. All the same, it has once achieved excellence. As the symbol of its age, it represents the technological and intellectual advancements of that time, and becomes firmly ensconced and immortalized as a link that connects to both the past and the future of human civilization. Meanwhile, Kodak's demise also carries a message, one about the destiny of technological culture: as technology is upgraded, then its culture has to undergo a process of transformation as well.

This has reminded me of the state of oil painting. Obviously it is not a technological culture, despite the fact that it contains technical and material elements. More importantly, at a time when digital image production is already highly developed, the ways and energies of traditional painting have increasingly come under scrutiny. The decline of western painting attests to this claim. Hence our repeated question 'what is it to be for painting in an image age?', in which propositions about the contemporary concerns and experimental quality of painting are repeatedly aired.

I paint sunflowers, in order to portray an entire sun-worshipping generation, namely the generation that underwent the Cultural Revolution. As the author Yu Hua once said, 'the sunflower is a common memory shared by all of us, an image capable of bringing tears to the eyes for this generation of Chinese'. The sunflower is apparently a poeticised image. Yet sunflower paintings are not about symbolism, nor do they stand in for ideology. Rather, they are the historic life portraiture of an entire generation. Such a presence is alive today and forever will be. It continues to depict the reality of an entire generation's historical experience and life's contour. With lively imagery that invokes the ancient poetic propositions of painting, it sets out to reconstruct our time's

Stempel ihrer Epoche, oder sind sogar untrennbar mit dieser verbunden. Kodaks Schicksal war auf Gedeih und Verderb an das Industriezeitalter gekettet: Als dieses in seiner Blüte stand, prosperierte Kodak, als der Strukturwandel einsetzte, ging es bergab. Doch das tut Kodaks Bedeutung keinen Abbruch: Als Symbol einer Epoche steht es für deren technischen, aber auch intellektuellen Fortschritt und ist damit ein wichtiges Glied in der langen Kette der menschlichen Zivilisation und hat seinen Platz in der Geschichte sicher. Gleichzeitig sagt uns Kodaks Ende auch etwas Wichtiges über die Beziehung zwischen Technologie und Kultur: In dem Maße, wie Technologien veralten und durch neue ersetzt werden, wandeln sich zwangsläufig die an sie geknüpften Kulturelemente.

Das bringt mich zur Malerei. Zwar ist diese offenkundig nicht direkt auf technologische Hilfsmittel angewiesen, jedoch spielen auch in ihr Technologie und Materialkunde eine gewisse Rolle; noch wichtiger ist jedoch der Einfluss der digitalen Bildindustrie. Ihre rasante Entwicklung stellt die traditionelle Malerei vor die Frage nach ihrer Daseinsberechtigung, wie es der Niedergang der westlichen Malerei anschaulich illustriert. Wir können daher gar nicht umhin, immer wieder die Frage nach dem Zweck der Malerei im Zeitalter der Bilderflut aufzuwerfen, nach dem aktuellen Interesse der Malerei und nach ihrem experimentellen Charakter.

Sie wissen, ich male Blumen – doch ich meine Menschen damit, die Menschen der „Sonnenblumengeneration", also die Generation derjenigen, die die Kulturrevolution am eigenen Leib erlebten. Vom Schriftsteller Yu Hua stammt der Satz: „Die Sonnenblumen haben sich in unser gemeinsames Gedächtnis eingebrannt, bei ihrem Anblick treten uns heiße Tränen in die Augen." Hierin ist die Sonnenblume natürlich ein poetisches Bild, doch ihre Darstellung bedeutet mehr als nur eine Chiffre

sensitivity in decline (Verfall). This constitutes the basic motif for this dialogue that our moderator has just mentioned.

I often come across international friends who keep asking me about the potential political intents in my aged sunflowers and sunflower fields. Today, I hope we are able to bypass the conventional discourse of 'East and West', and the ideological discourse constructed and perpetuated by the Cold War, in order to open up a new space for dialogue. I am convinced that misprisions inherent in the existing discourses have blinded us to the big picture of the reality, just as some *idées fixes* have concealed life itself and subdued the many rich and broad-based intellectual resources that we may possess.

Today we find ourselves engulfed in an age of digital and mass media, which have in various ways produced an endless amount of imagery that keep us encircled and entangled. On the one hand everything is made convenient for us. On the other hand, we come under the domination of technology. We are caught up between the Scylla and Charybdis of images and simulacra. The many Dispositifs of spectacle cut us into fragments that are either consumers or the consumed. We are losing daily the sensitivity to the entirety and depth of things. Such sensitivity is the only rescue from the vast seas of images. Yet with the on-going fragmentation and superficialisation of the subject, the sensitivity of our time is also in decline, which in turn gives rise to the decline of painting in question here. Therefore, the contemporary task, or renaissance, of painting is closely associated with the redemption of the contemporary sensitivity.

Here, I would like to offer a discussion about how painting could poetise historical experience from three perspectives. I want to return to the fountainhead of sensitivity with the

für einen bestimmten Bewusstseinszustand, denn in ihr erkennen wir das Lebensportrait einer ganzen Generation, ein Portrait, das auch zukünftig nichts von seiner Frische verlieren wird, denn in ihm materialisieren sich die Erfahrungen und Lebenslinien einer ganzen Epoche; dank dieser Frische wird es uns weiterhin dazu ermutigen, poetische Themen aus alter Zeit aufzugreifen ,um die im Zerfallen begriffenen Empfindungskraft in neue Formen zu gießen.

Ausländische Freunde fragen mich gerne nach der politischen Botschaft meiner verwelkten Sonnenblumen. Dazu möchte ich nur sagen, dass ich mir wünschte, wir würden endlich die aus dem alten Ost –West –Gegensatz sowie dem Kalten Krieg stammenden Denkschablonen hinter uns lassen und uns einen neuen Dialograum eröffnen. Ich bin der Meinung, dass vorgefertigte Begriffe stets zu schweren Missverständnissen führen und die Gesamtwirklichkeit verdecken. Voreingenommenheiten verschleiern das wahre Leben und hindern uns daran, aus einer lebendigen und reichen Inspirationsquelle zu schöpfen.

Wir leben heute in einem Zeitalter der digitalen Medien; Bilderfluten entstehen in Sekundenschnelle und bedrängen uns von allen Seiten. Vieles wird uns zwar dadurch erleichtert, auf der anderen Seite verlieren wir aber gleichzeitig den Blick für technische Meisterschaft. Wir stehen vor einem Ozean aus Bildern und sind doch gleichzeitig von Imitaten umgeben. Landschaftsinstallationen zerstückeln uns – wir sind Konsumierende und Konsumierte zugleich; dabei verlieren wir immer mehr die Fähigkeit zur ganzheitlichen Erfahrung der Gegenstände. Wir stehen vor einem Ozean aus Bildern, durch den nur der Kompass unserer Empfindungskraft uns hätte leiten können. Doch durch die Zersplitterung und Verflachung der Motive zerfällt auch diese. Direkte Folge davon ist der Niedergang der Malerei. Wenn sie jedoch in diesen Zeiten ihre

ancient, questioning and constructive spirit of painting.

I. Body and Experiential Image

In *My Name is Red*, Orhan Pamuk tells many stories about Persian miniatures as if with the mouth of a ghost. In the novel there is a parable about the drawing of a horse. Three miniaturists have been ordered to draw for the King the 'most beautiful horse in the world'. They have to try their best to please the king. One picks out a perfect work from an exquisite catalogue, and by cutting out the contours, he closely copies a horse. The second one does not even have to think twice to conjure up the horse that he has been painting thousands of times and that his predecessors had painted countless times. The third one, after moments of struggle, imagines the horse's presence there. He is reborn with the horse. As he paints a certain part of the horse, the corresponding part of his own body would be enlivened. Towards the end, his entire person is shaken to the core by the horse he has painted. Employing a paradoxical first person narrator, Pamuk carefully discloses the internal positions of the three painters.

The first artist's approach is that of technology, which stops at reproduction: when I draw a horse, I am just myself. That is all.
The second artist's approach is stylistic, which also stops at reproduction: when I draw a horse, I become the master of the past and myself at once.
The third artist's approach is approximate to that of ontology, which emphasises here and now and bodily 'experience': as I draw a horse I become that horse.
Apparently the third painter is closest to the real meaning of painting, and we term his approach that of 'experiential image'.

Legitimation und Vitalität bewahren will, dann gelingt dies nur, wenn sie sich der Aufgabe widmet, an der Wiederherstellung der Empfindungskraft mitzuwirken.

Ich möchte an dieser Stelle zeigen, wie wir durch Gestaltung einer aus alter Zeit ererbten skeptisch-schöpferischen Tradition zur Quelle des Empfindens zurückfinden können und anschließend die Frage untersuchen, wie die Malerei historische Erfahrungen poetisieren kann.

I. Der Körper und sein Bild

In dem Buch *Rot ist mein Name* des türkischen Schriftstellers Pamuk drehen sich viele der Geschichten um die persische Miniaturmalerei. In einer davon werden drei Miniaturmaler vom Sultan beauftragt, das schönste Pferd der Welt zu zeichnen. Die drei Maler machen sich mit Feuereifer ans Werk. Einer wählte unter den schönsten Pferdebildern, die er finden konnte, das Prächtigste aus und fertigte einen Durchschlag davon an. Der zweite ließ die unzähligen Bilder von Pferden, die er je gezeichnet hatte, vor seinem inneren Auge vorbeiziehen; dem Schönsten davon erlaubte er mit einem Lächeln auf den Lippen, vor sich auf dem Papier entstehen zu dürfen. Der dritte schließlich zögerte etwas, dann erblickte er das Pferd vor seinem inneren Auge und mit seinem eigenen Körper erlebte er dessen Geburt auf dem Papier nach. Am Ende ist dieser völlig erschüttert von seiner Pferdezeichnung. Pamuk verwendet hier die Ich-Perspektive, um das Innenleben der drei Maler zu beleuchten:

Der erste der Maler wählt eine rein technische Herangehensweise und beschränkt sich letztlich aufs Kopieren: Ein Pferd zu malen hat nichts mit mir persönlich zu tun, es ändert nichts an dem, was ich bin.

'Image' stands at the core of traditional Chinese hermeneutics. It is not a pure object, nor is it an object existing in pure consciousness. It is not ready-made, complete. Nor is it intangible, untraceable. 'Image' is a semblance that acts as a perceivable, tangible medium between object and subject. This medium offers a lively description of the hermeneutic and imaginative relationship between object and subject. Such 'image' is not a third party independent of object and subject. Rather it contains the life-form of the here and now in which both subject and object exist. Mediated by 'image', the physical-psychological 'experiential' grasp of life's entirety and implications can be termed 'experiential image'. Such a process combines both the physical body of the subject with the object in order to complete a certain transformation of life.

Such is a visible transformational process of life that relies on 'the body', which is not unlike a window. The painter can freely travel through it, sometimes looking outward from within, and vice versa. Just as Van Gogh's shoes. If you look outward, they are but a pair of shoes. If you look inward, then they constitutes a peasant's world. Our body now evolves into a pair of shoes to experience their harshness, and by extension the harshness of the peasant woman or Van Gogh's life. Meanwhile, the repeated strokes, the interweaving yellowish brown strokes, have yet again allowed all the people under the yoke of a harsh life to return to the pair of shoes with a suddenly activated image of harshness. All those speculations over their ownership (do they belong to a peasant woman, or to Van Gogh himself?) or over whether the two shoes were both for the left foot do not matter anymore. It has already evoked our sense of touch, and allowed us to experience, within the here and now, the image of the 'shoes' as a 'common experiencer'.

Der zweite Maler ist ein Stylist, aber auch er kommt über das Kopieren nicht hinaus: Durch das Malen des Pferdes verschmelze ich ein Stück weit mit den früheren Meistern und komme mir selbst näher.

Den Ansatz des dritten Malers könnte man als existenz-ialistisch bezeichnen, denn er betont das spontane „Einswerden" mit dem Objekt: Ein Pferd zu malen, bedeutet, ein Pferd zu werden.

Offensichtlich ist es der dritte der Maler, der die engste Verbindung zum Inhalt seiner Zeichnung besitzt. Diesen Zugang wollen wir als *ti xiang* (体象) bezeichnen. Das chinesische Schriftzeichen 象 (*xiang*) steht im Zentrum der traditionellen chinesischen Hermeneutik. Es bezieht sich weder eindeutig auf den Gegenstand noch aus-schließlich auf dessen geistiges Korrelat. Es handelt sich weder um etwas Geschaffenes, Fertiges, noch um etwas Substanzloses. xiang steht zwischen Subjekt und Objekt, es kann sowohl empfunden als auch beobachtet werden. Als solches liefert es uns eine Darstellung der assoziativ-hermeneutischen Beziehung zwischen Subjekt und Objekt. Jedoch ist *xiang* ebensowenig als etwas getrennt von Subjekt und Objekt Bestehendes zu denken. Vielmehr handelt es sich bei ihm um die lebendige Gestalt des Augenblicks, in der sowohl Subjekt als auch Objekt enthalten sind. Mit diesem *xiang* als Medium die Ganzheit und Tiefe des Lebens an Körper und Seele zu empfinden und zu erfassen – das nennen wir *ti xiang*. Dieser Prozess der Verschmelzung von Subjekt und Objekt kann mit gewissem Recht als Transformation des Lebens angesehen werden.

Hierbei handelt es sich um eine sichtbare Wandlung, die auf physischer Erfahrung basiert. Der Maler benutzt seinen Körper als Fenster in beide Richtungen, für die Innenschau genauso wie für die Außenschau. Nehmen wir zum Beispiel

II. Challenges and Transformations

Apple products can be found everywhere in our life, becoming perhaps the most active image of contemporary global society. The image / logo is at once an apple and a candle. Where does the shifting flame come from? From Apple itself. From 'apple' to 'candle', there is an elevation of 'image', as the flame comes from Apple and exhausts its life. Therefore, the elevation of 'image' is dependent on a certain deviation, certain challenges and resistance originating from within life. It is precisely such challenges that has emancipated life from the shackles of sensitivity and triggered transformation of new life-images. History of art testifies to the worthiness of such resistance. Shifts in modern experimental art reveal the force of resistance that comes with an independent mind. In our concerns with social reality, there always linger such complexes as tradition and innovation, identity and difference, spirituality and consumption. The key to the transformation of imagery and language lies in an independent attitude that challenges and reflects on the complexes and thereby conveying a kind of contemporary concern that is truly rooted in life and the grassroots. Therefore, the elevation of image is not a scheme or the objectification of such a scheme. Rather it is the offshoot of this involuntary challenge and resistance, a new life that has been transfigured and reborn after undergoing many complexes and nirvanas.

It is the same Orhan Pamuk, who, in his speech accepting the Nobel Prize in Literature, reminisced emotionally about his father's failing yet unstinting career as a writer as well as the story of father giving his manuscripts to him in a suitcase. His Nobel Lecture was titled 'My Father's Suitcase'. Pamuk wrote about his longing for the suitcase as well as his alertness to it. He knew what it contained, but found it difficult to open it

Van Goghs Schuhe: Äußerlich betrachtet lediglich einfache Fußbekleidung, in der Innenschau jedoch repräsentieren sie die bäuerliche Welt. Bei der Innenschau versetzen wir uns quasi körperlich in diese Schuhe, um deren Härte zu fühlen und an ihnen die Mühsal des Lebens einer Bäuerin oder gar die Bitterkeit Van Goghs eigenen Lebens nachzuempfinden. Jeder, der jemals Härte und Bitterkeit erfahren hat, wird sie in diesem Gewebe aus Pinselstrichen wiederfinden. Spekulationen darüber, ob es sich um die Schuhe einer Bäuerin oder Van Goghs eigene Schuhe, ein Paar oder zwei linke Schuhe handelt, sind dabei nicht wichtig, solange unser eigener Tastsinn erregt ist, solange wir in diesen Schuhen spontan einen Teil unserer eignen Biographie wiedererkennen.

II. Herausforderung und Transformation

Die Produkte der Firma Apple haben unseren Alltag fest im Griff und das Firmenlogo, der Apfel, ist zu größter Popularität gelangt. Wie ein Funke ist dieses Symbol übergesprungen und hat einen weltweiten Flächenbrand ausgelöst. Doch woher kam dieser Funke? Mir scheint, von Apple selbst, das ihn mittels des *xiang* mit seinem eigenen Leben genährt hat. Dieses *xiang* nämlich steht für eine innere Wandlung, eine Herausforderung und einen Widerstand inmitten des eigenen Lebens. Diese Herausforderung besteht darin, die beschränkte Empfindungskraft zu erweitern und dem Leben zu einer neuen Bildlichkeit zu verhelfen. Die Geschichte der Kunst vom Altertum bis heute bestätigt den Wert dieses Widerstandes, dessen autonome Kraft sich in den Wandlungen der modernen und aktuellen experimentellen Kunst widergespiegelt findet. Bei unserer Auseinandersetzung mit der Wirklichkeit sind stets Tradierung und Innovation, Identität und Differenz sowie Geist und Konsum miteinander verwoben. Sich diesen Verwicklungen autonom und reflektierend zu

easily. He was so afraid of opening father's suitcase, afraid that his father's certain boisterousness would intrude on his solitude, afraid that his father's exile style of writing would poison his independent experience of literature, of the local. In fact, he was perhaps afraid that his self-constructed place in the world and in his life, just as his place in literature, would come under intrusion. He was afraid that the suitcase would get in the way of his existence as a Turkish writer. In this suitcase, there are many messages and encounters from beyond the borders. There is also a lack and shortage of his father's generation's longing for a west-bound journey towards the centre of the world. As a member of the new-generation native writer, Pamuk's resistance and refusal are full of parabolic implications. We (including the younger generation) in China are no stranger to such resistance and struggle. It gathers up a certain non-Western-centred, local force of resistance and schemes for China's own cosmic construction.

III. Slow Processes and Intuitive Formation

In 2003, in the wilderness by the Sea of Marmara, I was suddenly confronted with an expanse of aged sunflowers under the setting sun. They struck me as cast from steel or copper and blended into the earth. They were facing the same direction, as the sun slowly set behind them. I thought I saw a legion of aged soldiers, or perhaps our own selves, the generation that once flowered and ceaselessly revolved around the sun. Instantly, all my experience with sunflowers, the collective destiny of that age, the vicissitudes of life, and the experiences that crossed my mind and deposited for decades, were revived. I saw an entire generation's life history brought back to life. I saw not only sunflowers, but also a poem, a wasteland of sunflowers. I caught myself of

stellen, Erkenntnisse zu destillieren, die in der Lebenspraxis fruchtbar und zur Grundlage verantwortlichen Handelns werden – das ist der Kern der Transformation, sowohl was Bild als auch was Sprache betrifft. Bei der Kultivierung des *xiang* handelt es sich daher nicht um die Umsetzung eines bestimmten Planes oder dessen materielles Resultat, sondern um das Produkt eines unwillkürlich und ungesteuert ablaufenden Prozesses, der sich aus Herausforderung und Widerstand zusammensetzt; eine Transformation und Wiedergeburt nach unzähligen Konflikten und Vernichtungen.

Um in diesem Zusammenhang noch einmal auf Pamuk zurückzukommen: In seiner berühmten Nobelpreisrede schreibt er von seinem Vater, der ein produktiver aber erfolgloser Schriftsteller gewesen war. In seinen späten Jahren schenkte er Pamuk einen Koffer, in dem er seine Manuskripte gesammelt hatte. In seiner Rede, die mit „Der Koffer meines Vaters" betitelt ist, beschreibt Pamuk die Faszination, die der Koffer auf ihn ausübt. Er weiß um seinen Inhalt, wagt aber nicht, ihn zu öffnen. Er fürchtet sich sogar davon, fürchtet, dass sein eigenes geordnetes und zurückgezogenes Schriftstellerdasein durcheinander gebracht würde und er selber die Autonomie über sein Schreiben verlieren könnte. Tatsächlich fürchtet er, dass sein Platz im Leben genauso erschüttert werden könnte wie seine Identität als Schriftsteller, als türkischer Schriftsteller. In dem Koffer schlummerten nämlich zahllose Erinnerungen seiner Vätergeneration, an die Rückschläge und Enttäuschungen auf deren Weg der Annäherung an den Westen, dem Zentrum der Welt. Artikuliert durch einen nicht-westlichen Schriftsteller der jüngeren Generation, dürften Pamuks Widerstand und Ablehnung im heutigen China auf Resonanz insbesondere bei den Jüngeren stoßen. Denn Pamuks Botschaft enthält ein lokales und nicht-westlich ausgerichtetes Widerstandspotenzial und ist damit

that particular season standing at the season's edge. I set out
my 'Sunflower Fields' series. Each creation brought me back
there, a locale with the setting sun and the calmness of Göt-
terdämmerung. That moment marked the starting point of my
memories about sunflower fiends, and the homeland of all the
subsequent images of sunflower fields.

In May 2012, my solo exhibition 'Re-Generation' was opened
at Staatliche Kunstsammlungen Dresden. In the centre of the
exhibition hall stood a sunflower field in which sunflowers
grew together with lotuses. They longed for the sun and
pointed towards the ceiling. On the wall opposite the field
was the oil painting 'Flower without Soil'. The black stalks
of the sunflower field formed a stark contrast with the white
stalks of 'Flower without Soil'. The greyish-blue cement of
the ceiling was just like the passing of time and washes down
the sunflower heads and spreads across the entire sunflower
field, whose fiery red pulls the sculptures and the paintings
together. Here ashes and fire are reborn together. 'Flower
without Soil' is a portrait of sun flowers on steel racks. In the
frame there are only sunflower heads, with no leaves or petals.
Seen from the outside, they are sunflowers. Deep within, they
are a generation turning their heads towards the Red Sun. I
stood there, as if stripped naked. Our bodies metamorphose
into the sunflowers in order to partake their vicissitudes and
those of an entire generation. Meanwhile, the palimpsest
of intersected brushstrokes brought all those vicissitudes
back to the sunflowers with abruptly activated historical
experience. It has awakened our physical 'involvement', and
'involve' us physically and emotionally in the assemblage of
sunflowers that are so filled with a multitude of emotions.

There are two prominent features to my sunflowers: first, they
are mostly aged sunflowers, seasoned with a tragic sentiment.

auch bedeutsam für ein in China sich eigenständig formendes
Weltverständnis.

III. Langsamkeit und direkte Anschauung

In Homers Odyssee kann der Schöpfer des Trojanischen
Pferdes nach gewonnenem Krieg nicht direkt in seine
Heimat zurückkehren, die Rückreise gerät zur Irrfahrt. Erst
nach insgesamt 20 äußerst beschwerlichen Jahren, nach
Verirrungen und Errettungen, trifft Odysseus wieder in Ithaka
ein. Das Wort „Errettung" besitzt hierbei eine starke spirituelle
Konnotation, es verweist auf eine Erweckung, eine Wiedergeburt. Odysseus Frau, Penelope, ist in Griechenland
auch als „die Weberin" bekannt. Um sich der zahlreichen
Freier zu erwehren, die sie während Odysseus Abwesenheit
bedrängten, gab sie als treue und kluge Ehefrau vor, ein
Leichentuch weben zu müssen. Während sie tagsüber daran
webte, trennte sie das Gewebte jedoch stets nachts wieder
heimlich auf, um von neuem beginnen zu können. Penelope
gilt daher als Sinnbild für Heimat, die ebenso immer wieder
neu erschaffen werden muss, wenn sie von Dauer sein soll.
Ob in Odysseus' Rückkehr und Errettungen oder in Penelopes
Weben, in beiden Fällen kommt eine Wertschätzung des
Langsamen, des Bedächtigen, eine Duldsamkeit gegenüber
dem Leben zum Ausdruck.

Diese Duldsamkeit findet sich auch beim Malen, denn
es handelt sich dabei um einen Schöpfungsprozess, der
sich über Jahre hinzieht und dennoch jedes Mal einen
neuen Anfang, eine Art Wiedergeburt darstellt. Der Maler
wischt dabei alles bisher Gemalte fort, er löscht alle bisher
gesehenen und verfestigten Bilder bei sich aus, stellt sich
wieder vor eine unberührte Fläche um eine Wiedergeburt zu
erleben, neue Vitalität freizusetzen.

Not that I don't like the glamorously sun-gilt sunflower fields, but that I always feel deeply torn. On the one hand I am passionate about life, about nature. On the other hand I feel helpless in the face of a brutality and brevity of life's cycles. Such passion, when fused with such a sense of helplessness, furnishes poets in the past two millennia with a tragic outlook. The poet's concerns are by extension those of his people. And the poet's tragic outlook is not confined to a singular self; rather it is commiseration with history. I paint, and I thrive in my solitude. It is perhaps comparable to an exile, a meditative practice, which, after many changes in fortune, is capable of experiencing the strifes and inconstancies of life, interspersed with melancholy. My callused hand is the result of excessive exertion while holding the brush. At the turn of spring many years ago, the callus formed almost a recess, as if shot through by a gun. Even up till now, each time I take up the brush, I feel a sting in my hand, a tinge of pain that never fails to excite me.

Second, my sunflowers come in the plural. You always see a field full of sunflowers, many stalks of them. The matrix of 800 sunflowers in the exhibition hall are cast in bronze and aluminium, chastened by fire. Its complication breeds constant change and its chaos and repetitions bring about life. Its moments of desperation exude excitement. These are the sunflowers of a collective, a generation, our generation. The most prominent feature of our generation is collectivism. We have witnessed two ruptures in value systems. We have joined the local production brigade (tu chadui) and the foreign production brigade (yang chadui) successively, and the two exiles have baptised us in fire. We then witnessed and experienced the rise of China. Individual fortunes and the destiny of our time overlap to such an extent that it gives birth to this kind of collectivity, which also defines my sunflower

Jedes Mal wieder von vorne anzufangen, sich ein ums andere Mal dieser Anspannung und Sorge auszusetzen, wirkt wie Medizin. Diese tägliche Dosis Medizin wirkt als Versprechen, das Versprechen auf Gesundung, sie ist aber auch ein Kokettieren mit der eigenen latenten Krankheit. Denn die menschliche Seele braucht dieses Kokettieren, um sich ihrer eigenen verborgenen Zustände zu vergewissern, diese aus der Dämmerung hervorzuziehen und zu erwecken. Malen ist genau dies: Die charmante Erweckung eines Versprechens.

Andererseits zeigt sich Malen aber auch häufig als ein blitzschnelles Erfassen des Moments, ein Erkennen der Dinge, die das Alltagsbewusstsein leicht übersieht. Man kann es insofern ein bisschen mit dem sprichwörtlichen Holen der Kastanien aus dem Feuer vergleichen: Genau beobachten und dann schnell zugreifen, doch nicht zu fest, um sich nicht zu verbrennen und nicht zu locker fassen, um die Chance nicht entgleiten zu lassen. Nur wenn man die Kastanien frisch und heiß genießt, entfalten sie ihr Aroma. So muss das Malen sein, nur so kann es Glanz und Aroma des Augenblickes einfangen. Der französische Philosoph Merleau-Ponty sagte einst: „Indem der Maler seinen Körper der Welt leiht, verwandelt er die Welt in Malerei." Malen bedeutet, den Gegenstand körperlich zu erleben und sich dabei einer ungewollten Herausforderung, einem unwillkürlichem Widerstand auszusetzen. Auf diese Art ist die Malerei in den universellen Schöpfungsprozess eingebunden - Malerei darf auf keinen Fall mit den Werkeinträgen in den Registern der Kunststammlungen verwechselt werden, oder mit Bildern, die entrückt an roten Museumswänden hängen. Durch eine derartige Verwaltbarkeit wird das Empfindungsvermögen der Menschen irregeleitet, die Erfahrung bleibt in der Oberfläche der Bildzeichen stecken, eine wirkliche Empfindungstiefe, die Körperliches und Seelisches verknüpft, wird verunmöglicht.

fields in an almost intractable way. The director of The Last Emperor, Bernardo Bertolucci said, 'Individuals are held hostage by history.' People are hijacked by the times in which they live, therefore in the depth of human language lingers a wordless memory. Just as a visitor to my exhibition wrote on the guestbook, 'the desolation of one or two stalks of sunflowers is desolation pure and simple. The desolation of a whole field of sunflowers is the destiny of a season, an entire generation.'

In 2009, my solo exhibition, 'The Redemption of a Sunflower Garden', was held in Shanghai Art Museum. In the following year, my other solo exhibition, 'To the Sunflower Field', was held in Zhejiang Art Museum. On both occasions, I noticed many of my peers gazing at the exhibits in tears, recounting their past to their children. The younger generations also discovered memories and experience of the time past. A youth wrote to tell me that in his hometown in the wasteland of Northwest China, there stood an endless stretch of sunflowers. At harvest time they would cut off the sunflower heads, leaving rows of stalks standing in the chilling winds, just like headless soldiers keeping watch on the hilltop. That would be the desolation of the earth after the harvest.

Of course, my sunflowers do not stop at historical memories of the past or reprises of hackneyed topics. In my sunflower fields, I have never stopped reflecting on how I could best deploy the embodied intelligence of painting towards the construction of a whole world. Such a world is not merely a landscape, but a commitment to humanist, spiritual values and their reconstruction. It is entwined with the formation of life undergoing measured evolution, with the birth of intuition of the here and now, with the heady mix of oblivion and existence, heart and eye, and with the sensitivity that relies on

Auf diese Weise verkümmern Bilder zu Schätzobjekten eines kühl taxierenden Blickes. Denn es sind unser Sprechen und der historische Gehalt eines Werkes, die ihm erst Lebenswärme verleihen. In einem Bild werden verstreute Gedanken gesammelt, unheimliche Begegnungen festgehalten. Die damit verbundene Imagination, die Empfindung von Schutzlosigkeit und Selbstvergessenheit inmitten tausenderlei ineinander verwobener Gefühle entzündet die künstlerische Leidenschaft und weckt ungeahnte transformative Kräfte. Diese Kräfte sind es, die dem Leben im Moment der Entfremdung höhere Qualität verleihen.

Malen ist eine behutsame Erfahrung des Werdens und gleichzeitig ein unmittelbarer Schaffensprozess. Sich dieser Empfindung wieder und wieder mit Haut und Haar aussetzen und die Eingebung aus diesen Momenten beziehen – das ist das Geheimnis der Malerei und das Schicksal des Malers. Aufgrund dieses stillen und gleichzeitig in einem Augenblick verdichteten Prozesses der körperlichen Erfahrung und unmittelbaren Gestaltung gleicht das Malen einem Floß, das gefährliche Stromschnellen überwindet, manches Mal zu kentern droht und doch den Maler fortträgt, in die Ferne, in sein eigenes Reich.

Vor kurzem wurde mein Sonnenblumenfeld in der Dresdner Staatlichen Kunstsammlung gezeigt. Ein Besucher bemerkte, die Sonnenblumen wirkten wie ein loderndes Flammenmeer. Und tatsächlich, Sonnenblumen erinnern mich an ein ständig brennendes Feuer - einerseits vernichtend, andererseits eine Quelle der Wiedergeburt. Die unauflösliche Verflochtenheit von Werden und Vergehen - in der Sonnenblume findet sie ihren erhebendsten poetischen Ausdruck

painting in its reconstruction of our time.

In the *Odyssey*, Odysseus, the inventor of the 'Trojan Horse' cannot return to his homeland. He almost gets lost on his return journey. As he returns to Ithaca after ten years, another ten years await him before he can really 'come home'. Between homecoming and homeland, there exist countless arrivals and departures as well as countless losses and redemptions. The word 'redemption' points to the soul. To describe saving someone from the fire we cannot use 'redemption', which implies reawakening and rebirth. Hence saving people from tribulation that is not spiritual in nature cannot be termed 'redemption'. Yet what is Penelope, the faithful wife of Odysseus, doing all these years? The name Penelope in Ancient Greek could mean 'weft'. And faced with many suitors with rather shady intentions, the faithful and wise wife designed the chicanery of 'weaving a burial shroud'. For three years she would weave during the day and undo part of the shroud at night. Penelope represents the local and the homely and the process of ceaseless dismantling and reconstruction. Odysseus's returns and redemptions as well as Penelope's constant undoing and weaving are all slow life-processes.

Painting is also one such slow life-process, of enduring construction (langjähriger Aufbau). In the meantime, each moment of painting is a kind of rebirth and regeneration, new Being-toward-death *(Sein zum Tode)*. The painter constantly erases what is already on the canvas and kills off the fore-thoughts and idées fixes in order to go through regeneration, a blossoming of new signs of life.

Such repeated beginnings bring the self into a constant tension, which is like a kind of pharmakon. The daily dose of pharmakon creates an expectation for health and recu-peration, as well as a titillation about the potential state of illness. Man's mind needs to face all sorts of titillation in order to stimulate the latencies and emancipate the self from an unenlightened state of mediocrity. Painting offers this kind of stimuli with overlapping expectations and titillations.

Approaches to painting often captures in the fastest way possible what has been neglected in ordinary states of things in order to grasp and comprehend them. It is not unlike snatching chestnuts from the fire. The roasting chestnuts make tempting noises over the flame. To snatch them from the fire one has to aim well, act quickly and hold firm. The piping-hot chestnut still burns in one's palm. One cannot hold too tight or throw it away. It has to be enjoyed in a whole piece while still warm. It tastes like fire, as all the flavours are encapsulated in this hotness. Painting is also like snatching chestnuts from the fire, as the painter has to make sure it radiates light and fragrance.

Maurice Merleau-Ponty said, 'once you lend your body to the world, the world is thus revealed.' Painting is imbued with the physicality of 'experiencing it with the body', a measured formation of life. Therefore painting remains a loop in the cycle of life's formation, rather than a kind of art documentation, or the patterns on the red-brick walls of the museums. It is precisely this ascription to patterns that has misled human sensitivity and restricted the painting experience to the surface of images and symbols, so that it becomes impossible to experience body-transplantation and synaesthesia. Such viewing of patterns has reduced seeing a painting to cold inspections. In fact, all language and their historical configuration of the subject carry the warmth of life. Painting records the traces of reflections on

life and certain unheimlich encounters. Such feelings, which have transcended imagination and lost its shelter and known nothing of their own location yet are entwined with many other feelings, fire up the passion of artistic creativity and contain certain unexpected transformational power. This transformational power would elevate life at the very moment of life's alienation.

Painting is a slow and measured life experience as well as an intuitive formation. It is precisely this slow and measured experience and intuitive formation, this repetitive insertion of self and the intuitive 'sudden transpiration' (plötzlich auf einmal durchgeschaut) that holds the secret and destiny of painting. It is precisely here, in this measured and instantaneous process of bodily experience and intuitive formation that painting sails through the treacherous waters like a raft to the faraway place that the painter can claim as his / her own.

As my works were exhibited in Dresden, someone said the sunflower fields were like flowing flames. Indeed, sunflowers always remind me of some enduring process of burning, which one the one hand is not unlike a ritual, and on the other hand the regeneration of life. If we collapse the ritual with the regeneration, we have a sacrament that reconstructs the poetics of life and death, overlapped and entwined.

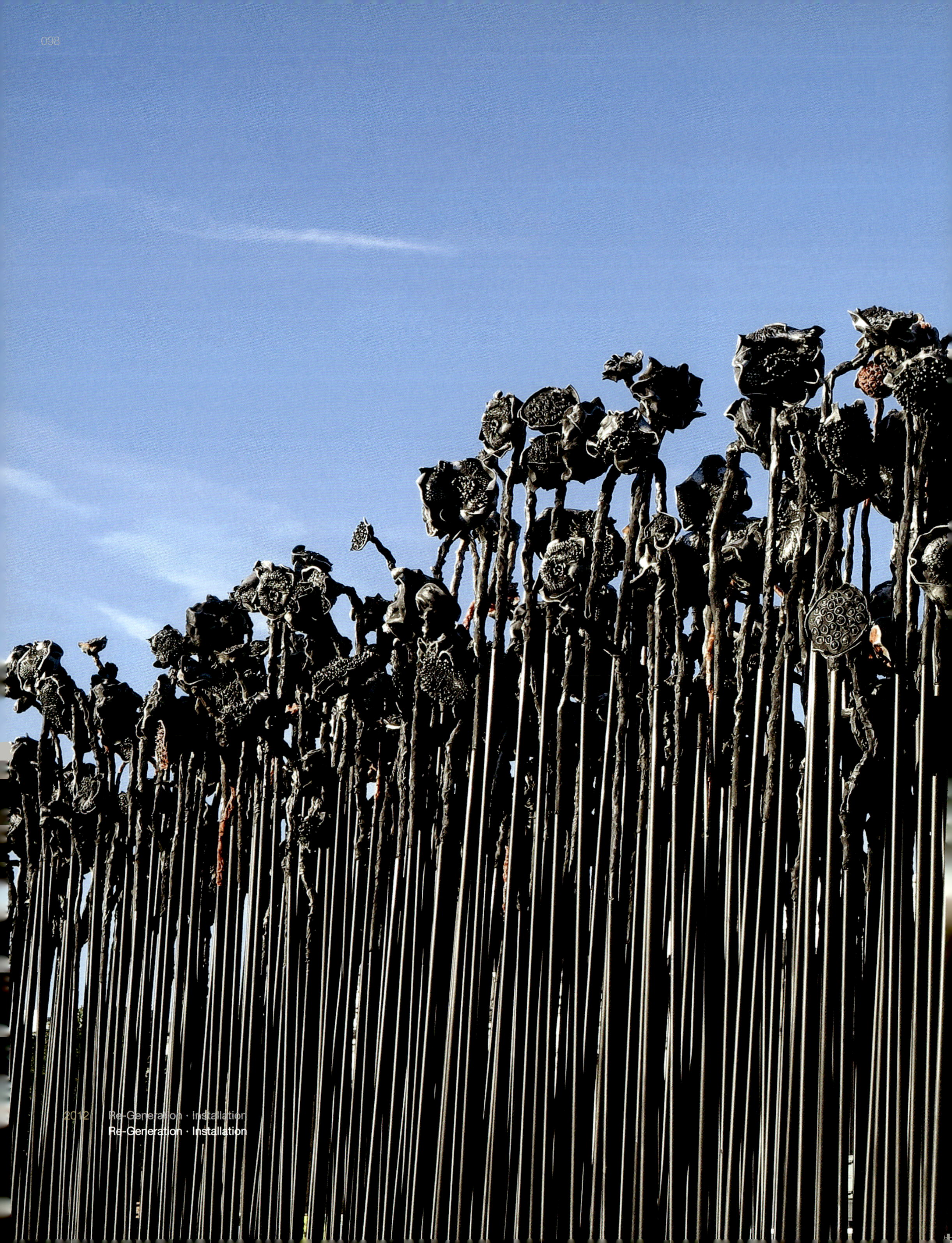

2012 · Re-Generation · Installation
Re-Generation · Installation

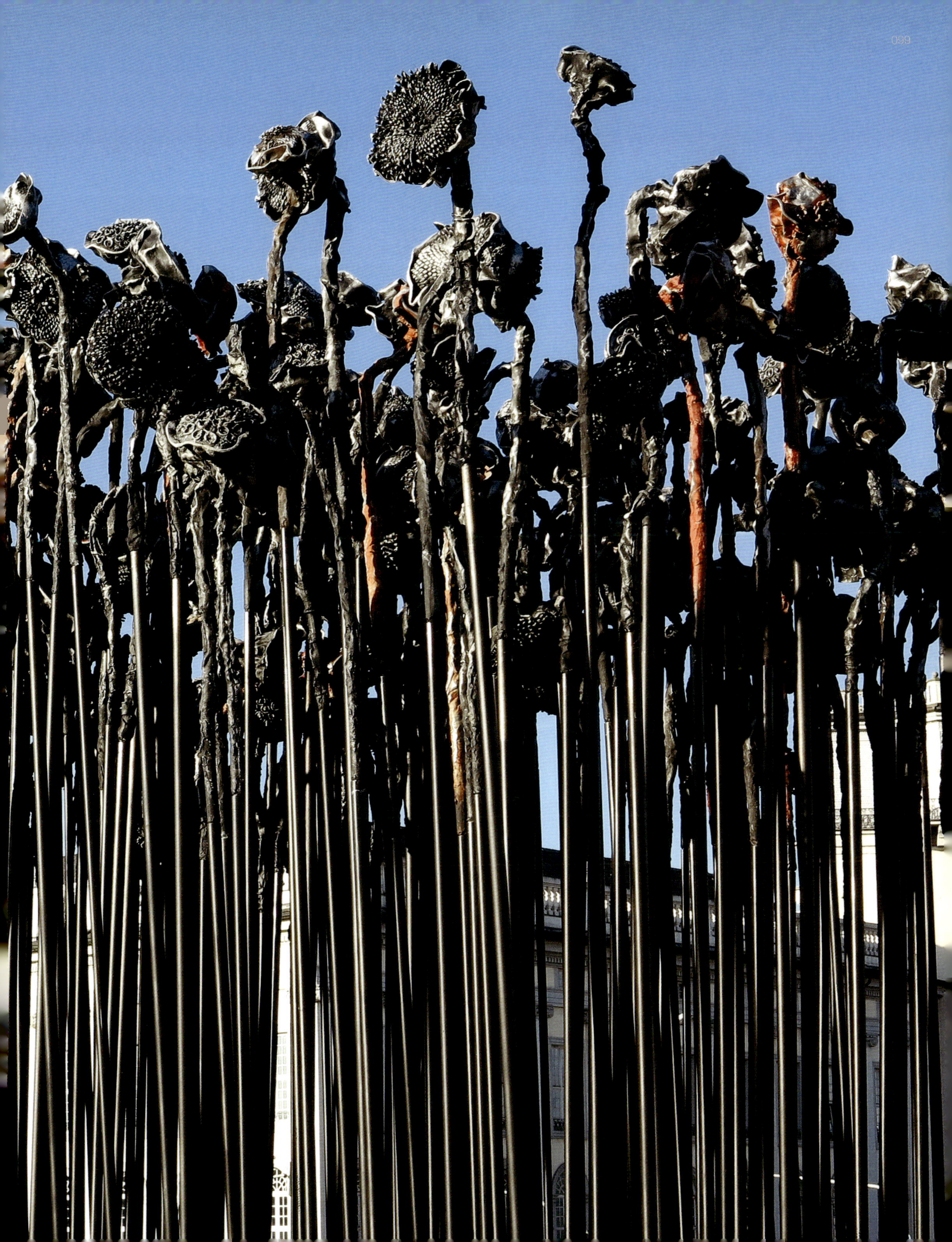

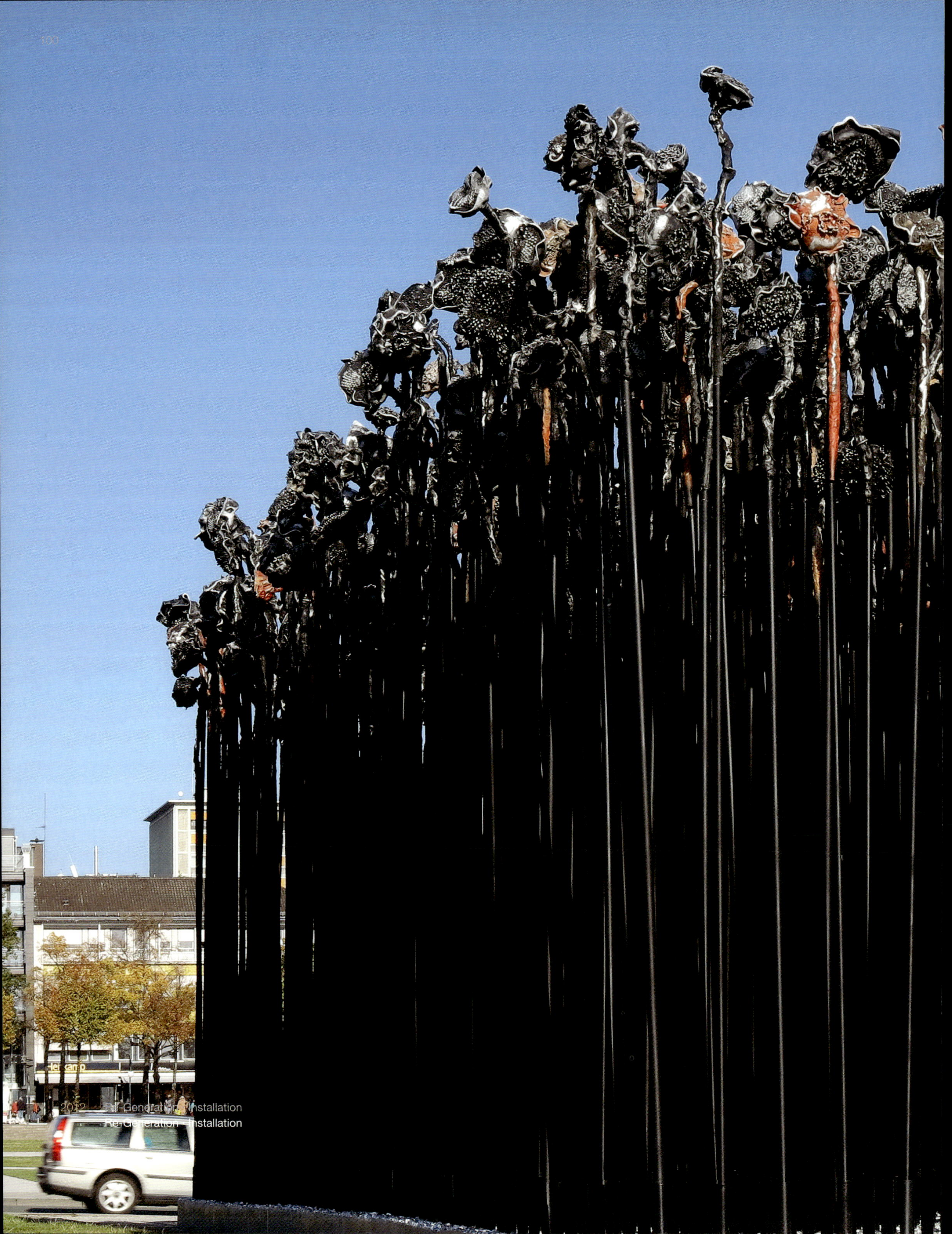

2012   1st Generation Installation
Re-Generation Installation

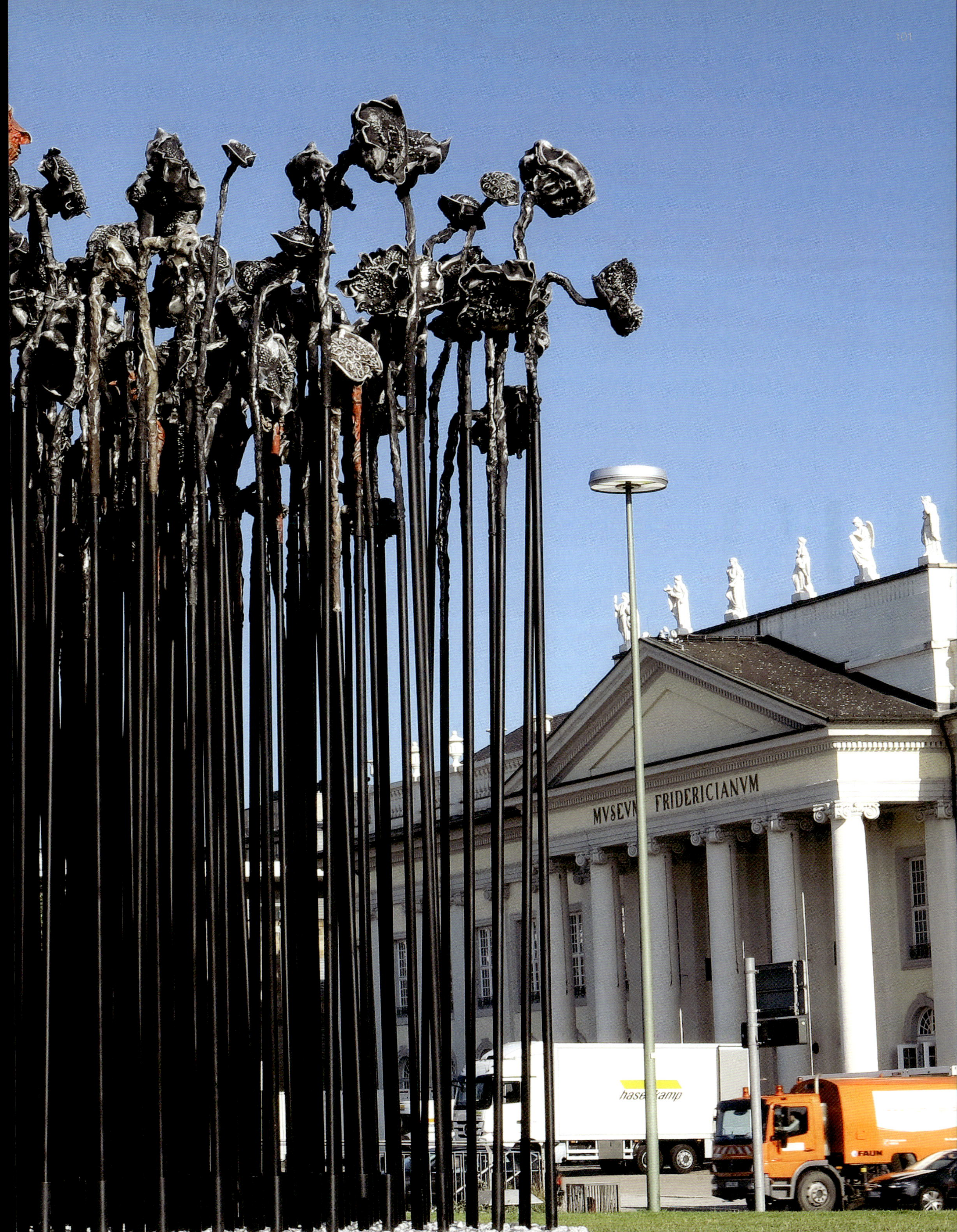
MVSEVM FRIDERICIANVM

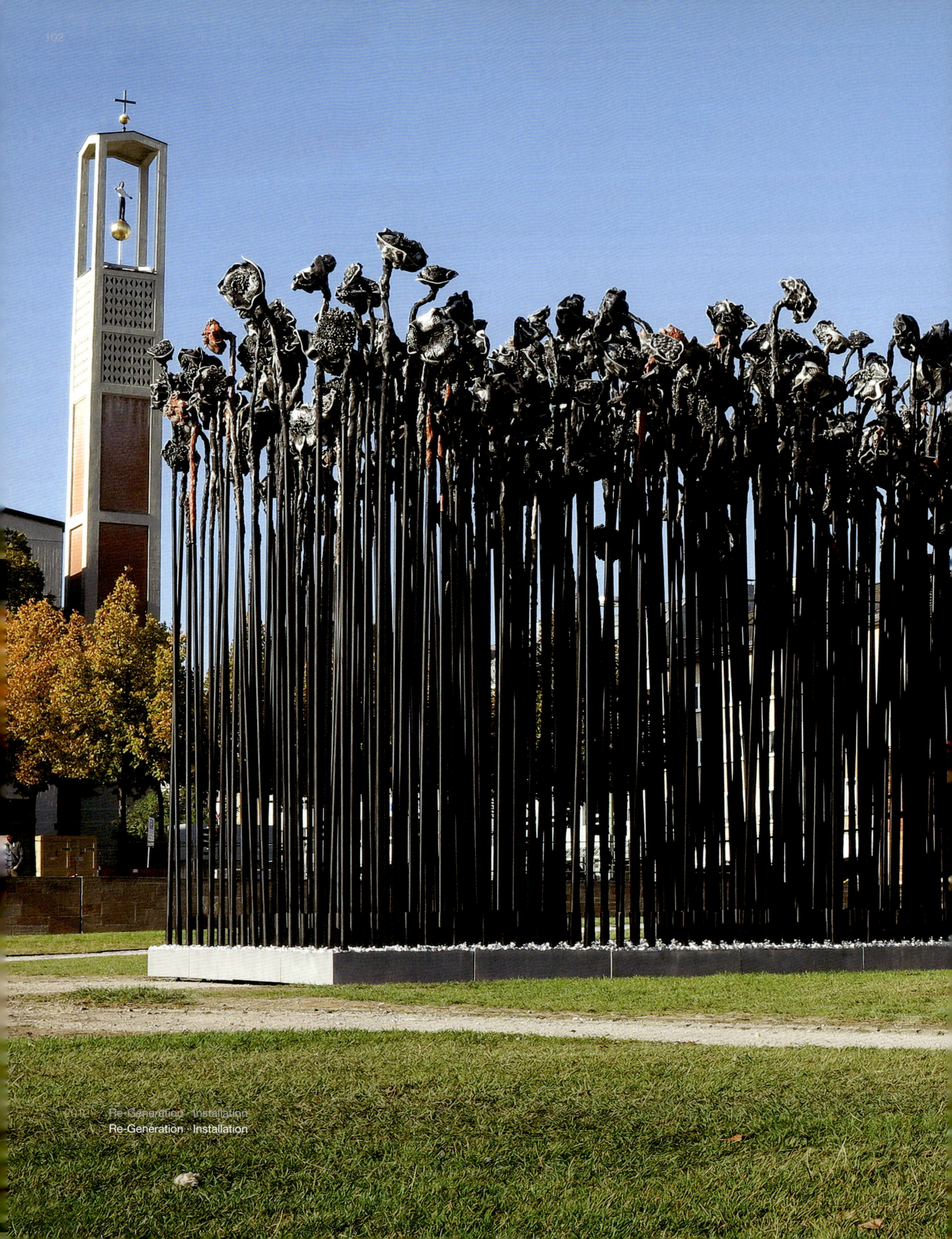

Re-Generation · Installation
Re-Generation · Installation

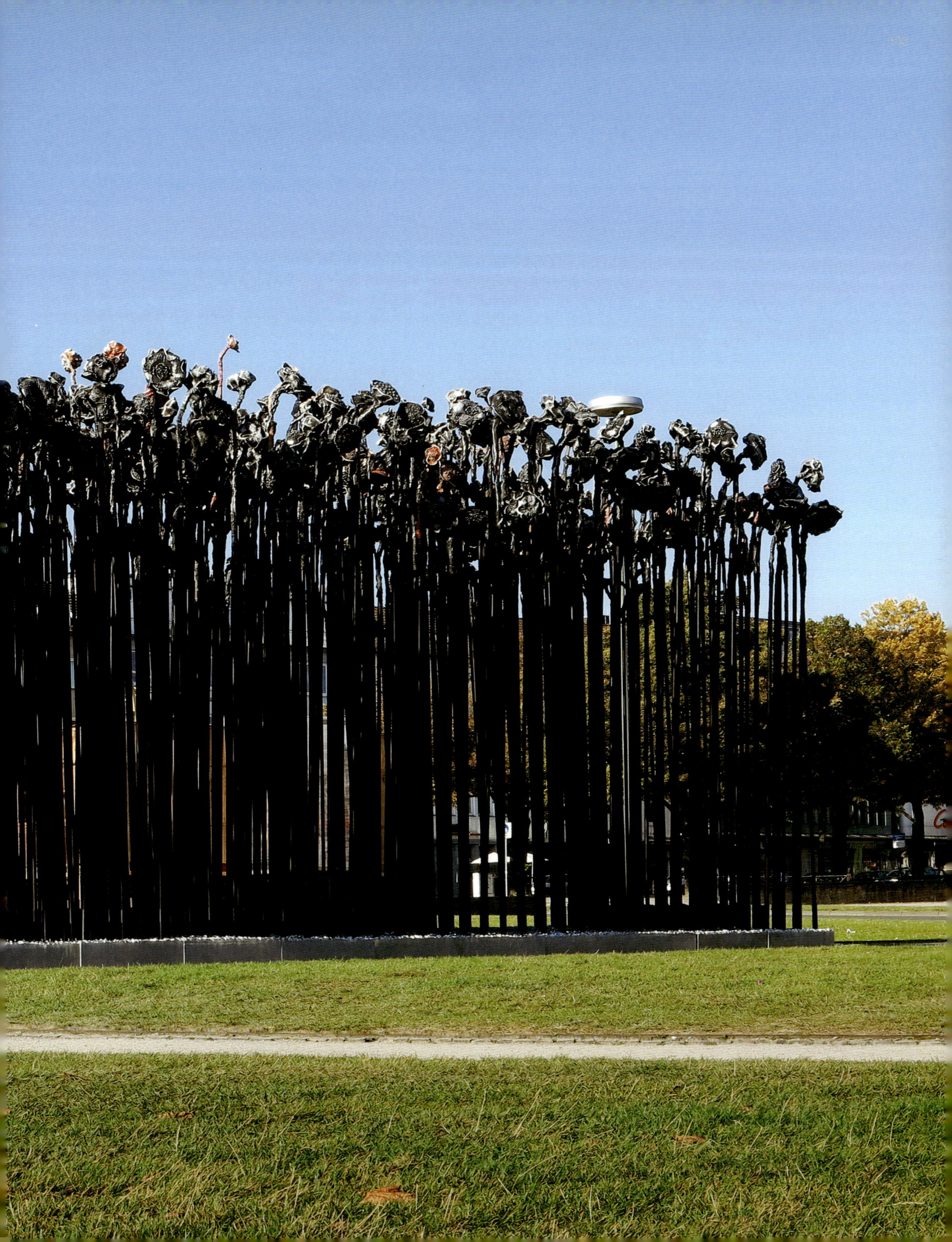

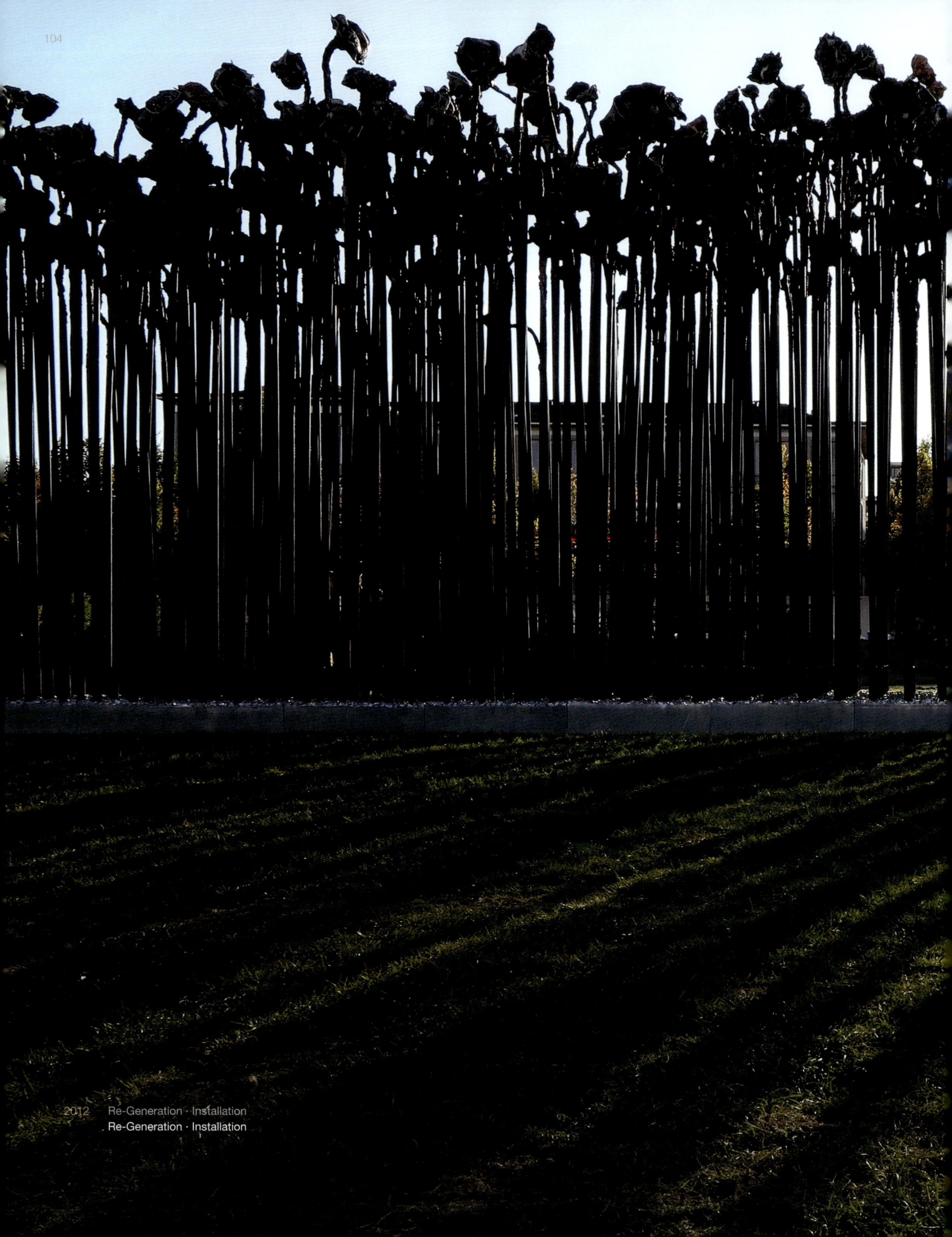

2012   Re-Generation · Installation
Re-Generation · Installation

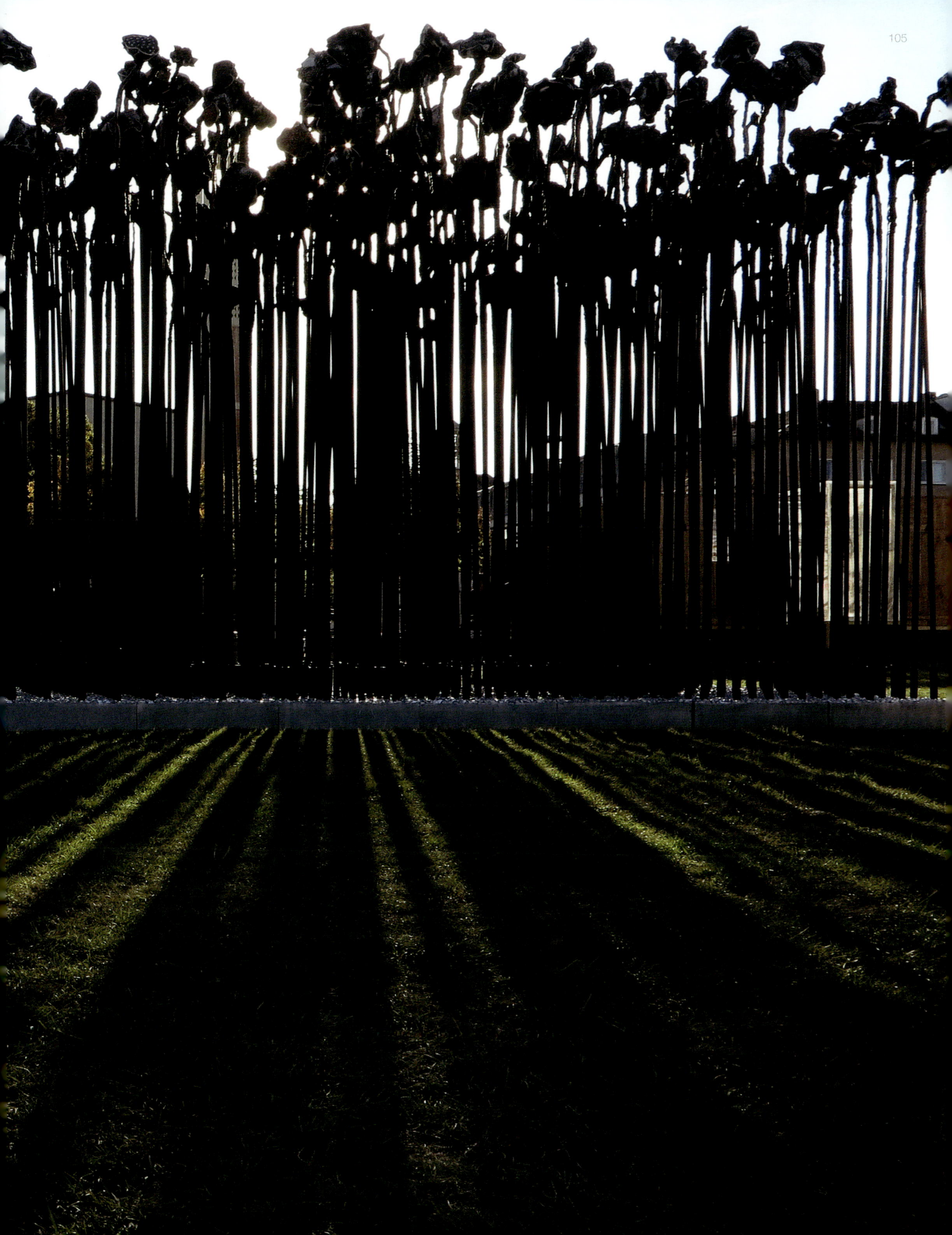

2012 Sunflower Lamp · Installation
Leuchtende Sonnenblumen · Installation

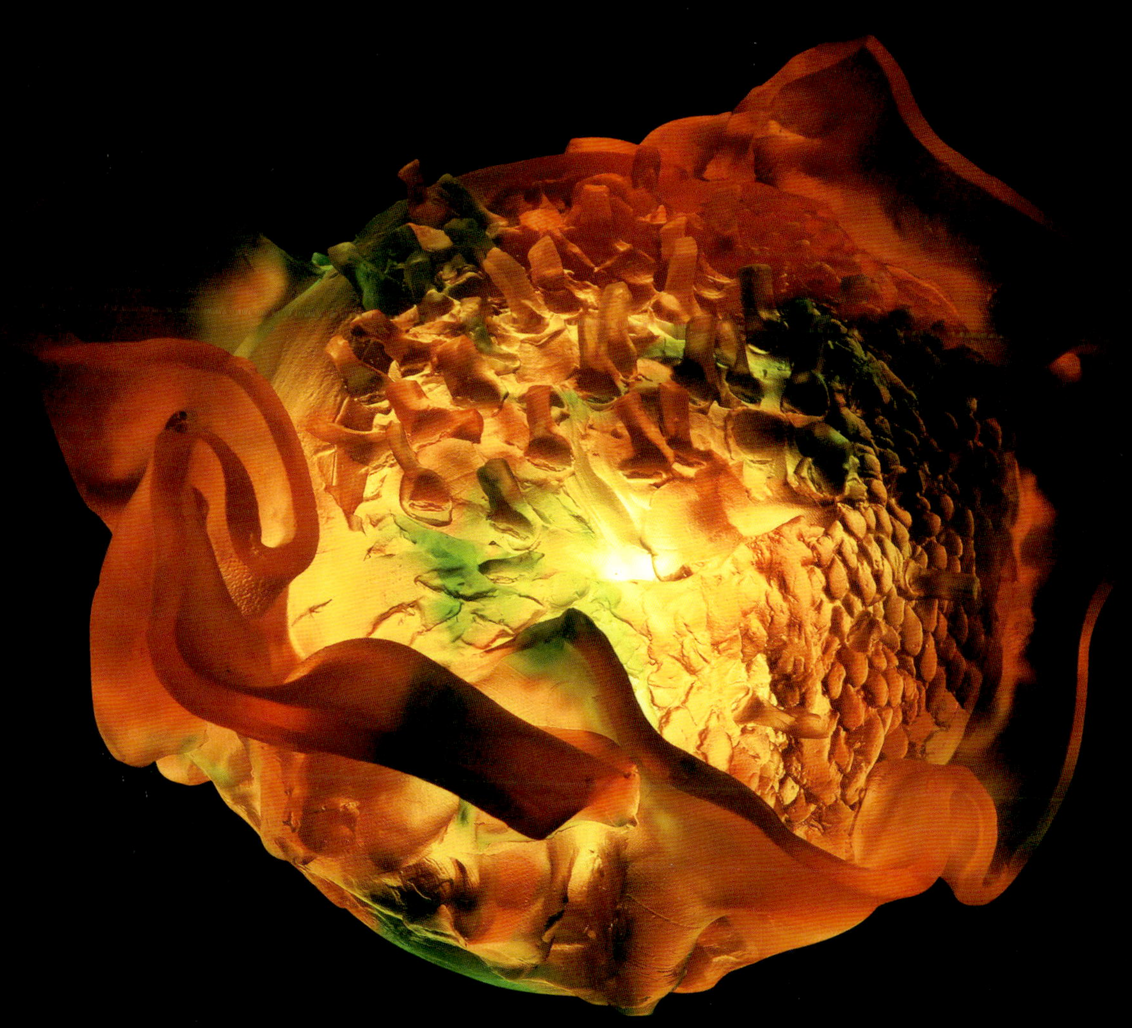

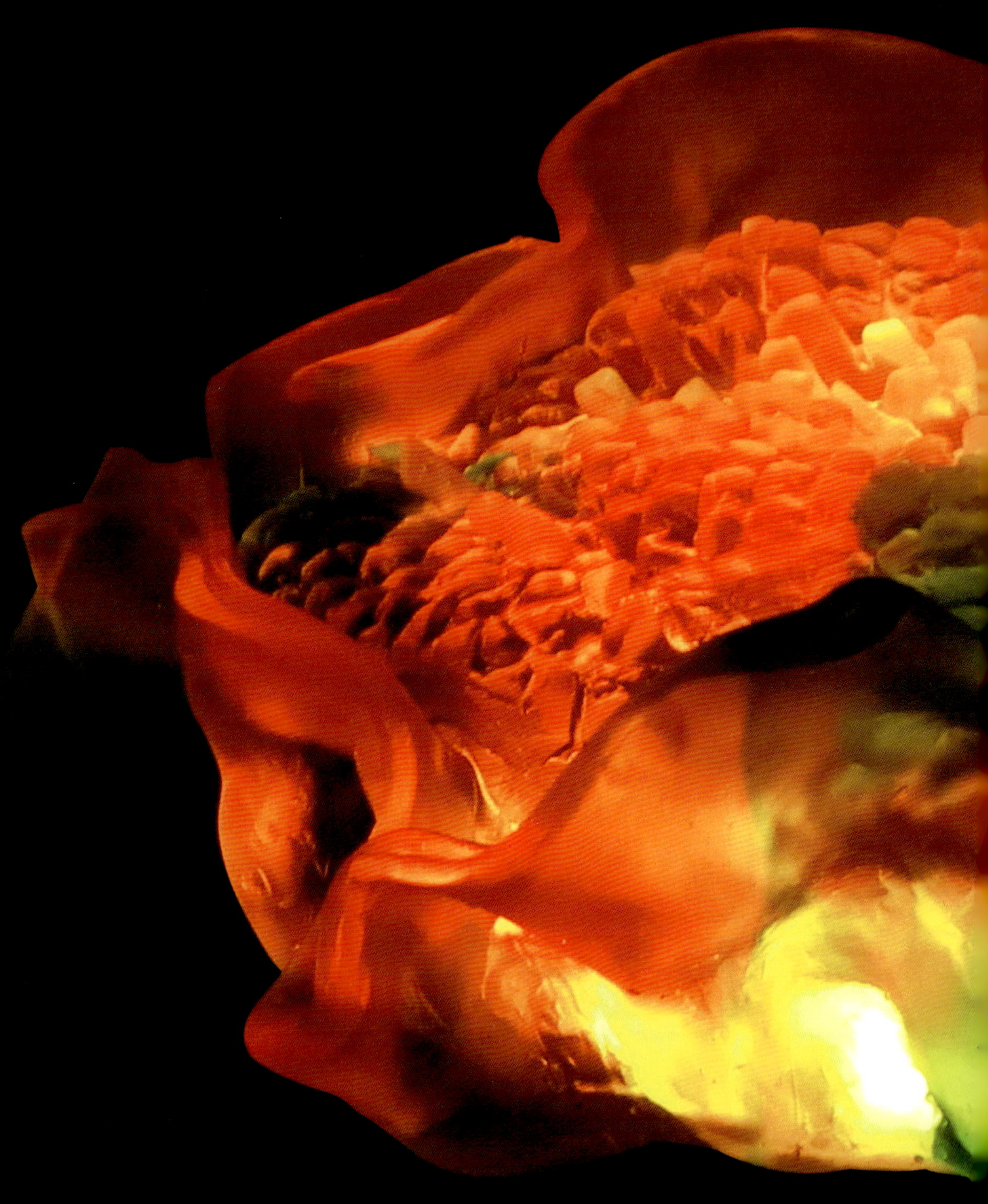

2012   Sunflower Lamp · Installation
Leuchtende Sonnenblumen · Installation

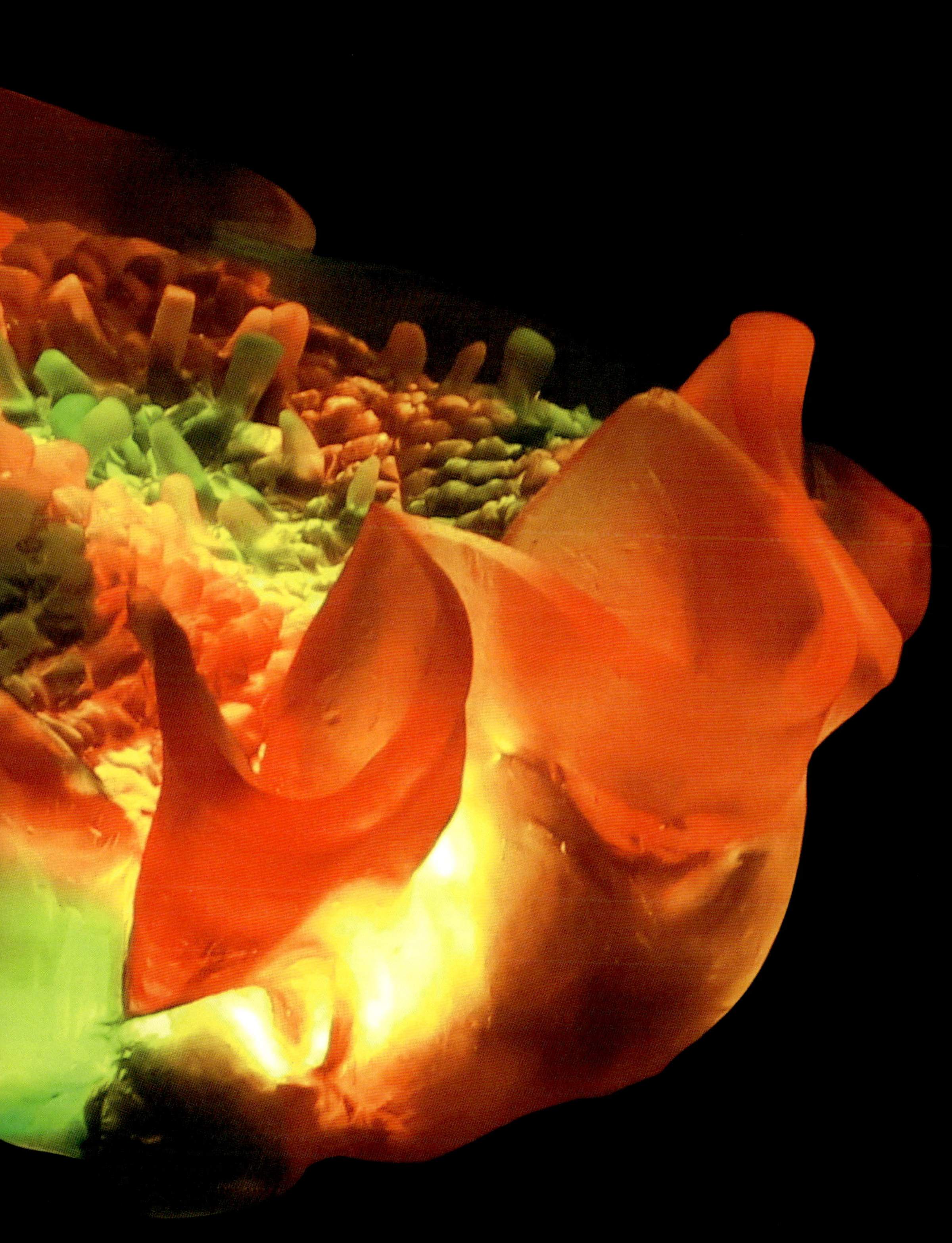

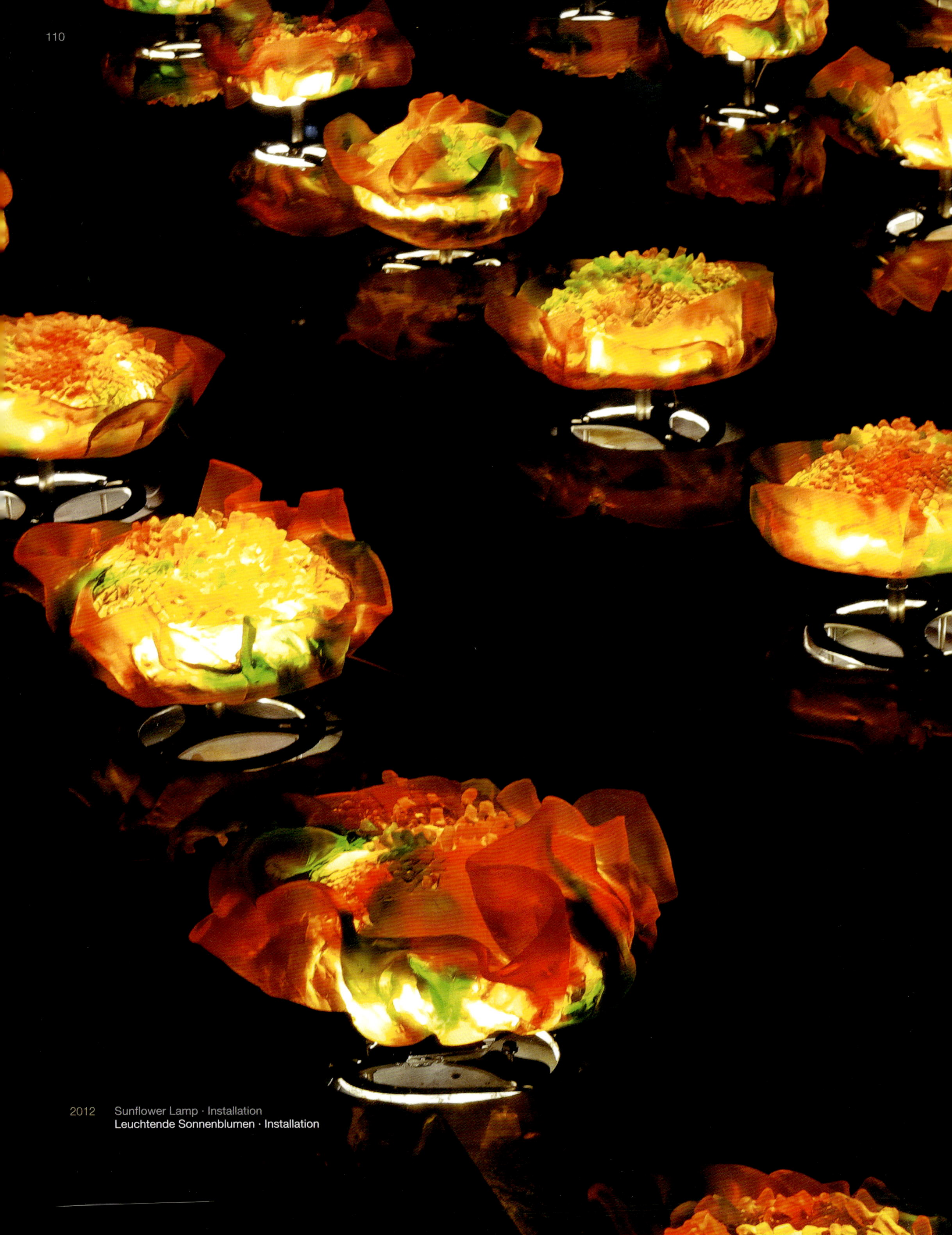

2012 Sunflower Lamp · Installation
Leuchtende Sonnenblumen · Installation

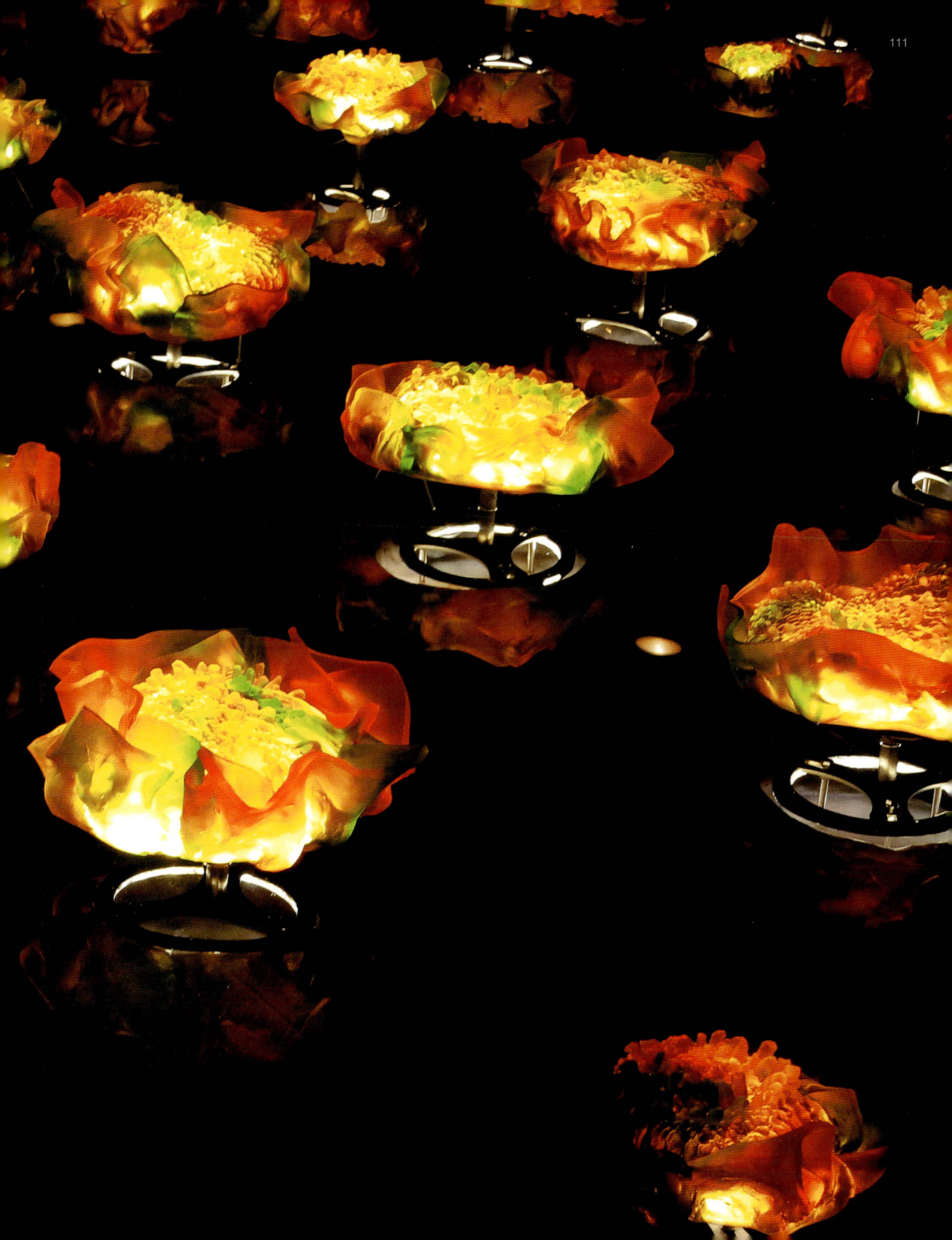

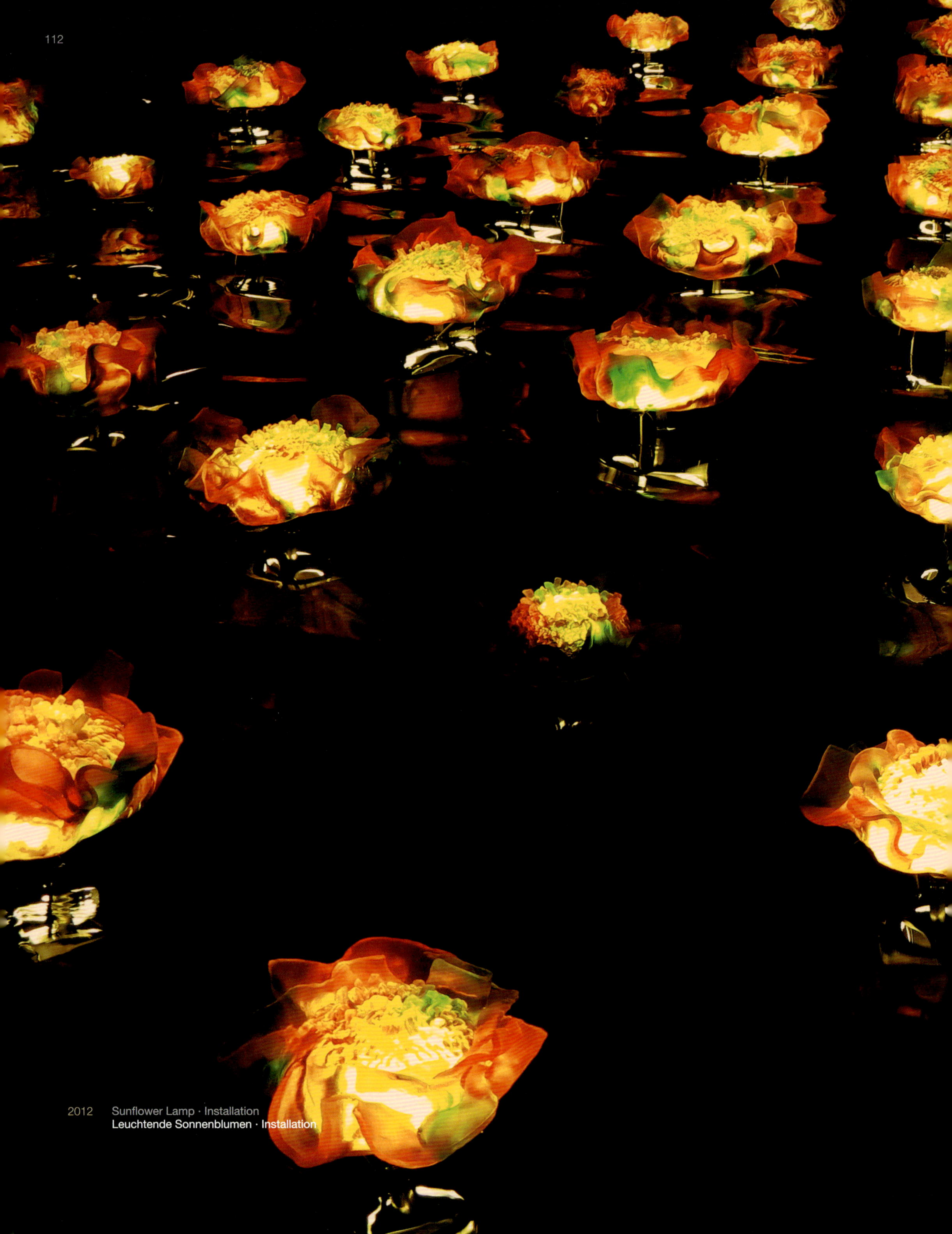

2012   Sunflower Lamp · Installation
Leuchtende Sonnenblumen · Installation

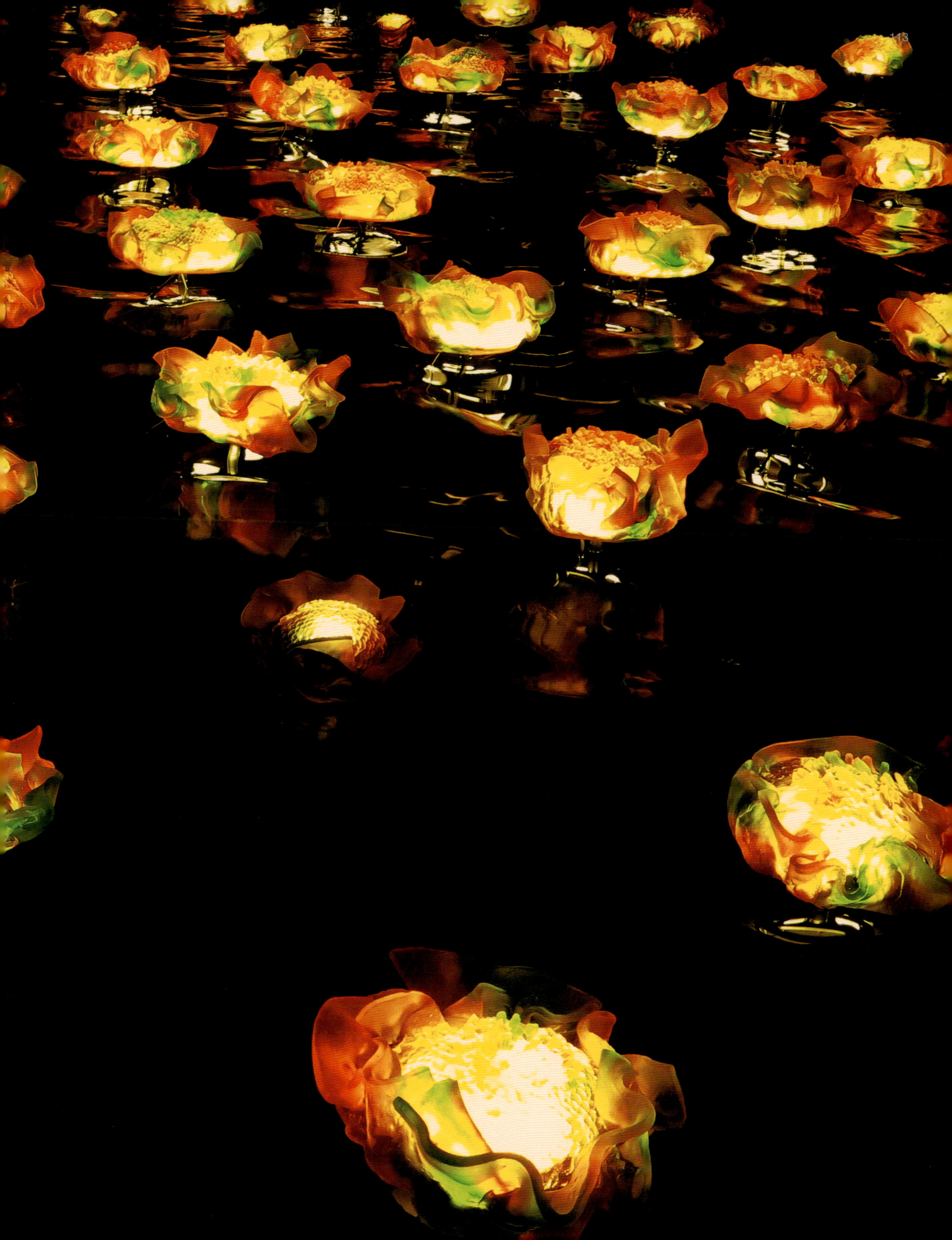

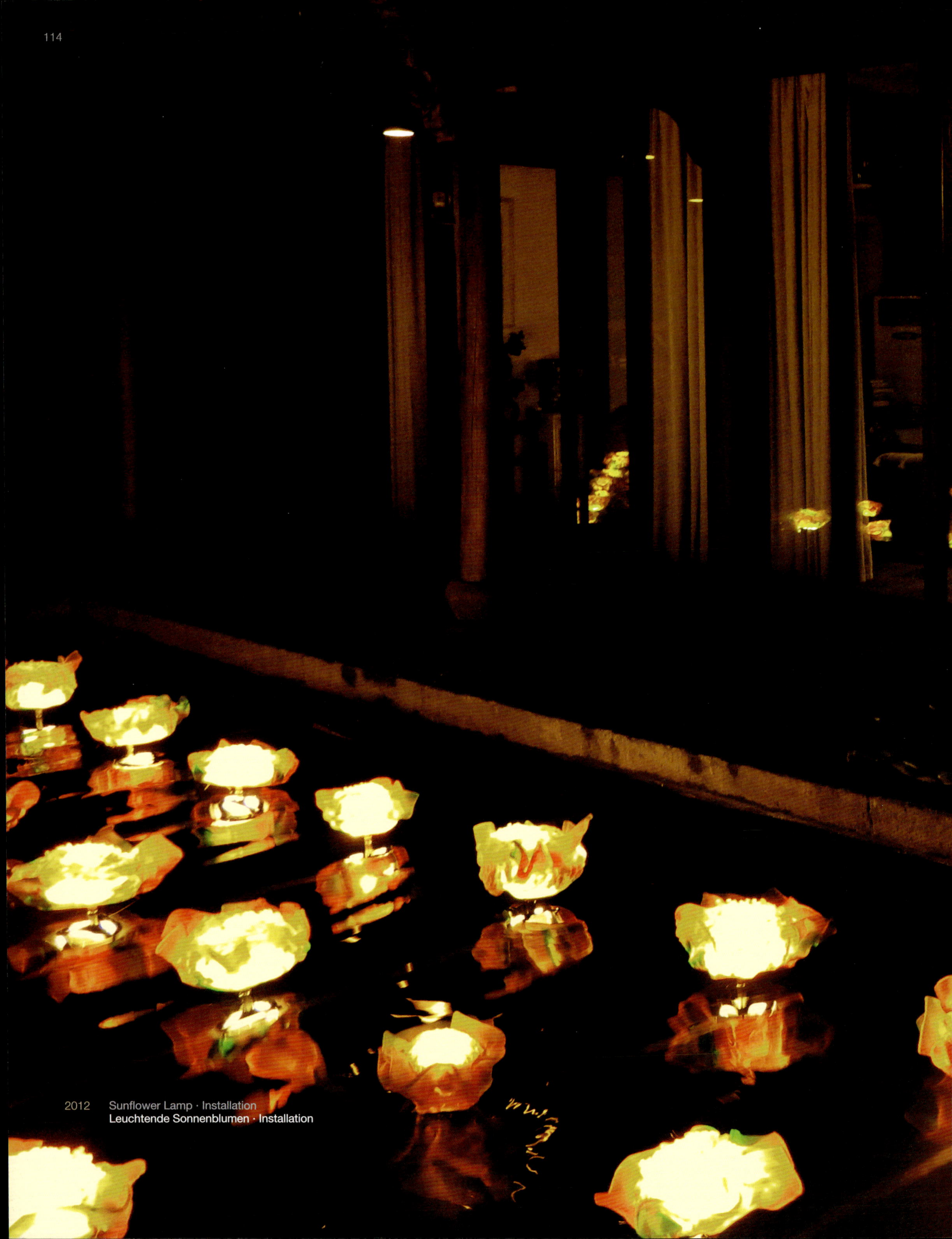

2012   Sunflower Lamp · Installation
Leuchtende Sonnenblumen · Installation

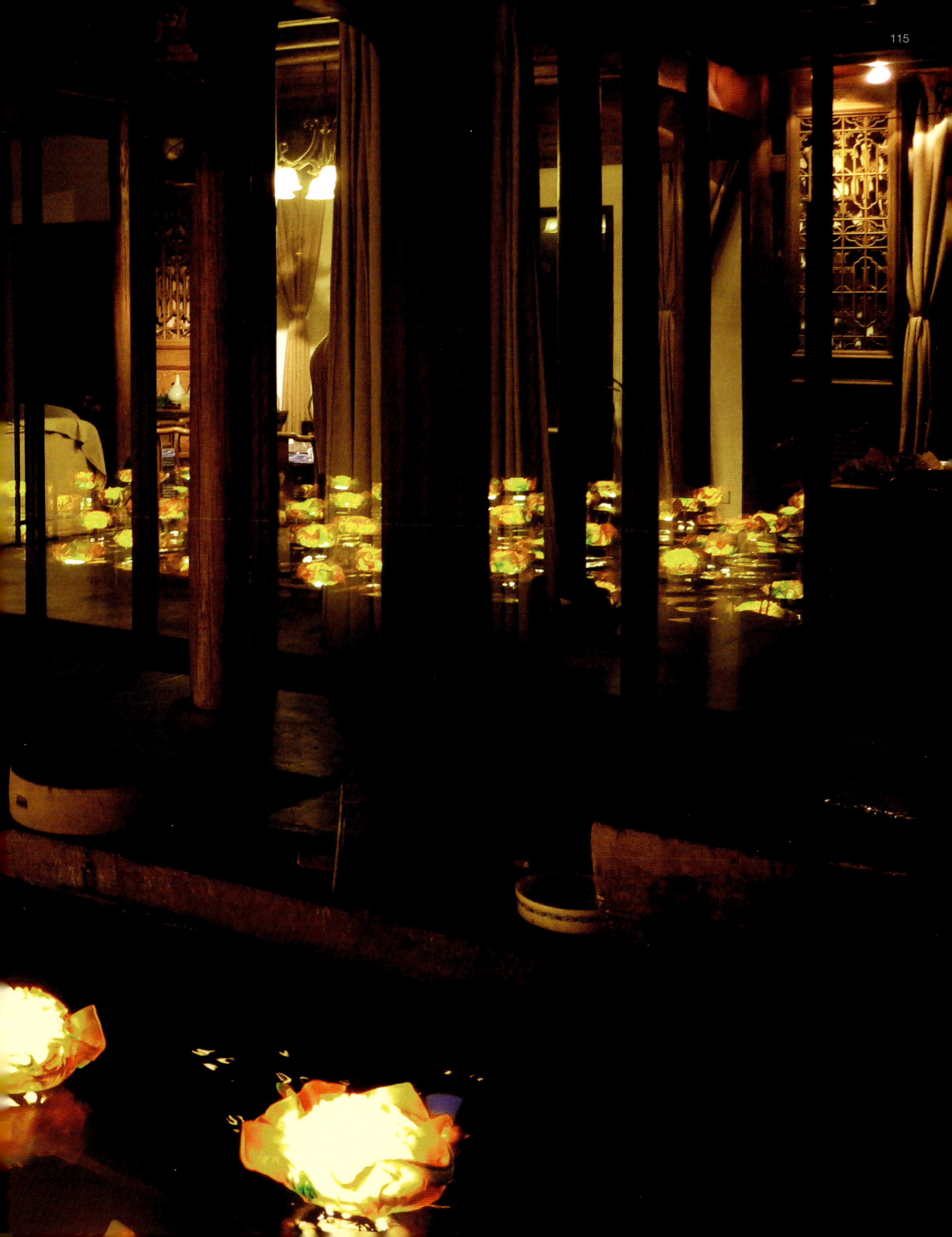

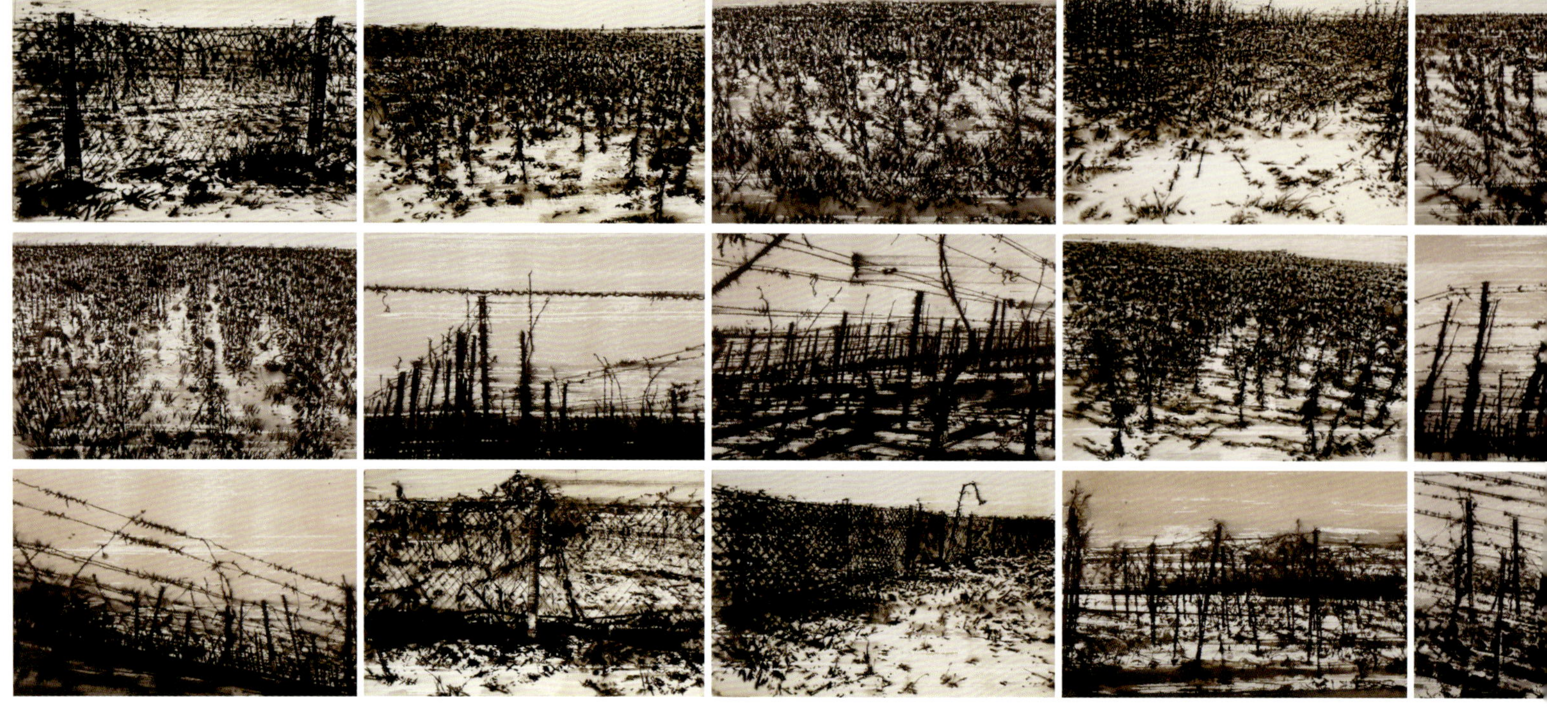

2005　Depths of Winter · Water Colour · 58cm×78cm×27
Die Tiefen des Winters · Aquarell · 58cm×78cm×27

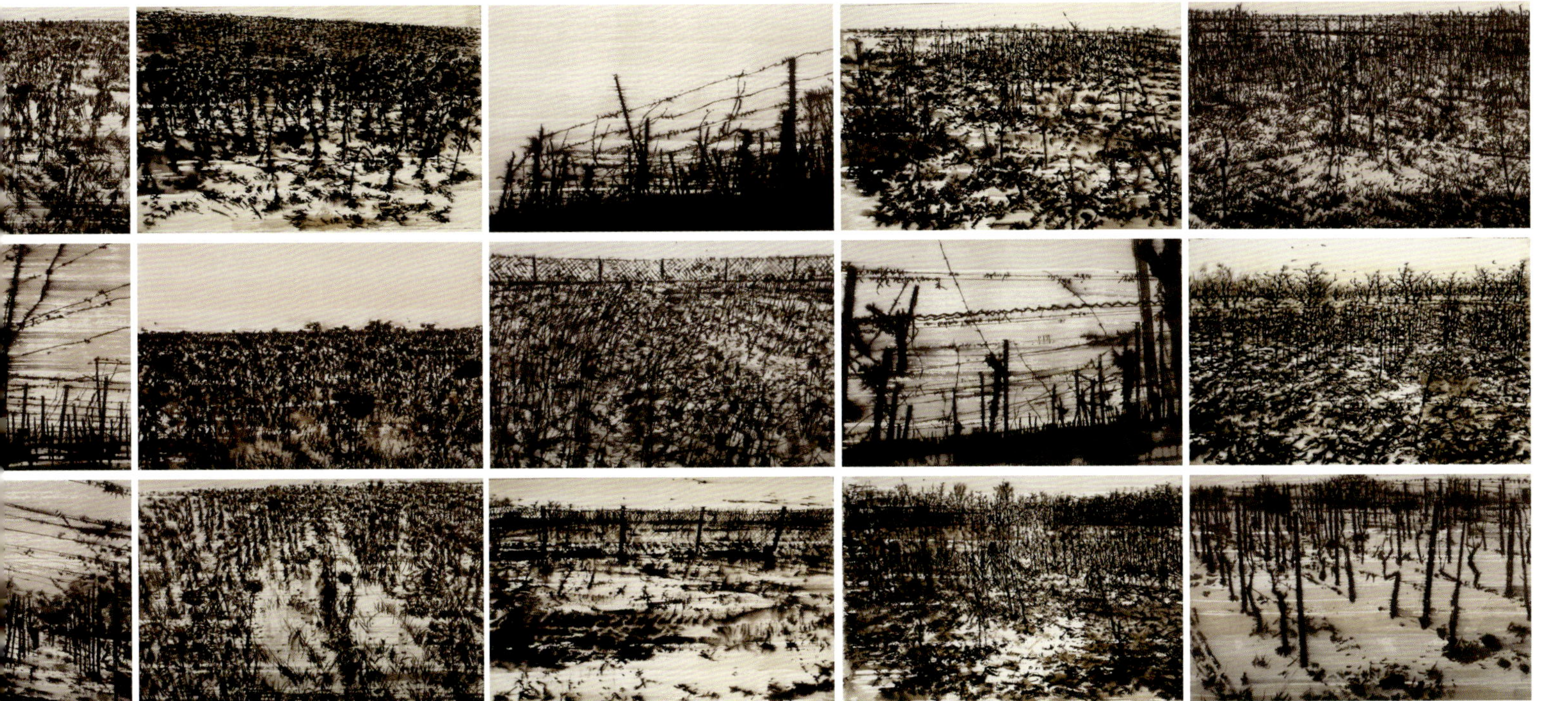

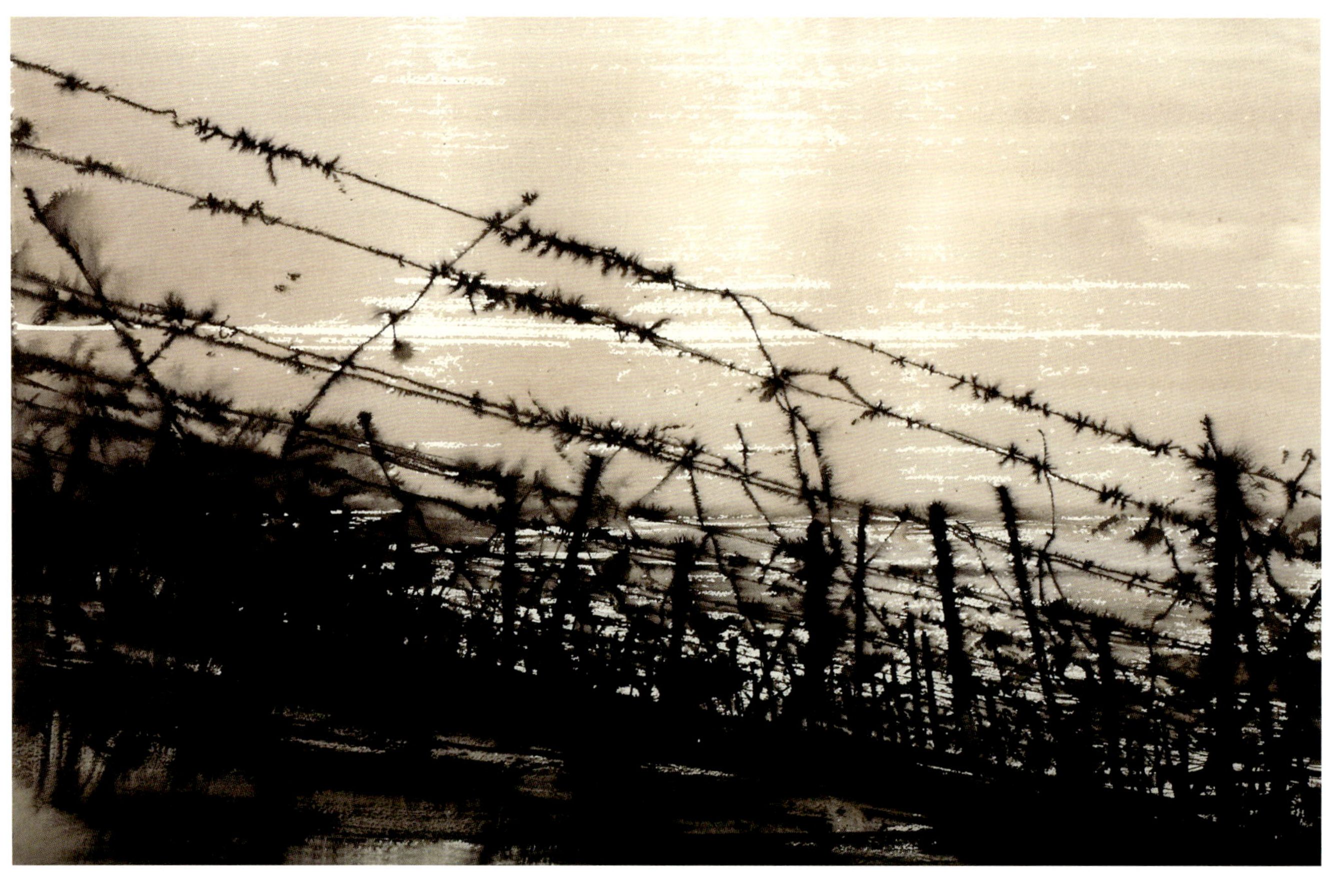

2005 Depths of Winter · Water Colour · 58cm×78cm×27
Die Tiefen des Winters · Aquarell · 58cm×78cm×27

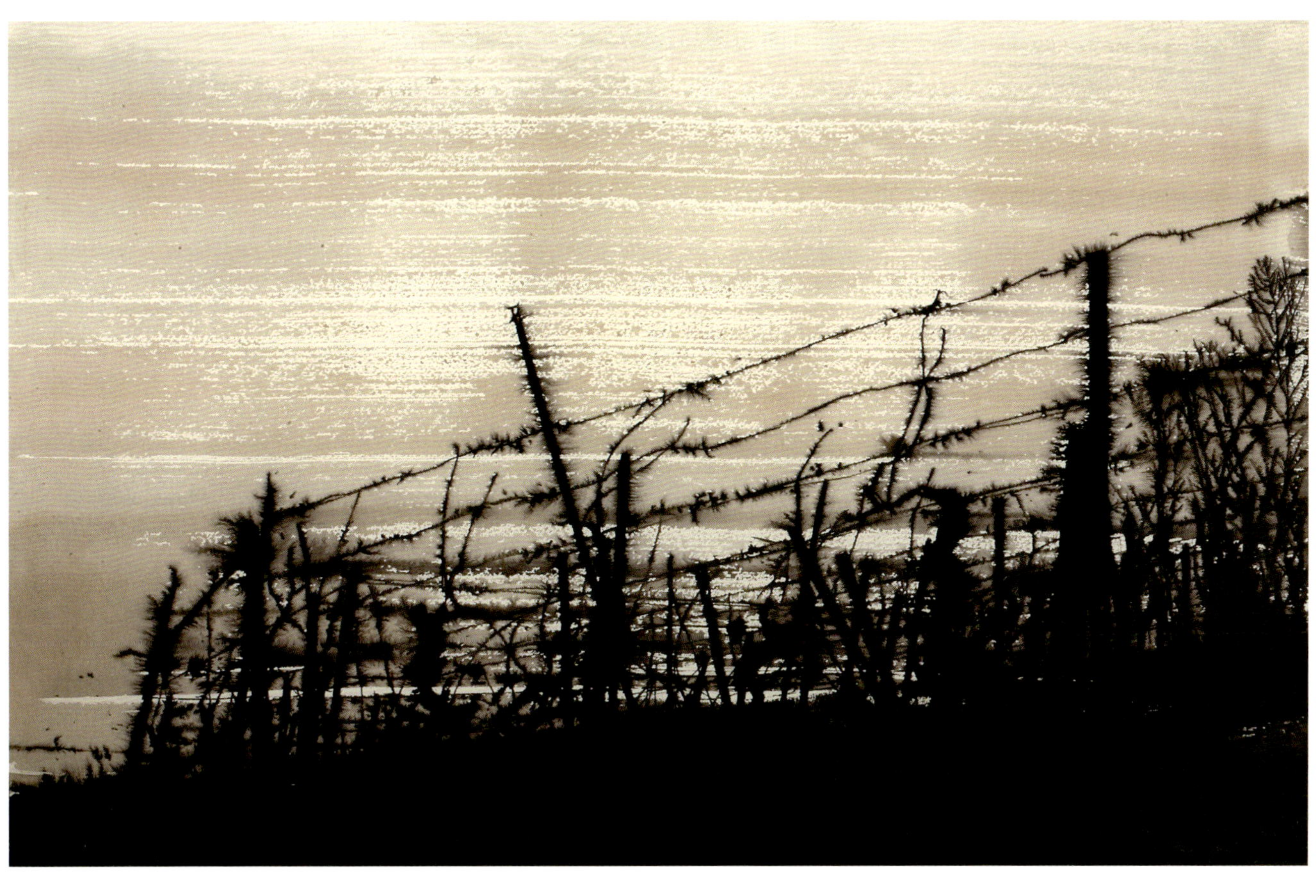

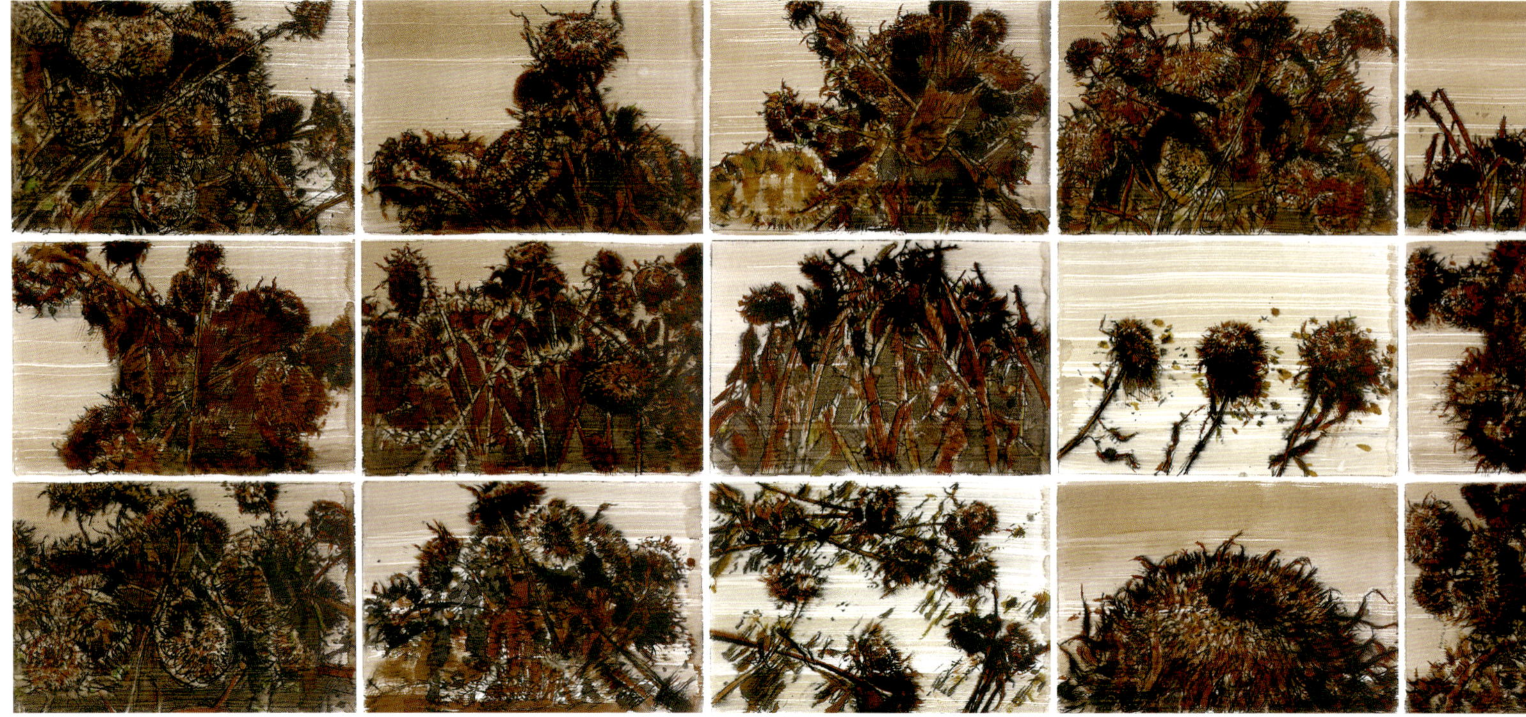

2008　Plant Sunflowers with a Painting Brush · Water Colour · 45cm×60cm×27
Mit einem Pinsel Sonnenblumen pflanzen · Aquarell · 45cm×60cm×27

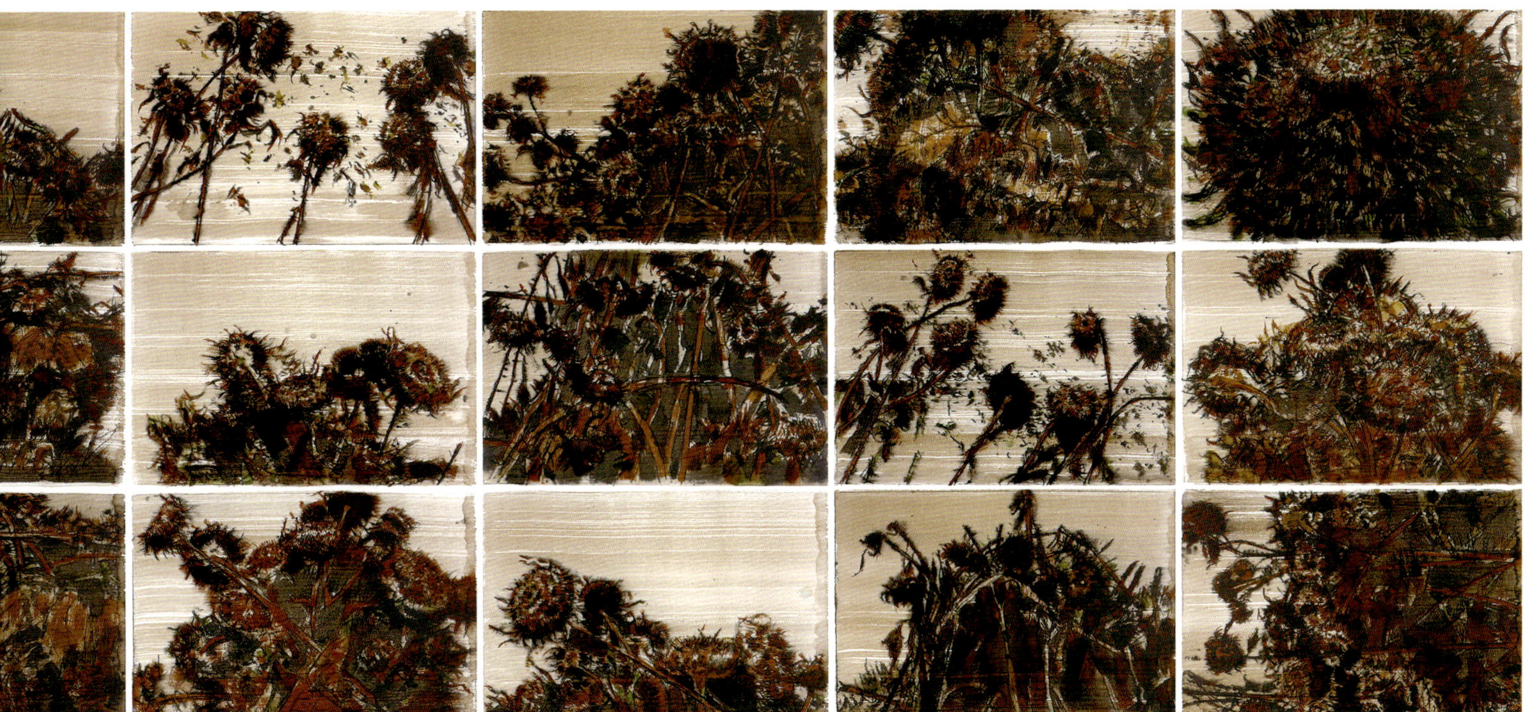

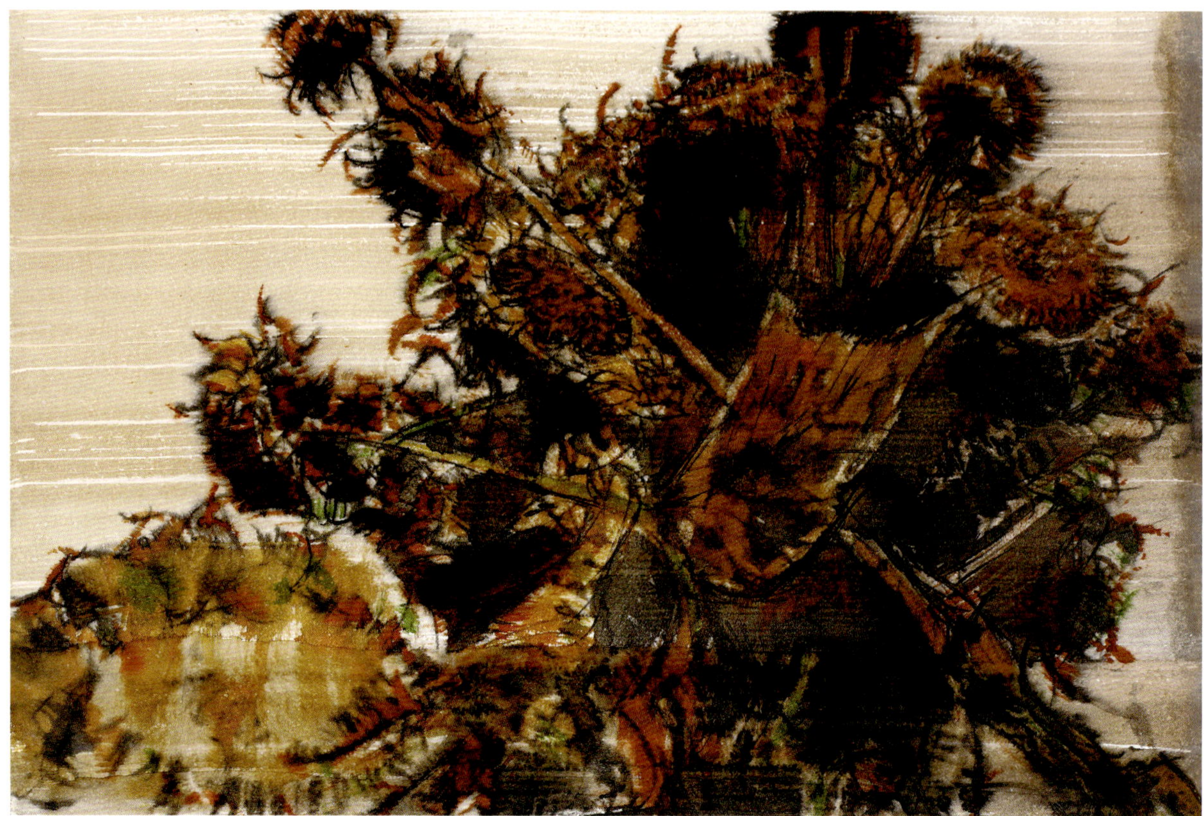

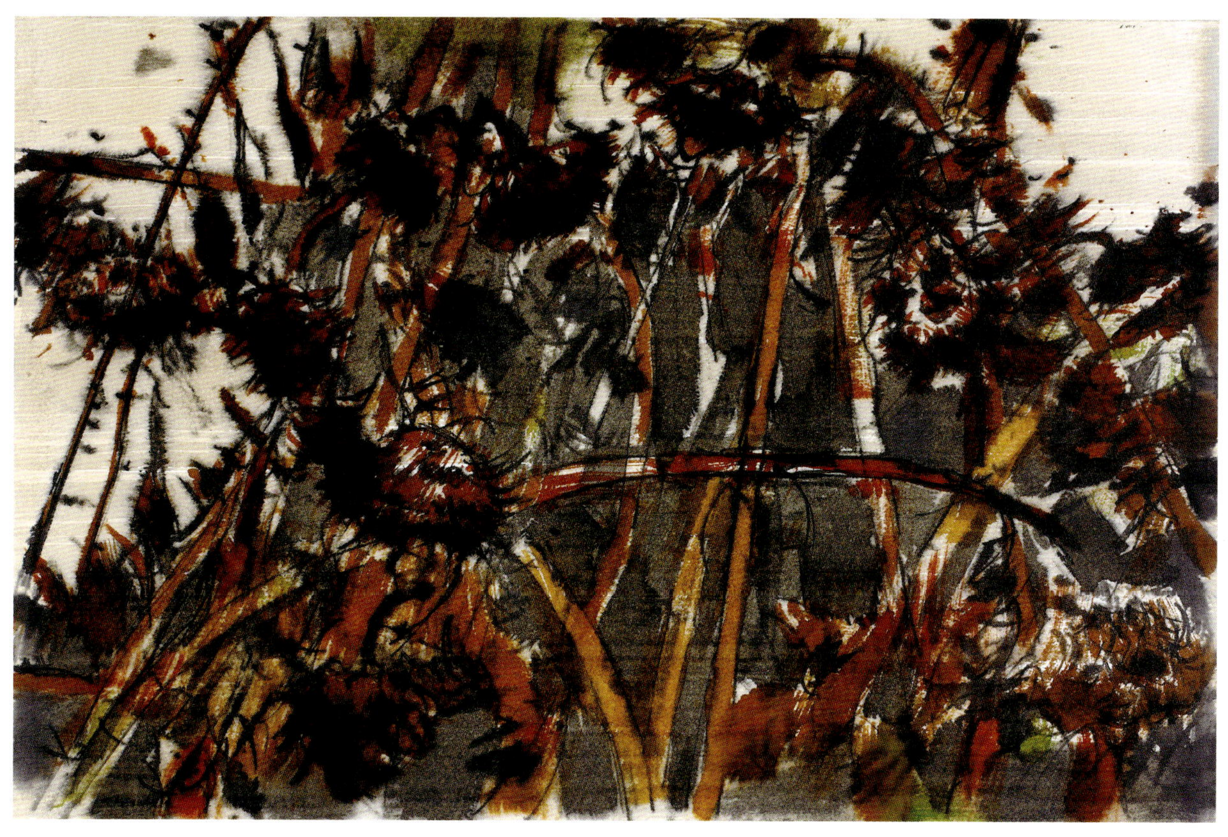

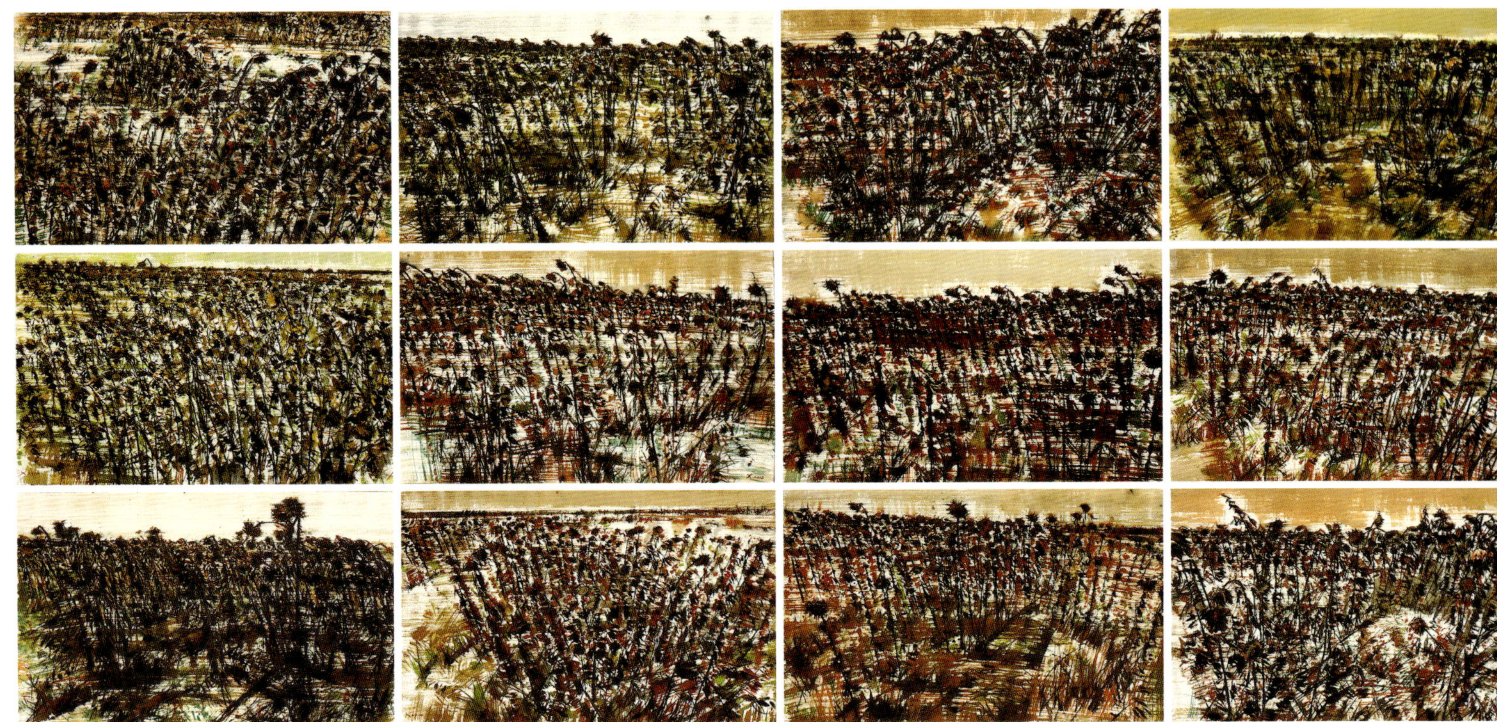

2012　Growth II· Water Colour · 58cm×78cm×24
Erwachsen II· Aquarell · 58cm×78cm×24

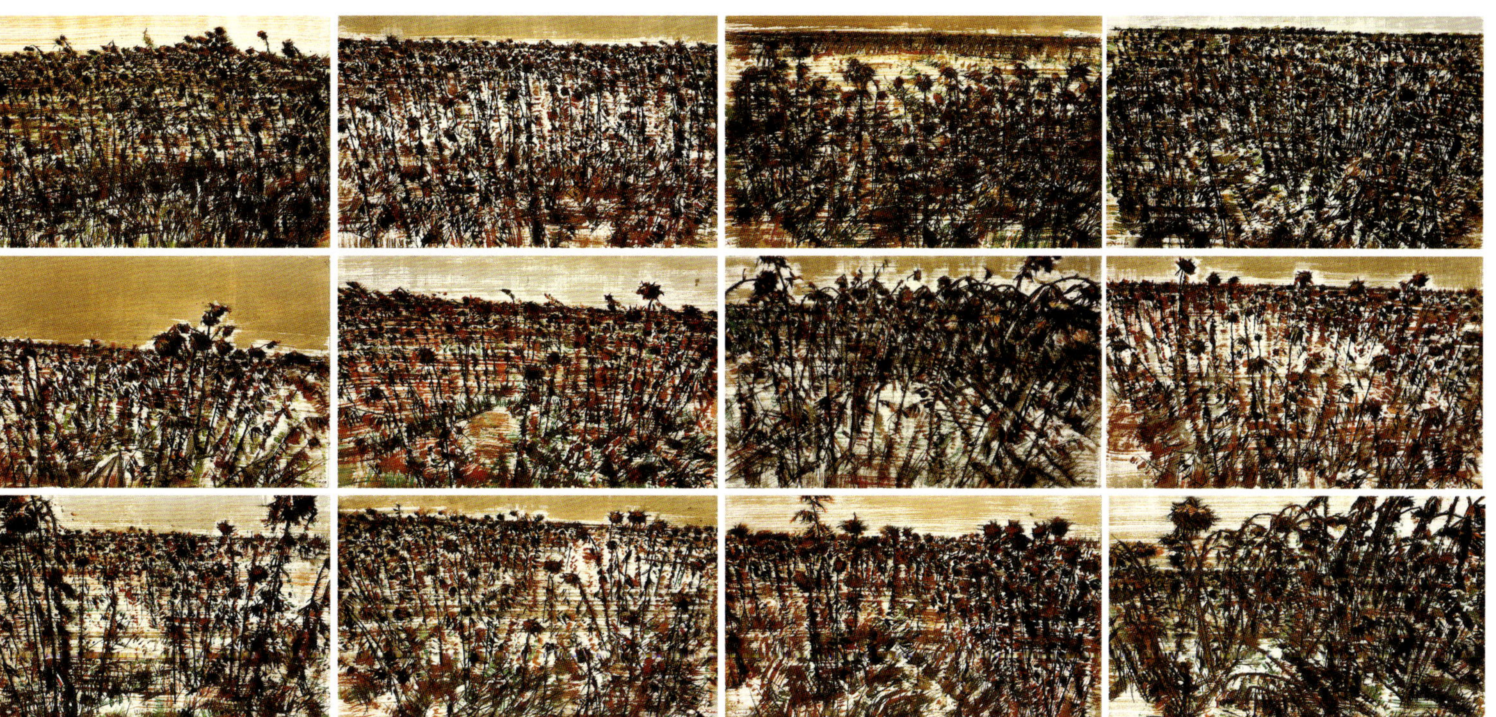

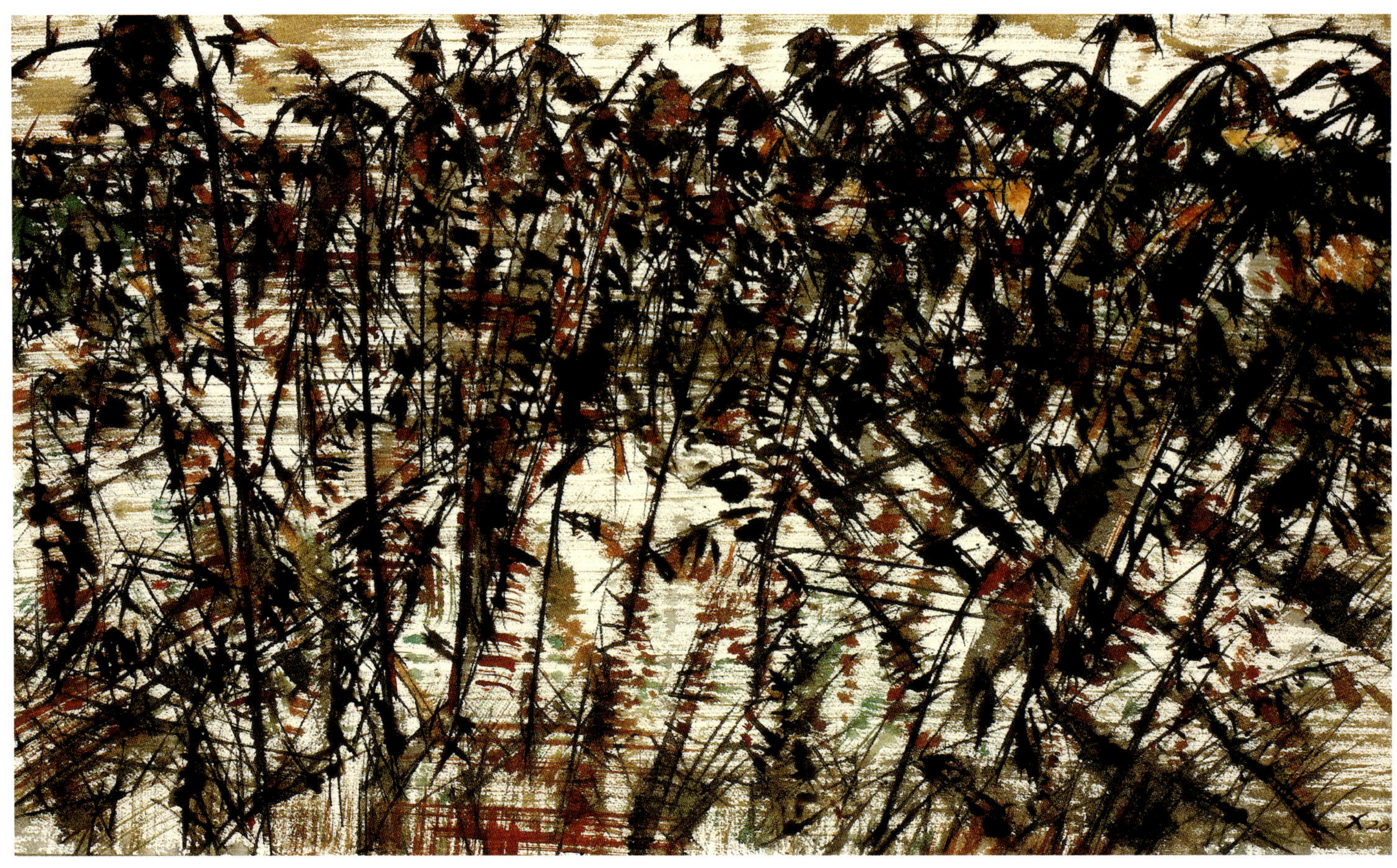

2012　Growth II· Water Colour · 58cm×78cm×24
Erwachsen II· Aquarell · 58cm×78cm×24

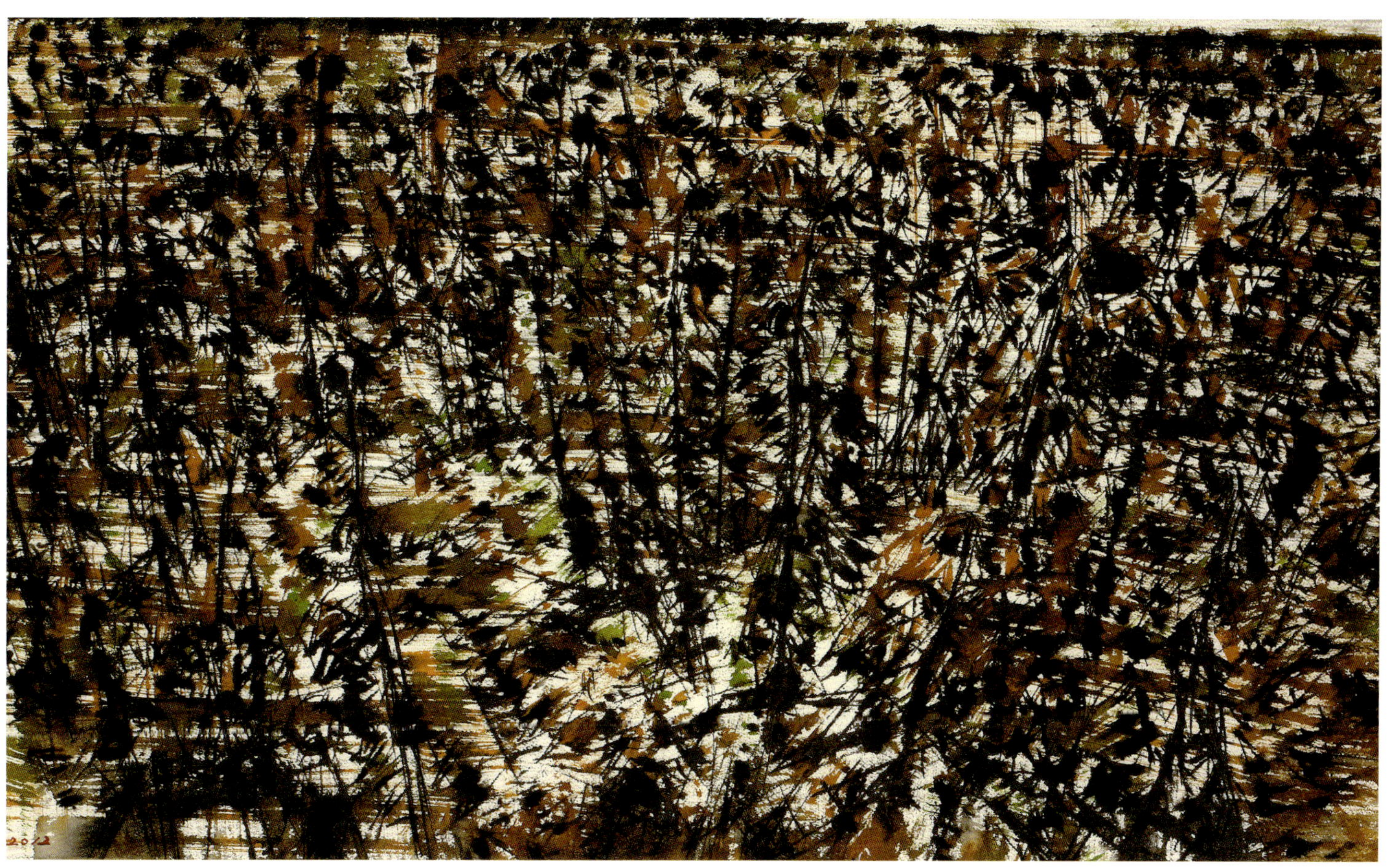

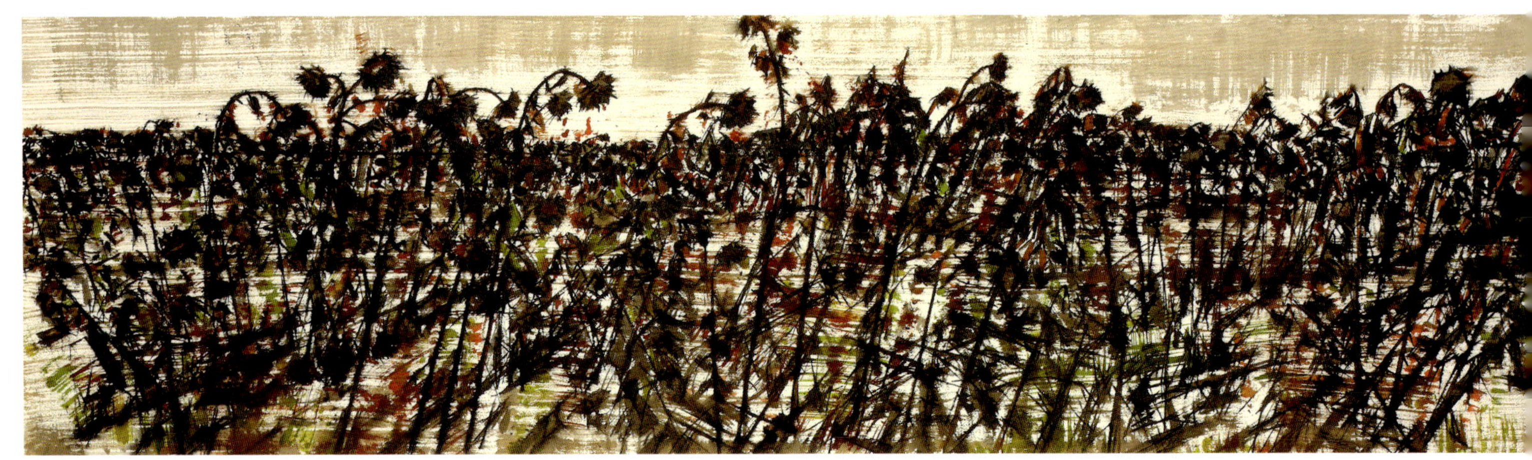

2012　The Wilderness II· Water Colour · 71cm×204cm×8
Die Wildnis II· Aquarell · 71cm×204cm×8

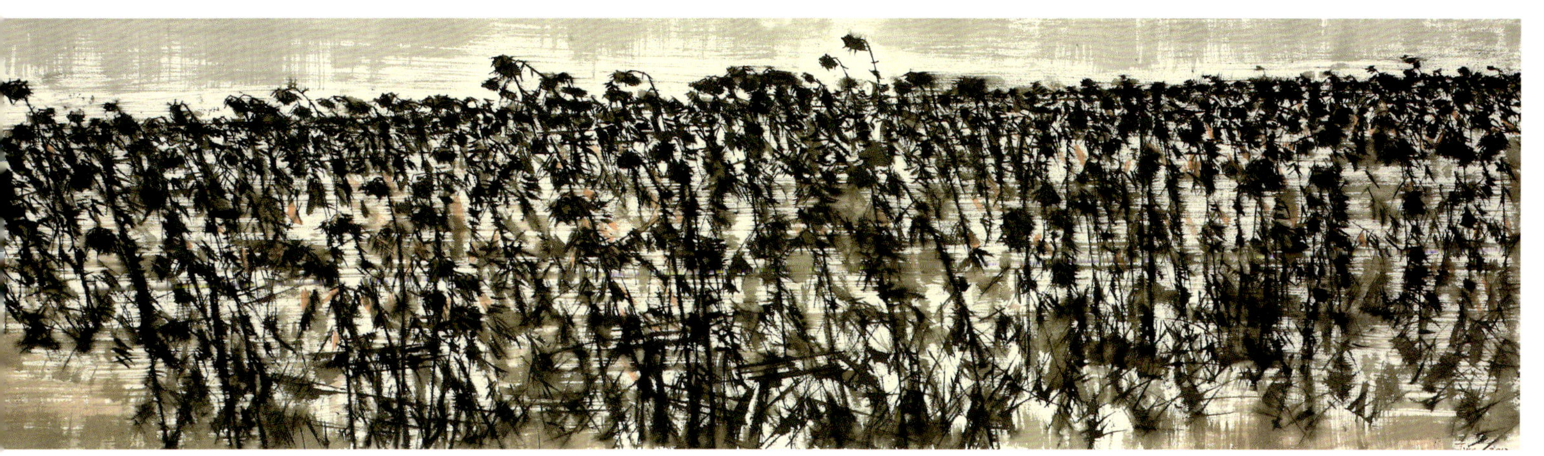

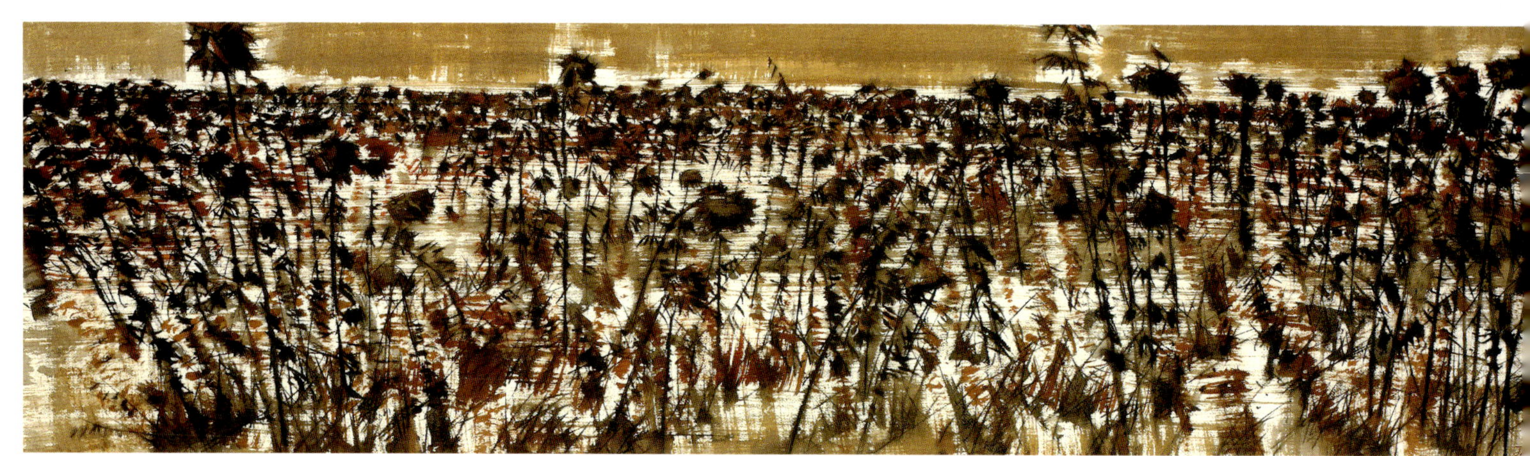

2012　The Wilderness II· Water Colour · 71cm×204cm×8
Die Wildnis II· Aquarell · 71cm×204cm×8

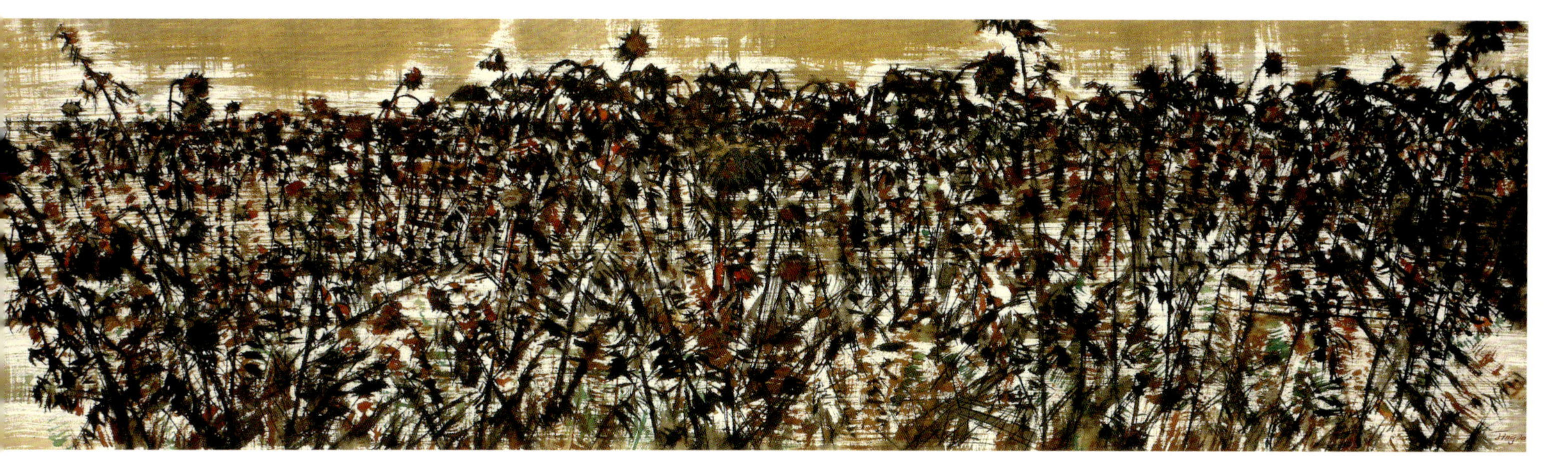

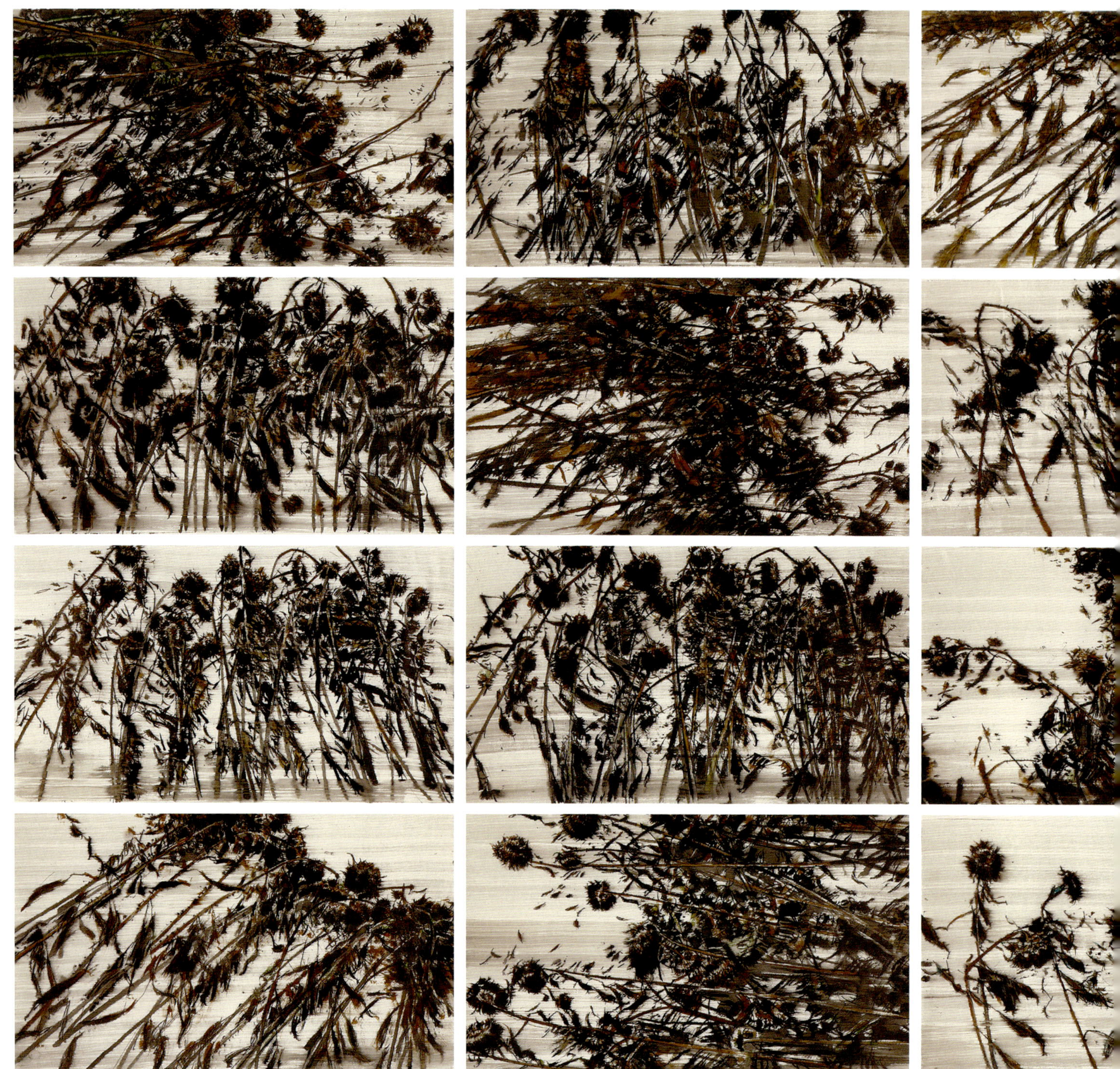

2008　Silence of the Sunflowers · Water Colour · 76cm×130cm×20
Stillleben——Die Sonnenblumen · Aquarell · 76cm×130cm×20

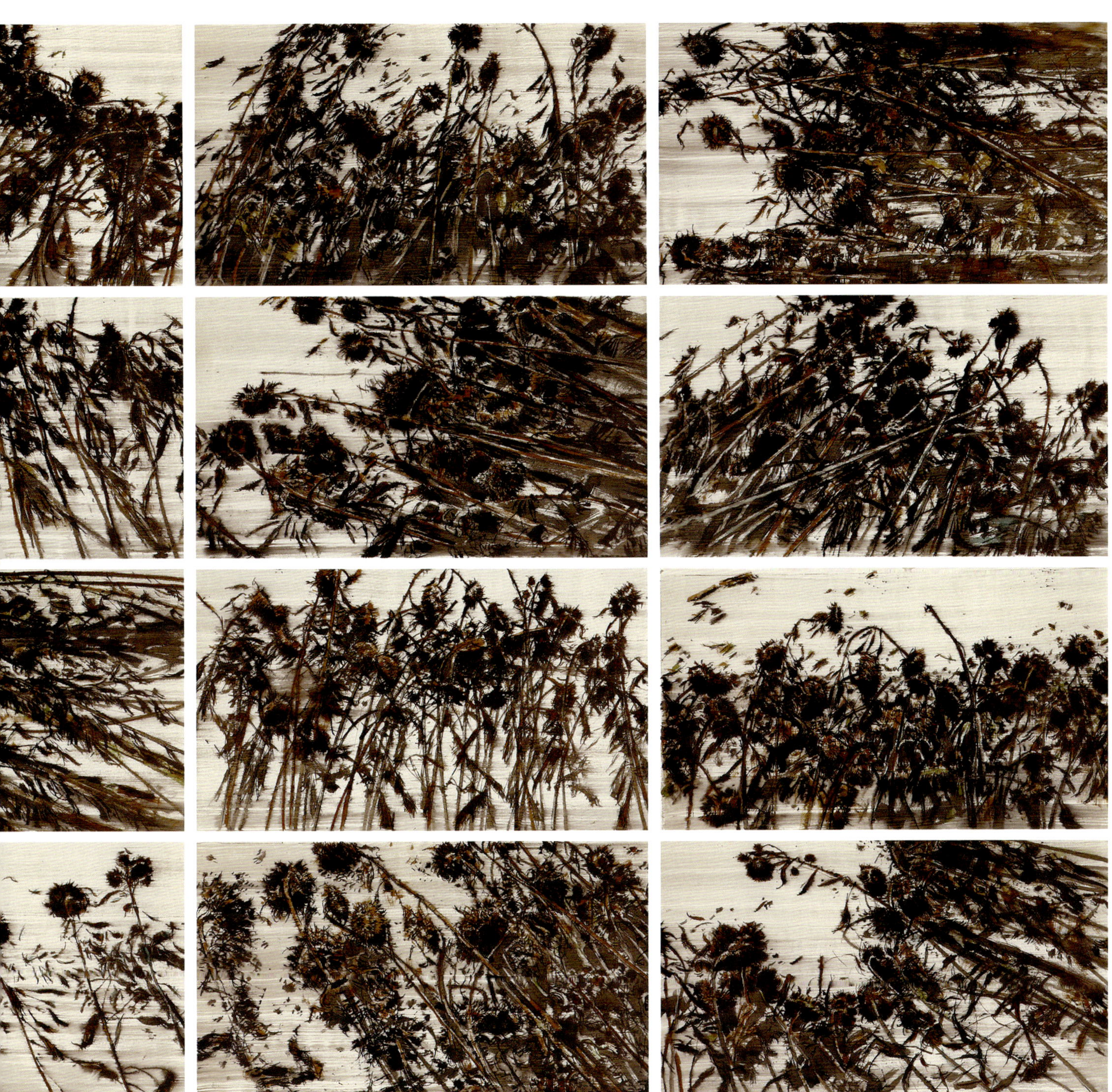

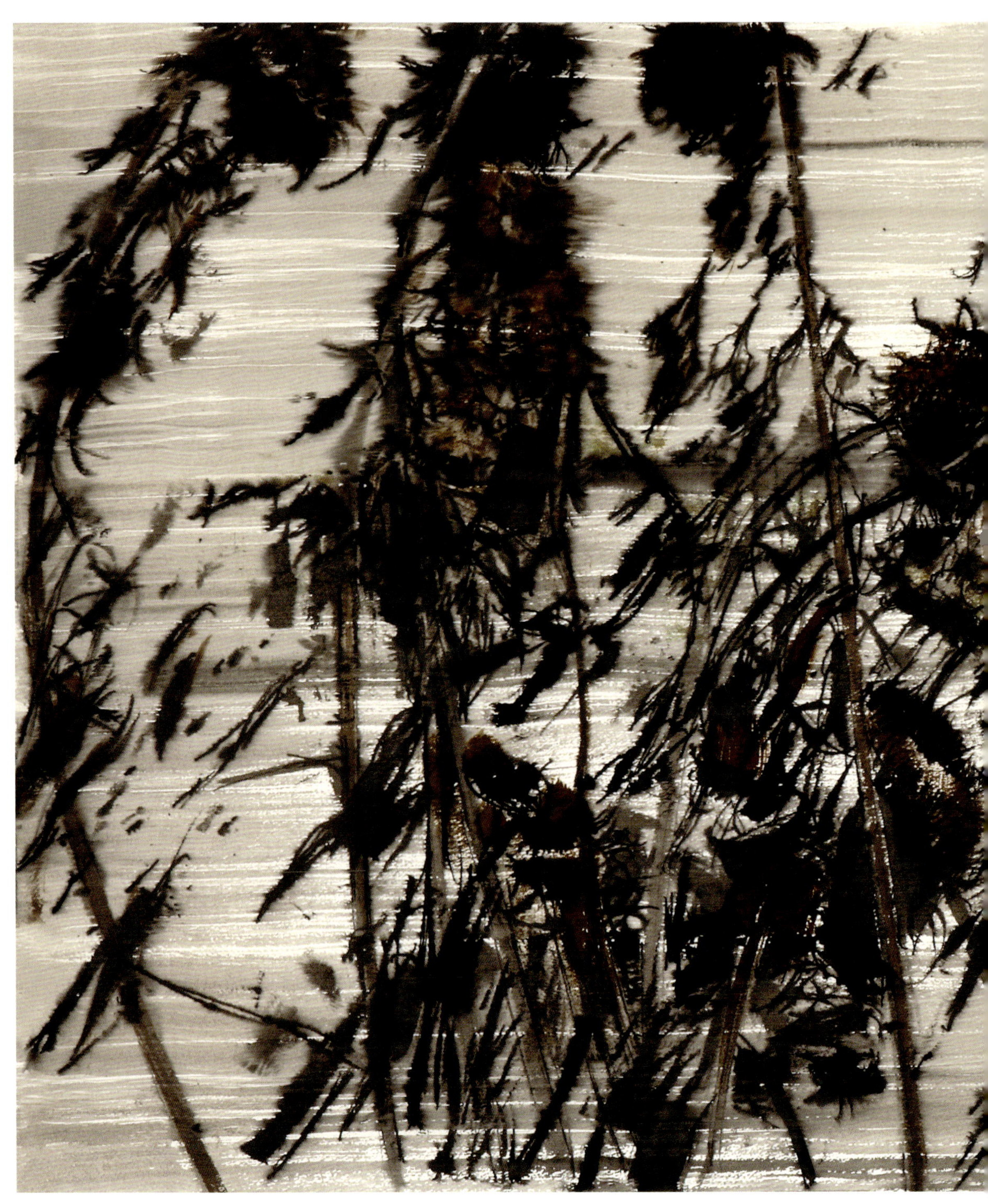

2008　Silence of the Sunflowers · Water Colour · 76cm×130cm×20
Stillleben——Die Sonnenblumen · Aquarell · 76cm×130cm×20

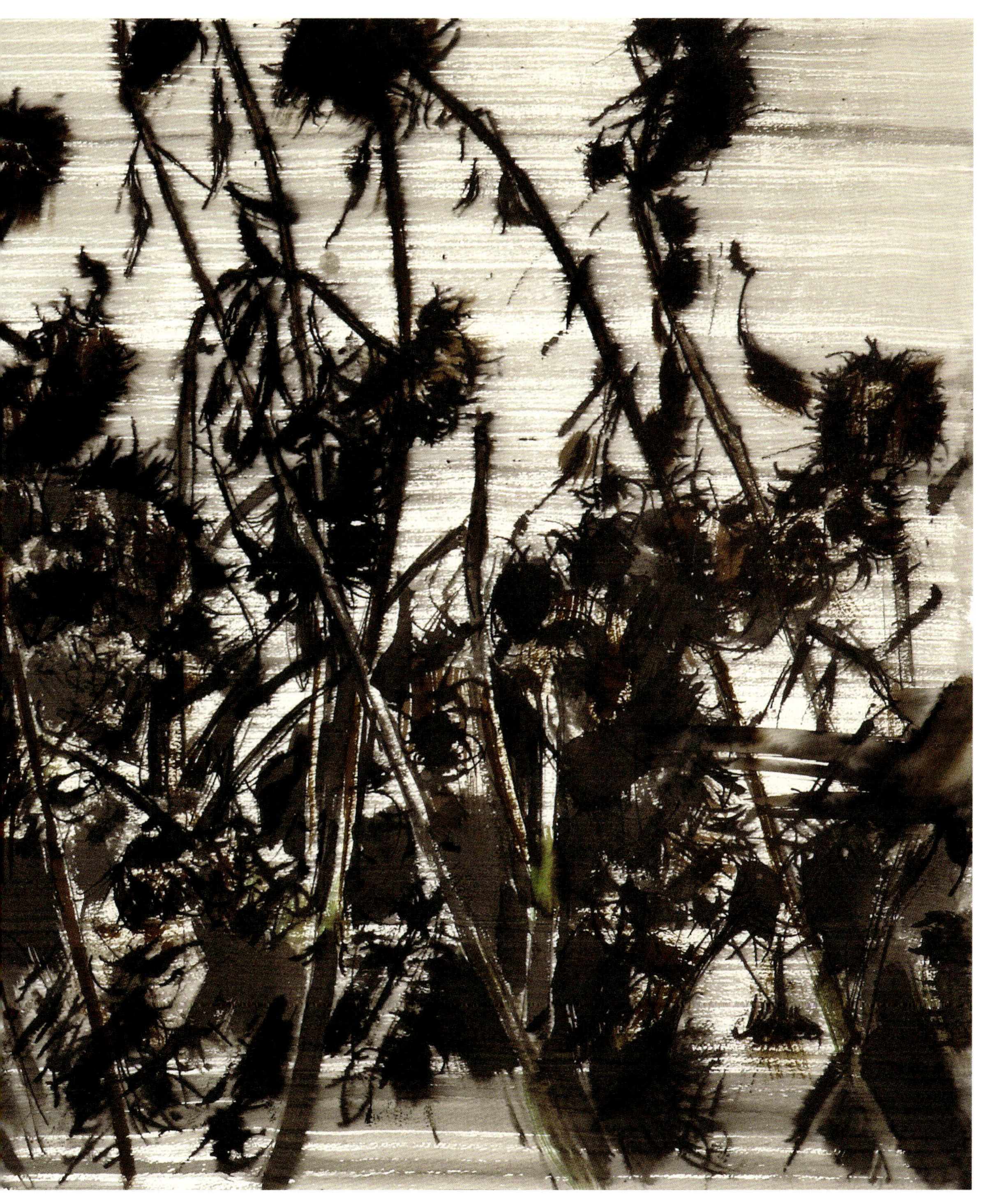

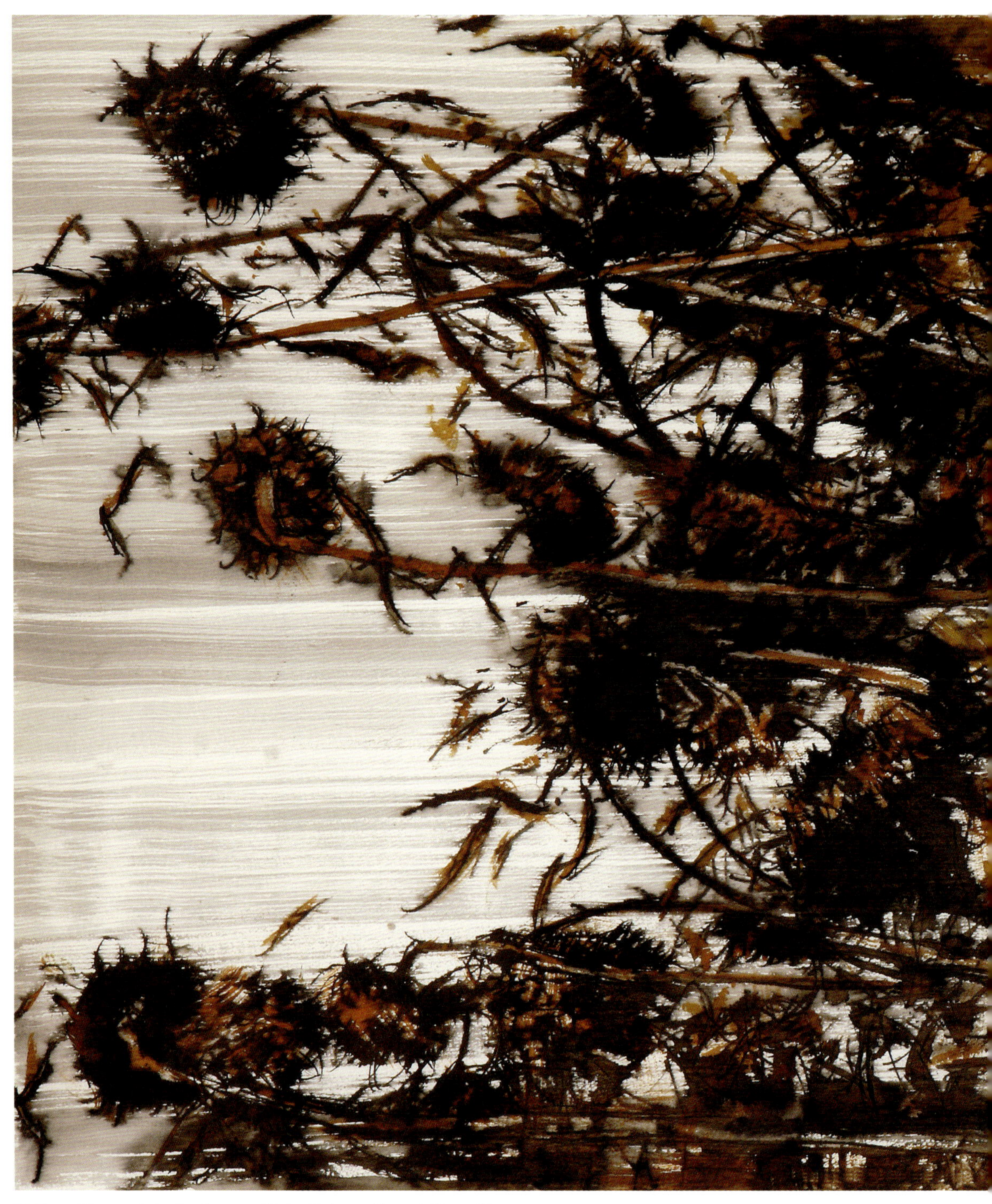

2008　Silence of the Sunflowers · Water Colour · 76cm×130cm×20
Stillleben——Die Sonnenblumen · Aquarell · 76cm×130cm×20

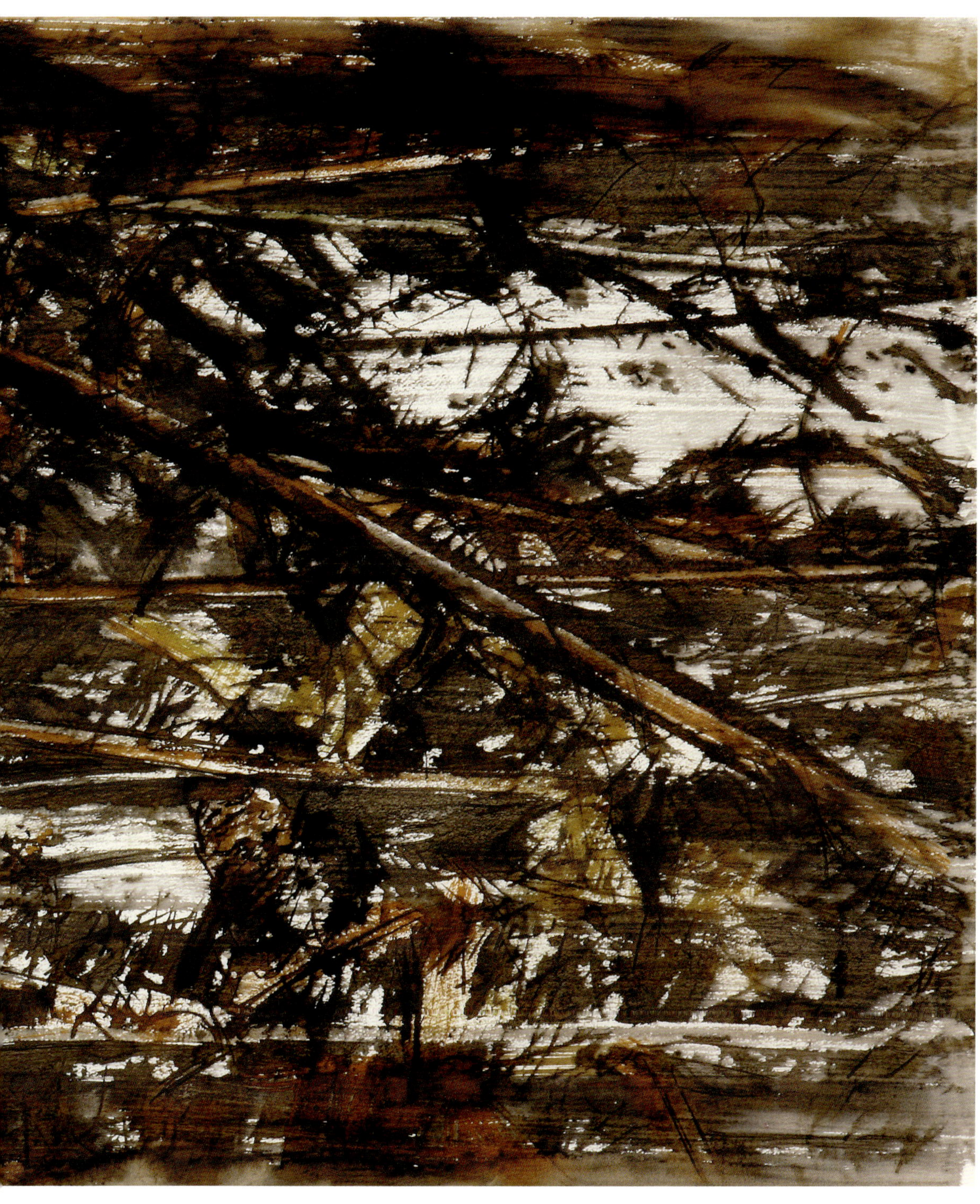

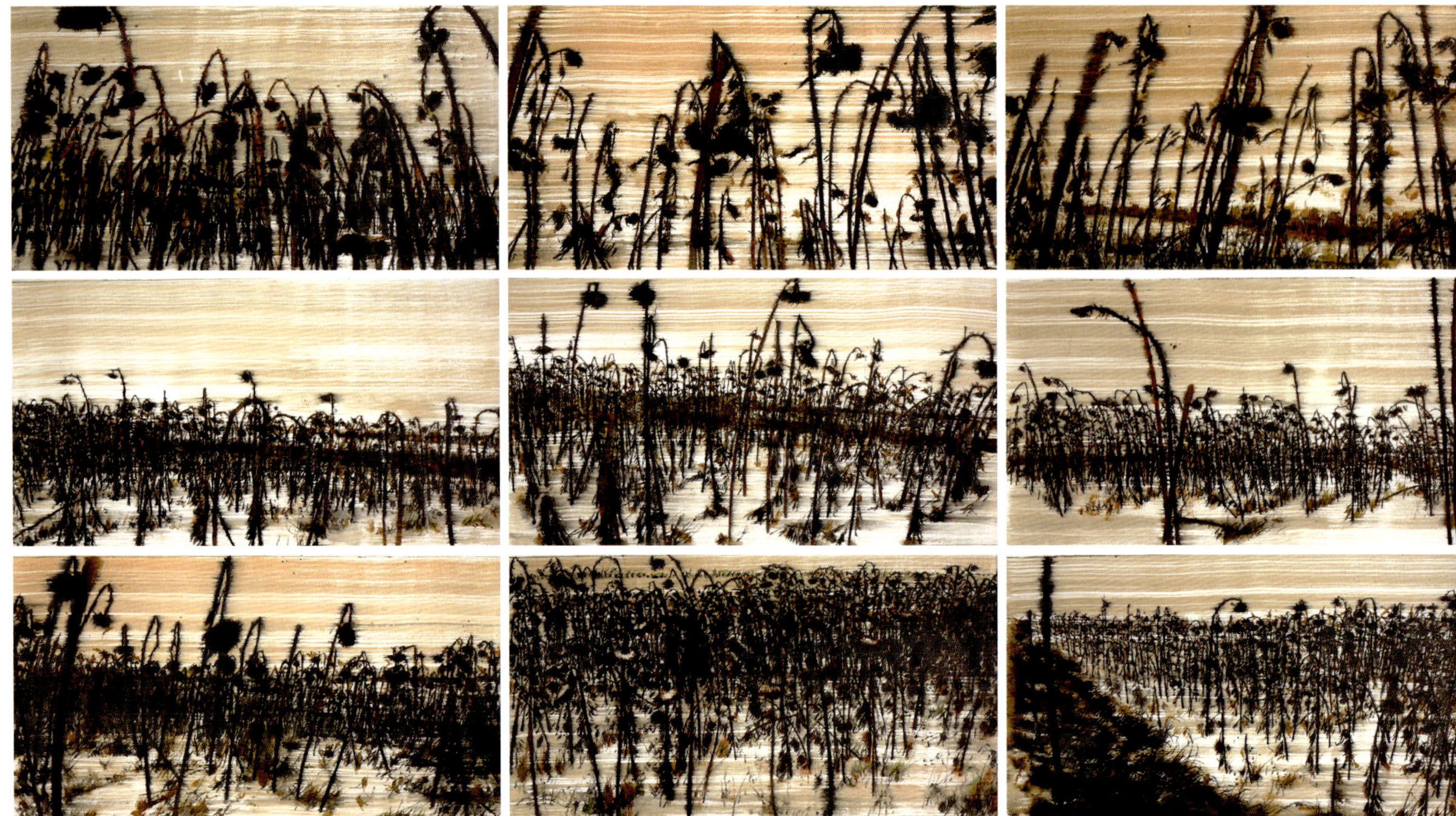

2008　Trip to the Far · Water Colour · 75cm×130cm×18
Fernreise · Aquarell · 75cm×130cm×18

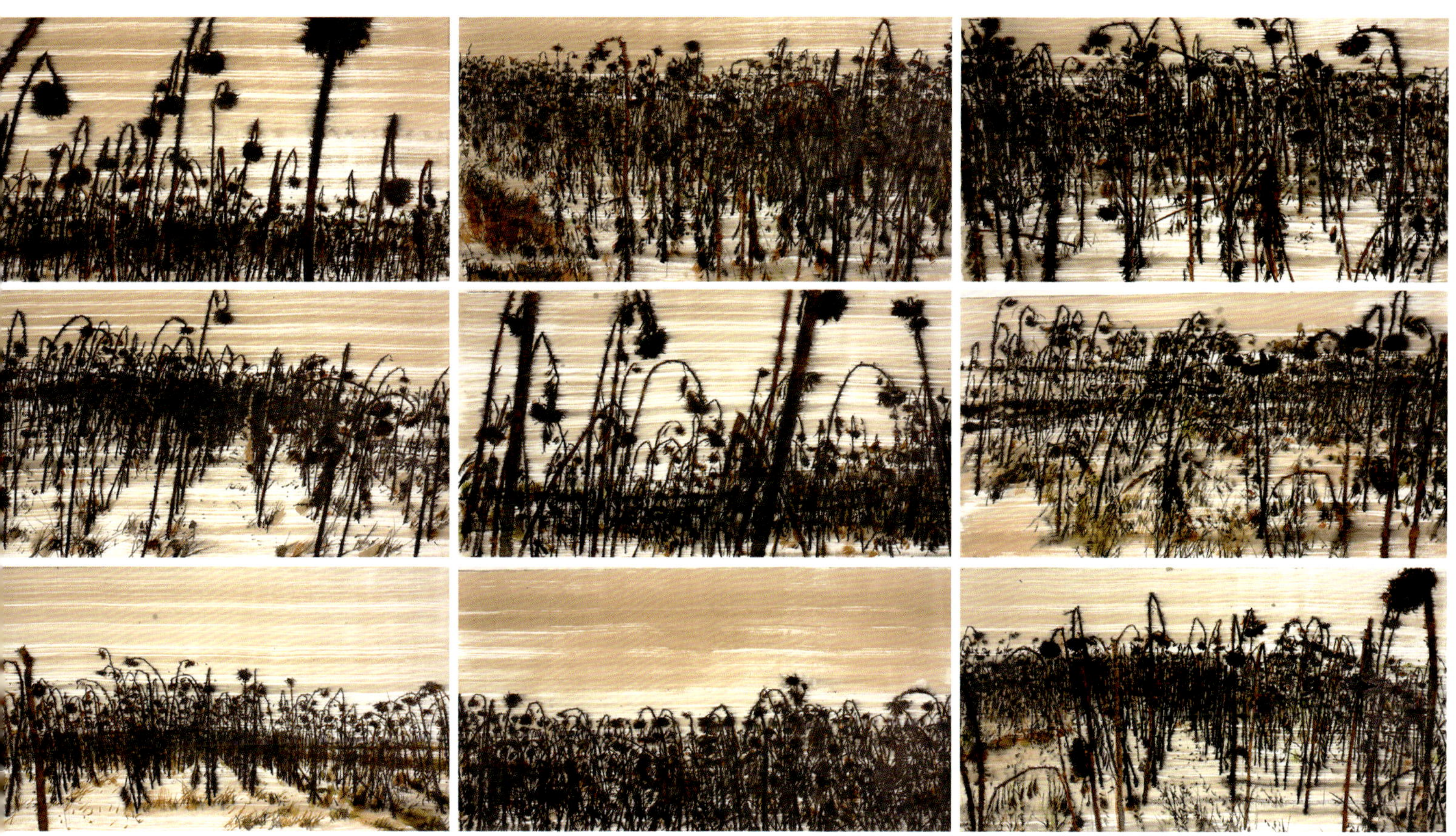

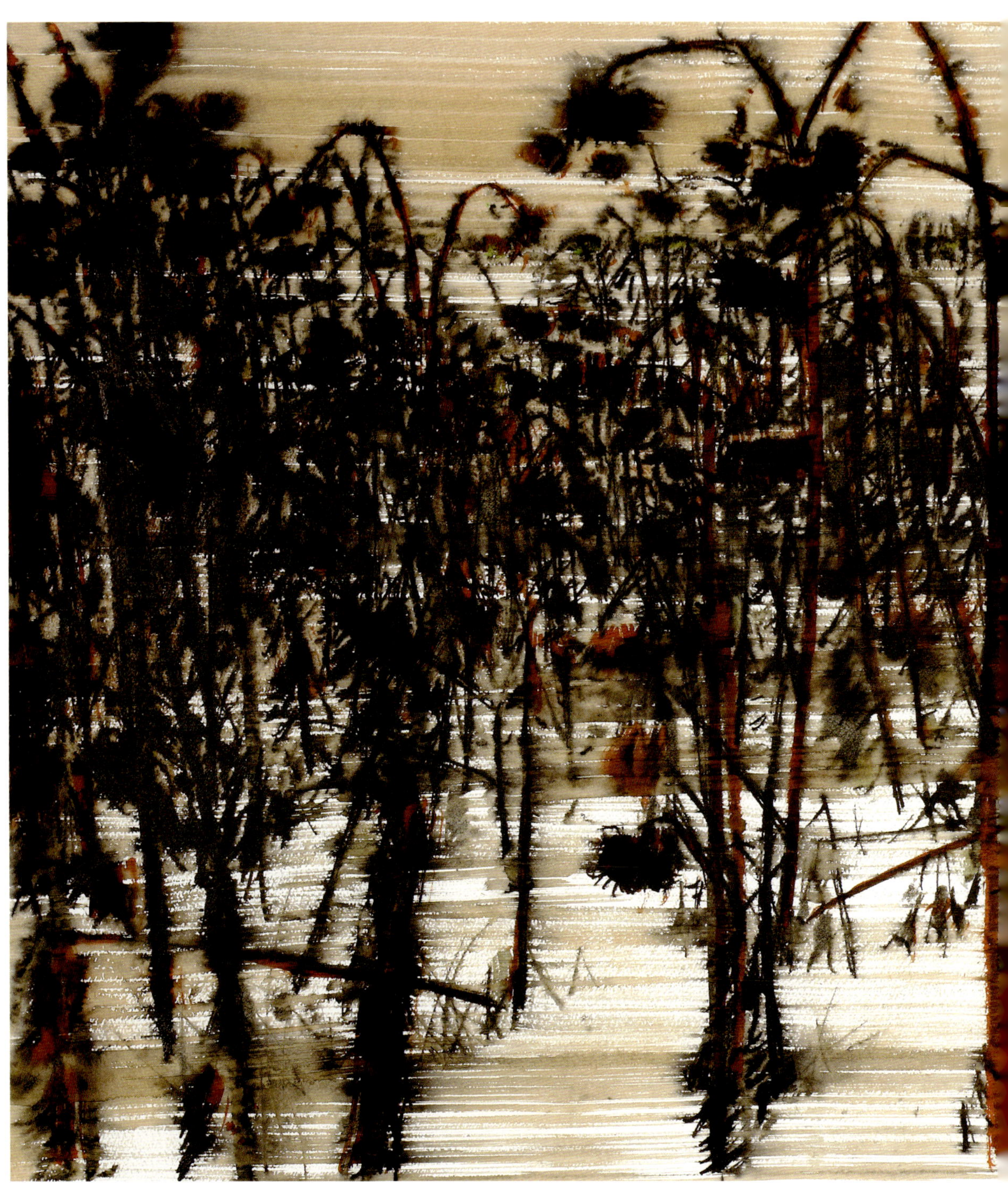

2008　Trip to the Far · Water Colour · 75cm×130cm×18
Fernreise · Aquarell · 75cm×130cm×18

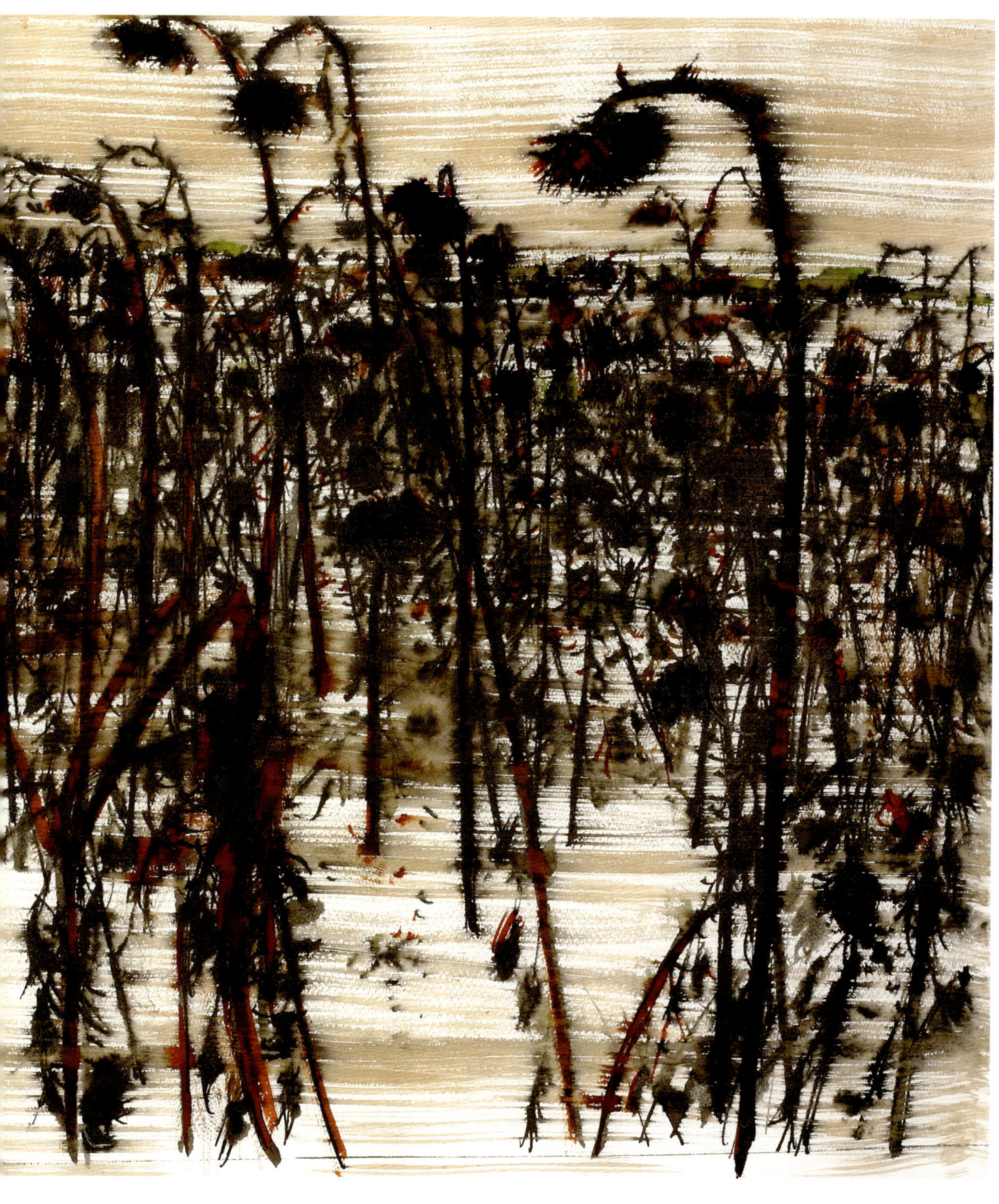

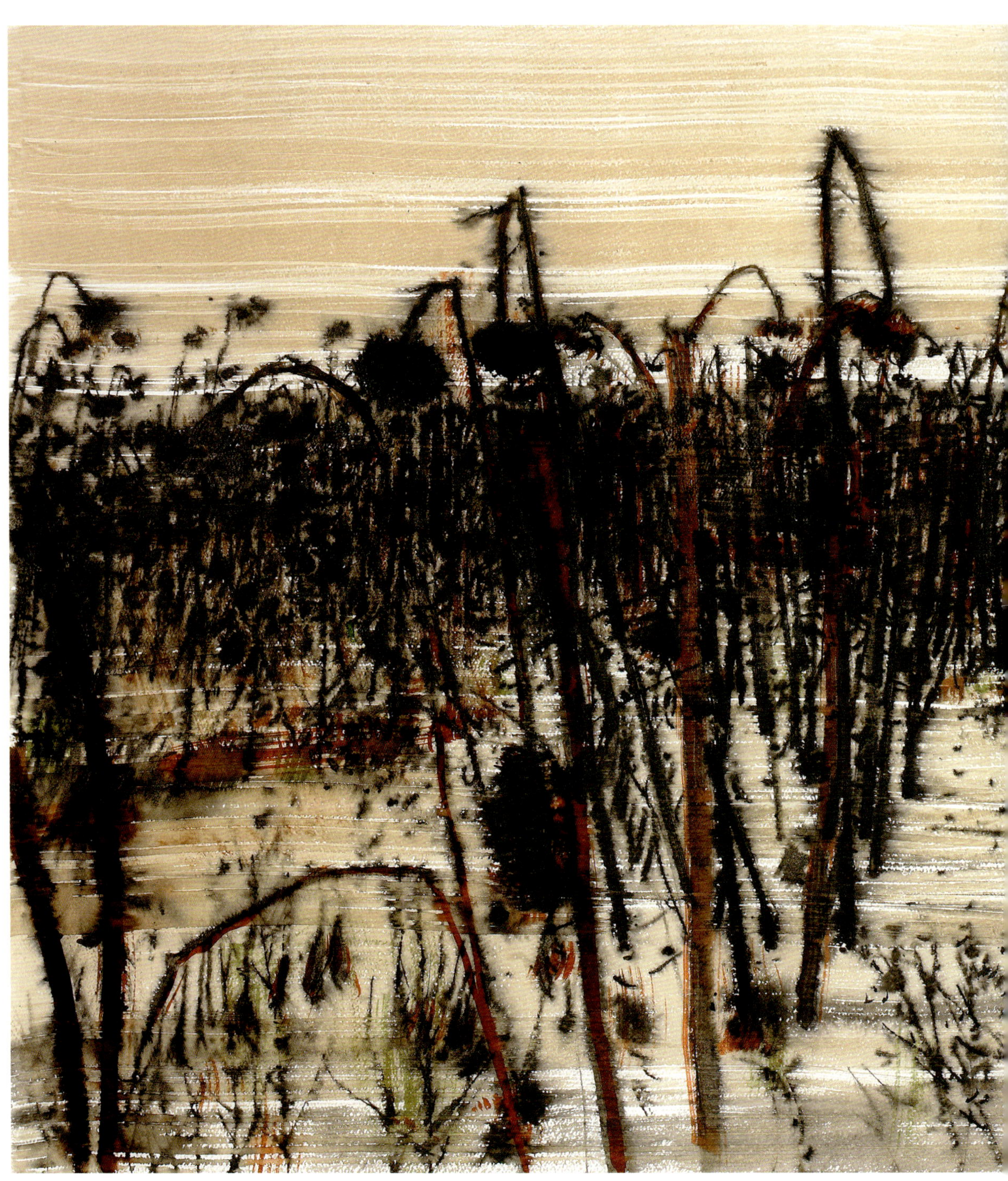

2008　Trip to the Far · Water Colour · 75cm×130cm×18
Fernreise · Aquarell · 75cm×130cm×18

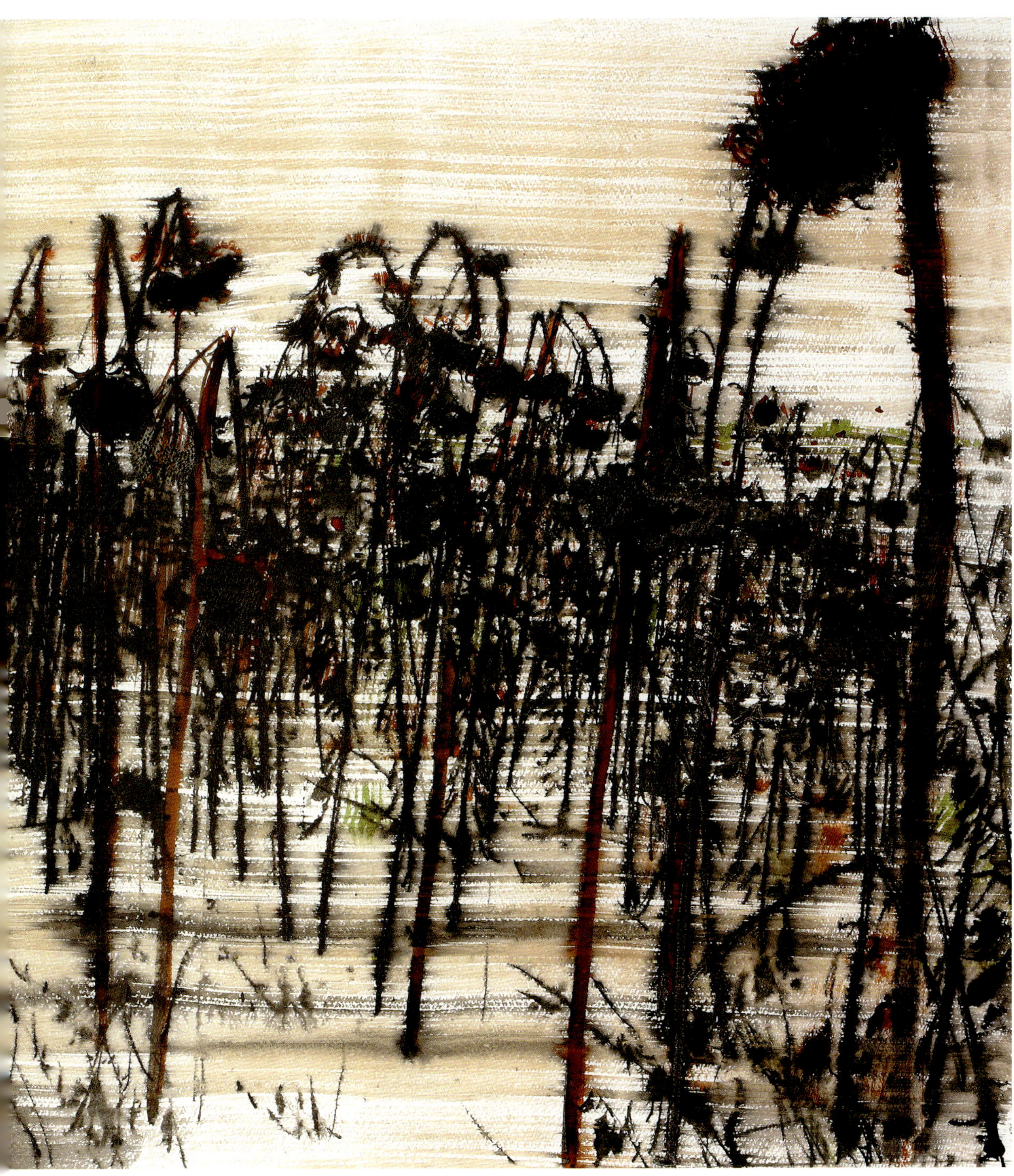

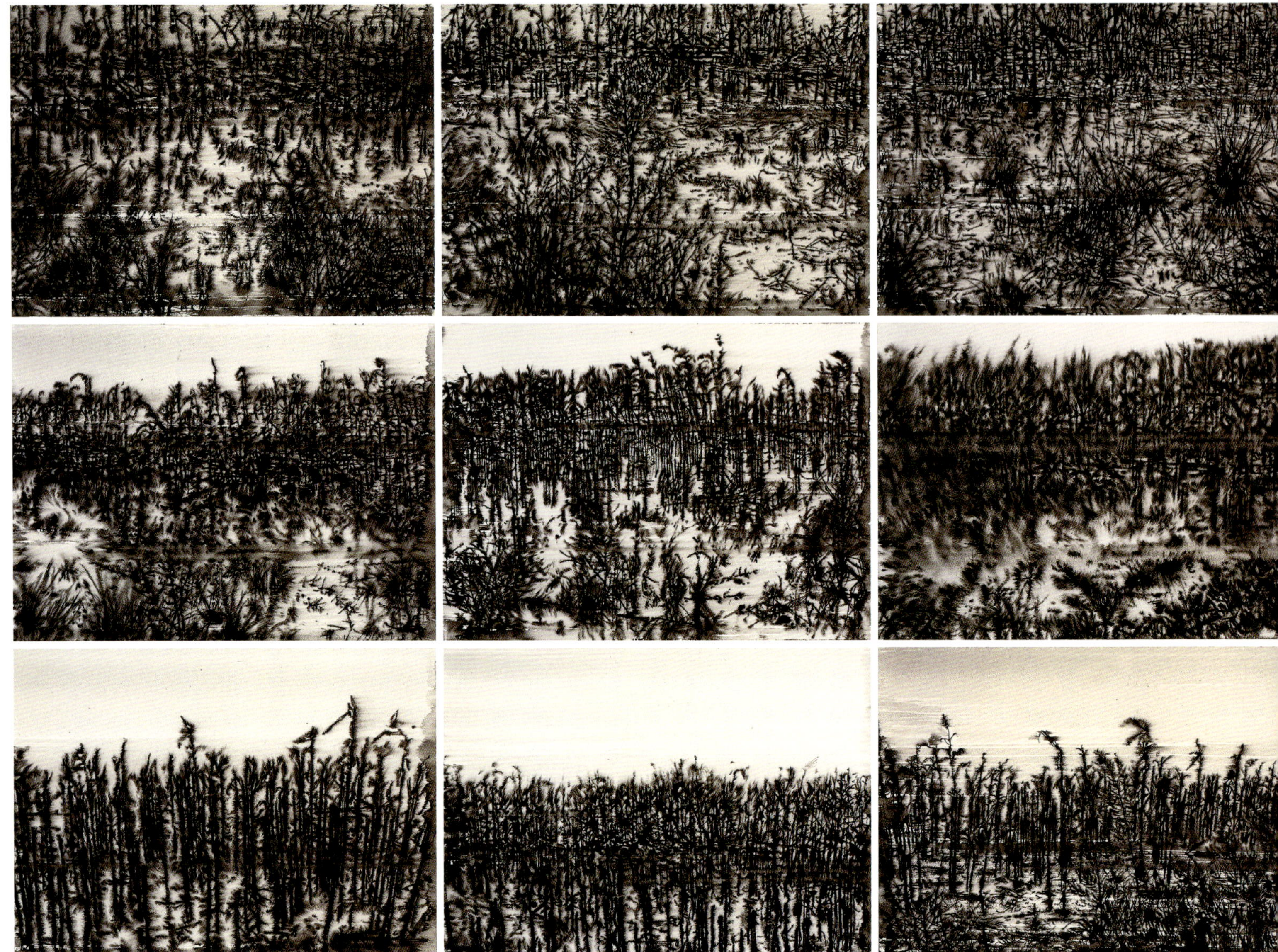

2005   Bulrush Pond I· Water Colour · 45cm×60cm×9
Blick auf den Schilf I· Aquarell · 45cm×60cm×9

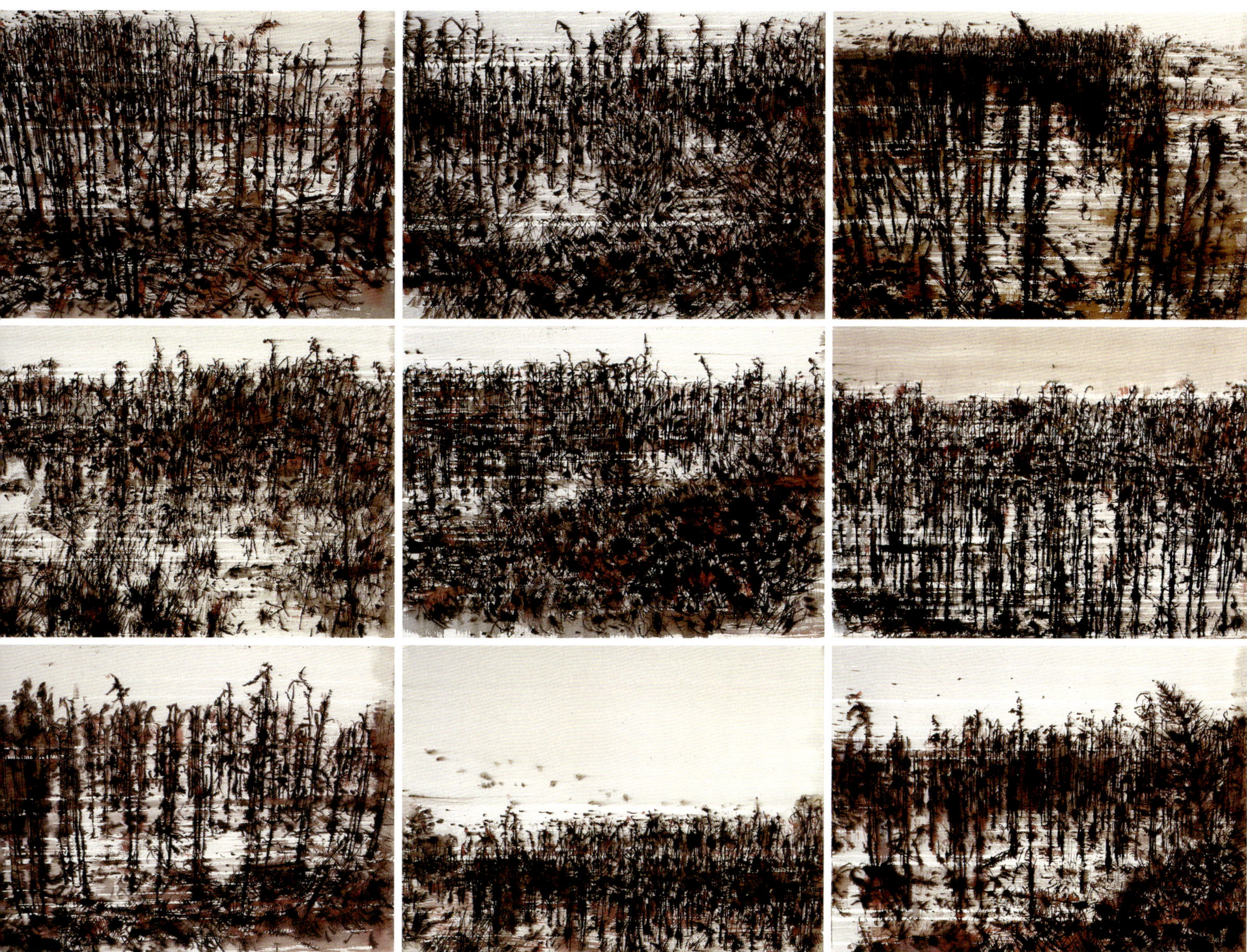

2005   Bulrush Pond II· Water Colour · 45cm×60cm×9
Blick auf den Schilf II· Aquarell · 45cm×60cm×9

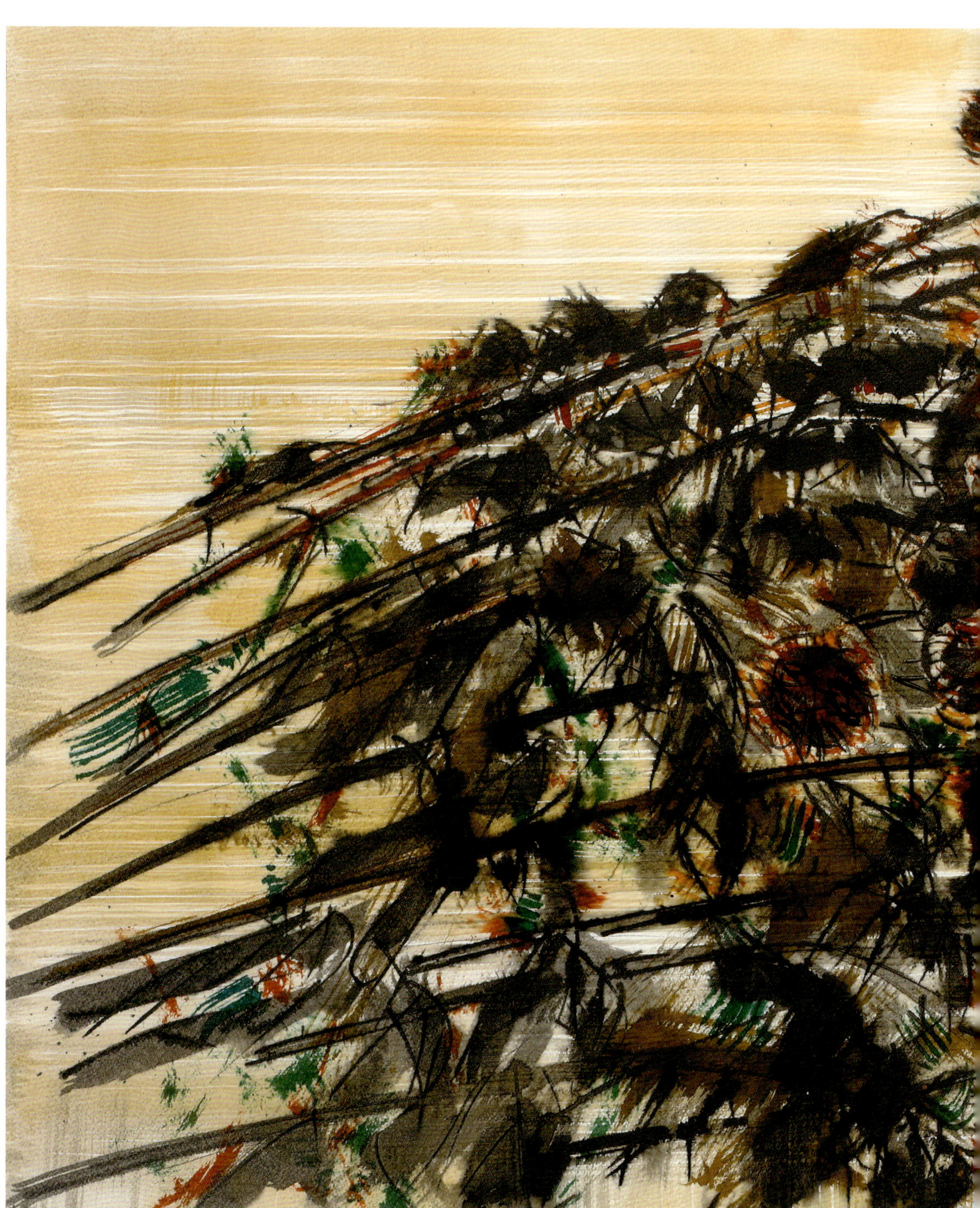

2012 Growth I· Water Colour · 58cm×78cm×8
Erwachsen I· Aquarell · 58cm×78cm×8

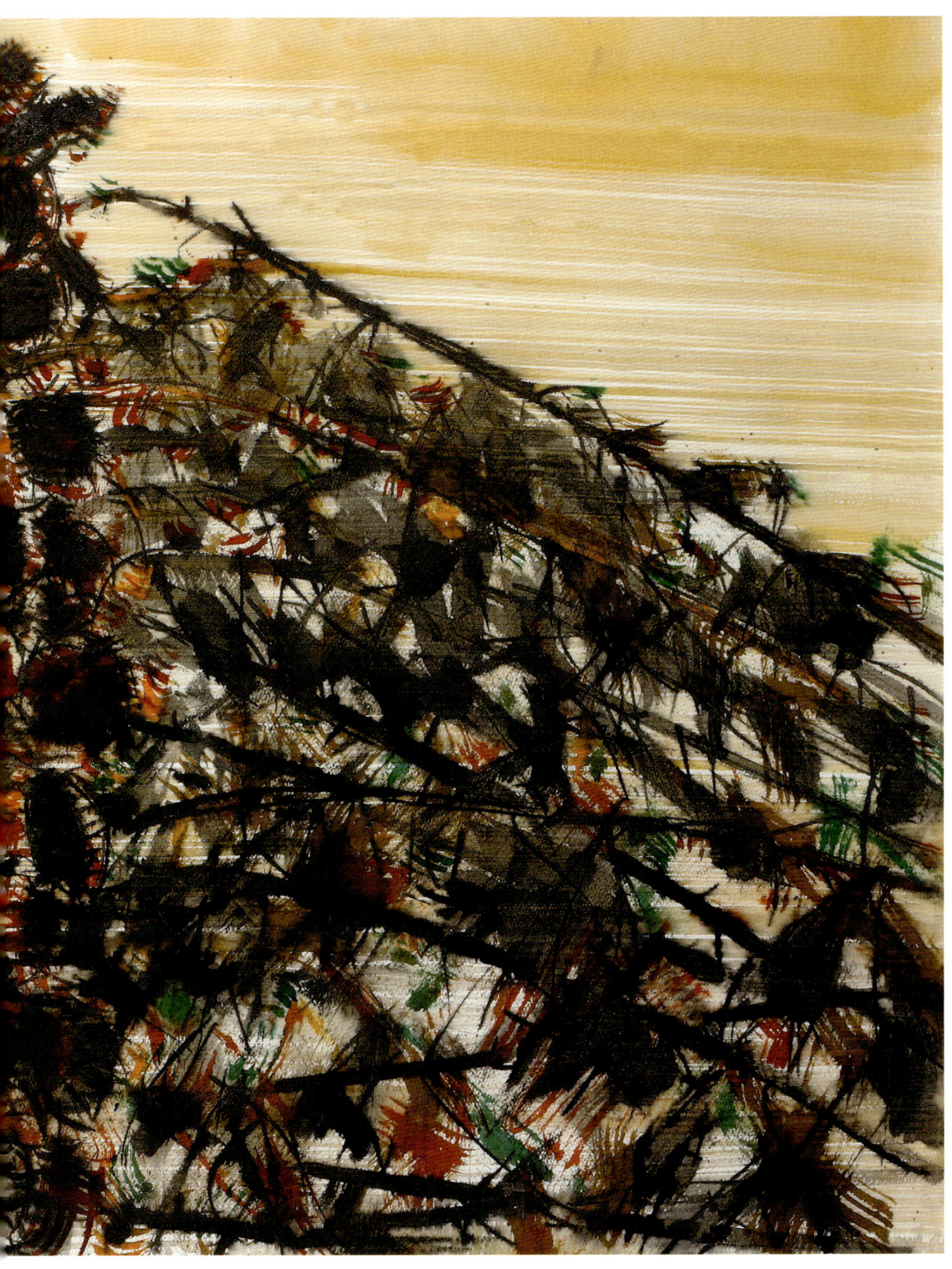

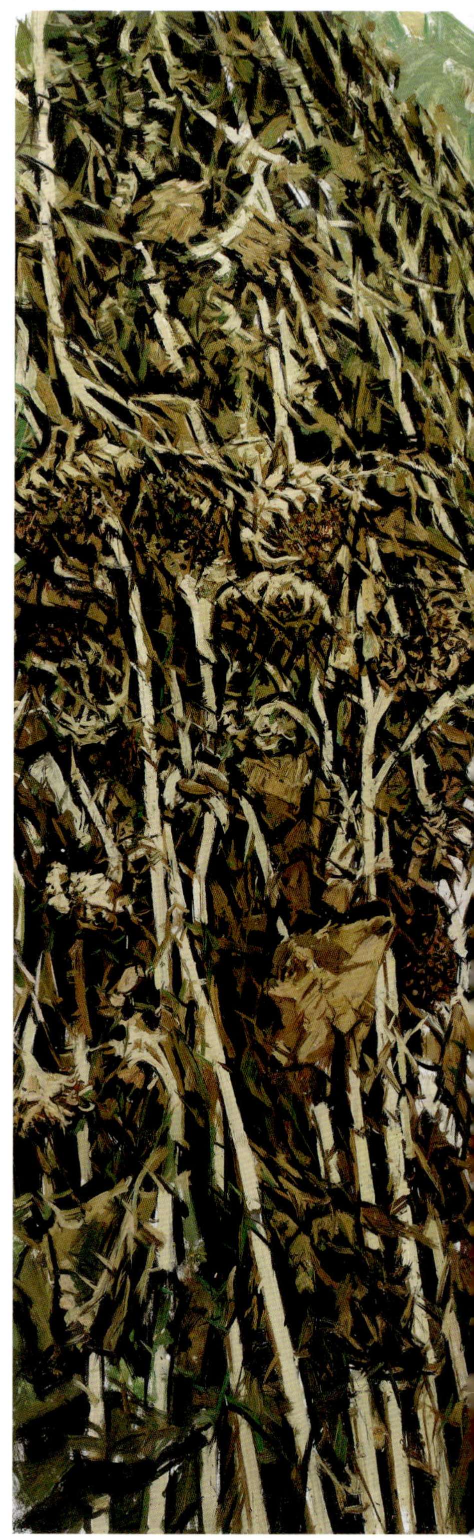

2012   Eight Tall Sunflowers · Oil Painting · 280cm×90cm×4
Acht Leinwände · Öl auf Leinwand · 280cm×90cm×4

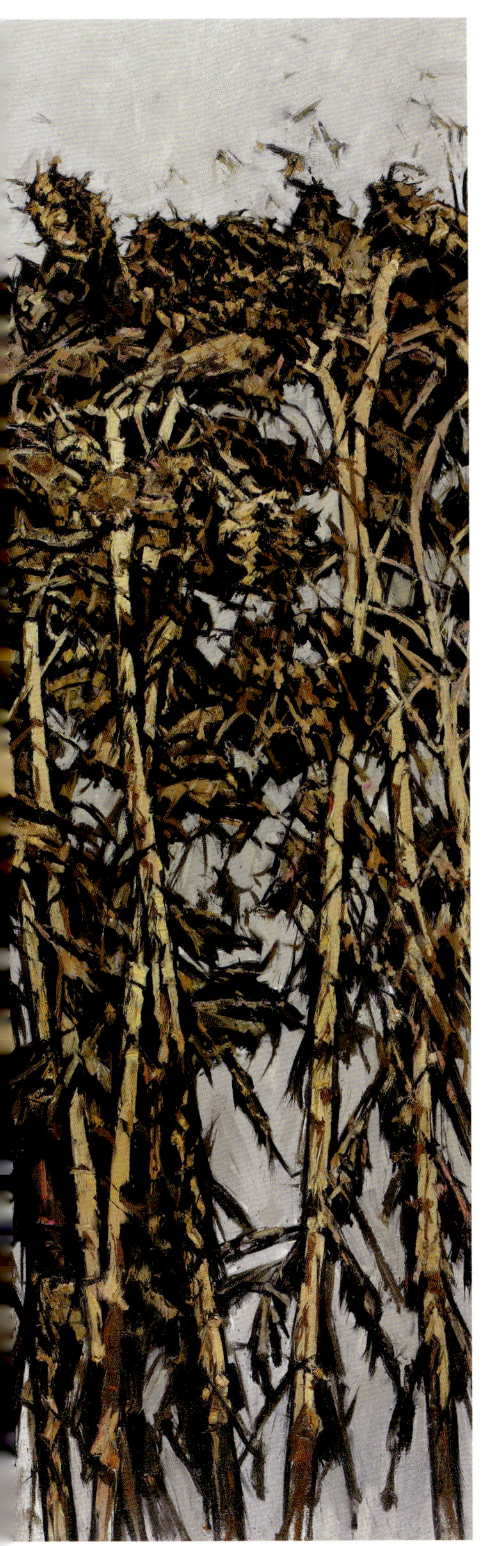
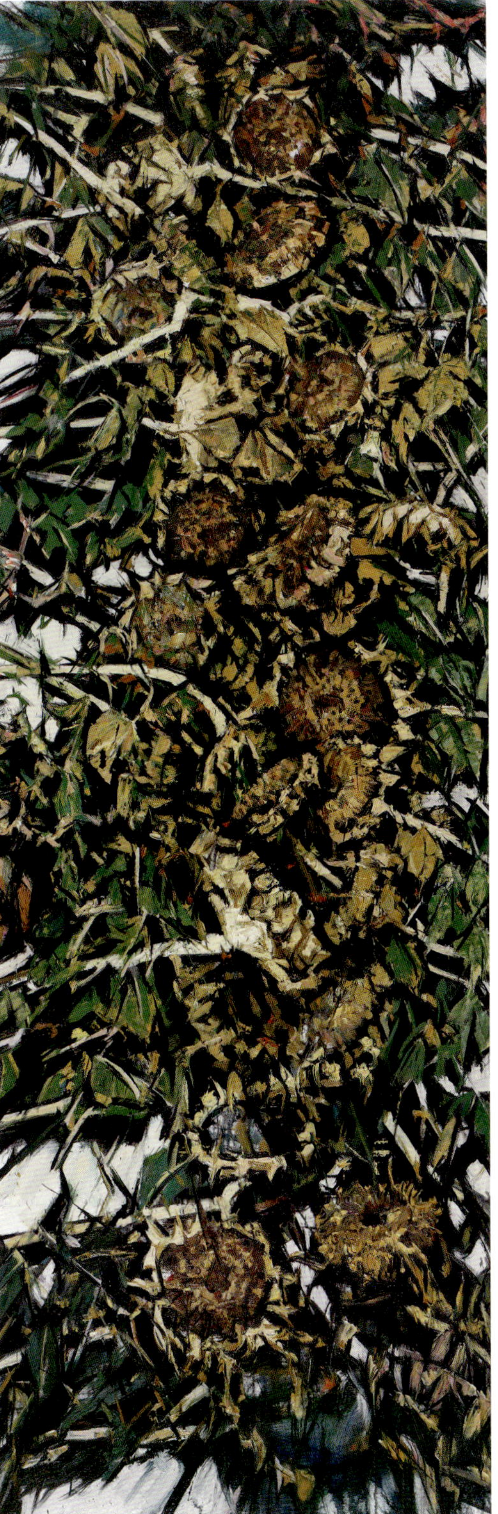
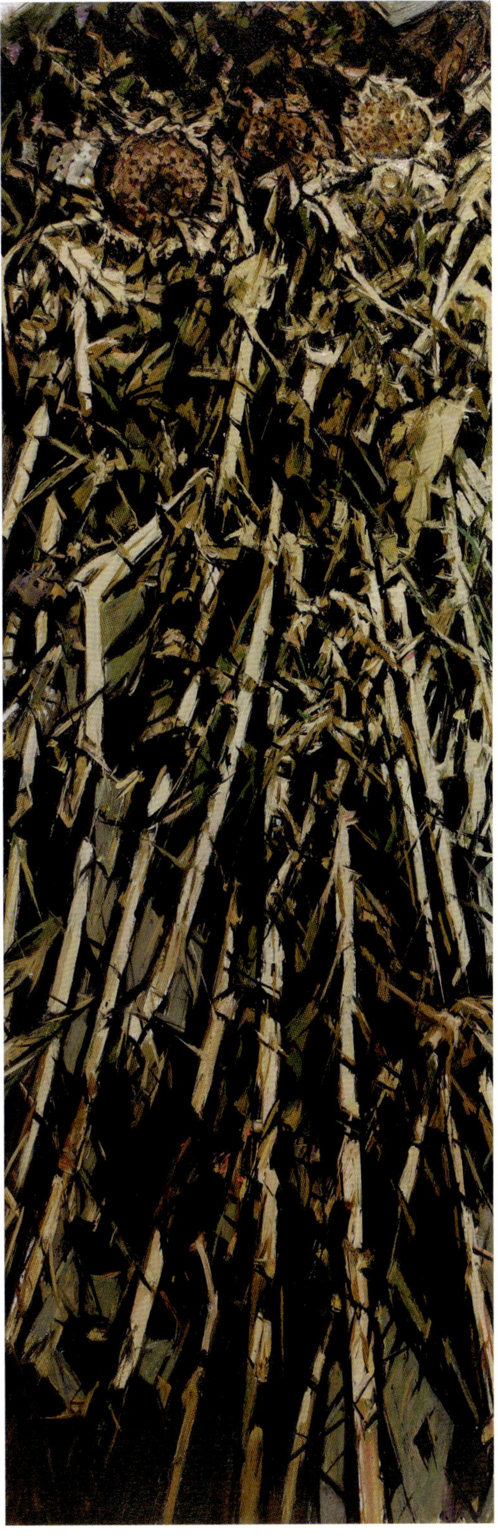

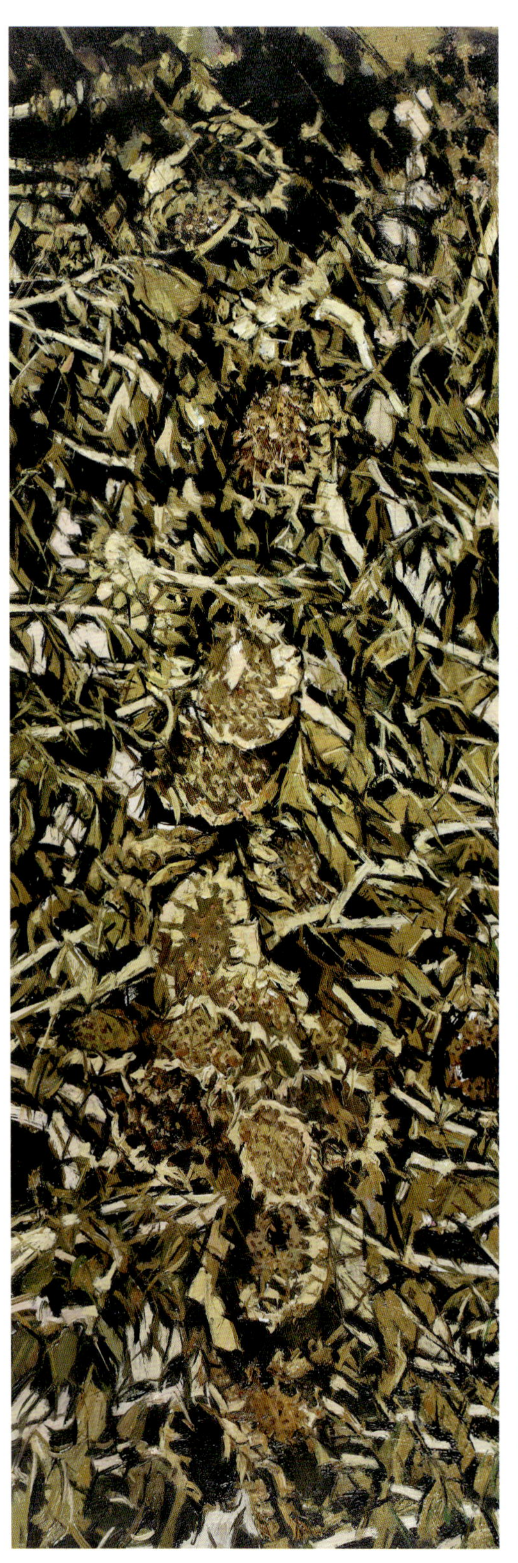
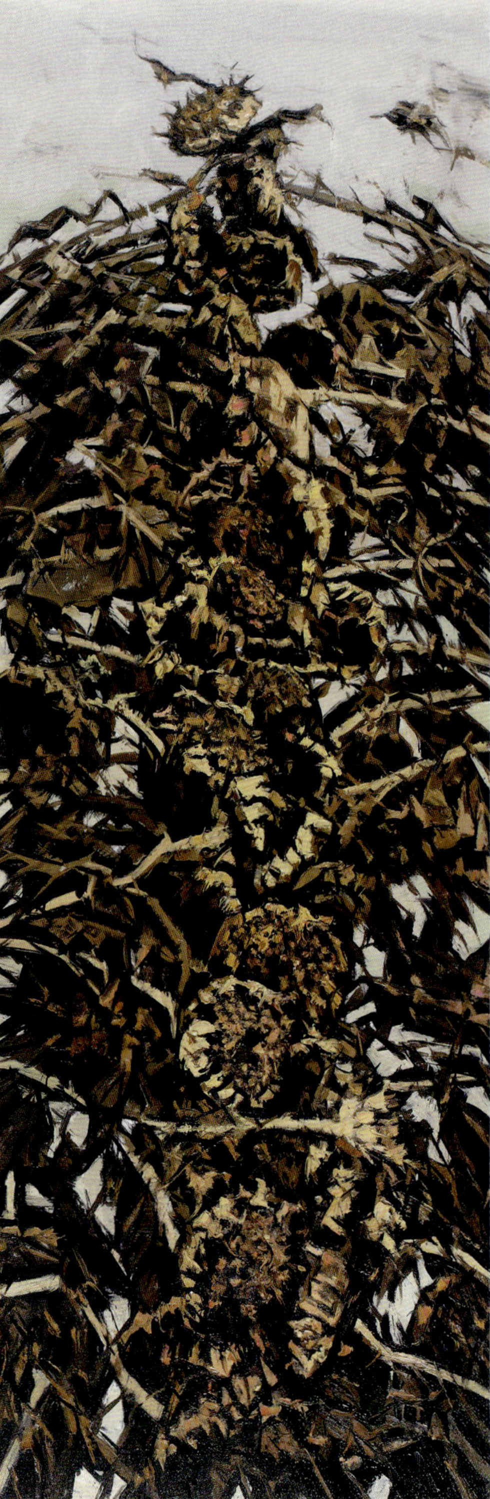
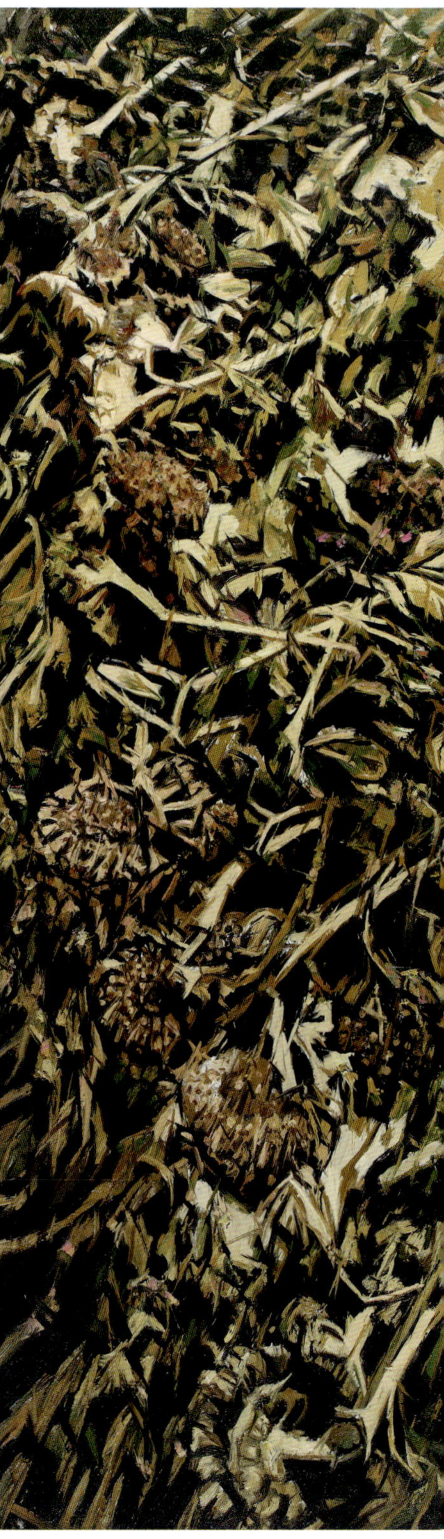

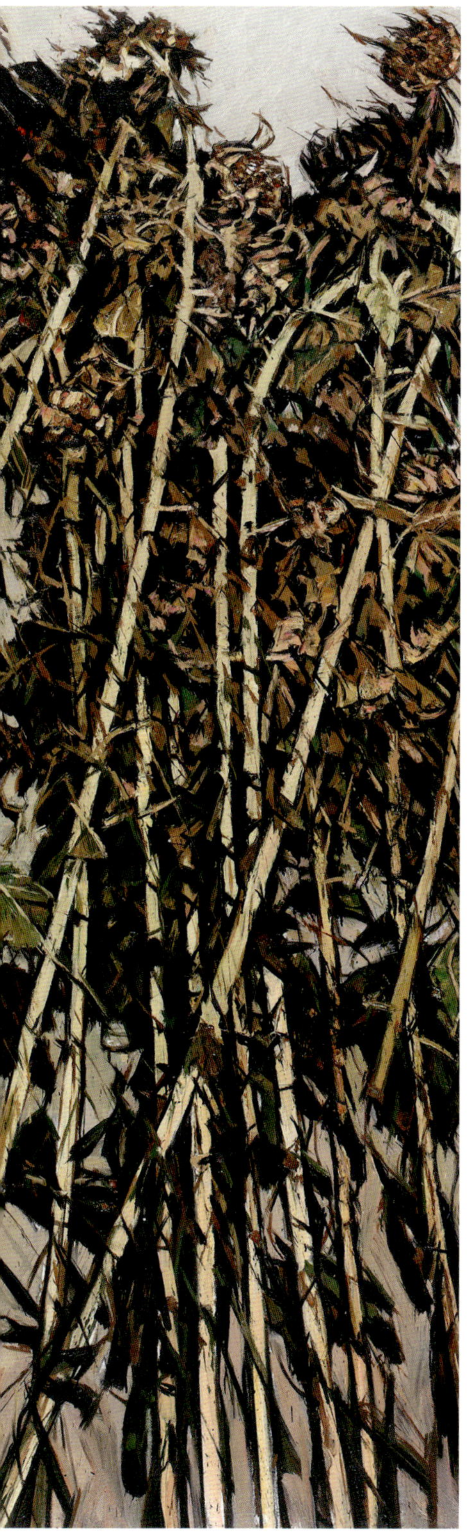

2012   Eight Tall Sunflowers · Oil Painting · 280cm×90cm×4
Acht Leinwände · Öl auf Leinwand · 280cm×90cm×4

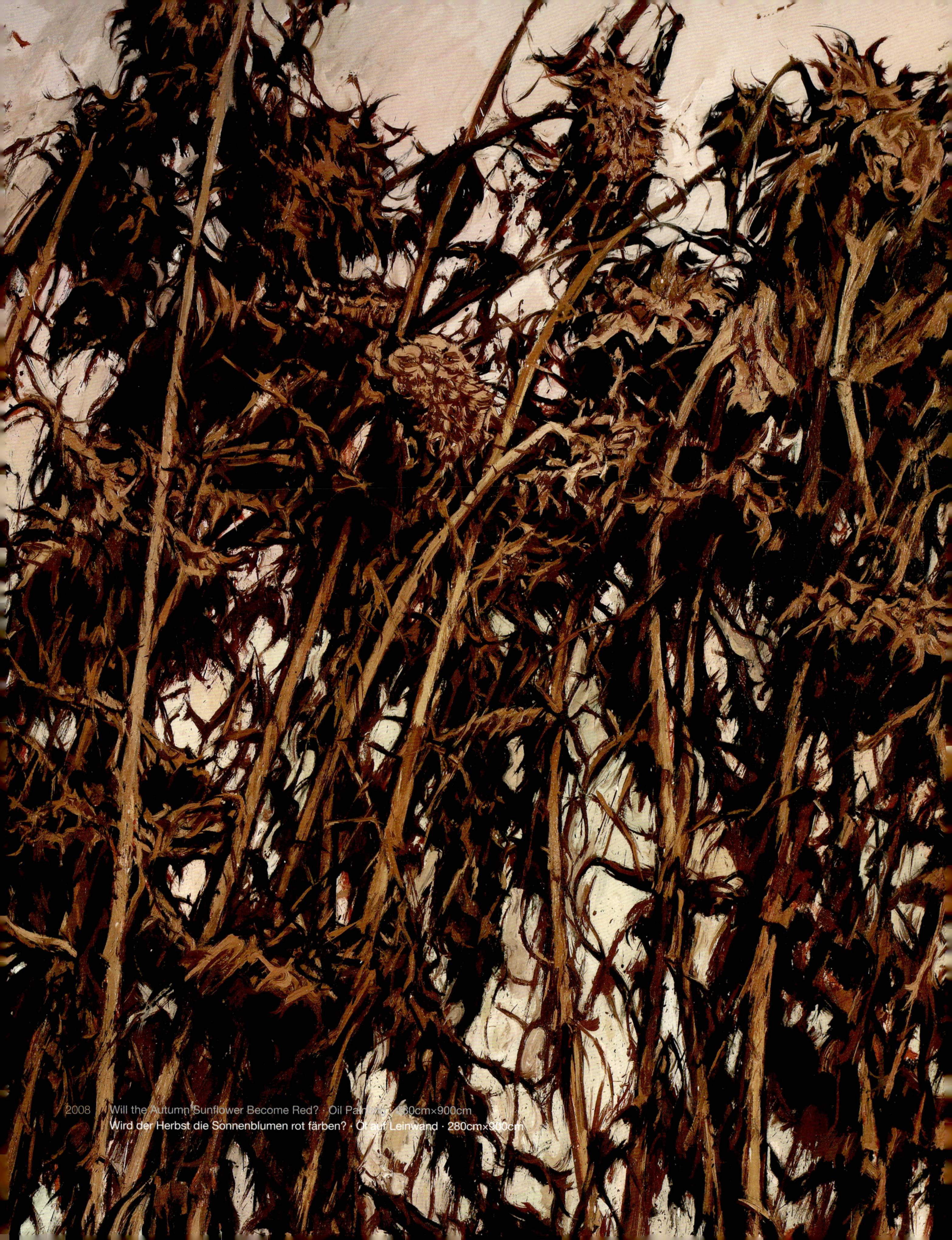

2008 · Will the Autumn Sunflower Become Red? · Oil Paint · 280cm×900cm
Wird der Herbst die Sonnenblumen rot färben? · Öt auf Leinwand · 280cm×900cm

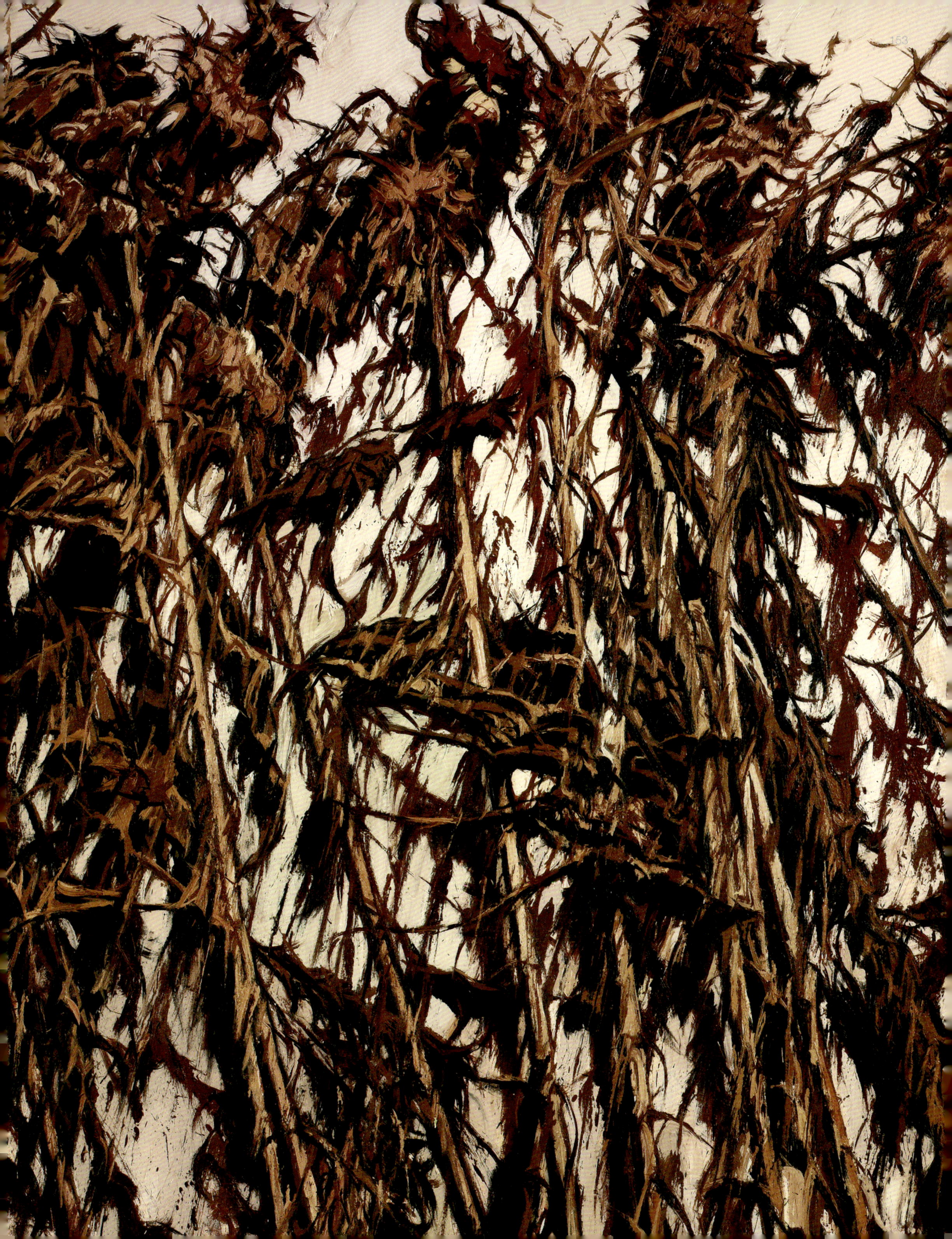

Wird der Herbst die Sonnenblumen rot färben? · Öl auf Leinwand · 280cm×900cm

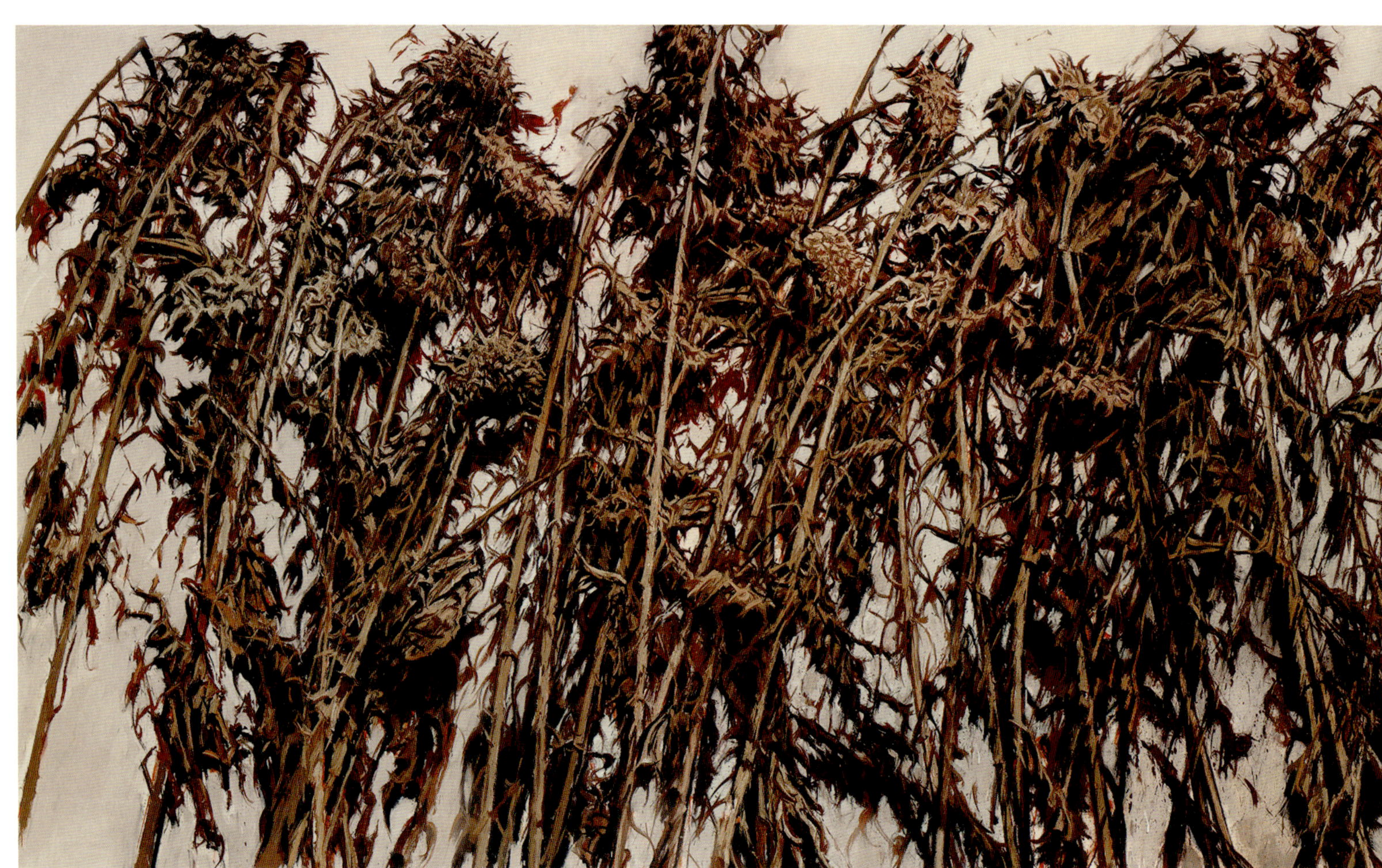

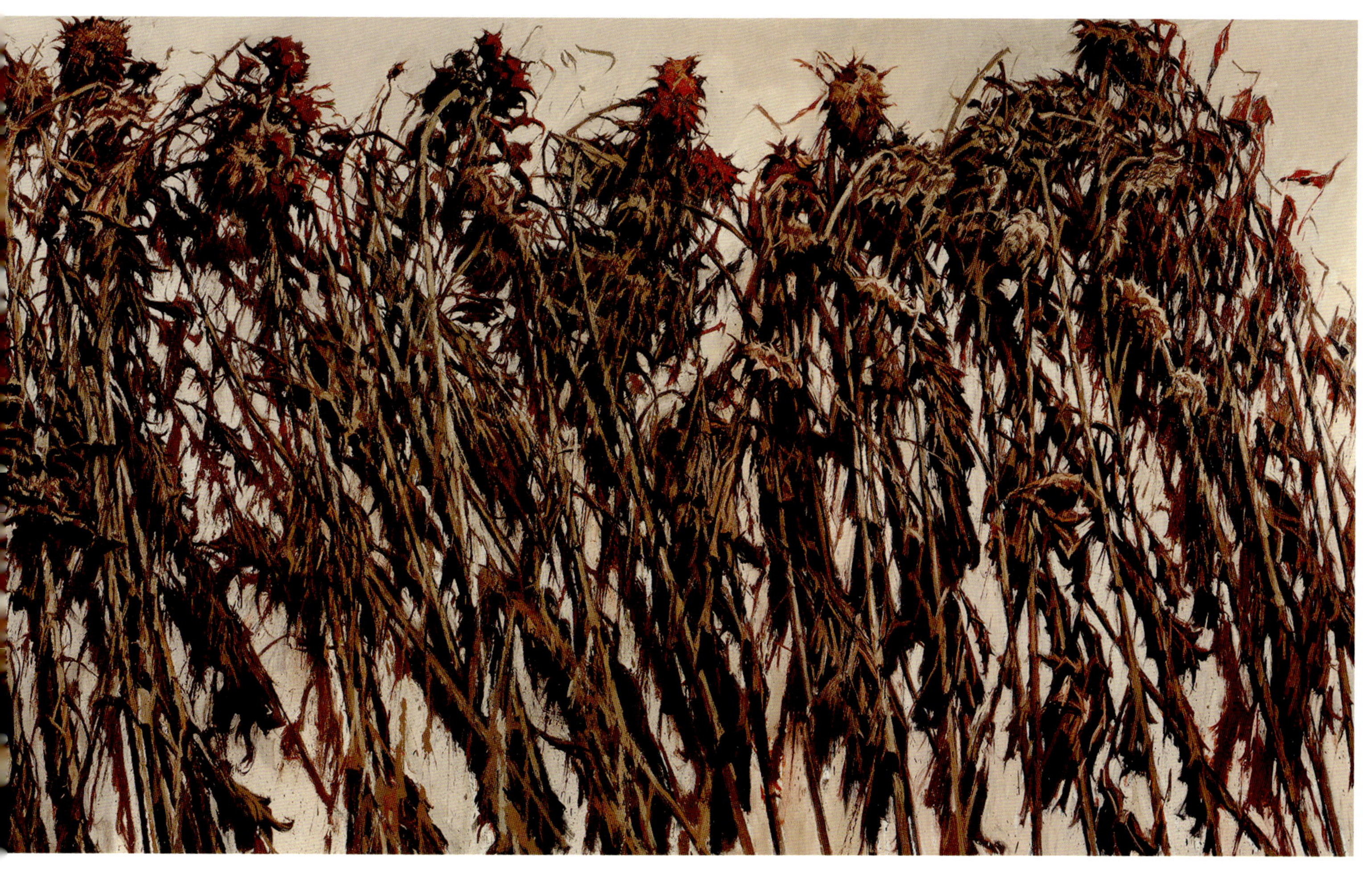

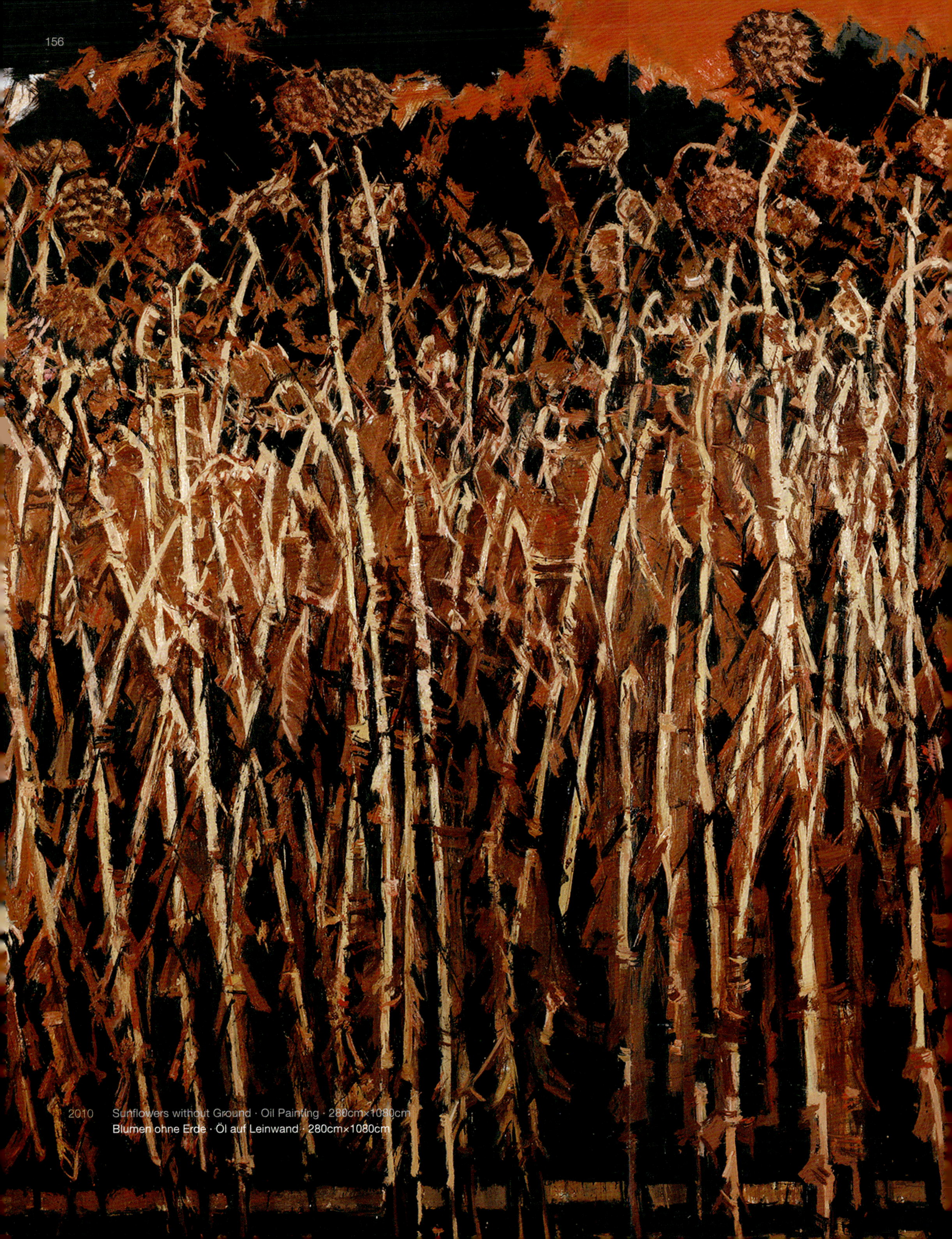

2010　Sunflowers without Ground · Oil Painting · 280cm×1080cm
Blumen ohne Erde · Öl auf Leinwand · 280cm×1080cm

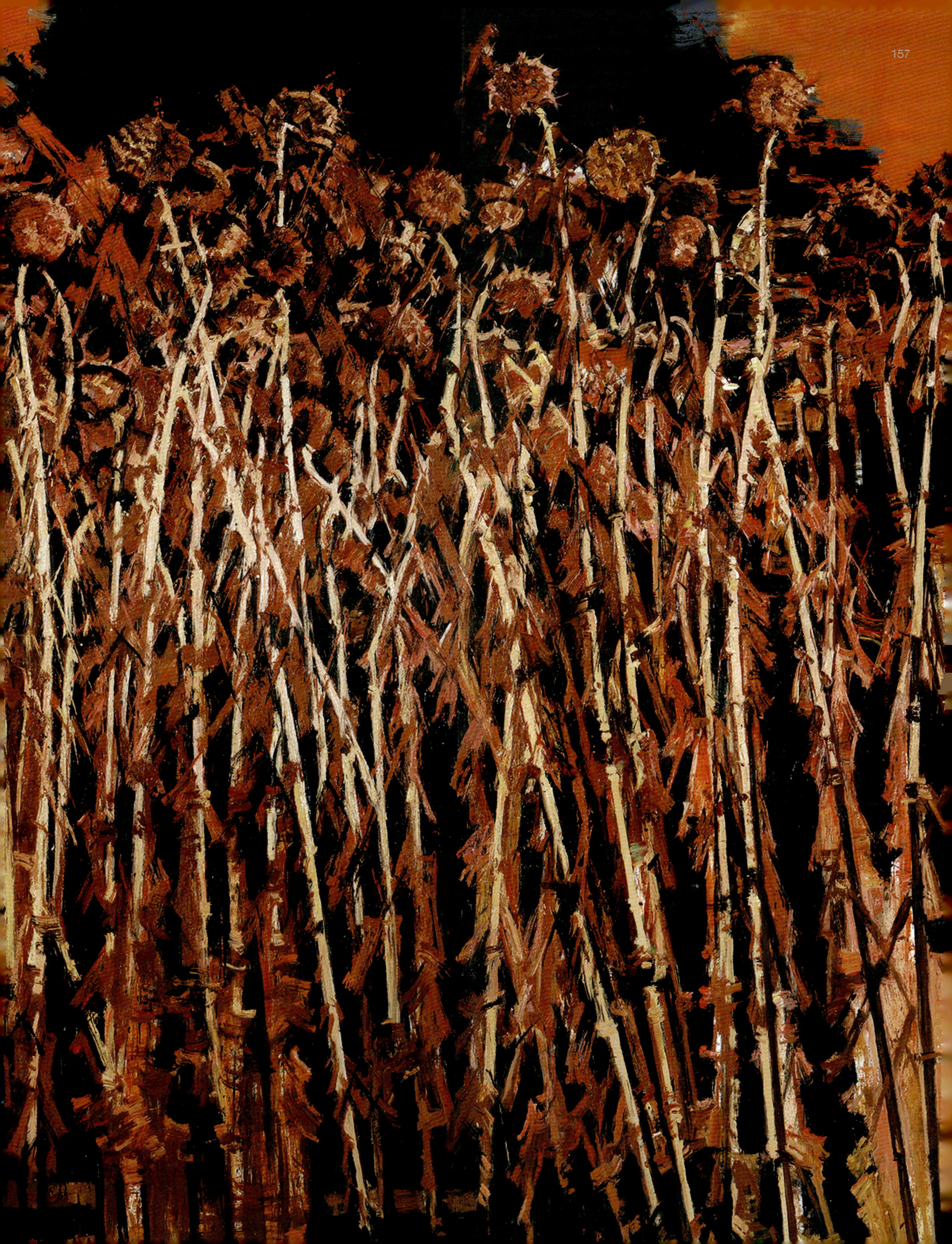

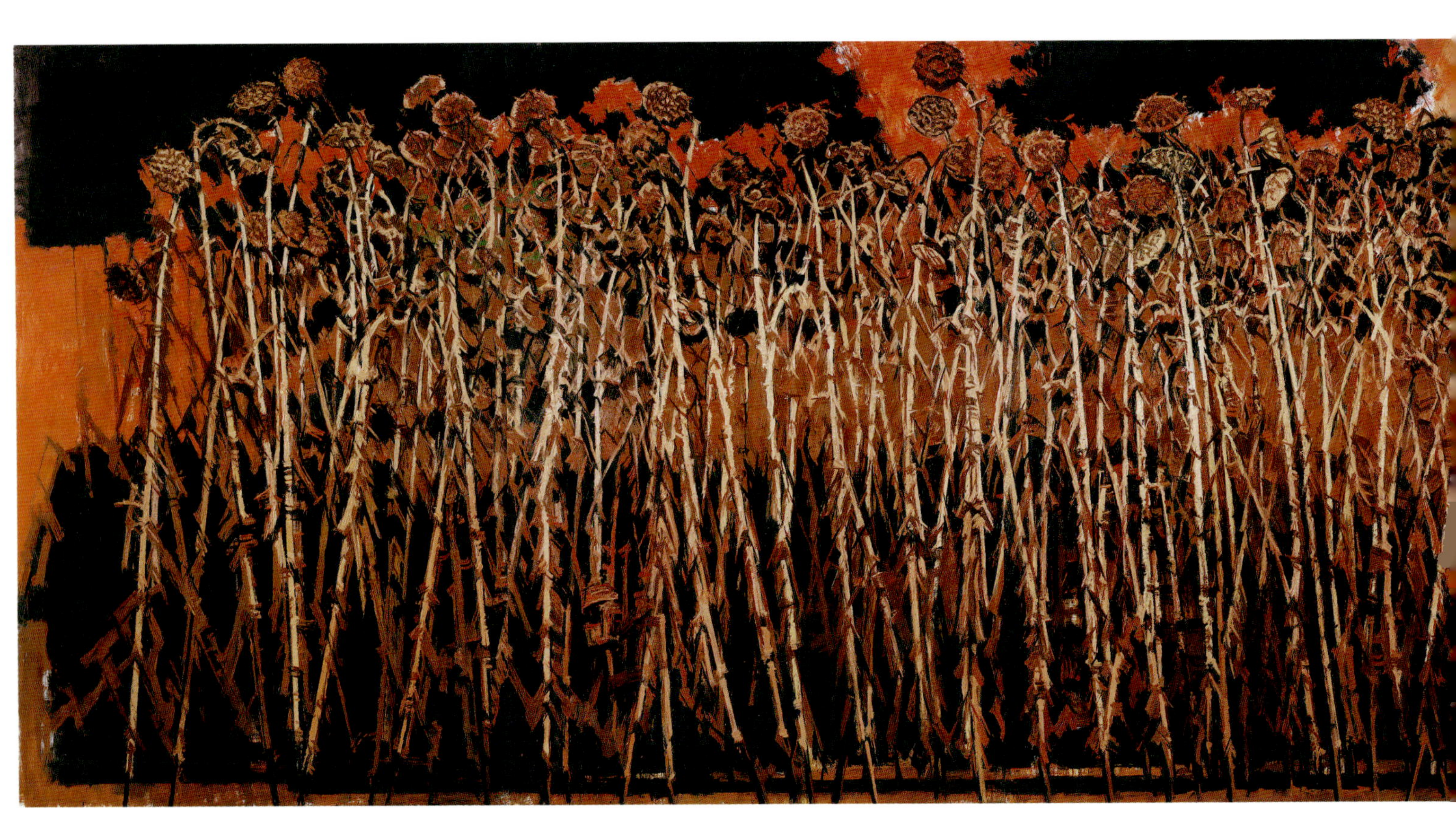

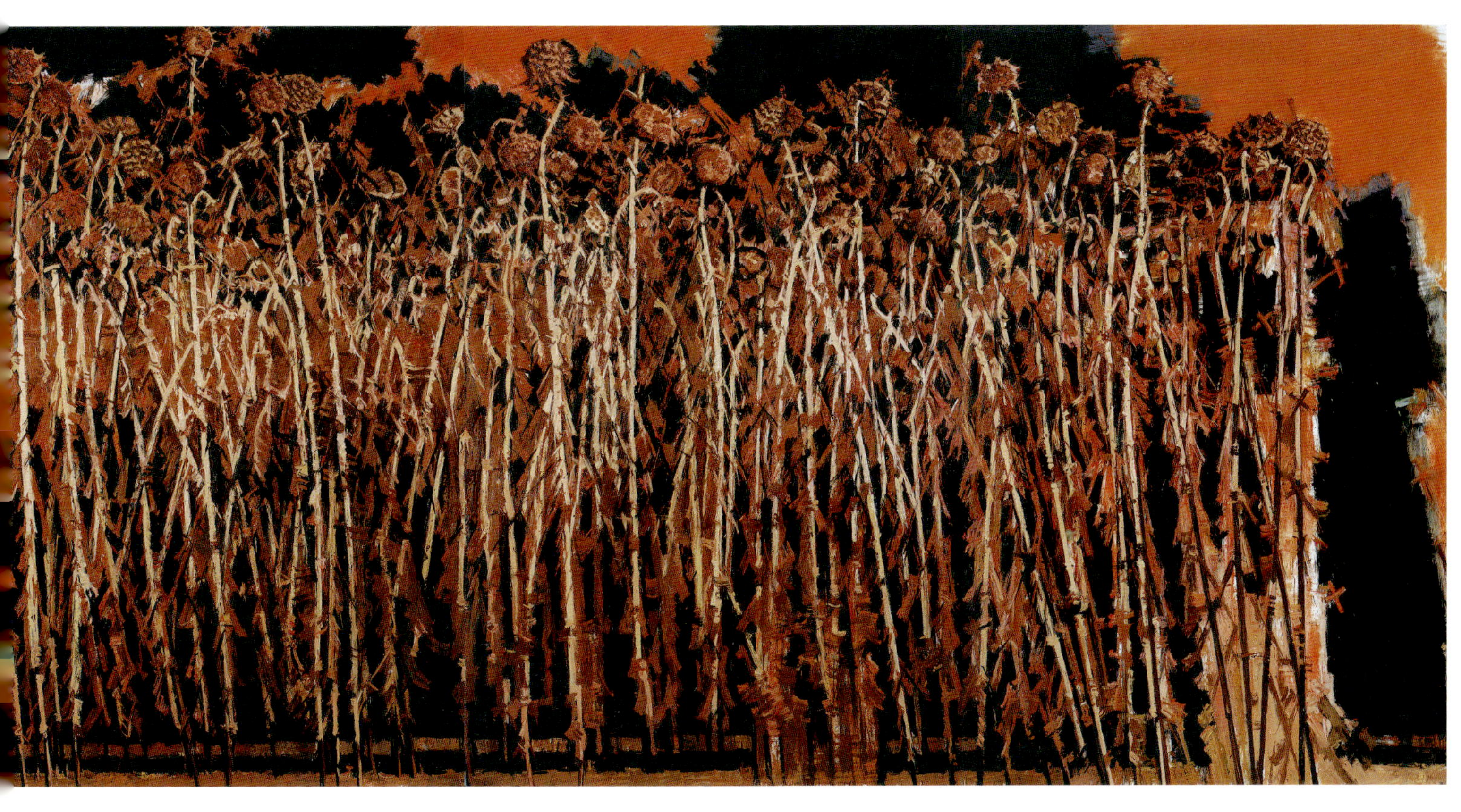

Xu Jiang

President of China Academy of Art, Professor of Oil Painting, President of China Oil Painting Society, Vice-President of China Artists Association. Member of the Education, Science, Culture and Public Health Committee, the National People's Congress. Member of China Federation of Literary and Art Circles, President of Zhejiang Federation of Literary and Art Circles.

After graduating in oil painting from China Academy of Art in the early 1980s, Xu Jiang went to the University of Fine Arts of Hamburg in the late 1980s for postgraduate study. He was invited to exhibit at international exhibitions such as the 2006 Venice Biennale, the 1998 Sao Paolo Art Biennial, the Asia-Pacific Triennial (Queensland, 1993), the 1996 Shanghai Biennale, the 1999 Fukuoka Biennale for Asian Art and the first Guangzhou Triennial (2002), as well as major academic exhibitions including 'Out of the National Ideology: Avant-garde Art of China' (Hamburg, 1995), 'Alors, le Chine?' (Paris, 2003), 'Contemporary Chinese Art Exhibition' (1995, Duisburg) and 'Landscape in Mind: Contemporary Chinese Landscape Art Exhibition' (2011, Washington DC).

He has been awarded, among others, Honorary Mention at the 2nd Beijing Biennale, the Lu Xun Art Award, and the Golden Prize at the 1997 China Art Exhibition. His recent series 'Sunflower Fields' has featured in his solo exhibitions in a few major museums in the country, including 'Vistas' (2006, National Art Museum of China and 2007, Guangdong Art Museum), 'The Redeemed Sunflower Fields' (2009, Shanghai Art Museum), 'To the Sunflower Fields' (2010, Zhejiang Art Museum), 'Most Sunflower Fields' (2011, Suzhou Museum), and 'Re-generation: Story of a Sunflower Field' (2012, Staatliche Kunstammlungen Dresden). His works have been included in the collections of many art museums internationally.

As a key driver of contemporary Chinese art, Xu Jiang has been behind the establishment of some of the major academic exhibition events in China, including the Shanghai Biennale, Guangzhou Triennial and Hangzhou Biennale for Calligraphy-Painting, Chinese Oil Painting Biennale. He has been chairing the academic committee of the Shanghai Biennale and curated Techniques of the Visible, Shanghai Biennale 2004, Living in Time: 29 Chinese Contemporary Artists (Berlin, 2001), Edges of the Earth: Migration of Contemporary Art and Regional Politics of Asia (Hangzhou, 2003), Writing / Non-writing, 2005 Hangzhou International Calligraphic Arts Festival, and the 1st Hangzhou Biennale for Calligraphy-Painting, 2010.

Among his many publications are his personal catalogues *The Redeemed Sunflower Fields* (2009), *Vistas: the Art of Xu Jiang* (2006), *The Earth* (2002), *Contemporary Art and Indigenous Culture* (2002), *Shanghai Mirages* (2001), *Urban Views* (2001) and *Paper, Chess, Art* (1995). He has also published collections of academic essays including *Vigil of One Meter* (2005) and *Sightseeing the City* (2005), *Nanshan Portraits* (2008), *Dismantling and Reconstruction* (2010), *The Sight of the University* (2010) and *The Visionary's Diary* (2010), *Words and Paintings* (2011). In addition he has also edited over 150 academic titles.

Exhibitions

1984 Sixth National Art Exhibition of China, Beijing

1987 Beyond the Open Door, USA

1988 Solo exhibition at the Hochscule für bildende Künste

Solo exhibition at the In Faust Gallery, Hamburg

1989 Hamburg Art Academy 1989 Exhibition and West German International Youth Art Group Exhibition

Solo exhibition at the Hamburg Kulturforum

Solo exhibition at the Lommel Gallery, Cologne

1990 Young Chinese Art, Saarbrücken National Museum of Art, Germany

1991 Second New Academic Exhibition, Hangzhou

1992 First Annual Chinese Oil Painting Exhibition, Hong Kong

Contemporary Young Sculptors Invitational Exhibition

Third Documentary Exhibition of Chinese Contemporary Art

1993 Asia Pacific Triennial, National Gallery, Queensland, Australia

Solo exhibition at Zee Stone Gallery, Hong Kong

1994 Second Chinese Oil Painting Exhibition; National Art Museum of China, Beijing

Chinese Art Critics' Annual Nomination Exhibition of Oil Painting, National Art Museum of China, Beijing

Exhibition of 12 Contemporary Chinese Oil Painters, New York and Los Angeles

1995 China's New Art, Hamburg

1996 The First Shanghai Biennale, Shanghai

1997 First Scholarly Invitational Exhibition of Contemporary Art, National Art Museum of China, Beijing

Great Exhibition of Chinese Art, National Art Museum of China, Beijing

1998 Sao Paulo Biennale

Between Abstraction and Representation, Taipei

1999 Fourteenth International Exhibition of Asian Art, Fukuoka Asian Art Museum, Japan

Ninth National Art Exhibition of China, National Art Museum of China, Beijing

2000 Gate of the Century: Invitational Exhibition of Chinese Art 1979-1999, Spain

Twentieth Century Chinese Oil Painting, National Art Museum of China, Beijing

2001 Landscapes of History: Exhibition of Xu Jiang, Berlin

Heaven & Earth: 2 Visions of China, Chicago Glass Curtain Gallery

New Image: Twenty Years of Contemporary Chinese Painting, National Art Museum of China, Beijing

The First Chengdu Biennial

Living in Time: 29 Chinese Contemporary Artists, Berlin

2002 Conceptual Images: 2002 Invitational Exhibition of Contemporary Chinese Oil Painting

Core of a Century: An Exhibition of 50 Contemporary Chinese Artists

2003 Parallel Time: Exhibition of Asian Contemporary Art, Hangzhou

Third Chinese Oil Painting Exhibition, National Art Museum of China, Beijing

2004 Alors la Chine? Centre Georges Pompidou, Paris

2004 First Wuhan Fine Arts Documentary Exhibition, Wuhan

2005 First International Beijing Biennale, National Art Museum of China, Beijing

2005 Second Chengdu Biennale

The Great River: A Retrospective of the New Era of Chinese Oil Painting, National Art Museum of China, Beijing

2006 Vistas: The Art of Xu Jiang, National Art Museum of China, Beijing

Microcosmos: Chinese Contemporary Art, Macau Art Museum

Intersections of History: Chinese Contemporary Art, National Museum of Art, Tehran

2007 Visions: The Art of Xu Jiang, Guangdong Museum of Art

The Hand for Cherishing "Paper", Italy

Far West: Four Artists between Germany and China

2008 Four Season: The 3rd China Media Art Festival, Hangzhou

Unpacking: Chinese Contemporary Art Exhibition, Hangzhou

Expand & Fusion — Chinese Oil Painting Exhibition, National Art Museum of China, Beijing

The Grist between the Stone: A meeting between Swedish and Chinese Contemporary Painting

2009 Redemption of a Sunflower Garden: New Works of Xu Jiang, Shanghai Art Museum

2010 Ttibutions to the Sunflower Fields ,Zhejiang Art Museum, Hangzhou

Dimention of Construction: Invitional Exhibiton of Chinese Contemporay Art, National Art Museum of China, Beijing

30 Years of Chinese Contemporary Art (1979-2009) , Minsheng Art Museum, Shanghai

2011 In the Depth of Sunflower Field , Suzhou Museum

Landscape in Mind: Contemporary Chinese Landscape Art Exhibition, Washington DC

Chinese Historical Context: Invitational Exhibition of Chinese Contemporary Art, Beijing Moca

Visuality: Exhibiton of Art and Phenomenology, Art Museum of CAA, Hangzhou

Sonet of Sunflower Field: Exhibition of Xu Jiang , Tina Keng Gallery, Taipei

2012 Gazing & Vision: French and Chinese Expressional Painters, Shanghai Art Museum

Re-generation: Story of a Sunflower Field, Staatliche Kunstammlungen Dresden

2013 Blossoming Spirits: Joint Exhibiton of Xu Jiang and Shihui, Ludwig Museum, Koblenz

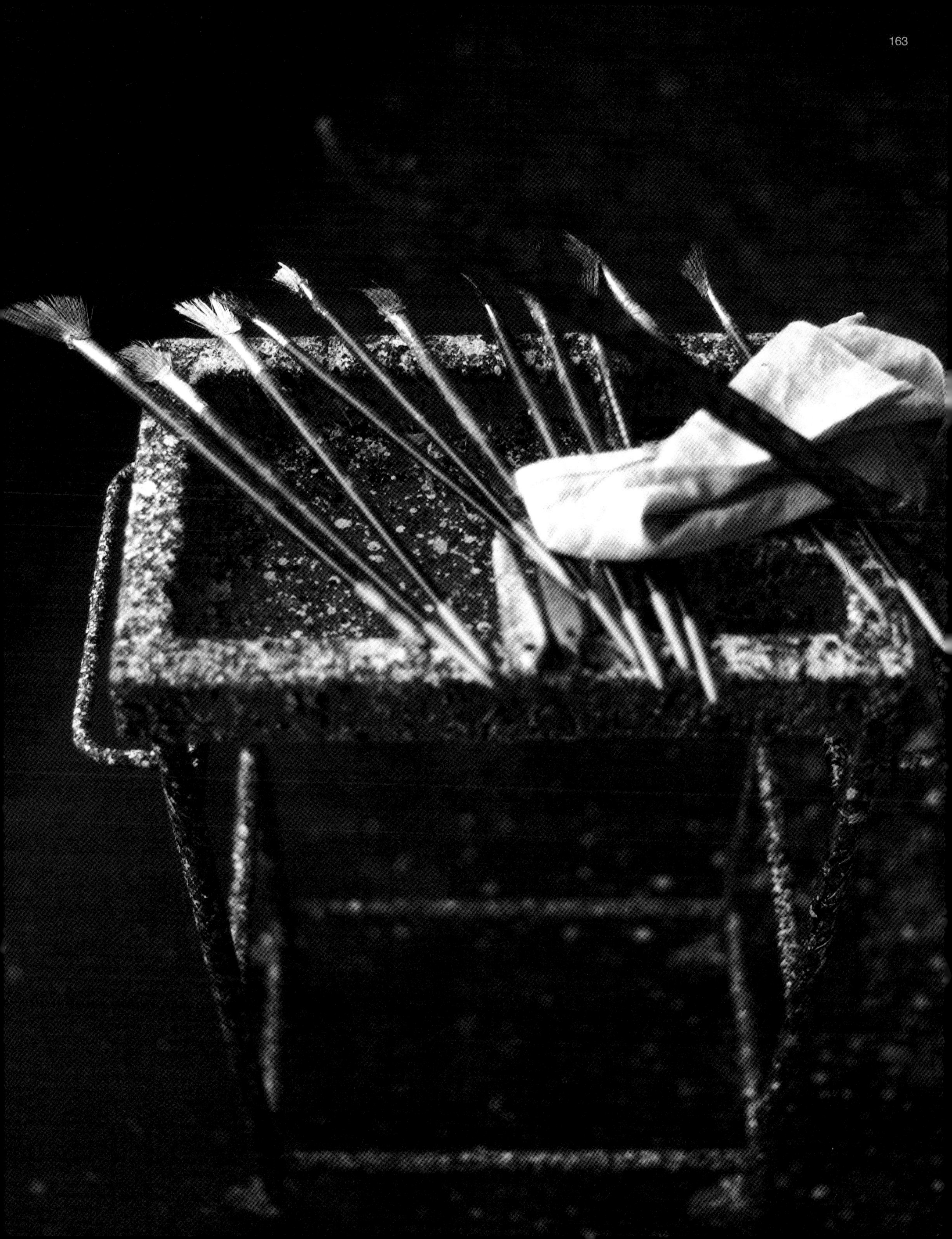

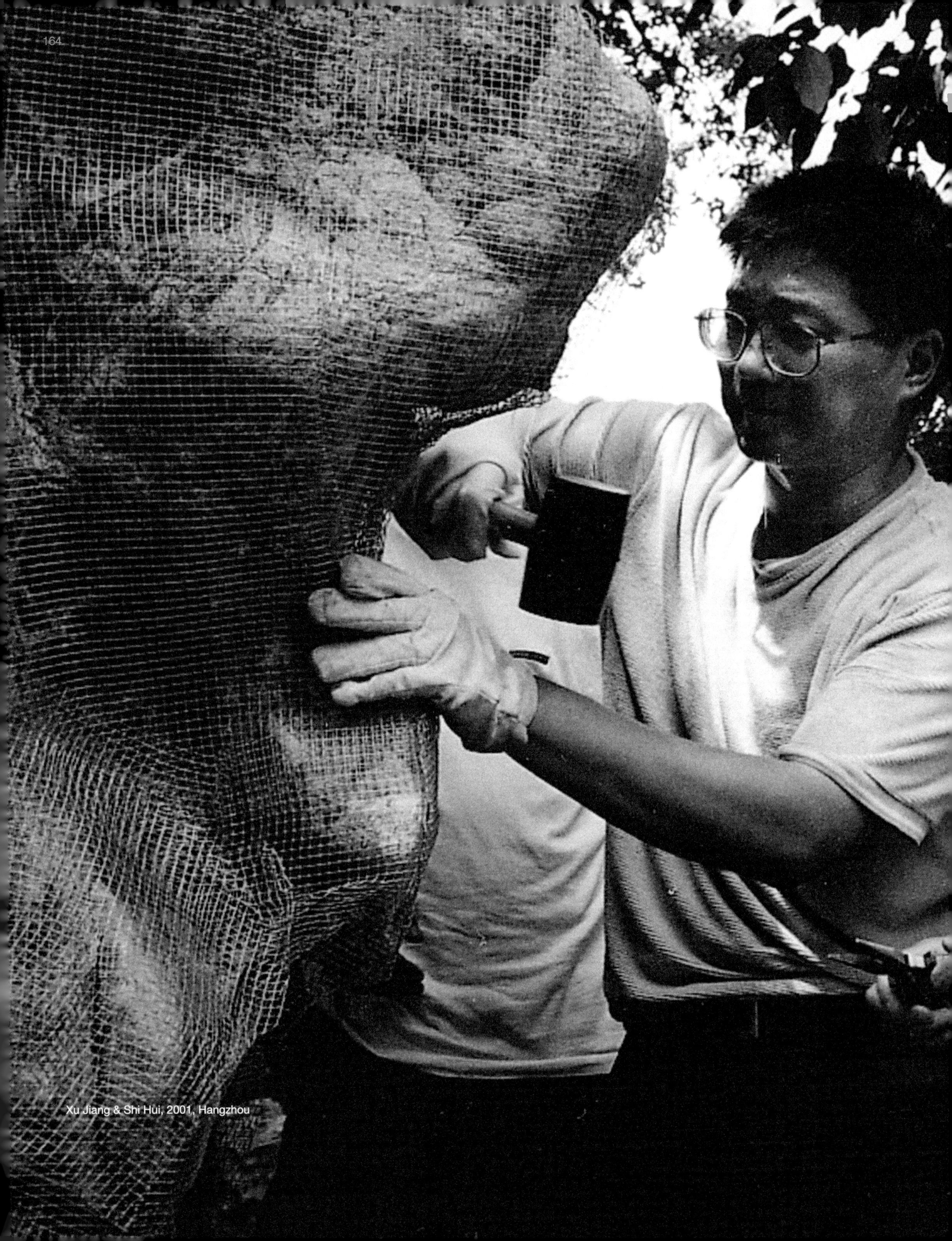

Xu Jiang & Shi Hui, 2001, Hangzhou

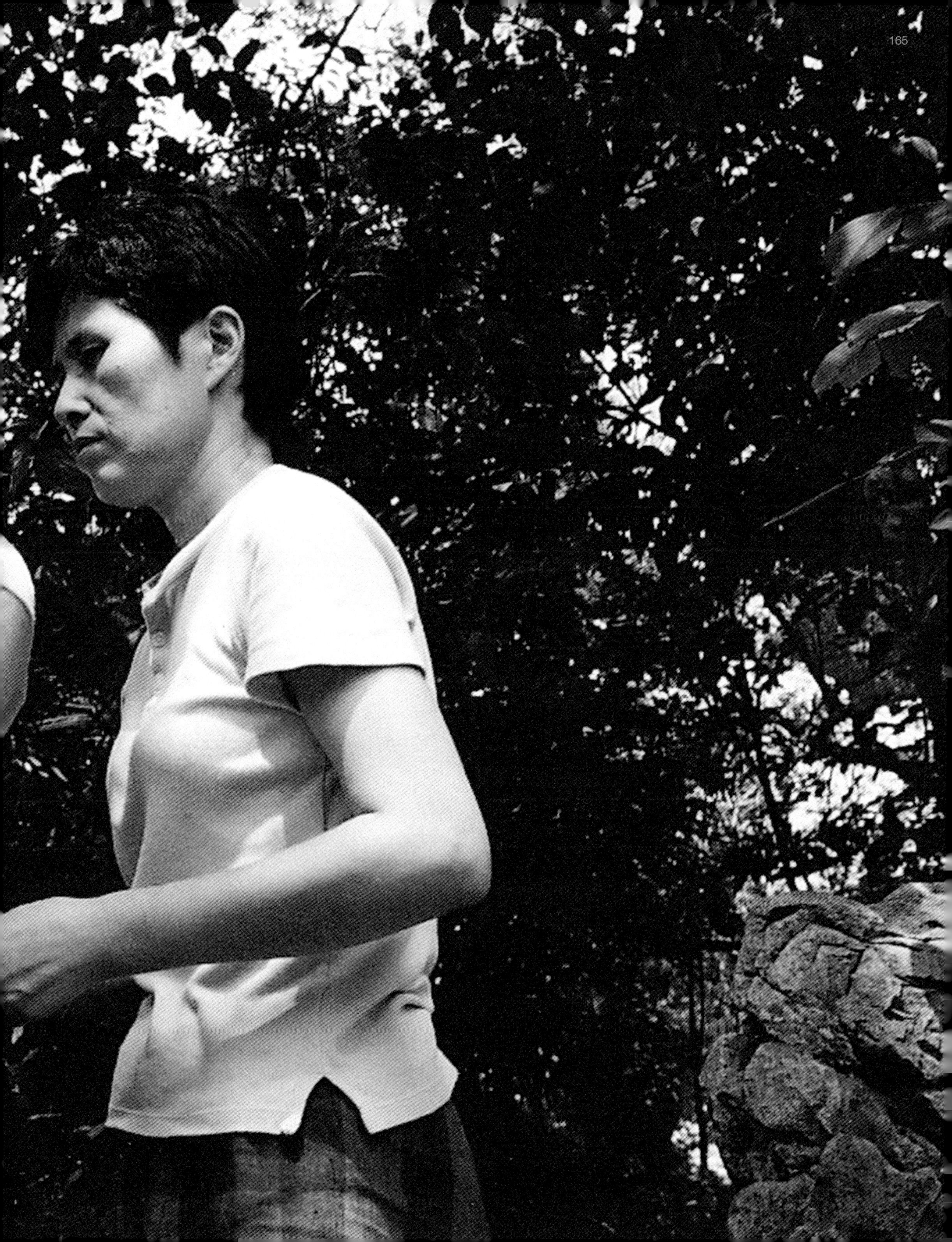

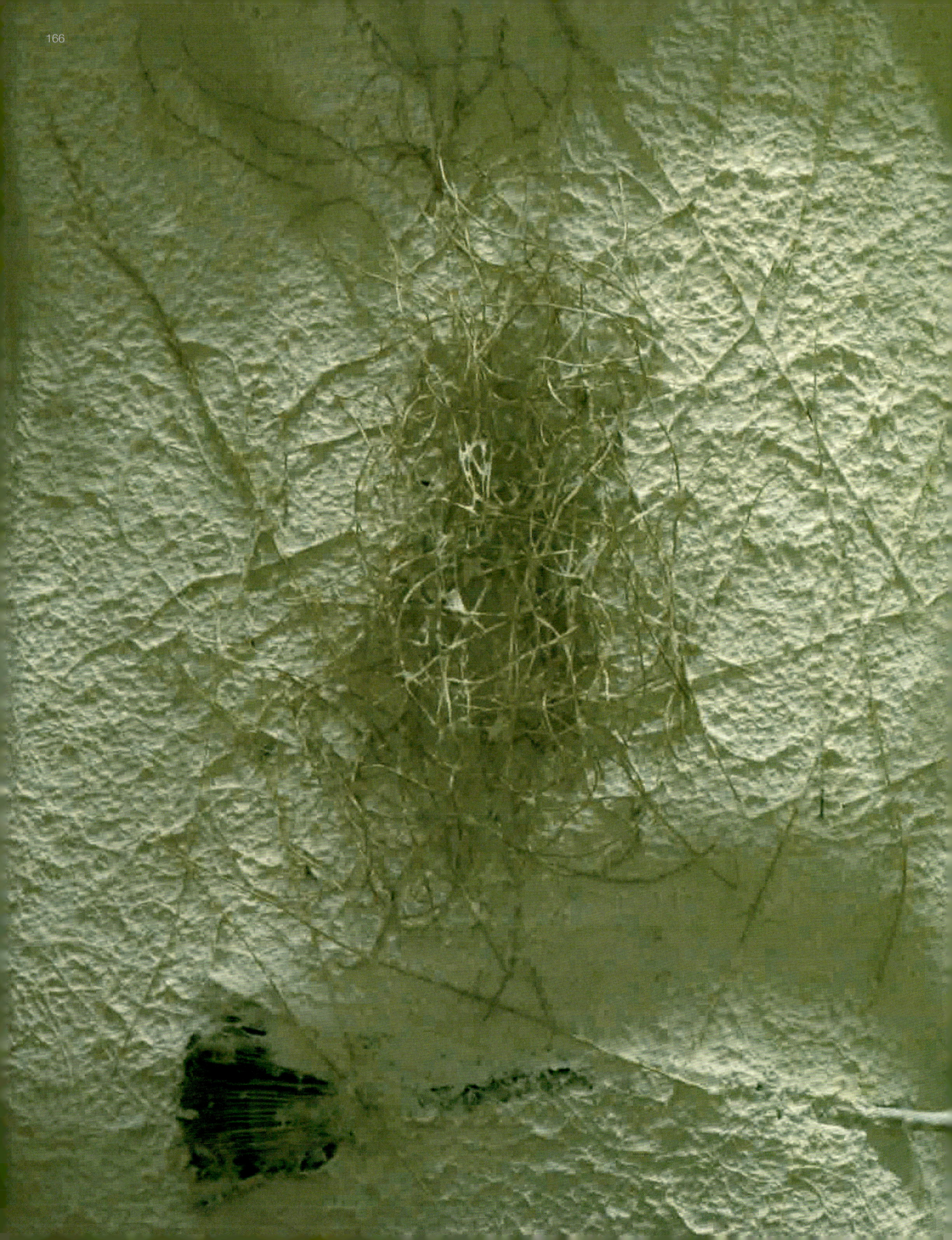

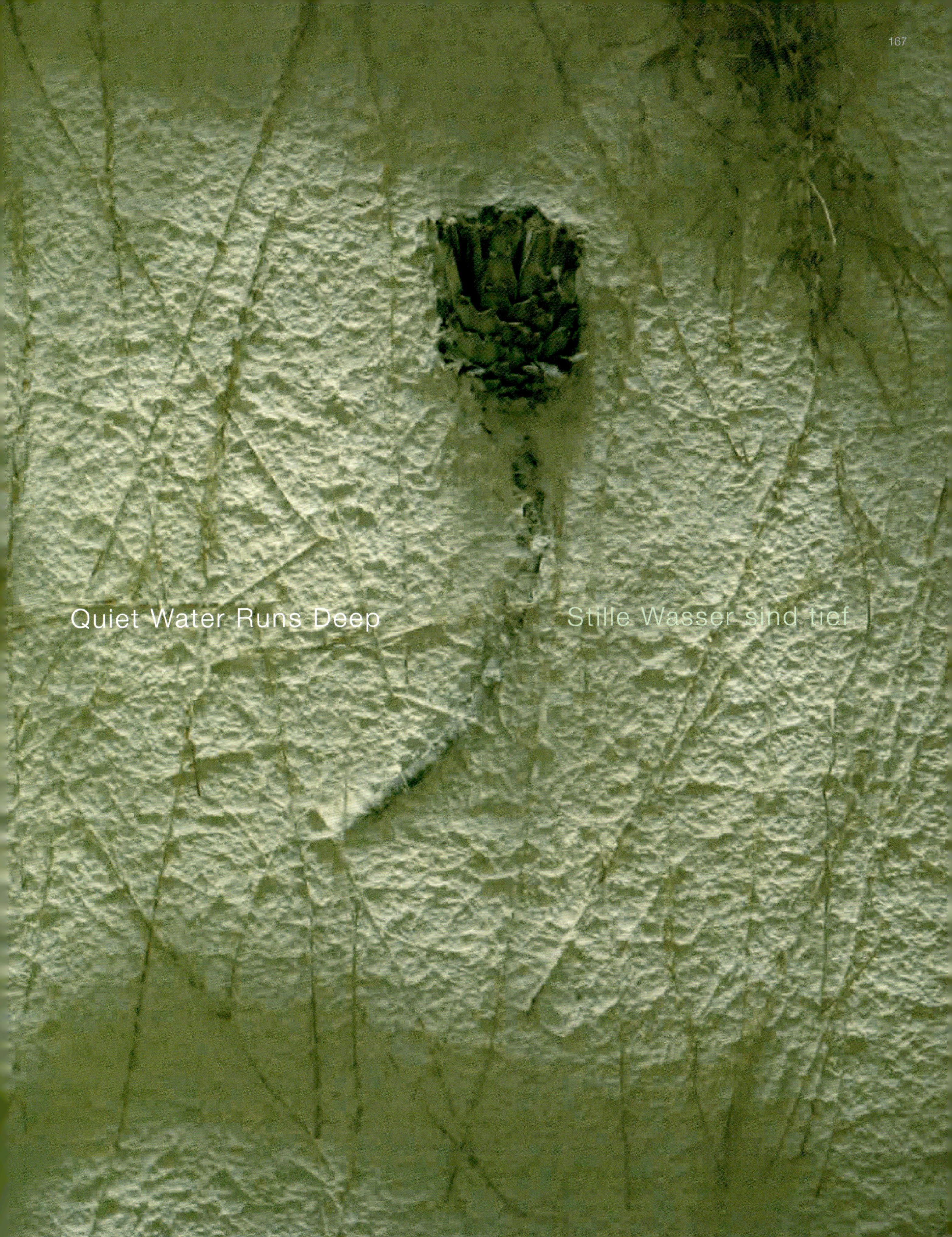

Quiet Water Runs Deep
Stille Wasser sind tief

From 'Spiritual Experience' to 'Cultural Experience'
The Art of Shi Hui
Fan Di'an

Von der „spirituellen Erfahrung" zum „kulturellen Erlebnis"
Die Kunst Shi Huis
Fan Di'an

In 2001, Shi Hui erected a paper-made literati rockery in the courtyard of Museum für Gegenwart (formerly the Hamburger Bahnhof) in Berlin. The title of the work is 'Fake Mountains: Visual Reflections in a Different Cultural Context'. As the title suggest, Shi Hui's work can be seen as the visual reflections within the complex cross-cultural context of contemporary art. Such reflections do not fall into scholarly metaphysics that is devoid of realistic concerns. Rather they permeate the feminine refinement and sensitivity that characterize her weaving and creativity.

In the complex transformations in contemporary Chinese art at the start of the 21st century, many artists have chosen to brave the conceptual wave and resort to innovative forms and experiment in medium. Such practices have constituted the full picture of Chinese art's march towards the contemporary. Shi Hui can be detected in this movement. From her works since the 1990s, the gestation process of each of her works is one that has consistently respected her own perceptions and the flowing orientation of her own psychological development. After completion, her works of course assume a 'shape', but do not come with an a priori 'form'. Her works are the result of

Im Jahr 2001 wurde ein Kunstfelsen aus Papier im Hof des Berliner Museums für Gegenwart (früher: Hamburger Bahnhof) aufgebaut. Der Titel des Werkes lautet: "Künstlicher Berg --- eine visuelle Reflexion in verschiedenen kulturellen Kontexten". Wie der Titel schon sagt, lässt sich Shi Huis Werk als eine visuelle Reflexion in einem transkulturellen Kontext der gegenwärtigen Kunst betrachten. Eine Reflexion, die eben nicht der unrealistischen Metaphysik der Gelehrten zuzuordnen ist, sondern sie gelangt durch die weibliche Empfindsamkeit hindurch, die ihr schöpferisches Weben umso mehr auszeichnet.

Im Zuge zahlreicher komplizierter Umwandlungen der chinesischen Kunst, die zu Beginn des 21.Jahrhunderts stattfanden, haben sich viele Künstler um eine neue Welle der Ideen, neue Kunstformen sowie Experimente mittels der Medien bemüht. Dies stellt einen Überblick über die Wege zur Moderne dar, welche die chinesische Kunst eingeschlagen hat. Shi Hui gehört ohne Zweifel auch zu jenen Künstlern. An allen von ihr seit 1990 geschaffenen Werken ist zu erkennen, dass die Künstlerin während der Entstehungphase großen Wert auf ihr Selbstgefühl und ihren Gedanken gelegt hat. Die

realization in an open-ended creative psychological space. Take the series of four groups of works titled 'Knots', which she completed during the 1990s. We cannot detect the formal conception prior to her hand starting the process of weaving. How they assume the eventual form was not the work of previously imagined forms. Rather it is the result of following the material's own trend of development at every turn of the weaving process. The works were not so much completed as fragments of her entire creative oeuvre, which she could not complete, but temporarily conclude. When she employs the language of weaving, the life of natural objects assumes an enlivened state and is awakened from its stupor to develop in an orderless way. What she affirms is the rather contingent forms of nature. Material objects start to display the colour of life under the nourishment of her emotions and sentiments. Therefore, names of the works in these series are not, and cannot be, 'cultural', but 'natural', such as 'Chains', 'Nests', 'Columns', and 'Flux'. If we locate her art within the landscape of Chinese art since the 1990s, then we can safely conclude that her respect for the intrinsic life value and natural characteristics of things in the 'linguistic turn' of Chinese art of the time characterised by 'anti-formalism' and the 'deconstruction of form'.

In the meantime, she has also reinforced this orientation from another angle, namely the combination of her work with the natural environment, which has enabled her work to inhabit the homeland in a larger space and find its 'form' in its relation with the natural environment. In this sense, her 1992 work 'Nests' provides a prime example. When the woven white half-ball touched the green grassland, the work attained its own space. Likewise, only when the rope-like 'Entwine' (1994-1995) wound around the tree, and when the slices of 'Traces' (2000) were placed in the shadow of

gefertigten Werken verfügen zwar über eine äußere Form, sie sind jedoch von jedem vorbestimmten Format befreit. Also sind sie die Ergebnisse der Verwirklichung der frei entwickelten Gedanken. Nehmen wir die vier aus 1990 stammenden Werke namens „Knoten" als ein Beispiel: man sieht eigentlich nur die finale Form der Werke, jedoch nicht die Ideen vor dem Weben und wie sie alle zur endgültigen Form gekommen sind. Sie sind nicht die Ergebnisse oder Verwirklichung vorgeregelter Intentionen, sondern das Weben entwickelt sich Schritt für Schritt. Die Werke sind in diesem Sinne nicht von ihr „gefertigt" worden, sondern eine Wiedergabe der Abschnitte der Schöpfung, die nie wirklich verwirklicht werden kann und deshalb nur vorübergehend zusammenfassend dargestellt ist. Denn jedesmal wenn sie die Sprache des Webens benutzt, wird jeder natürliche Gegenstand sofort ins Leben gerufen. Er wacht auf, entwickelt sich und befreit sich von jeder Ordnung. Alles, wofür sie plädiert, ist die Zufälligkeit der natürlichen Bewegung, die den Gegenständen durch das Ernähren mit Gefühlen den Schein von Lebendigkeit verleiht. Hierfür sind all die Namen ihrer derartigen Werke nicht „kulturell"--- sie können auch nicht „kulturell" sein. Stattdessen sind die Namen wie „Ketten", „Nester", „Säulen" oder „Ströme" eher „natürlich" geprägt. Stellt man ihre Werke in den Hintergrund der chinesischen Kunstwerke seit 1990, so erkennt man, dass die Idee der Künstlerin, den inneren Wert und die natürlichen Eigenschaften der Gegenstände hervor zu rufen, genau die von „Antiformalismus" wie „Dekonstruktion der Formen" geprägte „linguistische Umwandlung" zu dieser Zeit widerspiegelt.

Zur gleichen Zeit bekräftigt sie ihre Neigung aus einer anderen Perspektive, indem sie die Werke mit der natürlichen Umgebung in Verbindung setzt und den Werken somit eine „Heimat" darbietet. Dadurch wird den Werken eine Form

groves, did the works' theme and implications materialise. The approach of 'reconfiguring' 'form' in a large space that leads to the final completion of the work has left on her work a unique personal imprint. We may ask ourselves: Is she a weaving artist? Obviously not. Is she a sculptor? Perhaps not either. Is she an environment artist? No. In the use of materials, she is apparently not a member of the new media experiment movement, but her language is part of the wave of 'intermedia' art that is still under way today.

Shi Hui's artistic 'identity' can perhaps be clearly understood today. As a female artist, her feminism is clearly demonstrated in her choice of medium and the technique of weaving. Mr Fan Jingzhong and Ms Xu Hong have expressed their approval of the concentrated manual labour in the process of weaving (See *The Poetry of Modesty: A Catalogue of Works by Shi Hui*). Indeed, from the moment Shui Hui chose the white Chinese xuan paper as her main medium, she has never gone back. We can clearly discern her love for this medium, behind which lies an identification with the unique quality that marks the affinity between the medium and her own mind, as well as confidence in the contemporary transvaluation of traditional Chinese media. The latter is of greater significance, for in the age when Chinese art is overwhelmed by the medium categories and experience of the West, the Chinese artist's understanding and choice of medium is by itself a measurement of cultural cognisance. Shi Hui is no doubt sober about this. Likewise, the great amount of labour that goes into the process of her weaving is also able to demonstrate the sensitivity and pertinacity of the female artist. In addition, the fact that she regards the process of weaving as experiential can be termed as a 'postmodern pantheist' image interpretation. In this process, the spiritual experience is not manifested as responses to real objects, but also a

verliehen. „Nest" (1992) ist eines der frühesten Beispiele solcher Art. In dem Moment, wo die gewebte weiße Halbkugel auf die grüne Wiese fällt, wird das Raumgefühl des Werks sofort wahrgenommen. Gleiches gilt auch für folgende zwei Werke: Nur wenn das seilförmige „Umranken" die Bäume umschlingt und sich der scheibenförmige „Abdruck" im Schatten der Blätter befindet, können die übertragenen Deutungen zum Ausdruck gebracht werden. Ihre Werke sind deshalb durch ihre eigene Persönlichkeit geprägt, als dass die Künstlerin ihre Werke mittels „Rekonstruktion der Formen" vollendet. Manche mögen fragen, ob sie eine Weberin ist? Offensichtlich nicht. Ist sie denn eine Bildhauerin? Auch nicht. Eine Umweltkünstlerin? Ebenfalls nicht. Was die Verwendung von Materialien anbelangt, experimentiert sie zwar nicht mit neuen Medien, ihre Sprache weist dennoch die Eigenschaft der Intermedialität auf, die sich heutzutage so rasant entwickelt.

Shi Huis Identität als Künstlerin findet heute eindeutig Anerkennung. Als Künstlerin hat sie ihre feministischen Gedanken durch die Auswahl der Medien und die Art des Webens klar vorgestellt. Von Herrn Fan Jingzhong und Frau Xu Hong hat sie auch für ihre unübertreffliche Handarbeit, auf welche sie während des Webens großen Wert legt, viel Lob erhalten (siehe „Die Poesie der Bescheidenheit- -Werksammlung von Shi Hui"). Tatsächlich hat Shi Hui nie das weiße *Xuan*-Papier aufgegeben, nachdem sie es als ihr Hauptmedium festgelegt hatte. Daran ist ihre Vorliebe für das traditionelle chinesische Medium deutlich zu erkennen. Das hat wohl auch damit zu tun, dass sie sich dem von ihr selbst ausgewählten Material verbunden fühlt und dass sie an eine Neubewertung des traditionellen chinesischen Mediums glaubt. Das Letztere erweist sich als noch bedeutungsvoller in einer Zeit, in der die westlichen Medienarten und medialen Erfahrungen eine dominierende Rolle in der chinesischen

free self-consciousness, which seeks to realise its inner self-understanding while keeping the external in the reins. Strictly speaking, many of Shi Hui's works do not supply clearly identifiable meanings. Rather they offer an opportunity for the viewer to experience them. In this sense her female 'identity' is evident by implication but hidden from perception.

At the start of the new century, Shi Hui's art has undergone a series of transformations in comparison to the themes and forms of the 1990s, the most important of which could be summarised as the addition of 'cultural experience' to the expressive basis of 'spiritual experience'. In the Shanghai Biennale of 2000, her work 'Drift' allowed us a glimpse of the new developments in her art. The thickly-sliced shapes drifting in space did not give the impression of weightlessness. Rather it supplied a suspense of 'estrangement' to the viewer's visual psychology, as the spiritual representation of contemporary culture underlies the seeming appeal to visual forms. Mr Wu Hung apparently grasped its novelty and made the following comment, 'This is a postmodern sculpture. With irregular, hollowed-out shapes and their richly textured surfaces, the work attains a reinforced three-dimensionality. However, what matters most remains the drifting contrast between grandeur and fragility, which is a visual expressivity Shi Hui has been perfecting over the years.' From 'spiritual experience' to 'cultural experience', from 'natural environment' to 'cultural space', Shi Hui's art increasingly demonstrates a dialogic relationship with the loci of exhibition which are also the sites of culture.

Kunst spielen. Das Verstehen und die Auswahl der Medien durch die chinesischen Künstlern erweist sich an sich bereits als Maßstab kultureller Kenntnis. Darüber ist sich Shi Hui zweifellos im Klaren, außerdem ist sie durch ihre äußerst aufwändige Handarbeit im Akt des Webens berechtigt, Anerkennung für ihre natürliche Empfindsamkeit und Hartnäckigkeit zu empfangen. Darüber hinaus sieht sie den Webeprozess als einen Prozess des Erfahrungsammelns an, was wiederum als eine visuelle Interpretation eines „postmodernen Pantheisten" zu betrachten ist. In diesem Kontext ist die „psychologische Erfahrung" nicht nur die Widerspiegelung der Wahrnehmung der Gegenstände, sondern ein freies Selbstbewusstsein, ein Selbstverständnis, welches erst bei der Beherrschung der Gegenstände erzielt wird. Genau gesagt bieten viele von Shi Huis Werken keine eindeutigen Interpretationen, sie lassen die Betrachter sie selber wahrnehmen und fühlen. In diesem Sinne erweist sich ihre weibliche Identität in der Deutung als klar, aber vom Gefühl her versteckt.

Zu Beginn des neuen Jahrhunderts hat Shi Huis Kunst erneut Entwicklung erfahren. Eines der wichtigsten Charakteristika ist der Aufbau des „kulturellen Erlebnisses" auf der „geistigen Erfahrung". Im Jahr 2000 zeigte ihr Werk „Dahintreiben" auf der Biennale in Shanghai dem Publikum die neue Entwicklung in ihrer Kunst. Kurz nachdem man einen Blick auf eine Menge der großen, dicken Streifen geworfen hat, die schwebend im Raum stehen, hat man ein visuelles Verfremdungs-gefühl, denn die Form der Kunstwerke ist eigentlich nicht nur visuell auffällig, sondern sie sind im Kern eine aktuelle Widerspiegelung der gegenwärtigen Kultur. Herr Wu Hong, den das Werk begeisterte, kommentierte: „Dies ist eine postmoderne Skulptur, die durch unregelmäßige, hohle Form und üppig texturierte Oberfläche eine gestärkte Dreidimensionalität aufweist. Dabei ist zu bemerken, dass genau

der wechselnde, auffällige Kontrast zwischen Mächtigkeit und
Zerbrechlichkeit ein immer weiter elaboriertes Charakteristi-
kum im visuellen Ausdruck Shi Huis darstellt." Von „spiritueller
Erfahrung" hin zu einem „kulturellen Erlebnis", von „natürlicher
Umgebung" hin zu einem „kulturellen Raum" wird Shi Huis
Kunst besonders aufgrund Ihrer dialogischen Beziehung mit
den Ausstellungsstandorten - auch als Kulturfront bezeichnet
- geliebt und geschätzt.

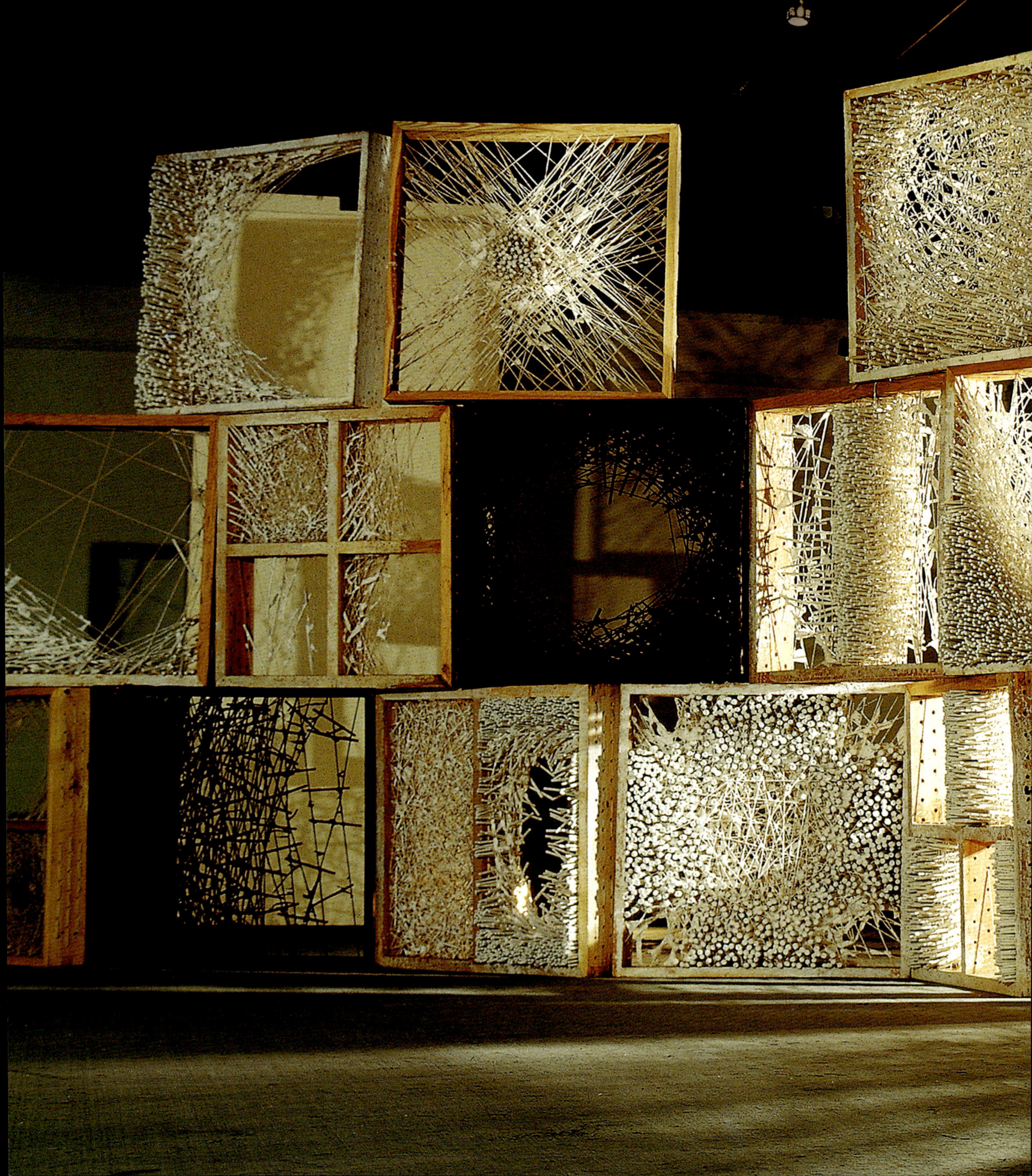

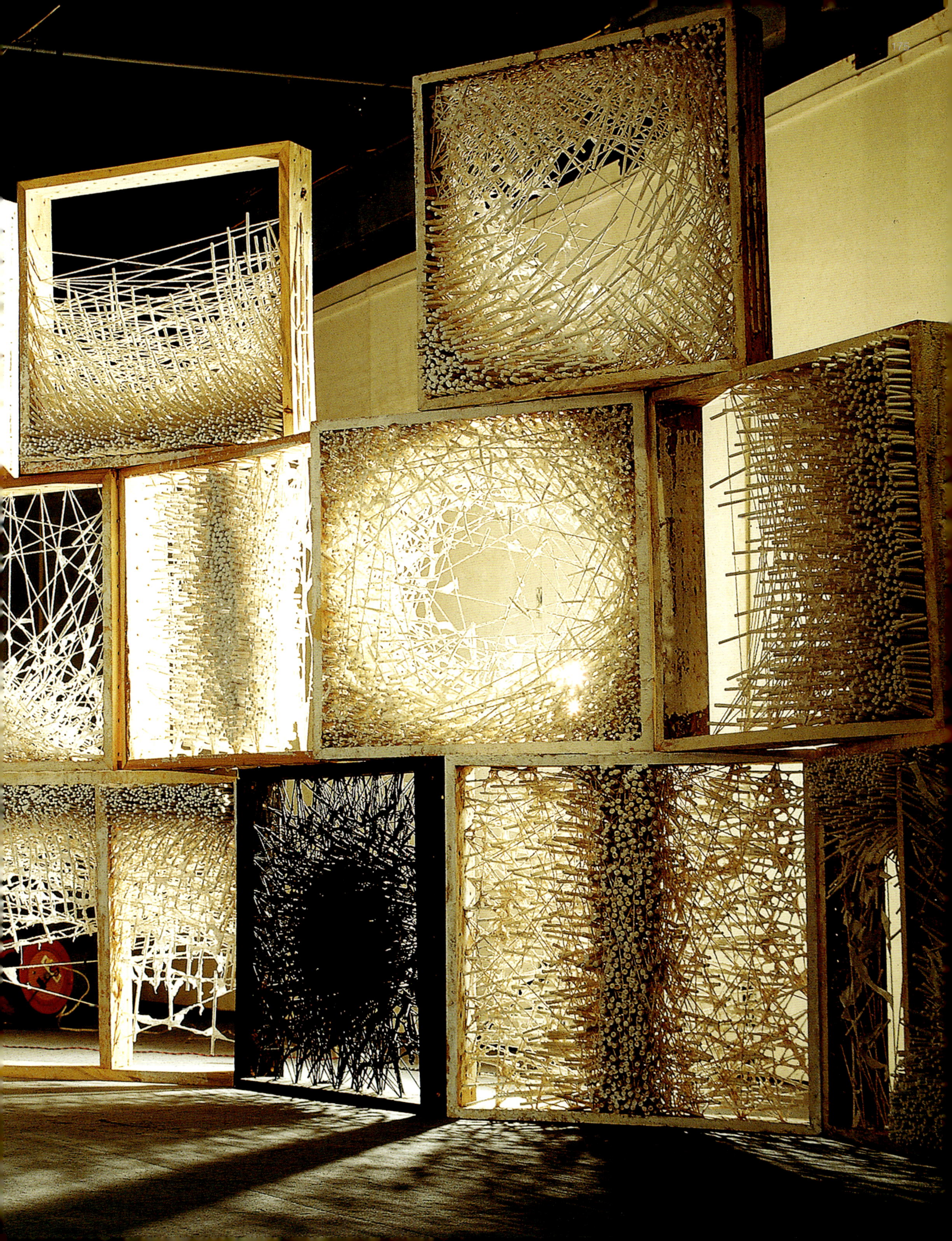

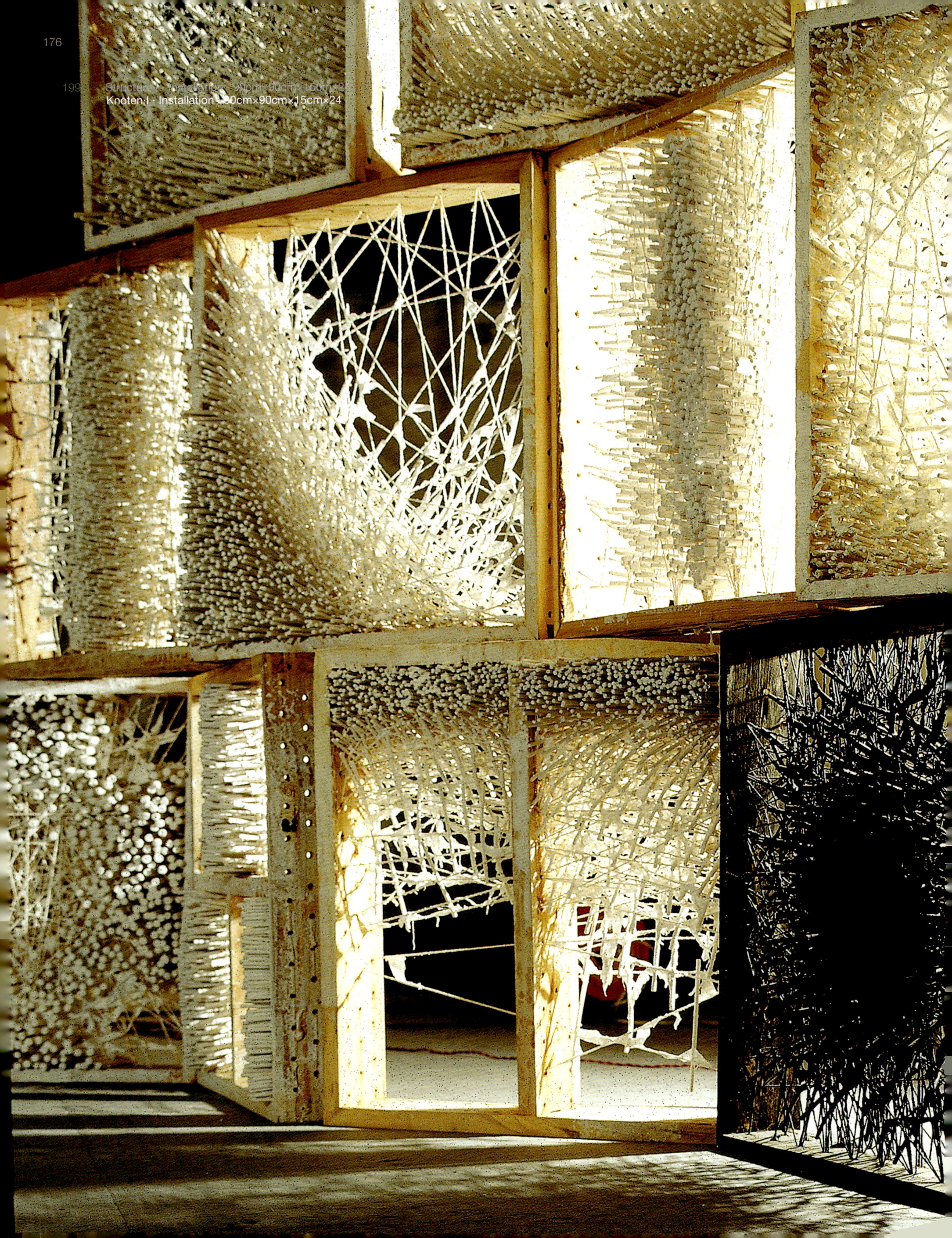

199
Structure·I · Installation · 90cm×90cm×15cm×24
Knoten·I · Installation · 90cm×90cm×15cm×24

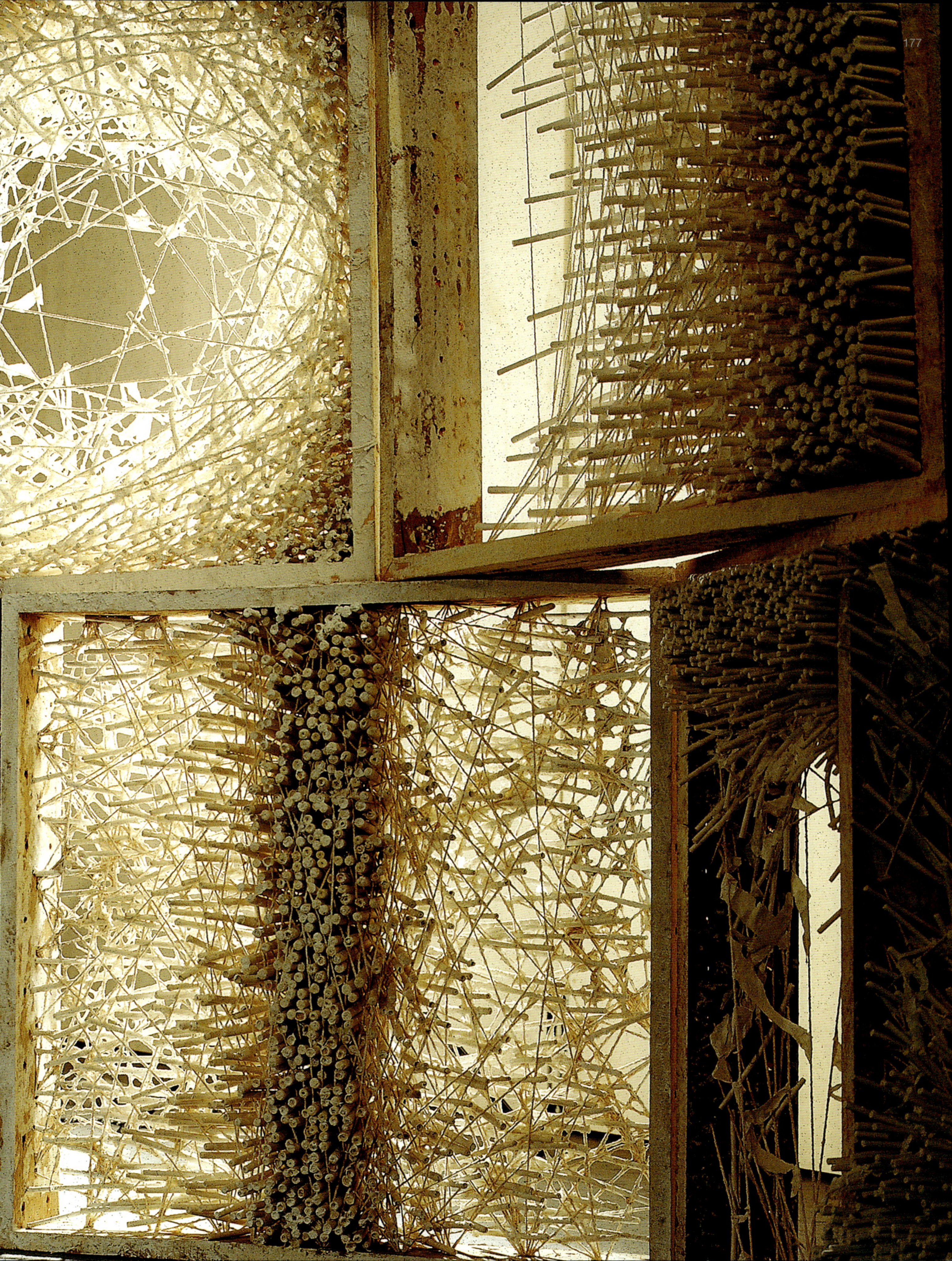

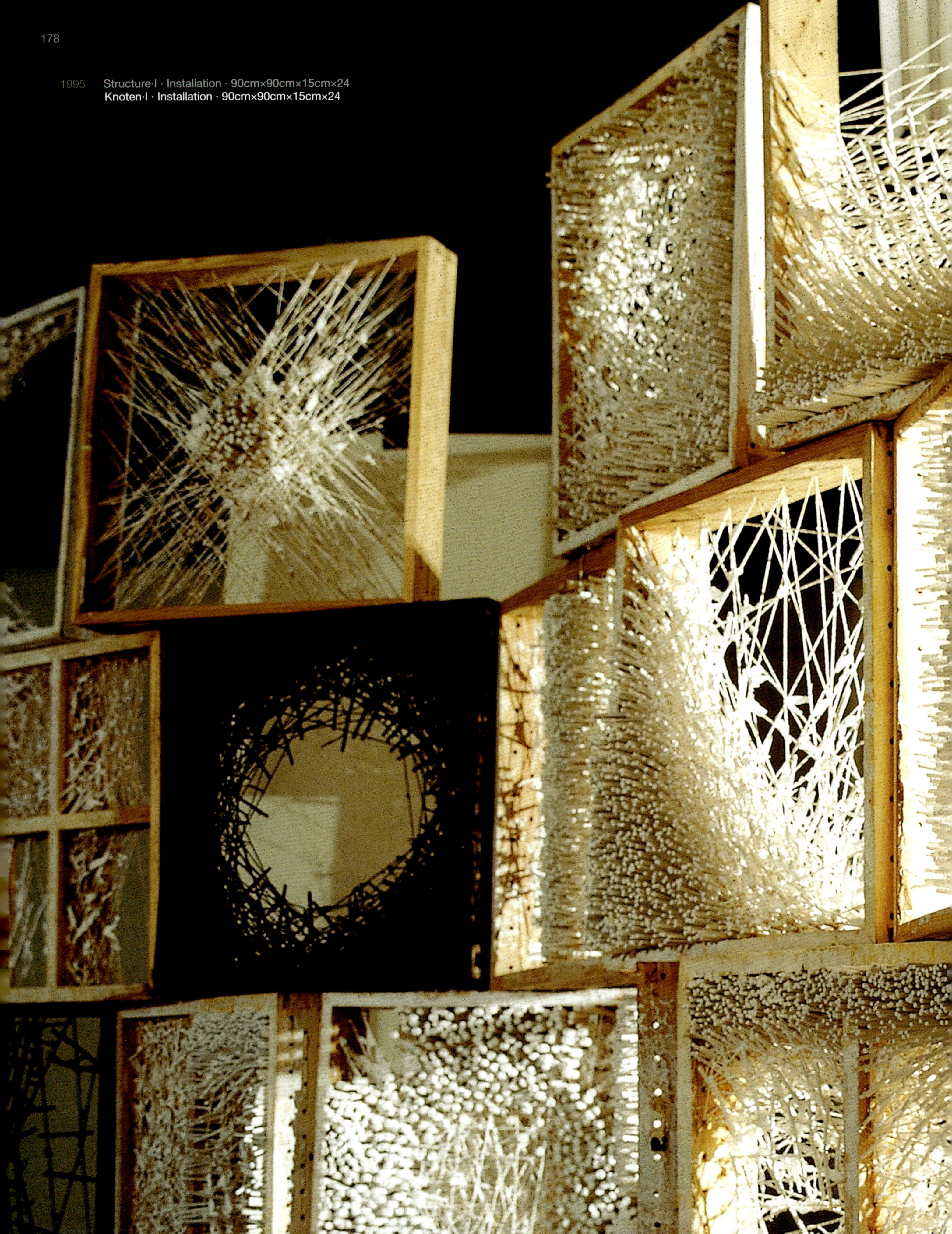

178
1995   Structure·I · Installation · 90cm×90cm×15cm×24
         Knoten·I · Installation · 90cm×90cm×15cm×24

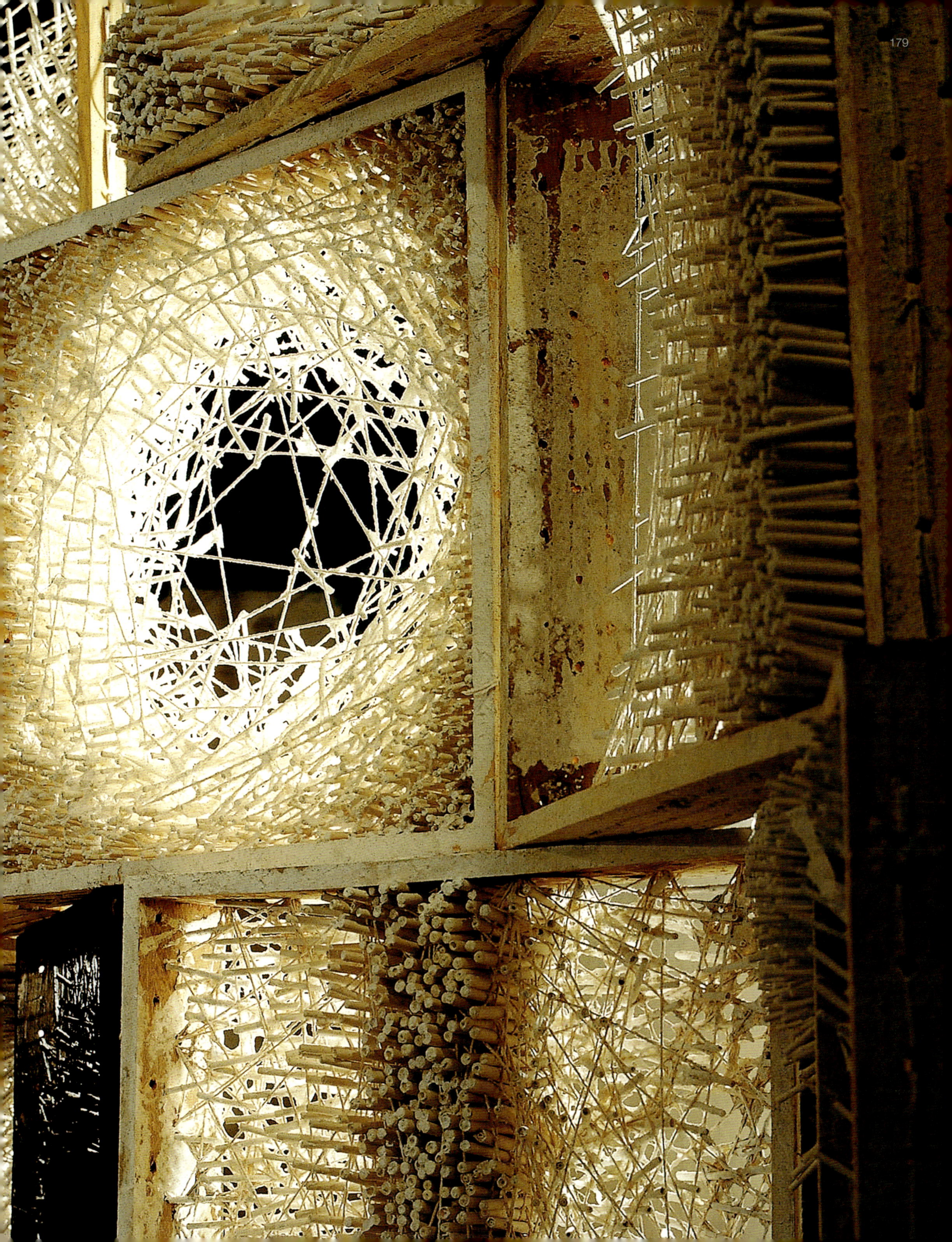

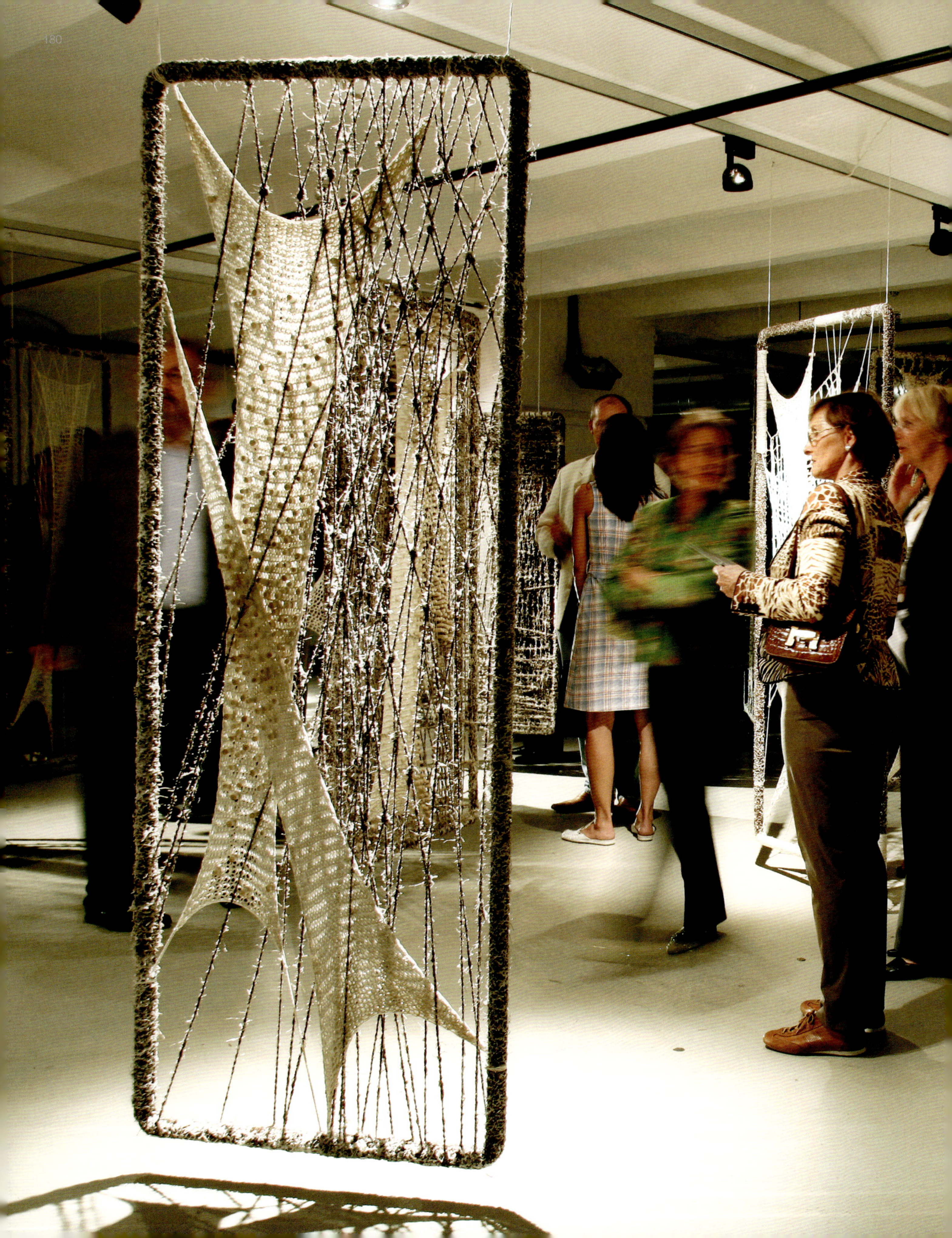

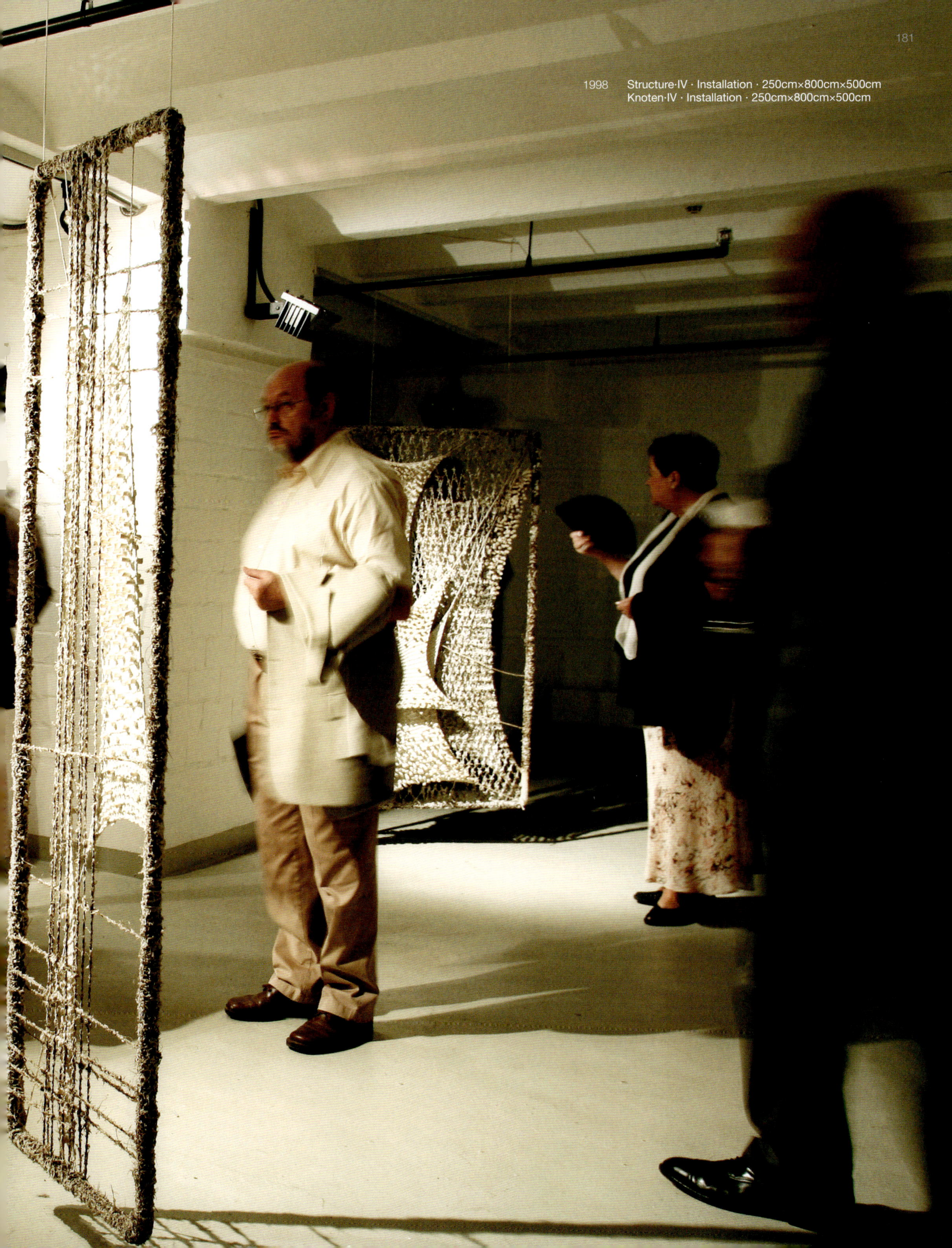
181
1998   Structure·IV · Installation · 250cm×800cm×500cm
Knoten·IV · Installation · 250cm×800cm×500cm

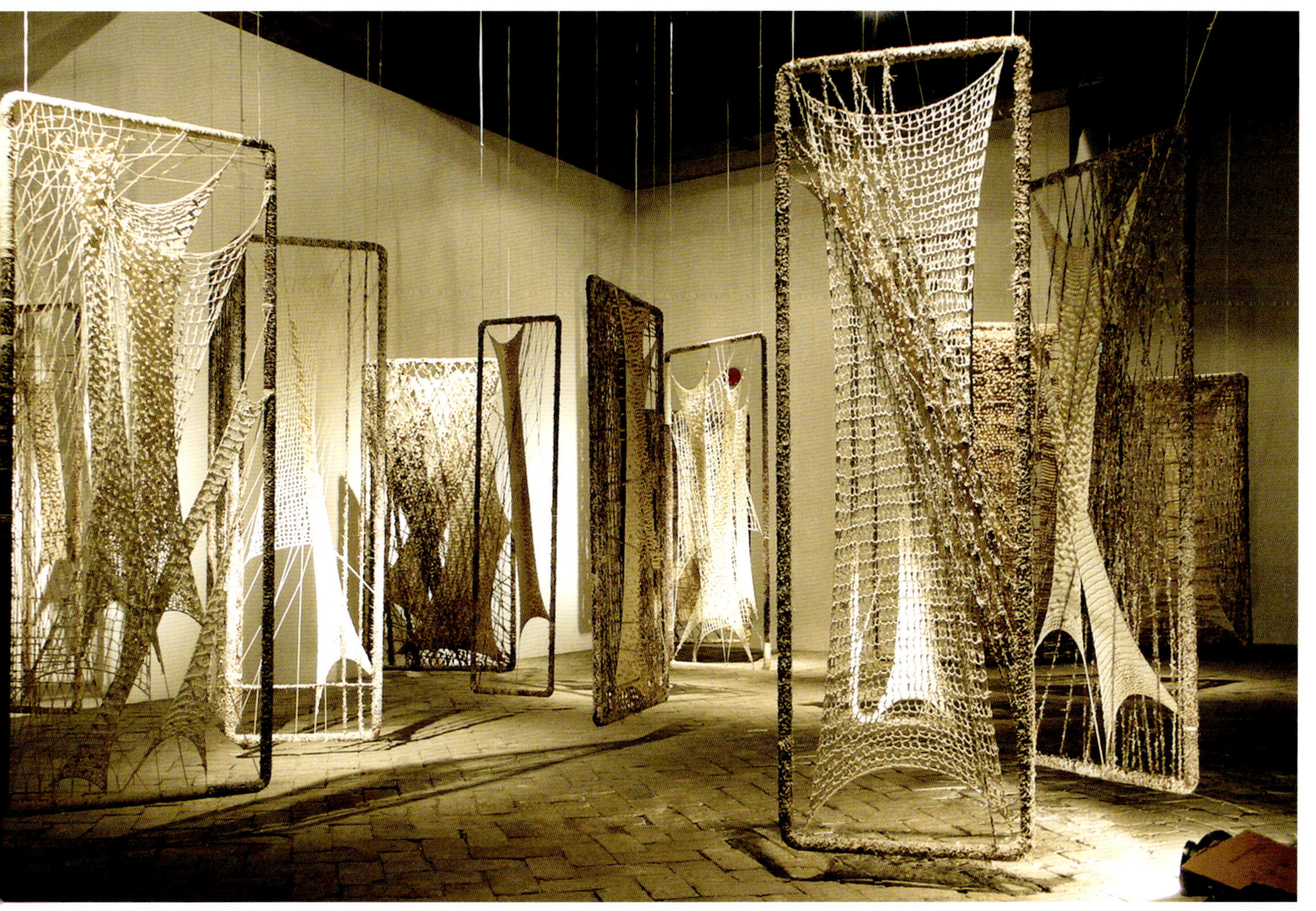

1998   Structure·IV · Installation · 250cm×800cm×500cm
Knoten·IV · Installation · 250cm×800cm×500cm

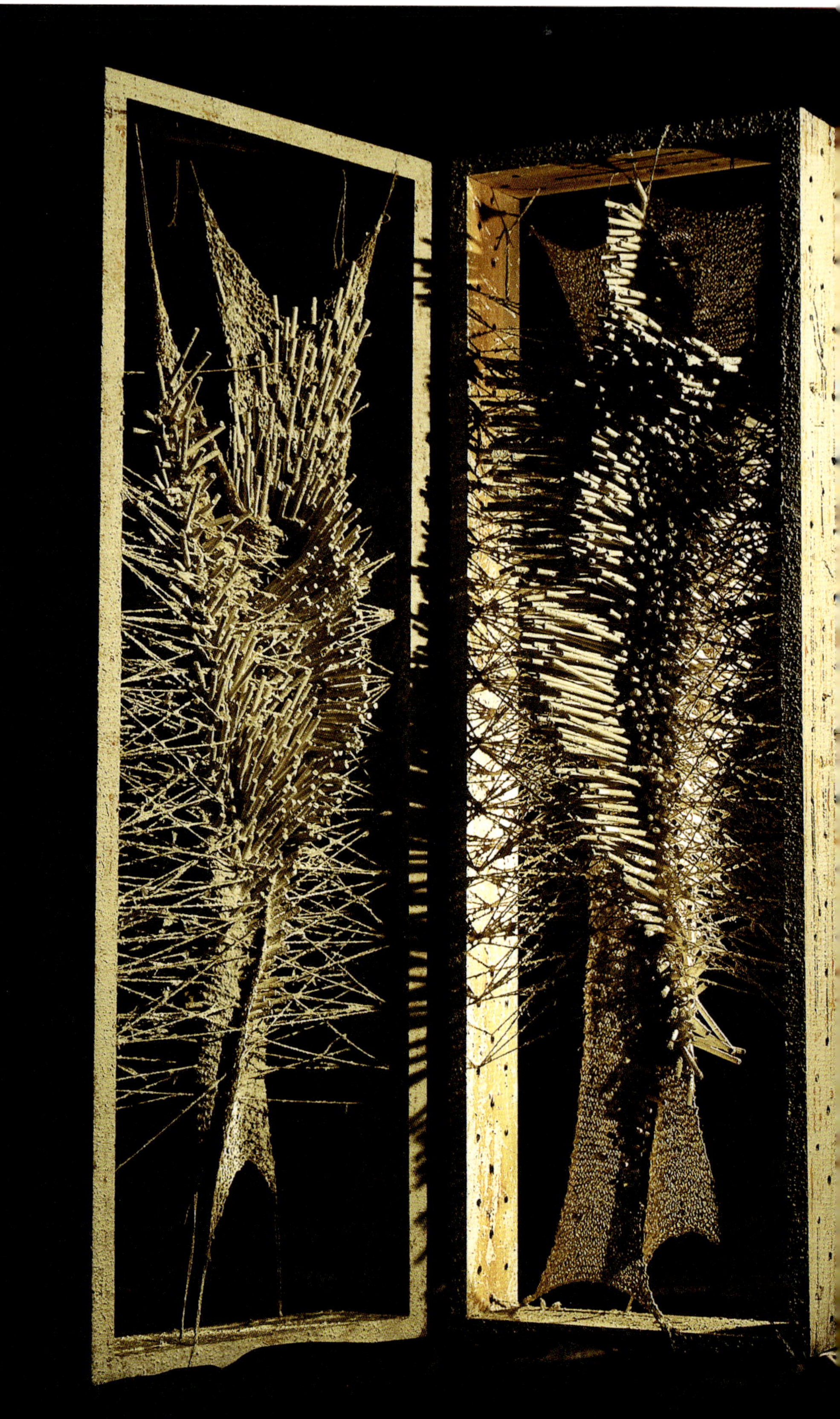

1996   Structure·II · Installation · 180cm×60cm×15cmx4
Knoten·II · Installation · 180cm×60cm×15cmx4

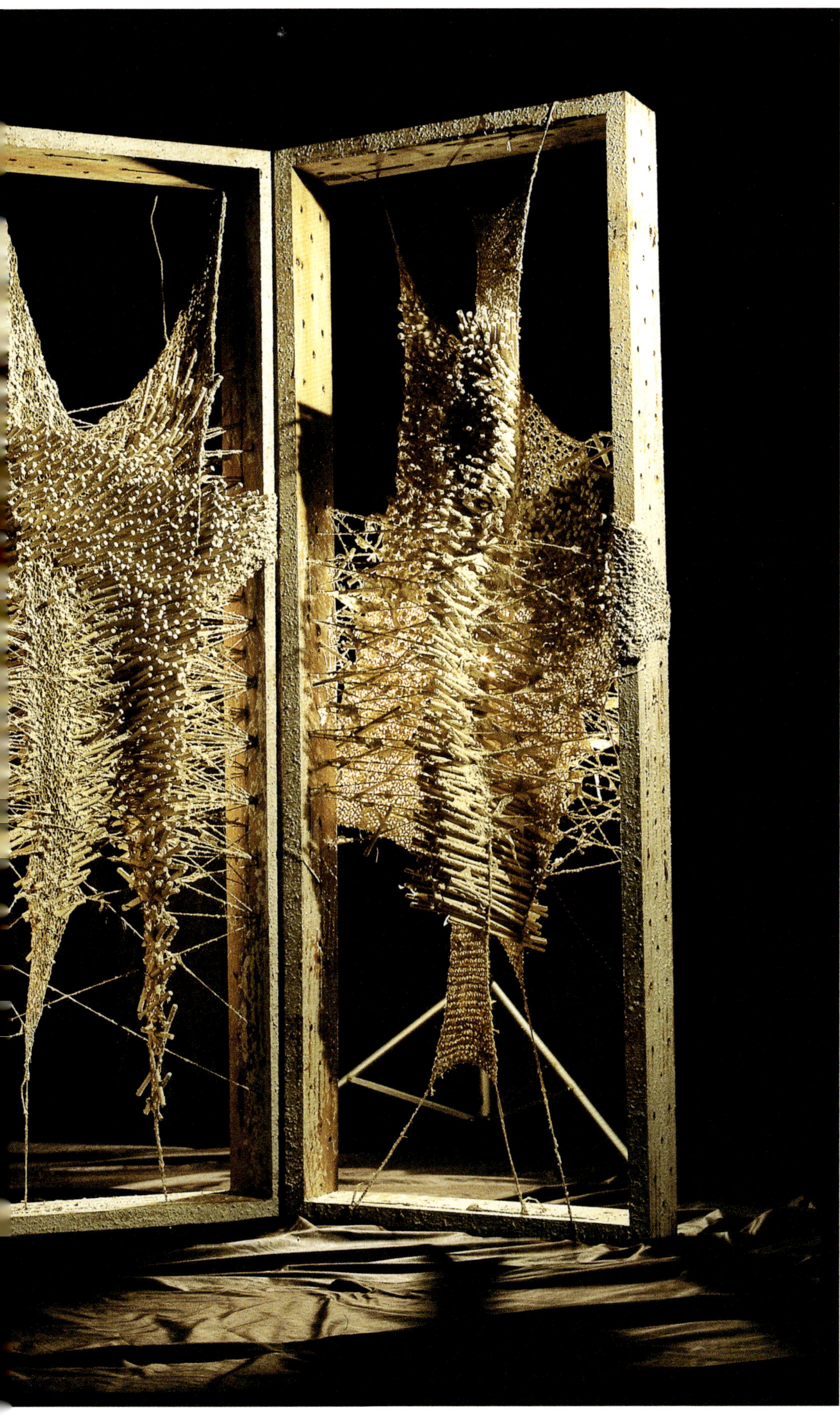

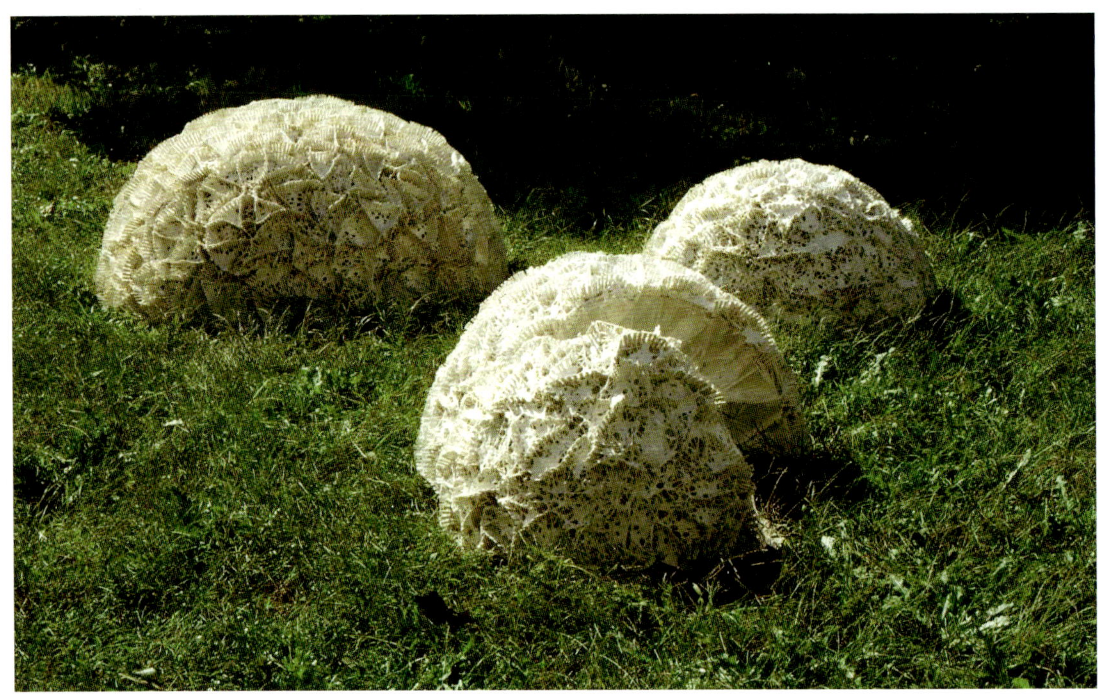

1992   Nest · Installation · 60cmx100cm, 60cmx80cm, 60cmx75cm
Nest · Installation · 60cmx100cm, 60cmx80cm, 60cmx75cm

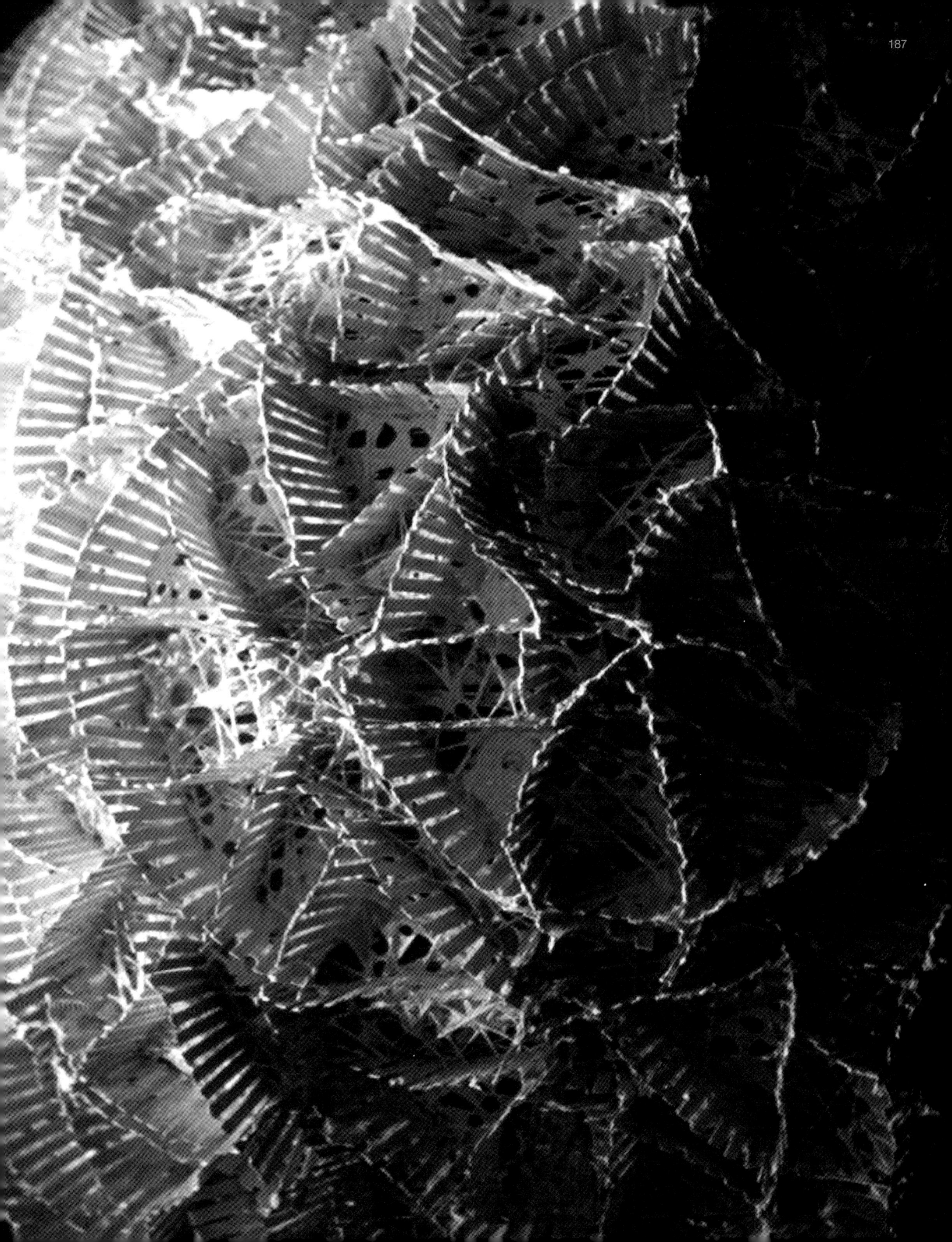

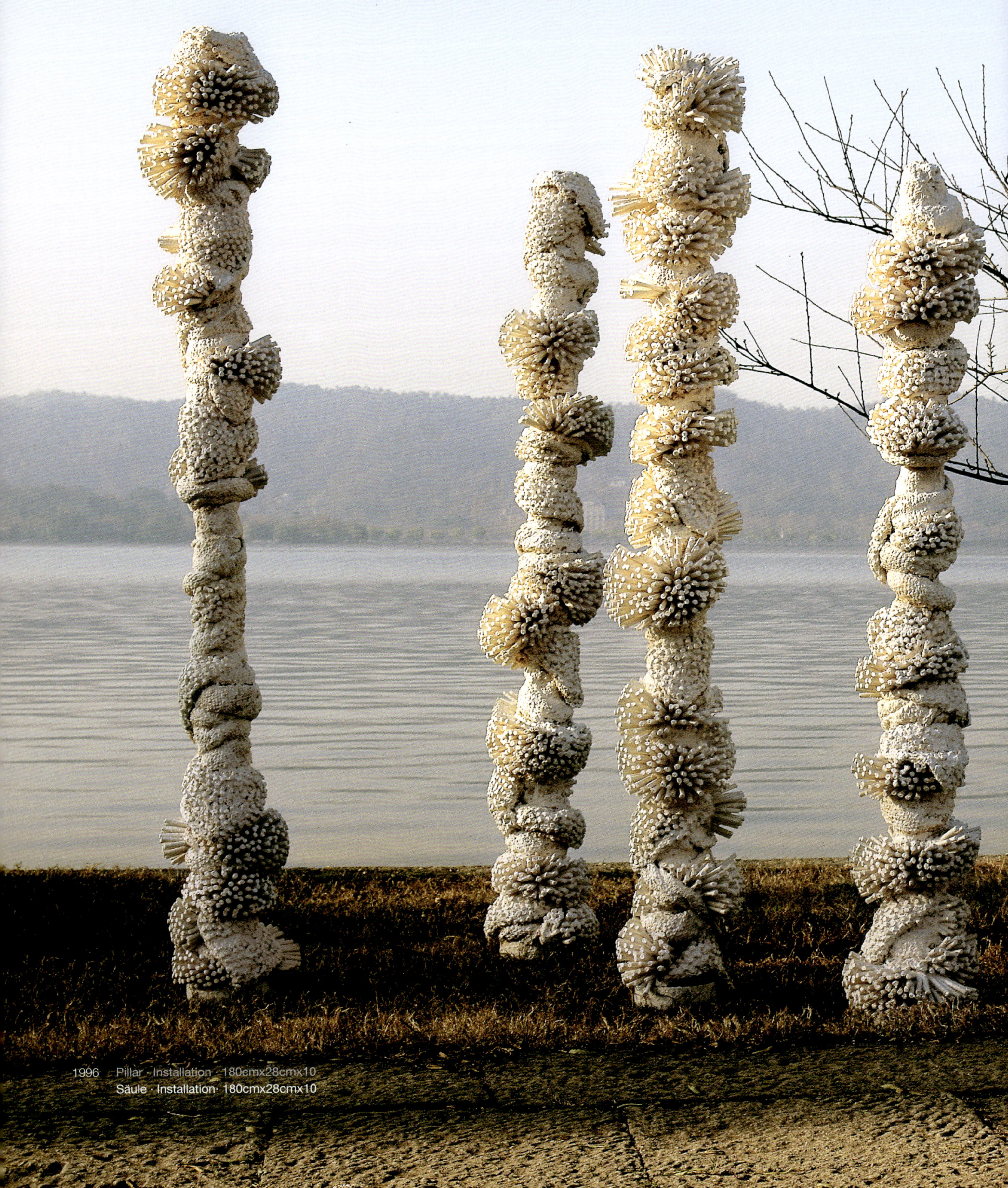

1996 · Pillar · Installation · 180cmx28cmx10
Säule · Installation · 180cmx28cmx10

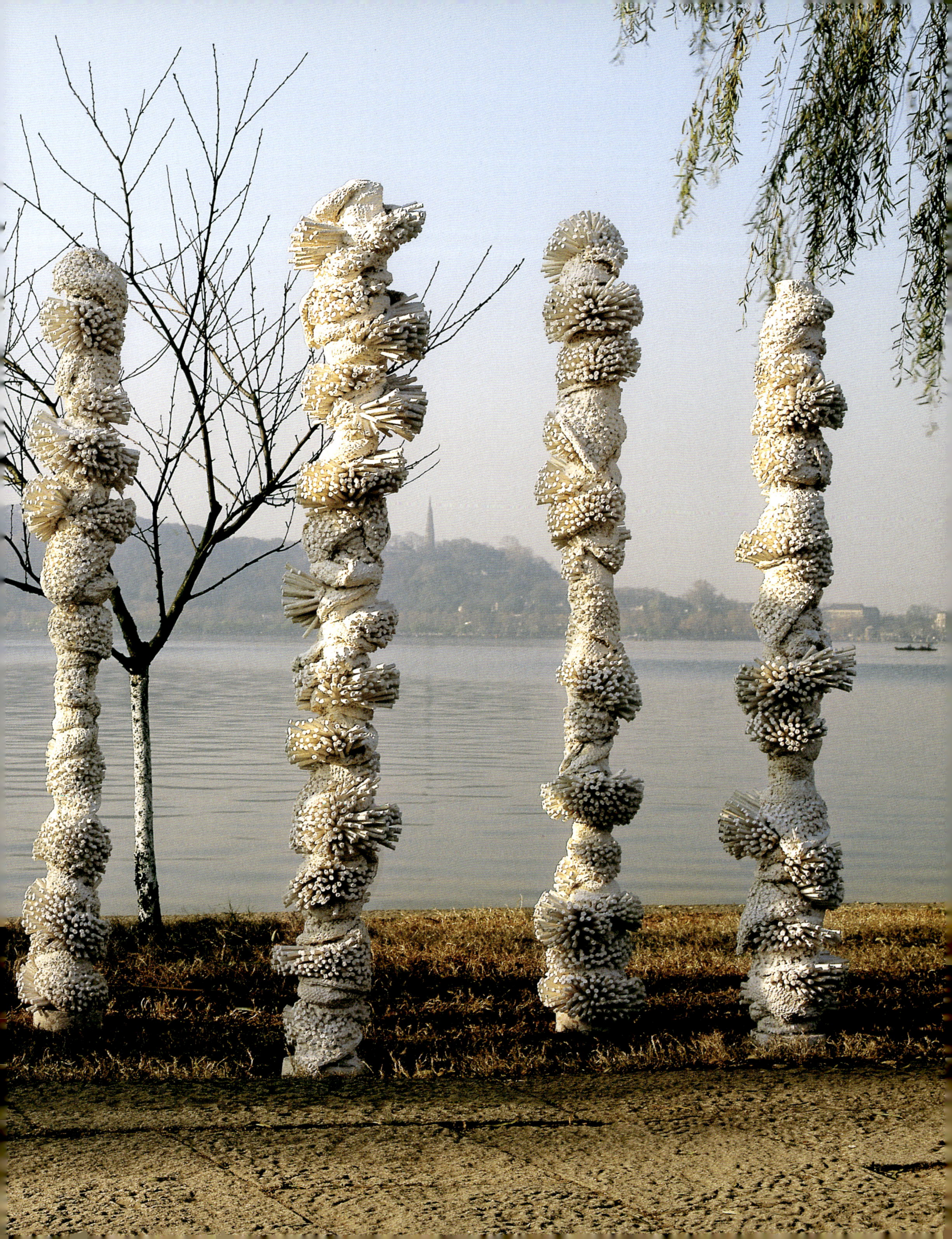

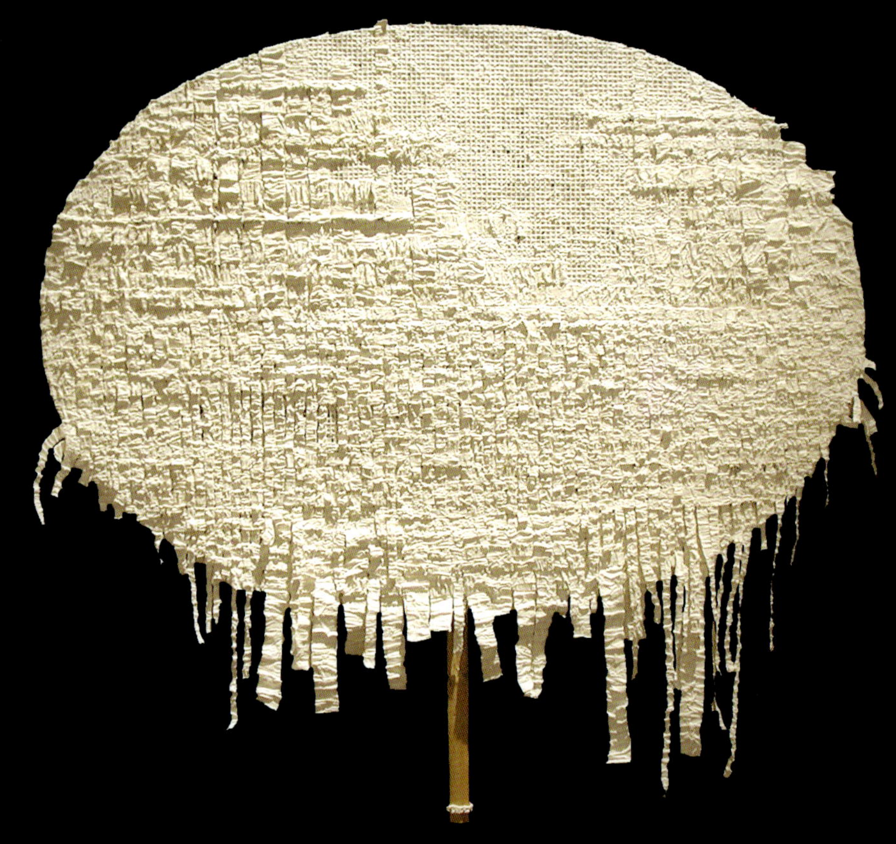

2002   Fan · Installationl· 80cm×110cm
Fächer · Installation · 80cm×110cm

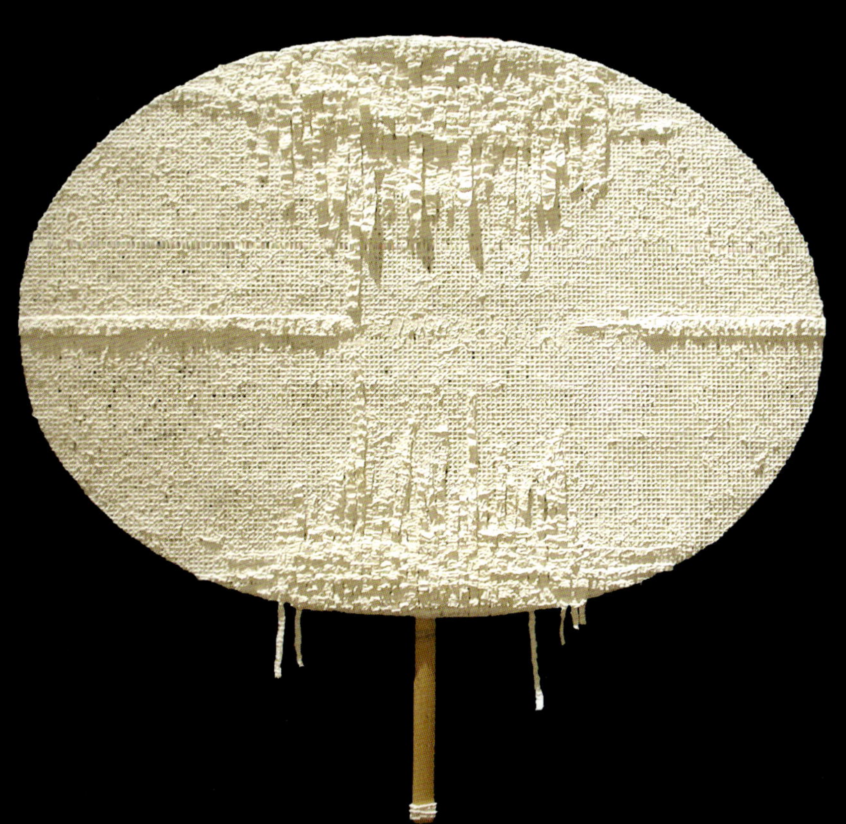

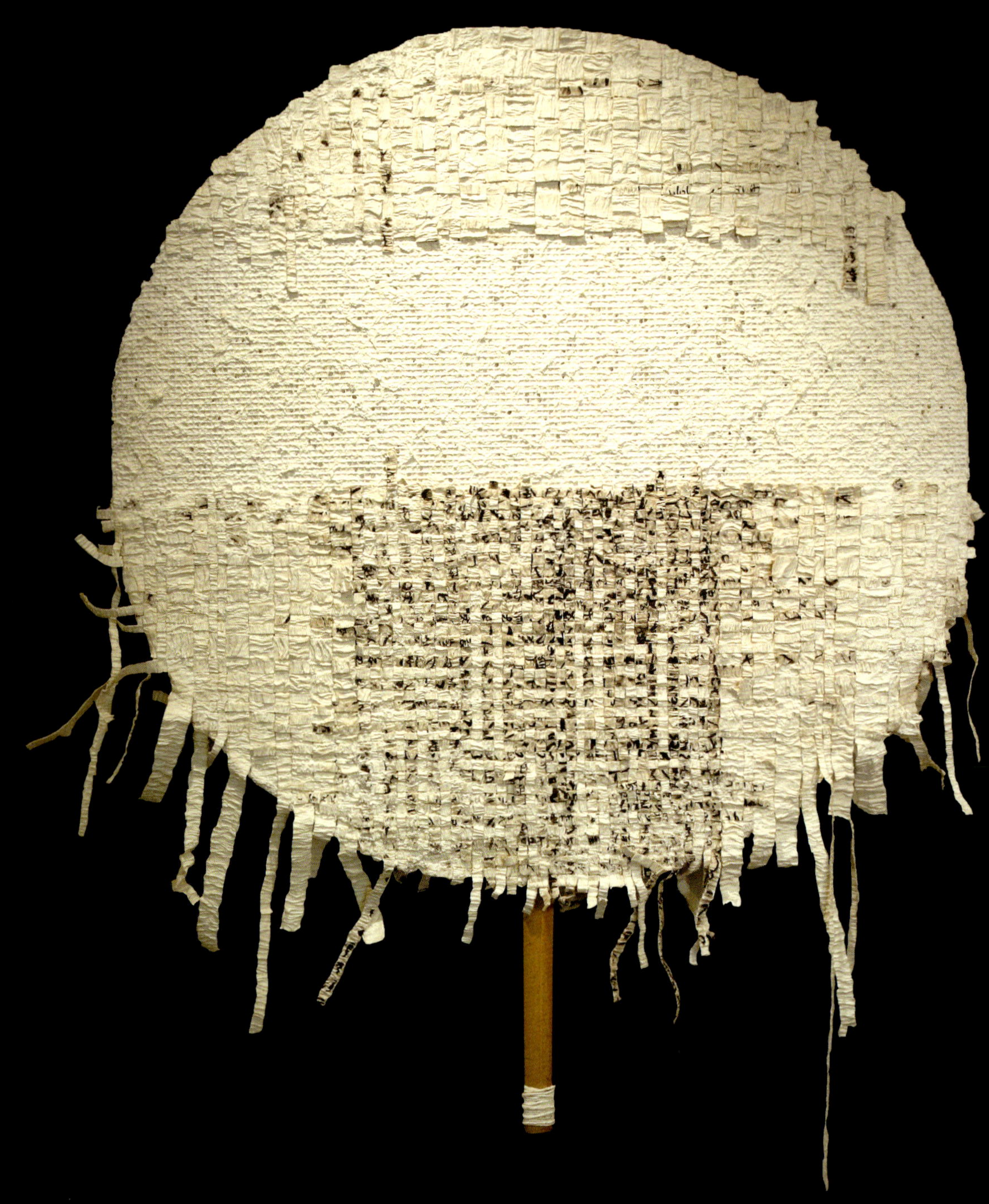

2006　Fan · Installationl · 92cm×92cm
Fächer · Installation · 92cm×92cm

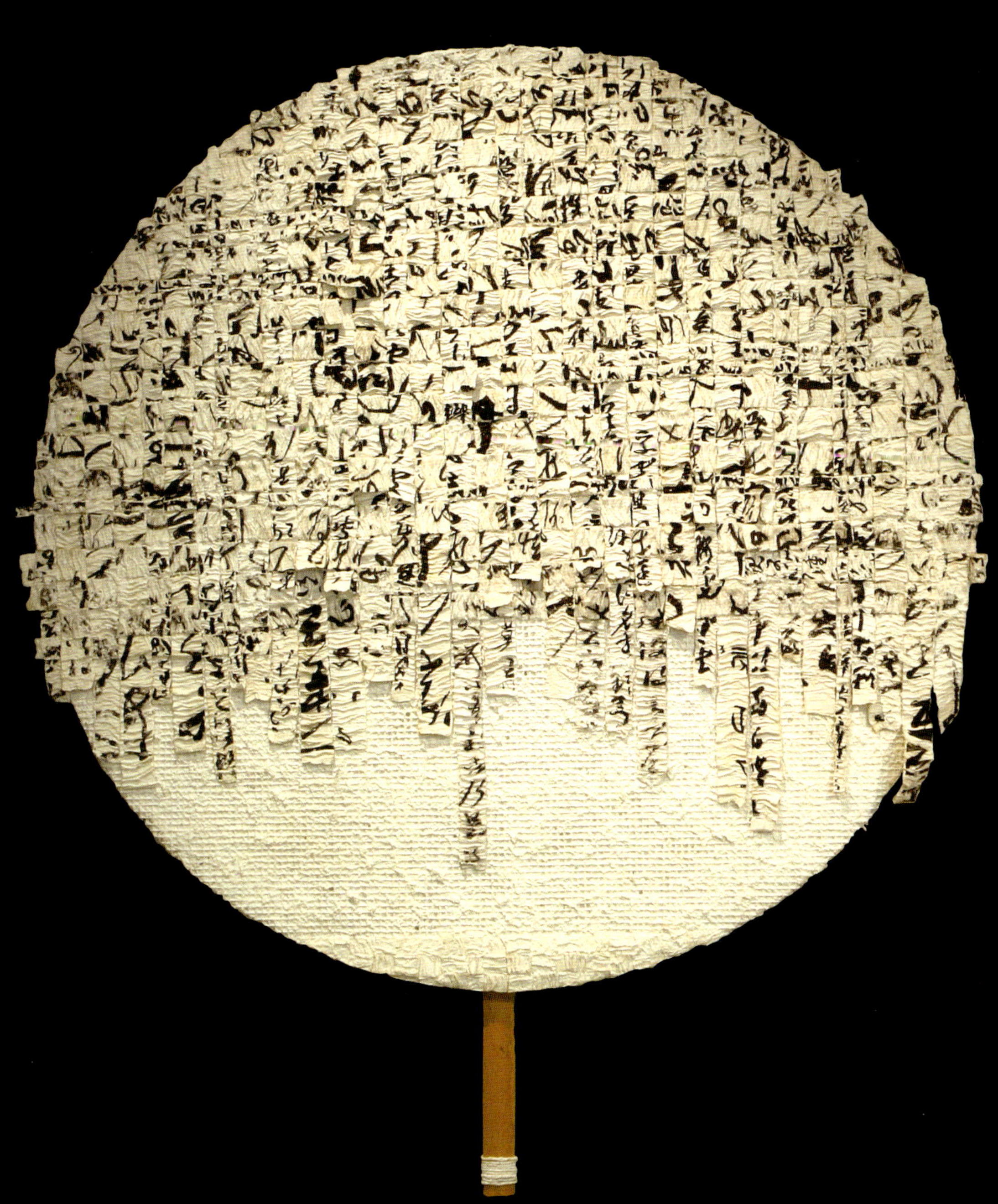

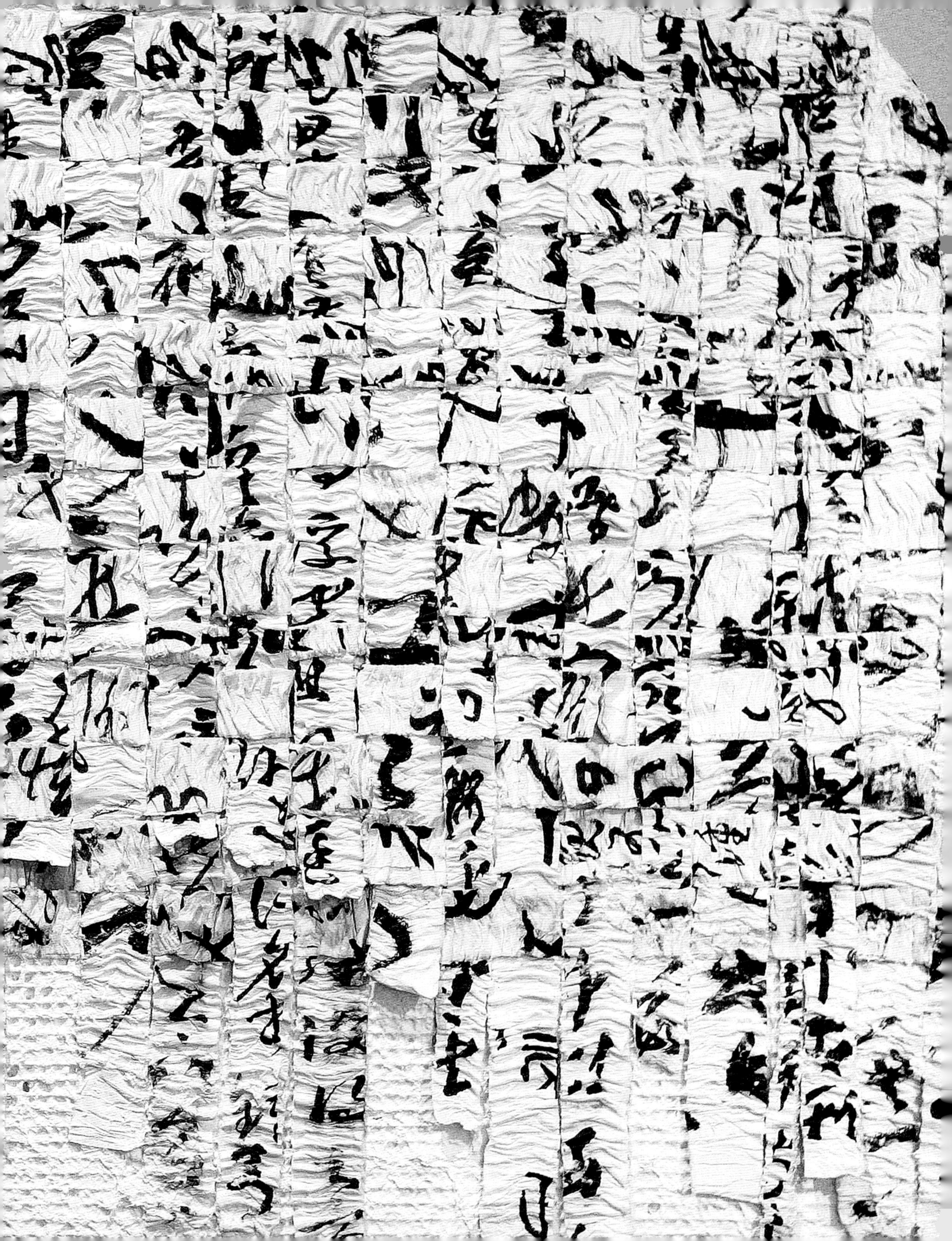

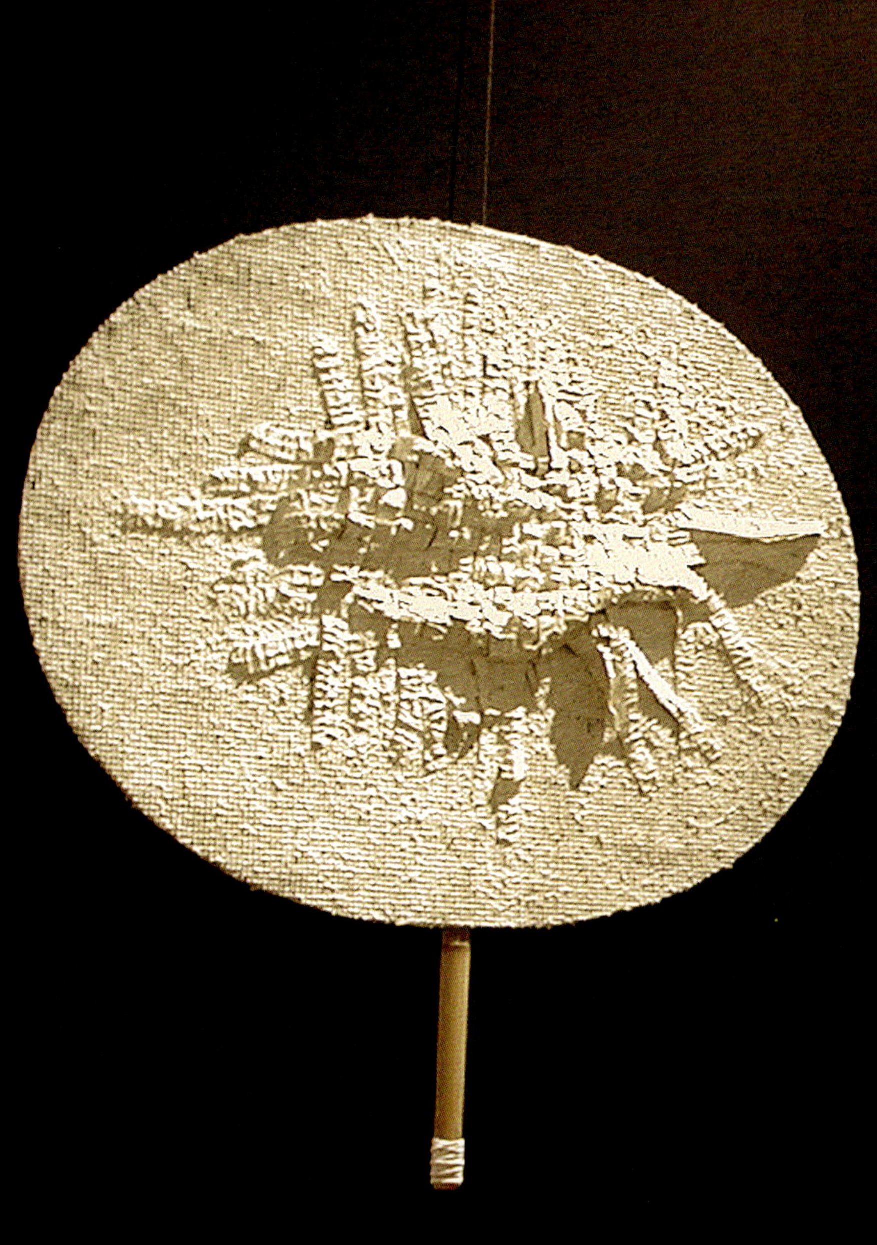

2002   Fan · Installationl· 80cm×110cm
        Fächer · Installation · 80cm×110cm

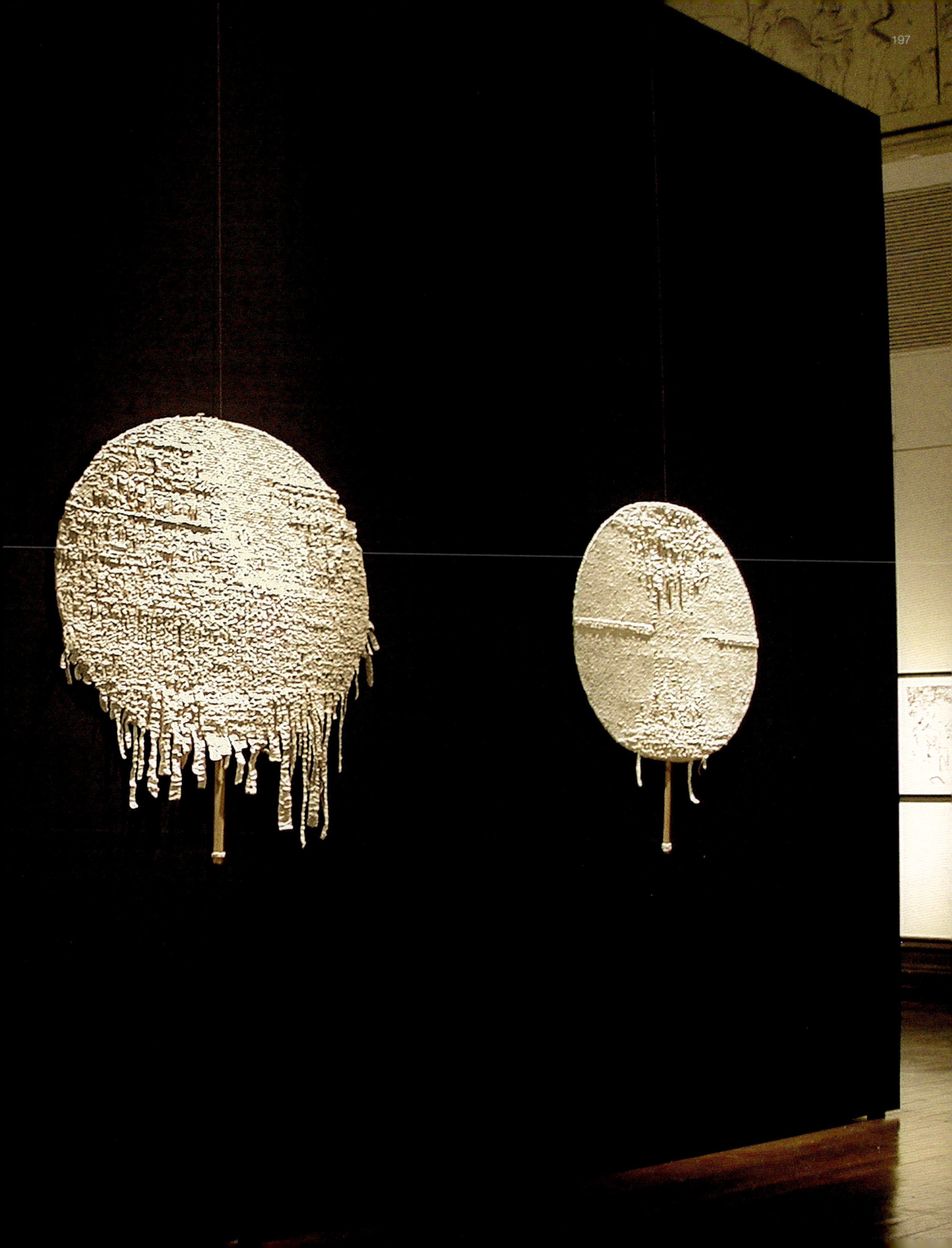

2012   Structure·V · Installation · 100cm×100cm×20cm×8
Knoten V · Installation · 100cm×100cm×20cm×8

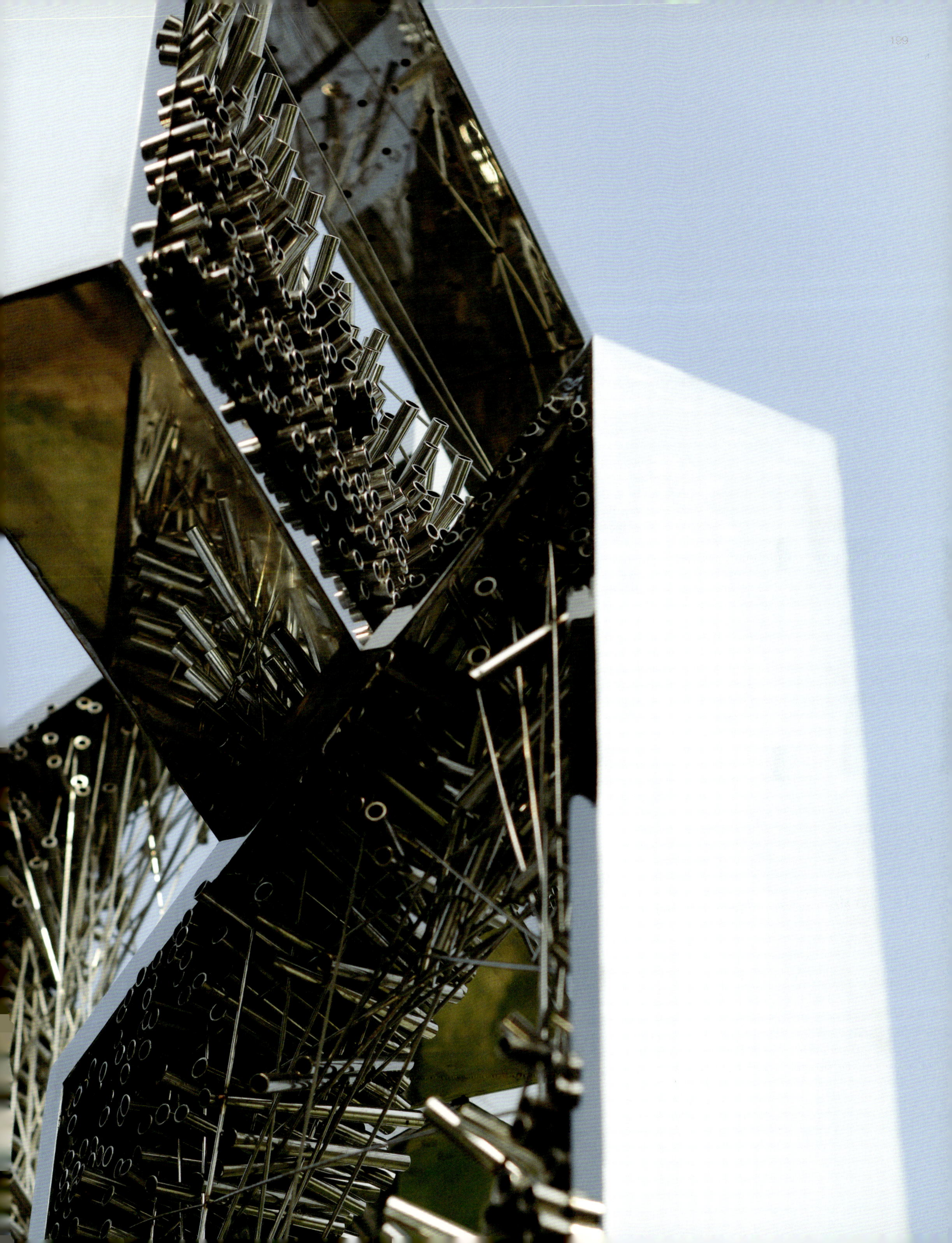

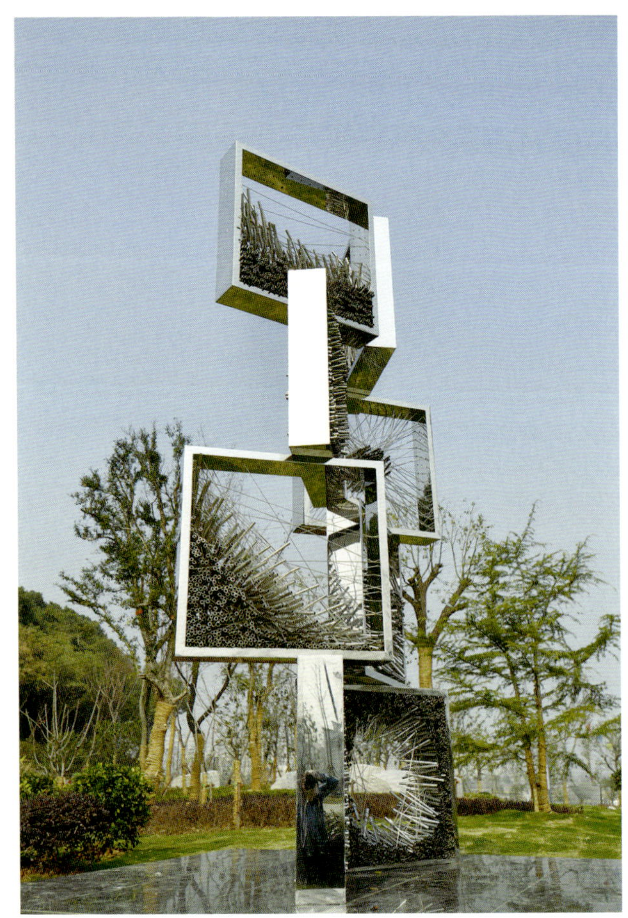

As a purely natural material, Chinese paper mache is something that pleases me deeply. The mache is white and clean, and its beguiling simplicity contains many potentials for change. Among the many ingredients of the paper pulp are bamboo and linen fibres, which lend it the resilient character. When presented in a fulfilled form, the paper mache implies an intrinsic 'resilience' under the soft white surface, which encompasses a characteristically Chinese aesthetic. Such resilience is also the quintessence of life that enables me to 'exist' within. What I would like to suggest, which I also would like to consistently practice in my own work, is that one needs to attend to the individual's grasp of material, and present the culture of a material as well as reflections on its life while conducting research about the material. (ShiHui)

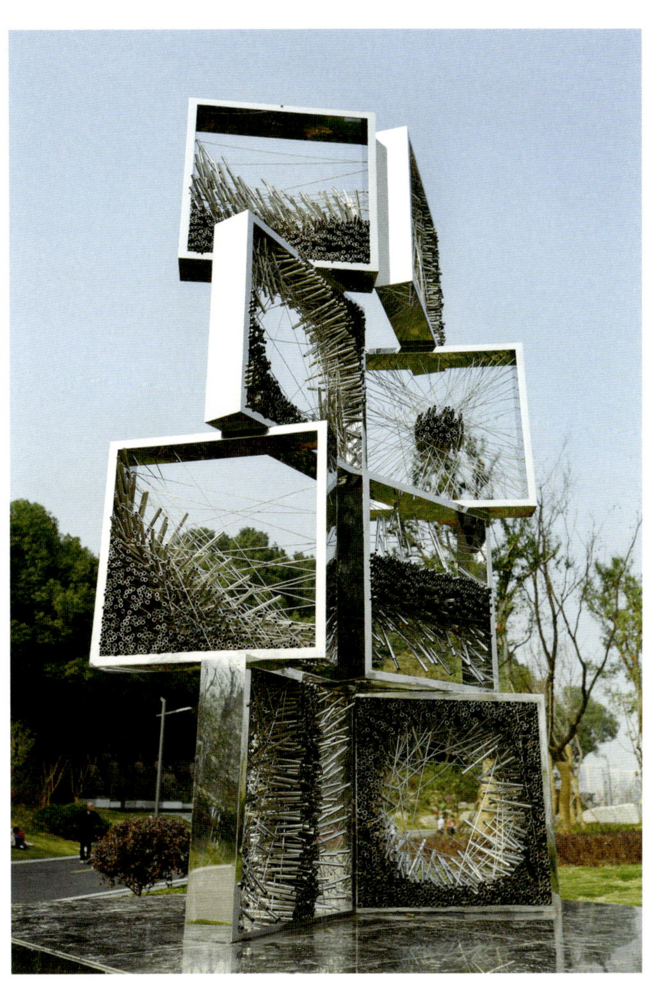

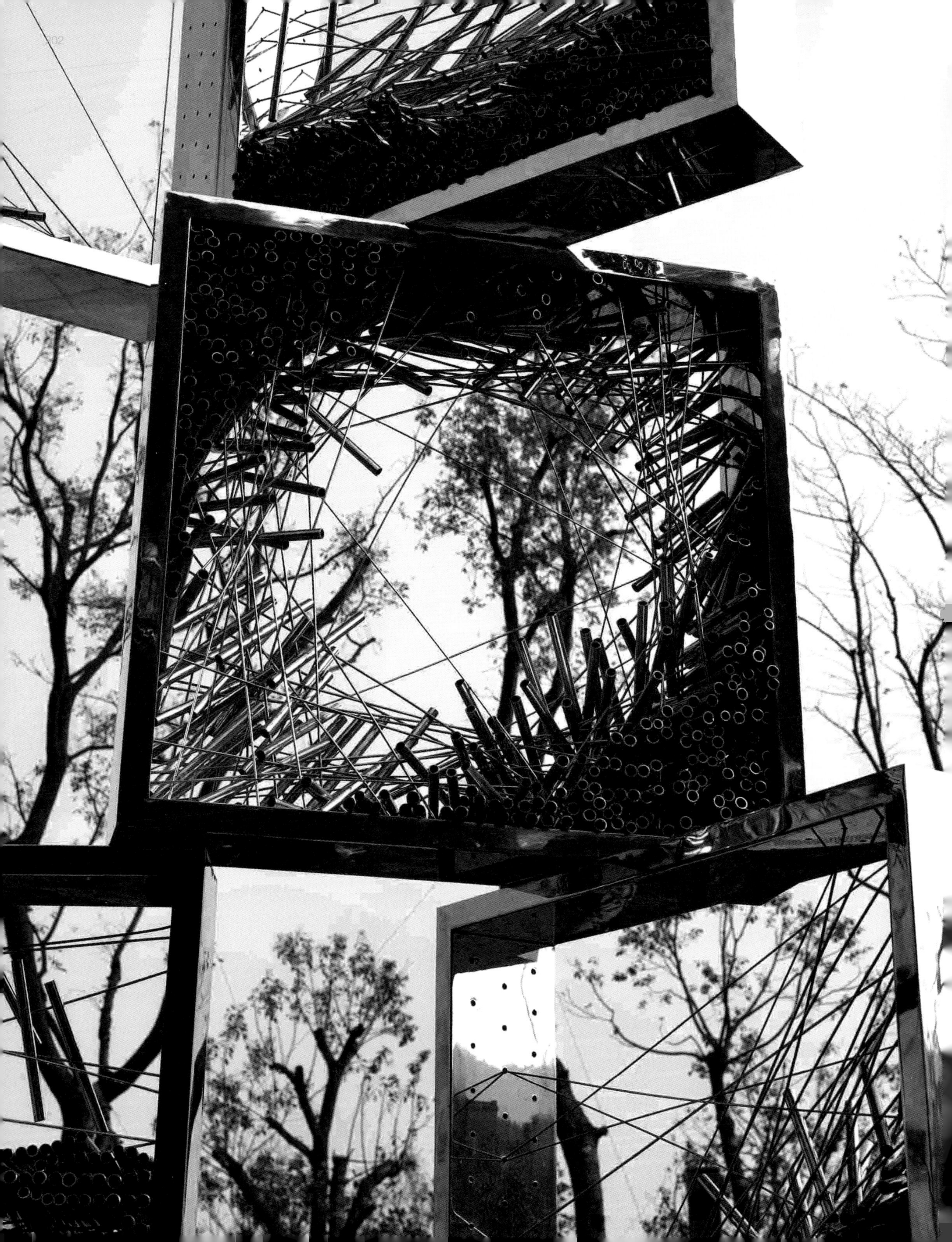

2012   Structure·V · Installation · 100cm×100cm×20cm×8
Knoten V · Installation · 100cm×100cm×20cm×8

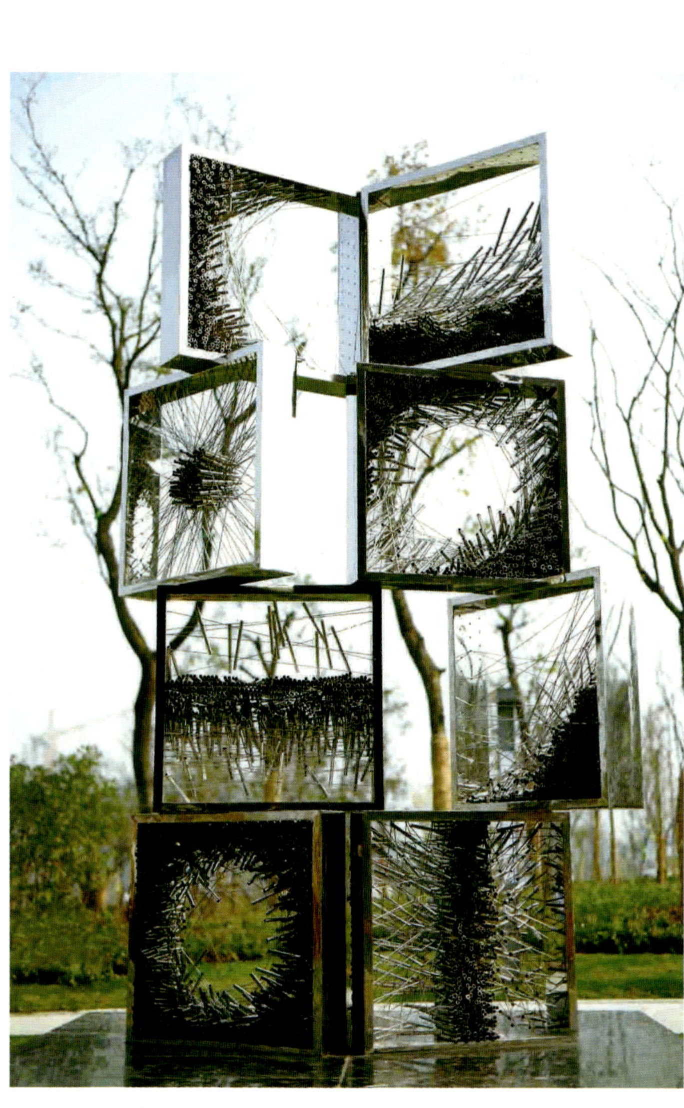

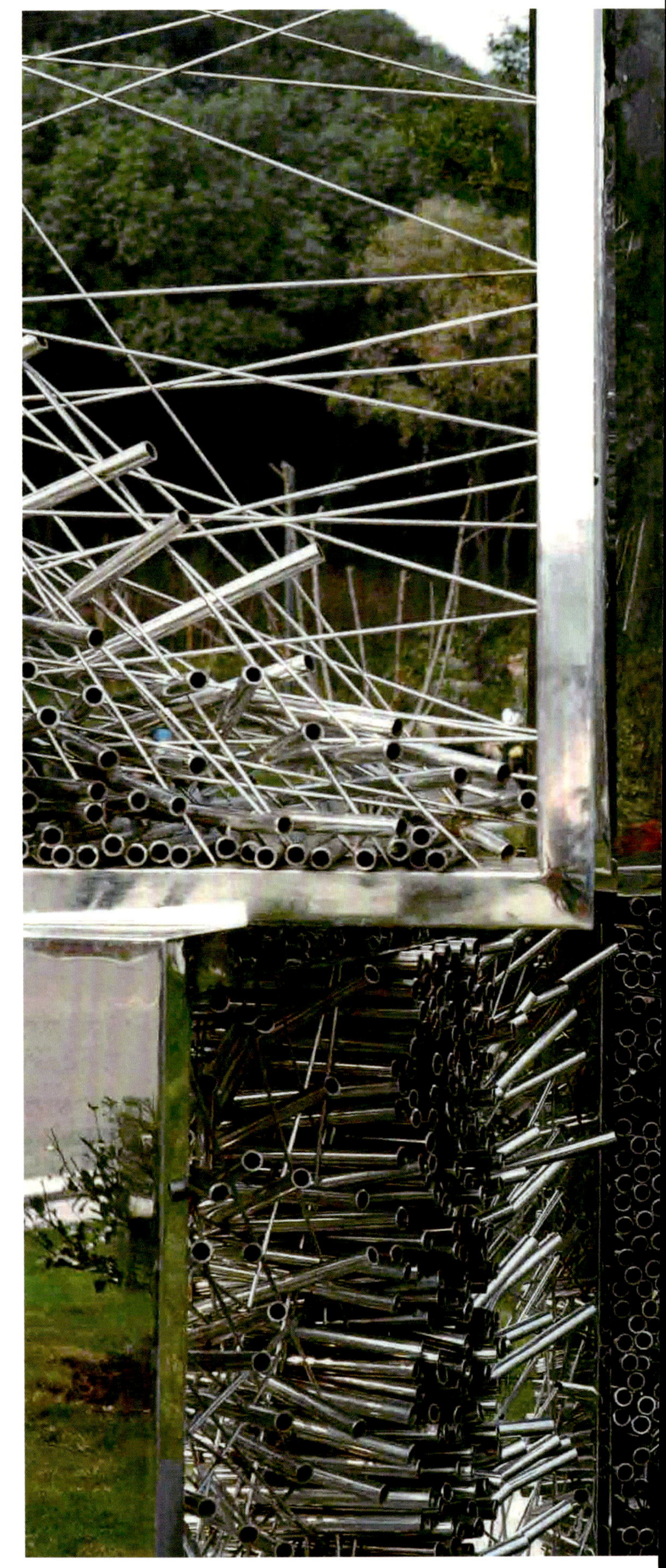

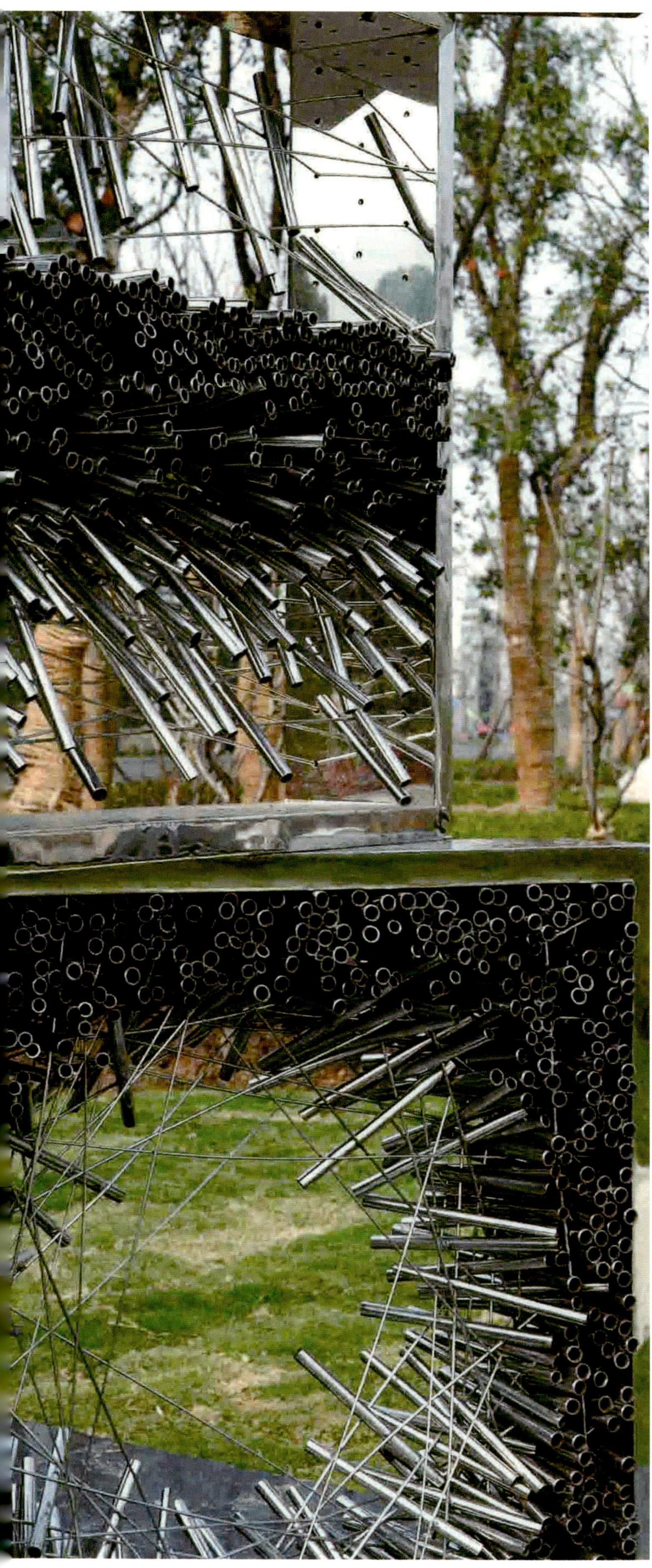

2012　Structure·V · Installation · 100cm×100cm×20cm×8
Knoten V · Installation · 100cm×100cm×20cm×8

Poetic Simplicity
Shi Hui's Work and its Overtone
Fan Jingzhong

Naive Dichtung
Konzept und Stil der Arbeiten Shi Huis
Fan Jingzhong

God has given us the wonderful art.
It will win the world and overcome nature,
While we have to endure labour and waiting.

Michelangelo

Gott erschuf die schöne Kunst.
Sie erfasst die Welt und die Natur als Ganzes.
Doch wir müssen Mühsal ertragen und uns in Geduld üben.

Michelangelo, Sonnet, 94.

I.

In speaking of Shi Hui's fibre art and soft sculpture, Xu Jiang mentioned her handwork several times, describing them as the"silent and complicated works". This reminds me of the motto inscribed on a photo of Franz List in the room of Alfred Brendel, the great contemporary pianist: "Art is beautiful and requires a great deal of hard work."I think that Xu's emphasis on the value of craftsmanship is a way of paying his respect to an old tradition that has faded away.This tradition was glorified by Cennino Cennini at the turn of the Middle Ages and the Modern Era in his *Il Libro dell'arte* which defines it as discovering and visualizing the invisible world with the hands and imagination of the artist. In his Paragone, Leonardo Da Vinci not only argues that the work of an artist is intellectually equal to that of the humanists, but also points out that the artist's inspiring hands are as powerful as God's, with which nothing can not be created.

This kind of celebrating craftsmanship can be found in our Chinese literature. For example, Zhuang Zi often extols the marvellous manual skills,which can only be achieved

I.

In seiner Einführung zu Shi Huis Werken der Faserkunst und weichen Skulpturen, kommt Xu Jiang gleich drei Mal auf die handarbeit-liche Herstellungspraxis der Künstlerin zu sprechen und bezeichnet dabei ihre Arbeit als stillschweigendes Projekt von unermesslichem Volumen. (siehe: „Skizzen zu Shi Huis Werken") Dieses lässt mich mir unweigerlich die einem sofort ins Auge springende deutschsprachige Textzeile neben Liszts Photo im Klavierzimmer des Pianisten Alfred Brendel ins Gedächtnis rufen: „Kunst ist schön, aber sie erfordert ein hohes Maß an harter Arbeit." Ich denke, Xu Jiang ist es daran gelegen, den Wert des Handwerks hervorzuheben. In der Tat ist es eine Respek-tbekundung gegenüber einer alten Tradition, die uns bereits sehr fern scheint.Diese Tradition wurde bereits an der Schwelle vom Mittelalter zur Neuzeit von einem großen Künstler, Cennino Cennini, in seinem „Il Libro dell'arte" gerühmt. Er legt darin dar, dass Künstler sich auf ihre Hände und Vorstellungskraft stützen, um so Verborgenes zu entdecken. In Leonardo Da Vincis „Paragone" wird nicht nur die Ansicht dargelegt, die Arbeit des Künstlers sei mit der des Literaten gleichzusetzen, sondern die Lobpreisung erreicht einen Höhepunkt im Vergleich des Künstlers mit Gott, denn auch er erschafft durch Hand und wirkt als Schöpfer allmächtig.

by years of practice. Despite the fact that many craftsmen may not have realized the ideal value of their work by hand, simply regarding it as routine task,stories as told by Zhuang Zi is the wonderful state of mind in which they create their works:ecstasy.This inspiring state helps the artist to transcend the limits of the reality he depicts and the media he uses,which often leads him to a realm of free spirit.

The works thus created may belong to what Johann Christoph Friedrich Schiller called the Simple Art, as opposed to the Sentimental Art. The latter is not composed, conveying a sense of intensity, in conflict with what is natural; it shows an insatiable desire, even with some destructive effect. For the simple artists, art is above all a form of natural expression. Their works move us by their naturalness, a touch of vivid reality, while the Sentimental art speaks us through the aid of ideas. The Simple art is a whole of grace and harmony, not only in perception but also in reason. In it the ability to feel and the sense of spontaneity is one, not yet being apart from each other in terms of their function. As Schiller said:

Everyone who gets pleasure from reading the simple poem will experience that one no longer feels empty if all his abili Times are devoted to the activities;we feel a sense of unity,without the need of differentiating what we have experienced.We not only enjoy our spiritual activities,but also appreciate the richness and gracefulness of our sensuality.However,our feelings triggered by the Sentimental Poems are very different…In a sentimental poet,the spirit completely lies in a state of movement,anxiety,hovering between opposite emotions.

It seems to me that Shi Hui's art can be classified as this

Was die Lobpreisung von handwerklicher Arbeit betrifft, findet sich in China eine andere Form der Darstellung. Im „Zhuangzi" stößt man laufend auf Beschreibungen von Handwerkstechniken. Was die Handwerkstradition betrifft, und obgleich sich viele Kunsthandwerker im Grunde nicht bewusst über den ideellen Wert ihrer Arbeit sind und ihrer Handfertigkeit schlicht mit der gewohnten Routine begegnen, stellt Zhuangzi in seiner Ausführung den Bewusstseinszustand des Künstlers in den Mittelpunkt und beschreibt diesen als einen Zustand der Ekstase. Das Ego überwindet die auferlegten Fesseln, das Bewusstsein löst die Bande zur Realität und das hervorgebrachte Werk ist folglich eine Art Ausformung der individuellen Erfahrungswerte.

Ein unter diesen Voraussetzungen entstandenes Werk entspricht der deutschen Tradition seit Schiller, und ist der naiven Kunst zuzuordnen. Die sogenannte naive Kunst steht der sentimentalischen Kunst antagonistisch gegenüber. Die sentimentalische Kunst ist nicht sanft und gemäßigt, sie ist spannungsgeladen und steht in Konflikt mit der Natur. Ihr zugrunde liegen Merkmale endlosen Verlangens bis hin zu Destruktion. Für die Vertreter der naiven Kunst ist Kunst in erster Linie eine natürliche Form des Ausdrucks. Solche Dichter rühren uns mit natürlicher, auf sinnlicher Wahrnehmung basierender Authentizität - einer lebendigen Vergegenwärtigung der Realität. Sentimentalische Dichter bemitteln sich des Mediums Vorstellungskraft, um uns zu bewegen. Die Betätigung der naiven Dichter bildet ein harmonisches und anmutiges Ganzes. Sinnlichkeit und Vernunft, Empfindungsvermögen und das spontane Vermögen, Initiative zu ergreifen sind nach wie vor aneinander gebunden. Wie Schiller ausführt:

Und das ist es auch, was jeder bei sich erfährt, wenn er sich beim Genusse naiver Dichtungen beobachtet. Er fühlt alle Kräfte seiner Menschheit in einem solchen Augenblick tätig, er bedarf nichts, or ist ein Ganzes in sich selbst; ohne etwas in seinem Gefühl zu unterscheiden, freut er sich zugleich seiner geistigen Tätigkeit und

simple style. If one reads her statement as follows, one will find they express precisely the same concept:

In my art, the language ofidea is far away from me, what I actually do is just to touch the materials in a state of mind which is easy and peaceful. During the course of my long time engagement in soft sculpture for years, I have developed a kind of sensitivity the texture of fibrous materials and a preference for its linear structure.

If one observes the artist at work, one will find that she is in a state which brings us back to Zhuang Zi's story that Gong Chui is able to draw by hands a perfect circle and rectangular shape without using any tools, whose fingers are incorporated with the objects as one, and need not any deliberation, as the mind is concentrated in what he is doing,forgetting all obstacles.Shi Hui says:

Once my hands touch these white, soft, flexible materials, I feel very comfortable and am in high spirit. Concentrating on doing things withthese materials, I can forget all the earthly trouble.

It is in this state of "forgetting" that the artist put her efforts and diligence to her works, which expresses a loft sense of simplicity and purity that Nature possesses. In other words, once her work is done, all the traces of her physical exertions disappear deep into the finished work itself.

II

The art practiced by Shi Hui is a kind of new art,which owes a lot to the contribution of the Bulgarian artist Maryn Varbanov with whom she had worked many years ago at the China Academy of Art in Hangzhou,where she is teaching. This genre was previously called the "Art of Hangings".

seines sinnlichen Lebens. Eine ganz andre Stimmung ist es, in die ihn der sentimentalische Dichter versetzt. [...] hier [ist] das Gemüt in Bewegung, es ist angespannt, es schwankt zwischen streitenden Gefühlen;

Meiner Ansicht nach ist Shi Huis Kunst dem naiven Stil zuzuordnen. Bei Betrachtung ihrer persönlichen Stellungnahme unten, scheint mir meine Annahme bestätigt.

In meiner Kunst scheint mir das Wort ‚Konzept' sehr fern. Alles, was ich in Wirklichkeit mache, ist, in einem ruhigen und gelassenen, völlig friedlichen Bewusstseinszustand das Material zu befühlen. All die Jahre der Arbeit an weichen Skulpturen haben mich hinsichtlich der Beschaffenheit von Faserstoffen sensibilisiert bzw. Präferenzen hervorgebracht. Dabei habe ich eine spezielle Vorliebe für lineare Strukturen entwickelt.

Indem wir aufmerksam ihrer Beschreibung des Zustandes im Zuge des kreativen Prozesses folgen, erhärtet sich die Annahme. Es erweckt ganz den Anschein als wolle sie uns in das Reich der lebhaften Erzählung des „Da Sheng" („Wer das Leben versteht") zurückführen. Obwohl sich ihr reichhaltiges Wissen auf die gegenwärtige Epoche bezieht, sagt Shi Hui:

Wenn meine Hände das strahlend-weiße, weiche Material berühren, durchströmt mich ein durch und durch behagliches Gefühl und meine Stimmung hebt sich. Im Zuge des Schaffensprozesses tauche ich physisch wie mental vollkommen in meine Arbeit ein, sodass ich alles um mich herum vergesse.

Es ist dieser Zustand der Ekstase, der den Künstler dazu befähigt, sich mit aller Willenskraft und harter Arbeit in sein Werk zu vertiefen, um uns so natürliche Naivität und Reinheit zu vermitteln. Die handwerkliche Arbeit verliert sich dabei in der Tiefe des Werkes.

but soon it feed itself from the confinement of the wall,it is greatly extended particularly in terms of its space. With this spatial liberation come such terms as "Fibre Art" and "Soft Sculpture",which further indicates the possibility of developing the"Art of Hangings" into a spatial form. However, Shi Hui has never deliberately pursued this line, the novelty of her work comes out of her making naturally: her works are always spatially fused with the earth, the plants, especially the sunshine.

One of Shi Hui's representative works, *The Nest*, gives full play to the fusion with the sunshine. *The Nest* is a life that has the potential power of growth; and this power helps it absorb the sunshine from every hole on the nest body. On the surface of the nest, we seem to see some dream—like shimmer, which gleams in the layers of meshes, leading the extension of the fibres, driving the derivation of the life. Lights strike on the white paper mache, trimmed with a charming tenderness, which makes life hopeful. It is in this way of simplicity that Shi composes the poetry of life in the melody of the sunshine.

The Trace is another expression of life. Shi Hui made a metaphor of eighteen pieces of boards. The ink trace on the boards conjures up the shadow and moss on the stones, then the fleeting time. Although Shi Hui has tried to get rid of the imagination of idea and emphasize the visual values themselves, although she wants people to feel her works directly with their sensory organs, just like reading the poetry of senses and the poetry of things, I still think thather work is deeply rooted in history, or in the thought that "Noidea but in things".

II.

Shi Hui beschäftigt sich mit einem gewissermaßen neuen Typus von Kunst. Dies verdankt sie ihrem bulgarischen Mentor, dem zu Recht gewürdigten Künstler Maryn Varbanov. Wie wir wissen, nennt sich diese Art von Kunst ursprünglich Tapisserie. Die Abkehr von der Wand als Präsentationsfläche in den siebziger Jahren, ebnete Schritt für Schritt den Weg für weitreichende gestalterische Freiheiten. Die Entstehung der Begriffe "Faserkunst" und "weiche Skulpturen" kennzeichnet die Tatsache, dass diese Art von Kunst im freien Raum nunmehr grenzenlose gestalterische Möglichkeiten gefunden hat. Als Vertreter der naiven Kunst war es Shi Hui nie daran gelegen, mit Kalkül nach Neuartigem zu streben. Zweifelsohne ergibt sich Originalität spontan. So sind Shi Huis Werke, was deren räumliche Gestaltung betrifft, immer eine Verschmelzung mit der Erde, mit Gras, mit Bäumen, speziell aber mit der Sonne.

Als nicht nur repräsentativstes Werk in diesem Kontext, sondern auch ohne Zweifel mitunter zentralstes im Schaffen der Künstlerin gilt das „Nest" in welchem das Charakteristikum des Verschmelzens mit der Sonne besonders subtil zum Ausdruck gebracht wird. Es ist ein glimmernder Schein, der sich Schicht für Schicht seinen Weg durch das Maschennetz bahnt, wobei er die Fasern scheinbar zu dehnen vermag. Monomerisch treibt er die Entfaltung des Nestes voran. Ab und an erscheint ein Flackern auf der membranartigen weißen Papierfasermasse. Die Risse im kugelförmigen Objekt verbreiten die Illusion von Stille und endloser Leere. Davon geht eine Art berauschende Faszination aus. Es scheint als sei eine zärtliche, noch schlaftrunkene Hoffnung erwacht. Vielleicht bedarf es eben gerade dieses zärtlichen Atems, um dem Leben Hoffnung ein zu hauchen.

Das Flackern der Lichtstrahlen ruft tiefste Gefühle wach. Die Naivität des Werkes gewinnt die Oberhand über jede blumig überladene Gestaltung. Aber dennoch unterscheidet sich das „Nest" sehr stark von „Kindred Spirits" der kanadischen

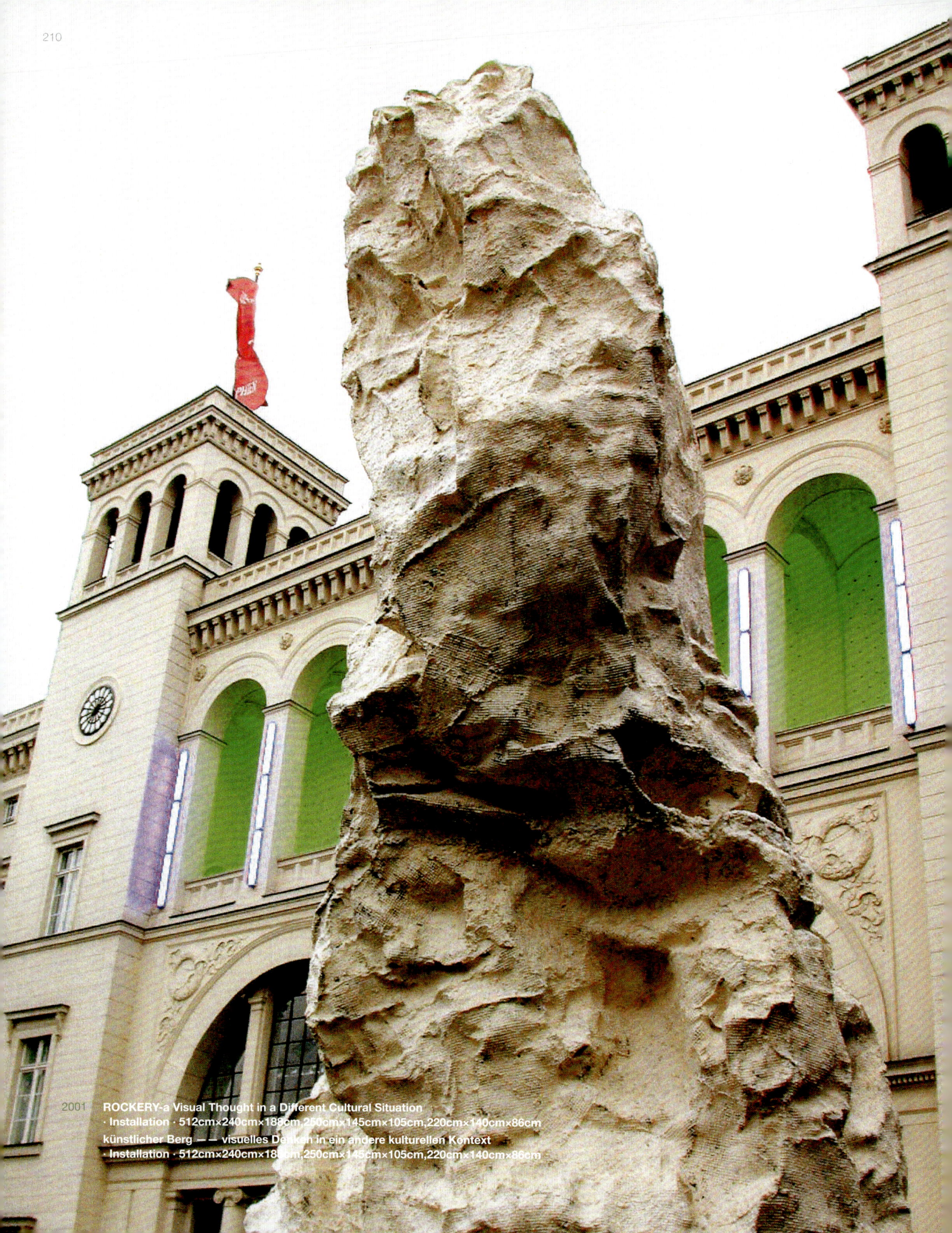

2001 **ROCKERY-a Visual Thought in a Different Cultural Situation**
· Installation · 512cm×240cm×188cm,250cm×145cm×105cm,220cm×140cm×86cm
künstlicher Berg —— visuelles Denken in ein andere kulturellen Kontext
· Installation · 512cm×240cm×188cm,250cm×145cm×105cm,220cm×140cm×86cm

Künstlerin Dawn MacNutt. Die nur schwach wahrnehmbare geheimnisvolle Stimmung wird in Letzterem durch Flackern von künstlichem Licht hervorgerufen. Das „Nest" unterscheidet sich auch von dem aus Bast gewobenen Werk „Hede (Stamen)" der finnischen Künstlerin Soili Arha. Obwohl dieses auch die Assoziation der Existenz von Leben hervorruft, scheint es eher so als gehe dieses Gefühl von der Entschlossenheit und Tatkraft einen Tunnel durch den Fels zu hauen aus. Shi Hui entgegen nutzt die Flut des Sonnenlichts um ein Gedicht vom Leben zu verfassen.

Gleichfalls aber in anderer Dimension schreibt auch das Werk „Scar" die Geschichte des Lebens. Aus achtzehn einfachen geometrischen Platten entsteht eine Metapher. Tuscheflecken bedingen die Assoziation von Flecken, die Sonne und Schatten auf Moos werfen und weiter die Assoziation zu den Spuren, die die verrinnende Zeit in einem Menschenleben hinterlässt. Obwohl ihr Werk beinahe gänzlich die konzipierte Assoziation ausschließt, werden keine Anstrengungen gescheut, den Wert des Visuellen an sich hervorzuheben, was den Betrachter, sich auf seine Sinne stützend, umgehend veranlasst, sich mit dem Werk zu identifizieren - ganz so wie in „poetry of senses" oder „poetry of things" oin Work eben mit den Sinnen erfahren.

Trotzdem denke ich, dass die Arbeit noch mehr in der Geschichte verwurzelt ist, oder aber möglicherweise in dem Gedanken „No ideas but in things". Nicht nur weil das als Material verwendete *Xuan*-Papier (Qualitätspapier für traditionelle Malerei und Kalligraphie aus Xuancheng, Provinz Anhui) schon einen dahingehenden Wink liefert, sondern auch weil ich überzeugt davon bin, dass ein großer Teil der Betrachter dieses Werkes sich das Gedicht „Recalling the Old Days at Mianchi" Su Dongpos ins Gedächtnis rufen werden. Das beliebte chinesische Sprichwort *„xue ni hong zhao"* („Die Spuren der Zeit") ist nämlich aus eben diesem Gedicht hervorgegangen. Es erklärt sich wahrscheinlich von selbst, wenn ich an dieser Stelle zum Vergleich ein Werk der Dichterin Amy Lowell zitiere:

Falling Snow

The snow whispers around me
And my wooden clogs
Leave holes behind me in the snow.
But no one will pass this way,
Seeking my footsteps.
And when the temple bell rings again
They will be covered and gone.

Dieses Gedicht ist reich an nachvollziehbaren sprachlichen Bildern, ein Kolorit genau wie in Shi Huis Werk. Der Glockenton am Ende des Gedichts manifestiert den im Denken der Autorin fest verwurzelten Humanismus. Einige Kritiker sind der Meinung, in diesem Gedicht spiegle sich Zeile für Zeile die Essenz des buddhistischen Glaubens wider. Es lässt einen unvermittelt an die folgende Maxime denken: „spontane Vereinigung um zu sein, um

zu gebären" und wir kommen letztendlich nicht umhin über die, dem Gesetz der Spontanität folgenden, achtzehn philosophischen Platten im Werk „Scar" nachzugrübeln.

Wenn wir Shi Huis Werke betrachten, stellt „Scar" einen Tagtraum dar. In ähnlicher Weise lässt die Reihe „Chan" („Wrap") den Betrachter die bizarren im Zwielicht am Seeufer zwischen grünem Peddingrohr und Lorbeer in voller Blüte stehenden Baumwollpflanzen singen hören. Jedes der Werke ist so rein und wahrhaftig, dass es gar nicht anders möglich ist, diese anders als von der Natur hervorgebrachte Produkte zu betrachten. Dennoch, sie sind kein Kind von Mutter Natur, sondern ein künstlerischer Geniestreich - anmutige Darstellungen, die Shi Hui Mutter Erde widmet. Exakt diese Art von Darstellung findet sich auch in vielen Gedichten:

Aus der Mitte des grünen, kräftigen, alten, abgebrochenen Zweiges erwächst der rein-weiße, anmutige Mai. („Im Mai erblüht der japanische Schnurbaum")

Möglicherweise ist in diesem Gedicht die bildliche Darstellung etwas zu durchschaubar. „They seem to be but are not flowers" eignet sich vielleicht sogar noch besser, um einen Vergleich zu „Chan" („Wrap") zu ziehen. Außerdem, wenn wir an Blumen denken, denken wir wahrscheinlich sofort an jene klassischen Meisterwerke mit humanistischen Zügen. Solche Meisterwerke finden sich in unserer alten Kultur zuhauf. Man erzählt sich, dass Tao Yuanming bei Wind und Regen, neben einem niedrigen Bambuszaun sitzend, sich mit wilden Chrysanthemen unterhält; Lin und Jing sich am in Nebel gehüllten Ufer des Westsees im duftbetörenden Hain von japanischen Aprikosen verlieren; Zhou Dunyi schlafend am Boot liegt, und im Traum mit dem Lotus eine metaphysische Einheit eingeht; Wir erzählen uns diese Anekdoten mit Freude, denn sie lassen uns die Lasten des Alltags vergessen und in eine andere Welt eintauchen. Shi Huis Reihe „Chan" („Wrap") ist völlig losgelöst von natürlicher Form und Struktur. Sie ist die Essenz aus Idee und Willenskraft und folgt einer sich auf Tastsinn und Sehvermögen stützenden Methode, die wiederum auf einem durch akribische Erforschung erlangten Verständnis gegenüber der Sonne und den Materialien basiert. Es verhält sich genau so, wie Immanuel Kant es dargelegt hat - als Ästhetik des Verstandes, weit entfernt von der emotionsgeladenen Tragik des Sentimentalismus.

Das Werk „Stone" präsentiert sich auf ganz neue Weise und markiert damit den Beginn eines neuen Abschnitts im Schaffen der Künstlerin, nämlich dem der Erforschung noch schlichterer Formen und Strukturen. Außerdem denke ich, dass „Stone" in der Geschichte weicher Skulpturen zweifellos das schlichteste und gegenständlichste Werk darstellt. Man könnte es höchstens noch mit „Kiefernadel" der polnischen Künstlerin Maria Komorowska oder aber der vasenförmigen Skulptur „Ohne Titel" der japanischen Künstlerin Katsuhiro Fujimura vergleichen. Die

The Twine series gives us an illusion of rare white flowers singing under the ivy, in the laurel clump. They are so pure that no one will doubt they are living creatures; however, they are products of mind, a beautiful image Shi Hui presents to the earth. When we think of flowers, many stories come into mind: Tao Yuanming, sitting on the little bamboo fence, talking with daisies in the light wind and drizzling rain; Lin Hejing, walking along the mistshrouded lake bank, was intoxicated with the shadow of the plum flowers; Zhou Dunyi, sleeping on a boat, merged into the sweet dream of lotus at the moonlight night. We take delight in relating these anecdotes of famous characters, because our thoughts are carried away afar from our boring daily life to a fairyland. Separated from the physical form, Shi Hui's *The Twine* series is a crystallization of thoughts and willpower. Shi Hui creates this kind of vision—touching approach after a rational study of sunshine and materials; this is what Kant called "rational aesthetics" without any sentimentality.

The Rock indicates that the artist has started a new way of creation--an exploration of simpler forms. In the history of soft sculpture's development, I think, *The Rock* is undoubtedly the simplest and most concrete work; probably, only *The Pine Needle* by the Polish artist Maria Komorowska and the jar-like thing of *the Untitled* by the Japanese Katsuhiro Fujimura can be compared with it. Shi Hui might be inspired by the traditional Chinese landscape painting when she produced *The Rock*, yet the paper mache, here is beyond its faltering and gives a feeling of stability and monumentality. We feel like this because the momentum of the rock shocks us,because we are inwardly enlightened mathematically by the volume and quality of the rock, which is functionally and descriptively meaningless. Nevertheless,this feeling depends on the

Inspiration zu „Stone" stammt mutmaßlich aus der chinesischen Landschaftsmalerei. Dennoch ist es keinesfalls diese Art von leichter, fließender Geschmeidigkeit der Landschaftsmalerei der südlichen Zong, die einen nachhaltigen Reiz auf uns auswirkt. Hier überkommt die weiche Papiermasse das ihr an sich innewohnende Charakteristikum und vermittelt ein marmornes Gefühl von Ruhe und Ausgeglichenheit, so würdevoll wie ein Denkmal. Diese Wahrnehmung wird durch die Wucht der schöpferischen Kraft der Künstlerin ausgelöst. Es sind Dimension und Beschaffenheit, die uns ähnlich mathematischer Gesetzmäßigkeiten diese tiefe Erkenntnis bringen. Dem Werk wohnen weder Zweckmäßigkeit noch Beschreibung inne. Die Empfindung ist allerdings abhängig vom Sonnenlicht. Sie stützt sich auf die würdevolle Silhouette, der sich Seite an Seite reihenden Schatten. Mit Hilfe des Sonnenlichts tritt sie noch reiner, noch ausgeprägter, noch schlichter in Erscheinung. Diese Tugenden hat die Künstlerin rein gestützt auf das natürliche Sonnenlicht prägnant hervorgebracht.

In vielerlei Hinsicht ist „Künstlicher Berg" eine Erweiterung zu „Stone". Sein Titel birgt ein Paradoxon. Möglicherweise ist dieses Werk noch spekulativer als „Stone". Es erinnert mich ein wenig an René Magrittes *Ceci n'est pas une pipe*. Das ist das zentrale Phänomen in Shi Huis jüngsten Arbeiten. Im Werk „Künstlicher Berg" sind typische chinesische Steinskulpturen in einem typisch westlichen Gebäude-innenhof platziert. Mittels dieser Dislokation von Kultur wird ein ganz spezieller Dialog zwischen Ost und West heraufbeschworen. In den Augen der Künstlerin soll es ein Appell zum Nachdenken sein. Dabei tritt uns sogleich die Beschreibung eines chinesischen Gartens in Goethes Theaterstück „Die Laune des Verliebten" ins Gedächtnis. Der chinesische Garten hatte einen starken Einfluss auf jene Epoche in Europa, wobei er durchaus auch kontroverse Beurteilungen erfuhr.

Dieses scheint heute kein Thema mehr zu sein. Allerdings sind Vertreter der modernen Zivilisationsforschung der Meinung, dass solche "Stimmungswelten" inzwischen bereits der Vergangenheit angehören und dadurch erst, argumentieren sie, hat Seele und

sunshine, on the clear shadow made by the profile in the faint shine, on the purer, clearer, simpler configuration, refined by the artist in the sun.

We might define *The Rockery* as a derivative of *The Rock*. The title is something paradoxical, reminding me of René Magritte's *Ceci n'est pas une pipe*. *The Rockery* may be more speculative than *The Trace* in connotative meaning; and this is something attractive in Shi Hui's recent works. A few pieces of typical Chinese rocks are put in a typical Western courtyard, thus oriental and occidental cultures go on a special discourse. Here, the artist intends to cause an uneasy contemplation in our mind. The work also associates itself with what Goethe called "Chinese Gothic pavilion and rockery" in *The Victory of Affection*. At that time, the Chinese garden had a great impact in Europe, but its appraisal was controversial.

Now, this problem seems to be self-evident. But the students of modern civilization think that the world of Stimmung, in which the soul and the object share a natural Übereinstimmen, has vanished. Based on the coordination among the objects, the soul raises an imaginative space to our minds, with the interacting objects, thus the recount of soul gets more poetic. Today, the objects have lost the sense of existence and remain only a calculation of their mutual relation. Then we won't feel that *The Rockew* is just proposed to create a visionary world. However, if the garden's design is an improvisation, the rocks are definitely playing the lead, with hue and shade, light and shadow, sound and noise harmonized simply, naturally well with the surroundings even in an exotic courtyard. We can't help considering that, behind the rocks, there might hide some delicate philosophy of order and regulation.

Objekt eine natürliche Übereinstimmung gefunden. Nach dem Grundsatz des Einklangs zwischen den Objekten, wird durch die interagierenden Objekte ein Raum geschaffen, der Assoziationen zulässt. Damit erhält eine "Schilderung" seine poetische Note. Heute haben viele Objekte bereits an Einzigartigkeit eingebüßt und funktionieren nur noch in Hochrechnung ihrer Beziehungen zu einander. Wenn wir vor diesem Hintergrund nochmals das Werk „Künstlicher Berg" betrachten, werden wir feststellen, dass es nichts wenlger tut als eine fiktive Welt zu schaffen. Dennoch, wenn wir davon ausgehen, dass das Anlegen eines Gartens an sich ein improvisiertes "Schauspiel" ist, dann nehmen offensichtlich die Steine die Hauptrolle darin ein. Ihr Farbton, ihr Spiel von Licht und Schatten, ihr Schall ist jeher unverändert und geht mit dem sie im exotischen Garten Umgebenden eine harmonische Einheit ein - ganz einfach und natürlich. Dies lässt uns nicht umhin darüber nachzusinnen, ob sich dahinter nicht vielleicht aller Art von Philosophie der harmonischen Ordnung verbirgt.

III.

In der grenzenlosen Natur folgt alles Leben einer gewissen Ordnung. Faserkunst oder weiche Skulpturen stellen in vielerlei Hinsicht eine bis ins Altertum zurückzuverfolgende Kunstfertigkeit des auf Ordnung beruhenden Arrangierens dar. Diese Kunst setzt voraus, dass der Künstler als Subjekt der objektiven Realität auftritt. Wenn man versucht die Dinge mathematisch in Relation zu setzen, bemerkt man, dass wie Zhuangzi in einigen seiner Ausführungen schildert, diese einer Relativität unterworfen sind. Je weiter und reichhaltiger der Umfang des Designs ist, desto mehr Einschränkungen ergeben sich bedingt durch die Obacht den Anforderungen zu entsprechen. Das Werk „Knoten" kann vielleicht nur verstanden werden, indem man es im Kontext dieser altertümlichen Parameter einer Ordnung der Dinge betrachtet.

„Knoten" ist eine Serie von Arbeiten, deren erstes Werk 1995 entstand. Darauf folgten nach und nach Fortsetzungen. Es zählt hinsichtlich seines Umfangs zu Shi Huis größtem Werk. Die

III

Everything in the world has its own order. Fibre art or soft sculpture, in a sense, is a skill of the order arrangement that can be traced back to ancient times. During the creation, the artists must obey the objective reality and work out the mathematical logic in space. Meanwhile, a design, which covers a wider and richer scope, should take into account of all kinds of possibilities and limitations. And only in the reference system of this ancient order arrangement can *The Structure* be comprehended properly, uniquely.

The Structure series, initially made in 1995, is the largest in scale of Shi Hui's works. The first set is made up of net, Chinese paper rolls and 22 huge frames with a method people apply to bed-making. However, it is from this ordinary process that Shi Hui extracts a new language of art. Different from the simply repeated work of bed-making, the coir ropes and wooden frames play a new game in which we see variations emerging from the simple order and regulation. When these forms stand up, we seem to be in a formation of net, which gives us an especially strange feeling of a new spatial structure; and we have never experienced this kind of new order before. Once we pay our attention to the details, we become to taste, as it were, a more colourful and more delicate variety of orders in the slanting light: profuse dots and lines making everything dainty and exquisite, sparkling and glittering, meanwhile mysterious and ingenious. There seems to be a flickering, constantly changing, hazy view which gives you a glimpse at a misty, deep and secluded valley; yet, there seem to be beams of sunshine falling down, giving out the silver light through thousands of leaves to weave a tranquil and a twinkling net on the ground. This poetic imagination

erste Arbeit dieser Serie besteht aus 22 riesigen, aneinander hängenden Holzrahmen, innerhalb eines jeden die fasrige Masse des *Xuan*-Papiers ein Netz spinnt. Dieses lehnt sich an die traditionelle Handwerkstechnik zur Bespannung eines Bettrahmens mit Palmstrick an. Zur Fixierung des Palmfaserseils wird dabei ein Holznagel verwendet. Und gerade aus dieser gewöhnlichen Handwerksarbeit hat Shi Hui eine neue künstlerische Sprache extrahiert. Mit dem auf fortlaufender Wiederholung beruhenden, schlichten Maschenwerk der Palmbett-bespannung hat dies nichts mehr gemein, denn Shi Huis Netzwerk orientiert sich nach neuen Bezugspunkten. Indem diese neuen Relationen unentwegt ausgenutzt und adjustiert werden, bedingt der ständige Wandel eine stetig sich fortentwickelnde Aufklärung der schlichten Ordnung. Wenn sich die Holzrahmen vor uns auftürmen, scheint es uns als wären wir Teil der Netzformation und wir erfahren eine Art bizarre, neue Raumarchitektur mit neuen Grenzen. Die neue Ordnung löst eine Selbsterfahrung aus, die wir so noch nie erlebt haben. Wenn wir unseren Blick auf die feinen Details der Arbeit richten, können wir unter dem schrägen Einfall der Sonnenstrahlen, noch mehr, noch raffiniertere Veränderungen der Ordnung wahrnehmen: Ein buntes Durcheinander an Punkten und Linien, fein verteilt, kunstvoll sich hindurchbohrend, glitzernd durchleuchtend, gleichzeitig aber schwierig auseinander zu halten, enigmatisch. Es erscheint wie eine verschwommene Szene eines Wechselspiels von hell und dunkel, das dich einen hastigen Blick in die dunstverhangenen düsteren Tiefen eines von Bergen überschatteten dunklen Tals werfen lässt. Abrupt, so scheint es, sendet die Sonne abermals Strahl für Strahl und das silberne Licht ergießt sich über die sich in zig-tausenden Formen präsentierenden Zweige und Blätter. Am Boden spinnt sich ein still flackerndes Netz. Diese Wahrnehmung ergibt sich aus Flut und Wandel der Sonneneinstrahlung. Sie ist voll von Poesie und mächtig diesen Moment zu erzeugen. Letztendlich ist sie aber doch mit Rolle um Rolle von *Xuan*-Papier herbeigeführt. Gerade die Bearbeitung des *Xuan*-Papiers offenbart im Zuge der handwerklichen und kreativen Umsetzung Grenzen was die stil-istische Verfeinerung durch den Künstler betrifft.

changes with the flow of lights, but what really cerates the picture are the Chinese paper rolls, with which the artist both expresses her ideas and shows her skills.

Thanks to the timehonoured culture, Chinese paper seems to be alive, breathing, working, full of latent ardour, marked on every fibre with the trace of time; also it seems to be an organic being, a phantom of some atmosphere. It is mainly because of the artist's sensibility to materials and cultural intuition that The Structure can bring out such a dainty and exquisite space and a gentle, full texture that endows the works a swirling glamour with dotty changes.

This cultural intuition is both the intuition to materials and the experience of complicated handwork and these are significant for the works of art. In the development of fibre art and soft sculpture, artists have been probing the secret of materials since l980's. Especially in 1985, at the l2th International Biennial of Tapestry in Lausanne, steel plate, metal pliers, plaster stone, sand ribbon and so on, all these modern materials became carriers of works. Till the1990's, more new ideas have emerged. Under this background, Shi Hui has come to realize the particular significance of common Chinese materials with a comparative view after years of trial and error. Not to mention Shi Hui devoted one and a half years to make *The Structure*, from her words we will understand how much effort she has put into it which vindicates her attitude towards art:

Exploring the mysterious spatial structure in the net constantly fascinates me. It is just like silkworm making its cocoon, spider weaving its web. In the recent 10 years, I take the simplest weaving

Wie wir wissen, ist weißes Papier nicht gleich weißes Papier. Zwischen herkömmlichem westlichem Papier und chinesischem *Xuan*-Papier liegt ein großer Unterschied. Dem *Xuan*-Papier wohnt die klassische chinesische Kultur inne. Es scheint lebendig. Es scheint zu atmen, zu arbeiten. Es scheint in sich Leidenschaft zu tragen. Es scheint die Zeit in seinen Fasern verborgen zu halten. Und indem es den Anschein macht, Existenz von Leben zu bergen, vermag es eine bestimmte Stimmung heraufzubeschwören. Der Grund, warum „Knoten" es vermag, den Raum so kunstvoll durchdrungen, das Gewebe so sanft und weich wie den ersten Schnee erscheinen zu lassen, liegt im schwelgenden ästhetischen Reiz, der sich durch den stetigen Wandel der punkthaften Muster des Gewebes ergibt. Dieses zeugt von einem hohen Grad an Sensibilität der Künstlerin gegenüber dem Material sowie ihrer kulturellen Intuition.

Diese kulturelle Intuition ist gleichzeitig auch die Intuition gegenüber dem Material sowie die durch Anfertigung eines so voluminösen Werkes in Handarbeit gewonnene persönliche Erfahrung. Auf diesen Grundlagen beruht das Werk. Die Entstehungsgeschichte der Faserkunst und der weichen Skulpturen reicht in die 80er Jahre des vergangenen Jahrhunderts zurück, von wo aus sich eine regelrechte Welle der Experimentierfreude unter den Künstlern ausbreitete. Speziell bei der „12th Lausanne International Biennial of Tapestry" bildeten so moderne Materialien wie unter anderen Stahlplatten, Metalle, Klammern und Gips die Grundlage der ausgestellten Arbeiten. In den 90er Jahren sind daraus neue Konzepte hervorgegangen. Vor diesem Hintergrund hat Shi Hui nach Jahren unermüd-lichen Experimentierens ein spezielles Verständnis gegenüber der den konventionellen, im chinesischen Alltag zur Anwendung gelangenden Materialen innewohnenden Bedeutung entwickelt. Bezug nehmend auf den unermesslichen Arbeitsaufwand, kann dennoch nicht behauptet werden, der Prozess hin zur Vollendung des ersten Werkes der Reihe „Knoten", an dem die Künstlerin ein ganzes Jahr gearbeitet hatte, stelle

skill as a starting point from which to develop a framework of contemporary significance. The making process really needs patience and tenacity. Sometimes, I really felt tired and wanted to have a rest, especially when the work was nearly finished and a sense of dullness made me fatigued. But when noticing some imperfect details, 1 was determined to hold on to continue the work.

Indeed, the manual labour is really toilsome, but it also unconsciously brings the artist into a realm where materials seem to Cooperate with hands and keep wandering about in the space. As acompensation for the artist's hard work, materials magically become a friend and an assistant of the artist, who reveals to her the secret of orders. When we are in front of The Structure, facing thousands of Chinese paper rolls the artist used, what Van Gogh called "a knotty problem" comes to our mind :

The mental effort of balancing the six essential colours: red, blue, yellow, orange, violet, green. This is work and cool calculation, when one's mind is utterly stretched like that of an actor on the stage in a difficult part, when one has to think of a thousand different things at a time within half an hour.

Don't think that I would ever artificially work myself into a feverish state. Rather remember that I am engrossed in a complicated calculus. . .

The so-called "calculation" springs up from time to time in such works as *The Structure*, and this "calculation" makes the artist feel that she could never express the material, space, texture and significance perlectly and harmoniously on her own alone. She might find not herself but something beyond her control guiding her hands. What on earth is the secret of balancing? No precise words could answer it. No wonder the humble artists always attribute it to the God's grace, which initially

vergeudete Zeit dar, speziell wenn wir ihre unten in einfachen Worten beschriebene Hingabe zur Kunst betrachten:

Ich finde es äußerst verlockend die mystischen Zwischenräume in unterschiedlichen Geweben zu erkunden. Ähnlich einer Seidenraupe die ihren Kokon spinnt, oder einer Spinne die ihr Netz webt. Seit zehn Jahren bemittle ich mich der einfachsten Webtechniken als Ausgangspunkt für meine Arbeiten. Im kontinuierlich voranschreitenden Verlauf der Geschichte versuche ich moderne Strukturen zu erschaffen. Es erfordert Geduld und Stärke. Manchmal ist es ermüdend und man möchte sich ausruhen, speziell wenn es auf die Endphase zugeht. Monotone Arbeit ist nun mal ermüdend. Auch wenn einem die Detailarbeit zu schaffen macht, muss man eben die Zähne zusammmen beißen und weiter machen.

In der Tat, Handwerksarbeit ist beschwerlich. Wie auch immer, die Handwerksarbeit führt den Künstler dazu, unbewusst seine Grenzen zu überschreiten. Die Materialien scheinen mit den Händen zu kooperieren und diese unermüdlich in Bewegung zu halten. Die Kompensation für seine Mühen, ist die Magie der Beziehung des Künstlers zum Material. Er hat in Letzterem einen Gesellen gewonnen, mit dessen Hilfe es ihm gelingt, die Mysterien der Ordnung offen darzulegen. Die anmutige, geschwungene Form des „Nests" ist der natürlichen Biegsamkeit des Bambus zu verdanken. Auch das Werk „Säule" nahm Ausgang von einer kreisenden Idee hinsichtlich einer Form, bis es nach drei Jahren kontinuierlichen Arbeitens zur Vollendung gebracht wurde. Wenn wir in das Netzwerk von „Knoten" eintauchen und die zig-tausenden Formen des *Xuan*-Papiers betrachten, die die Künstlerin geschaffen hat, wird uns automatisch bewusst, was Vincent van Gogh meinte als er vom heiklen Problem des Künstlers sprach:

Es ist eine mühevolle Arbeit, die Balance zwischen rot, blau, gelb, orange, violett, grün zu finden. Es bedarf großen Arbeitseinsatzes und nüchterner Analyse. In diesen Momenten zerbricht man sich den Kopf. Ähnlich einem Schauspieler der auf der Bühne in einer schwierigen Rolle steckt und innerhalb einer halben Stunde plötzlich

means the talent that the God besows on artists as well as the elegance of ideal beauty.

The idea of simplicity is an idea of grace, which is created by God directly or with the aid of artists. One of the ultimate goals of Shi Hui's labour is to give expression to this idea. Therefore, a modern artist she is, she does not mean to describe the complexity of the contemporary, especially the modern sensation of anxiety: on the contrary, her work is an expression of health, simplicity and purity. Her clear and limpid artistic language indicates an order that ever brightens the magnificent nature, This order is fine and exquisite, pure and innocent, sequential and plentiful: this order emphasizes our natural preference for plainness,thus we see a modern poet of simplicity beyond the charm of paper and delicacy of rope:the artist Shi Hui.

an hunderttausende Dinge gleichzeitig denken muss. Ihr braucht nicht zu glauben, dass ich euch einen Fanatismus vorspiele. Am Besten ihr berücksichtigt, dass ich ganz in mich versunken Berechnungen anstelle.

In Werken wie „Knoten" treten diese sogenannten „Berechnungen", von denen Vincent van Gogh spricht, zweifellos zahlreich zu Tage. Oftmals lässt es den Künstler sogar daran zweifeln im Stande zu sein aus eigener Kraft heraus Material, Raum, Struktur und Bedeutung in eine perfekte und harmonische Einheit bringen zu können. Möglicherweise denkt die Künstlerin auch, es wäre nicht sie selbst, sondern eine höhere Kraft, die ihre Hände lenkt. Was ist also das Geheimnis dieser Balance? Es ist unmöglich, dies präzise in Worte zu fassen. Nicht verwunderlich, dass bescheidene Künstler oftmals auf die Gunst der Götter verweisen. Wenn man diese Gunst als „grace" versteht, so impliziert seine ursprüngliche Bedeutung, dass die Götter den Künstler sowohl mit Talent als auch dem Ideal von Ästhetik und Grazie ausstatten.

Das Konzept von Naivität ist ein Konzept von „grace". Es ist von den Göttern hervorgebracht, oder anders gesagt, durch die von den Göttern gelenkten Hände des Künstlers hervorgebracht. Das oberste Ziel der umfassenden Arbeit, in die Shi Hui so viel investiert hat, ist es eben gerade dieses zu verkörpern. Folglich und wie unschwer zu erkennen, versucht Shi Hui, obwohl sie eine zeitgenössische Künstlerin ist, sich offensichtlich nicht darauf zu versteifen die komplexen Gefühle des modernen Menschen, speziell die Beklemmung, die der heutigen Zeit anhaftet, zum Ausdruck zu bringen. Viel mehr sind ihre Werke Ausdruck des Gefühls von Vitalität, Naivität und Reinheit. Sie bemittelt sich einer klaren und deutlichen künstlerischen Sprache um eine Ordnung darzustellen, in der sie der überquellenden, herrlichen Natur eine verständliche künstlerische Note verleiht - akribisch, ernst, reichhaltig und geregelt. Dies hebt mit Nachdruck unsere natürliche Veranlagung einer Vorliebe für Schlicht-heit hervor. In einer Welt von faszinierender Papierqualität und fragiler Fäden präsentiert sich Shi Hui als moderne naive Poetin.

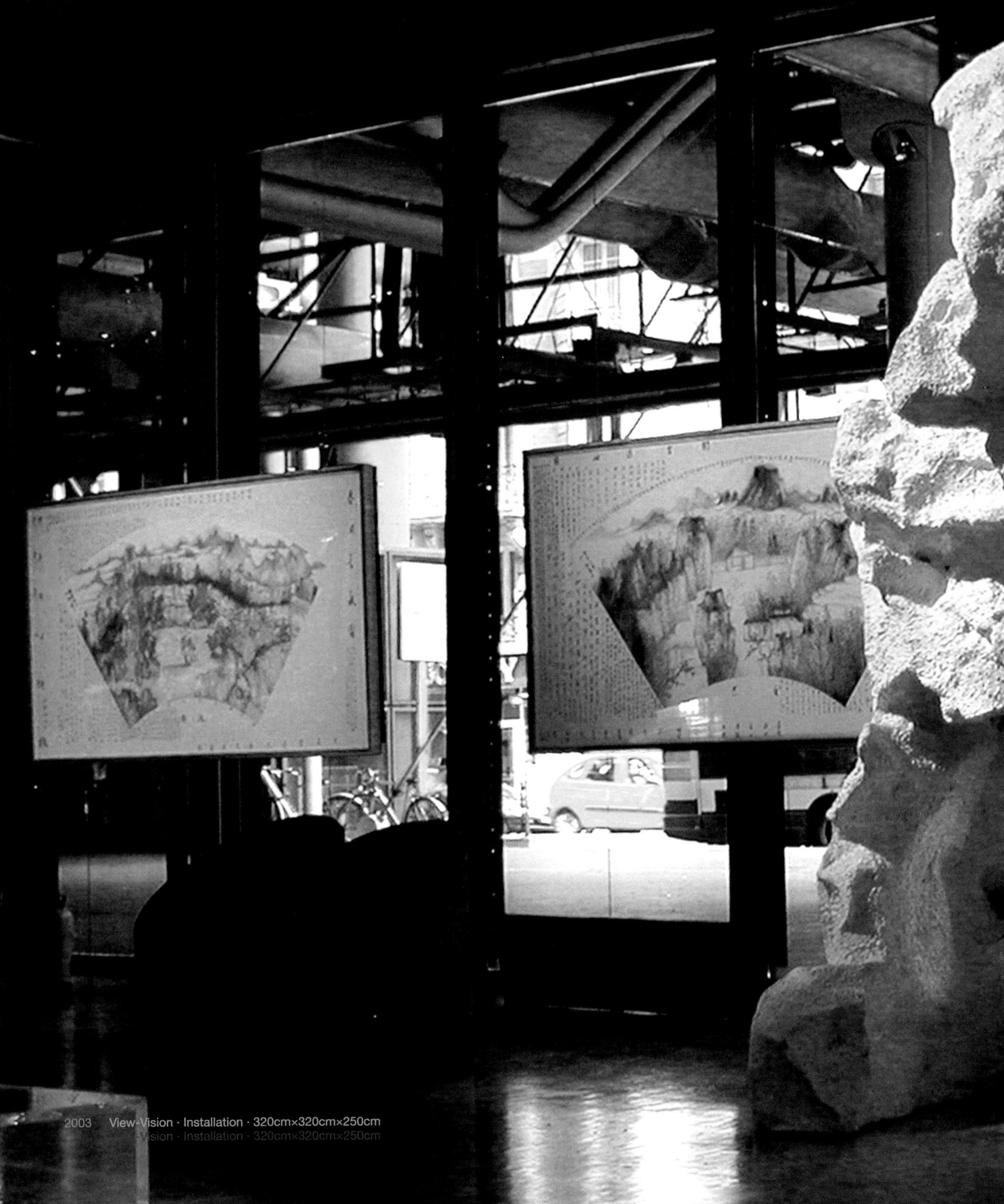

2003　View-Vision · Installation · 320cm×320cm×250cm

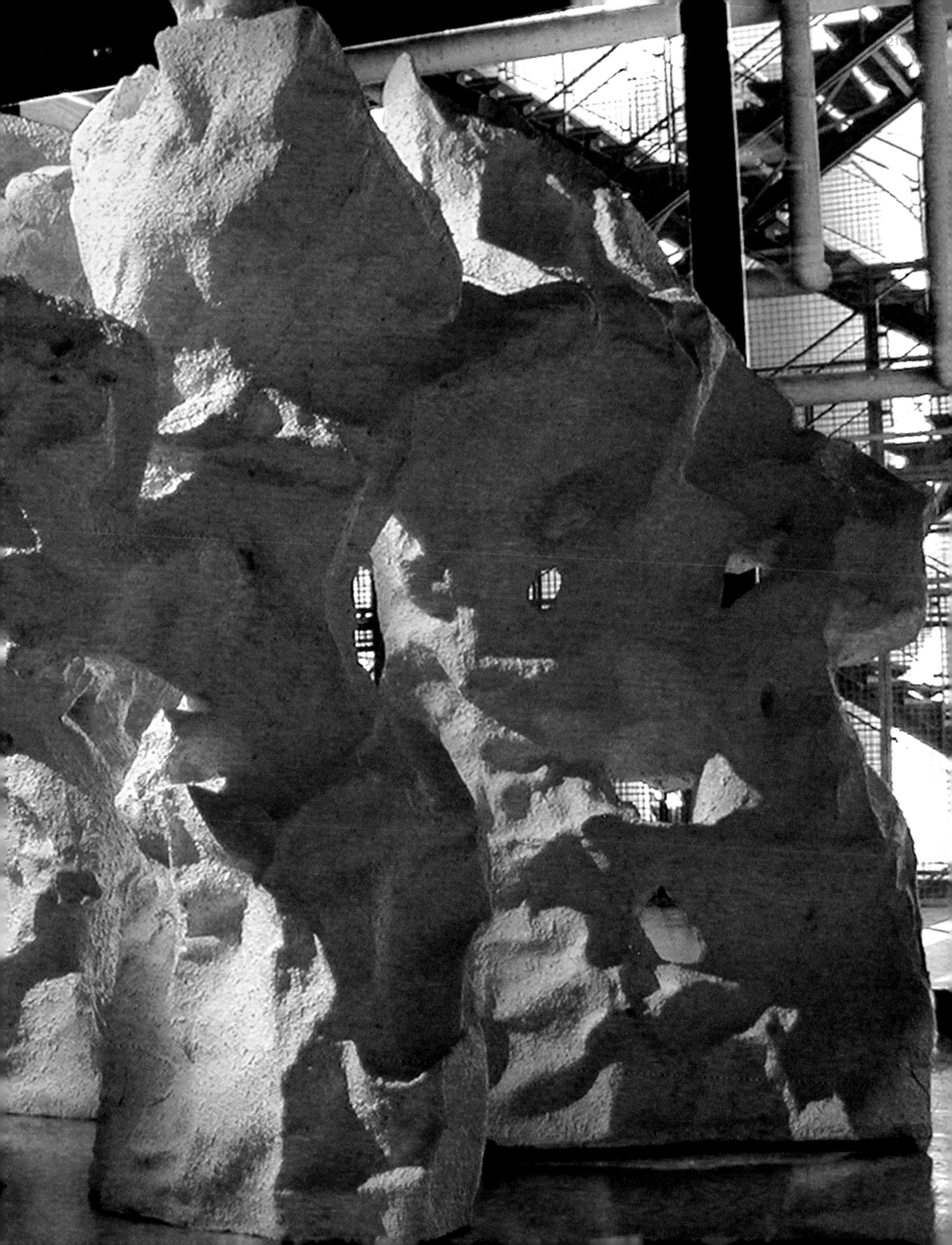

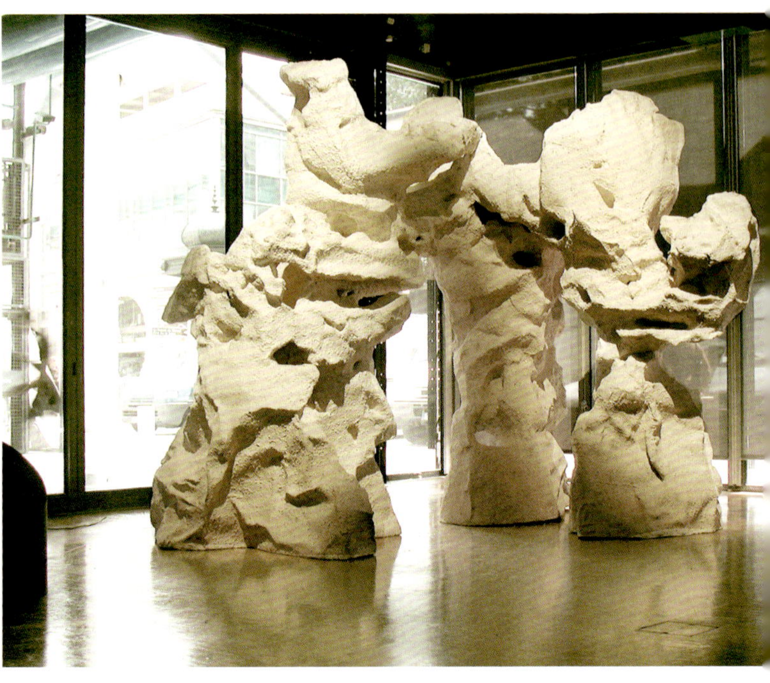

2003　View-Vision · Installation · 320cm×320cm×250cm
View-Vision · Installation · 320cm×320cm×250cm

Als rein natürliches Material befriedigt mich Papiermasse zutiefst. Sie ist weiß und sauber und ihre verführerische Schlichtheit birgt enormes Potential für Transformation. Unter den zahlreichen Stoffen, aus denen die Papiermasse besteht, finden sich Barnbus und Leinenfasern, die dem Endprodukt seine Widerstandsfähigkeit verleihen. Im Zuge des Formungsprozesses bis hin zur gewünschten Gestalt, tritt eine Art "zähes" Inneres unter dem elastischen weißen Äußeren zu Tage. Eben dieses elastisch wie auch zäh sein, entspricht dem chinesischen Sinnbild für Ästhetik. Diese Eigenschaften sind die Quintessenz des Lebens, die auch meine Existenz begründen. Ich denke, es ist nicht nur unerlässlich, einen individuellen Zugang zum Material zu finden, sondern sich im Zuge der Außeinandersetzung mit dem Material auch dessen Kultur zu widmen bzw. aber die eigene Lebenserfahrung miteinfliessen zu lassen. Diesen Ansatz versuche ich auch kontinuierlich in meiner Arbeit zu verfolgen. (ShiHui)

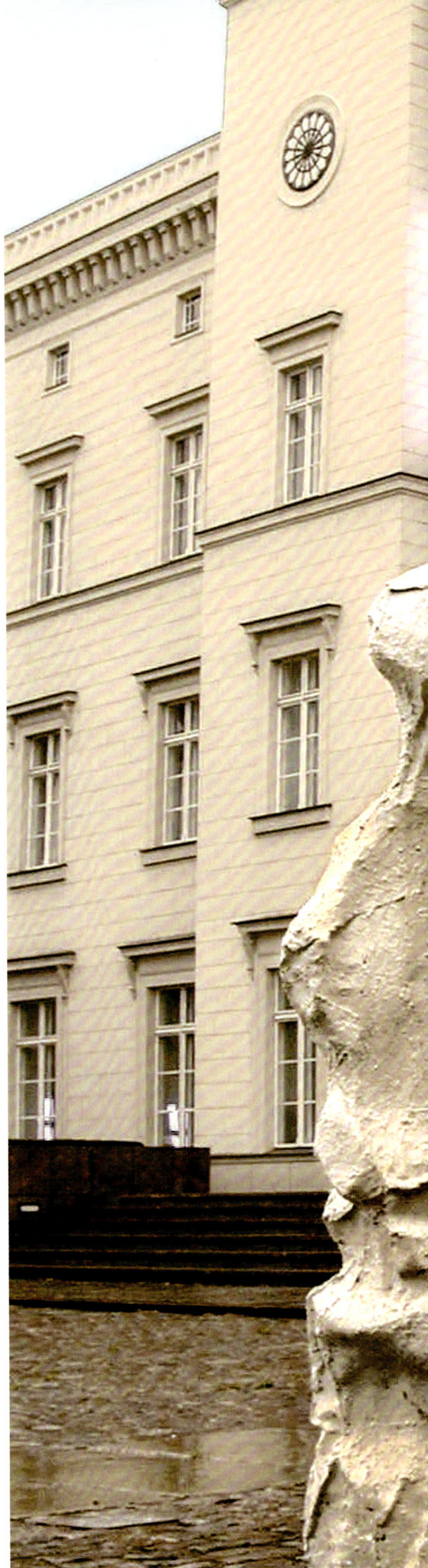

2001   ROCKERY-a Visual Thought in a Different Cultural Situation
· Installation · 512cm×240cm×188cm,250cm×145cm×105cm,220cm×140cm×86cm

künstlicher Berg —— visuelles Denken in ein andere kulturellen Kontext
· Installation · 512cm×240cm×188cm,250cm×145cm×105cm,220cm×140cm×86cm

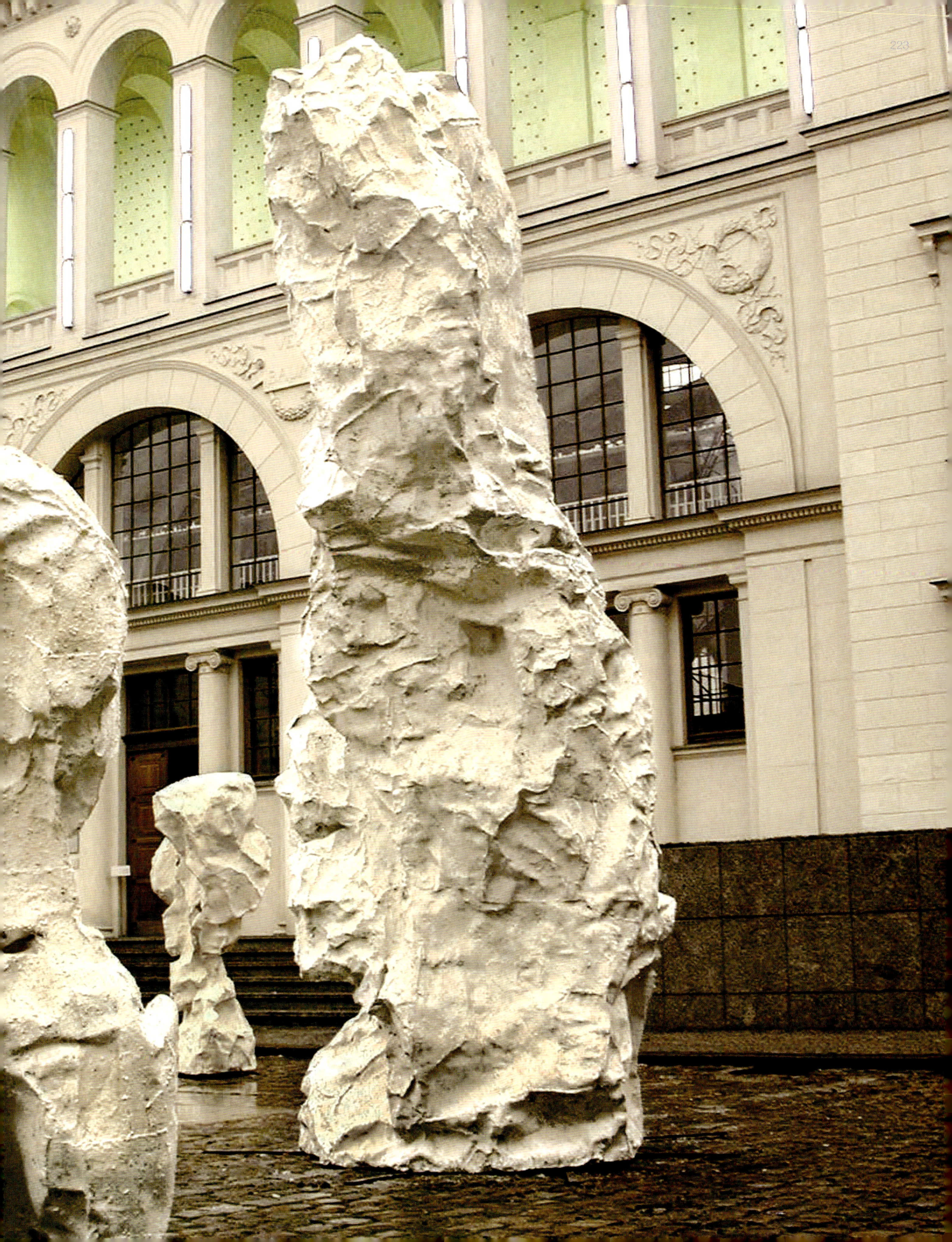

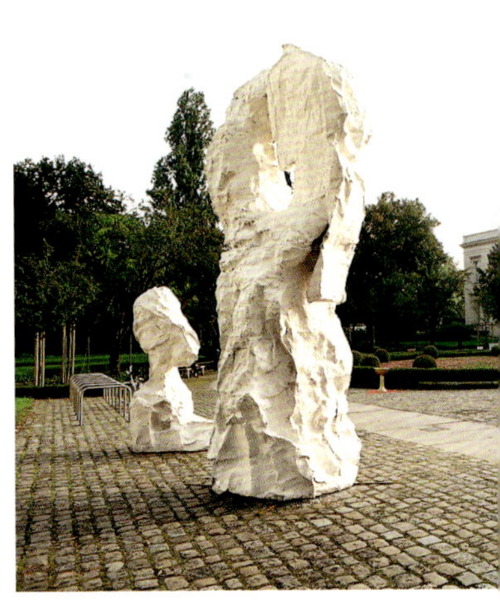

I am tempted to explore mystical spaces in
mesh structures. Just as the cocoon-spinning
silkworm and the web-weaving spider, I start with
the simplest weaving technique. In the process
of continuous exploration, I try to create new
frameworks in the modern sense. As the threads
of the frameworks unravel, space is intersected
into layered mesh, and paper rolls are inserted
into each individual grid. The membrane-like
paper mache encloses the traces of the thread.
The mix of linen threads, xuan paper and paper
mache has created a new form of gestation.

(ShiHui)

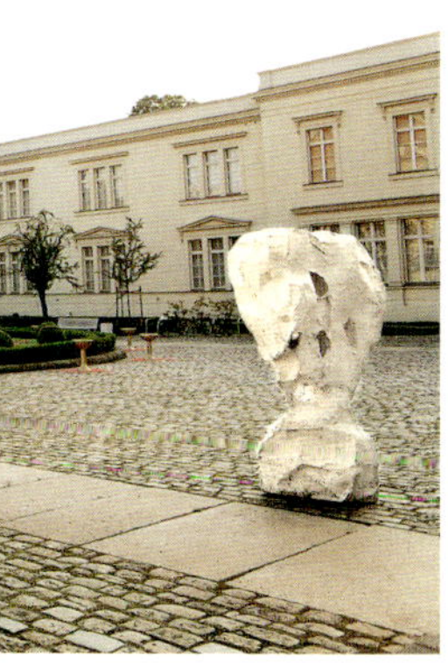

2001   ROCKERY-a Visual Thought in a Different Cultural Situation
· Installation · 512cm×240cm×188cm,250cm×145cm×105cm,220cm×140cm×86cm

künstlicher Berg —— Visuelle Reflexionen in unterschiedlichen kulturellen kontexten
· Installation · 512cm×240cm×188cm,250cm×145cm×105cm,220cm×140cm×86cm

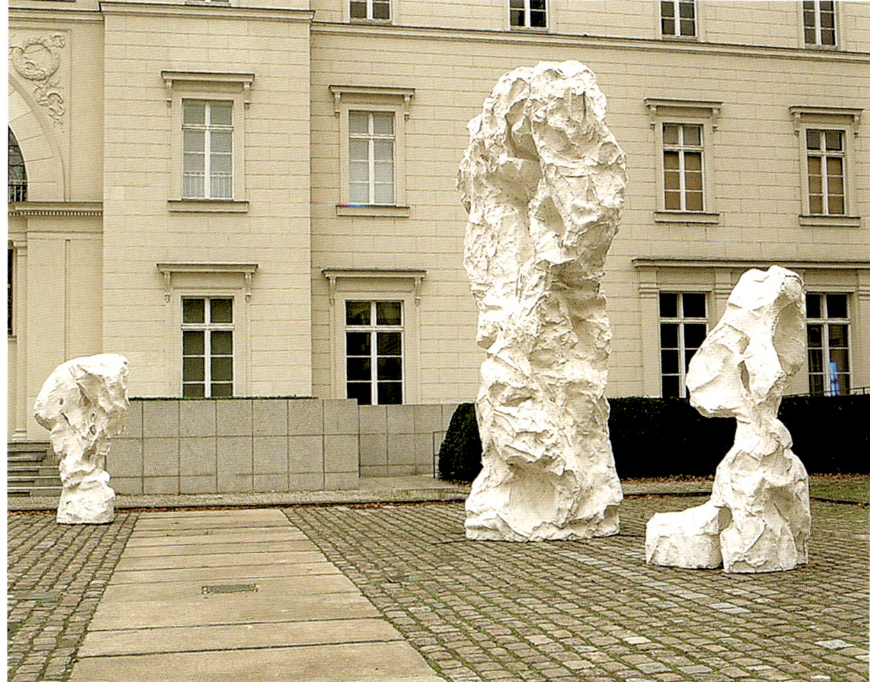

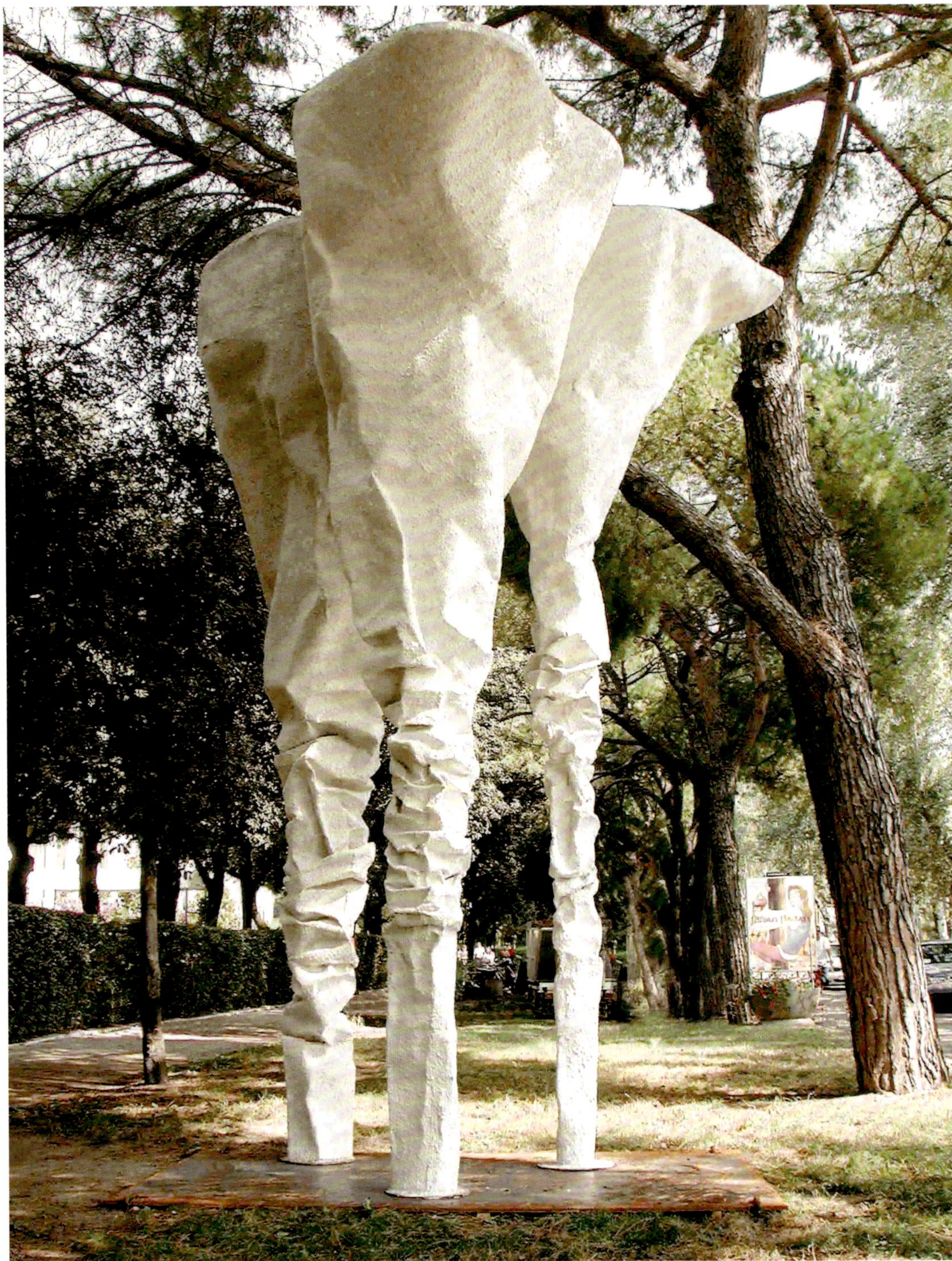

2002   Melt · Installation · 500cm×200cm×200cm×3
Schmelzen · Installation · 500cm×200cm×200cm×3

Ich finde es äußerst verlockend, die mystischen Zwischenräume in unterschiedlichen Geweben zu erkunden. Ähnlich einer Seidenraupe, die ihren Kokon spinnt, oder einer Spinne, die ihr Netz webt, beginne auch ich mit der einfachsten Technik. Im Zuge eines beständig voranschreitenden Erkundungsprozesses, versuche ich im Sinne von Modernität und Innovation immer neue Strukturen zu schaffen. Sobald sich die rahmengebende Grundstruktur hervor tut, bilden sich Freiräume im mehrschichtigen Gewebe, die ich mit Papierrollen stopfe. Die Mischung aus Leinenfäden, Xuan-Papier und Papiermasse hat eine neue Form von Reifeprozess hervorgebracht.

(ShiHui)

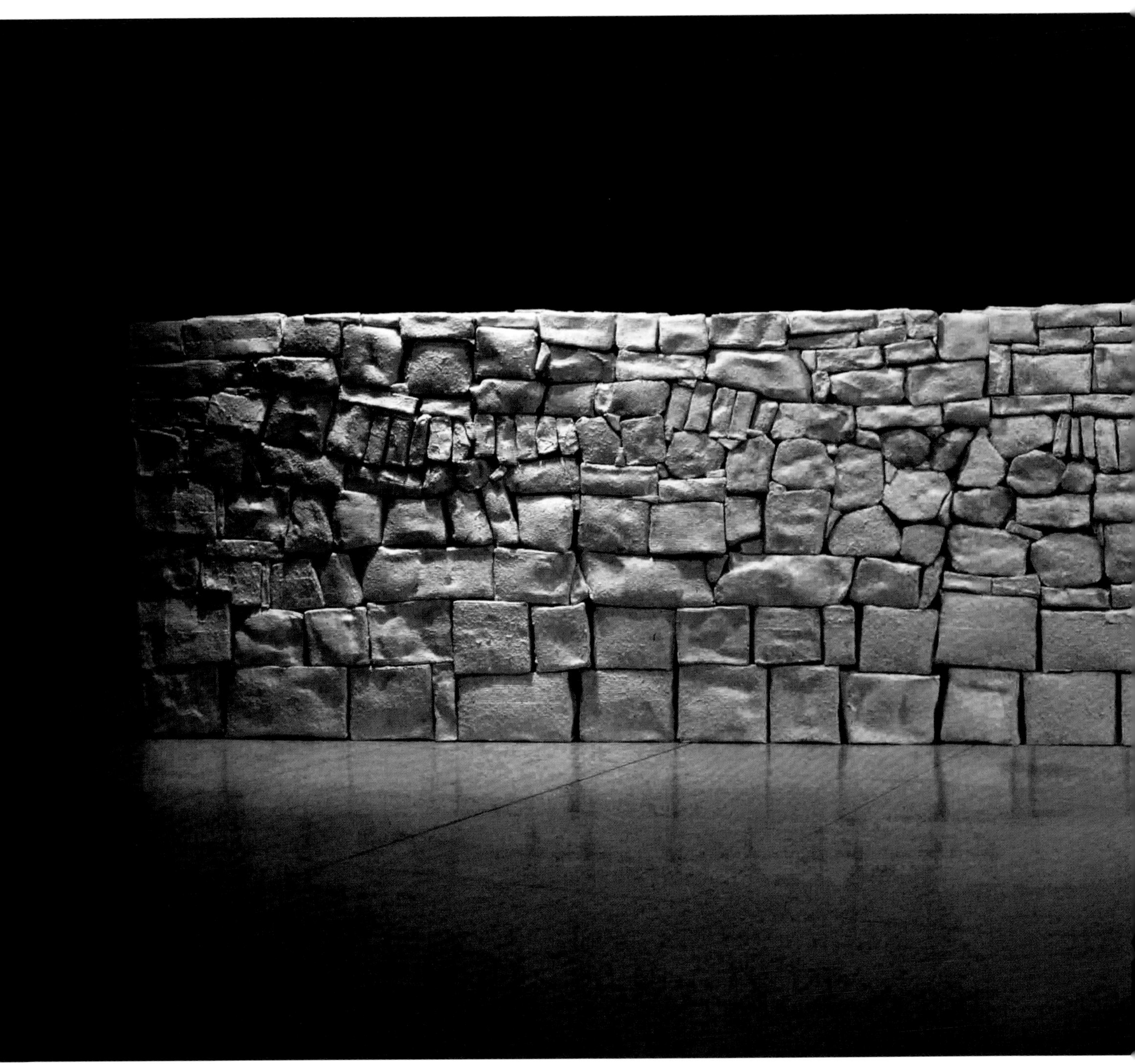

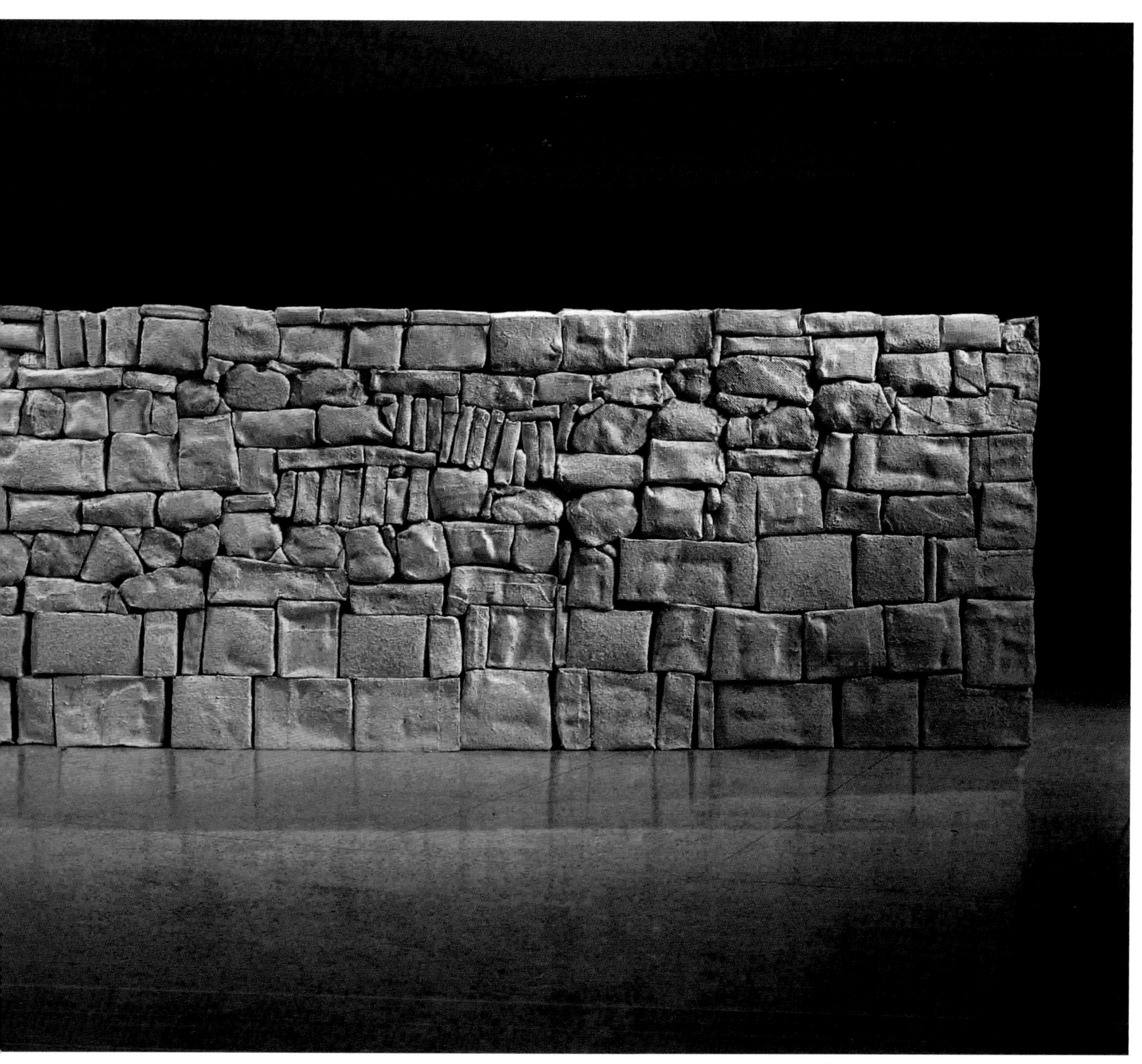

2003   Old Wall · Installation · 170cm×800cm×100cm
Wand · Installation · 170cm×800cm×100cm

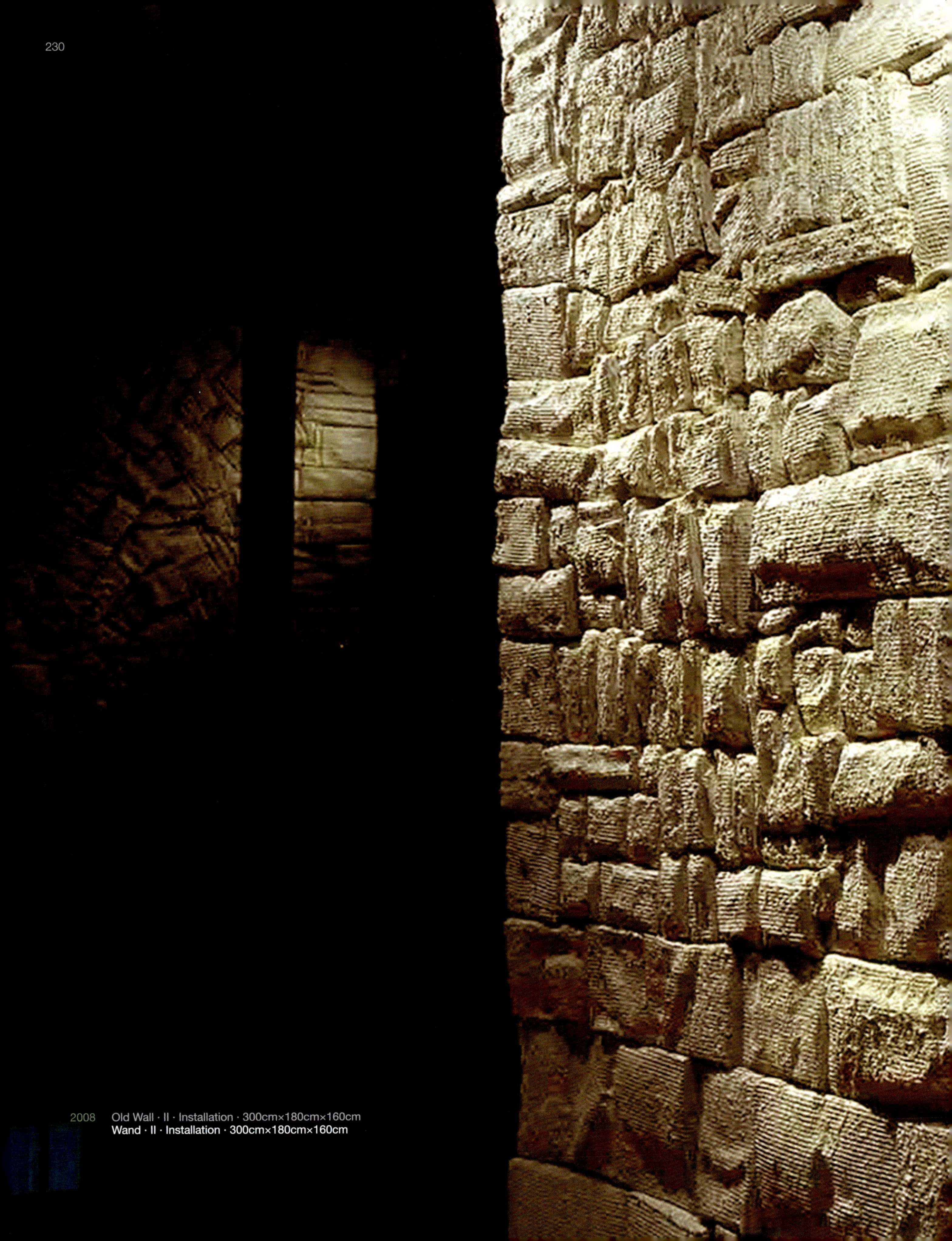

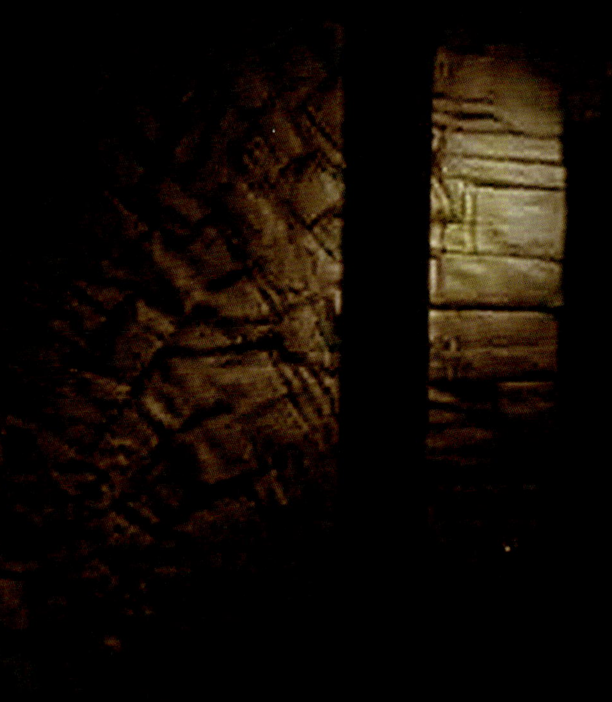

2008　Old Wall · II · Installation · 300cm×180cm×160cm
Wand · II · Installation · 300cm×180cm×160cm

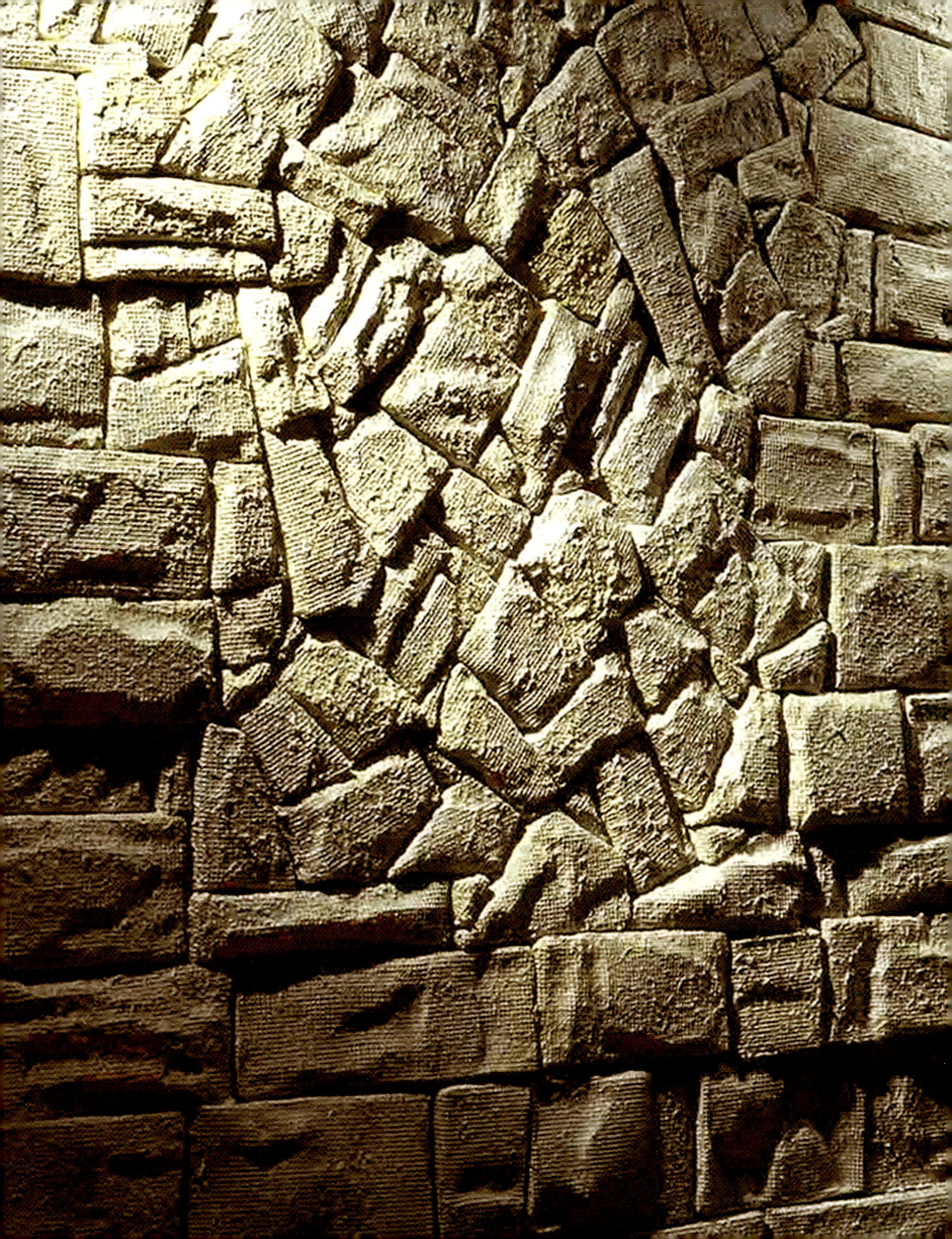

"Fibrous materials not only store the unique features of natural plant life, they also embody the ideal of synergy between nature and human life. The flexibility of bamboo strips, the pure whiteness of paper mache , the elasticity of cotton thread, they all represent this spark of vitality, which provokes a strong sense of familiarity. The way I create is characterised by a firm degree of randomness. By randomness I mean that there is a pure and simple, unconstrained relation between my physical labour and the form of gestation. Although I always have a vague expectation about the final outlook, from beginning to end, layer upon layer, the white fibre materials, which are shaping my works, are in a constant state of growth. Single entities of fibrous softness are continuously expanding. Gradually, they result into a general form, resembling a nest, a cocoon, a structure with holes inside. I am not sure whether these materials secretly refer to the womb from which all life emerges. Yet, the moment my formations are integrated into the larger environmental context, when they blend with the earth, the meadow, the trees, the sunlight, I always get this strong emotional feeling. I am overwhelmed by the poetry of life in nature."

(ShiHui)

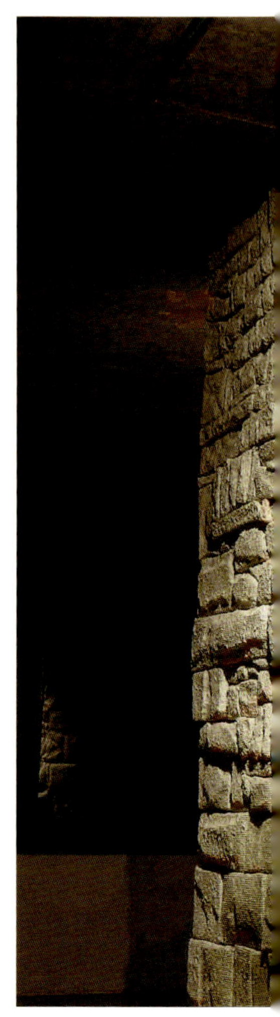

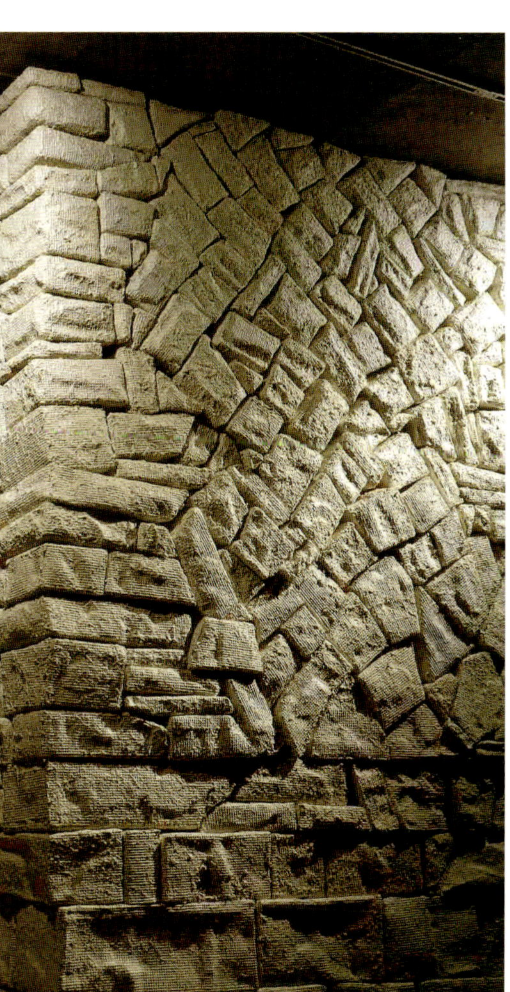

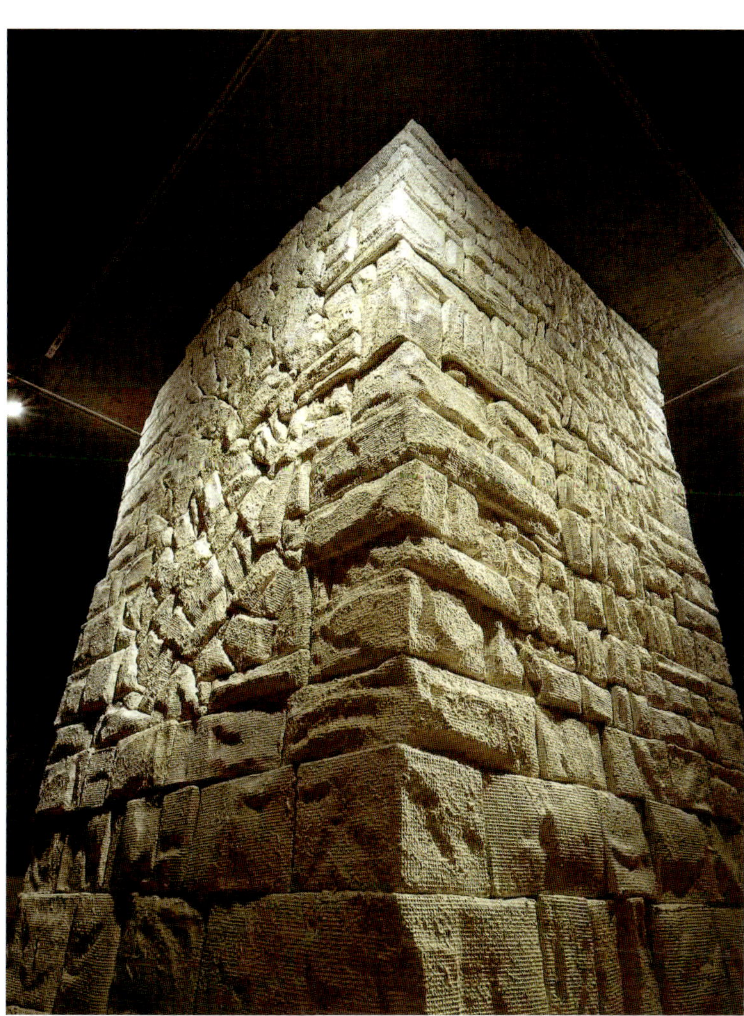

2003 Old Wall · II · Installation · 300cm×180cm×160cm
Wand · II · Installation · 300cm×180cm×160cm

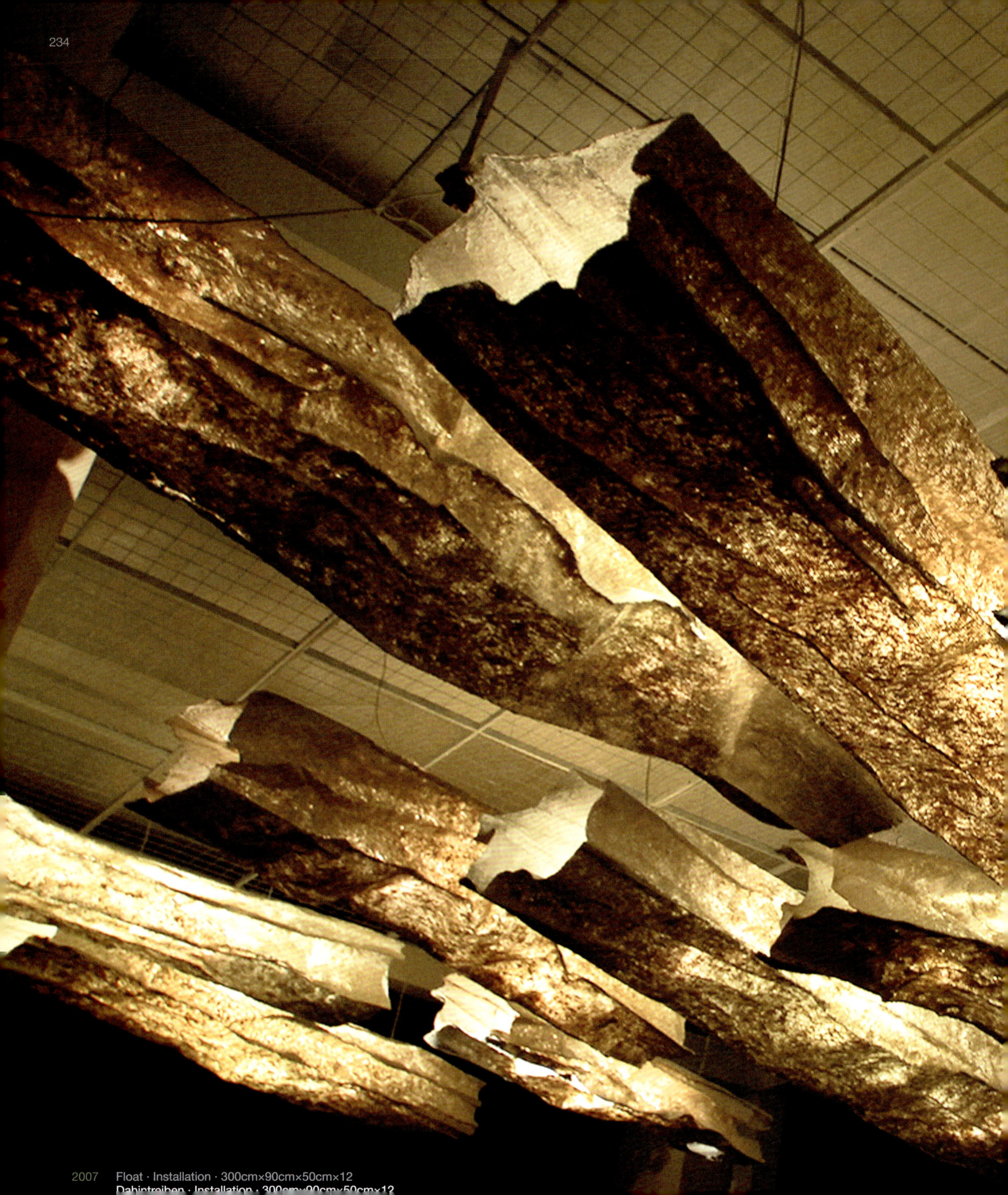

2007 Float · Installation · 300cm×90cm×50cm×12
Dahintreiben · Installation · 300cm×90cm×50cm×12

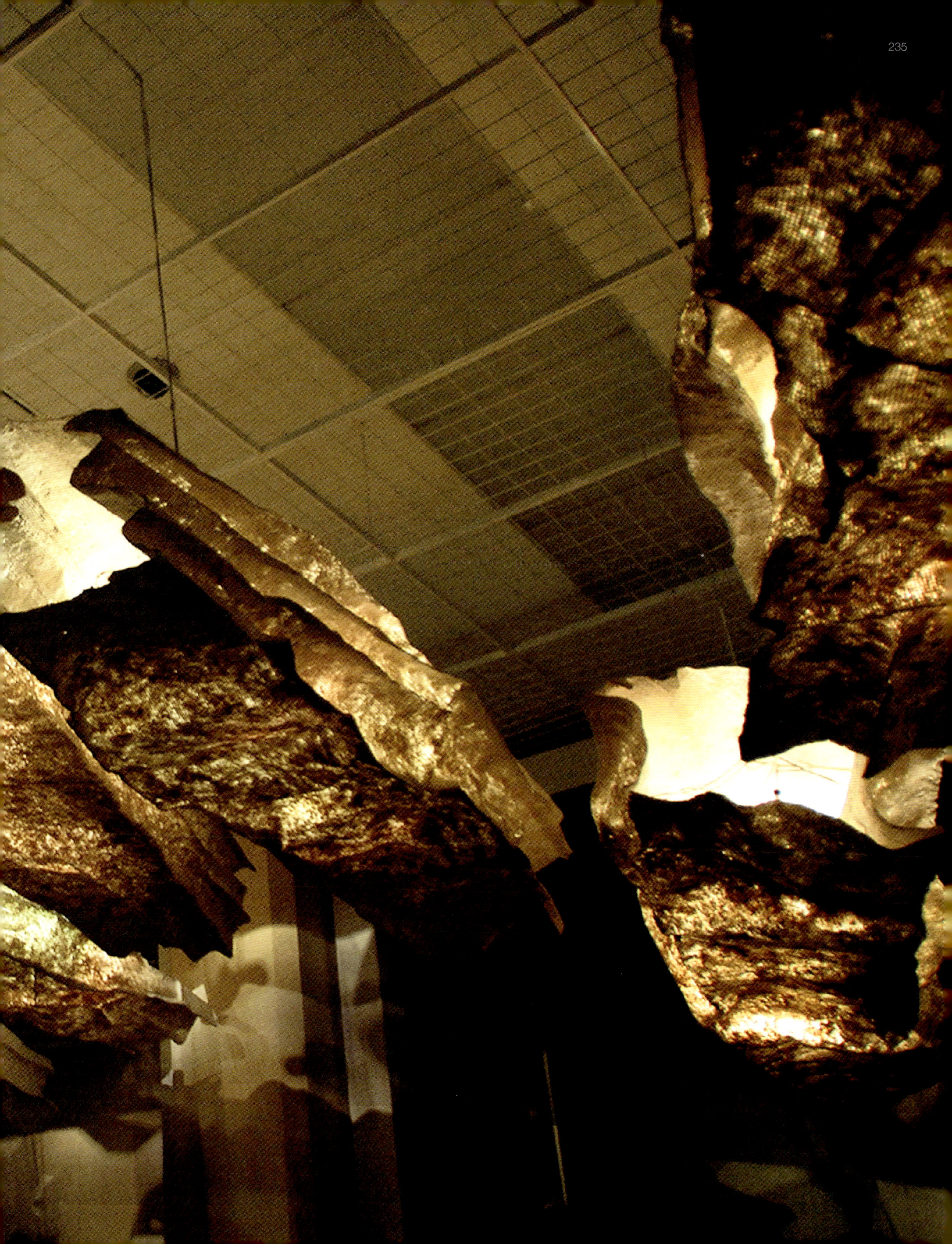

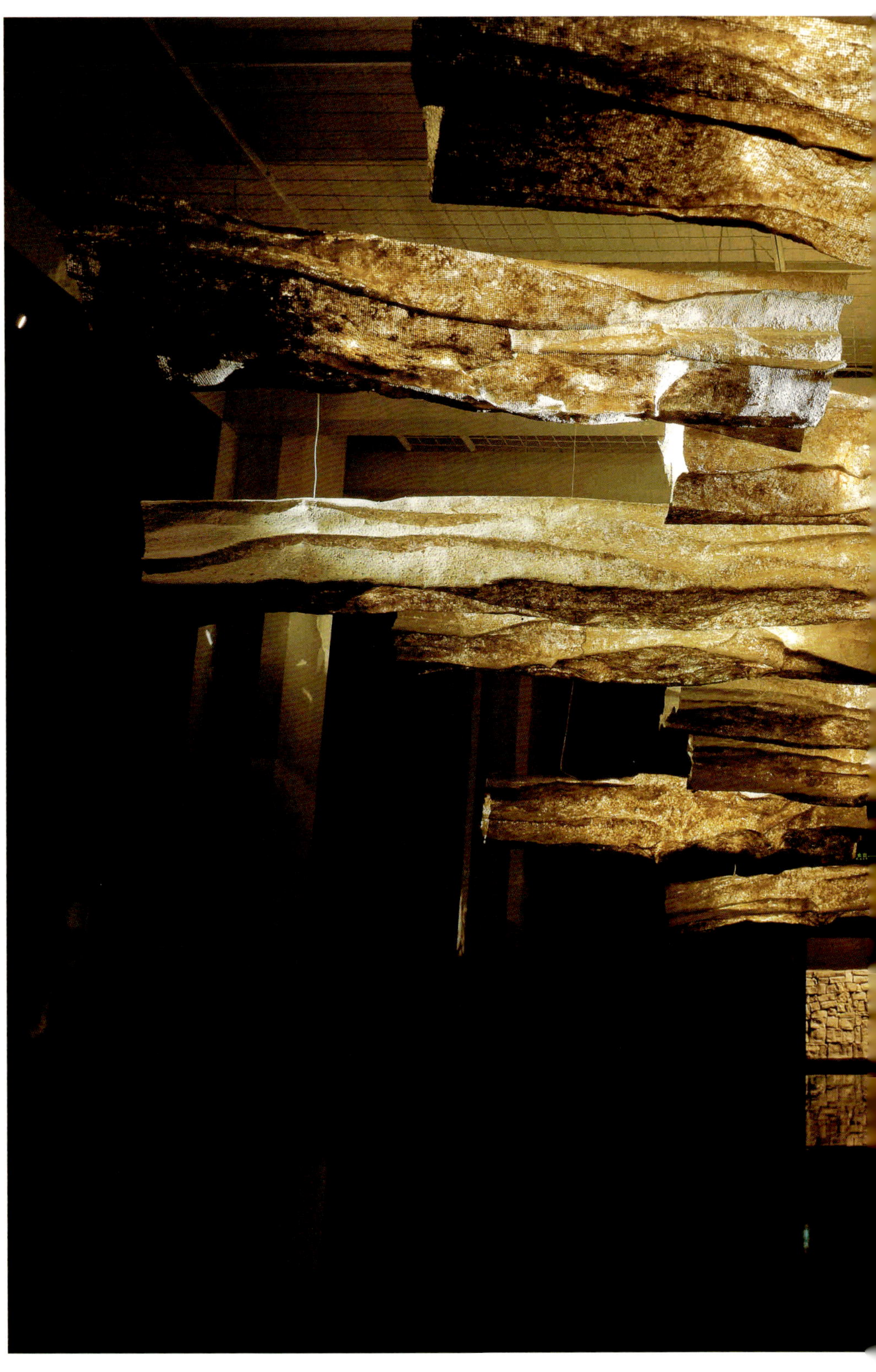

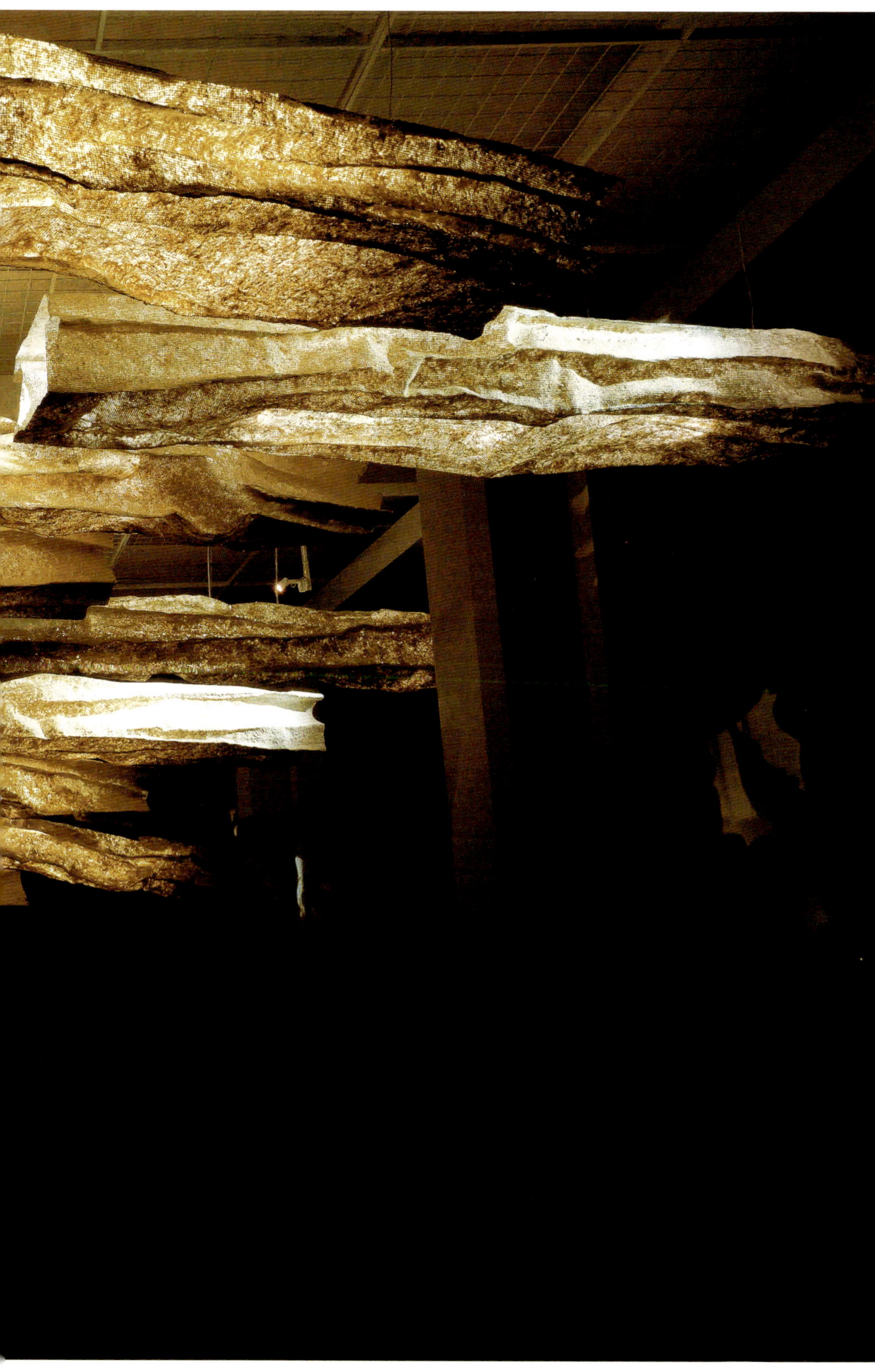

2007   Float · Installation · 300cm×90cm×50cm×12
Dahintreiben · Installation · 300cm×90cm×50cm×12

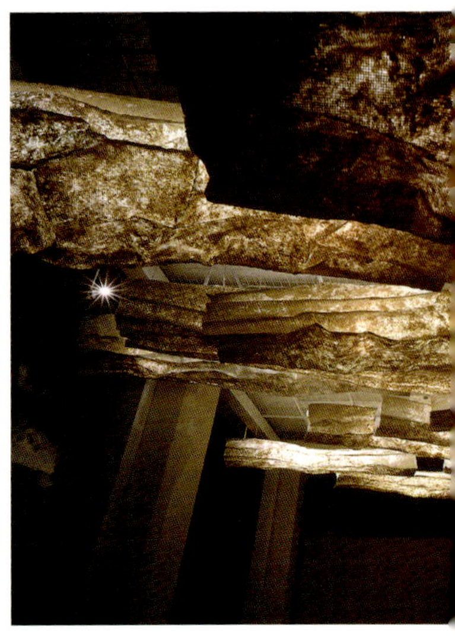

2007 Float · Installation · 300cm×90cm×50cm×12
Dahintreiben · Installation · 300cm×90cm×50cm×12

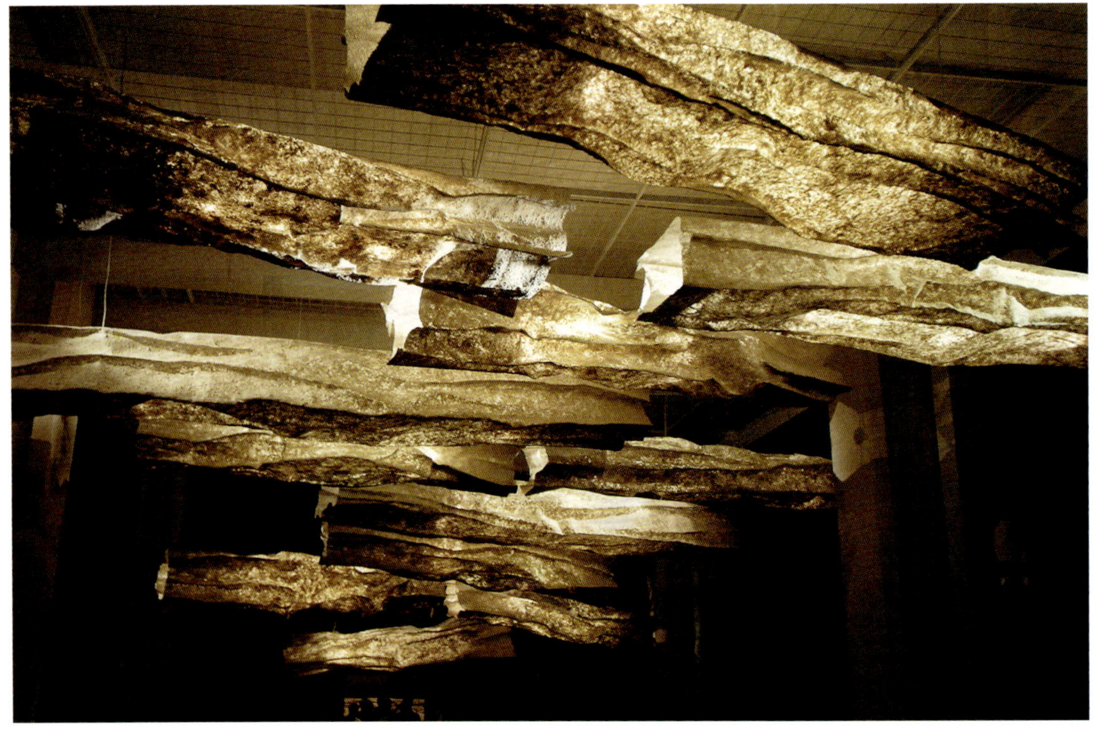

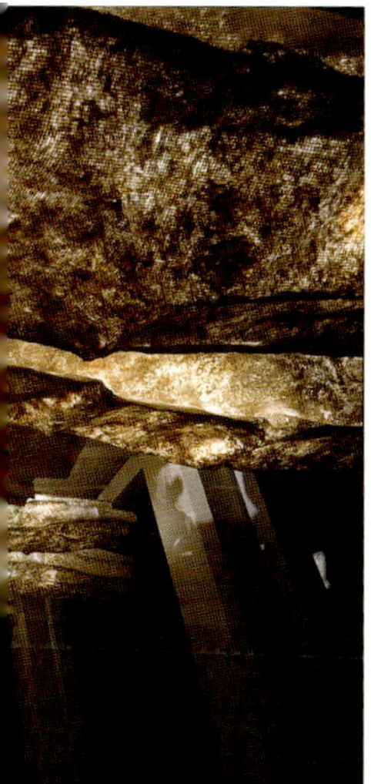

Fasermaterialien tragen nicht nur die einzigartigen Züge der natürlichen Pflanzenwelt in sich, sie verkörpern auch die Ideale der Synergie von Natur und menschlichem Leben. Die Federwirkung von Bambusstreifen, das rein Weiße der Papiermasse und die Elastizität von Baumwollfäden, sie alle repräsentieren den Funken von Vitalität, der uns ein so starkes Gefühl von Vertrautheit vermittelt. Meine Arbeit ist einem beständigen Grad an Zufälligkeit unterworfen. Unter Zufälligkeit meine ich ein reines und schlichtes, ungezwungenes Verhältnis zwischen physischer Arbeit und kreativem Reifeprozess. Obwohl ich immer nur eine vage Vorstellung vom Resultat habe, befinden sich die weißen Fasermaterialien, auf die ich mich stütze, von Anfang bis Ende, Schicht für Schicht, in einem konstanten Zustand des Wachstums. Einzelne Einheiten fasriger Weichheit entwickeln sich beständig weiter, bis sie die Form eines Nests, eines Kokons, einer Struktur mit Löchern annehmen. Ich bin mir nicht sicher, ob diese Materialien nicht insgeheim den Mutterleib, aus dem jegliches Menschenleben entspringt, darstellen. Wenn meine Installationen dann Integration in den Umgebungskontext finden, d.h., wenn sie in Kontakt mit Erde, Rasen, Bäumen und Sonnenlicht treten, überkommt mich immer ein sehr emotionales Gefühl: Ich bin überwältigt von der Poesie des Lebens und der Natur.

(ShiHui)

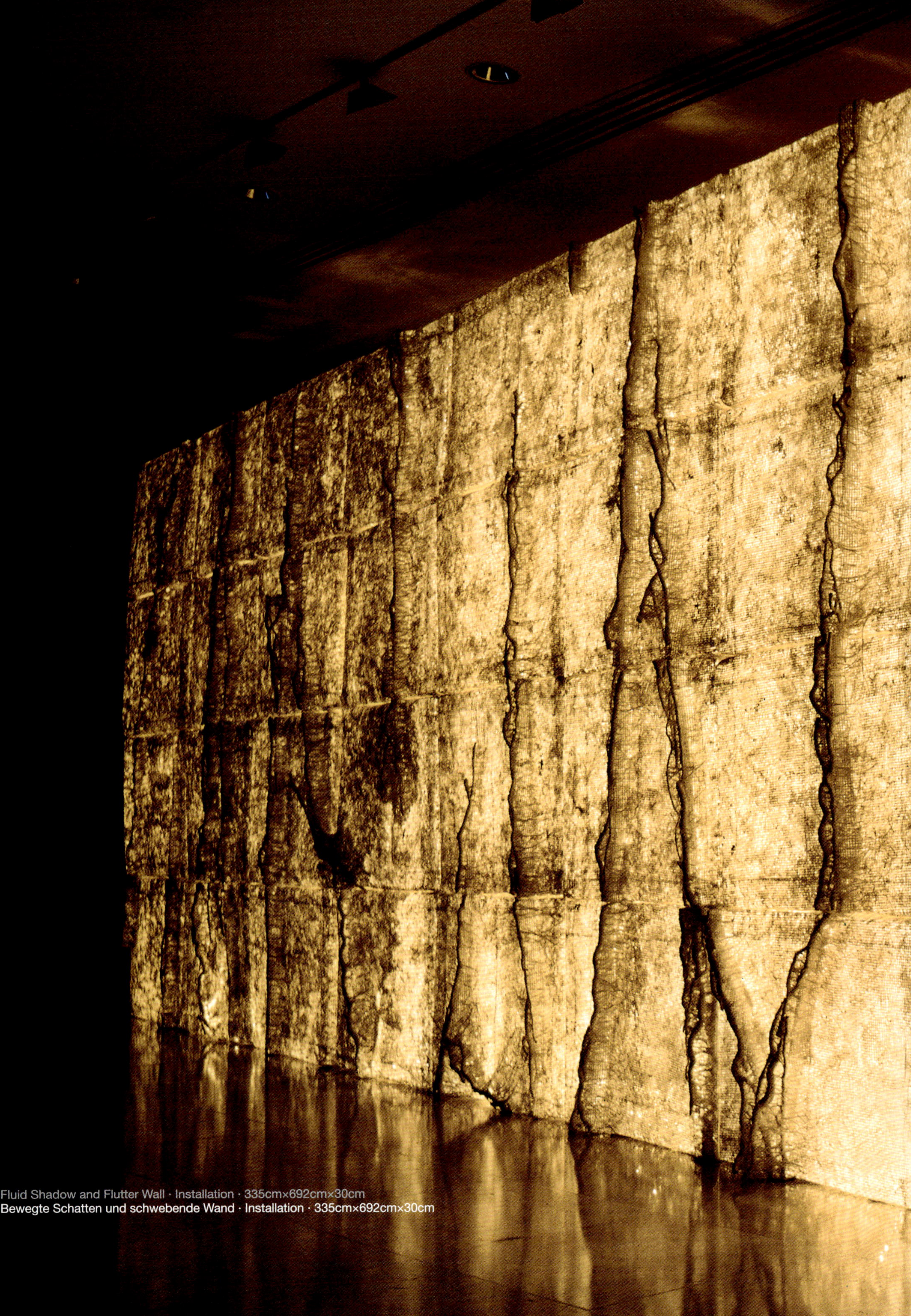

Fluid Shadow and Flutter Wall · Installation · 335cm×692cm×30cm
Bewegte Schatten und schwebende Wand · Installation · 335cm×692cm×30cm

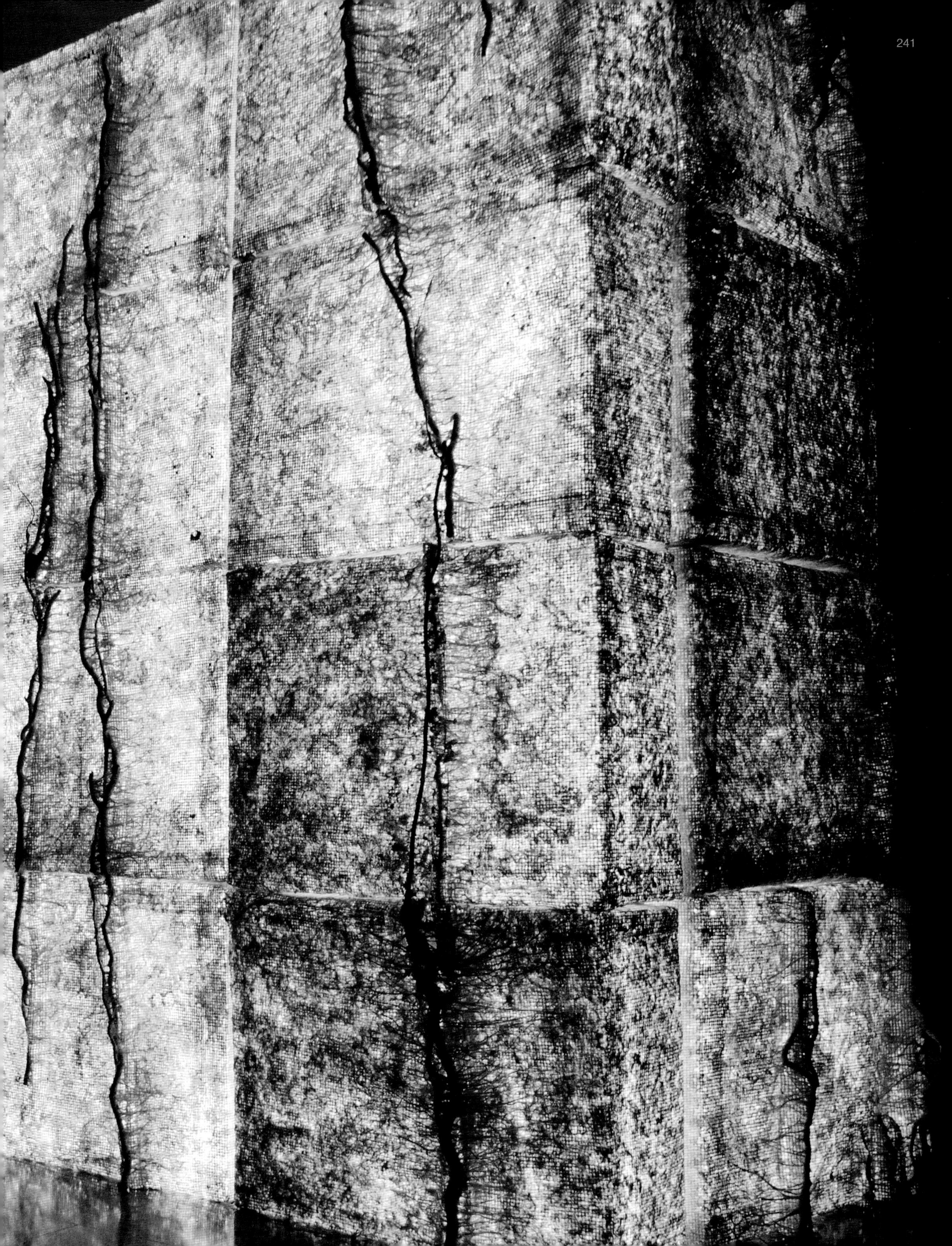

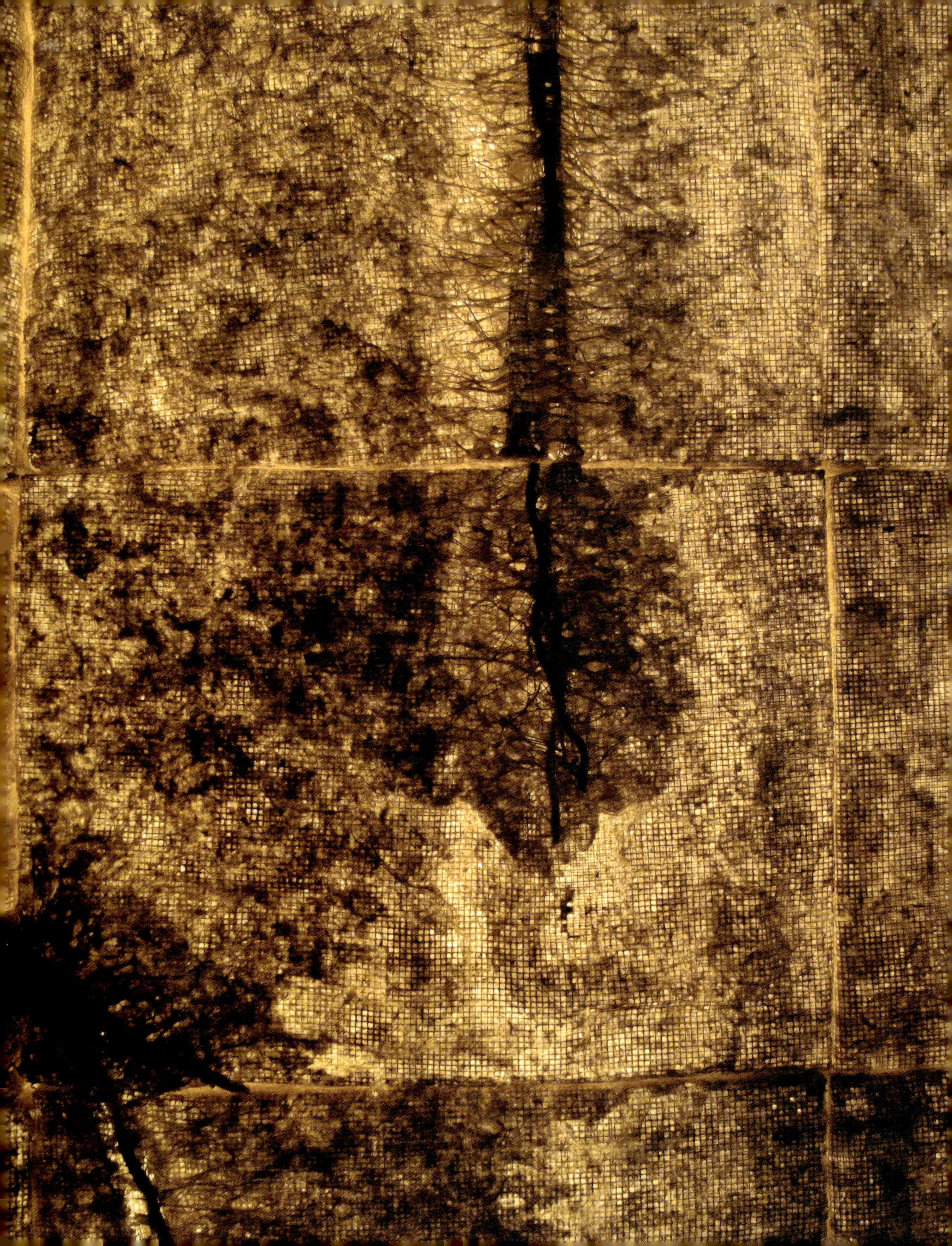

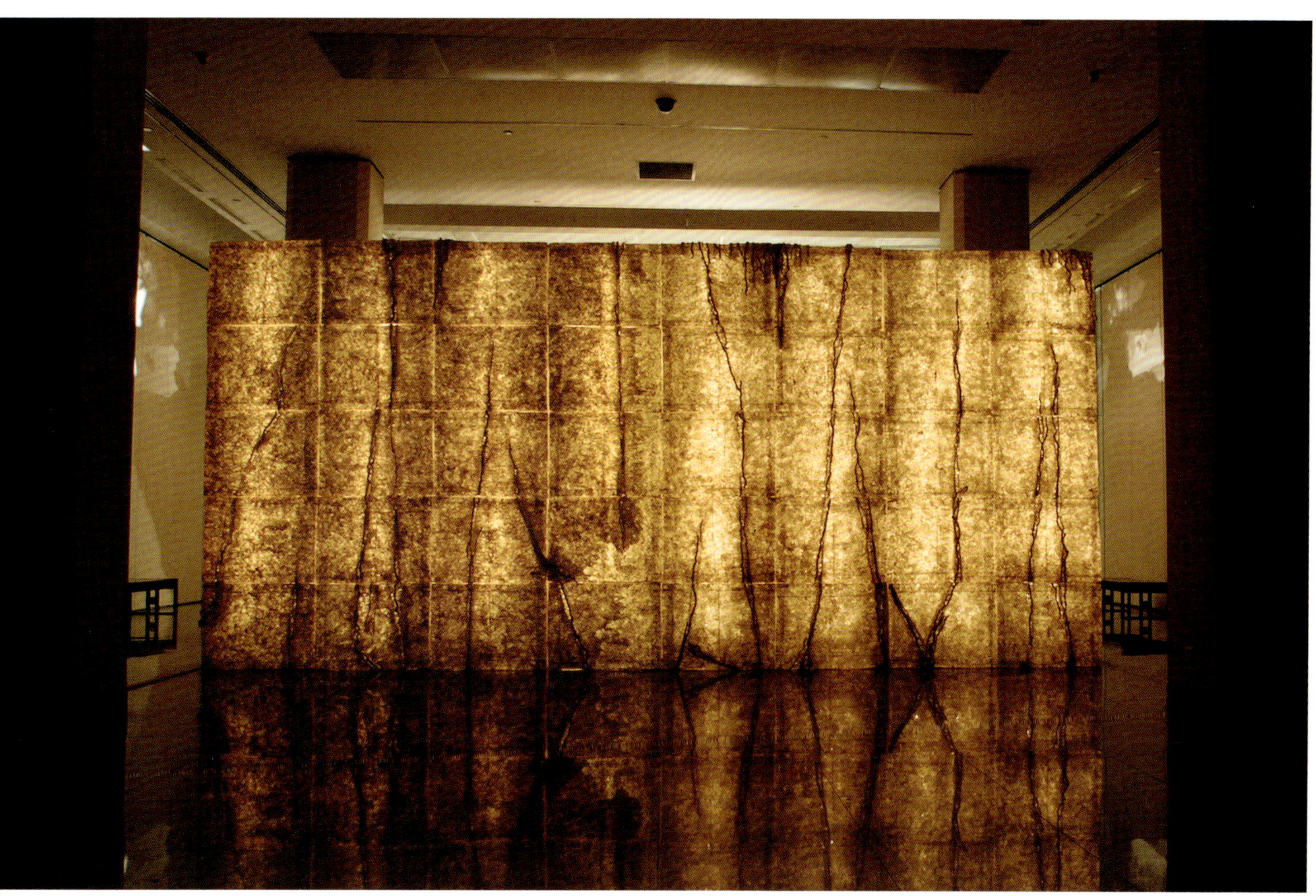

2007 Fluid Shadow and Flutter Wall · Installation · 335cm×692cm×30cm
Bewegte Schatten und schwebende Wand · Installation · 335cm×692cm×30cm

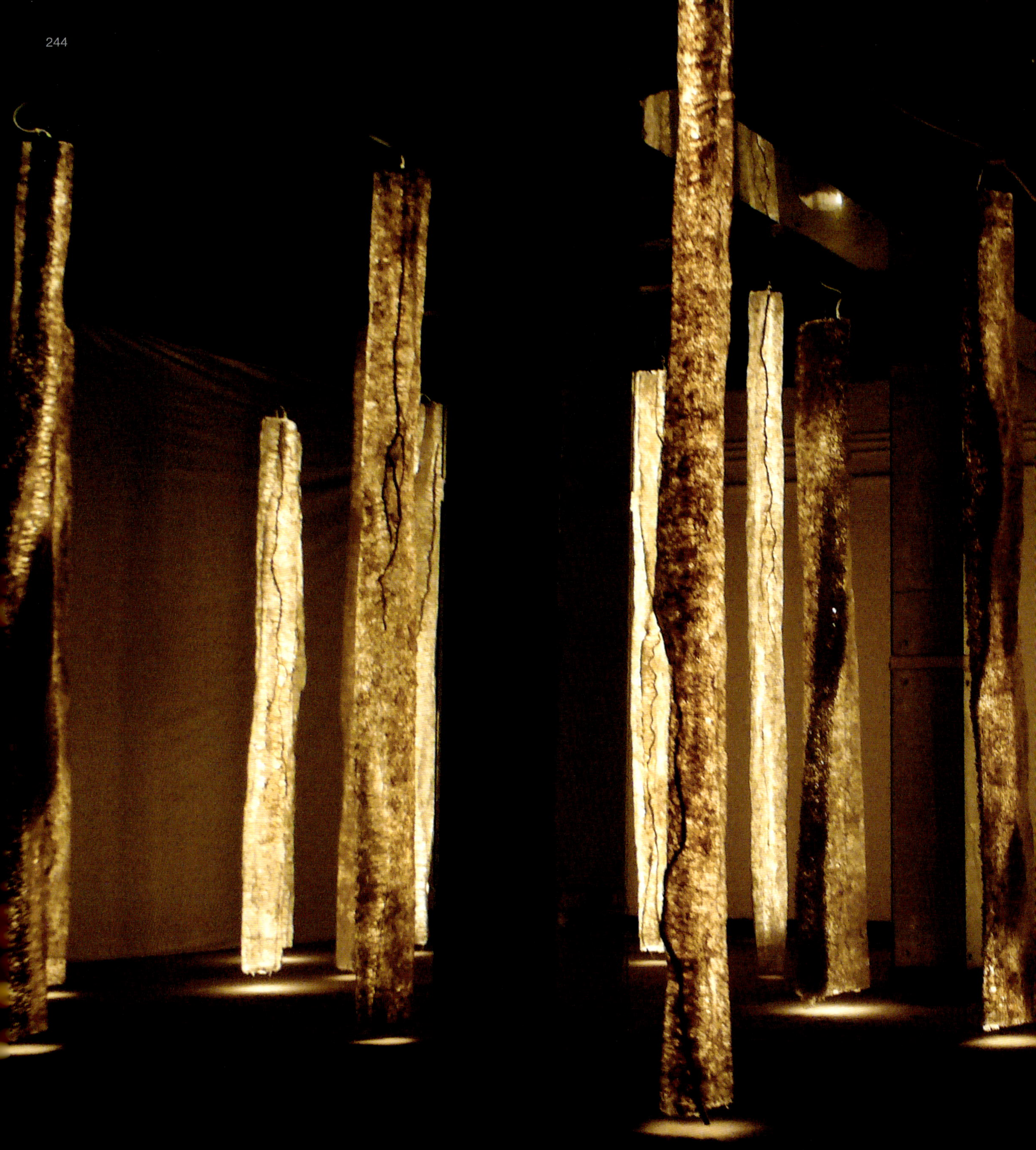

2007   Frozen Wind · Installation · 300cm×20cm×20cm×40
Gefrorener Wind · Installation · 300cm×20cm×20cm×40

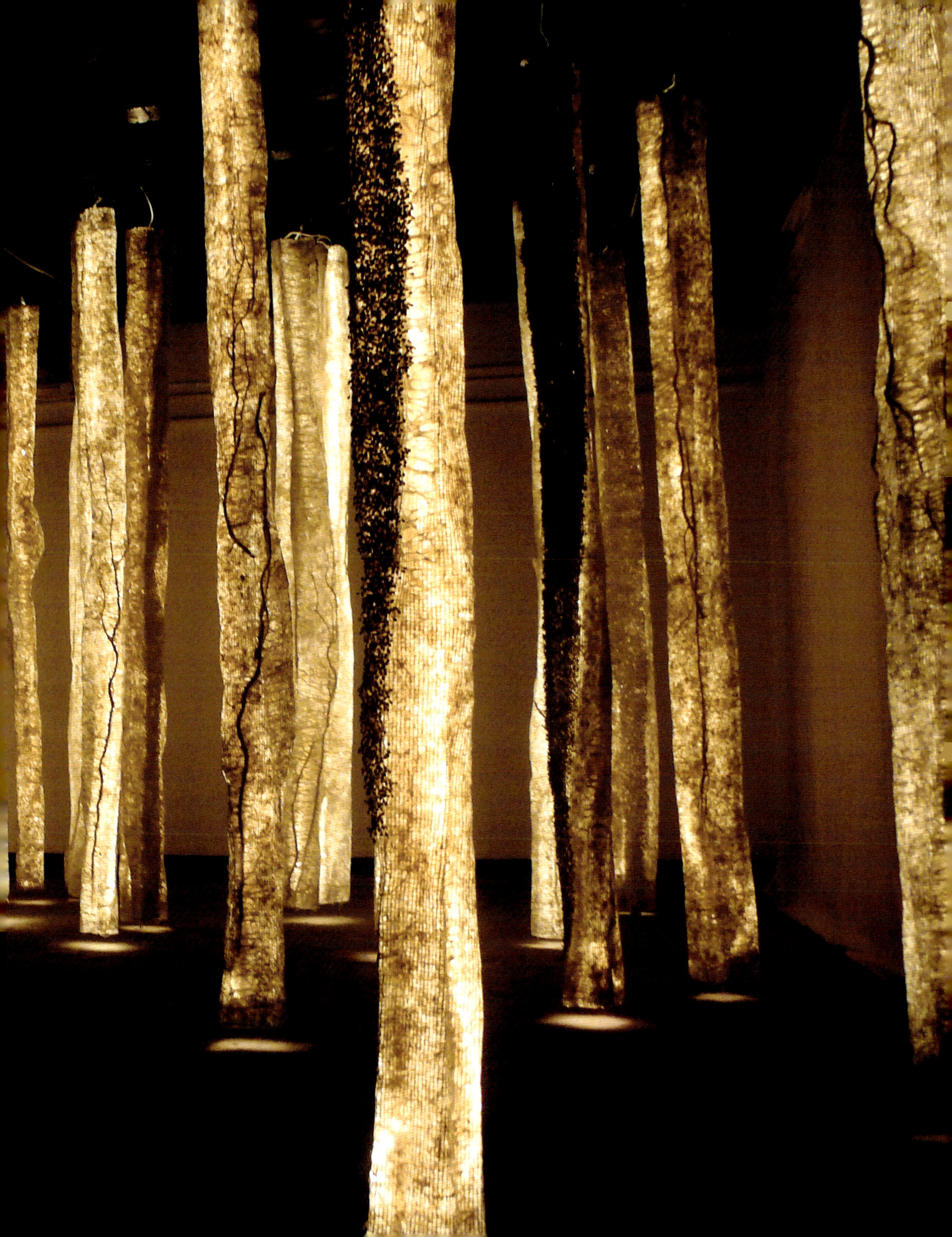

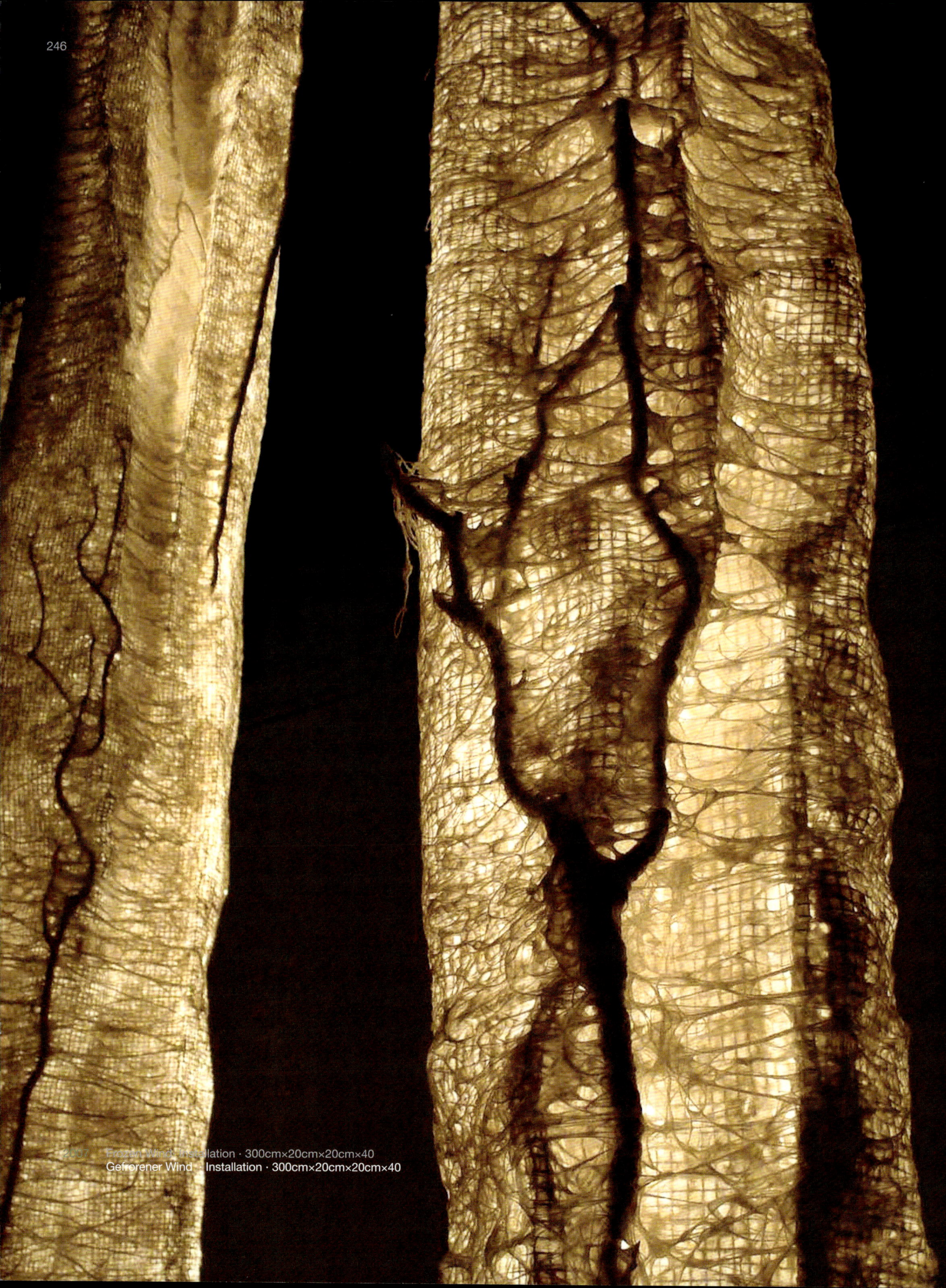

2007 · Frozen Wind · Installation · 300cm×20cm×20cm×40
Gefrorener Wind · Installation · 300cm×20cm×20cm×40

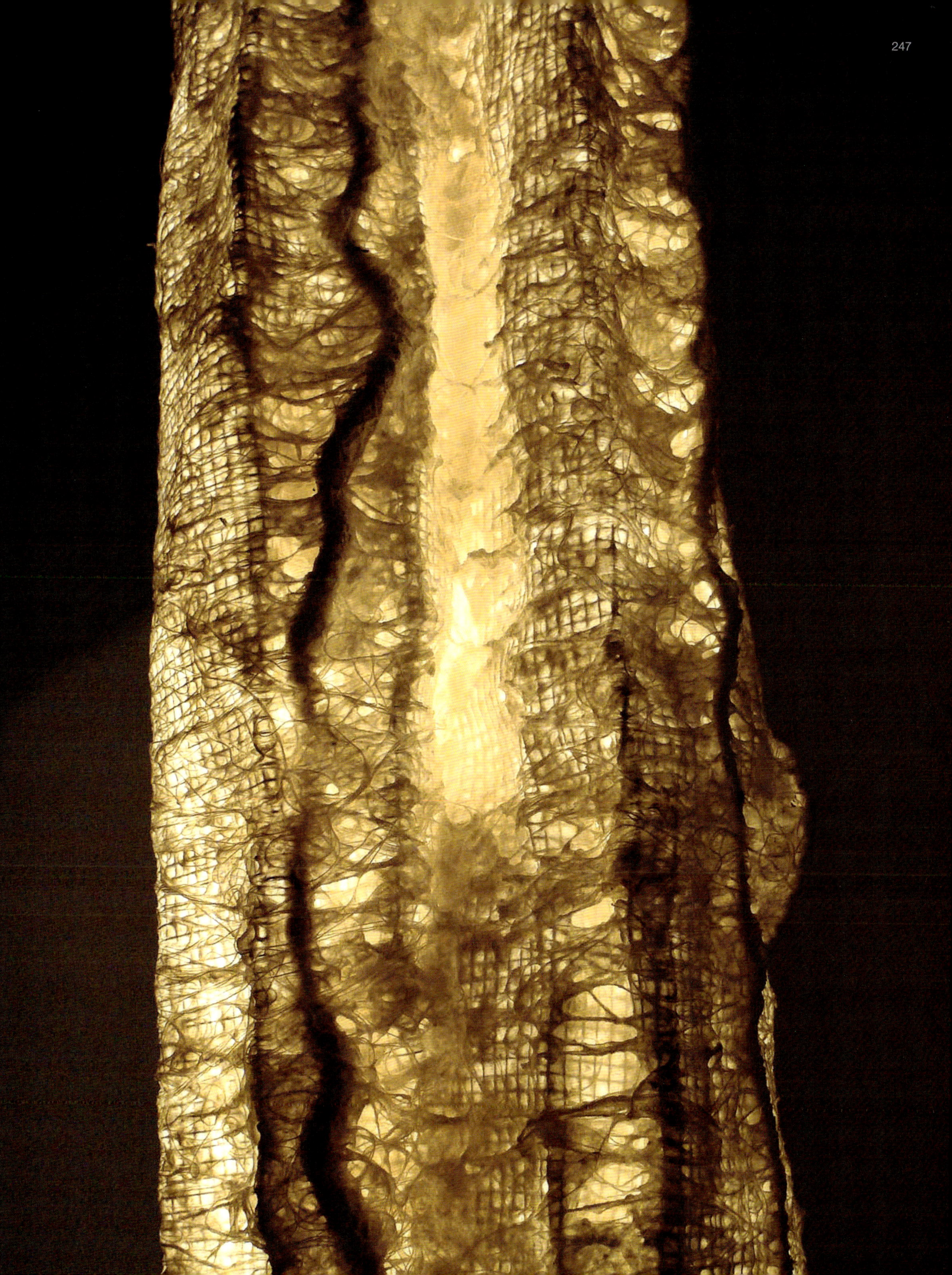

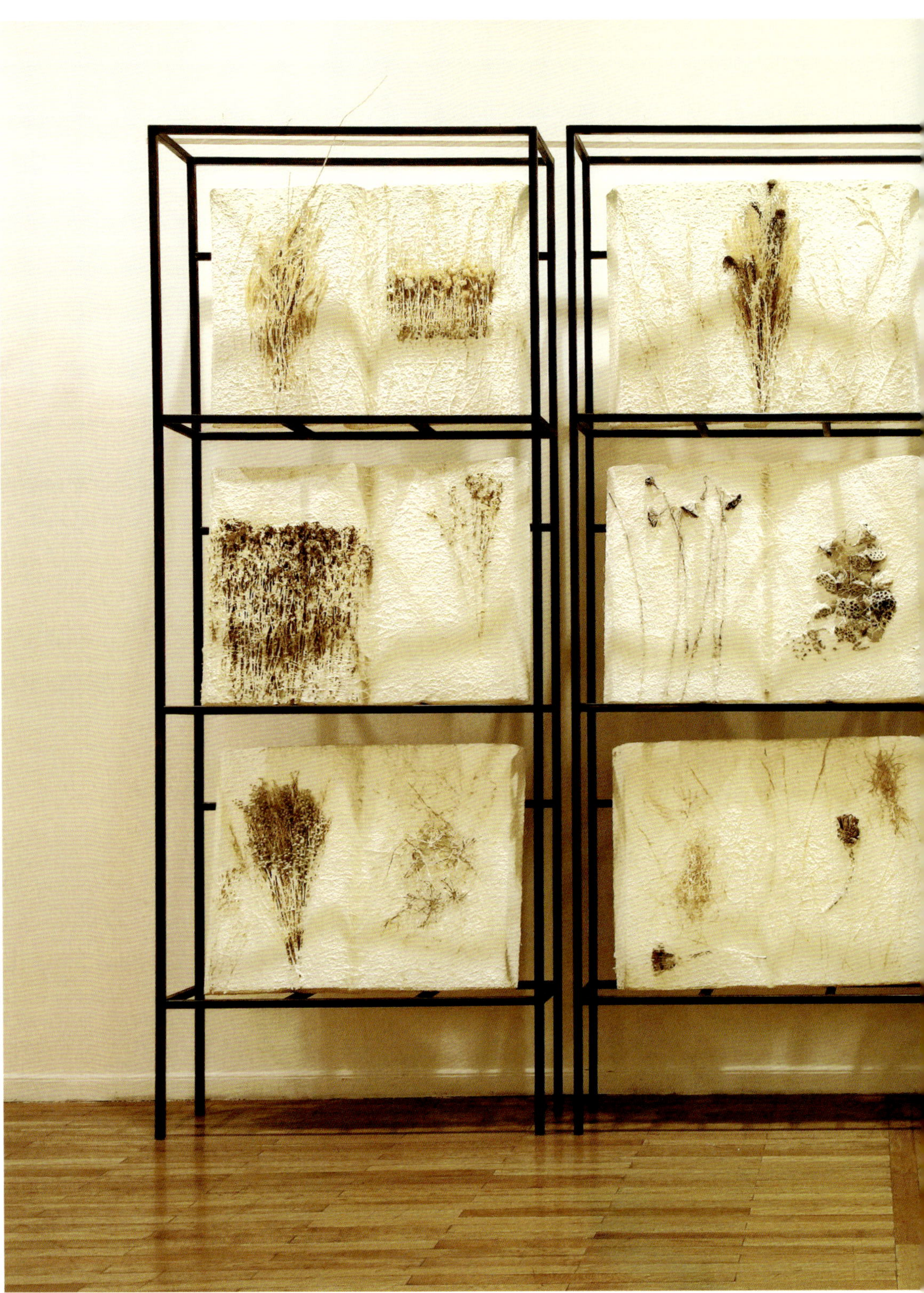

2009   Compendium of Materia Medica I · Installation · 360cm×145m×48cm×6
Das Buch heilender Kräuter I · Installation · 360cm×145cm×48cm×6

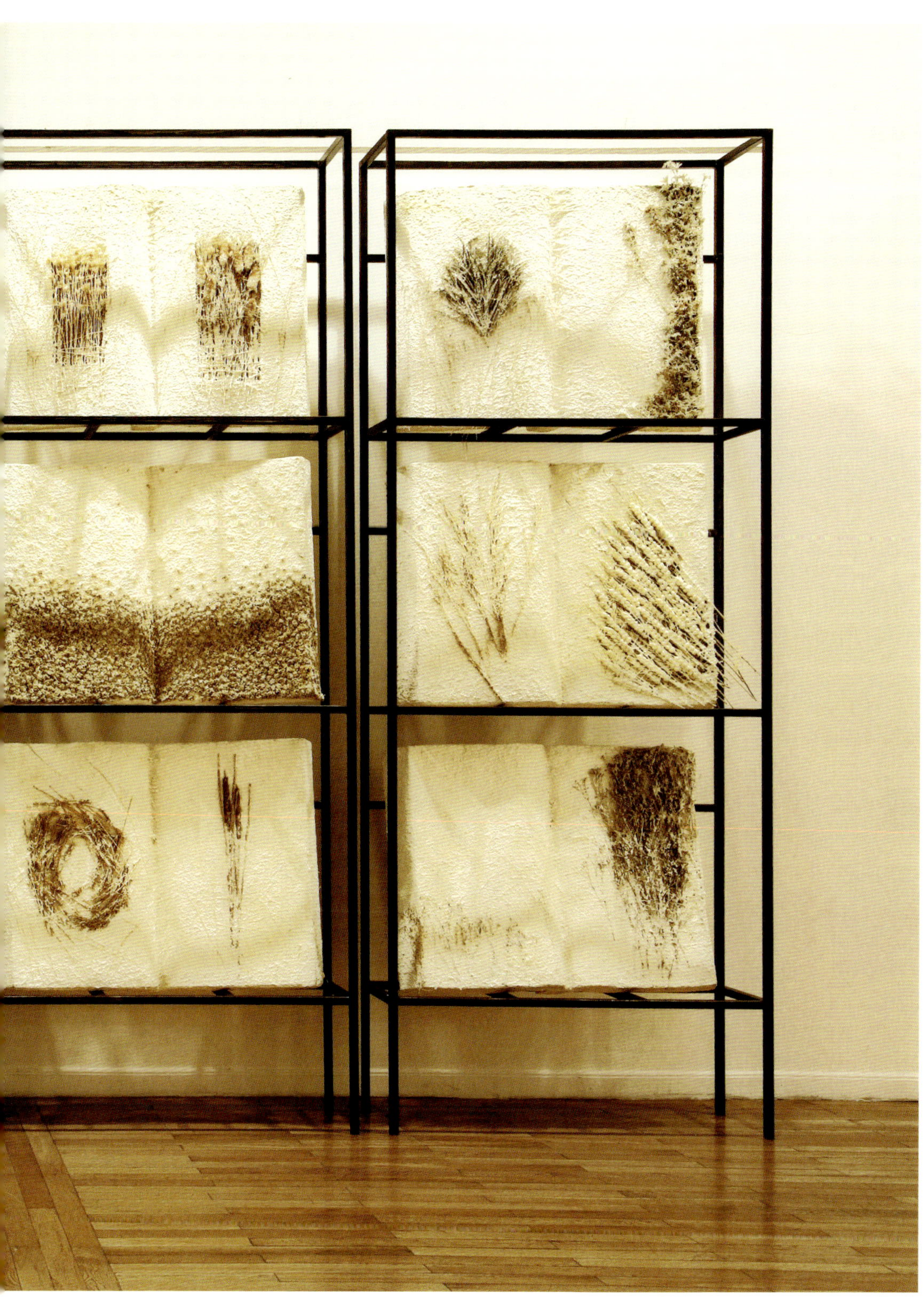

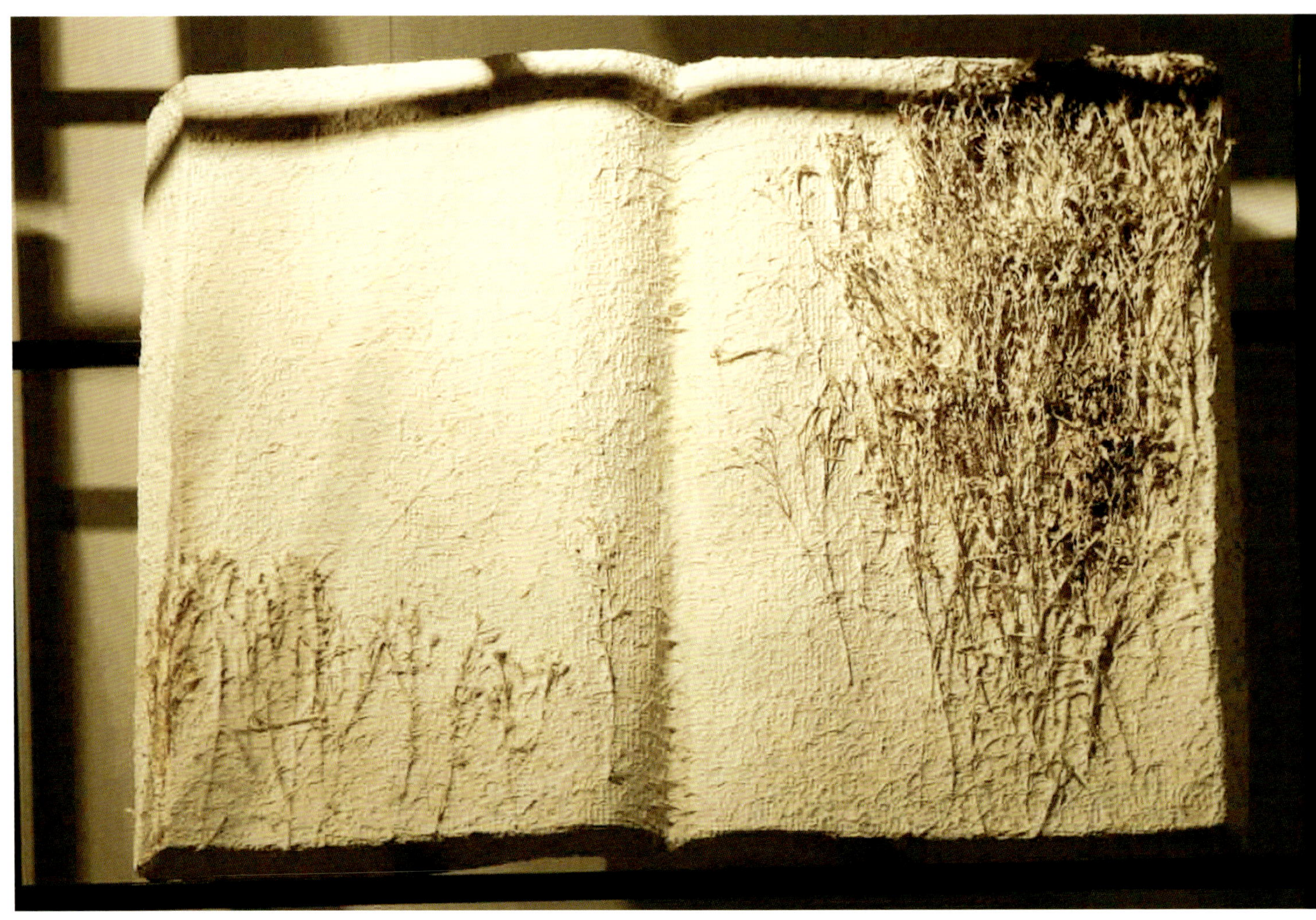

2009   Compendium of Materia Medica I · Installation · 360cm×145m×48cm×6
Das Buch heilender Kräuter I · Installation · 360cm×145cm×48cm×6

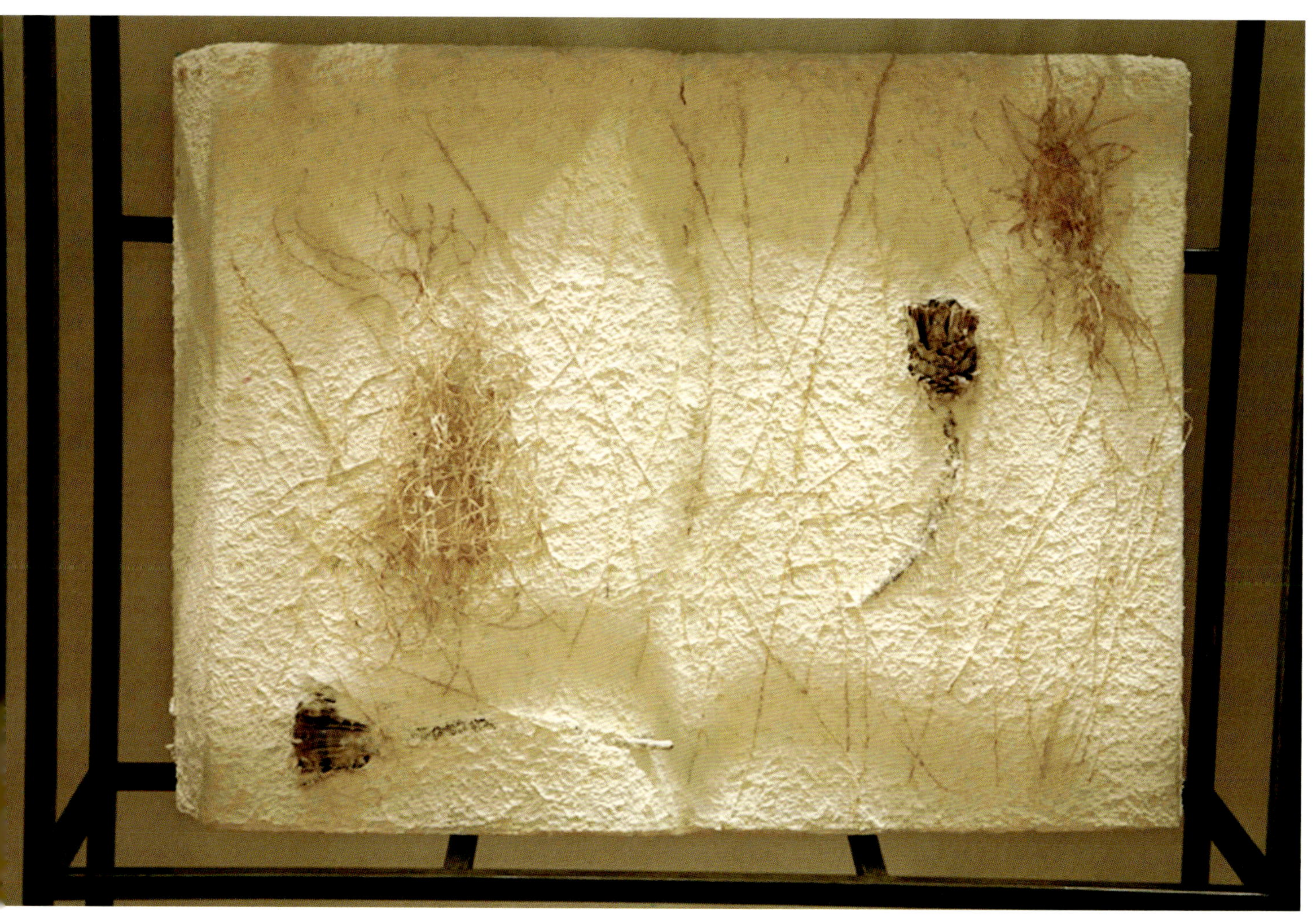

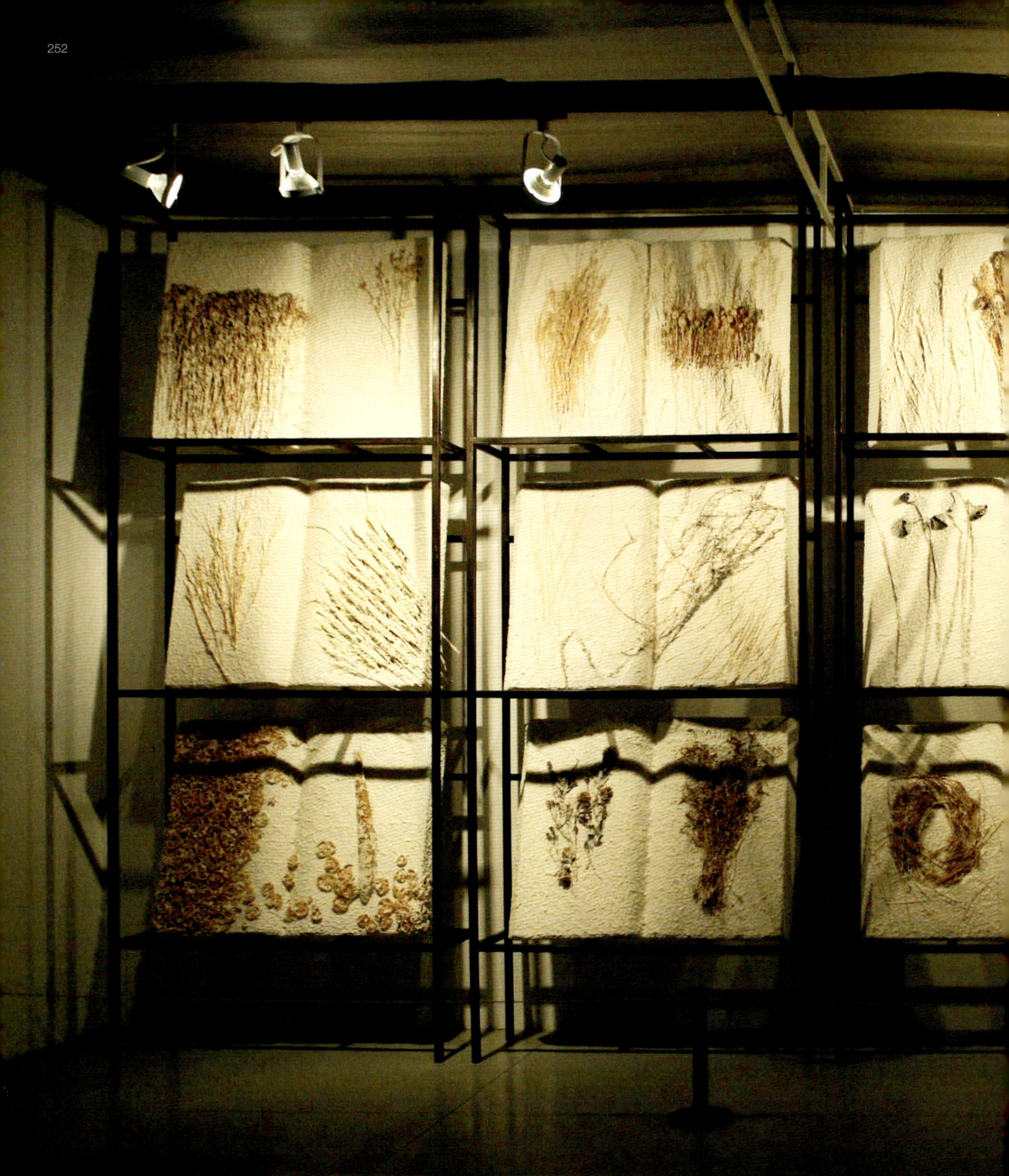

2009 Compendium of Materia Medica I · Installation · 360cm×145m×48cm×6
Das Buch heilender Kräuter I · Installation · 360cm×145cm×48cm×6

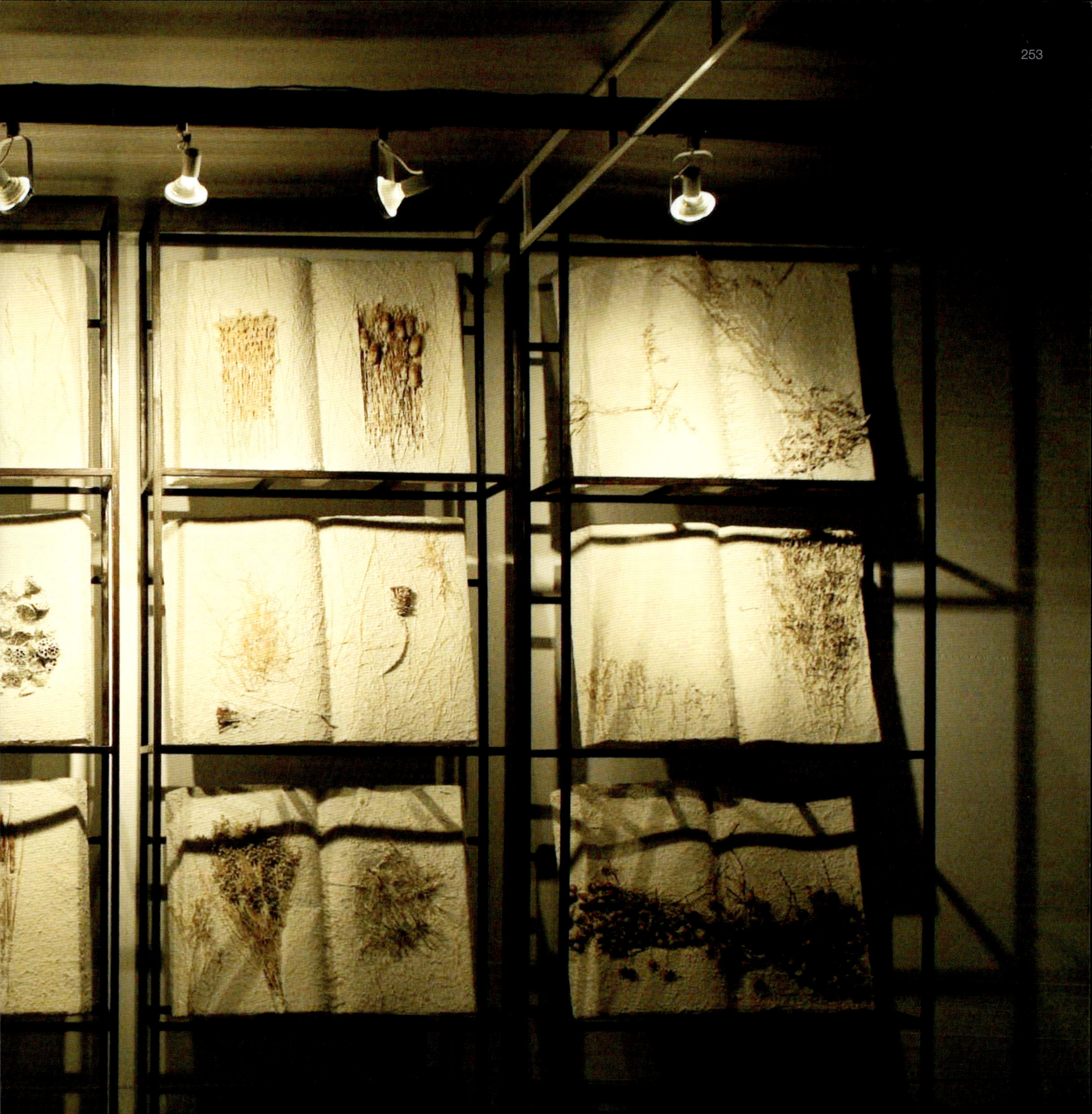

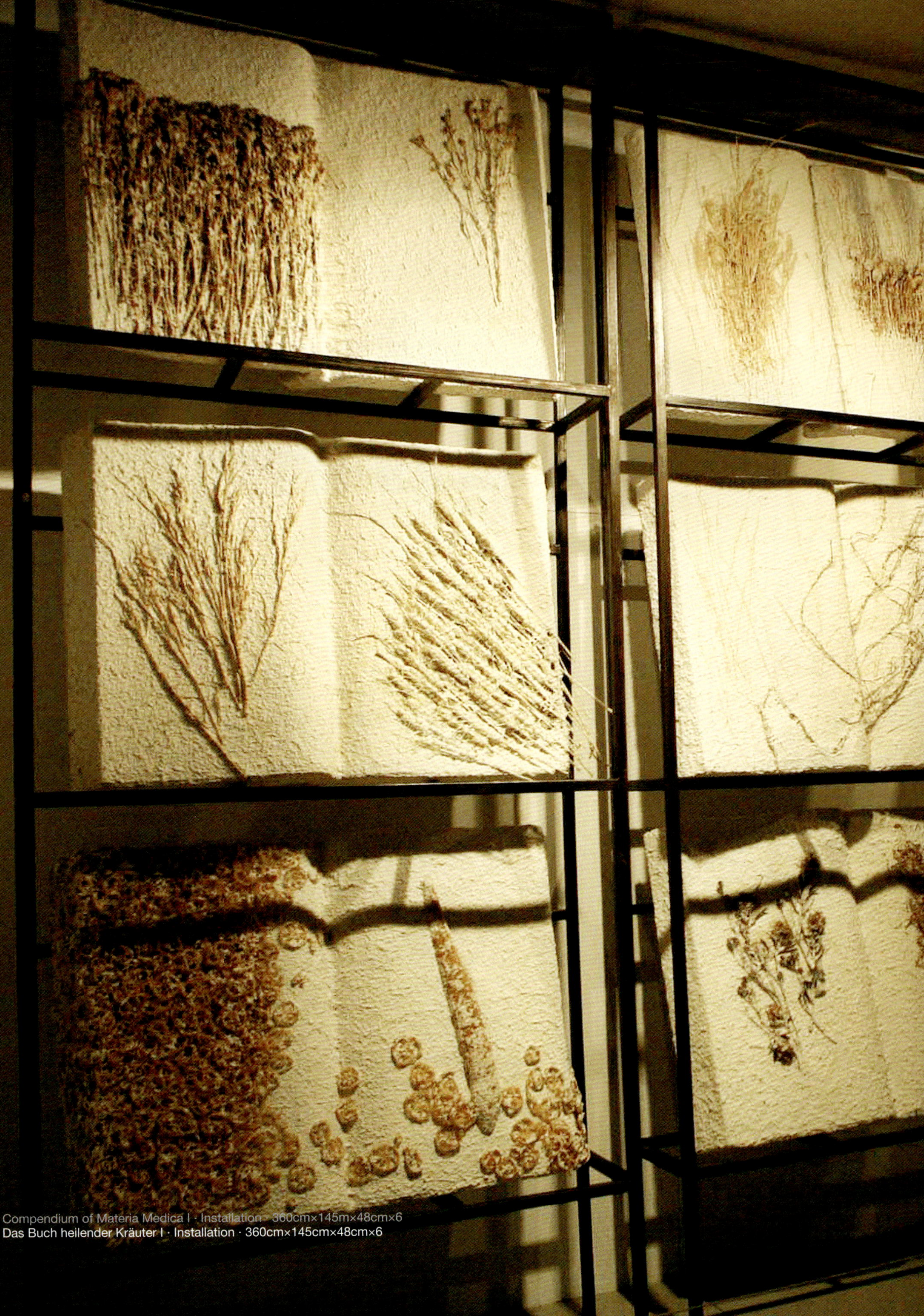

2009　Compendium of Materia Medica I · Installation · 360cm×145m×48cm×6
Das Buch heilender Kräuter I · Installation · 360cm×145cm×48cm×6

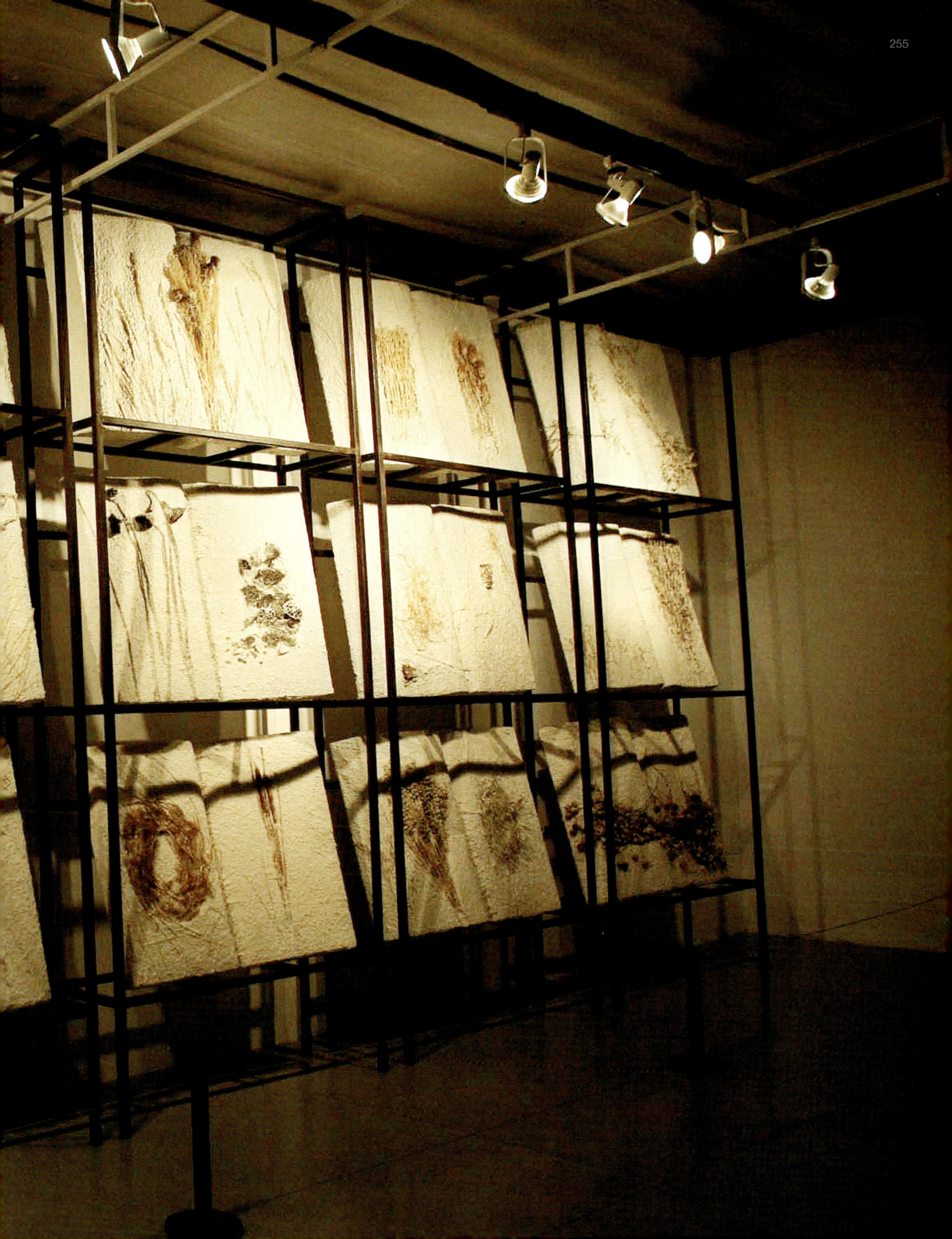

2009 Compendium of Materia Medica I · Installation · 360cm×145m×48cm×6
Das Buch heilender Kräuter I · Installation · 360cm×145cm×48cm×6

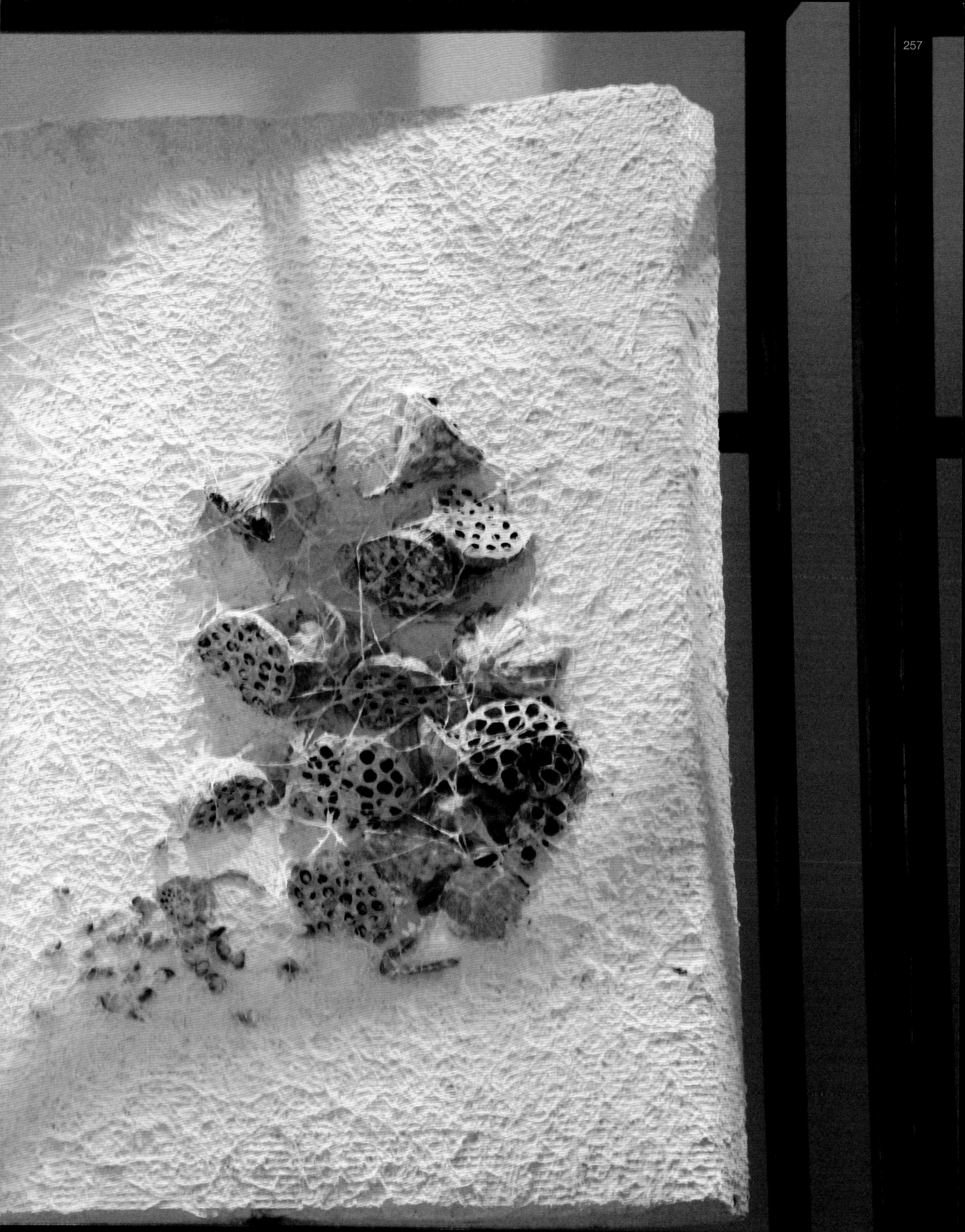

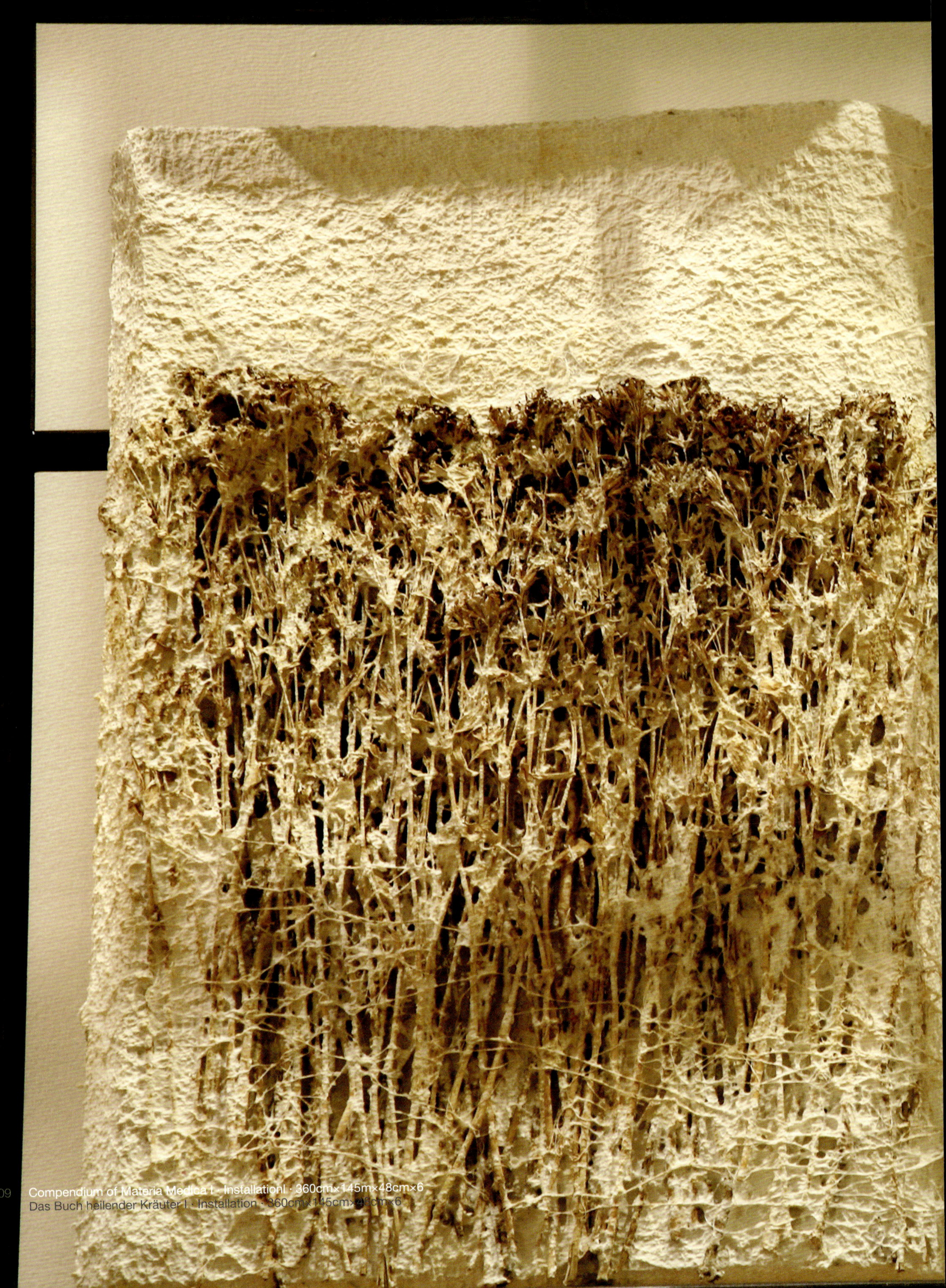

2009 Compendium of Materia Medica I · InstallationI · 360cm×145m×48cm×6
Das Buch heilender Kräuter I · Installation · 360cm×145cm×48cm×6

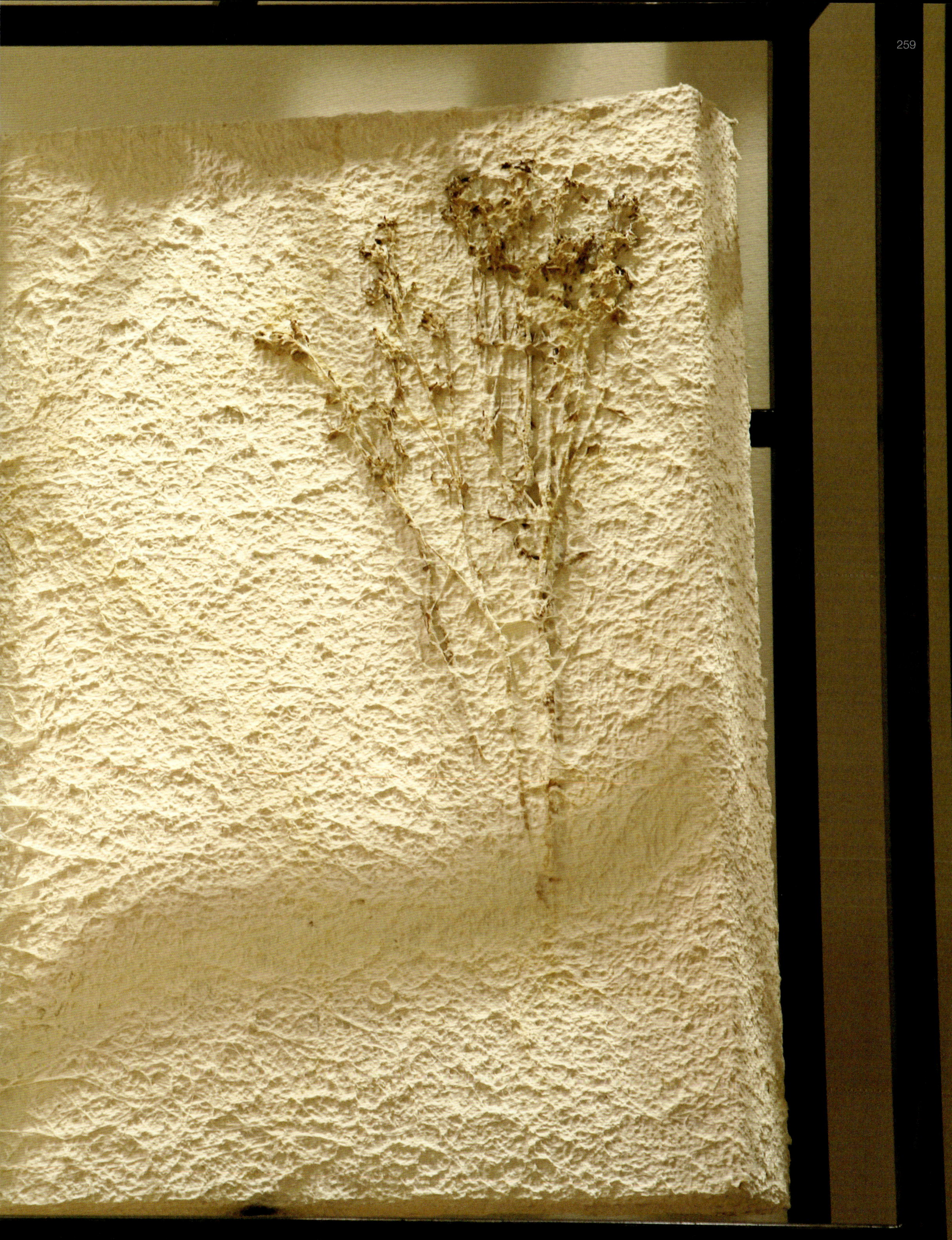

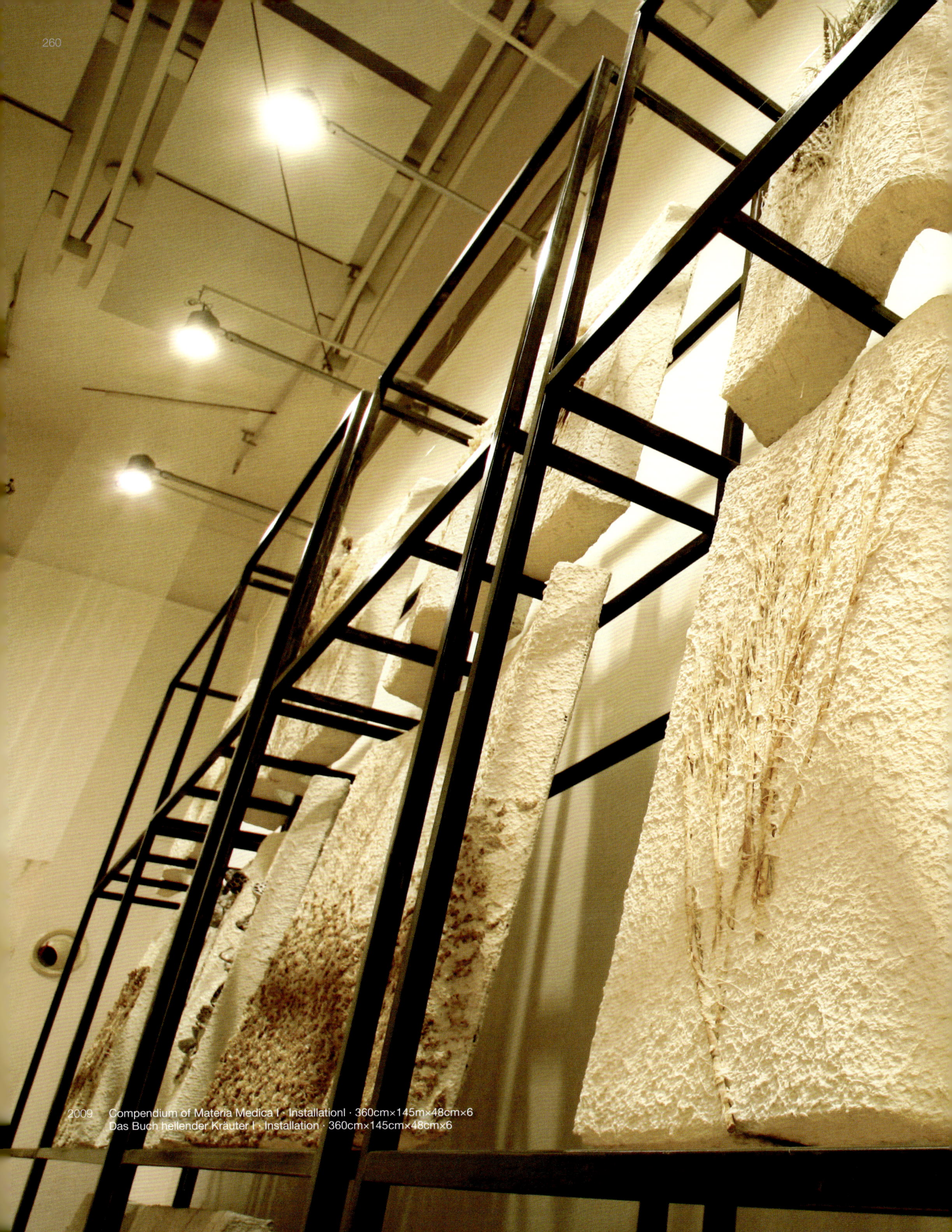

2009   Compendium of Materia Medica I · InstallationI · 360cm×145m×48cm×6
Das Buch heilender Kräuter I · Installation · 360cm×145cm×48cm×6

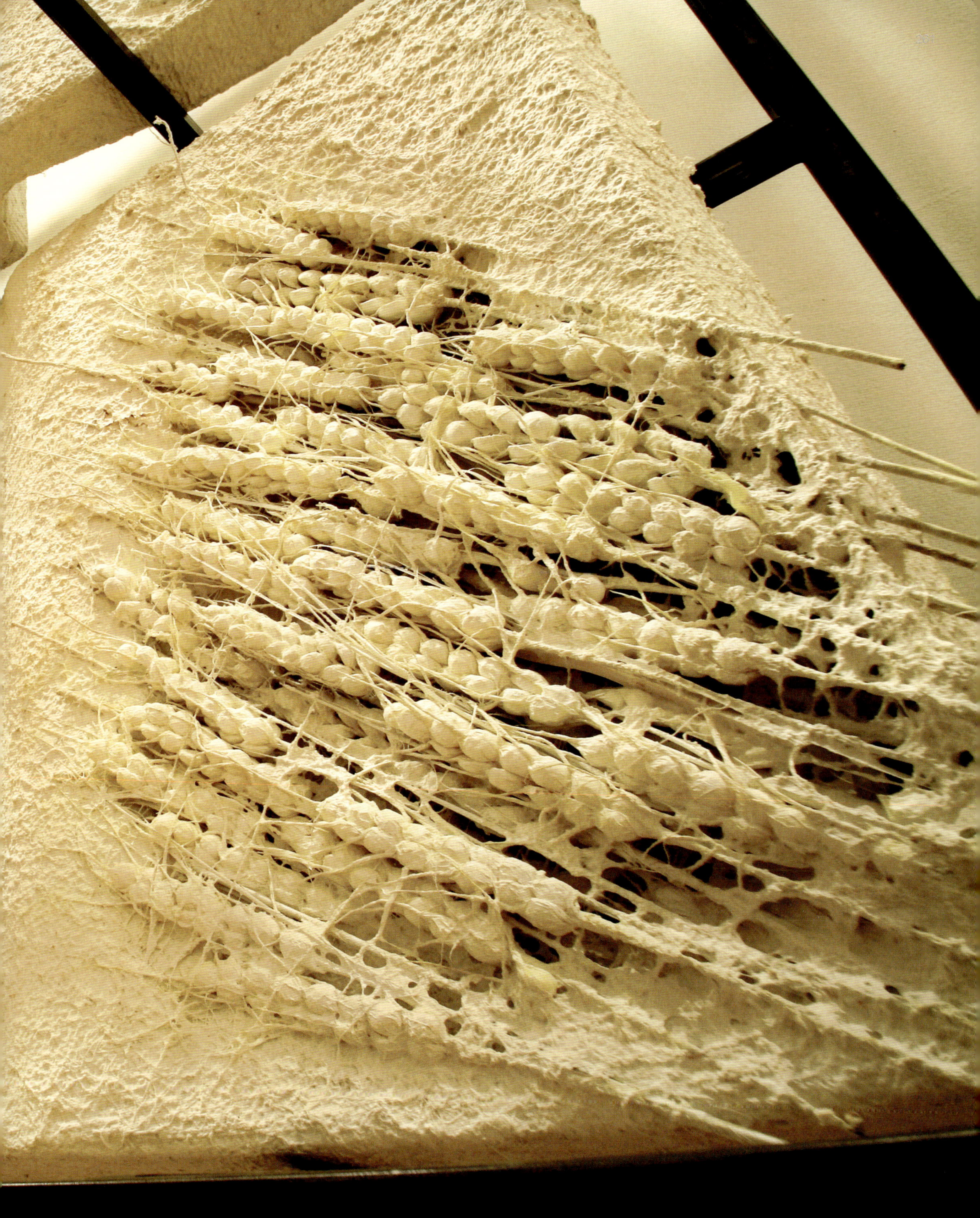

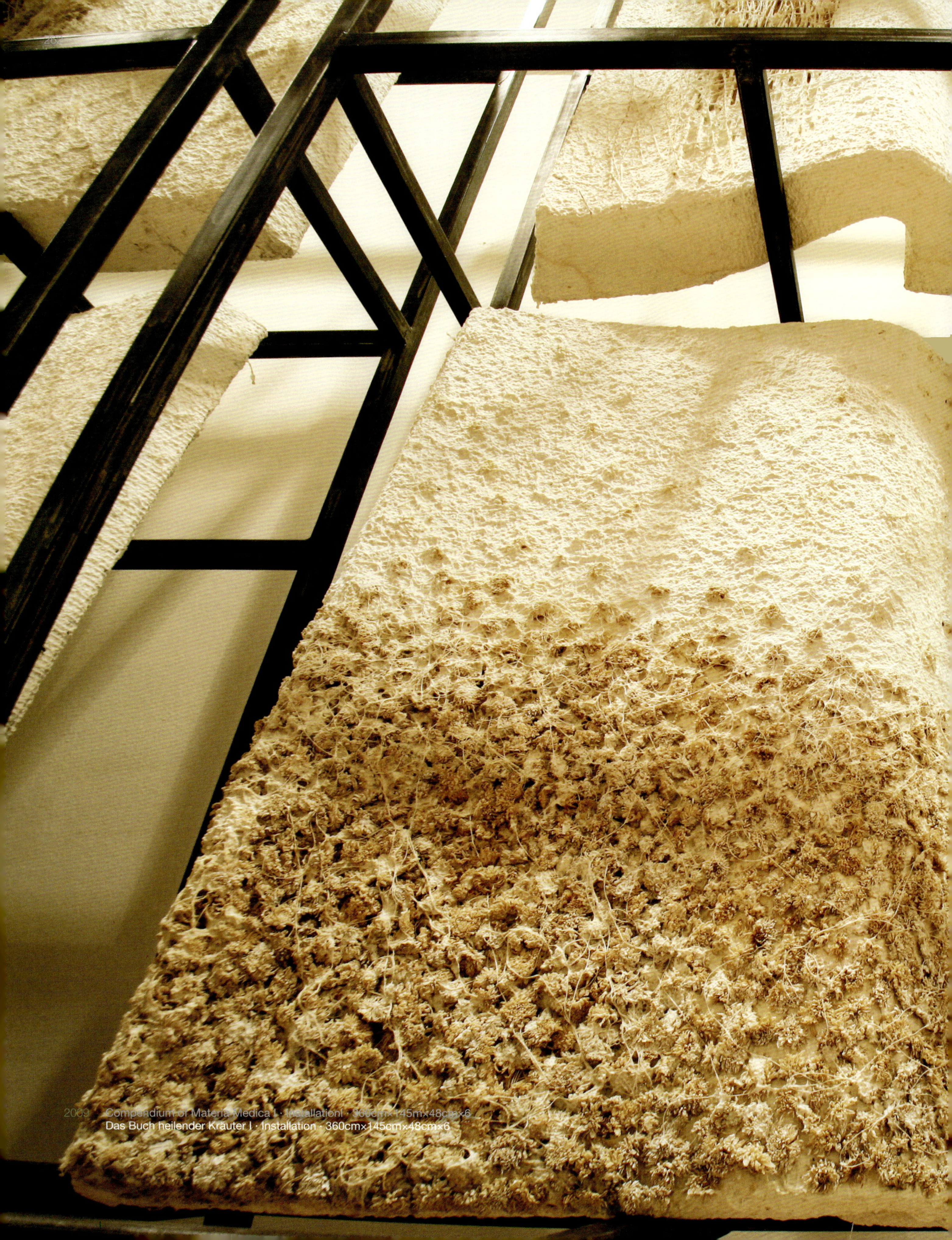

2009 · Compendium of Materia Medica I · Installationl · 360cm×145m×48cm×6
Das Buch heilender Kräuter I · Installation · 360cm×145cm×48cm×6

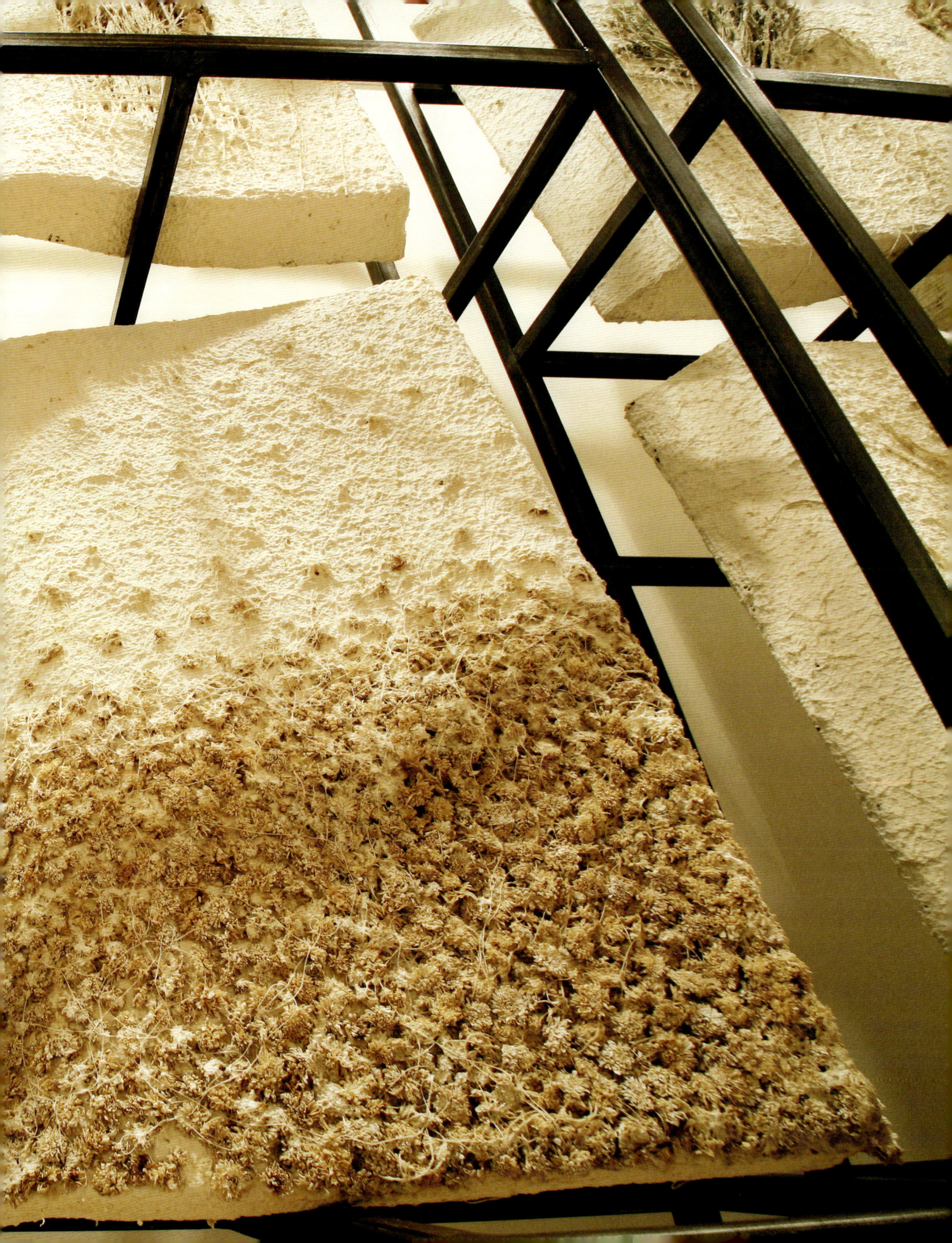

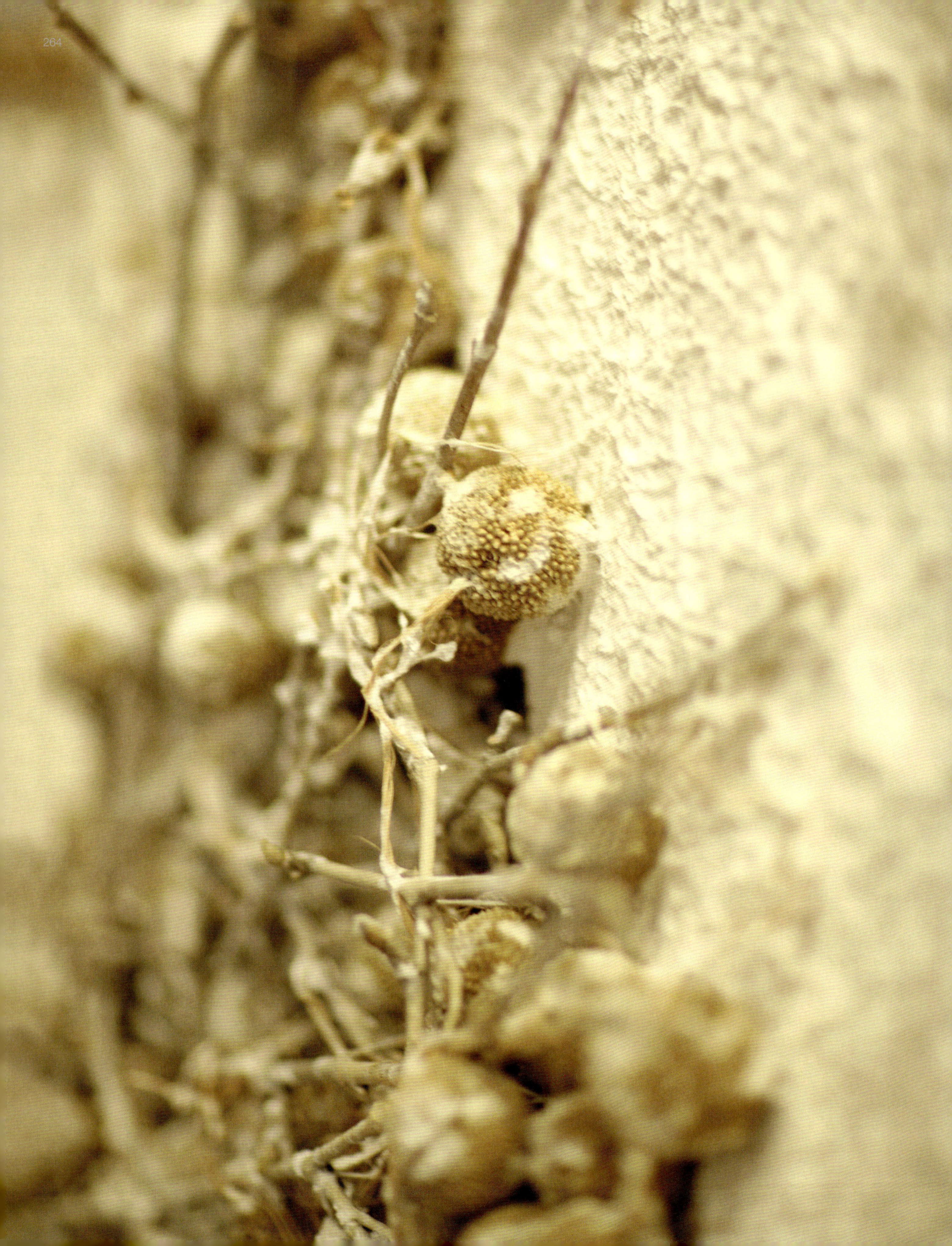

2009   Compendium of Materia Medica I · InstallationI · 360cm×145m×48cm×6
Das Buch heilender Kräuter I · Installation · 360cm×145cm×48cm×6

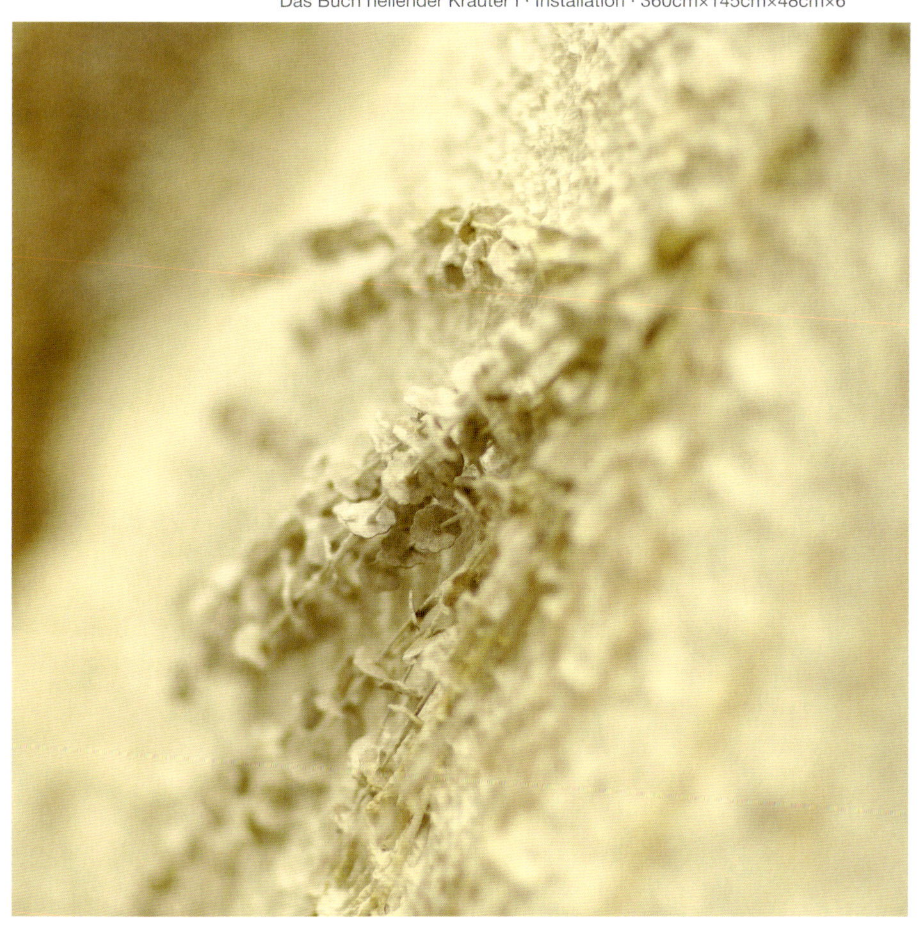

2009   Compendium of Materia Medica I · Installationl · 360cm×145m×48cm×6
Das Buch heilender Kräuter I · Installation · 360cm×145cm×48cm×6

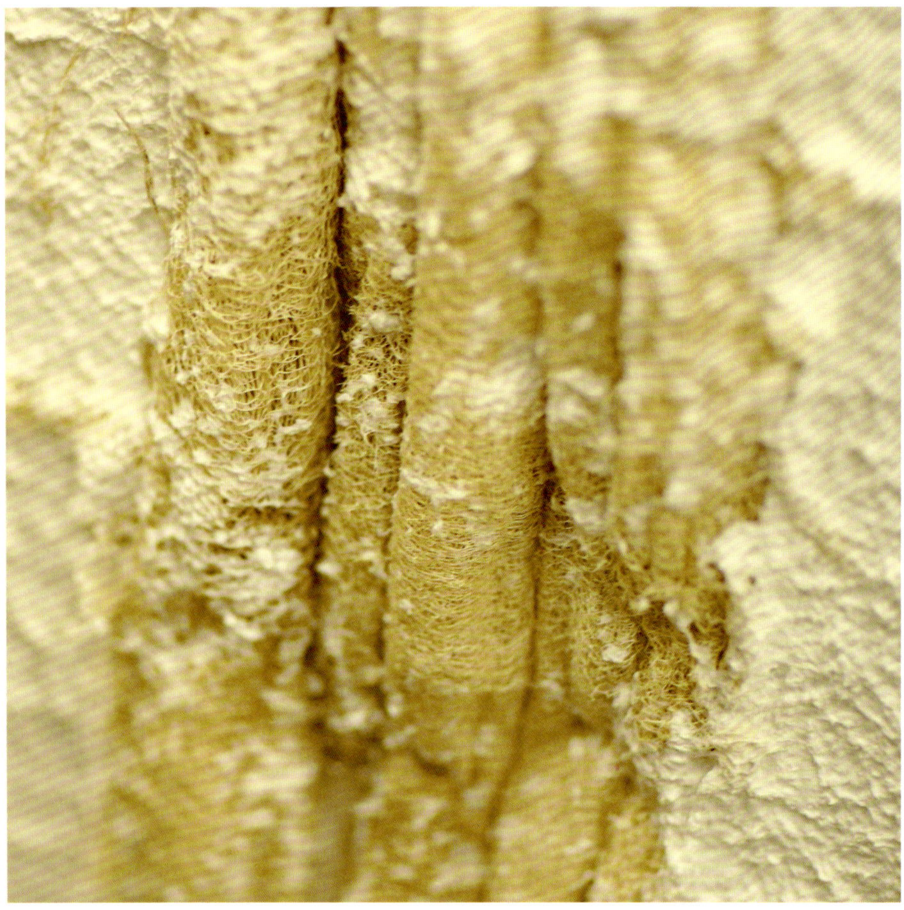

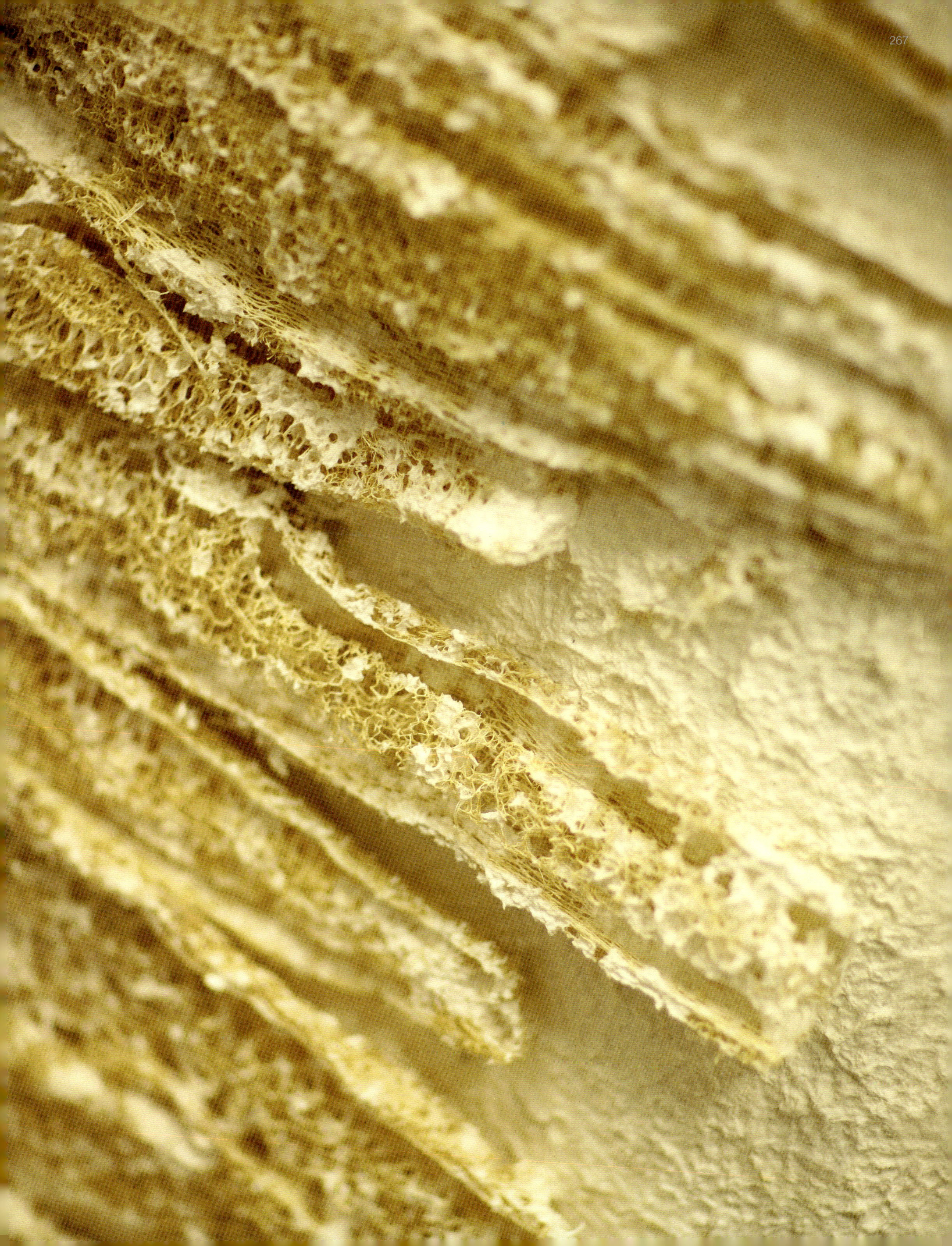

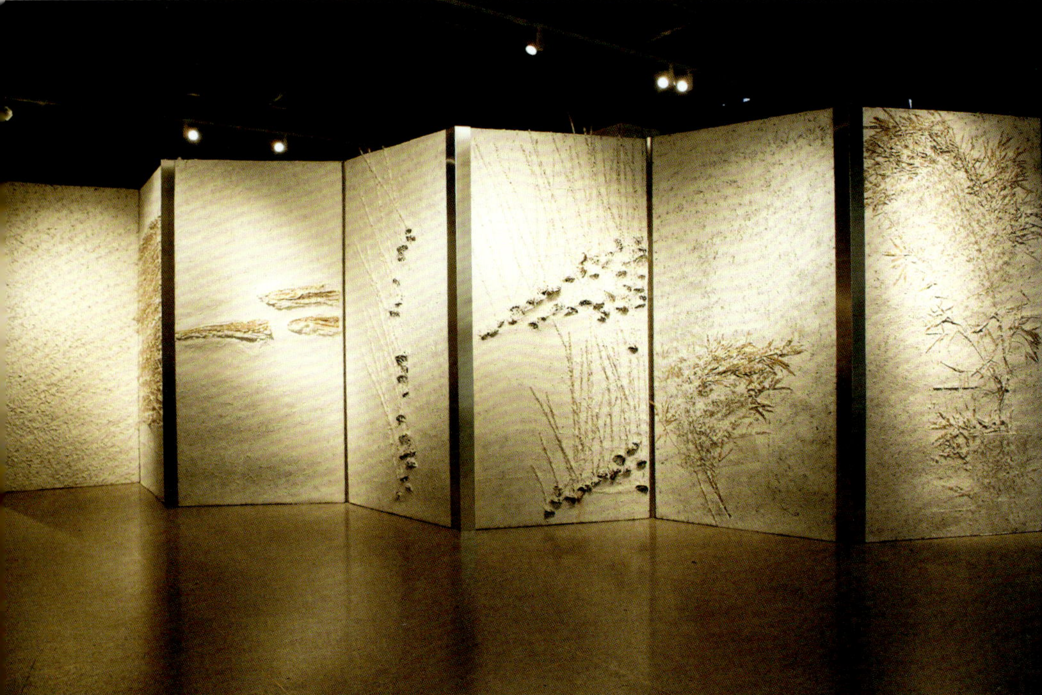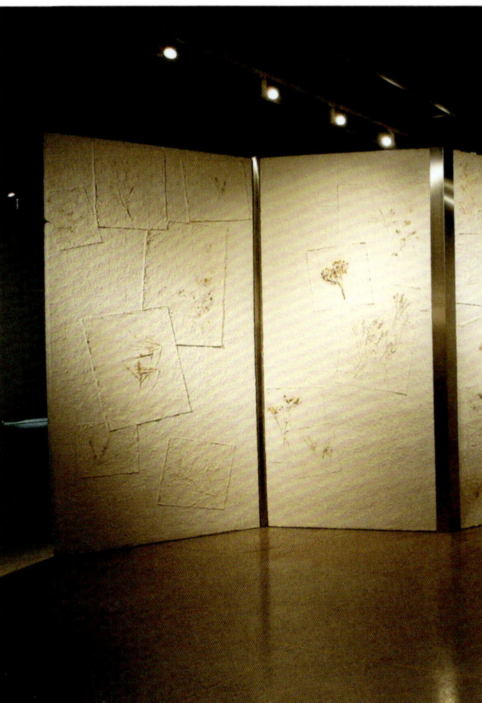

2012　Compendium of Materia Medica II · Installation · 250cm×120cm×8cm×7
Das Buch heilender Kräuter II · Installation · 250cm×120cm×8cm×7

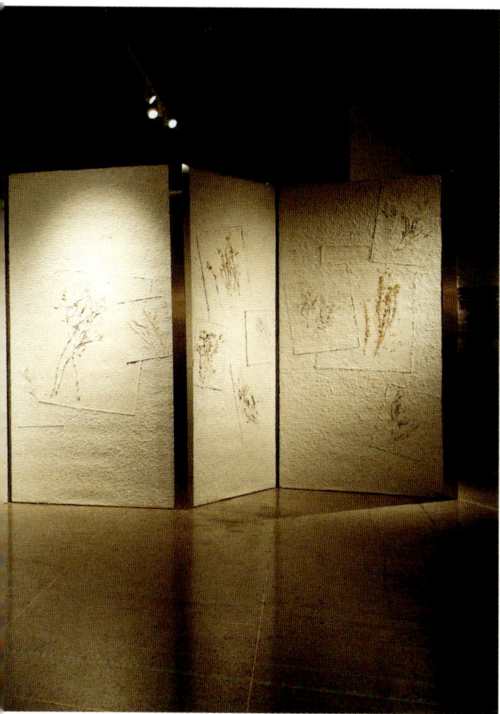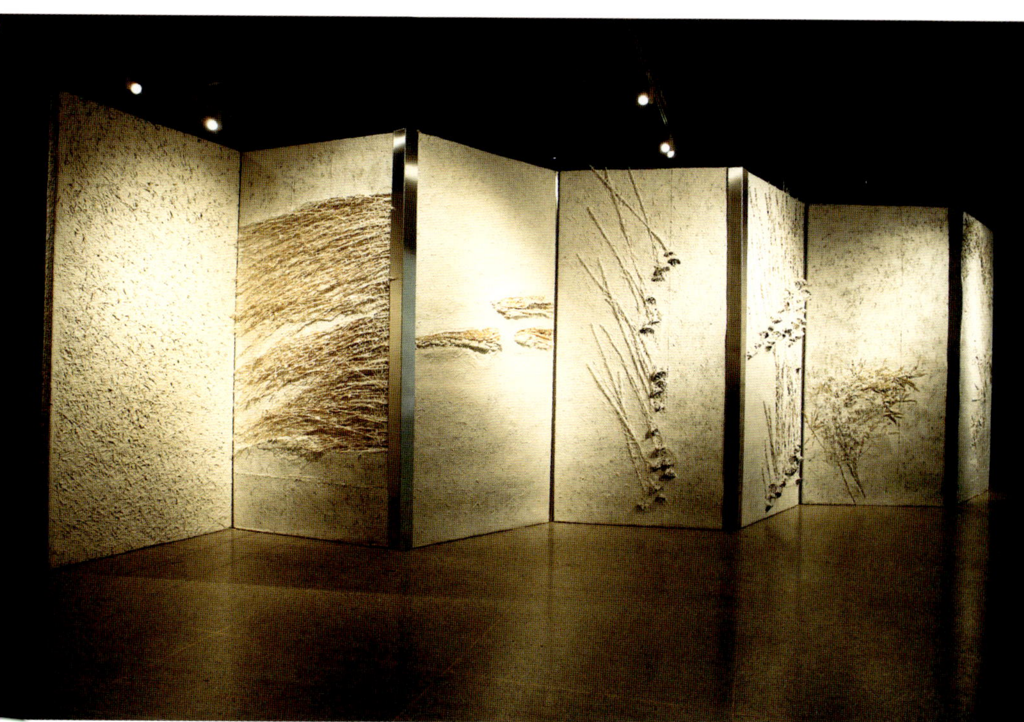

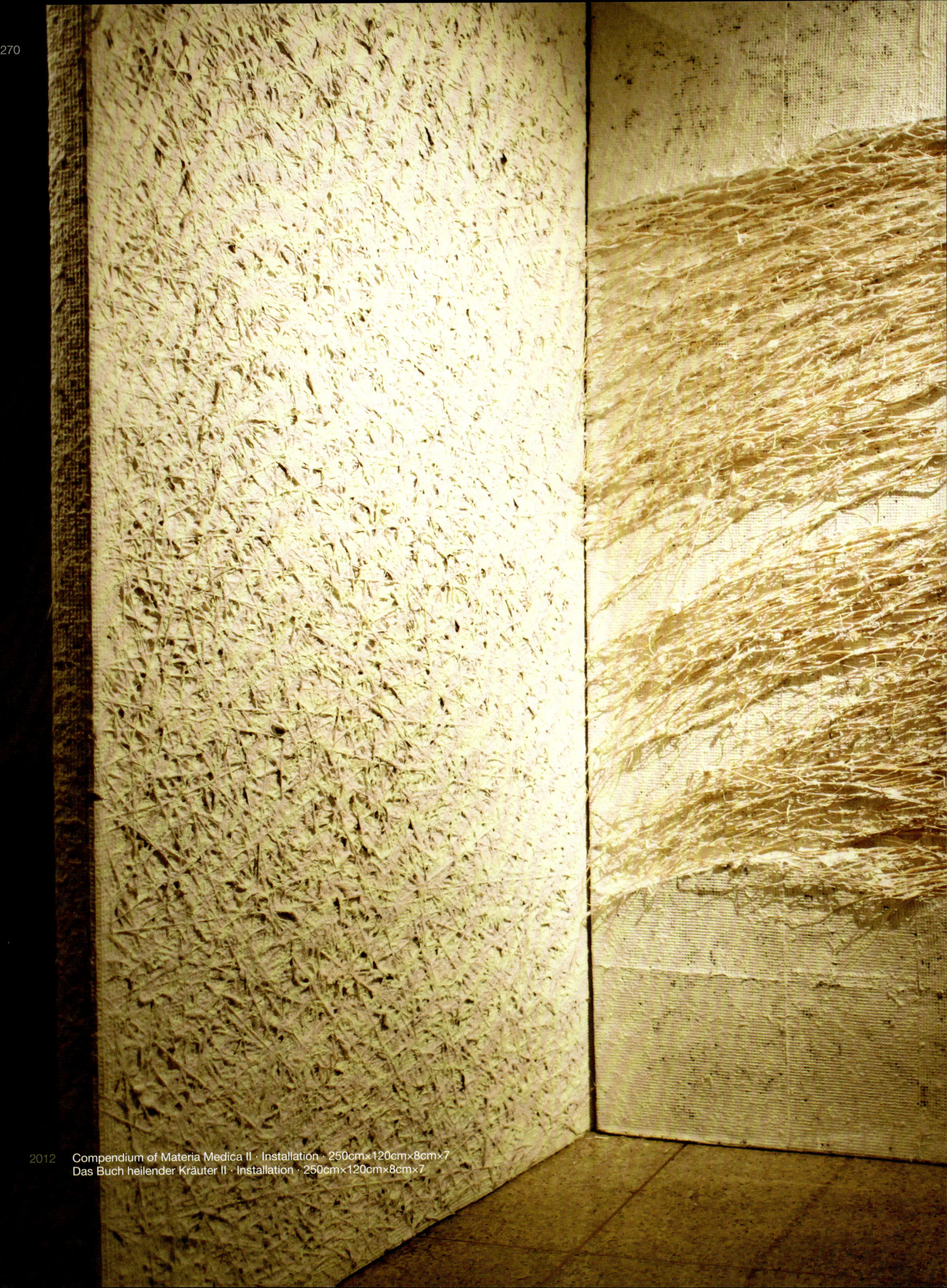

2012 Compendium of Materia Medica II · Installation · 250cm×120cm×8cm×7
Das Buch heilender Kräuter II · Installation · 250cm×120cm×8cm×7

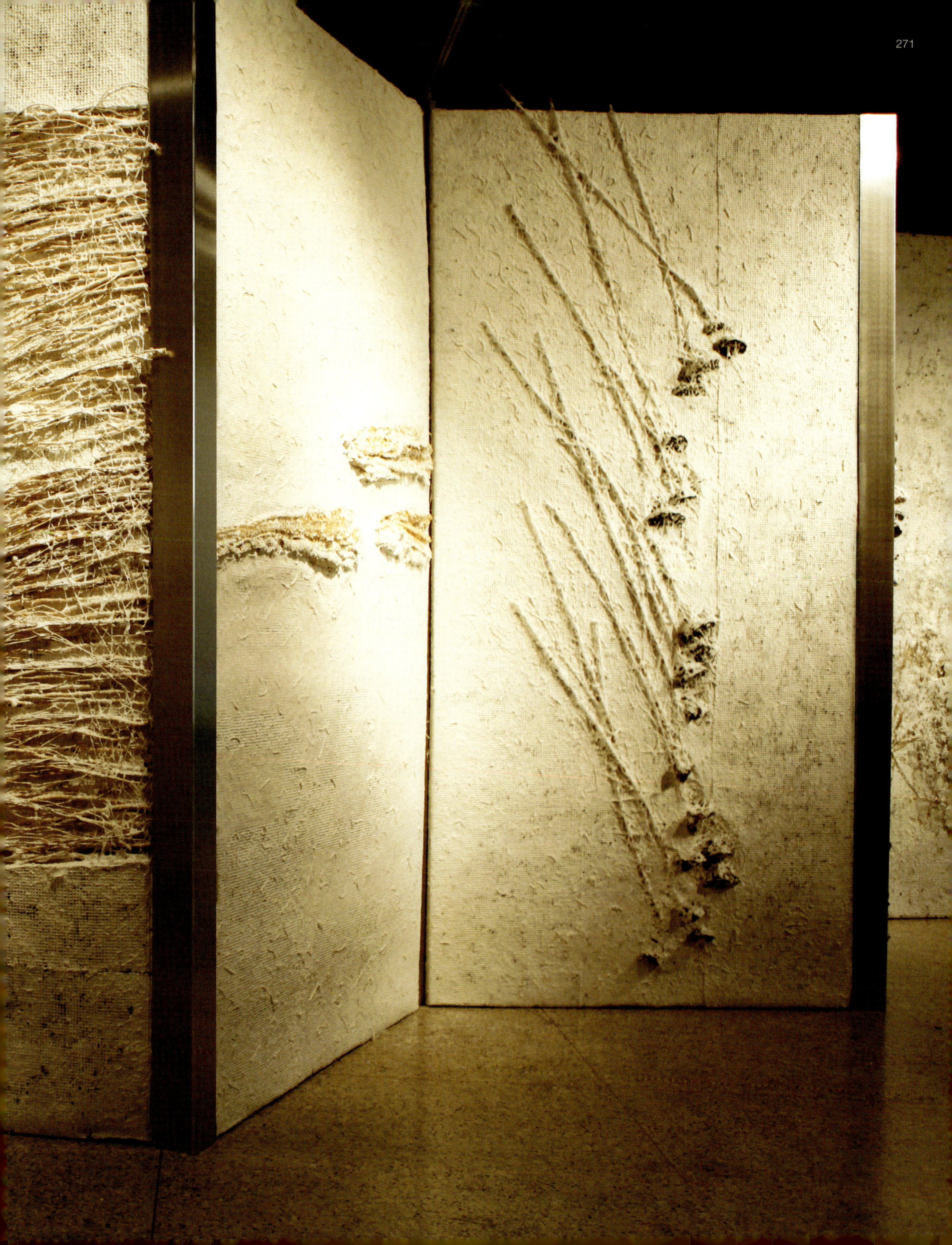

2012 Compendium of Materia Medica II · Installation · 250cm×120cm×8cm×7
Das Buch heilender Kräuter II · Installation · 250cm×120cm×8cm×7

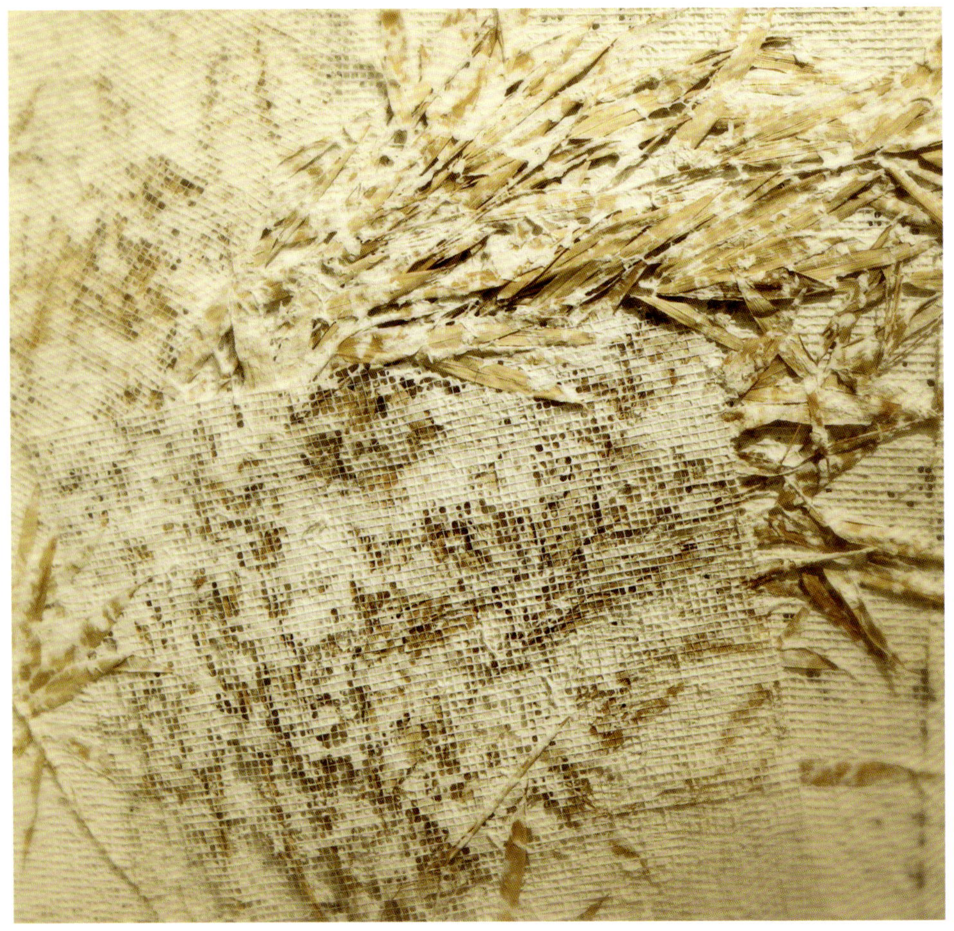

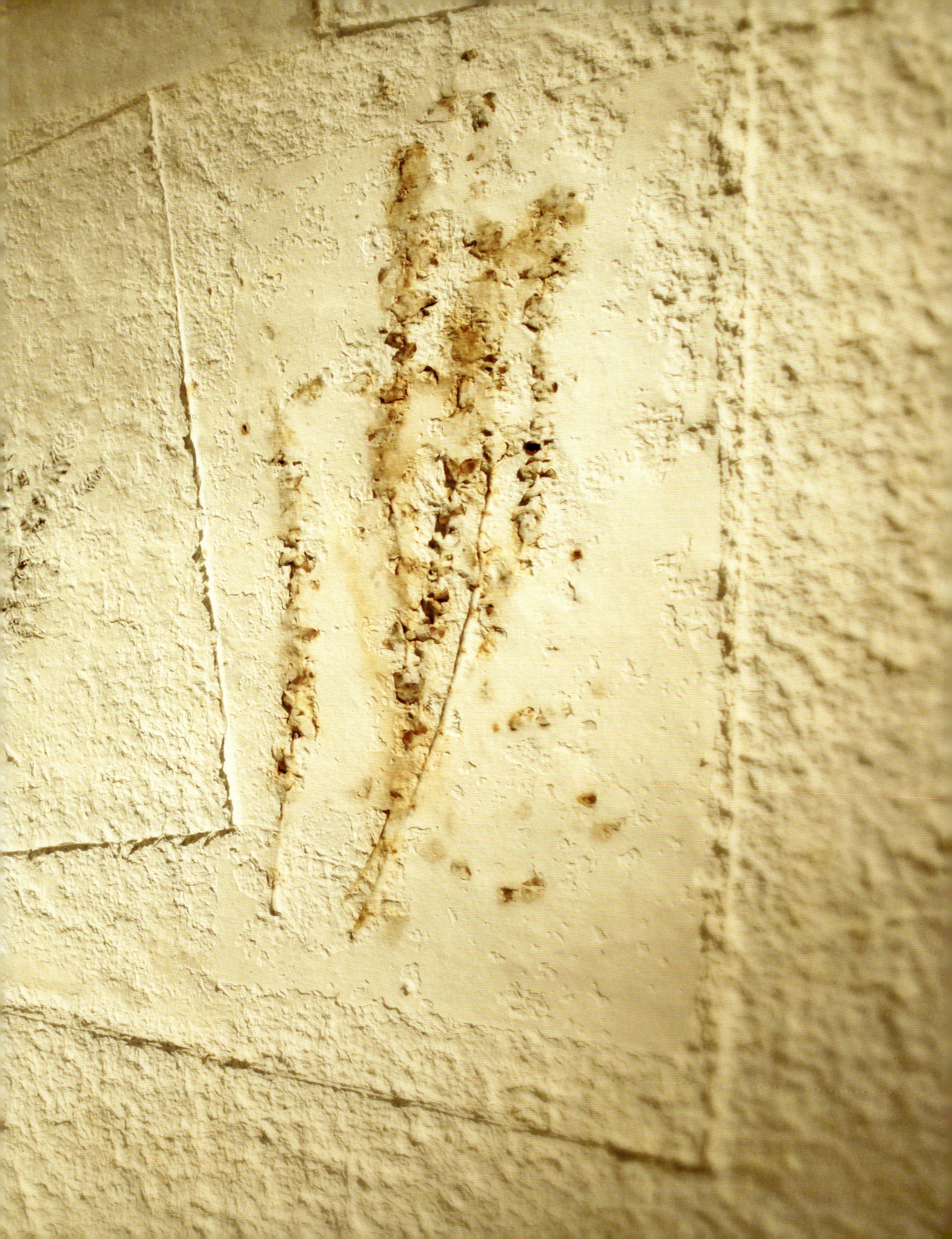

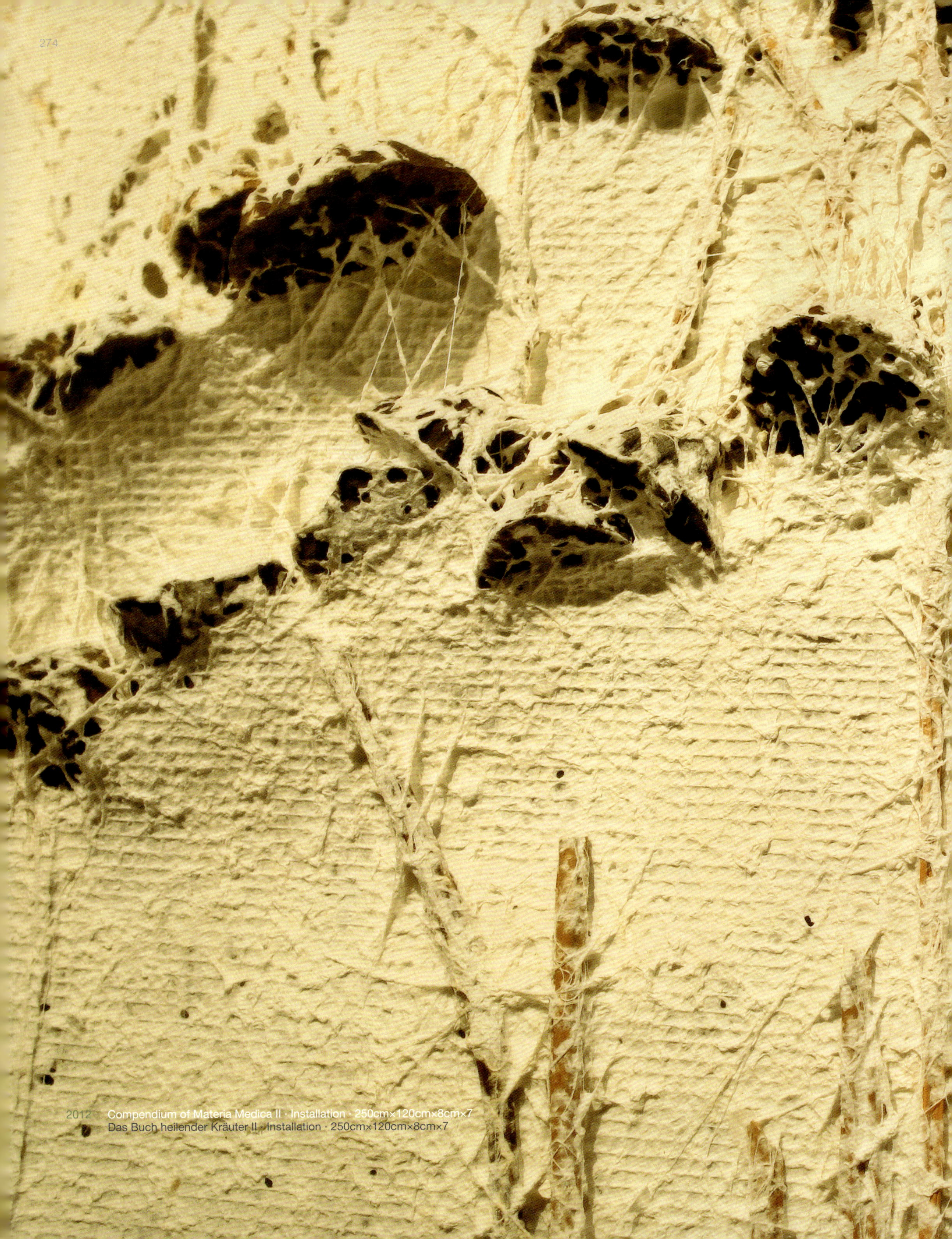

2012 Compendium of Materia Medica II · Installation · 250cm×120cm×8cm×7
Das Buch heilender Kräuter II · Installation · 250cm×120cm×8cm×7

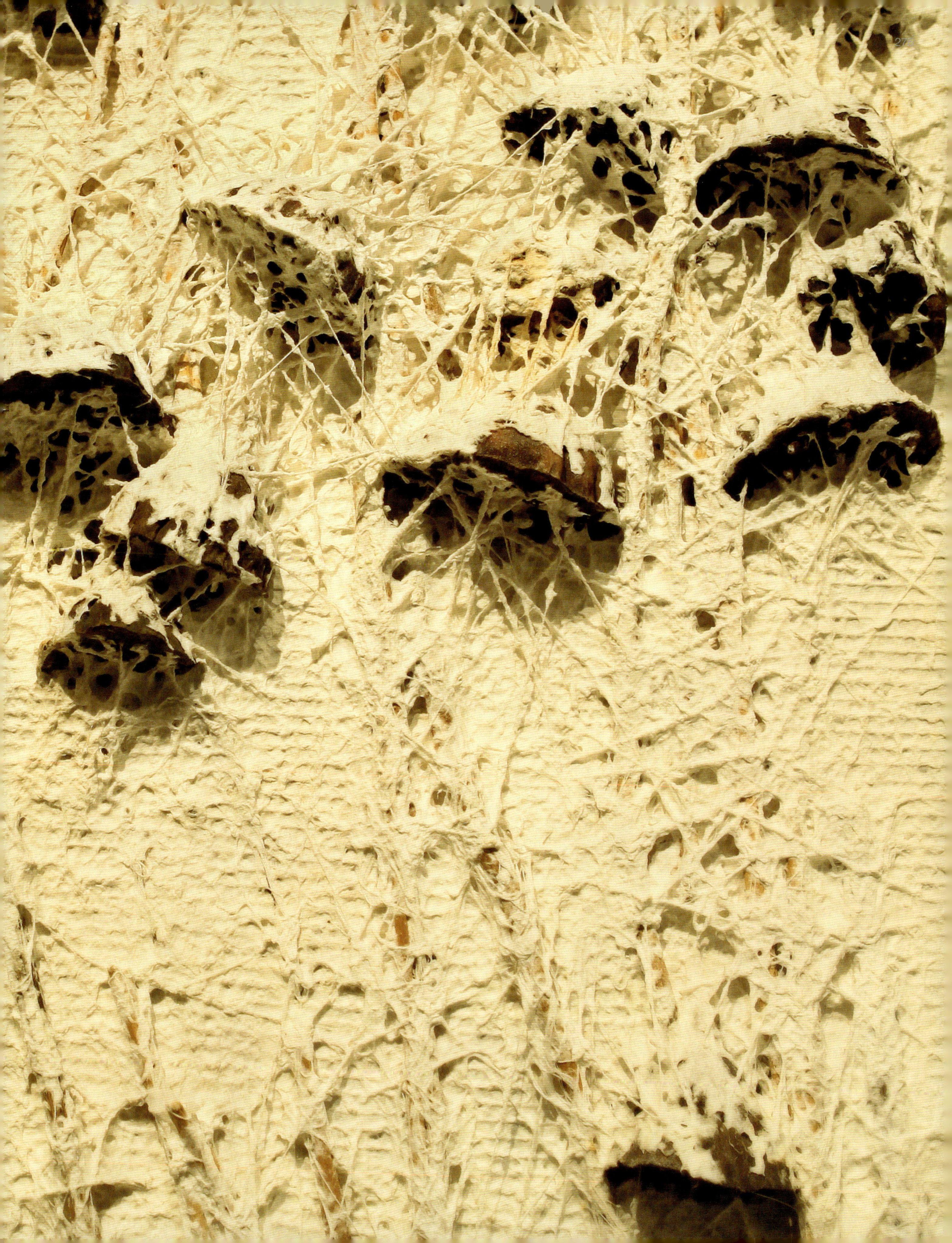

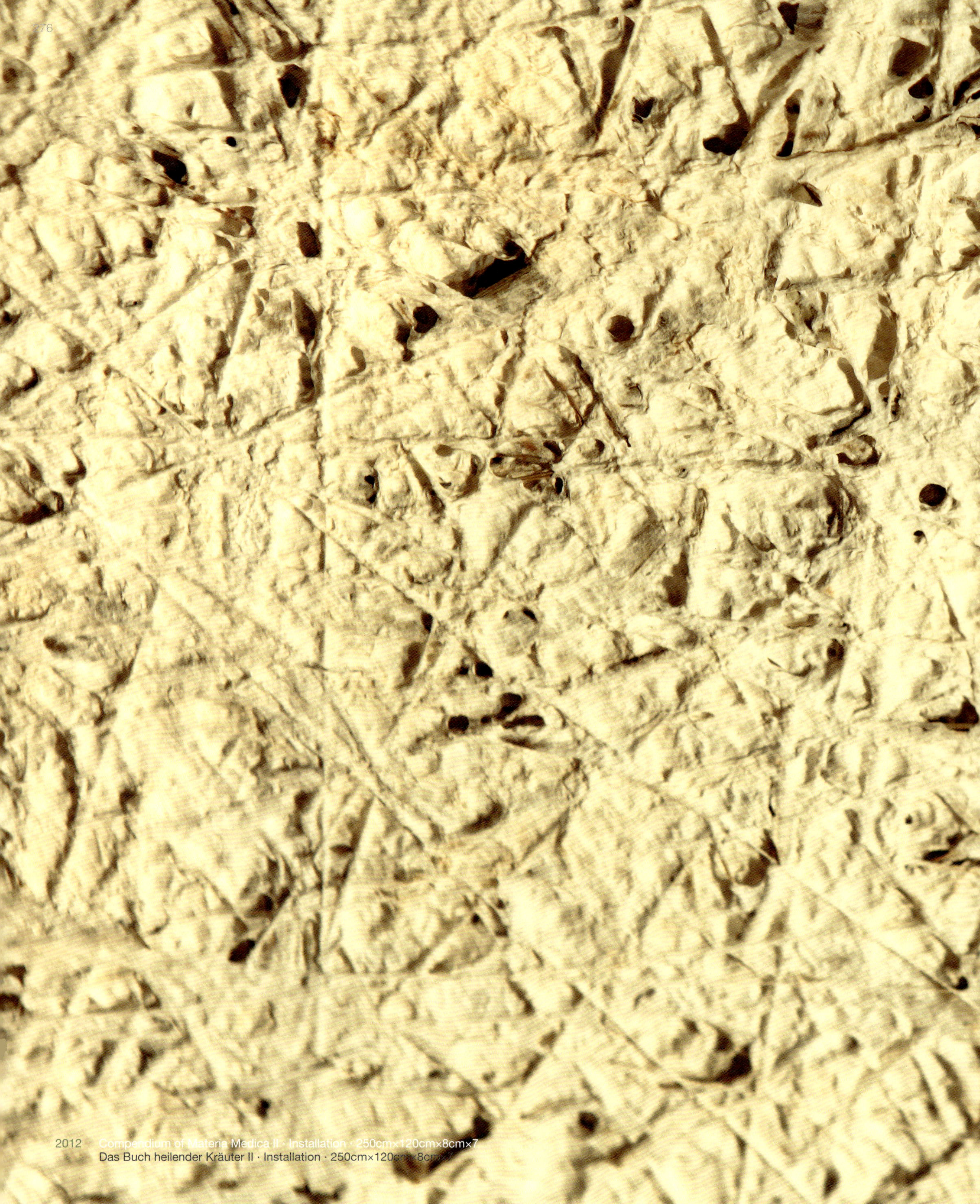

2012 · Compendium of Materia Medica II · Installation · 250cm×120cm×8cm×7
Das Buch heilender Kräuter II · Installation · 250cm×120cm×8cm×7

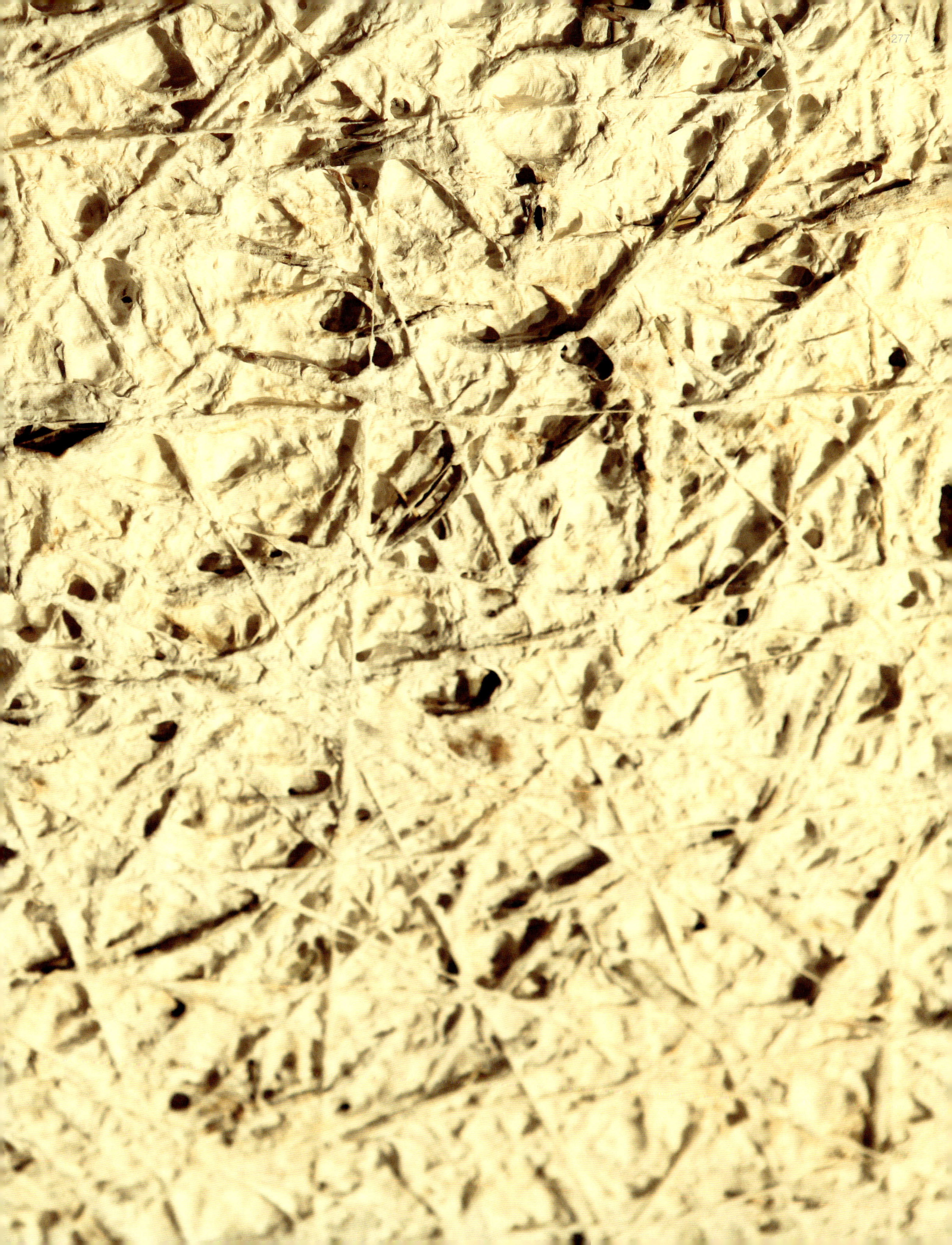

Shi Hui

Shi Hui was born in 1955 in Shanghai. In 1982, she graduated from the Zhejiang Academy of Art (now China Academy of Art), with a bachelor's degree in Dying and Weaving. While continuing her research and training at the Varbanov Tapestry Research Centre from 1986 to 1989, she was one of the pioneering Chinese contemporary fibre artists of the 1980s.

Shi Hui is a leading lady of Chinese contemporary art. The display of her collaborative work "Longevity" at the "13th International Lausanne Biennial of Contemporary Tapestry", in 1987, marked the breakthrough for contemporary Chinese tapestry art on the world scene.

Shi Hui's works represents a major evolution in visual language that took place in Chinese art since the 1990s. Showing deep respect for the intrinsic value and natural qualities of materials, her art genuinely embodies a "linguistic turn," which emphasises both "anti-form" and "restructured form".

For more than twenty years, Shi Hui has continued to push fibre art into new directions. Her work with cotton, canvas, rice paper, paper mache, and other materials exemplifies the characteristics of fiber, and has realised the Eastern spirit in contemporary art. Her works have been represented in many prestigious exhibitions, museums, and biennials, and have attracted a wide attention from the public.

Early works of Shi Hui were realised through flat and three-dimensional weaving. In the 1990s, her work broke free from the traditional frames of weaving. With web-like structures, she explored free space. Synthesising manual labor and a multitude of shapes inspired by natural life forms, she designed a new morphology of creation. Representative are her series "knot" and "Pillars". After 2000, with

works such as "Old Wall" and "Compendium of Materia Medica", Shi Hui reflects on the mediation between Chinese traditional culture and the contemporary environment.

Continuing to work with her favourite materials, Chinese paper and paper mache, Shi Hui obviously recognises the tacit bond between these traditional media and her spiritual self. It also mirrors her conviction of the important value that Chinese traditional media have, transformed in a present-day context. In the schema of Chinese contemporary art, Shi Hui's work has unique visual features. She expands traditional conceptions of weaving, and creates a structure of visual space. The process of weaving has become an experiental procedure, which visually develops as a kind of "postmodern animism".

Exhibitions

1987 The 13th International Biennial Art Tapestry Exhibition, Lausanne, Switzerland

1991 The First Documentary Exhibition of Contemporary Chinese Artists, Beijing & Nanjing, China

1992 The Chinese Contemporary Young Sculptors Invitational Exhibition, CNAFA Gallery, Hangzhou, China

The 92, International Art Festival—Earth and Fiber, Ankara, Turkey

1993 The Asia-Pacific Triennial, Queensland Art Gallery, Australia

1995 New Art From China, Hamburg, Germany

The 8th Installation Triennial of Tapestry, Lodz, Poland

Women Artists at the Academy , CNAFA Gallery, Hangzhou, China

1997 Showcasing International Art with a Focus on Contemporary Chinese Art, Art Beatus Gallery, Canada

Between Ego and Society, Exhibition of Contemporary Women Artists of China, Artemisia Gallery, Chicago, US

1998 Half of the Sky, Contemporary Chinese Women Artists , Bonn, Germany

JIANGNAN - Modern and Contemporary Art, From South of the Yangtze River, Vancouver, Canada

Century   Woman,Selected Works From the Exhibition,National Art Museum of China

Tradition · Reflection, China Contemporary Art Exhibition, Germany Embassy, Beijing

1999 Century Gate:1979-1999 China Invitational Exhibition, Chengdu, China

2000 Shanghai Spitit,2000 Shanghai Biennale, Shanghai Art Museum, China

Selected Contemporary Sculpture From China, Beijing, China

Exhibition of Paper and Pulp, Pusan Metropolitan Art Museum, Korea

Invited Exhibition on Contemporary Chinese Sculpture, Qingdao, China

2000 The West Lake International Sculpture Invitational Exhibition, Hangzhou, China

2001 Living in time: 29zeitgenossische Kunstler aus China, National Galerie im Hamburger Bahnhof Museum für Gegenwart, Berlin

Transplantation in Situ" The Fourth Shenzhen Contemporary Sculpture Exhibition, Shenzhen, China

Italy Asian-pacific International Biannual Contemporary Art Exhibition 2nd, Geneva National Contemporary Art Gallery, Genova, Italy

Heaven & Earth - Two Visions of CHINA, Columbia College Chicago Glass Curtain Gallery, US

2002 OPEN2002"The 5th International Exhibition of Sculptures and Installations in Venice-Lido

The First Guangzhou Triennial Reinterpretation: A Decade of Experimental Chinese Art(1990-2000), Guangdong Art Museum

Female Vision: Exhibition of Chinese Female Artists, Western Australia Museum

Paris-Pekin, Exhibition, Paris, France

2003 Alors , La Chine? Contemporary Chinese Art, Centre Pompidou, Paris, France

The First Beijing International Art Biennale, National Art Museum of China

2003 Parallel Time: Asian Contemporary Art Exhibition, China Academy of Art, Hangzhou, China

Open Sky: Contemporary Art Exhibition, Shanghai Duolun Museum of Modern Art

Metaphysics 2003: Shanghai Abstract Art Exhibition, Shanghai Art Museum

2004 Dream of the Dragon's Nation"Contemporary Art Exhibition from China , Irish Museum of Modern Art

2005 Metaphysics 2005: Black & White, Shanghai Art Museum Chengdu Biennale 2005

2006 Fluid Shadow and Flutter Wall" Solo Exhibition in Hamburg, Germany

2007 Martell Artists of the Year 2007, National Art Museum of China

What is Mono-ha?, Beijing Tokyo Art Projects

Linear: Chinese Abstract Art Exhibition, Creek Art, Shanghai

2008 China Gesture" The 1st Chinese Sculpture Exhibition, Xiamen, China

Our Future: Guy & Myriam Ullens Collection, UCCA, Beijing

Breath in Depth: Chinese Contemporary Female Art Exhibition, Creek Art, Shanghai

Chinese Garden for Living: Illusion into Reality, Pillnitz Palace, Dresden, Germany

Hypallage: The Post-Modern Mode of Chinese Contemporary Art, The OCT Contemporary Art Terminal, Shenzhen

2009 The Fifth Dimension — Art of Fiber and Space, He Xiangning Art Museum, Shenzhen/China MoCA, Shanghai

2010 Reshaping History Chinart from 2000 to 2009, Beijing,China

Nature of China — Contemporary Art Documenta, Suzhou,China

2011 Half The Sky — Women in the New Art of China , Westphal College Media Arts & Design Drexel University

Tao of Nature,Chinese Abstract Art Exhibition, MoCA, Shanghai,China

2012 Form of the Formless,Contemporary Art from China, Vorwerksallee, Budelsdorf,Germany

A Centenary Exhibition of Chinese Scupture, National Museum of China, Beijing

"Woman Road" Exhibition of Chinese and Korean Female Artists, 2012 Hwabong Gallery, Seoul

2013 Blossoming Spirits: Joint Exhibiton of Xu Jiang and Shihui, Ludwig Museum, Koblenz

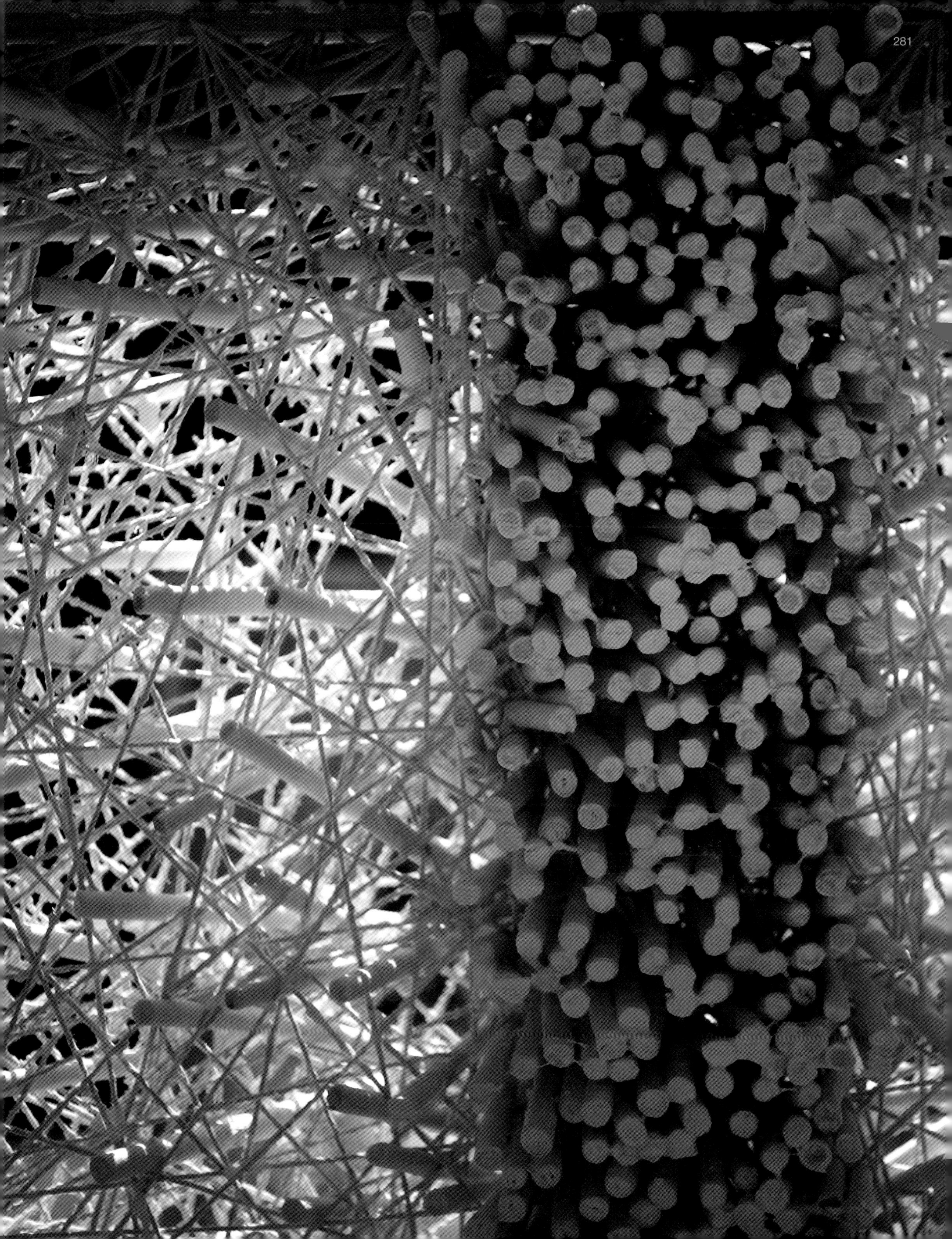

This catalogue was published
on the occasion of the exhibition
"Flourishing Spirits".

LUDWIGMUSEUM
im Deutschherrenhaus Koblenz

Editors: Beate Reifenscheid, Gao Shiming
Design & Layout: HEAVENS
Staff: Wang Xiaosong, Tang Suo, Gao Miye, Zhou Yincao
Text: Beate Reifenscheid P.7-23
    Gao Shiming P.25-33
    Claus Mewes P.35-39
    Xu Jiang P.43-55 P.86-97
    Fan Di'an P.169-173
    Fan Jingzhong P.206-273
    Shi Hui P.200 P.221 P.224 P.227 P.232 P.239
Translation: Ulrike Kniesner, Chen Heng
    Ingrid Fischer-Schreiber, Patrick Kühnel, Laoji Wang, Michael Wetzel
Proofreading: Ulrike Kniesner, Chen Heng, Gao Miye
Printing: Shanghai Artron Color Printing Co., Ltd.
Published by: Hirmer Publishers, Nymphenburger Strasse 84, 80636 Munich

Bibliographic information published by the Deutsche Nationalbibliothek
The Deutsche Nationalbibliothek lists this publication in the Deutsche Nationalbibliografie;
detailed bibliographic data available in the Internet at http://dnb.d-nb.de

ISBN 978-3-7774-2070-7
www.hirmerpublishers.com